Global Wesleyan Encyclopedia
of Biblical Theology

EDITORIAL COMMITTEE

ADVISORY COMMITTEE

Global Wesleyan
ENCYCLOPEDIA
of
BIBLICAL THEOLOGY

Robert D. Branson, PhD, Editor

ASSOCIATE EDITORS
Deirdre Brower-Latz, PhD
Sarah B. C. Derck, PhD
Wayne McCown, PhD

f·

THE FOUNDRY
PUBLISHING

Library of Congress Cataloging-in-Publication Data

Names: Branson, Robert, 1941- editor.
Title: Global Wesleyan encyclopedia of biblical theology / Robert D. Branson, editor ; associate editors, Deirdre Brower-Latz, Sarah B. C. Derck, Wayne McCown.
Description: Kansas City : The Foundry Publishing, 2020. | Includes bibliographical references and index. | Summary: "The purpose of the Global Wesleyan Encyclopedia of Biblical Theology is to define major biblical terms, themes, and concepts and offer a Wesleyan assessment of each. Also its intent is to reflect the global character of Christian faith by the choice of topics and the global character of the contributors. When appropriate, a theological assessment of the themes and concepts are offered. Finally, the book provides a guide for understanding the richness of the Wesleyan approach to interpreting Scripture"— Provided by publisher.
Identifiers: LCCN 2019030645 (print) | LCCN 2019030646 (ebook) | ISBN 9780834138230 (hardback) | ISBN 9780834138247 (ebook)
Subjects: LCSH: Bible—Theology—Encyclopedias. | Theology—Encyclopedias. | Wesleyan Church—Doctrines—Encyclopedias. | Holiness churches—Doctrines—Encyclopedias.
Classification: LCC BS440 .G563 2020 (print) | LCC BS440 (ebook) | DDC 230/.04103—dc23
LC record available at https://lccn.loc.gov/2019030645
LC ebook record available at https://lccn.loc.gov/2019030646

CONTENTS

PREFACE AND PURPOSE

In 2013 Beacon Hill Press (now the Foundry Publishing) published the *Global Wesleyan Dictionary of Theology*. Its contributors were drawn from the global family of Wesleyan churches, and their articles reflect the theological character of the Wesleyan tradition. It was immediately decided to begin work on a companion volume, the *Global Wesleyan Encyclopedia of Biblical Theology*. It is not the purpose of this volume to be narrowly sectarian, for the Wesleyan tradition is part of the broader spectrum of orthodox Christianity. Nor is this volume a dictionary of the Bible. There are a number of excellent works that fill that need. Rather, selected biblical themes and concepts are developed with a scholarly commitment to bring forth their meanings and their theological significances.

The purpose of the *Global Wesleyan Encyclopedia of Biblical Theology* is (1) to define major biblical terms, themes, and concepts and, where appropriate, to offer a characteristic Wesleyan assessment of each; (2) to reflect the global character of Christian faith by the choice of topics to be defined and by the global character of its contributors; (3) to offer when appropriate a theological assessment of the themes and concepts studied; and (4) to provide a guide for understanding the richness of the Wesleyan approach to interpreting Scripture and how it can help Christians in that tradition live and articulate their faith in a global context.

HOW TO USE THE ENCYCLOPEDIA

The encyclopedia has been designed to provide numerous ways to investigate a topic: (1) There is the essay itself in which the author discusses the topic. (2) In most of the essays some terms are in **bold**. These terms are treated elsewhere in the encyclopedia and constitute an internal cross-reference. (3) At the end of many essays there is a *See also* section that lists related topics defined in the encyclopedia. These topics constitute the encyclopedia's external cross-reference. (4) Resources for further study are listed at the end of most essays in a **Resources** section. Most of the resources are either books or journal articles. But some resources are located on the Internet. In these instances the website is identified. (5) The Scripture Index provides a ready reference to the scriptures authors have used to compose their essays. In citing the Psalms and a few other passages there is a difference between the numbering of the Hebrew Bible (HB) and the English translation. After listing the location of the translation, the location in the HB is placed in brackets.

CONTRIBUTORS

David A. Ackerman, PhD
Field Education Coordinator, Philippines and Micronesia
Church of the Nazarene
Manila, Philippines
Entries: **Conscience; Rest.**

Bill T. Arnold, PhD
Paul S. Amos Professor of Old Testament Interpretation
Asbury Theological Seminary
Wilmore, Kentucky
Entry: **Covenant.**

Neville Bartle, DMiss
Adjunct Professor in Folk Religions
Asia-Pacific Nazarene Theological Seminary
District Superintendent, Church of the Nazarene
Auckland, New Zealand
Entry: **Jesus's Victory over Sin and Death.**

David R. Bauer, PhD
Ralph Waldo Beeson Professor of Inductive Biblical Studies
Dean of the School of Biblical Interpretation
Asbury Theological Seminary
Wilmore, Kentucky
Entry: **Gospel of Matthew, Theology of.**

Stephen J. Bennett, PhD
Professor of Old Testament
Nyack College
Alliance Theological Seminary
Nyack, New York
Entry: **Completeness/Integrity.**

Brian T. Bernius, PhD
Associate Professor of Religion
Chair, Division of Religious and Ministerial Studies
Associate Professor of Old Testament and Near Eastern Studies
School of Theology and Ministry
Indian Wesleyan University
Marion, Indiana
Entries: **Idolatry; Prophets/Prophecy.**

Elaine A. Bernius, PhD
Associate Professor of Biblical Studies
School of Theology and Ministry
Indiana Wesleyan University
Marion, Indiana
Entry: **Image of God.**

P. Ben Boeckel, PhD
Adjunct Professor of Biblical Languages
Nazarene Theological Seminary
Associate Pastor
Richardson Church of the Nazarene
Dallas, Texas
Entry: **Evil.**

A. Wendell Bowes, PhD
Emeritus Professor of Old Testament
Northwest Nazarene University
Nampa, Idaho
Entry: **Wisdom, Theology of.**

Laurie J. Braaten, PhD
Emeritus Professor of Biblical Studies
Judson University
Elgin, Illinois
Entry: **Remnant.**

Clinton A. Branscombe, MRel
Associate Professor of Old Testament
Kingswood University
Sussex, New Brunswick, Canada
Entries: **Clean/Unclean; Compassion.**

Robert D. Branson, PhD
Emeritus Professor of Biblical Literature
Olivet Nazarene University
Bourbonnais, Illinois
Entries: **Fall, The; Hate; Miracles of Jesus.**

Kent Brower, PhD
Senior Research Fellow in Biblical Studies
Director of Research
Nazarene Theological College
Manchester, United Kingdom
Entry: **Holiness.**

Deirdre Brower-Latz, PhD
Principal, Senior Lecturer in Practical and Social Theology
Nazarene Theological College
Manchester, United Kingdom
Entry: **Leadership.**

Bart B. Bruehler, PhD
Associate Professor of New Testament
College of Adult and Professional Studies
Indiana Wesleyan University
Marion, Indiana
Entry: **Gospel.**

Filimão M. Chambo, DLitt et Phil
Regional Director, Africa Region
Church of the Nazarene
Johannesburg, South Africa
Entry: **Savior.**

Joseph Coleson, PhD
Professor of Old Testament
Director, MA (TS) Degree Program
Nazarene Theological Seminary
Kansas City, Missouri
Entry: **Creation.**

Rhonda G. Crutcher, PhD
Associate Pastor
Florida Keys Church of the Nazarene
District Missionary
South Florida District Church of the Nazarene
Key Largo, Florida
Entry: **Sanctification.**

John Culp, PhD
Professor of Philosophy Emeritus
Azusa Pacific University
Azusa, California
Entry: **Free Will.**

Sarah B. C. Derck, PhD
Assistant Professor of Old Testament
Houghton College
Houghton, New York
Entries: **Matriarchs; Sacred Space.**

Jenny DeVivo, PhD
Executive Director of Mission and Heritage
Saint Xavier University
Chicago, Illinois
Entry: **Peter, 1 and 2, Theology of.**

Timothy Dwyer, PhD
Professor of Bible and Ministry
Warner University
Lake Wales, Florida
Entry: **Sermon on the Mount.**

James O. Edlin, PhD
Professor of Biblical Literature and Languages
MidAmerica Nazarene University
Olathe, Kansas
Entry: **Land, Theology of the.**

J. Edward Ellis, PhD
Associate Professor of Biblical Literature
School of Theology and Christian Ministry
Olivet Nazarene University
Bourbonnais, Illinois
Entry: **Reconciliation.**

Brad Fipps, PhD
Professor of Religion
Southern Wesleyan University
Central, South Carolina
Entry: **Forgiveness, The Art and Necessity of.**

Dean Flemming, PhD
Professor of New Testament and Missions
MidAmerica Nazarene University
Olathe, Kansas
Entry: **Missional Hermeneutics.**

J. Russell Frazier, PhD
Senior Lecturer in Theology
Coordinator of the Doctor of Ministry Programme
Africa Nazarene University
Nairobi, Kenya
Entries: **Godliness/Godly; Parousia.**

Rob A. Fringer, PhD
Principal
Nazarene Theological College
Thornlands, Australia
Entry: **Regeneration/Rebirth.**

Ryan K. Giffin, MATS (PhD Candidate, Asbury Seminary)
Pastor
Village Community Church of the Nazarene
Kansas City, Kansas
Entry: **Honor-Shame Culture.**

Segbegnon Mathieu Gnonhossou, DMin
Adjunct Instructor
Eastern Kentucky University
Richmond, Kentucky
Entry: **Discipleship.**

Thomas Grafton, MA
(PhD Student in Biblical Studies)
Asbury Theological Seminary
Affiliate Faculty
Southwestern College
Winfield, Kansas
Entry: **Saints/Holy Ones.**

Timothy M. Green, PhD
Dean of the Millard Reed School of Theology and Christian Ministry
Professor of Old Testament Theology and Literature
Trevecca Nazarene University
Nashville, Tennessee
Entries: **Corporate Responsibility; Divination.**

Nabil Habibi, MA (PhD Candidate, University of Manchester)
Dean of Students
Nazarene Evangelical School
Sin el Fil, Lebanon
Entry: **Confession.**

Roger L. Hahn, PhD
Professor of New Testament
Willard H. Taylor Professor of Biblical Theology
Nazarene Theological Seminary
Kansas City, Missouri
Entry: **Kingdom of God/Heaven.**

Mawiyah Khazer Halasa, MA
Academic Dean
Professor of Pastoral Theology
Eastern Mediterranean Nazarene Bible College
Karak, Jordan
Entry: **Retribution.**

Ryan Hansen, PhD
Lead Pastor
Blakemore Church of the Nazarene
Nashville, Tennessee
Entry: **Witness of the Spirit.**

John E. Hartley, PhD
Distinguished Professor of Old Testament
Azusa Pacific Seminary
Azusa Pacific University
Azusa, California
Entry: **Helper.**

Nina Henrichs-Tarasenkova, PhD
Instructor
University of Portland
Portland, Oregon
Online Instructor
Asbury Theological Seminary
Wilmore, Kentucky
Entry: **Marriage.**

Drew S. Holland, MDiv (PhD Candidate, Asbury Seminary)
Associate Pastor
Huntsville First United Methodist Church
Huntsville, Alabama
Entry: **Redeem/Redeemer.**

Antonie Holleman, Drs
District Superintendent
Church of the Nazarene, the Netherlands
Zaandam, the Netherlands
Entry: **Election.**

Laura Sweat Holmes, PhD
Assistant Professor of New Testament
Seattle Pacific Seminary
Seattle Pacific University
Seattle, Washington
Entry: **Feminist Hermeneutics.**

Agnès Uwimana Ibanda, MA
Missionary with the Church of the Nazarene in the Africa Indian Ocean Field
Field Education Coordinator under Institut Théologique Nazaréen
Antananarivo, Madagascar
Entry: **Judgment.**

Andy Johnson, PhD
Professor of New Testament
Nazarene Theological Seminary
Kansas City, Missouri
Entry: **Theological Interpretation.**

Abson Prédestin Joseph, PhD
Associate Professor of New Testament
School of Theology and Ministry
Indiana Wesleyan University
Marion, Indiana
Entries: **Caribbean Hermeneutics; Communal Holiness.**

Simon Jothi, BD, MA (EdD Candidate, Trevecca Nazarene University)
Principal
South Asia Nazarene Bible College
Bangalore, India
Entry: **Fasting.**

Jorge L. Julca, DMin
President, Seminario Teológico Nazareno del Cono Sur
Regional Education Coordinator, South America Region
Church of the Nazarene
Buenos Aires, Argentina
Entries: **Inspiration of Scripture, Wesleyan Understanding of; Latin American
Hermeneutics.**

Brad E. Kelle, PhD
Professor of Old Testament and Hebrew
Point Loma Nazarene University
San Diego, California
Entry: **Righteousness.**

Thomas J. King, PhD
Professor of Old Testament
Nazarene Bible College
Colorado Springs, Colorado
Entry: **Sacrificial System.**

Steven J. Koskie, PhD
Pastor
Antioch United Methodist Church
Simsboro, Louisiana
Entry: **Wesleyan Hermeneutics.**

Kristina LaCelle-Peterson, PhD
Professor of Religion
Houghton College
Houghton, New York
Entry: **Justice, New Testament.**

Darin H. Land, PhD
Associate Professor of New Testament
Asia-Pacific Nazarene Theological Seminary
Taytay, Rizal, Philippians
Entry: **Remembering.**

Stephen J. Lennox, PhD
President
Kingswood University
Sussex, New Brunswick, Canada
Entries: **Festivals; Sacred Times.**

Roderick T. Leupp, PhD
Adjunct Instructor
Indiana Wesleyan University
Nazarene Bible College
Bartlesville, Oklahoma
Entry: **Predestination.**

Larisa Levicheva, PhD
Adjunct Professor of Christian Ministry
Indiana Wesleyan University
Marion, Indiana
Entries: **Poor/Poverty; Temptation/Test.**

Russell Lovett, PhD
Retired Missionary
Adjunct Instructor
Olivet Nazarene University
Bourbonnais, Illinois
Entry: **Faith.**

Kevin Twain Lowery, PhD
Professor of Theology and Philosophy
Chair, Department of Theology and Philosophy
Olivet Nazarene University
Bourbonnais, Illinois
Entry: **Biblical Ethics.**

Gilbert Lozano, PhD
Associate Professor of Biblical Studies
School of Theology
Anderson University
Anderson, Indiana
Entry: **Love.**

George Lyons, PhD
Emeritus Professor of New Testament
Northwest Nazarene University
Nampa, Idaho
Entry: **Grace.**

Kara J. Lyons-Pardue, PhD
Associate Professor of New Testament
School of Theology and Christian Ministry
Point Loma Nazarene University
San Diego, California
Entry: **Jesus and the Law.**

Kimberly S. Majeski, DMin
Associate Professor of Biblical Studies
School of Theology
Anderson University
Anderson, Indiana
Entries: **Eschatology; Women Leaders.**

William H. Malas Jr., PhD
Professor of Biblical Literature
Chair, Department of Religion
Eastern Nazarene College
Quincy, Massachusetts
Entry: **Incarnation.**

Steven T. Mann, PhD
Adjunct Professor of Biblical and Religious Studies
Azusa Pacific University
Azusa, California
Entry: **Holy Spirit.**

Jon Manning, MA
Instructor in New Testament
Point Loma Nazarene University
Azusa Pacific University
San Diego, California
Entry: **Patronage System.**

Gabi M. Markusse-Overduin, PhD
Teacher of New Testament
New Testament Chair of the Bible Cluster for the Curriculum Committee of European
    Nazarene College
Amersfoort, the Netherlands
Entry: **Afterlife.**

Troy W. Martin, PhD
Professor of Biblical Studies
Department of Religious Studies
Saint Xavier University
Chicago, Illinois
Entry: **Peter, 1 and 2, Theology of.**

Mónica Mastronardi de Fernández, DMin
Professor of Spiritual Formation and Pastoral Leadership
General Editor of the "School of Leadership" for the Mesoamerica Region
Seminario Nazareno de las Américas
San José, Costa Rica
Entry: **Call of God.**

Michael D. Matlock, PhD
Professor of Inductive Biblical Studies, Old Testament, and Early Judaism
Chair, Department of Inductive Biblical Studies
Asbury Theological Seminary
Wilmore, Kentucky
Entry: **Fear of the Lord/God.**

Stephanie Smith Matthews, MTS, MA
Assistant Professor of Old Testament
School of Theology and Christian Ministry
Point Loma Nazarene University
San Diego, California
Entry: **Mercy.**

Wayne McCown, PhD
Provost Emeritus, Roberts Wesleyan College
Founding Dean Emeritus, Northeastern Seminary
Roberts Wesleyan College
Rochester, New York
Entry: **Titles of Jesus.**

Kevin Mellish, PhD
Professor of Biblical Studies
School of Theology and Christian Ministry
Olivet Nazarene University
Bourbonnais, Illinois
Entry: **Jerusalem.**

Marty Alan Michelson, PhD
Professor of Old Testament
Southern Nazarene University
Bethany, Oklahoma
Entries: **Sacred Persons; Wrath of God.**

James C. Miller, PhD
Professor of Inductive Biblical Study and New Testament
Director, Center for the Study of World Christian Revitalization Movements
Asbury Theological Seminary
Orlando, Florida
Entry: **Church, The.**

Mitchel Modine, PhD
Professor of Old Testament
Asia-Pacific Nazarene Theological Seminary
Taytay, Rizal, Philippines
Entry: **Names of God.**

Frank M. Moore, PhD
General Editor
Church of the Nazarene
Global Ministry Center
Lenexa, Kansas
Entry: **Church, Mission of the.**

Gift Mtukwa, MA (PhD Candidate, University of Manchester)
Lecturer in Biblical Literature
Africa Nazarene University
Pastor
University Church of the Nazarene
Nairobi, Kenya
Entries: **Antichrist; Repentance.**

Larry Murphy, PhD
Professor of Biblical Literature
School of Theology and Christian Ministry
Olivet Nazarene University
Bourbonnais, Illinois
Entry: **Gospel of Mark, Theology of.**

Zablon John Nthamburi, PhD
Professor of Theology
Academic Registrar
Africa Nazarene University
Nairobi, Kenya
Entry: **African Context, Biblical Hermeneutics in the.**

Christopher D. O'Brien, MA (PhD Candidate, Fuller Theological Seminary)
Adjunct Professor of Theology and Director of Field Education
Roberts Wesleyan College
Rochester, New York
College and Young Adult Pastor, Pearce Church
North Chili, New York
Entry: **Demonic/Devil.**

Oh, Won Keun, PhD
Senior Pastor
Dae-Kwang Church of the Nazarene
Pyeongtaek, South Korea
Entry: **Belief/Believe.**

B. J. Oropeza, PhD
Professor of Biblical and Religious Studies
Department of Biblical and Religious Studies
Azusa Pacific University
Azusa, California
Entry: **Pauline Theology.**

Thomas E. Phillips, PhD
Dean of the Library
Claremont School of Theology
Claremont, California
Entries: **Resurrection; Works.**

H. Junia Pokrifka, PhD
Professor of Old Testament
Department of Biblical Studies
William Carey International University
Pasadena, California
Entries: **Messiah/Christ; Women in the Old Testament.**

Samuel M. Powell, PhD
Professor of Philosophy and Theology
School of Theology and Christian Ministry
Point Loma Nazarene University
San Diego, California
Entry: **Progressive Revelation.**

Daniel G. Powers, PhD
Cochairman of the Bible and Theology Department
Nazarene Bible College
Colorado Springs, Colorado
Entry: **Household Codes.**

Paulson Pulikottil, PhD
Senior Pastor
The Community of the Redeemed
Pune, India
Entries: **Indian Hermeneutics; Suffering.**

Stephen Riley, PhD
Assistant Professor of Old Testament and Hebrew
Northwest Nazarene University
Nampa, Idaho
Entry: **Justice, Old Testament.**

C. Michael Robbins, PhD
Azusa, California
Entry: **Gospel of John, Theology of.**

Barry L. Ross, PhD
Emeritus Professor of Old Testament
School of Theology
Anderson University
Anderson, Indiana
Entries: **Isaiah, Theology of; Peace; Word of God/Yahweh, The.**

Carol Rotz, DLitt et Phil
Retired Missionary
Adjunct Professor
Northwest Nazarene University
Nampa, Idaho
Entry: **Jesus's Ministry.**

David B. Schreiner, PhD
Assistant Professor of Old Testament
Wesley Biblical Seminary
Jackson, Mississippi
Entries: **Inheritance; Wilderness, Theology of.**

C. Jeanne Orjala Serrão, PhD
Professor of Biblical Literature
Dean, School of Theology and Philosophy
Mount Vernon Nazarene University
Mount Vernon, Ohio
Entry: **Hope.**

Brian C. Small, PhD
Pastor
Grand Rivers Pisgah United Methodist Church
Grand Rivers, Kentucky
Entry: **Hebrews, Theology of.**

David F. Smith, PhD
Professor of New Testament
School of Theology and Ministry
Indiana Wesleyan University
Marion, Indiana
Entry: **Slavery.**

Dan Spross, PhD
Emeritus Professor of Biblical Theology and Interpretation
Trevecca Nazarene University
Nashville, Tennessee
Entry: **Biblical Theology.**

Jeffrey Stackert, PhD
Associate Professor of Hebrew Bible
The Divinity School; also the College
University of Chicago
Chicago, Illinois
Entry: **Torah (Law, Instruction).**

Daryll Gordon Stanton, EdD
Senior Lecturer
Chair of the Department of Religion
Africa Nazarene University
Nairobi, Kenya
Entry: **Obedience.**

Lawson G. Stone, PhD
Professor of Old Testament
Asbury Theological Seminary
Wilmore, Kentucky
Entry: **Deuteronomic Theology.**

Jirair S. Tashjian, PhD
Professor Emeritus of New Testament
Southern Nazarene University
Bethany, Oklahoma
Entry: **Gifts of the Spirit.**

Richard P. Thompson, PhD
Professor of New Testament
Chair, Department of Philosophy and Religion
Director, Wesley Center Online
School of Theology and Christian Ministries
Northwest Nazarene University
Nampa, Idaho
Entries: **Luke-Acts, Theology of; Reader-Response Hermeneutics.**

Stéphane Tibi, MDiv
Eurasia Regional Education Coordinator
Church of the Nazarene
Büsingen am Hochrhein, Germany
Entry: **Holy Warfare.**

Külli Tõniste, PhD
Assistant Professor in Biblical Studies and Theology
Baltic Methodist Theological Seminary
Tallinn, Estonia
Entry: **Intertextuality, Hermeneutics of.**

Al Truesdale, PhD
Emeritus Professor of Philosophy of Religion and Christian Ethics
Nazarene Theological Seminary
Kansas City, Missouri
Entries: **Providence of God; Sin.**

Alex Varughese, PhD
Emeritus Professor of Old Testament
Mount Vernon Nazarene University
Mount Vernon, Ohio
Entry: **Jeremiah, Theology of.**

Robert W. Wall, ThD
Paul T. Walls Professor of Scripture and Wesleyan Studies
Seattle Pacific Seminary
Seattle Pacific University
Seattle, Washington
Entry: **Canonical Hermeneutics.**

Kenneth L. Waters Sr., PhD
Professor of New Testament
Associate Dean, Division of Religion and Philosophy
Associate Chaplain
Azusa Pacific University
Azusa, California
Entry: **Humility.**

Sarah Whittle, PhD, FHEA
Lecturer in Biblical Studies
Nazarene Theological College
Manchester, United Kingdom
Entry: **Justification.**

Wi, Mi Ja, PhD
Lecturer in Biblical Studies and Global Mission
Nazarene Theological College
Manchester, United Kingdom
Entry: **Asian Hermeneutics.**

Scott A. Williams, MA (PhD Student, Claremont School of Theology)
Associate Pastor
Foothill Community Free Methodist Church
Azusa, California
Entry: **Glory.**

Karen Strand Winslow, PhD
Professor of Biblical Studies
Chair of Biblical and Theological Studies
Director, Master of Arts (Theological Studies) Program
Azusa Pacific Seminary
Azusa Pacific University
Azusa, California
Entries: **Cosmology; Women's Roles in the Church.**

ENCYCLOPEDIA TOPICS
BY CATEGORY

BIBLE, GENERAL

Call of God
Creation
Eschatology
Faith
Forgiveness, The Art and Necessity of
Glory
Holy
    See Holiness; Holy Spirit; Holy
    Warfare.
Idolatry
Image of God
Inheritance
Judgment
Kingdom of God/Heaven
Law
    See Jesus and the Law; Torah (Law,
    Instruction).
Matriarchs
Obedience
Redeem/Redeemer
Repentance
Rest
Righteousness
Savior
Spirit
    See Holy Spirit.
Temptation/Test
Time(s)
    See Sacred Times.
Victory
    See Jesus's Victory over Sin and
    Death.
Word of God/Yahweh, The

BIBLE, NEW TESTAMENT

Afterlife
Antichrist
Confession

Demonic/Devil
Gifts of the Spirit
Gospel
Holy Spirit
Holy Warfare
Justice, New Testament
Justification
Reconciliation
Regeneration/Rebirth
Resurrection
Saints/Holy Ones
Spirit
    See Holy Spirit.
Witness of the Spirit
Women Leaders

BIBLE, OLD TESTAMENT

Clean/Unclean
Cosmology
Covenant
Fall, The
Fear of the Lord/God
Jerusalem
Justice, Old Testament
Names of God
Prophets/Prophecy
Remnant
Retribution
Women in the Old Testament
Wrath of God

CHURCH AND CULTURE

Biblical Ethics
Church, Mission of the
Communal Holiness
Discipleship
Ethics
    See Biblical Ethics.
Honor-Shame Culture

Household Codes
Leadership
Patronage System
Poor/Poverty
Slavery
Women's Roles in the Church

HERMENEUTICS

African Context, Biblical Hermeneutics
in the
Asian Hermeneutics
Canonical Hermeneutics
Caribbean Hermeneutics
Feminist Hermeneutics
Indian Hermeneutics
Intertextuality, Hermeneutics of
Latin American Hermeneutics
Missional Hermeneutics
Reader-Response Hermeneutics
Theological Interpretation
Wesleyan Hermeneutics

HUMAN QUALITIES

Compassion
Completeness/Integrity
Conscience
Corporate Responsibility
Free Will
Humility
Integrity
    See Completeness/Integrity.
Remembering

JESUS

Incarnation
Jesus and the Law
Jesus's Ministry
Jesus's Victory over Sin and Death
Messiah/Christ
Miracles of Jesus
Parousia
Second Coming
    See Parousia.
Sermon on the Mount
Titles of Jesus

RELIGIOUS ACTIVITIES

Divination
Fasting

Festivals
Sacrificial System

SACRED

Sacred Persons
Sacred Space
Sacred Times

THEOLOGY

Biblical Theology
Church, The
Election
Ethics
    See Biblical Ethics.
Evil
Inspiration of Scripture, Wesleyan
    Understanding of
Land, Theology of the
Marriage
Peace
Predestination
Progressive Revelation
Providence of God
Revelation
    See Progressive Revelation.
Sanctification
Suffering
Wilderness, Theology of
Wisdom, Theology of
Works

THEOLOGY OF BOOKS OR EPISTLES

Deuteronomic Theology
Gospel of John, Theology of
Gospel of Mark, Theology of
Gospel of Matthew, Theology of
Hebrews, Theology of
Isaiah, Theology of
Jeremiah, Theology of
Luke-Acts, Theology of
Pauline Theology
Peter, 1 and 2, Theology of
Torah (Law, Instruction)

WORD STUDIES

Belief/Believe ('āman, pisteuō)
Completeness/Integrity (tōm)
Godliness/Godly (ḥāsîd, eusebeia)

Grace (*ḥēn, charis*)

Hate (*śānē', miseō*)

Helper (*'ēzer*)

Holiness (*qdš, hagios*)

Hope (*elpis*)

Love (*'āhab, ḥesed, agapaō, phileō*)

Mercy (*eleos, eleeō*)

Parousia (*parousia*)

Sin (*ḥāṭā', pāša', 'āwōn, hamartia, adikia*)

ABBREVIATIONS*

GENERAL

AD	anno Domini (precedes date; equivalent to CE)
ANE	ancient Near East
AT	author's translation
BC	before Christ (follows date; equivalent to BCE)
BCE	before the Common Era
bk.	book
ca.	circa, about
CE	Common Era
cf.	*confer*, compare
ch(s).	chapter(s)
col(s).	column(s)
d.	died
e.g.	*exempli gratia*, for example
esp.	especially
etc.	*et cetera*, and the rest
f(f).	and the following one(s)
Fr.	French
Ger.	German
Gk.	Greek
HB	Hebrew Bible
Hebr.	Hebrew
i.e.	*id est*, that is
Lat.	Latin
lit.	literally
LXX	Septuagint
MS(S)	Manuscript(s)
MT	Masoretic Text (of the OT)
n(n).	note(s)
n.d.	no date
n.p.	no place; no publisher; no page
NT	New Testament
OT	Old Testament
para.	paragraph
pl.	plural
sec.	section
sg.	singular
s.v.	*sub verbo*, under the word
v(v).	verse(s)
x	following a number, times
YHWH	four consonant letters for the divine name transliterated Yahweh

---

*Abbreviations based on those given in *The SBL Handbook of Style*, ed. Patrick H. Alexander et al. (Peabody, MA: Hendrickson, 1999).

BIBLE TRANSLATIONS

AT	author's translation
CEB	Common English Bible
DRA	Douay-Rheims
ESV	English Standard Version
KJV	King James Version
NABRE	New American Bible (Revised Edition)
NASB	New American Standard Bible
NET	NET Bible (New English Translation)
NIV	New International Version
NKJV	New King James Version
NLT	New Living Translation
NRSV	New Revised Standard Version
RSV	Revised Standard Bible

PRINT CONVENTIONS

Bold font   refers to other encyclopedia topics

COMMENTARIES, DICTIONARIES, AND SERIES

AB   Anchor Bible.

ABD   *Anchor Bible Dictionary*. Edited by D. N. Freedman. 6 vols. New York: Doubleday, 1992.

ANTC   Abingdon New Testament Commentaries.

AOTC   Abingdon Old Testament Commentaries.

BEB   *Baker Encyclopedia of the Bible*. Edited by W. A. Elwell. 2 vols. Grand Rapids: Baker Book House, 1988.

DLNT   *Dictionary of the Later New Testament and Its Developments*. Edited by R. P. Martin and P. H. Davids. Downers Grove, IL: InterVarsity Press, 1997.

DPL   *Dictionary of Paul and His Letters*. Edited by G. F. Hawthorne and R. P. Martin. Downers Grove, IL: InterVarsity Press, 1993.

EDNT   *Exegetical Dictionary of the New Testament*. Edited by H. Balz and G. Schneider. 3 vols. Grand Rapids: Eerdmans, 1990-93.

FAT   Forschungen zum Alten Testament.

IBC   Interpretation: A Bible Commentary for Teaching and Preaching.

IDB   *The Interpreter's Dictionary of the Bible*. Edited by G. A. Buttrick. 4 vols. Nashville: Abingdon Press, 1962.

IDBSup *Interpreter's Dictionary of the Bible: Supplementary Volume*. Edited by K. Crim. Nashville: Abingdon Press, 1976.

ISBE   *International Standard Bible Encyclopedia*. Edited by G. W. Bromiley. 4 vols. Grand Rapids: Eerdmans, 1979-88.

JPSTC   Jewish Publication Society Torah Commentary.

JSNTSup Journal for the Study of the New Testament: Supplement Series.

JSOTSup Journal for the Study of the Old Testament: Supplement Series.

LBD   *Lexham Bible Dictionary*. Edited by J. D. Barry. Bellingham, WA: Lexham Press, 2015.

LTW   *Lexham Theological Wordbook*. Edited by D. Mangum, D. R. Brown, R. Klippenstein, and R. Hurst. Bellingham, WA: Lexham Press, 2014.

NBBC   New Beacon Bible Commentary.

NCBC   New Cambridge Bible Commentary.

NEAEHL   *The New Encyclopedia of Archaeological Excavations in the Holy Land*. Edited by E. Stern. 5 vols. Jerusalem: Israel Exploration Society, 1993–2008.

NIB   *The New Interpreter's Bible*.

NICNT   New International Commentary on the New Testament.

NICOT   New International Commentary on the Old Testament.

NIDB   *New Interpreter's Dictionary of the Bible*. Katharine Doob Sakenfield. 5 vols. Nashville: Abingdon Press, 2006-9.

NIDNTT   *New International Dictionary of New Testament Theology*. Edited by C. Brown. 4 vols. Grand Rapids: Zondervan, 1975-85.

NIDNTTE   *New International Dictionary of New Testament Theology and Exegesis*. Edited by M. Silva. 5 vols. Grand Rapids: Zondervan, 2014.

NIDOTTE   *New International Dictionary of Old Testament Theology and Exegesis*. Edited by W. A. VanGemeren. 5 vols. Grand Rapids: Zondervan, 1997.

NovTSup   Supplements to Novum Testamentum.

SBLMS   Society of Biblical Literature Monograph Series.

SNTSMS   Society for New Testament Studies Monograph Series.

TDNT   *Theological Dictionary of the New Testament*. Edited by G. Kittel and G. Friedrich. Translated by G. W. Bromiley. 10 vols. Grand Rapids: Eerdmans, 1964-76.

TDOT   *Theological Dictionary of the Old Testament*. Edited by G. J. Botterweck, H. Ringgren, and H. Fabry. Translated by J. T. Willis, G. W. Bromiley, D. E. Green, D. W. Stott. 15 vols. Grand Rapids: Eerdmans, 1974–.

TLNT   *Theological Lexicon of the New Testament*. C. Spicq. Translated and edited by J. D. Ernest. 3 vols. Peabody, MA: Hendrickson, 1994.

TLOT   *Theological Lexicon of the Old Testament*. Edited by E. Jenni, with assistance from C. Westermann. Translated by M. E. Biddle. 3 vols. Peabody, MA: Hendrickson, 1997.

TWOT   *Theological Wordbook of the Old Testament*. Edited by R. L. Harris and G. L. Archer Jr. 2 vols. Chicago: Moody Press, 1980.

VTSup   Supplements to Vetus Testamentum.

WBC   Word Biblical Commentary.

WUNT   Wissenschaftliche Untersuchungen zum Neuen Testament.

JOURNALS

BiBh   *Bible Bhashyam*

BibInt   *Biblical Interpretation*

BR   *Biblical Research*

BTB   *Biblical Theology Bulletin*

CBQ   *Catholic Biblical Quarterly*

CurTM   *Currents in Theology and Mission*

IJT   *Indian Journal of Theology*

JAOS   *Journal of the American Oriental Society*

JBL   *Journal of Biblical Literature*

Jeev   *Jeevadhara*

JSNT   *Journal for the Study of the New Testament*

JTI   *Journal of Theological Interpretation*

JTS   *Journal of Theological Studies*

TynBul   *Tyndale Bulletin*

VT   *Vetus Testamentum*

ABBREVIATIONS FOR THE BOOKS OF THE BIBLE

Old Testament

Gen.	Genesis	Neh.	Nehemiah	Hos.	Hosea
Exod.	Exodus	Esther	Esther	Joel	Joel
Lev.	Leviticus	Job	Job	Amos	Amos
Num.	Numbers	Ps. (pl. Pss.)	Psalms	Obad.	Obadiah
Deut.	Deuteronomy	Prov.	Proverbs	Jon.	Jonah
Josh.	Joshua	Eccles.	Ecclesiastes	Mic.	Micah
Judg.	Judges	Song of Sol.	Song of Songs	Nah.	Nahum
Ruth	Ruth	Isa.	Isaiah	Hab.	Habakkuk
1–2 Sam.	1–2 Samuel	Jer.	Jeremiah	Zeph.	Zephaniah
1–2 Kings	1–2 Kings	Lam.	Lamentations	Hag.	Haggai
1–2 Chron.	1–2 Chronicles	Ezek.	Ezekiel	Zech.	Zechariah
Ezra	Ezra	Dan.	Daniel	Mal.	Malachi

New Testament

Matt.	Matthew	Gal.	Galatians	Phlm.	Philemon
Mark	Mark	Eph.	Ephesians	Heb.	Hebrews
Luke	Luke	Phil.	Philippians	James	James
John	John	Col.	Colossians	1–2 Pet.	1–2 Peter
Acts	Acts	1–2 Thess.	1–2 Thessalonians	1–2–3 John	1–2–3 John
Rom.	Romans			Jude	Jude
1–2 Cor.	1–2 Corinthians	1–2 Tim.	1–2 Timothy	Rev.	Revelation
		Titus	Titus		

APOCRYPHA

1–2 Esd.	1–2 Esdras
1–2 Macc.	1–2 Maccabees
Sir.	Sirach/Ecclesiasticus
Wis.	Wisdom of Solomon

OLD TESTAMENT PSEUDEPIGRAPHA

2 Bar.	2 Baruch (Syriac Apocalypse)
1 En.	1 Enoch (Ethiopic Apocalypse)
2 En.	2 Enoch (Slavonic Apocalypse)
Jos. Asen.	Joseph and Aseneth
Jub.	Jubilees
L.A.B.	Liber antiquitatum biblicarum (Pseudo-Philo)

DEAD SEA SCROLLS

1Qap Gen	Genesis Apocryphon
1QM	Milḥamah or War Scroll
1QS	Serek Hayaḥad or Rule of the Community
4Q394	Miqṣat Ma'aśê ha-Torah
4Q510	Shirot or Songs of the Sage

JOSEPHUS

Ant.	Jewish Antiquities

APOSTOLIC FATHERS

Mart. Pol.   *Martyrdom of Polycarp*

OTHER ANCIENT WRITINGS

Appian
  Bell. civ.   *Bella civilia*
Aristotle
  Gen. an.   *De generatione animalium*
  Part. an.   *De partibus animalium*
  Pol.   *Politica*
Plato
  Tim.   *Timaeus*
Plutarch
  Phoc.   *Phocion*
  Reg. imp.   *Regnum et imperatorum apophthegmata*
    apophth.
Xenophon
  Hell.   *Hellenica*

TRANSLITERATION OF HEBREW AND GREEK

Hebrew Consonant Transliteration

Hebrew/ Aramaic	Letter	English
א	*alef*	ʾ
ב	*bet*	*b*
ג	*gimel*	*g*
ד	*dalet*	*d*
ה	*he*	*h*
ו	*vav*	*v* or *w*
ז	*zayin*	*z*
ח	*khet*	*ḥ*
ט	*tet*	*ṭ*
י	*yod*	*y*
כ/ך	*kaf*	*k*
ל	*lamed*	*l*
מ/ם	*mem*	*m*
נ/ן	*nun*	*n*
ס	*samek*	*s*
ע	*ayin*	ʿ
פ/ף	*pe*	*p; f* (spirant)
צ/ץ	*tsade*	*ṣ*
ק	*qof*	*q*
ר	*resh*	*r*
שׂ	*sin*	*ś*
שׁ	*shin*	*š*
ת	*tav*	*t; th* (spirant)

Greek Transliteration

Greek	Letter	English
α	*alpha*	*a*
β	*bēta*	*b*
γ	*gamma*	*g*
γ	*gamma nasal*	*n* (before γ, κ, ξ, χ)
δ	*delta*	*d*
ε	*epsilon*	*e*
ζ	*zēta*	*z*
η	*ēta*	*ē*
θ	*thēta*	*th*
ι	*iōta*	*i*
κ	*kappa*	*k*
λ	*lambda*	*l*
μ	*mu*	*m*
ν	*nu*	*n*
ξ	*xi*	*x*
ο	*omicron*	*o*
π	*pi*	*p*
ρ	*rhō*	*r*
ρ	initial *rhō*	*rh*
σ/ς	*sigma*	*s*
τ	*tau*	*t*
υ	*upsilon*	*y*
υ	*upsilon*	*u* (in diphthongs: *au, eu, ēu, ou, ui*)
φ	*phi*	*ph*
χ	*chi*	*ch*
ψ	*psi*	*ps*
ω	*ōmega*	*ō*
ʽ	rough breathing	*h* (before initial vowels or diphthongs)

INTRODUCING THE WESLEYAN HERMENEUTICAL TRADITION

In many ways John Wesley (1703-91) was a man of his time. He was an Anglican priest with Protestant views about the Bible, its divine inspiration, and its authority for the church's faith and practice. Yet he was also Catholic in his valuing of the teachings of the early church fathers. Wesley was a child of the Enlightenment, accepting that what one believed should be intellectually reasonable in matters of science as well as in matters of faith and the interpretation of Scripture. However, Wesley rejected the Church of England's Calvinist theology of predestination. Instead, he followed the teaching of Jacobus Arminius that all people receive prevenient grace by the Holy Spirit, which enables them to respond to God and God's gift of salvation.

Although Wesley was a product of his day, his theological emphases inherently provided a starting point for interpreting Scripture different from that of others. While Calvinist interpretations of the Bible were deeply influenced by the theological emphasis on God's sovereignty, Wesley maintained that the ultimate purpose of Scripture is to bring all humanity to salvation. Wesley understood all Scripture in general to be soteriological in focus: the entire Bible, from Genesis to Revelation, reveals God's saving work that calls all persons to repentance, reconciliation, and forgiveness.

Of crucial importance to Wesley was an understanding of the Bible as the church's "rule of faith" or, as he put it, the "analogy of faith." Many Protestants tended to emphasize New Testament teachings over those of the Old Testament, but Wesley insisted on a return to a more literal or plain sense of Scripture, which was based on the *whole* Christian Bible—that is, *both* Testaments. Not unaware of differences between specific texts (e.g., the four Gospels) or Testaments, he contended there to be core theological themes that were found throughout the Christian canon: justification and sanctification, divine grace, love for God and others, and holiness of heart and life. Wesley described such themes as a "way of salvation," since it was God's grace that would lead to holy living. Thus a significant characteristic of a Wesleyan approach to biblical interpretation is the earnest search for potential meaning(s) from a biblical passage that may call for or challenge a special understanding of salvation (i.e., holy living) among Wesleyan worshippers.

Wesley's views on God's guidance of the biblical authors reflected orthodox positions of his day. He affirmed God's inspiration or the "assistance" of the Holy Spirit, so that God's message was faithfully transmitted by those writers. At the same time, Wesley also noted the *human* role of those same authors in the writing of the biblical texts, seeing the texts as products of the collaboration between God and human authors. This accounts for differences in wording, literary style, and personality that appear in various texts, as well as many Old Testament texts that may have been written over extended periods by several authors. Although Wesley affirmed the trustworthiness of Scripture despite some challenges that came with the early rise of historical criticism, he also welcomed the scholarly historical-critical study of the Bible, since his own work appropriated both textual-critical and historical methods to interpret selected passages.

Whereas many theological traditions emphasize the important role of divine inspiration in the origin of the biblical texts, Wesley took this matter one step further. In his comments on 2 Timothy 3:16-17 in his *Explanatory Notes upon the New Testament*, he declared that readers of the Bible also need the same Spirit both to help them understand what they are reading and to bring that same passage alive in their contemporary setting. In other words, as important as the inspiration of biblical authors may be for the trustworthiness of the Bible, Wesley also contended that church readers need similar assistance from the Spirit to hear the Scriptures speak again in a fresh way for a new day. Some describe this as "double inspiration," since this depicts inspiration in a dual sense: initially, when the writing occurred, and then, at the time of reading. Each instance of inspiration may be deemed both distinct and contextual. Both relate to the same text, but, like God's breath in the first human (Gen. 2:7), both require God's Spirit to breathe life into the words for them to speak effectively in different contexts. From Wesley's perspective, the Spirit enables readers of Scripture, within the context of the church, to hear a divine word through these sacred texts—a word that may guide them in living a holy life. Such a word would speak to their situation and culture in life. Such a fresh meaning of Scripture would also be in keeping with reason, which would help them understand God's gift of salvation, redemption, holiness, and sanctification.

Interpretive approaches to Scripture that focus on pastoral concerns and emphasize the readers' response in living more than their acquisition of mere biblical knowledge correspond with Wesley's consideration of experience within the realm of salvation. Wesley was not interested in interpretations that merely offered new ways to speak about old biblical words. His concern was that interpretations of Scripture would lead to the experience of God's grace in one's life and, therefore, holy living. Wesley also allowed for the possibility that the church's collective experience might clarify how Scripture has been interpreted.

But since experience is often varied in nature, Wesley stressed the importance of reading and discussing Scripture with others (e.g., Sermon 39, "Catholic Spirit," sec. 1, para. 4).

Much has changed in the methods and practices of biblical interpretation since Wesley's day. Yet his theological descendants are indebted to him for theological and interpretive trajectories that still shape and define aspects of the Wesleyan biblical-hermeneutical tradition, despite diverse methods that arise out of contemporary biblical scholarship.

First, the Wesleyan emphasis on the role of the Spirit within the reading and interpretive process reimagines reading and study as an encounter with God. Modern interpretive approaches tend to objectify the biblical text. But the Wesleyan tradition has long affirmed what contemporary approaches now recognize: interpretation involves more than just the biblical text and an uninfluenced reader. Rather, readers of Scripture must be open to the Spirit of God speaking through these texts and not be merely intent on understanding the "words on the page." Such interpretation will not ignore textual details but will also account for other *extratextual* contributions to the process.

Second (and related to the first), the Wesleyan emphasis on the Spirit's work within the church accentuates the context of reading Scripture *as* the church. The Wesleyan hermeneutical tradition recognizes and understands its context, which shapes these readings of Scripture (see above). Thus it recognizes that the Christian canon addresses the people of God to help form and shape them as God's people, to instruct them about how to treat one another as God's people, and to guide them in dealing with other peoples.

Third, the Wesleyan hermeneutical tradition assumes that the outcome and confirmation of the interpretation of the Bible is the faithful response to sacred Scripture by its interpreters. Interpretation is more than merely the rearticulation of what a passage could mean; it is ultimately a faithful response to God's grace, to which the Scriptures give witness, as the church embodies that grace in its ongoing life of holiness, characterized by love: love of God and love of others.

Richard P. Thompson, PhD
Professor of New Testament
Chair, Department of Philosophy and Religion
Director, Wesley Center Online
School of Theology and Christian Ministries
Northwest Nazarene University
Nampa, Idaho

Robert D. Branson, PhD
Emeritus Professor of Biblical Literature
Olivet Nazarene University
Bourbonnais, Illinois

Aa

AFRICAN CONTEXT, BIBLICAL HERMENEUTICS IN THE

Hermeneutics is the science of studying passages of the Bible within their proper contexts in order to derive the intended meaning. Context is crucial to the understanding of a biblical passage. Context in this instance refers to historical, structural, cultural, and linguistic settings. Context also infers that we must interpret a passage in the light of the whole biblical book and indeed the entire Bible. It is Scripture that sheds light on other passages of Scripture. Hermeneutics helps us to approximate the intended meaning and phraseology of the original author and to avoid using the lens of our own individual bias when reading the Bible.

The OT is closer to the African context than is the NT. Stories from the OT are more easily understood by Africans, since their worldview is similar to that encountered in OT times. Books such as the Psalms, Proverbs, Prophetic Books, and 1 and 2 Kings draw an immediate symbolic parallel with the African religious milieu.

The hermeneutical task, however, demands that when a translator translates the Bible into African languages, he or she must use cultural tools. Many of the original translations, however, were done by missionaries who at times were not well versed with the indigenous languages, metaphors, idioms, and cultures. For instance, translating the term "God" according to the cultural understanding of a supreme deity has led many times to mistaken renderings, resulting in the misunderstanding of the whole concept.

The Bible describes people who were from different cultural backgrounds: herders, agriculturists, city dwellers, village folks. Some were **slaves**, and others were rulers. In biblical interpretation we need first to place ourselves in their cultural modes. Then using the cultural parallels with our own contemporary setting, the text of the Bible may be translated with more meaning for our situation.

African Christians understand that when they read the Bible, they are entering into a long period of Christian tradition during which time the canon was developed and was brought to a close. They recognize it as truly the inspired **Word of God**. Following the Christian tradition concerning the efficacy of the canon and the realization that Christian councils put a stamp of authority on every stage of its development, the Bible becomes the inspired Word of God that has authority above indigenous traditions. It is not just literature but is foremost the inspired Word, which is authoritative for African Christians and as such influences their human endeavors and existence.

Being God's self-revelation to humankind, the Bible becomes a norm by which African Christians reflect their relationship with God and with each other. In this sense **inspiration** does not mean that they take the Bible literally or irrationally, but it means they must expect to discover God's challenges to them and to find meaning for their lives and **hopes**.

Vernacular Translations of Scripture

The Bible has been translated into many African languages. The translation of the Bible continues to be an important task in evangelization. It becomes the medium through which biblical hermeneutics is promulgated at the grass roots, because translation carries with it the process of enculturation as a way of acquiring exegetical skills. This process exposes the Bible to the practices of the local culture and worldview. For in the process of translation, African views become the medium of expressing deep biblical truths about God and our relationship to God and humanity. Indigenous concepts have to be discovered as well as local words for "God" and "divine mystery." The importance of the Bible to African communities cannot be overestimated. Often, portions of the Bible became the prime readers for literacy. Through the translated Scriptures, God addresses people in their own language, using their own metaphors. Africans identify with this God who reveals himself through their language as one who is concerned about their history, well-being, and future.

David Barrett detects a certain hermeneutical independence when the Bible is translated into local languages. He draws a link between the translation of the Bible and the initiation of some indigenous churches. In communities where the complete Bible has been translated, more indigenous churches appear to have emerged. The main reason is that translation helps a particular community grasp the deepest meaning of a biblical passage and thus transform it into a deeper theological manifestation (1968, 109).

The Bible is highly esteemed by the African Christian community and provides a strong medium through which Christian **faith** is propagated. Its authority has penetrated deep into the spiritual, cultural, and social life of African communities that are pervaded by a strong conviction that the **Holy Spirit** gives ordinary people **wisdom** and power to interpret the Bible as well as discern its deeper spiritual meaning. Many **believe** that everything in the Bible is true and reliable. They have, particularly within charismatic groups, a special yearning for mystical experiences. The hermeneutical task in the translation of Scripture tries to bridge the historical, cultural, and linguistic gaps that would inevitably hinder a reader from drawing out the actual and authentic meaning of a passage.

Pneumatology in African Hermeneutics

Many of the African churches (including locally instituted churches) have a bias toward Pentecostalism. The Holy Spirit features prominently in many sermons and Bible study sessions. Their theological orientation is tinged with Pentecostal traits. The Holy Spirit manifests himself in dreams, visions, prophecies, healing, and worship. Charismatic **gifts of the Spirit** inspire Christians to serve others through their devotion in evangelism, **repentance**, and the building up of the community of believers (Gk., *koinōnia*). The Spirit makes it possible for people from different socioeconomic and cultural backgrounds to hear the Word of God speak to them in their natural surroundings.

Through the prompting of the Holy Spirit, the African churches have endeavored to interpret the Bible in order to make it more relevant to their communities in their contemporary situations. Although Africans accept and revere the centrality of Jesus Christ, they are inextricably linked to the cultural and religious traditions that inform their values, insights, and philosophical traits. These values are incorporated in exegetical practices in an attempt to bring out genuine African interpretations. For the biblical exegete to be true to the task, he or she must place the text in its historical context and also do the hermeneutical work of placing it in the contemporary situation.

The Spirit of God leads interpreters to unfold the mysteries of the Bible for the situation of the hearer instead of trying to transpose the hearer into the times of the Bible. Preachers in African-instituted churches have learned skills to apply biblical texts to the real-life situations of the people. Their hearers thereby readily identify themselves with the message and try to discern the will of God. In such free interpretation of the Bible lies the danger of the preacher reading into the passage his or her own thoughts rather than reading the meaning out of the passage.

The Bible has had great influence even among people with little or no religious inclination. Being a relatively new phenomenon in many parts of Africa (translations belong to the nineteenth and twentieth centuries, during the era of modern Christian missions), the Bible has influenced many communities, some of which are not yet Christian. What has captured the imagination of many people is the Bible's bias for **justice,** popularly known as the "option for the **poor**." Jesus's mission has been understood to mean that he came to emancipate all those who find themselves on the periphery of society. The proclamation of the **gospel** leads to the wholeness of life, for the gospel cannot be complete in a situation where injustice (social and economic) prevails.

Centrality of Scripture

To the church in Africa, the Bible is the central and primary source of God's revelation. The OT appears to be more popular than does the NT, even though the parables and miracle stories are given special prominence. The Epistle of James has strong appeal to African preachers because it portrays the importance of applying faith to daily living. In it they see the practical struggle between light and darkness, faith and unbelief, **sacred** and profane.

The exodus motif has been used by many groups, particularly within the African-instituted churches. They believe that just as God liberated the Israelites in their hour of need, he will likewise liberate those undergoing perilous moments. The Bible is depicted as a book that supports and upholds what is appropriate within the African traditions and practices. The example of Jesus healing others has taken a central place in worship because wholeness is juxtaposed with **holiness**. In order to be **holy**, one has to be made whole; Jesus must **forgive sins** before performing an act of healing.

African-Instituted Churches

Among the African-instituted churches, the Bible is often interpreted freely in sermons. Sermons are teaching sessions, and a three-hour sermon is not unusual. For example, an elder from an African-instituted church in Nairobi, Kenya, preached a sermon based on Exodus 4, concerning the calling of Moses. He described the background of the text, explaining Moses's upbringing as that of a prince in Pharaoh's court, emphasizing that Moses was brought up by royalty and lacked nothing. He was, therefore, reluctant to answer God's call to liberate his people from bondage. The elder reminded the congregation members that they, too, were in bondage in various ways. Some were unemployed, lacked a good education, or did not have decent shelter. Some lacked food, while others were sick. He reminded them that they needed a Moses in their midst. God had heard their cries and would soon send a Moses if they fixed their faith and trust in him. Many people were able to identify with the message that addressed their contemporary situations. The elder's hermeneutical interpretation was a rereading of the biblical text within an existential context that made the biblical message relevant and real.

Another exposition was done on John 4:1-42. Verse 12 was highlighted because it mentioned ancestors. In Africa ancestral veneration is strong. The Samaritan woman valued her ancestors, whose deeds and heroic benevolence were worthy of remembrance. The concept of ancestor worship held the key to the interpretation of the story. The reference to Jacob as an ancestor depicted the woman's devotion and reverence to her culture and tradition. Jesus succeeded in demonstrating that in line with ancestor Jacob, he brought life to those who encountered him.

The preacher emphasized that the people must hold on to Jesus as their proto-ancestor just as their forefathers held on to their ancestors for sustenance. The African Christians' experience of ancestorhood makes them feel that they are indeed part of the great Christian family with a rich heritage.

Conclusion

When Africans read the Bible, there are certain themes that become of greater interest: the themes of healing and wholeness, physical and spiritual well-being, the reality of sin and its alienation, curses and blessings, and the need to seek holiness. The theme of justice in the midst of oppression is also becoming prominent.

Biblical hermeneutics in Africa involves the art of demonstrating that the Bible is a living and practical book; hence Bible study cannot be meaningful unless there is practical life experience. In the Bible, Africans experience the acts of God that impinge on their lives in a mundane and practical manner.

While it can be said that Africans respond to the biblical message within their socioeconomic and religious milieu, the message is dynamic and influences the whole community. African Christians will continue to interpret the Bible within their own context, since God speaks to them directly using their language, idioms, metaphors, and culture. The Bible is alive in Africa. It continues to influence and transform the lives of individuals and communities.

Resources

Barrett, David B. *Schism and Renewal in Africa: An Analysis of Six Thousand Contemporary Religious Movements.* Nairobi, KE: Oxford Press, 1968.

Bujo, Bénézet. *African Theology in the 21st Century: The Contribution of the Pioneers.* Nairobi, KE: Paulines Publications, 2003.

Daneel, M. L. "African Independent Church Pneumatology and the Salvation of All Creation." *International Review of Missions* 82, no. 326 (1993): 147.

Gibellini, Rosino. *Paths of African Theology.* Maryknoll, NY: Orbis Books, 1994.

Healey, Joseph, and Donald Sybertz. *Towards an African Narrative Theology.* Nairobi, KE: Paulines Publications, 1996.

Kanyoro, R. A. "Translation Research Strategy for Africa." *Bible Translator* 34, no. 1 (1983): 101.

Kemdirim, Protus. "The Samaritan Woman: An Apostle of Ancestorhood." *Voice from the Third World: Interfaith Dialogue Listening to African Voices* 28, no. 2 (2005): 128.

Magesa, Laurenti. *Christian Ethics in Africa.* Nairobi, KE: Acton Publishers, 2002.

Nthamburi, Zablon. *The African Church at the Crossroads: A Strategy for Indigenization.* Nairobi, KE: Uzima Press, 1991.

Nthamburi, Zablon, and Douglas Waruta. "Biblical Hermeneutics in African Instituted Churches." Pages 40-57 in *The Bible in African Christianity.* Nairobi, KE: Acton Publishers, 1997.

Sanneh, Lamin. *Translating the Message: The Missionary Impact on Culture.* Maryknoll, NY: Orbis Books, 2009.

Setiloane, Gabriel. *African Theology: An Introduction.* Johannesburg, ZA: Skotaville Publishers, 1986.

Turner, Harold W. *Profile through Preaching: A Study of the Sermon Texts Used in a West African Independent Church.* London: Edinburgh House Press, 1965.

West, Gerald, and Musa Dube, eds. *The Bible in Africa: Transactions, Trajectories, and Trends.* Leiden, NL: E. J. Brill, 2000.

ZABLON JOHN NTHAMBURI, PHD

AFTERLIFE

The OT reflects an ancient Semitic view of spatial reality with three tiers: the realm of heaven, the realm of the living, and the realm of the dead. While their neighboring peoples were concerned with navigating the various influences that both the realm of heaven and the realm of the dead had on the realm in which they lived, the Israelites were called by Yahweh to keep their focus on life. The **Torah** prohibits the Israelites from the worship of other gods (Exod. 20:3; 34:14; Deut. 12:30-31) as well as from contacting the dead through mediums (Deut. 18:10-13). Although bodily contact with the deceased was obviously necessary to some extent, it rendered the living ritually **unclean** for a certain amount of days (see Num. 19:11-22). God's people were to be focused on God and on life.

And so the OT does not directly answer the question that many today ask: What happens when we, when I, die? It does, however, reflect a belief that life continues on beyond the grave.

The realm of the dead is referred to as *Sheol,* often translated into English as "the pit" (i.e., Ps. 30:9 [10 HB]), physically located in the depths of the earth. One of the most vivid pictures in the Bible is given in the book of Numbers, where the earth opens up and swallows alive the rebellious Korah, Dathan, and Abiram; their families; and all they own (16:27-33). Sheol is bleak and silent. Worms (Job 24:19-20) and decay (Ps. 16:10) are associated with it. Sheol's inhabitants are apathetic (Eccl. 9:10) and cannot praise God (Ps. 6:5 [6 HB]; 31:17 [18 HB]). And yet, Jonah can say that he cried out to the Lord from the depths of Sheol and was heard (Jon. 2:2 [3 HB]). And the psalmist proclaims that even if one would go down to Sheol, God would be present (Ps. 139:8).

Communication between the realm of the living and the realm of the dead is portrayed in the unique story of King Saul requiring a medium to call up Samuel in order to ask him for advice. While there are instances portrayed in the OT in which breath was returned to lifeless bodies (see 1 Kings 17:19-22; 2 Kings 4:32-36), in this situation Samuel did not return to life but communicated to King Saul from the realm of the dead (1 Sam. 28:3-25).

Later writers reflect a belief in postmortem **judgment** and a **resurrection** from Sheol. Daniel 12:2, perhaps reflecting Isaiah 25:8 and 26:19, indicates this succinctly: "Multitudes who sleep in the dust of the earth will awake:

some to everlasting life, others to shame and everlasting contempt" (NIV). These texts model the logical consequences of the OT belief in the **righteousness** and **mercy** of God in the face of extreme **suffering**. Despite the borders between life and death that humans experience, vindication will come for God's people who live according to God's heart.

This belief in an ultimate judgment and resurrection is also reflected in the writings of the NT. Jesus discussed the issue of resurrection with the Sadducees, who did not believe in a resurrection, claiming that those who had passed before were yet alive (Mark 12:18-27). The grieving Martha confessed her faith in the ultimate resurrection of her brother, Lazarus, when Jesus told her that her brother would live (John 11:23-24). The idea of an ultimate vindication of God's people is expressed with echoes of Daniel 7 and in Mark 13:24-27 (see also Matt. 24; Luke 21:25-28). The parables in Matthew 25 express this vindication as an ultimate judgment for all nations, in which the result is either happiness in the presence of God (vv. 23, 46b) or separation from God (vv. 30, 46a). The ultimate verdict is determined by how people use that which was entrusted to them (Luke 16:19-31).

While a modern reader might be sensitive to the temporal dimension of Jesus's response to the penitent criminal crucified with him ("today you will be with me in paradise" [Luke 23:43, NIV]), Luke's focus may be more on the words "with me." The request of the criminal had been for Jesus to remember him. Jesus's reply transcends mere remembrance; the man will actually be with Jesus. The Gospel narratives show Jesus consistently together with his followers. Death does not change this.

Paul affirmed the general resurrection on the basis of the resurrection of Jesus Christ. Because it had been confirmed by several witnesses that Jesus had indeed been resurrected, it could be deduced that all who belong to him will also be resurrected from the dead (1 Cor. 15:23). The body that is subject to decay will be removed in death, and a new body will be given that is not subject to decay. A resurrection without a body is unthinkable.

The biblical view of the afterlife cannot be separated from the total narrative of God's redemptive presence with humanity. Death is never portrayed in the Bible as a good thing. The various descriptions of Sheol in the OT attest to this. However, God is good and is portrayed consistently as faithful even beyond the grave. The God who covenants himself to humanity through Jesus Christ's death has covenanted himself to be with humanity through death into eternal life through the resurrection of Jesus Christ. While no human, including the biblical writers, has ever known exactly what will meet him or her on the other side of the grave, the biblical **faith** is that no human needs ever to make the transition alone.

See also Cosmology; Covenant; Creation; Hope; Remembering.

Resources

Clark-Soles, Jaime. *Death and the Afterlife in the New Testament.* New York: T and T Clark, 2006.

Johnston, Philip S. *Shades of Sheol: Death and Afterlife in the Old Testament.* Nottingham, UK: Apollos, 2002.

Raphael, Simcha Paull. *Jewish Views of the Afterlife.* 2nd ed. Lanham, MD: Rowman and Littlefield, 2009.

Wright, N. T. *Surprised by Hope: Rethinking Heaven, the Resurrection, and the Mission of the Church.* New York: HarperCollins, 2008.

GABI M. MARKUSSE-OVERDUIN, PHD

ANTICHRIST

The Greek word *antichristos* is made up of the prefix *anti* and the noun *christos* ("anointed one" or "**messiah**"). *Anti* can mean both "in the place of" and "against." It is related to *pseudochristos* (false Christ) and *antitheos* (against God).

Even though we do not have the word "antichrist" in the OT, the OT provides the background for NT usage. The **prophecy** of Daniel speaks of the beast that is against God (Dan. 7:25; 8:25). Daniel also foretold of the "abomination that causes desolation" (11:31, NIV) and described the actions of a king, an *antitheos*, most likely Antiochus IV Epiphanes, who would disregard God and his temple (vv. 31-38).

In the NT, Jesus warned his disciples that false messiahs and **prophets** would come. The Greek word translated "false messiahs" (Mark 13:22) is *pseudochristoi*, a variation of *antichristoi*. Paul warned that the "man of lawlessness" (*anthrōpos tēs anomias*), an agent of Satan, would exalt himself above God and take his position. However, even he is destined for destruction (2 Thess. 2:3, 8-12).

The word "antichrist" is only found in 1 and 2 John. John announced that many antichrists have already come (1 John 2:18) and that they denied that Jesus is the unique Son of God, the Christ (v. 22). They were led by a spirit that does not **believe** Jesus is from God (4:3), and they were deceivers (2 John v. 7). In contrast to the Synoptic **Gospels** and Paul's writings, there is not just one antichrist but a plurality of antichrists. These antichrists were not just against Christ but actually presumed to be Christ.

The concept of antichrists finds its fullest expression in the book of Revelation, where the beast becomes the "embodiment of **evil**." Revelation reflects the beast envisioned by Daniel, which is worshipped as a god by those who do not follow the Lamb of God (ch. 13). The dragon gives the beast its authority (v. 5). However, God and the Lamb have the final word on the fate of the beast and Satan behind it. **Wrath** awaits both Satan and those who follow him (17:11, 14).

Resources

Farrell, Hobert K., and Donald M. Lake. "Antichrist." Pages 118-19 in *BEB*.

Frankemölle, H. "*Anti*." Pages 108-9 in vol. 1 of *EDNT*.

Grundmann, Walter. "χρίω, χριστός, ἀντίχριστος, χρῖσμα, χριστιανός." Pages 493-580 in vol. 9 of *TDNT*.

Kauder, E. "ἀντίχριστος." Pages 124-26 in vol. 4 of *NIDNTT*.

Rist, M. "Antichrist." Pages 175-78 in vol. 1 of *IDB*.

Thielman, Frank. *Theology of the New Testament: A Canonical and Synthetic Approach*. Grand Rapids: Zondervan, 2005.

Williamson, Rick. *1, 2, and 3 John*. NBBC. Kansas City: Beacon Hill Press of Kansas City, 2010.

GIFT MTUKWA, MA

ASIAN HERMENEUTICS

In any quest of Asian biblical interpretation, one must acknowledge the cultural and religious diversity and the socioeconomic and historico-political complexity of Asia and its people. There are several contextual issues germane to Asian hermeneutics. First, Asia has long been a place with scriptures of major world religions (Hinduism, Buddhism, Islam), including highly developed philosophical teachings (Confucianism, Taoism) and a deep cultural heritage. Second, socioeconomic **poverty** and disparity is a day-to-day reality in many parts of Asia. Third, colonization by imperial powers is a shared experience of Asian countries.

Given these realities and the issues arising from them, Asian hermeneutics seeks to read the Bible in ways that are relevant to the Asian settings. At the same time, it uses Asian contexts to illuminate the Bible. Thus Asian biblical interpretation stresses dialogic ways of interacting between text and context, and transformative aspects of texts in praxis.

In reaction to Western critical hermeneutical methods and in search of indigenous Asian hermeneutics, Asian biblical interpreters have developed various approaches either reflecting Asia's past religio-cultural traditions or applying Asia's present contexts to interpret the Bible. In this article, five Asian hermeneutical approaches are discussed: (1) cross-textual; (2) cross-cultural; (3) contextual (liberation); (4) postcolonial; (5) Asian feminist.

Five Approaches in Asian Biblical Hermeneutics

Cross-Textual. The cross-textual approach seeks to put the Bible and Asian scriptures such as the Vedas (Hinduism) and the sutras (Buddhism) side by side as dialogical partners for mutual enrichment of the texts. Archie C. C. Lee, a proponent of cross-textual hermeneutics, argues that the Bible needs to be appropriated in the light of Asian religio-cultural texts in order to be read critically and relevantly in multi-scriptural Asian settings and to be reclaimed as an Asian scripture (2008). In doing so, the exclusiveness and authority of the Bible over against other texts is challenged. Thus the emphasis is shifted toward its relatedness to other texts in order to accommodate the Bible to Asian Christians and to broaden the dialogue from intrafaith among minority Christians to interfaith among diverse religious communities of Asia. For instance, the proximity of **wisdom** literature in the Hebrew Bible to Buddhist teachings is used to find common ground for interfaith dialogue. Similar texts or religious concepts of the Bible and other Asian texts are contrasted to illuminate the distinctiveness of the Bible.

Cross-textual hermeneutics is necessary and legitimate in multi-scriptural Asian settings because it encourages Christians to engage with the biblical texts to construct meanings through the Asian lens. However, there seems to be a huge distance between the cross-textual hermeneutics practiced by scholars and the approaches to the Bible practiced by ordinary Asian Christian Bible readers. The authority of the Bible is rarely challenged among Asian Christians. For some, their reading is akin to a Western fundamentalist approach that focuses on inerrancy. For others, it means that the Bible is the touchstone of doctrine and practice. Moreover, acknowledging religious texts of Asia as **sacred** to Asian Christian **faith** communities differs from placing the Bible as just one among many divinely inspired texts. Finally, cross-textual hermeneutics underestimates Asian people's oral religious traditions and marginalizes the less educated majority from religious dialogues due to highly academic approaches to the texts.

Cross-Cultural. The cross-cultural approach, taking the rich oral tradition and the illiterate reality of many people into account, recognizes that God has been speaking to Asians through Asia's cultural diversity. In its understanding of the biblical texts, cross-cultural hermeneutics seeks to read the Bible through cultural elements, such as folktales, tribal values, or Confucian ethos, many of which are in fact the underlying bases of Asian mentality. Similar to a cross-textual approach, it embraces Asian cultures to construct the meaning(s) of biblical texts relevant to Asians and to bridge the gap between the foreignness of Christianity and Asian identity by using vernacular traditions and popular teachings. For example, the Chinese creation myth is compared with the Genesis **creation** account (Gen. 1–2). The significance of benevolence in Confucianism is paralleled with *agapē* (Gk., "love") in Christianity. Ancestor worship in Korean and Chinese contexts, which was once indiscriminately condemned as pagan and idolatrous, is reappraised through critical engagements with the text and cultural settings of filial piety (cf. 1 Cor. 8). Community-oriented tribal values are also revisited in Asians' biblical reading.

With multicultural sensitivity, cross-cultural hermeneutics reassesses the Asian cultural heritage to shed fresh light on the meaning(s) of the Bible. Nevertheless, it tends to idealize the indigenous traditions and its uncritical use of cultural elements in biblical interpretation can result in syncretism. One of the key questions in using cross-textual and cross-cultural approaches is this: Does the Bible offer anything distinctive and unique? To be precise, is the Bible even necessary for Asians if the religious, philosophical, or cultural traditions of Asia provide sufficient answers to essential issues?

Contextual. The contextual (liberation) approach emerges in response to social, economic, and political situations of Asia in line with liberation theology in Latin America and black theology in Africa. The biblical **image of God** as the protector and liberator of the oppressed and Jesus's **suffering** and identification with the **poor** become keys for liberation hermeneutics as it particularly speaks to the experience of poverty and the socioeconomic disparity of Asian people. Thus liberation hermeneutics in Asia, such as the *minjung* (the powerless and dispossessed mass) in Korea, the *burakumin* (outcast and discriminated communities) in Japan, and the *dalit* (oppressed caste people) in India, applies the texts to Asian contexts or vice versa.

Minjung hermeneutics reads the Bible through the eyes of the oppressed minjung. Byung-Mu Ahn, while employing historical criticism in reading the Bible, understands the *ochlos* (Gk., "crowd") in Mark's Gospel who follow Jesus and with whom Jesus stands from the perspective of minjung in a Korean historico-political context. *Burakumin* are common village people, often referred to as an outcast group. The Japanese call them *eta*, which literally means "much pollution." Religious and cultural discrimination against them in terms of purity and impurity is challenged in the light of Jesus's identification with the so-called sinners in the Gospels.

Dalit hermeneutics in India reads the texts from the counter-Brahmanism or status quo perspective. In doing so, it not only seeks to liberate dalit people but also challenges the deeply rooted caste structure in India. M. Gnanavaram's reading of the Good Samaritan narrative (Luke 10) highlights the role of the religiously and culturally marginalized Samaritan in the story in comparison with the dalits in India (1993).

Asian liberation hermeneutics has developed in response to the experience of people situated in particular times and places of Asia. Thus it has its limitations when applied generally. Nevertheless, its effort to bring the marginalized into the subject of God's history continues to challenge the many oppressive realities in Asia.

Postcolonial. The postcolonial approach, strongly advocated by R. S. Sugirtharajah, emerges in Asian countries once colonized either by European powers or by imperial Japan. It employs a hermeneutics of suspicion that sees the Bible as a text loaded with colonial intentions. Sugirtharajah contends that the utmost goal of postcolonial hermeneutics is to identify the embedded colonial codes and ideologies that lie behind the text and to reconstruct meanings as articulated by the once-colonized (1999, 18-22). In doing this, it subverts the traditional meaning of the text. It differs from the previous three approaches because it is not looking for the meaning(s) of the text or the relevance of the text limited to particular Asian contexts. It rather concerns a new identity construction that is shaped through the interaction of values and ideas in the process of postcolonial reading.

Postcolonial scriptural reading finds the endorsement of assimilation in the Persian imperial context of the book of Esther. It also seeks to hear the protest voice that is overlooked or silenced. In its subversive reading of the parable of the tenants (Matt. 21; Mark 12; Luke 20), postcolonial hermeneutics brings the perspective of the tenants to the front. Hence, a postcolonial approach opens up the hermeneutical possibility of hearing an independent voice from Asian biblical interpreters as the third world's Bible readers.

Asian Feminist. Alongside postcolonial hermeneutics, the Asian feminist approach not only questions colonial ideology entangled in the texts but also underscores its interplay of gender, race, and colonial status. The history of colonization by imperial powers implicates sexual exploitation of Asian women. Due to their female and Asian identity, Asian Christian women face multilayered oppression in their reading of the Bible: (1) from patriarchal texts of the Bible; (2) from patriarchal contexts of their own culture and society, shaped by (neo-) Confucianism particularly in Korea where Christianity and biblical interpretation are deeply rooted in appreciating doubly patriarchal forces; and (3) from socioeconomic marginalization, in addition to the common colonized experience. In the context of this reality, Asian feminist hermeneutics seeks to decolonize and depatriarchalize the texts to construct liberative and counter-narrative readings.

With sensitivity to colonial power and gender, Asian feminist hermeneutics, on the one hand, draws particular attention to Gentile women such as Hagar, an Egyptian slave, and Rahab, a Canaanite prostitute. Kwok Pui-lan challenges the way in which race and sexuality are frequently symbolized as evil in the Bible. Kwok illustrates the story of Rahab (Josh. 2) as a typical example of the double colonization of woman read from the perspective of native women of the colonized nation (2005, 77-99). East Asian feminists read the Bible against the double suppression of women. Thus they find patriarchy to be the hermeneutical key to biblical interpretation. The proximity between patriarchy embedded in the Bible and Confucian ideology embedded in their culture is deployed in their analysis of the text. Most importantly, Asian feminist hermeneutics becomes more aware of hearing the voice of ordinary women and their telling of the biblical story.

Challenges in Asian Hermeneutics

In postmodern Asia, biblical interpretation is no longer simply a matter of overcoming the alienation between biblical texts and Asian religions or people. Globalization brings far more diversity to Asia. Asian hermeneutics needs to take seriously Asian diaspora communities across the world and a hybrid of Asian culture. With this, there remain several challenges.

First, the goal of Asian hermeneutics should not be to react against the global hermeneutical discourse but to contribute to it. The task for Asian Christians is to discover how to utilize various hermeneutical practices with their Asian-ness to enrich the global community.

Second, the formation of Christian identity in the process of doing Asian hermeneutics is important. The question is not "How can an Asian claim her true Christian identity without losing the other?" but "How can Christian identity make her truly Asian and vice versa?"

Third, the authority of the Bible in Asia stands between two extremes: Asian hermeneutics in academia and Asian Christians in practice. The former relativizes the Bible as one of many truths and thus strips it of its distinctiveness as the revelatory Scripture of God. The latter upholds a fundamentalist approach to the Bible that deprives it of its dynamic to challenge Asian Christians where they are as Asians. The task for Asian hermeneutics is to reaffirm both the distinctive and the dynamic nature of the Bible.

See also Communal Holiness; Feminist Hermeneutics.

Resources

Gnanavaram, M. "'Dalit Theology' and the Parable of the Good Samaritan." *JSNT* 50 (1993): 59-83.

Kim, Yung Suk, and Jin-Ho Kim, eds. *Reading Minjung Theology in the Twenty-First Century: Selected Writings by Ahn Byung-Mu and Modern Critical Responses.* Eugene, OR: Wipf and Stock, 2013.

Kwok, Pui-lan. *Postcolonial Imagination and Feminist Theology.* Louisville, KY: Westminster John Knox Press, 2005.

Lee, Archie C. C. "Cross-Textual Hermeneutics and Identity in Multi-scriptural Asia." Pages 179-204 in *Christian Theology in Asia: Emerging Forms and Themes.* Edited by Sebastian Kim. Cambridge, UK: Cambridge University Press, 2008.

Rajumar, Peniel. *Dalit Theology and Dalit Liberation: Problems, Paradigms and Possibilities.* Farnham, UK: Ashgate, 2010.

Sugirtharajah, R. S. *Asian Biblical Hermeneutics and Postcolonialism: Contesting the Interpretations.* Sheffield, UK: Sheffield Academic Press, 1999.

———. "Introduction, and Some Thoughts on Asian Biblical Hermeneutics." *BibInt* 2, no. 3 (1994): 251-63.

———, ed. *Voices from the Margin: Interpreting the Bible in the Third World.* Maryknoll, NY: Orbis Books, 2006.

WI, MI JA, PHD

Bb

BELIEF/BELIEVE (*'āman, pisteuō*)

The concept of belief is grounded in the idea of conviction or certainty. In the Bible, belief is usually understood as one's trust in God and his **covenant**. This restores the right relationship with God that was once broken by the unbelief of the first man, Adam.

The OT concept of belief is expressed by the Hebrew root *'mn* and its related terms. The verb *'āman* conveys either the state or the act of believing something or someone as reliable. Objects of the verb vary, such as ideas, facts, words, people, or deities that can be considered trustworthy. When God is the object of belief, God, rather than the believer, takes the initiative by revealing himself. Such revelation provokes the **fear of God** and necessitates one's responsive act of believing. One's belief, based upon this true fear of God, leads to a constant obedient response to God's words. Abraham's act of believing, portrayed as a lifelong **obedience**, is demonstrated in Genesis through his fear of God (22:12).

In the causative stem (hiphil), *'āman* is used to indicate "the repeated or continuing act of believing" in God and his word, illustrated by Abraham (15:6). By his belief, Abraham was reckoned righteous. Although the verb occurs for the first time in this narrative, it is not the first time Abraham had shown his trust in God. Abraham had consistently accepted God as reliable, and obediently responded to God's words from the beginning of their encounter (12:1-4). As is the case with other biblical figures, the action of belief precedes or surpasses the vocabulary of belief.

In the passive stem (niphal), *'āman* is used to denote "faithfulness" as a personal characteristic of Abraham. Abraham's life proved to be one that made a firm commitment to God's words, which became the basis not only for Abraham's **righteousness** but also for God's faithfulness to his promise (Gen. 22:12ff.). In this way, the Bible highlights true belief on the basis of true **fear of God** as a decisive condition for righteousness and as an essential attribute of the realization of God's covenant promise.

This idea of faithfulness is elaborated by the noun *'ĕmûnâ*, which refers to "firmness" or "fidelity" possessed by God (Deut. 32:4; Isa. 11:5), or those who are in right relationship with God (1 Sam. 26:23; Prov. 28:20). The most significant theological use of *'ĕmûnâ* is Habakkuk 2:4*b*, "the righteous shall live by his **faith**." Here *'ĕmûnâ* refers to an unshaken trust in God as an eternal requisite for the life of the righteous (Rom. 1:17). The word *'ĕmet* may also indicate "dependability" or "faithfulness" (Exod. 18:21; Neh. 7:2).

In line with the OT, the concept of belief in the NT is related to this question: Within the theological framework of the covenant, who are the righteous who will inherit God's promise along with Abraham? By making frequent connections to the OT references, the NT resolves the problem concerning the identity of the righteous through the interpretation of belief in Christ Jesus.

The NT concept of belief is represented by the Greek verb *pisteuō* and its related terms that shed light on the significance of one's act of believing in Christ and in the fulfillment of God's covenant promise. The NT follows the LXX in using the verb *pisteuō* as the Greek counterpart of the Hebrew verb *'āman*.

The verb *pisteuō* indicates belief in the truthfulness of the **gospel** (Mark 1:15; Acts 4:4), trust in God (Rom. 4:24; Titus 3:8), and trust in Christ (John 2:11; 3:16-18; Rom. 3:22; Gal. 2:16). In the causative form, the verb refers to the act of being confident about something reliable (2 Tim. 3:14). The noun *pistis* refers to either the state of or the act of believing and is frequently used to denote one's belief in God (1 Thess. 1:8; 1 Pet. 1:21), in Christ (Eph. 1:15), or in the truth (2 Thess. 2:13). Most significantly, the word is used to defend the position that a person is justified, not by the works of the **law**, but by faith (Rom. 3:28).

New Testament writers frequently refer to the OT account of Abraham's act of believing as a decisive exemplar of "righteousness by faith." Abraham made every effort to secure his continuing faith-based **obedience** to God's words in the context of the covenant relationship. In this way, NT writers characterize belief as that which is proven in obedience to God and as one's proper response to God's promise (Rom. 4:13-16; Gal. 3:14, 22). This is an essential condition of the realization of God's covenant promise in Christ (Rom. 4:21).

In conclusion, belief in God becomes the basis for one's right relationship with God within the context of covenant relationship. As a result of belief, one is reckoned righteous based upon the eternal covenant with God, which is not only promised but also fulfilled (Gen. 15:6; Rom. 3:28). Furthermore, belief in God continues to work as the underlying principle for the living out of a commitment to God and his word (Ezek. 18:5; Hab. 2:4*b*; Rom. 1:17). True belief enables one to recover not only a right relationship with God but also righteous living in the world.

See also Jesus and the Law; Reconciliation; Word of God/Yahweh, The; Works.

Resources
Fenlason, Aaron C. "Belief." *LTW*.
Hamilton, Victor P. *The Book of Genesis: Chapters 1-17*. NICOT. Grand Rapids: Eerdmans, 1990.
Longenecker, Bruce W. *The Triumph of Abraham's God: The Transformation of Identity in Galatians*. Nashville: Abingdon Press, 1998.
Moberly, R. W. L. "Abraham's Righteousness (Genesis XV 6)." In *Studies in the Pentateuch*. VTSup 41. Leiden, NL: E. J. Brill, 1990.
Moxnes, Halvor. *Theology in Conflict: Studies in Paul's Understanding of God in Romans*. NovTSup 53. Leiden, NL: E. J. Brill, 1980.
Wenham, Gordon J. *Genesis 1–15*. WBC, vol. 1. Waco, TX: Word Books, 1987.
Wright, N. T. *The Climax of the Covenant: Christ and the Law in Pauline Theology*. Minneapolis: Fortress Press, 1991.

OH, WON KEUN, PHD

BIBLICAL ETHICS

Ethical issues are addressed in Scripture in several ways. There are discourses that provide broad principles that everyone should follow (e.g., the **Sermon on the Mount**), statements made in specific contexts (e.g., Pauline admonishments), and narratives that illustrate both what to do and what not to do.

Functions of Biblical Ethics
Biblical ethics served several purposes for its authors and original readers. The overarching goal was to build relationships with God and others. Since God desires the best for his creatures, helpful actions are consistent with God's moral character, and harmful actions run contrary to it. Consequently, our attitudes and actions can bring us closer to God (and others) or they can separate us.

Biblical ethics stresses character formation to solidify helpful attitudes and actions into patterns. The concept of the **image of God** reflects this. Humanity was created with the capacity to reflect the character of God (Gen. 1:26-27; 2 Pet. 1:4). Consequently, biblical ethics has both relational and ontological aspects that are interrelated.

Another notable function of biblical ethics is group identity. Particular practices and behaviors (e.g., circumcision, Nazirite vows) were intended to make group members identifiable. The theological rationale for this was to present a positive witness of the group's shared faith. Having a shared identity is endemic to all groups. It creates a bond between group members, increasing cohesion and morale, but it can also engender negative attitudes such as exclusivism, judgmentalism, arrogance, and hatred. Group identity is thus one of the more controversial aspects of religion. Misplaced zeal is a fertile breeding ground for legalism, violence, and pettiness, especially when it is rooted in something considered to be authoritative, such as Scripture or tradition.

Consequently, we must distinguish between ethics and social taboos, even in biblical ethics. Some actions and attitudes are helpful or harmful, while others merely reflect group identity. Consider Jesus's keeping of the Sabbath (e.g., Mark 2:23–3:6) and the **Jerusalem** council over circumcision (Acts 15:1-35).

Gradual Shift in Emphases over Time

Several emphases of biblical ethics changed over time, especially in the OT, which spans a large period. These were, at least in part, adaptations to the culture's more general move away from fatalism. The biblical authors increasingly attributed the state of affairs in the world to human control. This affected their ethics in several respects.

First, there was a shift from corporate to personal responsibility. After all, if humans have greater control than what had been previously thought, they have greater ethical responsibility. In the earlier biblical writings, especially the Decalogue, God promised to reward and punish the group for the behavior of individuals (e.g., Exod. 20:5-6; 34:7; Num. 14:18). This included families, tribes, cities, and entire nations. Families were destined to reap the rewards and pay the penalties for up to four generations. Sometimes the group itself was sufficiently corrupt to justify destroying it completely, as in the flood of Noah (Gen. 6–9) and the destruction of Sodom and Gomorrah (chs. 18–19). In other instances God punished the group for the disobedience of one, such as Achan, who kept some of the Jericho plunder (Josh. 7), and David, who took a census (2 Sam. 24).

Compare these with passages such as Ezekiel 18. Here group accountability is no longer the prevailing standard. Instead, children and parents are responsible for their individual behaviors. Likewise, it could no longer be assumed that success is a reward from God or that woe and trials are a sign of God's punishment. This point is poignantly made in the book of Job (see ch. 21). Later, Jesus's healing of the man born blind reinforced this point (John 9).

Second, biblical ethics gradually replaced its earlier emphasis on corporate rules with an emphasis on personal **conscience**. The biblical authors began to see the state of the world as more contingent on human behavior, and this required individuals to develop moral discernment. Mere group conformity was no longer sufficient. Prescribing one-size-fits-all rules would no longer be adequate. The biblical authors realized that the complexity of matters cannot be adequately addressed in a simple list of rules. A good illustration of this is the gradual refinement of their views concerning **marriage** and divorce. Note the nuance that Jesus adds to their understanding (Matt.

5:27-32; 19:3-12), his unwillingness to punish the Samaritan woman (John 4:1-42) or the woman caught in adultery (8:2-11). Paul continued this, such as his expansion of the grounds for divorce (1 Cor. 7).

As the biblical authors began to ascribe less to fatalism, they began to be more optimistic about influencing, even reforming, the attitudes and behaviors of individuals. This resulted in a movement from punishment to **forgiveness**. Compare the stories of Abraham (Gen. 18) and Moses (Exod. 32) pleading for God to show **mercy** to others with the much later story of Jonah, in which God wanted to forgive, but Jonah did not. The stress on forgiveness continued to increase throughout the Gospels (e.g., Matt. 5–7; 18:21-22) and the rest of the NT.

These shifts reflect the reality that ethics is more complex than a simple choice to obey or disobey. In this way, the story of Adam and Eve eating from the Tree of the Knowledge of Good and Evil (Gen. 2–3) illustrates the state of innocence that was lost as human beings began to understand that matters of right and wrong are as complex as the situations we judge, particularly in light of the many causes that shape them. The biblical authors still held firm beliefs about God's ultimate control over everything (e.g., Isa. 45:7). However, quietly accepting **evil** without question no longer seemed satisfactory. Instead, they began to wonder why God allowed bad things to happen, because they wanted to better understand what God wanted them to do about it (e.g., Job; James 1).

Applying Biblical Ethics Today

For the biblical authors, ethics was a dynamic enterprise, not a static one. This is why Judaism developed a multifaceted rabbinic tradition for ethical and theological reflection. It is also why Christianity has historically relied on ecumenically developed creeds and on the writings of the early church fathers as resources for scriptural interpretation. Even within the NT itself, there are extended conversations over the relationship between law and **grace**, because those authors knew that the core values of Christianity need to be continually adapted and applied to new contexts.

The Wesleyan tradition recognizes the dynamic nature of scriptural interpretation, so it emphasizes tradition, reason, and experience as resources for that task. Along with Scripture itself, these elements together provide a holistic and balanced biblical hermeneutic that is well suited for applying biblical ethics to contemporary situations.

We can only do **justice** to biblical ethics when we view it within its historical and cultural development and approach it in a manner consistent with the biblical authors themselves. The core values of the biblical authors are still relevant today, and yet our context is continually changing. Fortunately, the Bible doesn't stop at merely offering rigid prescriptions. Instead, it provides us with trajectories developed within a dynamic tradition of ethical reflection.

See also Communal Holiness; Creation; Fall, The; Jesus and the Law.

KEVIN TWAIN LOWERY, PHD

BIBLICAL THEOLOGY

Biblical theology can be defined as the coherent articulation and expression of the Bible's specific texts into a larger conceptual unity. The conceptual unity of each particular text is understood as a part of an ever-larger theological unity, ultimately embracing the context of all Scripture. The focus of the subject matter of that particular theological entity intentionally moves in three distinct directions.

Beginning with *the world within the text,* biblical theology seeks to clarify the theology that is expressed within a particular text as it is understood within its broader biblical context. The text must be closely read and studied within its historical context as well as within its literary setting to gain a theological understanding of it.

In an effort to better understand the thought world expressed within the text, the focus next shifts to *the world behind the text,* seeking greater understanding and illumination of the theology that shaped and formed the author, editor, or redactor of that particular text, as well as the original intended audience addressed within the world of that text. Such focus aids in understanding what the text was saying to its audience.

Finally, the focus shifts to *the world in front of the text.* The theology produced in front of the text as it is read and heard within the faith community has ongoing implications for that community. The response of those who receive and appropriate the implications of what they have heard produces a new theological reality that shapes the ongoing life of that faith community.

All three areas of focus—*within* the text, *behind* the text, and *in front of* the text—should be integrated in developing a thorough biblical theology.

The academic discipline of biblical theology is a complex and interesting hybrid of two significant disciplines that at best mutually inform each other—namely, biblical studies and theological studies. The discipline of biblical studies is typically subdivided between OT and NT. Because OT and NT studies tend to be discreet within the academy, a comprehensive biblical theology is developed far less frequently than an OT theology or NT theology.

The academic discipline of theological studies is equally complex. Systematic theology primarily utilizes current philosophical categories for organizing and synthesizing theological understanding, usually drawing heavily from biblical texts that are thematically collated within the structures determined by the overarching system or grid being used. Dogmatic theology typically creates a system determined by a dominant creedal or theological faith affirmation. Philosophical theology usually incorporates a particular way of thinking drawn from current philosophical models as the basis for constructing a theological system. Historical theology carefully examines the traditional biblical interpretations and theological understandings that have shaped and formed previous faith communities, usually in a linear and progressive way from the distant past up to the present. Practical theology examines biblical, systematic, and historical theologies in order to enable the church to carry out its current mission in the world through faithful practices and applications of those theologies.

What makes the biblical-theology hybrid interesting is not merely the complexity of the two primary parts, Bible and theology, but also the diversity of emphases that ensue when the two are put together into a unitary whole. A variety of approaches, methods, and understandings of particular theological concepts within the biblical text began as soon as multiple texts were created, collected, and utilized within ancient faith communities. Some of these approaches and methods are as old as the biblical text itself!

The oldest method of doing biblical theology began within the time frame of biblical texts themselves as some members of a later faith community reexamined and critiqued the theological understanding of a prior community, or at least their faithfulness in putting that understanding into practice.

From the return out of exile until the establishment of Second Temple Judaism, rabbinic Jewish interpreters of the OT developed the method of midrash that would examine older texts piece by piece and seek to work each of them into a contemporary theological framework to help the people of God embrace and understand how God had been working among them from the beginning. This work culminated in the Mishnah and the Talmud.

Early Christian authors such as **Paul**, James, **Matthew**, and **John** were quite at home with this particular theological method, utilizing it often in the process of creating the NT documents.

The early **church** fathers continued utilizing a form of midrash as a proof-text methodology that sought to provide justification for theological concepts by creating a catalog of texts that supported and undergirded particular theological assertions.

As creeds became more and more normative for orthodox theology, dogmatic theology began to provide the structure of an overall understanding of the Bible. The texts that most strongly supported creedal affirmations were given the most emphasis because they were understood as the foundations of the **faith**. Lesser texts were given less emphasis in the theological understanding of the church and its traditions.

With the burgeoning of the historical-critical method in biblical studies in the nineteenth century, new methods of doing biblical theology were developed. Thematic biblical theologies emerged from extensive word studies that enabled the tracking of major or dominant themes throughout one or both Testaments. Accepting the sharp chasm created by the distinction between biblical theology and systematic theology, most of these efforts worked synchronically.

Synchronic biblical theologies operate from the perspective that there is a core belief or concept within a biblical book or testament or the entire Bible around which the basic theology of the whole revolves or develops. These concepts emerge from the close reading of the text itself, so they are not superimposed from outside the text; instead, they let the text provide the norm governing the organization of the theological system advanced. They are neither derivatives of a philosophical system nor the product of a dogmatically established formulation.

Many biblical theologies produced in the mid-twentieth century followed this methodological path. Yet the determination of a theological center seemed highly subjective, as evidenced by the numerous competing centers that soon emerged. **Covenant**, divine design, divine presence, **election, creation** (and eventually, re-creation), **kingdom of God**, salvation history, and lordship were all put forward as determinative centers for doing biblical theology. Some of these proposed centers worked very well for major sections of a testament or the entire Bible, but most seemed to ignore some significant texts or force them into very artificial constructs. Noting the difficulty of establishing an accepted center, many synchronic NT theologies worked sequentially from Matthew to Revelation.

Diachronic biblical theologies emerged shortly thereafter and operated from the perspective that there were longitudinal trajectories that developed *through time*. These biblical theologies structured their work beginning with the earliest faith expressions and affirmations to their final forms in the latest eras represented at the closing of the respective canons. The telling and the subsequent retelling of events, actions, reactions, and responses throughout the generations show the dynamic development of the biblical faith through time as history moves ever forward.

In diachronic biblical theology the people of God continue to give theological shape to the texts that in turn continue shaping them. The method works best where the history of the text and the history within the text can be readily identified. When the text itself has an ambiguous historical context, fitting it into any era is difficult. The method also tends at times to blur the lines between history and theology.

The collapse of historical certainty as the basis for theological development in the 1970s led to the cessation of publication of any major biblical theologies for the next two decades. The impasse was finally overcome in the last decade of the twentieth century with two major OT methodological movements that propelled biblical theology forward. Canonical context and communal narrative marked the resumption of productive work in the field.

Communal narrative works explicitly with an understanding of the biblical text as a polyvalent communal narrative. Despite the many and varied voices, the text remains a narrative developed in and for the community. Communal narrative operates implicitly with a diachronic methodology that sees major concepts and ideas shaped and reshaped in the ongoing life of the community, with a strong emphasis on social implications and applications as theological narrative continues to be told and retold.

Communal narrative focuses on the community gathered *in front of* the text and readily critiques communal shortcomings. However, at times narratives are read in ways to make the current faith community hostile to the traditional faith community as a historical and social entity. The primary focus of communal narrative is to move away from the historical context of biblical texts and locate the theological thrust of all texts in front of contemporary readers.

For canonical context, the established parameters of the classical Christian canon as a whole become the shaping force for the contemporary community of faith. While there are diverse witnesses, there is one unitary Christian canon. Each particular text must be heard and read in the light of the whole biblical text. Theology does indeed develop in its understanding through time, yet canonical shaping works in both directions, not always simply from older to newer, from the OT to the NT, but also from the NT back to the OT read as Christian Scripture. The primary unifying factor for the community doing biblical theology together was that they were indeed a faith community.

The largest challenge to canonical context as a method is the immensity of the task of letting the entire canon shape the theological thrust of each particular text. The entire body of text is massive. This method requires OT scholars to carefully study NT texts as well. It requires NT scholars to thoroughly examine OT texts beyond their use as quotations in the NT so that they might better understand the theology of the entire canon.

With the complexity and variety of texts, approaches, and methodologies available in the realm of biblical theology as a hybrid discipline, there are several challenging issues to be addressed.

First, is there a single unitary biblical theology at all? Can there be a finished product that does justice to all of the diverse voices expressed in the totality of Scripture? Or are there only multiple biblical theologies?

Second, is the primary function of biblical theology merely analytical and descriptive, suggestive but not declarative? Or does the descriptive analysis provide the basis for the prescriptive and the normative, and if so, can the biblical theologian be the one to give voice to that reality for the church and for the world?

Third, how does the context of the theologian shape the theological understanding that can be garnered from reading and hearing the biblical texts with other members of the broader Christian community? In an era of multiple ideologically defined "communities" who find identity in gender, race, ethnicity, or economic and social strata, is biblical theology to be specially tailored to suit their group needs at the expense of a greater community awareness?

Finally, what is the better venue for doing biblical theology, the academy or the church? Perhaps the best biblical theology that is still yet to come will happen when the minister, the scholar, and the layperson all come together to listen to the Bible together and think theologically for the sake of the church.

See also Communal Holiness; Progressive Revelation.

Resources

Adam, A. K. M., Stephen E. Fowl, Kevin J. Vanhoozer, and Francis Watson. *Reading Scripture with the Church: Toward a Hermeneutic for Theological Interpretation.* Grand Rapids: Baker Academic, 2006.

Barr, James. *The Concept of Biblical Theology: An Old Testament Perspective.* Minneapolis: Fortress Press, 1999.

Brueggemann, Walter. *Theology of the Old Testament: Testimony, Dispute, Advocacy.* Minneapolis: Fortress Press, 1997.

Childs, Brevard S. *Biblical Theology in Crisis.* Philadelphia: Westminster Press, 1970.

———. *Biblical Theology of the Old and New Testaments: Theological Reflection on the Christian Bible.* Minneapolis: Fortress Press, 1992.

Davis, Ellen F., and Richard B. Hays, eds. *The Art of Reading Scripture.* Grand Rapids: Eerdmans, 2003.

Kraftchick, Steven J., Charles D. Myers, and Ben C. Ollenburger, eds. *Biblical Theology: Problems and Perspectives.* Nashville: Abingdon Press, 1995.

Ollenburger, Ben C., Elmer A. Martens, and Gerhard Hasel, eds. *The Flowering of Old Testament Theology: A Reader in Twentieth-Century Old Testament Theology.* Winona Lake, IN: Eisenbrauns, 1992.

Stuhlmacher, Peter. *How to Do Biblical Theology.* Allison Park, PA: Pickwick, 1995.

DAN SPROSS, PHD

Cc

CALL OF GOD

Throughout the Bible, we find that God chooses certain people or groups of people to serve him and his purposes. God calls certain parts of the **creation** by name (Gen. 1:5; Ps. 147:4; Isa. 40:26), but this call can also be directed to persons, families, or people groups (Israel: Deut. 4:37; prophets: 1 Sam. 3; Gentiles: Isa. 55:5; the church: 1 Pet. 2:9) to entrust them with specific tasks. Because humans have **free will**, they can reject or accept God's call. Rejection can bring consequences or punishment (Ps. 81:11-12 [13-14 HB]; Isa. 65:12; Jer. 7:13-15).

The purpose of God's call varies with the recipient.

The Universal Call to Salvation. An invitation is given to all human generations to abandon **sin** and accept the new, **holy**, and eternal life Jesus Christ freely offered through the cross (Isa. 1:18; Matt. 11:28; John 3:16-17; Rev. 3:19-20; 22:17). It is a call to the heart of every human being through the work of the **Holy Spirit**'s prevenient **grace** (John 6:44; 16:8) and through the proclamation of the Word in the ministry of the **church** (Matt. 28:19-20; Rom. 10:17).

*The Call to **Discipleship**.* Those who accept the invitation to salvation, and who belong to God's people, the church (Gk., *ekklēsia*), are called to "belong to Christ" (2 Cor. 10:7, NIV); that is, to follow him as disciples (Luke 6:13), surrendering their lives completely to his lordship. This is a call to continuous growth, having as a goal the model of Jesus Christ's holy life (Eph. 4:13).

The Call to Be a Community. First Abraham's family (Isa. 41:8-9) and then the whole nation of Israel (Deut. 7:6-8) were called by God to be his people, through whom the **Savior** would be born. Israel was chosen to be the holy people of God, called to live in **holiness** among the nations, bearing witness to the one true God (Lev. 11:45; Isa. 49:6-7). Members of the church, the new Israel, share the same vocation, since they are called to be servants and priests of God to the world (1 Pet. 2:9). To carry out this ministry of restoration, the church is vested with the power and gifts of the Holy Spirit (Rom. 12:3-8; 1 Cor. 12–14; Eph. 4:7-16; 1 Pet. 4:10-11).

The Individual Call to Ministry. To be servants (ministers) of Jesus Christ is a calling shared by all the redeemed, through different occupations. The service or ministry to which one is called is an expression of worship; therefore, it is not limited to activities related to the church, but embraces each and every one of the various occupations a child of God carries out in daily life. In the Bible, God called individuals such as Abraham (Gen. 12:1-3), Moses (Exod. 3:4), Isaiah (Isa. 6:8), and Paul (Acts 26:16). The assigned offices or functions vary throughout Scripture: spiritual leader (Exod. 3:9-10), **prophet** (John 1:6-8), missionary/apostle (Rom. 1:1; Gal. 1:15), artisan (Exod. 31:2), and mother (Gen. 18:12-14; Luke 1:28), among others. All these entrusted functions contribute to the development of God's redemptive plan (Eph. 4:7-16).

Church leaders are responsible for helping people to recognize and respond positively to the call of God (vv. 11-13). This preparation requires a context of positive relationships, patient **love**, and intercessory prayer. God created his children for "good **works**" (Eph. 2:10, NIV; see also 1 Cor. 7:22), and being engaged in them produces joy (Ps. 100:1-2).

The call to fulfill a special service in the body of Christ is for all God's children (1 Cor. 12:5-31), not just for professional ministers such as pastors and missionaries. The **gifts of the Spirit** are distributed to all members of the church, so that everyone fulfills a special and individual function. Multiple ministries are needed to meet the varied needs of the church and the world (Luke 4:18-19; John 14:12). Since ministry meets needs and these vary according to the times and contexts, the church will always need to promote creative ministries and train disciples of the Lord to serve in new, specialized functions.

While there is no ministry more important than another, the ministry of "pastor and teacher"—grammatically linked together in the Greek text of Ephesians 4:11—is principal, because it coordinates and nourishes all other ministries (vv. 11-13). For John Wesley, candidates for the pastoral ministry had to display these qualities: full assurance of the call, a real experience of salvation, the indwelling love of God, a healthy and clear understanding of spiritual and ecclesiastical affairs, the gifts and abilities pastoral ministry requires, and the fruit of conversion ([1872] 1978, 324-25; see also John 15:16).

Resources

Brown, Guillermo. *Ministrando juntos: Un modelo para líderes en la iglesia local.* San José, CR: AIBC, 1989.
Patterson, Ben. *El servir a Dios.* Miami, FL: Vida, 1984.

Taylor, Richard S. *Diccionario teológico Beacon*. Kansas City: Casa Nazarena de Publicaciones, 1994.

Vine, W. E. *Diccionario Expositivo de palabras del Antiguo y Nuevo Testamento exhaustivo de Vine*. Nashville: Grupo Nelson, 2007.

Wesley, John. *The Works of John Wesley*. Vol. 8. 3rd ed. London: Wesleyan Methodist Book Room, 1872. Reprint, Kansas City: Beacon Hill Press of Kansas City, 1978.

Yoder, John Howard. *El ministerio de todos: Creciendo hacia la plenitud en Cristo*. Guatemala City: Semilla-Clara, 1995.

MÓNICA MASTRONARDI DE FERNÁNDEZ, DMIN

CANONICAL HERMENEUTICS

A recent development in the study of biblical hermeneutics, called canonical hermeneutics, underscores two elements that distinguish it from other contemporary strategies of biblical interpretation.

1. Forming the Christian Faith

First, practitioners of a canonical approach to Scripture underscore the ecclesial address of its interpretation and practice. The purpose of Bible study is to retrieve materials that are formative of Christian **faith** and life and that are also performative in Christian worship, catechesis, mission, and personal devotions toward that holy end.

Significantly, canonical hermeneutics pays close attention to a *pneumatology* of Scripture in which biblical texts are studied as acts of worship in the company of the **Holy Spirit**, trusting that worshipful acts of interpretation serve the divine economy as a sanctified and sanctifying means of God's grace. The effects of receiving and digesting this sacrament of the Word are illumination and guidance by the Spirit that targets covenant-keeping discipleship in witness of the living Jesus. In this sense, canonical hermeneutics sponsors an *ecclesial* orientation to any theological explanation of Scripture's enduring authority and its authorized practices. The principal address of Scripture is to the **church**; there would be no Scripture to study without the community that formed and preserved it.

2. The Church's Formation of the Canon

Second, this emphasis on ecclesial practices is reflected in the deployment of biblical criticisms to study closely the phenomena of Scripture's formation when certain apostolic writings were providentially received, preserved, and collected into discrete collections and then canonized to form the church's Scripture. Canonical hermeneutics sponsors a critical interest in Scripture's production, which is decisive for understanding the intentions of its ongoing practice as God's Word for God's people. In this sense, the real point of a biblical text's origins is not the moment of its composition but the postbiblical moment of the church's canonization of its final (i.e., canonical) form. If the original communicative intentions of a text control how it is read today, then this approach registers these intentions, not by the presumed intentions of its author or first readers, but by the intentions of those subsequent readers who first received that text and then read it as Scripture. Moreover, the church's postbiblical reception of those apostolic writings is then recognized as inspired by the Holy Spirit, and thus canonization was based less on who wrote them (i.e., on their authorship) and more on their congruence with the apostolic witness to Jesus and the sanctifying results of their practice within the one holy catholic and apostolic church.

Tracking the History of a Text

A theology of Scripture cued by Scripture's providential formation and ongoing function as the church's canon forges the orienting concerns and practices of canonical hermeneutics. The resurgence of interest in the patristic use of Scripture is in part prompted by the examples it provides of how and why texts were used during the period when the biblical canon was formed. In response to rival movements, the church's interpretation of Scripture from the second to the fourth century is ordered by the apostolic witness of Jesus in response to the need for a common standard to settle a variety of epistemic and ecclesial crises. The substance of what the apostles saw and heard of Jesus was recalled, mostly by the texts that they wrote and their communities preserved, and translated into a working grammar of faith—a "rule of faith." This rule of faith not only supplied the interpretive key by which the church was able to recognize those texts suitable to canonize but also guided the church's performances of them to form a faithful people—in Tertullian's phrase, a *gubernaculum interpretationis* (Lat., "governor for interpretation").

The growing importance of a text's history of interpretation when considered as a testimony to its ongoing relevance also reflects the growing interest in a theological interpretation of Scripture. Tracking the history of a biblical text registers its capacity to convey different meanings to different readers. Yet the faithful interpreter's appropriation of this history is hardly arbitrary. His or her constant concern is that both the content and consequence of a text's interpretation coheres with the church's apostolic rule of faith. Theological stability and life-giving adaptability are indispensable characteristics of any faithful interpretation of a sacred text.

Scripture's Two Testaments

Canonical hermeneutics proceeds from the vital recognition that Scripture's two Testaments form an interpenetrating whole. This unity should not deny the profound diversity among biblical witnesses or the historical particularity of each. Rather the formation of a single biblical canon under the providence of one God for the formation of one holy church forges the critical recognition that the production of Scripture in its final form creates the context in which diverse texts are read together, text with co-text, within the literary boundary of a single book that the Spirit produced and continues to use in forming Christians who know and **love** God.

For example, while Jesus accepted the God to whom Israel's Scripture bore witness, he found new and different implications and applications for his disciples that challenged traditional interpretations (cf. Matt. 5:17-48). Indeed, the existential necessity and eschatological urgency of God's word, mediated by this textual *traditium*, is formative of theological understanding, yet constantly requires every faithful reader to seek out from the old, old **gospel** story those new meanings (*traditio*) that are adaptable to the life of today's believers who continue to submit to Scripture's instruction as a word from the Lord God Almighty.

Scripture Approached as a Shaped Text

The canonical process produced a sacred Scripture of aesthetic excellence. Each canonical collection or volume of books is designed to perform certain roles within the canonical whole. The sequence of collections and even the arrangement and titles given to books within these canonical collections are not arbitrary but purposeful of their use in forming faithful people. Theological interpretation includes these nontextual elements as laden with meaning. For example, the title "To the Hebrews" was given to this anonymous letter long after it was written as the address of those who continue to read it as Scripture. Consider the placement of the fourfold Gospel at the head of the NT canon (even though hardly the first books written) to grant it theological priority. Within this Gospel, Matthew is placed and read first at least in part because it effectively helps readers transition from old to new. Like the artist who resists producing artifacts for "art's sake" but rather artifacts that evoke constructive responses from viewers, theological interpretation seeks after full meanings that accomplish Scripture's holy ends.

ROBERT W. WALL, THD

CARIBBEAN HERMENEUTICS

Caribbean hermeneutics refers to the ways Caribbean readers approach Scripture and the reasons for these ways. This definition is rooted in two premises. First, social location plays an important role in the way one reads and interprets Scripture. Second, hermeneutics is concerned with not only how one reads but also why one reads a certain way. What follows is both a description of the nature of Caribbean hermeneutics and a proposal for what it could and should be.

Caribbean hermeneutics is multifaceted at its core. The Caribbean is home to many cultures and subcultures. While its inhabitants share similar experiences and memories of displacement and diasporic existence—**slavery** and liberation, colonialism and emancipation, economic struggles and development, political oppression and resistance, and inequality and social activism—the stories and histories that shape Caribbean identity are diverse and nuanced.

In addition, the differences in language and geographic space (e.g., French: Haiti, Martinique, Guadeloupe; English: Jamaica, Trinidad and Tobago, Barbados; Spanish: Cuba, Puerto Rico; and Dutch: Curaçao, Bonaire, Saint Martin) account for differences in the social and theological imagery that undergirds differing approaches to the text. For example, readers from Jamaica, who are attuned to the realities of Rastafarianism, in their appropriation of the Psalms will be keen to raise certain hermeneutical questions that readers from Haiti may be unaware of or take for granted. This diversity is also partly rooted in colonialism. The divergence in worldview and modus operandi of the French, British, Dutch, Portuguese, and Spanish/Latin cultures continues to be felt in how people from different islands relate to one another, how they theologize, and how they interpret life.

Notwithstanding, there are characteristics that are at the core of the ways and the reasons a diverse Caribbean population approaches the task of interpretation in a particular manner.

Caribbean hermeneutics is communal. Caribbean readers benefit greatly from their ability to read texts in community and for the sake of the community. They are able to identify the ecclesial implications of their reading and gain insights that are otherwise not readily apparent to readers who are not as attentive to communal perspectives. The strength of the family unit and the bond of the extended-family system in Caribbean cultures create a sense of community whose impact is felt in the interpretive process.

From this perspective, the hermeneutical task consists of a dialogue between the reader and the text, between the individual and his or her community, and between communities. This is a process that is rooted in, promotes, and strengthens ecclesiology. It is not a linear process where one travels to the text to discover meanings that may or may not be applicable, but a process where the reader/community journeys to the world of the text and is willing to dwell there and be transformed by it. It is a process in which the text is reading the person at the same time as the person is reading the text. In addition, there is accountability between the reader and his or her community. As that community shows dependence on the **Holy Spirit**, it grows and flourishes in a manner that builds trust and fruitful interpretive collaboration.

The affinities between Caribbean and biblical cultures—that is, **honor and shame**, **patronage** and reciprocity, patriarchy, and hospitality—create a helpful familiarity with the setting, facilitate this embodiment, and enable the Caribbean reader to take seriously the claims Scripture makes on his or her life. The following exhortation is a case in point.

My brothers and sisters, what good is it if people say they have **faith** but do nothing to show it? Claiming to have faith can't save anyone, can it? Imagine a brother or sister who is naked and never has enough food to eat. What if one of you said, "Go in **peace**! Stay warm! Have a nice meal!"? What good is it if you don't actually give them what their body needs? (James 2:14-16, CEB)

Practicing this exhortation does not require questioning how and in what context such appeal is applicable. Rather, the Caribbean reader would be asking, What resources do I have available, and how do I provide the help needed? For example, it is common practice in Haiti to leave a portion of the family meal available in case a neighbor, a stranger, or someone in need was to visit during or after a meal. People do not need an invitation to visit one another. It is part of life. Therefore, it is inhospitable to bid a visitor farewell without offering him or her a meal. In the larger context of the life of the local **church**, a benevolent fund is often set aside to provide a weekly stipend to widows and the needy among the congregation.

Caribbean hermeneutics is subversive. The lingering effects of the hurt and oppression of colonialism are often felt in the hermeneutical process. They are expressed in liberation, postcolonial, and resistance readings. Some Caribbean readers often approach the text with suspicion because it is difficult to reconcile the fact that this same text was used to oppress, enslave, and subdue for centuries. Others view the text as a construct of the oppressor's own social and theological imagination.

The hermeneutical task, therefore, to some extent consists of deconstructing and reconstructing the text to highlight and push against the oppressor's interpretive shortcomings. Subversive hermeneutics at times maintains a strong "us versus them" approach and is sometimes guilty of the same selective, suspicious, and harmful hermeneutical practices that it is pushing against. However, this process also involves the appropriation of texts that show God's heart for the oppressed to substantiate the claim that God is on the side of the oppressed. In addition, it takes seriously the different voices that are present in a text and is intentional about bringing awareness to minority voices and perspectives.

Caribbean hermeneutics is contextual. The hermeneutical acumen of Caribbean readers has been shaped to some extent through the interaction with American and European missionaries, on the one hand, and through the educational formation of Caribbean students at institutions in North America and Europe, on the other hand. The (imported) methodologies and hermeneutical systems that are predominant in academic circles and among the educated laity are socially constructed. Therefore, they do not necessarily take into consideration the location and experience of Caribbean readers. Consequently, in addition to being subversive, Caribbean hermeneutics by necessity is (i.e., must be) contextual. Caribbean readers from time to time must reimagine their understanding of the text and even of the hermeneutical process itself. The hermeneutical task consists of readers paying close attention to the things that make them who they are and demonstrating an awareness of how those things impact their reading lenses.

Caribbean hermeneutics is Scripture based. The most important characteristic of Caribbean hermeneutics is that it approaches the Bible as Christian Scripture. The text of the Bible does not exist in a vacuum. The Bible is given by God to the **church** for the church's edification and theological transformation. Caribbean readers tend to focus on the Bible in its final literary form. This does not negate the importance of text-critical issues (form, source, and historicity); it simply relegates them to their proper (i.e., secondary) order.

Caribbean hermeneutics is embodied. The act of reading is not simply a philosophical exercise where the search for meaning is carried out for its own sake. The challenges conveyed by the text are truths that are (and need to be) lived, experienced, and embodied daily. The hermeneutical task is undertaken to understand how to make sense of life in the midst of turmoil; how to experience God in the midst of difficulties, pains, and tragedies; and how to show gratitude for provision and live with contentment. Here again the similarities between Israel and the Caribbean experience enable readers to see themselves in the stories of God's actions on behalf of his people: **slavery** and emancipation; exile, displacement, and protection in diaspora; and **suffering** and vindication. Caribbean readers are able to identify with the sufferings, celebrate the power of God to deliver his children, and anticipate their own vindication. In this state, the questions they raise have less to do with principles that can be gathered from the text than with the kinds of behaviors, attitudes, and habits of the heart that one must display to experience God's redeeming power. The end goal of the hermeneutical task is on being and becoming.

See also Communal Holiness.

Resources

Brueggemann, Walter. *Interpretation and Obedience: From Faithful Reading to Faithful Living*. Minneapolis: Fortress Press, 1991.

Keener, Craig, and M. Daniel Carroll R., eds. *Global Voices: Reading the Bible in the Majority World*. Peabody, MA: Hendrickson, 2013.

Murrell, N. Samuel. "Hermeneutics as Interpretation, Part 2: Contextual Truths in Sub-Version Preaching." *Caribbean Journal of Evangelical Theology* 3 (June 1999): 48-64.

Segovia, Fernando, and Mary Ann Tolbert, eds. *Reading from This Place*. Vol. 2, *Social Location and Biblical Interpretation in Global Perspective*. Minneapolis: Fortress Press, 1995.

Thomas, Oral. "A Resistant Biblical Hermeneutic within the Caribbean." *Black Theology: An International Journal* 6, no. 3 (September 2008): 330-42.

Westphal, Merold. *Whose Community? Which Interpretation? Philosophical Hermeneutics for the Church.* Grand Rapids: Baker Academic, 2009.

ABSON PRÉDESTIN JOSEPH, PHD

CHURCH, MISSION OF THE

Attention to this subject focuses not on the church that has a mission but rather on the mission that the church has as its champion. The entire sweep of Scripture presents readers with the story of God. More specifically, readers encounter the heart of our loving heavenly Father on a mission to restore relationship with every man, woman, youth, and child on earth.

Eden's garden provided the backdrop for the story's beginning. God created Adam and Eve, placed them in a perfect environment, and anticipated relationship as they walked and talked together "in the cool of the day" (Gen. 3:8, NIV). Humanity's self-sovereignty disrupted God's plan. Consequences included forbidden knowledge, ejection from the garden of Eden, and broken fellowship with God.

Not satisfied to leave humanity in their fallen condition, the Father immediately began a mission to restore relationship with his children. He revealed a plan in Genesis 3:15, before Adam and Eve departed from the garden, that would mend their broken fellowship. From the moment God spoke those words until today, the Father's restless heart has been on a mission to bring every lost person home.

Genesis 1–11 unfolds this mission as the Creator worked with all humanity. The focus narrowed in Genesis 12 to one family, Abraham and Sarah. This focused attention did not represent divine interest only in Abraham, Sarah, and their descendants. God's first **covenant** with Abraham in verse 3 emphasized that "all peoples on earth will be blessed through you" (NIV). God repeated this global interest in all humanity in Genesis 18:18 and 22:18.

Readers find God's concern for all humanity in covenants throughout the OT. God shared his heart's desire with Moses in Exodus 19:6. The Hebrew people would be "a kingdom of priests and a holy nation" (NIV), not as an exclusive divine privilege, but that they might take the message of God's love to all earth's inhabitants.

Old Testament **prophets** especially understood the divine mission. Isaiah represented the prophets well when he called attention to the message of the "Holy One of Israel" (Isa. 55:5, NIV). God invited all of humanity to seek and call upon him so that he might have **mercy** and freely pardon all who forsook their wicked ways and returned to him (vv. 5-7).

A proper perspective on the Jonah narrative in the book named for God's reluctant minister to Nineveh calls attention not to Jonah but to the restless Father's heart reaching out to an entire people group with whom he desired relationship. God's **love** for Nineveh's citizens illustrates one example of divine love for all earth's inhabitants. God, not Jonah, is the true missionary in the story.

The NT sheds additional light on God's searching heart. Jesus painted the clearest picture ever imagined of the Father on a mission to restore relationship with his people. Our Lord spoke of a shepherd who could not be satisfied with ninety-nine sheep safely in the fold. The shepherd left the safety of the protected walls and searched every hill and valley until he found the one remaining lost sheep. Bringing it home, he said to "his friends and neighbors . . . , 'Rejoice with me; I have found my lost sheep'" (Luke 15:6, NIV).

Jesus reminded his hearers of the Father's incredible love and desire to bestow eternal life on everyone who would accept Christ (John 3:16-17). His statement refers, not to a limited mission to a select number of individuals, but to a universal invitation to every member of the human family. Jesus preached and taught the mission invitation throughout his earthly ministry. Before he returned to his Father, he challenged his followers to join in this divine mission in Matthew 28:19-20, known as the Great Commission. Christ's command to go into the world and share God's message of love remains the mission of his church until he comes again.

The word "**incarnation**" means "in the flesh." The word most often refers to Jesus coming to the world to continue the mission of the Father in restoring lost people to divine relationship (John 1:14; 3:16). Jesus, the sent One, now sends his followers: "As the Father has sent me, I am sending you" (20:21, NIV). Therefore, incarnation now includes the movement of the body of Christ into the world challenged with God's mission and impacting both individuals and communities *in the flesh*.

Transformation of both individuals and communities occurs as the **Holy Spirit** gives purpose and direction to Christ's disciples in bringing God's message of love, **forgiveness**, and restoration to everyone. The Spirit supplies both the passion and vision for fulfilling the Great Commission. He also speaks to the hearts of individuals about **righteousness** and **judgment** (John 16:8-11) to bring them to the Father's heart.

The church's incarnational mission continues in discipling new believers in the Christian **faith**. **Repentance**, faith in Christ, and baptism mark the beginning of this lifelong process. Instruction directs believers toward the goal of Christlikeness (Matt. 28:19-20; 2 Cor. 3:18; Phil. 2:1-11; 1 John 3:2). The Holy Spirit guides **discipleship** efforts (John 16:12-15; Rom. 8:1-17). The Spirit matures new disciples into disciple makers who further God's mission in the world.

Because God's dream for the Hebrew people to become "a kingdom of priests and a holy nation" (Exod. 19:6, NIV) for reaching the world did not materialize, he challenged the church with his dream. The book of Acts tells the story of the early church participating in God's global mission. Christ's disciples took the good news of Christ Jesus to **Jerusalem**, Judea, Samaria, and the Gentile world of that day. Luke described Christ's work through his body of believers in twenty-eight chapters. That does not complete the story, however. It only begins it, for God's Holy Spirit has been writing Acts chapter 29 throughout church history. The work of the Spirit continues today. God's mission desires "all people to be saved" (1 Tim. 2:4, NIV). He invites every disciple of Christ to join in that global mission.

See also Afterlife; Fall, The; Holiness; Reconciliation; Sin.

FRANK M. MOORE, PHD

CHURCH, THE

The NT concept of the church, its nature, and its mission cannot be understood apart from its deep roots in the OT. This article thus examines two OT passages that form the critical backdrop for understanding the church in the NT, before surveying the NT evidence itself.

Old Testament

The origins and mission of a people called to be God's own began with **God's call** of Abram (Gen. 12:1-3). Three features of this call are worth noting for our purposes. First, God made promises to Abram, but they were conditioned on Abram's trust in God. Second, God promised to raise a great people through Abram's offspring. The trajectory toward a full-fledged people of God began here. Third, through Abram and his descendants God promised that "all peoples on earth will be blessed through you" (v. 3, NIV).

The mention of "peoples" ties these promises to the Babel episode (ch. 11) when God scattered the nations, an act of **judgment** that culminated the long chronicle of woe resulting from human **sin**. God's promised actions involving Abram and his descendants will remedy the consequences of human sin chronicled in Genesis 3-11.

The promises to Abram define the nature and mission of a people called to be God's own: to become a great people and to be a channel of God's blessing to all peoples. In doing so, these promises set the agenda for the larger contours of the grand narrative of Scripture that follows. As Christopher J. H. Wright has noted, God's words to Abram deserve the title "The Great Commission" for the people of God (2006, 214).

The second formative text, Exodus 19:4-6, states Israel's identity and purpose in a succinct programmatic fashion at the pivotal moment before the presentation of the **covenant** beginning in Exodus 20. God reminded the Israelites that they owed their existence to God's gracious saving initiative. God had brought them out of **slavery** in Egypt by a mighty act of divine deliverance. Moreover, that rescue was personal: God had brought them out of Egypt "to myself" (19:4, NIV). Then God laid down an all-important condition: as with Abram, the covenant would succeed only if the Israelites obeyed God. Should they do so, three results would follow. First, they would be God's special possession among the nations (v. 5). Second, they would be a "kingdom of priests" to God (v. 6*a*, NIV). As such, the Israelites would occupy a missional place, mediating between God and the nations. They would function as a channel of blessing to the nations as promised to Abram in Genesis 12. Finally, they would be a "holy nation" (Exod. 19:6*a*, NIV). The Israelites would be set apart for God and for God's purposes in a twofold sense. They would be **holy** by virtue of God *declaring* them as set apart. But they would also be called to *actualize* holiness in daily life as they lived in **obedience** to God (v. 5). In summary, Exodus 19:4-6 further specifies Israel's missional and ethical charge. As God's special possession, the Israelites were to function as priests to the nations while embodying a life set apart for God.

These themes from Genesis 12 and Exodus 19 echo throughout the OT and into the NT, functioning to define God's people. For example, Peter interpreted post-Pentecost events in terms of God's covenant with Abraham concerning Israel and the nations (Acts 3:25; see also Paul in Rom. 4:17). Furthermore, few themes resound throughout Scripture as much as does **holiness**. In many ways, the extended treatment of holiness in Leviticus 19 can be understood as an exposition of Exodus 19:6 (Wright 2006, 214). But this theme continues into the NT in multiple ways, not least when Paul describes his auditors in terms of holiness (e.g., 1 Cor. 1:2; cf. 1 Pet. 2:9).

New Testament

Drawing on diverse themes within the OT **prophets**, especially Isaiah, the **Gospels** defined Jesus's mission in terms of restoring Israel after its destruction by the Assyrians and Babylonians centuries earlier. For example, see how the long opening sections of Matthew and Luke narrate the story of Jesus into the larger history of Israel.

Within the Gospels, Jesus called disciples to follow him. Among those disciples stood one central group known as the Twelve. This numbered group represented the twelve tribes of a restored Israel. Thus at the heart of Jesus's ministry we find **communal** concerns, specifically the formation of a restored people of God.

As with the descriptions of the people of God in the OT, the people in the NT bear a distinct character. Matthew's **Sermon on the Mount** (Matt. 5–7) provides the most vivid and well-known description of the moral norms of the people formed around Jesus. Although the term translated "church" occurs only twice in the four Gospels (Matt. 16:18; 18:17), a concern for the people of God and the traits that define them remain central throughout.

With the Acts of the Apostles and the NT letters, we find a more developed understanding of what we call the church. Multiple themes can be identified that describe the nature and **mission of the church**. Here we can only provide a small sampling of the evidence.

The Church Is a Worshipping Community. After Jesus's ascension, his followers continued to meet in the temple courts and around meals for prayer and worship (Acts 2:46-47). Perhaps no picture of the church in the NT surpasses the scenes of worship in the heavenly throne room found in Revelation 4–5 and 7.

The Church Is a Multination Community. The mission of God's people from the beginning has been to serve as the channel of God's blessing to the peoples of the earth. The NT vision for the church consisted precisely of a single people drawn from all peoples or nations. Based on the evidence of Romans and Galatians, one of the central struggles of Paul's ministry was defining the conditions by which the nations (the "Gentiles") would be considered part of the church. Once again, the scenes of heavenly worship in Revelation specifically mention that people "from every nation, tribe, people and language" (7:9, NIV) will be gathered in worship before the throne of God.

The Church Is a Christlike Community. The holiness and character of the church is patterned after the life modeled by Jesus. In Philippians 2:5, Paul exhorted the Philippians to have the same "mind" that was in Jesus Christ. Paul then spelled out how Jesus embodied that mind (or mind-set) through a life that refused to exploit the **honor** and position that was rightfully his, to such a degree that he actually died on a cross for them (vv. 6-8). As a result of this choice on Jesus's part, God the Father honored him by raising him from the dead and seating him at God's own right hand as coruler over all (vv. 9-11). Paul then provided additional examples of this mind-set in Timothy (vv. 19-24), Epaphroditus (vv. 25-30), and himself (3:4-11). Finally, he exhorted the Philippians to imitate him and those like him (v. 17). His point was that the Philippians collectively were to embody the mind-set modeled for them by Jesus Christ.

The Church Is a Disciple-Making Community. If Matthew's Gospel is known for Jesus's final charge to "make disciples of all nations" (28:19), we find the disciple-making process alive and well in the Pauline letters. In 2 Timothy 2:2, Timothy is reminded to entrust what he has learned to others who will then teach others the same.

The Church Is a Holy Spirit–Led Community. The **Holy Spirit** equips and guides the church. The church's **leadership** functions on the basis of the **gifts** provided by the Holy Spirit for various ministries (e.g., Eph. 4:7-13).

In summary, the church is the multination missional community of God's people, existing on the basis of God's gracious and saving initiative, formed into the likeness of Jesus Christ, led by and equipped by the Holy Spirit, existing in a climate of worship as it makes disciples of all nations. The specific forms it takes as it lives into these realities depends on the specific contexts in which it finds itself.

Two final questions persist. Debates continue around the definition of the church in relation to the **kingdom of God**. Furthermore, the relationship between the NT church and Israel remains unresolved. This is a matter of great concern in light of the virulent Christian supersessionism (i.e., the belief that the new covenant in Jesus Christ supersedes the old covenant) in the decades preceding the Holocaust in central Europe.

See also Biblical Ethics; Grace; Resurrection.

Resources

Goldingay, John. *Biblical Theology: The God of the Christian Scriptures.* Downers Grove, IL: IVP Academic, 2016.

———. "Israel." Pages 173-253 in *Israel's Faith.* Vol. 2 of *Old Testament Theology.* Downers Grove, IL: IVP Academic, 2006.

Snyder, Howard A. *The Community of the King.* 2nd ed. Downers Grove, IL: InterVarsity Press, 2004.

Wells, Jo Bailey. *God's Holy People: A Theme in Biblical Theology.* JSOTSup 305. Sheffield, UK: Sheffield Academic Press, 2000.

Wright, Christopher J. H. *The Mission of God: Unlocking the Bible's Grand Narrative.* Downers Grove, IL: IVP Academic, 2006.

JAMES C. MILLER, PHD

CLEAN/UNCLEAN

Modern readers often misunderstand the biblical terms "clean" and "unclean" as primarily concerned with hygiene and roughly synonymous with the terms "clean" and "dirty." The NIV frequently adds "ceremonially" to counteract this connection to hygiene. In ancient thought, "clean" and "unclean" were often paired with the terms "holy" and "common" (Lev. 10:10; Ezek. 22:23, 26). To declare something clean meant it was fit for sacred service; anything declared unclean was not fit.

Old Testament

While the NIV uses the word "clean" to translate about a dozen Hebrew words, one root (*ṭhr*) accounts for the vast majority of occurrences, appearing a little over 200 times. Its primary meaning is "to be clean; to cleanse, purify, pronounce clean." The term translated "unclean" by the NIV (*ṭmʾ*) occurs 281 times, meaning "to become unclean; to defile, desecrate."

These terms are not evenly distributed in the OT. Leviticus has just over half (150) of the occurrences of "unclean" (*ṭmʾ*). Adding Ezekiel (43), Numbers (37), and Deuteronomy (10) increases the amount to 85 percent in four books. The distribution of "clean" (*ṭhr*) is slightly different. Leviticus still has the most (74), Exodus is next (29), followed by Numbers (19) and then Ezekiel (16). These four books account for two-thirds of all occurrences.

The OT speaks of both **holiness** and uncleanness as contagious. Since God is the ultimate source of holiness, wherever God is present, the place is **holy**. When God appeared to Moses at the burning bush, Moses removed his sandals because he was standing on holy ground (Exod. 3:5; cf. Josh. 5:15). Objects that were used in the worship of God needed to the cleansed and thus made fit for sacred use (Exod. 29:37; 40:9-10; Lev. 8:10). Those who met with God needed to be cleansed so that they would be fit for sacred service (Isa. 6:5-7).

The OT lists several categories that could make a person or object clean or unclean. The most common related to death. Touching an animal carcass (Lev. 5:2-3; 11:31-35) made a person unclean. Touching a human corpse also made a person unclean (Num. 19:11). Nazirites would have to restart their vows over from the beginning if someone died in their presence (6:9-12). When a person died, someone must dispose of the body and thus become unclean. Priests who were unclean could not fulfill their priestly function; therefore, they should only make themselves unclean for a close relative (Lev. 21:1-4). The high priest would be made unclean simply by being in the same place as a dead body (v. 11).

Eating unclean animals would also make someone unclean. All prohibited birds were either predators or carrion eaters—that is, eaters of flesh (11:13-19). Clean animals were rendered unclean if they were found dead or killed by other animals (17:15).

Other causes included certain skin diseases (13:1-46), menstruation (15:19-23), childbirth (12:2-6), and abnormal bodily discharges (15:1-15). Mold made fabric or houses unclean (13:47-59; 14:33-57). All of these could also be seen as symbols of death. In the case of menstruation and childbirth, loss of blood suggested loss of life. Uncleanness after sexual relations (15:18) may have been due to the loss of bodily fluid.

Some of the things that rendered a person unclean cannot be so easily connected with death. For example, rabbits and camels were prohibited, but they are not flesh eaters. These may have simply been set as a test of loyalty for the Israelites.

Uncleanness was dealt with in varying ways. Some types were cleansed by washing, some lasted to the end of the day, and others lasted for a week or longer. Skin diseases or abnormal bodily discharges lasted as long as the condition continued. Many forms of uncleanness would not be fully cleansed without making one or more **sacrificial** offerings.

The annual Day of Atonement was a special day of general cleansing (16:1-34). On that day, offerings were made for the high priest and his own household, for the people as a whole, and even for the tabernacle and all its furnishings.

New Testament

The NT uses one primary Greek root for "clean" or "pure" (*katharos*), which occurs 112 times. Of these occurrences, a prefix is used over 40 times to negate the meaning: "unclean" or "impure" (i.e., *akathartos*). Unlike the OT, these terms are fairly well distributed in the NT, occurring in twenty of the twenty-seven books. In the NT, the emphasis is about going beyond specific laws to highlight the intent of such regulations and also to return to a state of cleanness.

In the OT, uncleanness was frequently connected with death. However, instead of avoiding those who were unclean, Jesus restored life and health. Jairus's daughter was raised to life, and the woman subjected to bleeding was healed through contact with Jesus (Mark 5:22-42).

Uncleanness became a point of dispute between Jesus and the religious leaders, whose traditions had grown beyond the OT legislation. For example, in the area of handwashing, Jesus stressed the importance of following the intent of commands (Mark 7:1-23; Luke 11:37-41).

Similarly, dietary laws should not be seen as an end in themselves. "Jesus declared all foods clean" (Mark 7:19, NIV), for what was more important was what came out of a person (Rom. 14:20). Peter's vision of many animals, some "unclean," and his visit at the house of Cornelius (Acts 10) showed that Gentiles should not be excluded due to their non-Jewish status. Those that **feared God** would be accepted by God (11:18). Paul summarized the internal nature of cleanness this way: "To the pure, all things are pure, but to those who are corrupted and do not **believe**, nothing is pure" (Titus 1:15, NIV).

Resources

Averbeck, Richard. "Clean and Unclean." Pages 477-86 in vol. 4 of *NIDOTTE*.
Babcock, Bryan C. "Clean and Unclean." In *LBD*.
Snyder, Benjamin J. "Clean and Unclean." In *LTW*.
Wenham, G. J. "Clean and Unclean." Pages 210-12 in *New Bible Dictionary*. Downers Grove, IL: InterVarsity Press, 1996.

CLINTON A. BRANSCOMBE, MREL

COMMUNAL HOLINESS

God exists in community and reveals himself to humanity as Father, Son, and **Holy Spirit**. God's **holiness** is communal because it is a shared attribute within the Godhead and because **God calls** humanity to be in relationship with him and invites us to partake in his holiness.

In the OT, the plurality of the Godhead is evident in the use of the Hebrew *ʾĕlōhîm*, a plural substantive, as a proper name for God. The language attested to in the **creation** account, "let us make . . ." (Gen. 1:26, NIV), and in the Babel narrative, "let us go down . . ." (11:6-7, NIV), further supports this. In the Babel narrative, the first person plural follows the use of YHWH as the name for God. This unity of plurality (*Yahweh 'ĕlōhîm*) is attested even in the monotheistic text par excellence (Deut. 6:4-5).

The primary term used to convey God's holiness is the Hebrew substantive *qōdeš* and its derivatives. Whereas this word is multifaceted in its development, usage, and applications, the concept became closely connected with the divine. God in his very essence is holy, the source of holiness (Exod. 15:11; Lev. 19:2; 20:3; 22:2; 1 Sam. 2:2; Pss. 22:3 [4 HB]; 33:21; 103:1; Isa. 6:3; 12:6). God revealed himself to Israel as a holy God (Exod. 3:5; Isa. 17:7; 29:19; Jer. 50:29), who delivered and called Israel to partake in his holiness (Exod. 19:6; Lev. 19:2; 22:32; Deut. 7:1-6; 26:18-19).

Holiness is intrinsically communal because it finds its expression within the context of God's covenantal relationship with his people. How an individual lives out his or her holy **obedience** to Yahweh's commands can only take place within the framework of shared and lived existence. The relationship with YHWH determined the boundaries and behavior Israel as a nation needed to maintain internally, in the Israelites' relationships with one another, and externally, in the nation's relationships with other nations (Exod. 20:1–23:19; Deut. 27–30).

Another term used to convey communal holiness is the Hebrew word *tāmîm*, rendered by the Greek word *teleios* in the LXX. It conveys and is connected to ideas of blamelessness, **righteousness**, and purity. It describes devotion to God expressed in the relationship between God and the righteous (e.g., Gen. 6:9; 17:1; Deut. 18:13; 2 Sam. 22:24-26; Pss. 15:1-5; 101:2-8). It also qualifies the trust that is established in a loyal relationship between persons (e.g., to act with **integrity** [Judg. 9:16, 19]).

The communal aspect of holiness is evident even when the individual is in focus. In Genesis 6:9 Noah's perfection was established on the basis of his lifestyle *among* his generation. In 2 Samuel 22:24-26, David sang praises to God for delivering him from his enemies and credited his integrity/perfection as the reason God acted on his behalf. There, the language of perfection, rendered by the Greek *amōmos* in the LXX, is equated with righteousness, refraining from iniquity, and being pure in God's sight. Finally, in Deuteronomy 18:13, the community of Israel is addressed collectively and urged to be perfect—completely devoted to YHWH. Its devotion to God, a sign of obedience, was demonstrated through a lifestyle and set of practices that underscored its differences over against the other nations around it.

The word *tāmîm* is also used to describe the way of the Lord (Deut. 32:4; 2 Sam. 22:31; Ps. 18:30 [31 HB]). The metaphor of "walking in the way(s) of Yahweh" exhorts individuals and corporate Israel to embody a lifestyle that **honors** God by obeying his precepts (Gen. 17:1-2; Deut. 10:12; 11:22; Josh. 22:5; 1 Kings 8:58, AT). "To walk in the ways of the LORD" is to commune with him, to **love** and obey him. It is to live righteously and blamelessly in his eyes and in one's dealings with other human beings.

In the NT, these concepts (*hagios, teleios, amōmos*) are appropriated in a way that demonstrates continuity with the OT. Jesus challenged his followers to embody the perfection that is characteristic of their heavenly Father (Matt. 5:48). Jesus's words were a summary statement of teachings aimed to reshape the audience's understanding of a life together that honors God the Father. They also are followed by warnings and exhortations on how to display one's righteousness in relationships with other persons (6:1–7:29). By linking the fatherhood of God with holiness, Jesus strengthened the communal nature of the concept. Perfection is born of a shared experience of belonging to the family of God. It is motivated by a desire to **honor** God and to represent him faithfully. It is expressed tangibly in daily actions and interactions.

The **Gospels**' portrayal of Jesus provides a picture of **holiness** in action. Jesus is identified as "the Holy One of God" (Mark 1:24; Luke 4:34; John 6:69, NIV). His holiness is rooted in the fact that Mary's conception of him was the work of the Holy Spirit (Luke 1:35). Further, God's declaration of being pleased with Jesus and the anointing of the Holy Spirit at his baptism attested to the holiness he possessed and would impart to his followers (Matt. 3:13-17; Mark 1:9-11; Luke 3:21-22; John 17:17-19; 20:22).

Jesus redefined the boundaries of **cleanness** and **uncleanness**. He engaged and interacted with the spheres of uncleanness to impart his holiness to the people he encountered by welcoming them into fellowship, forgiving their **sins**, reversing their sicknesses, restoring them to right relationship with God and their neighbors, and challenging them to honor God the Father by adopting a new way of life.

In the letter to the Ephesians, "to be holy and blameless" is identified as the purpose of God's **election** (1:3-4, NIV). The same language is used later to describe the **church** as being a corporate entity and having a corporate identity in relation to Christ (5:27). This communal understanding of holiness is attested elsewhere in Romans 12:1-2, where the cultic imagery is merged with that of plurality in unity: "present *your bodies* as *a* living, holy, pleasing *sacrifice* to God" (AT, emphasis added). The apostle described what this act of worship looks like in daily life (Rom. 12:3–15:6; cf. Col. 3:12-17).

In the letter of James, the theme of holiness is grounded partly in his discussion of the concepts of purity and perfection. The use of *teleios* (1:4, 17, 25; 3:2), *teleō* (2:8), and *teleioō* (2:22) is **ethical** in nature and communal in its outworking. For example, perfection is achieved when a person is able to control his or her speech (3:2). It is also at work in those who abide in and act according to the perfect law of liberty. Perfection finds its expression in what James described as religion that is pure and unblemished in the sight of God the Father—namely, to care for the widows and orphans in their affliction and to keep oneself from being defiled by the world (1:25-27, author's paraphrase). In 1 Peter, the concept of holiness contains ethical and communal characteristics and is also firmly rooted in the OT. For example, as in Deuteronomy 18:13, the Epistle is replete with the language of nonconformity, obedience to God, purification, and devotion to God that the elect living in the diaspora must display (e.g., 1 Pet. 1:17, 22-23; 2:11-17; 3:8-12; 4:1-6). Further, the author drew on Leviticus 19:2 and used it as a basis for his exhortation (1 Pet. 1:14-16). Leviticus 19 contains the guidelines God had set forward for community life in Israel. In appropriating this text, the author of 1 Peter is suggesting that as the people of Israel were called to display God's character in everyday life, so members of the present community are required to display behavior that is characteristic of those who now are members of God's family. In addition, as Israel was set apart to show the nations the way to God, so the community is expected to **witness** God's **grace** and lovingkindness to the people around it, even its detractors. The image of the "living stones" built as a "spiritual house" and constituting a "holy priesthood" in 2:5 (NIV) also contributes to this understanding. The "spiritual house" is reminiscent of the temple where God dwelt and fellowshipped with his people. This highlights the community's corporate identity, its relationship with God, and the role it plays toward the world.

See also Biblical Ethics; Reconciliation; Works.

Resources
Brower, Kent E., and Andy Johnson, eds. *Holiness and Ecclesiology in the New Testament.* Grand Rapids: Eerdmans, 2007.

Hübner, Hans. "τέλειος." Pages 342-44 in vol. 3 of *EDNT.*

Joseph, Abson Prédestin. "Social Holiness in James and 1 Peter." Pages 29-40 in *Holy Imagination: Rethinking Social Holiness.* Edited by Nathan Crawford, Jonathan Dodrill, and David Wilson. Lexington, KY: Emeth Press, 2015.

Kuhn, Karl Georg, and Otto Procksch. "ἅγιος." Pages 88-110 in vol. 1 of *TDNT.*

Naudé, Jackie A. "קדשׁ." Pages 877-87 in vol. 3 of *NIDOTTE.*

Olivier, J. P. J. "תמם." Pages 306-8 in vol. 4 of *NIDOTTE.*

Wright, David P., and Robert Hodgson Jr. "Holiness." Pages 237-54 in vol. 3 of *ABD.*

ABSON PRÉDESTIN JOSEPH, PHD

COMPASSION

Exodus 34:6 declares, "The LORD, the LORD, the compassionate and gracious God, slow to anger, abounding in love and faithfulness" (NIV; see also 2 Chron. 30:9; Neh. 9:17; Pss. 86:15; 103:8; 111:4; 145:8; Joel 2:13; Jon. 4:2). After the divine name, the first attribute is "compassionate" (Hebr., *raḥûm*) followed by "gracious" (Hebr., *ḥannûn*). These adjectives, while also used of humans, are most often applied to God and usually appear together, although the order varies. The original root behind *raḥûm* was *reḥem*, meaning "womb." This reflects a deep-seated parental (not merely maternal) **love** and concern. "As a father has compassion on his children, so the Lord has compassion on those who fear him" (Ps. 103:13, NIV).

Divine compassion is more than a sentimental response; it evokes action. "But the Lord was gracious [*hānan*] to them and had compassion [*rāham*] and showed concern for them because of his **covenant** with Abraham, Isaac and Jacob. To this day he has been unwilling to destroy them or banish them from his presence" (2 Kings 13:23, NIV). Compassion may be shown through a delay in sending **judgment** or in renewal after an extended period of difficulty: "Then the Lord your God will restore your fortunes and have compassion [*rāham*] on you and gather you again from all the nations where he scattered you" (Deut. 30:3, NIV).

Another related term, *hāmal* (spare; pity), occurs slightly less frequently than *rāham*. In about one third of its occurrences, God is the active subject: "'On the day when I act,' says the Lord Almighty, 'they will be my treasured possession. I will spare [*hāmal*] them, just as a father has compassion and spares [*hāmal*] his son who serves him'" (Mal. 3:17, NIV).

In the Septuagint, various forms of the Greek root *eleos* (mercy) were most commonly used to translate these Hebrew terms. In the NT, Jesus used *eleos* to rebuke the Pharisees: "You have neglected the more important matters of the **law**—**justice, mercy** and faithfulness" (Matt. 23:23, NIV). Like its Hebrew counterparts, *eleos* is not simply an emotional reaction but also involves action. When people requested healing, they asked that Jesus "have mercy" (Matt. 15:22; Mark 10:47; Luke 18:38-39, NIV).

Exclusive to the Gospels is *splanchnizomai*, meaning "have pity" or "feel compassion." This term also includes action. When Jesus "saw a large crowd, he had compassion on them and healed their sick" (Matt. 14:14, NIV). When the father saw his lost son, he was "filled with compassion for him; he ran to his son" (Luke 15:20, NIV).

A third Greek term, *oiktirmōn* (compassionate), occurs in one verse in the Gospels: "Be merciful, just as you Father is merciful" (Luke 6:36, NIV). Paul used *oiktirmōn* (pl. of *oiktirmos* [compassion]) to speak of God's action, which in turn required a response: "In view of God's mercy . . . offer your bodies as a living **sacrifice**" (Rom. 12:1, NIV; see also Phil. 2:1-2). The concept of compassion is never simply an emotion but also an active response.

See also Fear of the Lord/God; Grace.

CLINTON A. BRANSCOMBE, MREL

COMPLETENESS/INTEGRITY (*tōm*)

The Hebrew verb for "to complete" or "to finish" is *tāmam* (Strong 1990, no. H8552). Solomon "completed" or "finished" the work to overlay the interior of the temple with gold (1 Kings 6:22, author's paraphrase). The noun is *tōm*, "completeness" (no. H8537). The Hebrew language is verb driven, and thus there are sixty-four occurrences of this verb, and a fewer number of the noun form (twenty-eight occurrences). Hebrew nouns are usually based on verbs, so the noun is literally "completeness" or "fullness." Metaphorically, it is primarily "integrity" or "innocence" and can also mean "safety," "prosperity," or "truth." There is an overlap of meaning with the noun *šālôm* (no. H7965), which is based on a different verb that also means "to complete" (no. H7999; e.g., 1 Kings 7:51).

1. *Completeness, Fullness.* Out of twenty-eight occurrences of *tōm*, only two have the literal meaning of "completeness" or "fullness." In Job 21:23, Job laments the failure of the doctrine of **retribution**. According to this doctrine, the righteous should live a long and prosperous life, while the wicked should be cut short. Instead, Job observed that the wicked often live long lives, dying in peace, "full of strength" or "completely strong" (AT; lit. "in bone of his completeness"—specifically, "bone" is related to a verb meaning "to be strong" [Strong 1990, no. H6105]; see below for the possibility that this occurrence should be understood as "prosperity").

The second literal usage is in Isaiah 47:9, which is an oracle against Babylon. According to the oracle, Babylon would become both childless and a widow in one day. This childlessness and widowhood will be "complete" (lit., "as their completeness"; "in full measure," NIV).

2. *Integrity, Innocence.* Nineteen times, *tōm* is used metaphorically to mean "integrity" or "innocence." The word is often used in the phrase "integrity of heart," suggesting that the metaphorical use comes from the idea of having a full or complete heart (Gen. 20:5, 6; 1 Kings 9:4; Pss. 78:72; 101:2). "Heart" in Hebrew signifies the organ of thinking, will, or attitude. Ancient Hebrews had no conception of the function of the brain.

Integrity is not only an attitude (as suggested by the connection with "heart") but also an action. This is suggested by the connection with walking (or "way"). This is an important concept in Psalm 26, which mentions it twice: "I have walked in my integrity" (vv. 1, 11, ESV; see also Job 4:6; Ps. 101:2; Prov. 2:7; 10:9; 19:1; 20:7; 28:6). The Bible often uses the metaphor of a path to describe conduct (e.g., Ps. 119:105).

Integrity is sometimes paralleled with **righteousness** and contrasted with wickedness. Hebrew poetry operates by placing lines in parallel, rather than rhyming. This means that the parallel line can give a hint to the meaning of the first line (in synonymous parallelism; and the opposite is true with antithetical parallelism). Psalms 7:8 [9 HB] and 25:21 connect integrity with parallel lines of righteousness and uprightness.

Elsewhere, wickedness is in the parallel line. Integrity is contrasted with iniquity (Prov. 10:29), **sin** (13:6), perverse speech or action (19:1; 28:6).

While integrity can be an attitude or an action, it can also be the lack of malice in the sense of innocence or even ignorance. Pharaoh's punishment for marrying Sarah was mitigated because of his innocence, for he thought that Sarah was Abraham's sister (Gen. 20:5, 6; see also 2 Sam. 15:11). He was innocent by reason of ignorance. In a couple of places, ignorance is the main nuance. The archer who shot King Ahab did so "at random." He was not trying to kill the king, since he did not recognize him on account of his disguise (1 Kings 22:34; 2 Chron. 18:33).

In one place, integrity is parallel with "skill." This reflects a broader definition of wisdom in the Bible, which includes both integrity and skill (Ps. 78:72). **Wisdom** is more than intellectual prowess. It is primarily the action of making godly choices, hence its close connection with righteousness. However, it is broad enough to include the skill required of the tabernacle artisans (Exod. 31:6).

3. *Safety, Prosperity.* One or two occurrences of *tōm* signify "safety" or "prosperity." Although there is little in the context to make a certain determination, this definition is shared by the similar word *šālôm*, which also comes from a verb meaning "to complete" or "to finish." In the verse before Psalm 41:12 [13 HB], the psalmist praised God for his safety from enemies, then declares "you uphold me in my *safety*" (AT; "Because of my *integrity* you uphold me" [NIV]; emphasis added).

The definition of "prosperity" may be present in Job 21:23, where *tōm* is usually taken in its literal meaning of "completeness" or "fullness" ("full vigor" [NIV]). The context is the wicked prospering and living long (Job 21:7-16). So the idea of prosperity fits the flow of thought, with the sense that "one person dies in prosperity of health" (v. 23, AT).

4. *Truth.* Although the etymology is uncertain, six times what appears to be the plural of *tōm* (*tummîm* [Strong 1990, no. H8550]) is used to signify the divining equipment (cf. *'urîm* [no. H224]) used by the priesthood (Exod. 28:30; Lev. 8:8; Deut. 33:8; Ezra 2:63; Neh. 7:65). Most English versions leave the words untranslated: "Urim and Thummim" (NIV). Douay-Rheims follows the ancient Greek version (LXX) and translates the words "the rational [breastplate] of judgment doctrine [*'urîm*] and truth [*tummîm*]" (e.g., Exod. 38:30). The word *'urîm* is the plural of the word "light." This makes the names of the priestly articles "light and truth," which is reasonable for articles that are used for divination, even though the exact nature of these articles is unknown.

See also Divination.

Resources

Gerstenberger, E. "תמם *tmm* to be complete." Pages 1424-28 in vol. 3 of *TLOT*.
Olivier, J. P. J. "תמם." Pages 306-8 in vol. 4 of *NIDOTTE*.
Strong, James. *The New Strong's Exhaustive Concordance of the Bible.* Nashville: Thomas Nelson, 1990.

STEPHEN J. BENNETT, PHD

CONFESSION

Confession in the Bible is the declaration of a truth that relates to praising God, repenting of a sin, or converting to the way of Christ.

As for confession of sin, the most common terms used in the OT are the Hebrew verbs *yādâ* (Lev. 16:21) and *nāgad* (Ps. 38:18 [19 HB]). *Yādâ* is used for both praise to God and confession of sin. In the NT the Greek verb *exomologeō* (Mark 1:5) means "to confess one's sin." The Greek verb *homologeō* (1 John 1:9), which also means "to confess," interestingly has a communal aspect of speaking together.

Acts of confession of sin abound in the Bible. The first story involves Adam and Eve refusing to confess their sin before God, which leads to the breaking of relationship with him (Gen. 3:10-13). The characters in the Bible struggle between confession of sin and praise to God, on the one hand, and pride in oneself and rebellion toward God, on the other hand.

Three major characteristics of confession of sin can be observed within the Bible. First, just as confession or praise is done after God's saving acts, confession of sin is usually done after the people of God experience his **judgment** or his **holiness** and power. The people in the **wilderness** confessed their sins after God declared that they would not enter the promised land (Num. 14:40). Nehemiah confessed the sins of his people after hearing of the desolation of **Jerusalem** (Neh. 1:6-9). Job was silenced as God listed his mighty works in **creation** and was moved to declare his **repentance** (Job 40:1–42:6). The Prodigal Son decided to return to his father and confess after experiencing the humiliation of separation from him (Luke 15:17-21).

Second, though confession of **sin** is sometimes personal, it is usually done, if not communal, by a priest, **prophet**, or king on behalf of the entire people. During the Day of Atonement, the high priest would confess the sins of all the people on the head of the goat to be sent into the wilderness (Lev. 16:21). King Hezekiah cleaned the temple and confessed the sins of his fathers (2 Chron. 29:6). Ezra mourned and confessed that his people had turned away from God by marrying the Gentiles (Ezra 9:4-7, 10-15). Daniel, too, confessed with tears the rebellion of his people (Dan. 9:5-15).

Finally, confession of sin is usually part of the act of worship to God. The Psalms, some of which were used in communal worship, abound in confessions of **sin** (Pss. 32, 40, 51, and 130). Isaiah confessed the sins of his people in the temple as he witnessed the worship of the seraphim (Isa. 6:3-5). After his confession in the presence of God, he was sent out to do God's work (vv. 8-13). James, in his final advice for the **church**, lists communal confession of sins as one of the practices of the people of God (James 5:16).

See also Communal Holiness; Fall, The; Festivals; Sacred Times; Sacrificial System.

NABIL HABIBI, MA

CONSCIENCE

The English word comes from the Latin *conscientia*, sharing "knowledge with" another or oneself. No Hebrew word shares linguistic similarities with the English. The OT uses various images for the inner person, the most common being "heart" (*lēb*). The heart is where decisions are made for how a person lives. Negatively, one may experience inner pain after violating God's will or **law**, or impulsively doing something without considering the consequences (1 Sam. 25:31). David's heart was struck with pain after realizing the consequences of his actions (24:5; 2 Sam. 24:10).

Positively, the heart can be pure before God as demonstrated by **integrity** and honesty (Ps. 24:4), resulting in blessings from God (73:1). **Righteousness** leads to a blameless heart (Job 27:6). Faithfully walking with God brings a peaceful heart (2 Kings 20:3). Blamelessness results from hiding **God's word** in the heart so that it can be recalled as a moral guide (Ps. 40:8 [9 HB]; 119:11). This growing sensitivity to God's word will move one to **obedience** (Deut. 30:14). David was a man after God's own heart because he followed God's will and developed a heart sensitive to God (1 Sam. 13:14; Acts 13:22).

Another metaphor translated "conscience" is the kidney (*kělāyôt*). God knows the motives of the inner person (Jer. 17:10). God tests the righteous **integrity** of the kidneys along with the mind or heart (Pss. 7:8-9 [9-10 HB]; 26:2; Jer. 11:20; 20:12). The inner person responds to God's instruction (Ps. 16:7). The kidneys may also experience pain in disobedience (73:21).

The etymology of the Greek *syneidēsis* is similar to the Latin and means "knowing together with" someone or as a form of self-awareness, which may lead to embracing virtues or avoiding vices. Of the thirty occurrences in the NT, twenty-two are found in **Pauline** letters. The word is not found in the **Gospels**.

The conscience is a gift of God and a way God communicates his will to us. The conscience may be strong or weak, determined by the amount of knowledge it has and what a person does with this knowledge (1 Cor. 8:7, 10). This knowledge comes from nature (Rom. 2:15), **grace** (2 Cor. 1:12), and community (Heb. 10:22-25), which provide standards for making judgments. Rejecting God's direct or indirect **revelation** leads to a "seared" insensitivity to **evil** (1 Tim. 4:2, NIV; Titus 1:15).

The goal of the conscience is to know and obey God's will (1 Tim. 1:5). To do this, it must be cleansed by the blood of Christ (Heb. 9:14) and cooperate with God's grace through the **Holy Spirit** (Rom. 9:1). Obedient **faith** opens our minds to renewal into the **image** of Christ (Rom. 12:1-2; 1 Cor.

2:16), making it possible to follow God's **law** written on the heart through the new **covenant** (Heb. 8:10; 10:16). The result will be a good or clear conscience (Acts 24:16; 1 Tim. 3:9; Heb. 13:18; 1 Pet 3:16).

See also Biblical Ethics; Communal Holiness.

DAVID A. ACKERMAN, PHD

CORPORATE RESPONSIBILITY

Corporate responsibility refers to the interdependent and mutual relationship that exists between an individual and the larger community to which the individual belongs. Biblical texts depict the effects of individual actions upon the larger community. Both divine retribution upon a community and human retribution upon a group within the community can result from a single person's crime. Israel's futile attempt in capturing Ai resulted from Achan's taking war spoils out of Jericho. Although other members of the community had not personally participated in Achan's act, the text describes his action in corporate language: "The Israelites broke faith in regard to the devoted things" (Josh. 7:1, NRSV). Achan's family suffered death as a result of his act (vv. 19-26; see also 2 Sam 21:1-14 for the retribution upon Saul's family for Saul's action). Prophets announced judgment upon entire nations due to the transgression of specific individuals or groups such as priests, prophets, or rulers. The Deuteronomistic writer attributed Judah's exile to the sins of a single king, Manasseh (2 Kings 24:3-4).

In contrast to those biblical texts that hold an entire community responsible for the acts of an individual, other texts insist that the individual alone be held accountable for his or her actions. Deuteronomic law stipulates that "parents shall not be put to death for their children, nor shall children be put to death for their parents" (Deut. 24:16, NRSV). Overturning the proverb "The parents have eaten sour grapes, and the children's teeth are set on edge" (Jer. 31:29 and Ezek. 18:2, NRSV), Jeremiah and Ezekiel insist that "only the person who sins . . . shall die" (Ezek. 18:4, NRSV; Jer. 31:30).

In attempting to reconcile what appears to be contrasting perspectives on the relationship between the individual and the corporate entity, OT scholar H. Wheeler Robinson proposed that ancient Israel's thinking evolved from an early notion of corporate personality to a later understanding of individualism. Robinson argued that early Israel did not perceive the individual to be a distinct and separate entity from the corporate entity (e.g., the family, community, or nation to which the individual belonged). As the community was present in a single member, retribution upon the community could result from the act of an individual. In order to reconcile the understanding of corporate personality with other biblical texts that emphasize individual retribution, Robinson proposed that a more sophisticated, more logical, and morally superior understanding of the individual had evolved by the time of the eighth-century prophets. Over time, this understanding replaced the notion of corporate personality. Each individual was ultimately viewed as a distinct and separate entity responsible only for his or her actions.

Subsequent analyses of biblical texts raised significant objections to the notions of both corporate personality and radical individualism in the Bible. Neither early nor later biblical texts deny the individual as having a separate and unique identity within the community. Neither do texts portray the individual as lacking awareness of being a distinct entity within the larger corporate entity. Biblical texts assume that individual actions could and did have either direct or indirect effects upon the community to which the individual belongs and thus do not portray a radical, privatized individualism.

Both ancient Israel and the early Christian community viewed the individual as participating in a symbiotic and interdependent relationship of solidarity with other individuals and with the community at large. Corporate life affected individuals who composed the community, while individual actions affected the community to which the individuals belonged. Within this intricate web of mutual relationality, the individual shared responsibility for other individuals and for the community at large. Likewise, the community shared responsibility for the individuals who composed it.

Three categories of corporate responsibility may be distinguished: affecting, generational, and representative.

Affecting Responsibility. As **covenant** communities, both ancient Israel and the early **church** understood that individual action is not merely a privatized or isolated event. As the identity of an individual encompassed other persons (e.g., parent with child, king with people, neighbor with neighbor, patron with client, citizen with noncitizen), those other persons and the corporate entity itself both affected and were affected by the individual. Social and judicial regulations stipulated the manner in which individuals and the community were to engage appropriately within this intricate web of communal relationality.

The apostle Paul's metaphor of the church as a physical body (1 Cor. 12) demonstrates the affecting nature of covenantal corporate responsibility. Individuals compose a corporate body that is larger than and that gives defining context to the individual member. Nevertheless, the individual member does not lose his or her uniqueness or function within that body. While no member can isolate himself or herself or another member from the body, each member is responsible to the other: "If one member suffers, all suffer together with it; if one member is honored, all rejoice together with it" (v. 26, NRSV).

Generational Responsibility. Corporate responsibility crosses generational lines as one generation influences subsequent generations either for good or bad. Each generation is responsible to testify to Yahweh's faithfulness to the succeeding generation (Exod. 12:26-27; Deut. 6:7; 11:19; Josh. 4:19-24). A generation not present at an event is capable of confessing Yahweh's deeds as if it were present with the first generation (Deut. 26:5-10). Biblical Israel was also keenly aware of the manner in which one generation's actions have residual consequences upon successive generations (Exod. 34:7; Num. 14:18).

Representative Responsibility. Literarily and theologically, biblical texts identify certain individuals with a corporate entity in such a way that the narrative of the individual is representative of the larger group. The individual is the embodiment of the group so that the group becomes the extension of the individual. This literary-theological representation is apparent in such narratives as Jacob (for Israel) and Adam (for humanity). As the apostle Paul viewed Jesus Christ as the second Adam through whom a new humanity has begun, the community of Christ's followers, the church, becomes the extension of Christ himself.

The biblical notion of corporate responsibility challenges, on the one hand, a radical, privatized individualism in which the community is merely an assemblage of independent persons and, on the other hand, an excessive communalism in which the individual is absorbed into the corporate entity so that the individual forfeits his or her distinctiveness within the community. John Wesley's statement regarding "solitary religion" echoes this biblical concept of corporate responsibility: "'Holy solitaries' is a phrase no more consistent with the **gospel** than holy adulterers. The gospel of Christ knows of no religion but social; no **holiness** but social holiness" (1739, viii).

See also Communal Holiness.

Resources

Kaminsky, Joel S. "Corporate Responsibility." Pages 285-87 in *Eerdmans Dictionary of the Bible*. Edited by David Noel Freedman, Allen C. Myers, and Astrid B. Beck. Grand Rapids: Eerdmans, 2000.

———. *Corporate Responsibility in the Hebrew Bible*. JSOTSup 196. Sheffield, UK: Sheffield Academic Press, 1995.

———. "The Sins of the Fathers: A Theological Investigation of the Biblical Tension between Corporate and Individual Retribution." *Judaism: A Quarterly Journal of Jewish Life and Thought* 46, no. 3 (1997): 319-32.

Robinson, H. Wheeler. *Corporate Personality in Ancient Israel*. Rev. ed. Edinburgh: T and T Clark, 1991.

Rogerson, John W. "The Hebrew Conception of Corporate Personality: A Re-examination." *JTS* 21 (1970): 1-16.

Sang-Won (Aaron) Son. *Corporate Elements in Pauline Anthropology*. Fort Worth: Pontifical Bible Institute, 2001.

Wesley, John, and Charles Wesley. *Hymns and Sacred Poems*. London: William Strahan, 1739.

TIMOTHY M. GREEN, PHD

COSMOLOGY

"Cosmology" is a term used to denote a developed perspective on the known and imagined world, its parts, and their relationships to one another. Biblical cosmology is the view of the world represented in the Bible and held by those who produced it and their early audiences. This includes their views of physical and metaphysical elements, the natural and supernatural aspects of life as they experienced and imagined it.

These writers, like their contemporaries, used their senses to experience nature and the divine. The cosmologies they transmitted in authoritative texts were based upon this and what they inherited through their ancestors, all of whom sought to explain and interpret what they knew or assumed to be true.

The producers of the Bible had sensory abilities just as we moderns do. They, too, observed the wonders of the heavens and the earth (Pss. 24:1-2; 104:10-26). However, in important ways their explanations were not the same as ours. They had no telescopes through which to peer into distant galaxies, no knowledge of how atmospheric conditions affect our weather, and no microscopes for examining cellular tissue. They did not possess the tools or methods modern archaeologists use for unsealing records found in fossils, rock formations, and artifacts located in ancient layers of sediment. The Bible was produced and received as Scripture long before modern science began to influence our understanding of the vast natural order.

This means that the biblical writers did not realize that the light of the sun took eight minutes to reach them or that the stars that blanketed the night sky reflected light that originated billions of light years away in **space** and **time**. They did not know that the ground on which they stood was part of a planet that was part of a solar system within a galaxy that was only one of hundreds of billions of galaxies. Nonetheless, they stood in awe of the wonders of **creation** and expressed **faith** in their creator God, whom they did know.

Although the Bible does not present what moderns would call a scientific cosmology, and we cannot search it for explanations about realities unknown to the writers (such as dinosaurs and the death of stars), many sections of it present a *logia* or an understanding of the *cosmos*, the world they inhabited. This is expressed or assumed in many places throughout both Testaments. Genesis 1, Isaiah 40:12-28, and Job 38–39 provide particularly rich illustrations of biblical cosmology, which, like other ancient cosmologies, involves order based on observable spatial considerations, particularly the vertical axis. The Bible's most basic cosmology includes the "**land**" (Hebr. *ʾereṣ* translated "earth") that lies under the "sky" or "heavens" (Hebr., *šāmayim*), and waters that are below the land or earth. Lower elements, within and under the land or earth, could be imagined. When humans died, if buried in the earth, they were thought to transgress lower, to an **afterlife** in Sheol, an even lower region (1 Sam. 2:6; Ps. 18:5 [6 HB]; Isa. 38:18).

In Genesis 1:9, the "dry land" (Hebr., *hayyabbāšâ*) named "land" or "earth" (*'ereṣ*; v. 10) emerged from waters that remained under the "dome" or "firmament" (Hebr., *rāqîa'*) named "sky" or "heavens" (*šāmayim*; v. 8), the divider of waters mentioned in verses 6-7 (cf. Ezek. 1:22, 26). The sun, moon, and stars were situated in the *rāqîa'*, now *šāmayim*, above the land (Gen. 1:14); the land is the source of creepers and beasts (v. 24), the habitation of humans (vv. 26-30), and the nurturer of all land creatures. The waters above the *rāqîa'* or *šāmayim* were the source of rain, hail, and snow (7:11; Job 38:22). The waters under the earth were the source of seas, rivers, lakes, and floods and the habitation of all sea creatures (Gen. 1:20-22; 7:11).

The creator of all this (and of humans who create cosmologies) was God, who spoke light, the sky, dry land, the sun and moon, and creatures into existence. God named the emerging elements and structured them to order day and night, seasons, and years; to bring forth inhabitants (1:14-20, 24); and to feed the creatures, including the humans that God made in God's own **image** (vv. 26-30).

This three-storied cosmology is also depicted in one strand of the flood story (7:11; 8:2) and assumed elsewhere. Passages in the **Wisdom** literature envision pillars holding the land or earth above the subterranean rivers and waters (Job 38:4-6; Ps. 104:5). Wisdom itself plays a part in creation in Proverbs 8:22-31 (later taken up and applied to Christ in John 1 and Col. 1). The emphasis in Isaiah 40 is on incomparable YHWH, the everlasting God, creator of the ends of the earth and all its creatures (cf. Job 38-39).

Regarding creator-creature relationships within the biblical cosmology, YHWH, Israel's God, is exalted—the highest figure in the hierarchy of the biblical cosmos relationally and in the heavens spatially. Nonetheless, in the biblical story, YHWH found ways to reveal intention, **hope**, despair, and need and to encounter, **love**, and deliver humans. YHWH, God Most High, the **Holy** One, the everlasting Creator, portrayed in the Bible as dwelling in the highest heavens (1 Kings 8:27-30; Ps. 11:4), wished to dwell with people on their land (Ps. 74:2; Joel 3:17-18).

The NT writers assumed the physical and metaphysical cosmology of the OT Scriptures (Matt. 16:18-19; Rev. 5:3, 13). They affirmed that Christ Jesus, in whom God was fully incarnate, is Lord, creator, and sustainer of his world (John 1:1-18 [Logos]; 1 Cor. 8:6; Phil. 2:6-7; Col. 1:15-20). They proclaimed that in Jesus of Nazareth, beginning as the infant son of Mary, God became fully human while remaining fully God: "Very, truly, I tell you, before Abraham was, I am" (John 8:58, NRSV). Jesus, like his Father, exercised authority over elements of nature and all powers inhabiting the cosmic realms (Ps. 96:4-6; Mark 4:35–5:19).

Eventually, Jesus submitted to death but, after his redemptive **suffering**, was raised to the heavens by God, while remaining with earthbound people through his **Spirit**. Jesus prepares a place for them (John 14:1-3) and will bring a new **Jerusalem**, where he will dwell and make all things new (Rev. 21:1-5). Thus the NT variously depicts a unification of the realms of heaven and earth, calling for unity among God's people through their knowledge of God and love for others.

See also Incarnation; Names of God; Parousia; Resurrection.

KAREN STRAND WINSLOW, PHD

COVENANT

This important concept in biblical thought first appears when God promised to make a covenant (Hebr., *bĕrît*) with Noah (Gen. 6:18; cf. 9:9-17). Our English terms "covenant" and "testament" are inadequate to express the theological richness of the notion as found in Scripture. At its core is a reference to a simple binding relationship between two parties. It quickly takes on a much richer and more complex significance because of its recurrence throughout the Bible and because it often also connotes the self-imposed obligations accepted by parties of the relationship, implying at times the concept of a pledge (Deut. 26:17-19). Indeed, the concept itself becomes so central to biblical thought, it serves as *the* organizing principle of the Bible, giving us two "Testaments" since the days of Melito of Sardis in Greek (died ca. AD 180) and Tertullian in Latin (died ca. AD 230), a usage found embedded in the Bible itself (Luke 22:20; 2 Cor. 3:6, 14).

The Hebrew term *bĕrît* occurs 285 times in the OT, and its Greek counterpart, *diathēkē*, 33 times in the NT. The latter denoted "last will and testament" in Hellenistic times. But the LXX used it so frequently for the Hebrew *bĕrît* that *diathēkē* in the NT took on the theological nuances and significances of the OT usage.

Some readers speak of an Edenic or **creation** covenant as the first biblical covenant. However, the term "covenant" does not appear in Genesis 1–3. To frame God's relationship with Adam and Eve as a covenant is a theological imposition upon the text often driven by a preconceived notion of "dispensations." The first biblical covenant is God's commitment to save Noah and his family from the floodwaters (6:18; 9:9-17). This Noahic covenant includes obligations on Noah's part, since he was required to follow God's instructions for the building of the ark, to make preparations for the flood, and to avoid blood guilt in the future (9:5-6). The covenant includes God's promise to refrain from cataclysmic floods in the future—a promise marked for all time by the rainbow, which became a sign of the covenant. This universal covenant establishes God's program of general revelation for all humanity and provides a context for the other covenants, which will introduce more specific, special revelation.

The second covenant is that between God and Abraham (chs. 15, 17). In a blood ritual, God confirmed the **land** promise to Abraham, in which he "made a covenant" with him (15:18, NIV). The first paragraph of Genesis 15 is also a confirmation of the seed promise (vv. 1-6; cf. 12:7). In a subsequent passage, God changed the patriarch's name, from Abram to Abraham, and gave circumcision (17:1-22), parallel to Noah's rainbow, as an identifying marker of the covenant relationship. Like the Noahic covenant, this patriarchal covenant contains promissory elements that seem at first glance to be unconditional; God will make Abraham exceedingly fruitful, an "everlasting covenant" (vv. 7, 13, 19, NIV), which is similar to God's promise not to flood the earth again. In this case, the patriarch's obligations are summarized in the stipulations "walk before me faithfully and be blameless" (v. 1, NIV) and in the practice of circumcision as acceptance of his part in the covenant (vv. 9-14, 23-27). In this Abrahamic covenant, more has been revealed to fewer; the universal scope of the first covenant has been replaced with the individual concerns of a wandering nomad. Note also that the all-encompassing Noahic covenant was never nullified, marked by its rainbow sign in perpetuity. Therefore, the Abrahamic covenant does not supersede it but instead builds upon it.

The third covenant of the OT is the Mosaic, in which the scope widens to the national level. The principles of the ancestral family covenant are applied here to national Israel. More than general formulaic or literary parallels, the Abrahamic covenant is the hermeneutical key to the rest of the Pentateuch (Exod. 2:23-25) and has a genetic theological connection with God's deliverance of Israel from bondage in Egypt and the Mosaic covenant (3:6, 15). The patriarchal and Mosaic covenants are therefore organically connected, making them closer to each other than either is to the universal covenant of Noah. Here the conditions of the covenant are clarified in elaborate stipulations—the **laws** of God, detailed in the Ten Commandments and their applications and crystallized as the **Torah** in Deuteronomy.

The relationship between Yahweh and Israel in the Mosaic covenant is a confirmation and fulfillment of the promises to Abraham and demonstrates the faithfulness of God. After redeeming the Israelites from **slavery** in Egypt, God revealed more of his nature to them, established a unique relationship with them, and promised again to fulfill the land promise (Exod. 6:6-8). Israel's essential nature as a missionary nation was clarified as part of this covenant; now defined as a priestly kingdom, Israel would serve as mediator between God and the nations, thus fulfilling again the promises to Abraham (Gen. 12:2-3; Exod. 19:5-6).

The fourth covenant in the OT's narrative framework is the Davidic covenant (2 Sam. 7; cf. also 23:5; 1 Kings 8:24; 2 Chron. 7:18; 13:5; 21:7; Pss. 89:1-4 [2-5 HB]; 132:11-18). Here we move again from the broad national scope of the Mosaic covenant to the royal family itself, through which Yahweh promised a dominant and permanent kingdom. God ensured a son of David upon the throne in **Jerusalem**. This permanency of **God's kingdom** is the promissory element of the Davidic covenant and has been taken by some to be an unconditional covenant, especially because of the "forever" language used to describe it (2 Sam. 7:13, 16, NIV). However, "forever" in this context can be misleading and needs to be balanced with other references stating the continuance of the Davidic dynasty as clearly conditional (1 Kings 8:25; 9:4-5; Ps. 132:11-18).

Other contrasts between the Mosaic and Davidic covenants have been assumed, taking the Davidic as pushing the Mosaic covenant into the background, superseding it in some way. In this interpretation, the Davidic covenant is taken as a new, everlasting, unconditional covenant in contrast to the older, outmoded, conditional Mosaic covenant. However, the promises to David cannot be elevated over the **law** of Moses. To do so fails to appreciate the historical embeddedness of the covenants in their narrative contexts at the expense of the sameness of those covenants. The OT evinces a basic organic unity in the program of covenants, through which God has revealed his essential nature to ancient Israel. Each of these covenants is, at one and the same moment, different but similar to the preceding ones; none supersedes the others. Their whole is greater than the sum of their individual parts.

The OT itself recognizes these iterations of divine covenants as incomplete. Ultimately, God promised through his **prophets** a "new covenant" (Jer. 31:31, NIV) in which the law will be internalized and knowledge of God will be intimate and purifying (vv. 32-34; cf. Ezek. 36:26-28; 37:26-28). Such **holiness** of heart and hands (Wesley's "inward and outward" holiness, involving both inner transformation and outward, ethical dimensions) was the objective of all these OT covenants. Yet the OT points forward to a day when the covenants will be renewed, restored, and offered to all humanity through David's greater Son, by means of the blood of the new covenant (Mark 14:24; Luke 22:20). This new covenant through the life, ministry, and death of the **Messiah** makes his followers "ministers of a new covenant" (2 Cor. 3:6, NIV) in which the **glory** of God is revealed (vv. 7-18).

Scholars have long recognized that modern-language equivalents, such as the English word "covenant," are inadequate to capture the rich multifaceted dimensions of the biblical concept. Because of its wide range of significances, some have mistakenly argued that in certain contexts of the OT, "covenant" connotes the unilateral, unconditional, and unbreakable promise of God. At times, scholars have distinguished between "promissory" and "obligatory" covenants, taking the Abrahamic and Davidic covenants as promissory and comparable to ANE royal land grants. The Mosaic covenant is obligatory and more akin to ancient political treaties.

Since the days of Walther Eichrodt, most scholars have acknowledged that in both profane ANE usage and the Bible's religious usage, covenant should always be thought of as a bilateral relationship. Further, biblical covenants, like their ANE counterparts, are binary, and most are asymmetrical. "Binary" means that covenants are not simply mutual agreements between two parties but agreements that consist of two elements: promise and obligation. Some covenants emphasize the promises while hardly mentioning the obligations of the parties involved. These are usually identified as promissory covenants. By contrast, others leave the promissory elements implicit and are primarily obligatory covenants. Thus the term "unconditional" is misleading because all covenants are both promissory and obligatory by definition, although either component may be left entirely implicit in the language describing a covenant.

The burden of maintaining such relationships is almost always unequally distributed (genuine parity agreements are rare), but we must not forget that covenants are, in essence, two-sided relationships. Covenants are better understood as asymmetrical, with the Abrahamic and Davidic covenants stressing the promises of the powerful party (God), and the Mosaic covenant stressing the responsibilities of the weaker party (Israel). In this sense, there are no unconditional covenants in the Bible, but at times God is said to emphasize through "eternal" promises (that is, into perpetuity) his intentions for humanity.

Such promises associated with the covenants may be considered extrapolations of the benefits of those covenants into the future for the perpetual edification of humanity. Specific and narrow promises—salvation through the flood waters (Noah), the promises of land and seed (Abraham), and the promise of a Davidic dynasty (David)—were the immediate promises of the covenants. Those covenants were by definition conditioned upon human obligations. But each covenant also bore additional divine obligations in perpetuity for the edification of all humanity.

Some in the **church** have debated whether there is one covenant with multiple applications or numerous covenants. So-called covenant theologians assume that the biblical covenants have an organically unified character, while advocates of classical dispensationalism assume that there are a number of distinct dispensations (often seven), each governed by its own covenant. The idea of dispensations with distinct covenants assumes a particular eschatological perspective that is foreign to Wesleyan thought. Wesleyans tend to focus on the unity between the Bible's two Testaments; it is thus more natural to think of the continuity of the OT's four covenants, illustrating that covenants may be developed and adapted, but not superseded. The Mosaic covenant does not make null and void the Abrahamic covenant, no more than Zion (Davidic) supersedes Sinai (Mosaic). The distinctions between the OT covenants are differences of degree rather than kind. Ultimately then, the NT builds upon and assumes the OT, without nullifying or replacing it.

In sum, the biblical concept of covenant establishes a relationship between two parties, where such relationship did not exist previously. The idea appears to have begun in early Israel as a solemn ritual involving animal sacrifice and oaths in order to ensure obligations on the part of one or both parties. Sometime in Israel's history, the concept was layered with a relatively standard ANE political treaty. For example, Israel's King Ahab entered a trade agreement (*bĕrît*) with the Aramean King Ben-Hadad, based on an uneasy détente between their two armies and an agreement to allow commerce in each other's capital cities, Samaria and Damascus (1 Kings 20:34).

The covenant concept found expansion in political settings between suzerains and vassals in many ANE political treaties, which then became a rich and pliable metaphor in the hands of Israel's theologians to describe its relationship with Yahweh. In this form, the covenant structure appears to have been used to give organizational arrangement to the book of Deuteronomy and perhaps individual passages such as the book of the covenant (Exod. 20–23) and the Shechemite covenant (Josh. 24). Ultimately, then, the concept of covenant becomes more than a metaphor in the NT, as it comes to describe the salvific atoning work of the Messiah and the essential hope of the church.

See also Biblical Ethics; Deuteronomic Theology; Fall, The; Incarnation; Progressive Revelation.

Resources

Arnold, Bill T. *Genesis*. NCBC. Cambridge, UK: Cambridge University Press, 2009.
Eichrodt, Walther. *Theology of the Old Testament*. Translated by J. A. Baker. 2 vols. The Old Testament Library. Philadelphia: Westminster Press, 1961.
Knoppers, Gary N. "Ancient Near Eastern Royal Grants and the Davidic Covenant: A Parallel?" *JAOS* 116, no. 4 (1996): 670-97.

BILL T. ARNOLD, PHD

CREATION

Christian theology understands God as the only uncreated and transcendent Being. Thus the term "creation" refers to all that is not God—what God the Creator has brought into being or has made possible. A biblical theology of creation also encompasses God's continuous sustaining **providence**, as well as God's ultimate restoration and renewal of all the earthly creation from the sweeping damage inflicted upon it by humankind turning away from God.

Most Christians, including Wesleyans, intend to interpret Scripture attuned to the guidance of Scripture itself. Yet the Bible's creation texts come from a thought world different in many ways from our own modern-postmodern era—especially on issues we think of as requiring a scientific approach. Thus we may find some of our a priori assumptions to be at odds with an authentic interpretation of these ancient texts. If so, a Wesleyan commitment should lead us to adjust our assumptions, rather than the texts' own intentions.

Genesis 1

Genesis 1:1 affirms that "God created the heavens and the earth" (NIV). Verse 2 brings the focus earthward; heavenly entities are mentioned again only in relation to the earth. Introducing the framework of the week—six days of work followed by a šabbāt (Hebr., "ceasing")—Genesis 1 presents a trifold pairing of a complex of functions and functionaries: light and light-bearers (days one and four); skies, seas and sky, and sea creatures and birds (days two and five); dry land and land creatures (days three and six).

Recent scholarship has shown the natural and intended analogues of Genesis 1 are the creation accounts of Israel's ANE neighbors. The clearest literary comparisons are with the epic hymn Enuma Elish, which, in its Babylonian version, celebrates the building and inauguration of the temple of Marduk, the "creator god." Reading Genesis 1 carefully, in the indisputably ANE context of its origin, reveals its intended subject: the inauguration of God's chosen cosmic temple, the earth. It relates a functional rather than a material ontology. That is, Genesis 1 reports not merely the initial creation of matter and material entities but also the assignment of their functions in, for, and/or with respect to God's temple, the earth. This accords with the known cosmological interests of the ANE world, including Israel.

Genesis 1, though, is not imitation; it is correction. Israel's neighbors were polytheistic, worshipping many of the entities and processes of the natural world as gods and goddesses. For example, verse 2 represents the primeval waters, not as an untamable, terrifying, and lethal goddess who must be slain—as the Enuma Elish presents her—but as an absolute stillness waiting on God's initiative. Verses 14-19 invalidates worship of the heavenly bodies in favor of the God who made them and, more importantly for Genesis 1, gave them their functions as light-bearers and regulators-markers of time for the earth and its denizens.

Much like in poetry and poetic prose, Genesis 1 is phenomenological, depicting entities and events as we experience and/or observe them. The sky is not a "bowl" (Hebr., rāqîaʿ; v. 7) but, with an unobstructed view around the horizon, it looks like one. From any one location on earth, the waters do appear to be gathered together into one place, so the dry land can appear (v. 9). Genesis 1, together with all the Bible's creation texts, is God centered, earth centered, and human centered. The Bible is not antiscientific, but its interests lie elsewhere. They are theological, anthropological, and eschatological interests, understood as God's redemption and restoration of all God's good creation, including but not limited to the earth's human inhabitants.

Genesis 2–3

That Genesis 2 is a different account is obvious from the statement of verse 4a: "These are the tôlĕdôt [accounts] of the heavens and the earth" (AT). It functions here as a transitional statement from God's establishment of the Sabbath (vv. 1-3) to a more detailed account of God's making of the 'ādām (Hebr., "human"). God first "formed" (Hebr., yāṣar) a single 'ādām, prepared him to understand God's intention that humans would live in community, and only then differentiated the lone 'ādām into two, male and female. By every literary canon (including the literature of the ANE), the two successive accounts of Genesis 1–2 establish the theological tenet that humans are the climax of God's earthly creation.

Genesis 3 reports the humans' choice to reject the God who made them, only to find that breaking that relationship also broke or badly damaged every other relationship. God's eschatological intentions for creation are revealed already in God's promise to the woman, tendered indirectly through the promise that her seed would crush the serpent's head (v. 15).

Isaiah, the Psalms, Job, and Revelation

One theological imperative of a comprehensive biblical theology is that God's creation and eschatological intentions are inseparably linked. As surely as God initially created everything "very good" (Gen. 1:31, NIV), so will God see to it that creation is restored, made new (Rev. 21:5). Seen in this light, every line of the Bible concerns creation. Some sections and pericopes, though, are creation texts, directly and intentionally.

Isaiah uses creation vocabulary, and references creation themes extensively. The Hebrew verb bārā' (create) is not the only marker of creation language, but it is an important one. Isaiah used it twenty-one times, more frequently than any other biblical book, and only Genesis 1:1–2:4 (7x) has a greater concentration of occurrences than Isaiah 45 (6x). Just as important in Isaiah, especially in chapters 40–66, are the vocabulary, images, themes, and metaphors having to do with creation, redemption, renewal, or re-creation. Vivid examples include chapters 11, 25 (part of the so-called little apocalypse, chs. 24–27), 35, 40, 48–49, 61, 65. Comprehensively, we should understand Isaiah as asserting that only God the transcendent Creator can re-create what human perverseness has marred or destroyed—and God intends to do just that.

A significant number of the Psalms are explicitly creation themed, in whole or in part. Among the better known are Psalm 8 ("When I consider . . ." [vv. 3ff., NASB]), Psalm 19 ("The heavens are telling . . ." [vv. 1ff., NASB]), Psalm 24 ("The earth is the LORD's . . ." [vv. 1ff., NASB]), Psalm 100 ("It is He who has made us . . ." [v. 3, NASB]), and Psalm 139 ("I am fearfully and wonderfully made . . ." [vv. 14ff., NASB]). Psalm 104, an elegant and eloquent hymn in praise of Yahweh as Creator and Provider, is particularly important; that it is partially sourced in an Egyptian hymn to Aton, the sun god of the Amarna revolution, proves only that purloined property *can* be restored to its rightful Owner.

Job referenced God as Creator in two of his speeches, chapters 10 and 26. Much more exalted and compelling are the monologues of God's long-awaited response at the end of the book, chapters 38–39 and 40–41. In searching rhetorical questions and vivid word pictures, these chapters make the case for God as visionary Creator and compassionate Provider. They reveal that God takes joy in creating intricately, majestically, and well. This is true even in the quarters of the earth the ancients considered empty and useless and of God's creatures that most either disregarded or regarded only with trepidation.

If the chronological arc of God's purposes in creation is from creation to redemption to eschatological fulfillment, the visions of John the Revelator constitute a glimpse of the *telos* (Gk., "goal"). "Behold, I am making all things new" (Rev. 21:5, NASB) is a creation statement. Chapters 21–22 are lyrical, infused with emotional power, and steeped in the eschatological perspective first voiced in Isaiah and Ezekiel. John saw, not the primeval garden from which the ancient pair were expelled, but **Jerusalem** the **holy** city—the representative and the abode of the **saints**, the bride of Christ. Moreover, the Tree of Life, to which the flaming sword had prevented access, is multiplied, lining both sides of the river of life flowing out from under the throne of God, and freely approached by anyone within the city.

The Whole of Scripture

We must be content with mentioning only a handful of the creation-significant words, lines, themes, and instructions contained within the rest of the Bible's pages. The legal material of the Pentateuch or **Torah** (Hebr., *tôrâ*, "instruction") essentially is God teaching ancient Israel how to live together as an agrarian subsistence-village culture and economy. To sustain such a life in God's intended *šālôm* (Hebr., "**peace**," "wholeness," and "plenty") means the Torah is instruction in creation care, broadly conceived: trust in God's protection from external threats; living harmoniously, even with the cranky neighbor; protecting and promoting the welfare of the family, the field, the fruit trees, and the flocks; reverential and joyful worship of the God who provides all; instruction of the next generations in faithfulness to Yahweh and in avoiding imitation of Israel's pagan neighbors in their worship of God's creation—all these, and more, comprise the Torah's creation concerns.

Even the theological history of the Former **Prophets** (Joshua, Judges, 1 and 2 Samuel, and 1 and 2 Kings) contains explicit notices of God as Lord of creation. Prominent among them are God's cosmic interventions in battle on Israel's behalf (Josh. 10); Deborah's song of victory (Judg. 5); Elijah's confrontation with Baal's prophets on Mount Carmel (1 Kings 18:16-45);

and God's destruction of the Assyrian army besieging Jerusalem (2 Kings 19:20-35). The God of creation is also the God of history. God does not often intervene directly but is well able and ready to do so when both God's creation and historical purposes are served.

Besides Isaiah, others of the Latter Prophets (Jeremiah, Ezekiel, and the Twelve or Minor Prophets) also voice creation and re-creation themes. Apocalyptic literature is eschatological by definition. Ezekiel 40–48 comprises a sweeping apocalyptic vision, ending with the most succinct possible expression of the eschatological **hope**, "Yahweh is there" (48:35, AT). Amos vividly extols God as Creator (5:8-9) and as Restorer of Israel's *šālôm* in the renewed provision of agricultural abundance (9:13-15). Hosea 2 announces God's removal of divine sustenance from faithless Israel and then woos Israel again with an abundance benefitting all creation.

Proverbs extols **Wisdom** as God's handmaid in creation (8:22-31). Before and after that passage, creation is a regular and multifaceted subject of the wisdom teacher's ponderings and maxims. The five books of the Megillot (Ruth, Song of Songs, Ecclesiastes, Lamentations, Esther), following Proverbs in the order of the Hebrew Bible, are replete with creation themes and notes—major and minor, explicit and implicit. A single example must suffice: In a literary *inclusio*, Ruth 1:6 reports that "God had visited his people to give them food," while 4:13 says, "God gave [Ruth] conception, and she bore a son" (AT). In ancient Israel, faithful villagers (peasants) knew God as creator-provider of food for life and as creator-bestower of new life in the womb.

In the NT outside the book of Revelation, creation language focuses primarily on Jesus Christ. A signal text is John 1:1-3, identifying Jesus as the *Logos* who was "with God" and "was God," and through whom "all things became" (AT). Matthew 8:23-27; Mark 4:35-41; Luke 8:22-25—all report Jesus calming a storm on the Sea of Galilee, demonstrating the power of the Creator to command the creation. Acts 14:8-18 records Paul and Barnabas in Lystra deflecting worship from themselves to God as creator of all. In Romans 8:18-22, Paul says that "all creation [*ktisis*] groans" (v. 22, AT), awaiting its redemption or release. The Christ hymn of Colossians 1:15-20 extols Jesus the Christ as Creator and Sustainer.

Creation, redemption, and renewal are the backdrop of the entire NT, as they are of the OT.

Theological Themes

From the primal creation narratives of Genesis 1–2 emerge many of the paramount theological understandings traceable throughout the Scriptures:

- God is the transcendent and immanent creator of all.
- God created humans ('*ādām*) in and as the **image of God** (Lat., *imago Dei*).
- A major part of human vocation is stewardship and creation care.

- Concomitantly, all honest work is to be esteemed, not disdained.
- Creation originates and validates our common identity markers: name, place, and vocation.
- God intends humans to live in harmonious relationships, reflecting the image of God.
- God intends humans to be jointly autonomous under God. By God's standards in creation and redemption, human relationships are inherently nonhierarchical. This includes gender equality.

The human choice of alienation from God resulted in the marring and/or breaking of all earthly relationships as well. God's response is the redemption and renewal effected by Jesus's death and **resurrection**. Thus the trajectory and *telos* of the Scriptures—explicitly, implicitly, and in toto—is the story of God's good creation redeemed and restored: "Behold, I am making all things new" (Rev. 21:5, NASB).

See also Biblical Theology; Communal Holiness; Cosmology; Eschatology; Fall, The; Prophets/Prophecy; Wesleyan Hermeneutics; Wisdom, Theology of.

JOSEPH COLESON, PHD

Dd

DEMONIC/DEVIL

Although concepts of the demonic and the Devil or Satan are rejected in much of contemporary thought, Scripture depicts them as present realities. Whether interpreted as supernatural or mythical figures, Christians have traditionally understood them as the cause of **evil**, **suffering**, and unfaithfulness in the world. Moreover, the Devil or Satan has had a prominent role in Christian tradition as the one to blame for humanity's **fall** (Gen. 3) and is often depicted as God's archenemy, who is equally wise, all-powerful, and omnipresent. But how does Scripture define the nature of the demonic and the Devil or Satan in the world?

The OT has little to say about the demonic, but the demonic figures that are mentioned are "demons" (Hebr., *šēdîm*; Gk., *daimonia*) and "goat demons" (Hebr., *śĕ'îrîm*). These terms are used to describe the new or false gods worshipped by the Israelites (Lev. 17:7; Deut. 32:17; 2 Chron. 11:15; Ps. 106:37). Isaiah also describes the presence of "goat demons" as part of God's **judgment** on the nations (13:21; 34:14). Other figures in the OT that have been interpreted as "demonic" include wild animals (Isa. 13:21; 34:14), the leech (Prov. 30:15), Azazel (Lev. 16:8), and Lilith (Isa. 34:14). However, the precise nature and role of the demonic is not clearly developed in the OT.

Although "satan" (Hebr., *śāṭān*; Gk., *satan*) in the NT refers to a proper name, the use of this term in the OT, for both human and divine figures, has the general meaning of "adversary," "accuser," or "obstructer." The only instance when "satan" is possibly a proper name is in 1 Chronicles 21:1, when David is tempted to take a census (cf. 2 Sam. 24:1). In other instances, though, "satan" more generally refers to an office such as the "accuser" who appears before the Lord and is ready to accuse Joshua the high priest (Zech. 3:1-2) or the psalmist's call on God to provide an "accuser" to bring the psalmist's abuser to **justice** (Ps. 109:6). Job 1–2 reveals an exchange between

God and one of God's heavenly beings, "the satan," who accuses Job and carries out Job's trials and tribulations within the boundaries set by God.

The OT also defines "adversary" in the sense of being one's opponent as in the case of David (1 Sam. 29:4; see 2 Sam. 19:22 [23]), Hadad (1 Kings 11:14), and Rezon (vv. 23, 25). In Numbers, the angel of Yahweh functions as Balaam's adversary by obstructing his path (22:22, 32). According to the OT, nonhuman devils and satans are part of God's heavenly court and function as adversaries and accusers within the boundaries set by God.

The concepts of the demonic and the Devil or Satan become more associated with evil opposition to God during the intertestamental period. They function as God's antagonists who battle with God and attempt to foil God's plans by causing unfaithfulness, sickness, suffering, and destruction in the world. The Qumran community, for instance, viewed demonic spirits as messengers of destruction (4Q510 1:5), punishers of the wicked (1QS 4:12), and the cause behind people living in darkness (1QM 13:12). In *1 Enoch* and *Jubilees*, evil spirits and demonic figures inflict harm on people (*1 En.* 15:8-11), cause sickness (*Jub.* 10:11-13), lead people astray (v. 1), and cause destruction in the world (*1 En.* 15:8-11).

There are also several satanic figures mentioned in intertestamental texts that lead the demonic figures and forces against God. For instance, *1 Enoch* identifies Semjaza as a leader of the fallen angels who convinces them to make a mutual agreement to have children with human women (6:3). Later in the text of *1 Enoch*, the evil spirits of Azazel and Satan are condemned for leading people astray, and as a result, they will be thrown into the fiery abyss on the day of judgment (54:1-6). Similar to the role of the "satan" in Job, Mastema is a leader of the evil spirits (*Jub.* 10:1-14; 11:1-5; 19:28) who requests that God test Abraham's **faith** by having him **sacrifice** his son Isaac (17:16-18). God responds by shaming Mastema, who then consequently falls from the heavenly realm. These intertestamental texts reveal a growing recognition that the demonic have leaders who lead the charge against God and cause unfaithfulness.

In the NT, the terms "devil" (Gk., *diabolos*) and "satan" (Gk., *satan*) become proper names for the "evil one" (Gk., *ponēros*; Matt. 13:19) who rules over demons (9:34) and this world (John 12:31; 14:30; 16:11; 1 John 5:19). As God's adversary, the Devil or Satan challenges God's reign by means of tempting Jesus (Matt. 4:1-11), convincing Judas's heart to betray Jesus (John 13:2), keeping the **gospel** from unbelievers (Luke 8:12), causing illness (13:11-16), oppressing humanity (Acts 10:38), deceiving the world (Rev. 12:9), and leading people astray (2 Cor. 11:14; Eph. 4:27; 1 Tim. 3:6-7; 1 Pet. 5:8). The Devil, moreover, has the power of death (Heb. 2:14), but not over God's children (1 John 5:18).

The concept of the demonic in the NT primarily appears in the form of "demons" (Gk., *daimonia*) and "**unclean** spirits" (Gk., *pneumata akatharta*; e.g., Mark 1:23). According to the NT, "demons" and "unclean spirits" (the terms are interchangeable) do the work of the Devil or Satan (Matt. 9:34; 12:24; Mark 3:22) and are associated with, though not always the cause of (Mark 1:32), the presence of violent behavior (5:1-5), illnesses (Matt. 10:1; Luke 8:2), blindness (Matt. 12:22), muteness (9:32-33), physical disabilities (Luke 13:11), and seizures (9:39).

Although the demonic and the Devil or Satan continue to work against God's reign in the world, Scripture bears witness to Jesus who came "to destroy the works of the devil" (1 John 3:8, NASB). This is evident in Jesus proclaiming the gospel (Mark 1:15), healing the sick (1:34), performing exorcisms (5:1-20), offering life (John 6:27, 35), and overcoming death via the **resurrection** (1 Cor. 15:20-28). By doing these **works**, Jesus confronts and overcomes the evil work of the demonic and the Devil or Satan, whom in the last days Jesus will cast into "eternal fire" (Matt. 25:41, NASB; Rev. 20:10). Thus whether one interprets the demonic and the Devil or Satan supernaturally or mythically, Scripture invites its readers to participate in the reality where God has defeated the power of **evil** in the world through the life, death, and **resurrection** of Jesus.

See also Temptation/Test.

Resource

Oldridge, Darren. *The Devil: A Very Short Introduction*. Oxford, UK: Oxford University Press, 2012.

CHRISTOPHER D. O'BRIEN, MA

DEUTERONOMIC THEOLOGY

Scholars use the term "Deuteronomic" to denote features of the book of Deuteronomy, and "Deuteronomistic" for other parts of the OT imitative or derivative of Deuteronomy. Joshua–Kings (exclusive of Ruth)—namely, the Former Prophets of the Hebrew canon—is a continuous narrative with stylistic similarities and themes rooted in Deuteronomy and is thus called the Deuteronomistic History (DH). This entry focuses on Deuteronomic theology but will make illustrative reference also to DH.

Deuteronomic theology is marked by a rhetorical situation highlighting Moses's final address to the Israelites in Moab after the forty years of wilderness wandering. During that time, all members of the community over twenty—that is, all adults who witnessed the Exodus—died for their rebellion against God in the wilderness (Num. 13–14). The audience thus consisted of persons under sixty who were youths when God pronounced judgment on the Exodus generation and mainly those less than forty who had been born in the wilderness. Thus Deuteronomy addressed a new generation who did not witness the great redemptive acts of God in Egypt but had lived under the shadow of judgment. God's saving action was in the past; the promised land was a barely discernible future.

With such a dark heritage, Moses reminded this generation that not even the direct experience of the miraculous saving power of God insured against a future rebellion against God. That would require more than deliverance from Egypt. It would require a transformation of the essential nature of the community and its members. This distinctive vision of the audience proved fertile for later generations of Israelites.

In the late seventh century BC, during the reign of Josiah, Deuteronomy spoke uniquely to Judeans who had seen the legacy of the righteous king Hezekiah obliterated by the abominable king Manasseh. The book of Deuteronomy, evidently discovered in the temple, guided Josiah's religious reforms (2 Kings 22–23).

In the exile, a new generation, born in Babylonia, who had not even seen their homes in Israel and Judah, turned to Deuteronomy to probe their experience for an explanation of their loss. It produced the DH, whose final scene occurred in the mid-sixth century BC. Like the audience of Deuteronomy, Judean exiles had only their predecessors' **sin** and **judgment** behind them, with a formidable challenge of building new homes in the promised land looming ahead of them. There are seven characteristics of Deuteronomic theology, however, that gave them hope.

1. The Singularity of Yahweh

To this audience, Deuteronomy offered a distinctive message that also resonates through the DH, the singularity of Yahweh, expressed in the Shema (Deut. 6:4). This was no mere ideological monotheism, but a passionate polemic against pagan gods as well as deviant Israelite understandings of Yahweh. Deuteronomy envisions Israel's seduction into the service of pagan gods as a genuine threat. The distinctive expression "Yahweh our/your God" encapsulates this passion. The Deuteronomistic passages in the DH reflect this concern by emphasizing every deviation of the Hebrews from the strict worship of Yahweh.

2. Love for Yahweh

Deuteronomy highlights a single comprehensive demand: wholehearted **love** for Yahweh expressed by constant preoccupation with serving him. This striking demand, that Yahweh not only be obeyed but also loved, addresses the emotions and loyalties, thus distinguishing Deuteronomy and Deuteronomistic literature from the rest of the OT. The demand to love Yahweh epitomizes Deuteronomy's stress on the heart as the locus of religious rectitude. Attitudes such as the fear of Yahweh, remembering Yahweh, scrupulous listening to Yahweh, the sin of forgetting Yahweh—all focus on the heart, to which Deuteronomy refers incessantly. While the Priestly traditions of the Pentateuch strove to ensure Israel's constant and comprehensive liturgical fitness, Deuteronomy pressed for an equally comprehensive moral and spiritual orientation. The piety of Deuteronomy has as its most striking, even if gruesome, emblem the circumcised heart (10:16; 30:6).

Deuteronomy did not merely explain the **law** to an untutored audience but also urged the Hebrews to internalize the law. This purpose produces the characteristic style of Deuteronomy, which is a warm rhetorical appeal rather than the absolute pronouncements of direct divine revelation. Joshua–Kings clearly pursues Deuteronomy's concern for wholehearted, loving **obedience** to Yahweh. Not only did the writer duly note which kings "did what was right in the eyes of Yahweh" (e.g., 1 Kings 15:11, AT), but the writer often noted as well the extent of the kings' sincerity and enthusiasm.

3. Unity of the People of God

Deuteronomy stresses the undiluted identity and unity of the people of God. Externally, Deuteronomy stresses that Israel was one people clearly defined over against the surrounding Canaanite culture. Israel must remain constantly vigilant in avoiding any compromise with the Canaanite culture. Internally, Deuteronomy repeatedly emphasizes the solidarity that the Israelites must maintain with one another. Deuteronomy scarcely acknowledges the division of Israel into twelve tribes but constantly speaks of fellow Israelites as "your kin" (e.g., "your Israelite kin" [3:18, NRSV]).

This emphasis on the clarity of Israel's identity both externally and internally also dominates the DH. Throughout these books the sin of syncretism with Canaanite culture finds repeated notice and careful documentation. Likewise, the DH evinces horror at the division of Israel. The secession of the northern tribes was, for this historian, the unpardonable crime, the political counterpart to their abandoning Yahweh to serve other gods.

4. Single Sacrificial Site

Deuteronomy limits all sacrifice to a single site to be chosen by Yahweh (ch. 12). Many of the laws in Deuteronomy implement the practical implications of this centralization law. In Genesis–Numbers all slaughter of animals is sacred and must occur at an altar. Deuteronomy, by contrast, realizes that centralization of sacrifice renders this expectation impracticable. Deuteronomy licenses the "profane" slaughter of animals solely for eating (12:20-27).

Implementation of this law entailed the closure and even destruction of many sanctuaries where Yahweh had been worshipped through sacrifice, thus putting a large number of local clergy out of work. Deuteronomy addresses this problem by repeatedly reminding the reader to show charity toward the Levites.

The DH emphasizes centralized worship with its repeated differentiation between Yahweh-worshipping and idol-worshipping kings. It also distinguishes between Yahwistic kings who failed to implement centralization, despite their acknowledged **righteousness**, and the only two kings—Hezekiah and Josiah—who did implement it. These two kings added to their overall righteousness the virtue of taking down the "high places."

Two kinds of high places appear in the DH. One is the scene of pagan worship. The author would not have approved of kings who tolerated pagan worship. The failure of "righteous" kings to remove the high places indicates these sites were sanctuaries of Yahweh (1 Sam. 9:12, 19; 1 Kings 3:2-4). Such worship, though Yahwistic, failed to pass the Deuteronomistic test of centralization.

The primary criterion for this one sanctuary was Yahweh's placement of his name there. Rather than referring to some mystical or symbolic presence, the language of "placing the name" directly, according to Richter, derives from Akkadian idioms in which conquering kings asserted their authority over new territories by "placing [their] names" via an inscribed monument (2002, 207-17).

5. Scriptural Orientation

Deuteronomy is distinctive among the Pentateuchal books in having an explicitly scriptural orientation. First, the speaker in Deuteronomy clearly offers this material as the authoritative summary and interpretation of the entire Mosaic **Torah** for the new setting of life in Canaan. References to "this law" refer specifically to Deuteronomy as a book (e.g., 1:5; 17:18-19). This literary self-awareness and expectation that the book itself would be used as a norm and reference distinguishes Deuteronomy from Genesis–Numbers.

Scattered references to writing notwithstanding, Genesis–Numbers envision the will of God to be known by the Hebrews mainly as a part of their general cultural awareness, through oral tradition or priestly instruction. Seldom do written documents appear in Genesis–Numbers as a regularly consulted rule of **faith** for Yahweh's people, as "scripture." Deuteronomy, however, displays a strong orientation toward scripturally regulated religion. The king was to keep a written "copy of this law" (17:18, NRSV) that he was to read constantly in order to rule in the fear of God.

The DH displays a marked concern precisely for this lawbook-oriented piety. The book of Joshua assigns the book of the law a pivotal place in the settlement of Canaan. Joshua was charged to meditate on the book of the law constantly, patterning his entire life on its precepts (Josh. 1:8). Once Jericho and Ai fell, the people gathered and Joshua read from the law, bringing the first stage of the conquest to a climax (8:30-35). At the end of the book, Joshua once again emphasized the book of the law as the criterion for Israel's continued enjoyment of the gift of the **land** (23:6; 24:26).

The book of the law then drops out of the narrative and does not occur again in this programmatic role until the reform of Josiah (2 Kings 22–23), when the book was rediscovered and Josiah responded appropriately with penitent sorrow, establishing the book of the law as the criterion for Judah's life.

6. Centrality of Moses

Deuteronomy stresses the centrality of Moses as the mediator between Yahweh and Israel. All claims to mediate the will of God must stand in the Mosaic succession. Deuteronomy provides for this continuation of the Mosaic role in at least three forms. One is the book of the law of Moses. Joshua 1:1-9 opens with the divine declaration that Moses was dead. It moves quickly then to urge on Joshua the constant study of "this book of the law" (v. 8, NASB) as the condition for Joshua's replicating Moses's career.

The second vehicle for continuing the Mosaic influence is the king, who must be subservient to the Mosaic law book. Most significant, however, is Moses's declaration that "Yahweh will raise up a prophet like me" for the Israelites (Deut. 18:15, AT). The true **prophet** in Deuteronomy carries on the exclusive mediatorial role of Moses (vv. 16-19).

Two features stand out in Deuteronomy's discussion of prophecy. First, the prophet must hew strictly to the Deuteronomic demand for purity of worship (v. 20). This strict content criterion takes primacy even over supernatural signs and wonders (13:1-5). Second, the criterion of fulfilled prophecy, especially threats, marks the true prophet (18:22).

Unsurprisingly, the DH manifests this concern for prophecy and these two criteria. Frequently in Kings, reference is made to prophets of other deities, especially in the northern kingdom, in contrast to the true prophets of Yahweh, who are frequently depicted as standing alone. Gerhard von Rad demonstrated that a detailed network of prophecy and fulfillment binds the DH into a complete whole (1953). The narrative thus relates how Yahweh worked in history through his word and how Yahweh's word actually makes history.

7. The Deuteronomic Style

The distinctiveness of the Deuteronomic style is hard to overstate. The prose is sonorous, bordering on monotonous but for its elevated content. Synonyms accumulate to drive home the point of the speaker, and scores of unique turns of phrase demarcate this style.

The presence in the DH of so many of these distinctive phrases and ideas justifies the conclusion that a writer consciously imitating Deuteronomy had a critical role in shaping Joshua–Kings, as argued programmatically by Martin Noth (1981, 13-26). His model was later elaborated in two forms: one suggested two editions of the DH, Josianic and exilic, and the other was mainly proposed by German scholars, who discerned three or more complex stages of composition during and after the exile.

Deuteronomic theology, urging on the people of God a wholehearted love and uncompromising loyalty to God, has provided a rich fund of images and language for the Wesleyan theological tradition to express and refine its emphasis on the challenges of inward and outward human transformation under divine **grace**.

Resources

Nelson, Richard. *The Double Redaction of the Deuteronomistic History.* JSOTSup 18. Sheffield, UK: JSOT Press, 1981.

Noth, Martin. *The Deuteronomistic History.* 2nd ed. JSOTSup 15. Sheffield, UK: JSOT Press, 1981.

Rad, Gerhard von. "The Deuteronomistic Theology of History in the Books of Kings." Pages 74-91 in *Studies in Deuteronomy.* London: SCM, 1953.

Richter, Sandra. *The Deuteronomistic History and the Name Theology.* Berlin: Walter de Gruyter, 2002.

Weinfeld, Moshe. *Deuteronomy and the Deuteronomic School.* Oxford, UK: Clarendon Press, 1972.

LAWSON G. STONE, PHD

DISCIPLESHIP

Discipleship is the way of life that characterizes those called disciples. The word "disciple" has roots in the Latin word *discipulus.* The Greek noun *mathētēs* may mean "pupil," "learner," or "follower," and the Hebrew verb *lāmad* to "teach" or "learn."

New Testament

In addition to the noun *mathētēs,* the verb *manthanō* means "to learn." The words appear often in the NT, over 270 times in the Gospels and Acts. Culturally *mathētēs* refers to someone who attaches himself to another person in order to acquire abstract and practical knowledge. The NT uses "disciple" to designate those faithful toward a contemporary figure (e.g., the disciples of John in Matt. 11:2; Mark 2:18; 6:29; Luke 5.33; the disciples of Jesus in John 1:37; 4:31), toward a historical human figure (e.g., the disciples of Moses in John 9:28), and toward a movement (e.g., the disciples of the Pharisees in Matt 22:16; Mark 2:18). In Scripture, being a disciple has distinctive features, all rooted in the OT and in relation to contemporary realities.

Old Testament

In the OT the basic meaning of the verb *lāmad* is "to instruct." It is used in the sense of corporate (Deut. 4:14; 5:1; 20:18; 2 Chron. 17:7-9; Ezra 7:10; Hos. 10:11) and personal (Pss. 18:34 [35 HB]; 25:4-9; 119:35; Prov. 30:3; Jer. 31:34) appeal or desire to learn, teach, and receive instruction in order to form right dispositions of fear and service in covenantal relationship with God. This OT use perhaps lies behind Matthew 28:19, which has neither "make" nor "disciples" but simply the verb "disciple."

Across Scripture

This OT vision informs the NT vision of discipleship beyond the use of *mathētēs* and calls attention to other words associated with disciples. Discipleship invites followers to submit to their teacher and to "go behind" him (Gk., *akoloutheō*) or "to pursue" him to every place to learn from him. This pursuit results from God's initiative in inviting and calling humanity both in the OT (Gen. 3:9; 12:4-8; Exod. 3:4-10) and in the NT (Matt. 9:9; 19:21; Mark 1:17; 3:13). Closely associated with *akoloutheō* is *opisō*, which is used for "behind" or "after" and often found with active verbs to express the disciple's intentional subordination to his teacher. In the LXX, this Greek term is used to call God's people to follow after God (Deut. 13:4) and God's prophets (1 Kings 19:20-21) instead of following baals or other gods (Judg. 2:12; Jer. 2:23); in the NT, this call is reiterated by Jesus (Matt. 16:24; Mark 1:17; 8:34; Luke 9:23; John 1:43, 12:26), who could thus be perceived as God or as God's agent to follow. Closely related to "going behind" or "going after" is the Greek term *mimeomai*, meaning "to imitate" or "to emulate" a person or an example. A resolute following of Jesus results in imitating Jesus's life and ministry (Mark 3:14-15; Luke 6:40) including his cruciformity (Matt. 16:24; Mark 8:34; Luke 9:23; John 16:33). Furthermore, while "disciple" is absent from the Epistles, discipleship is present in the sense of turning believers into imitators of God and God's agents (1 Cor. 4:16; 11:1; Eph. 5:1; Phil. 3:17; Heb. 6:12).

Purpose and Nature

Discipleship fulfills God's mission fully embodied by Jesus as the agent of the kingdom (Gk., *basileia*) of God or heaven on earth (Matt. 4:23; 9:35; Mark 1:15; Luke 4:43; 8:1), understood in its first-century setting as a corporate entity under God's own rule. In God's kingdom discipleship is meant, not as a means to escape this world, but as a means to be fully present. Thus Jesus chose and called his coagents around the life of discipleship. The decadent nature of the world and the sorry fate of persons and communities suggest that discipleship must be thoroughgoing, countercultural, and deeply rooted in a new way of life. This experience happens with the disciples, who are called to a reconstruction of self within multiple relationships, a change of loyalty, and a tangible manifestation of transformed dispositions and attitudes. Thus discipleship is a call to live fully in the complexity of this world in light of the inaugurated **kingdom of God**.

Context and Content

Rooted in Hebraic **faith**, discipleship is a contextual whole-life embrace of God's mission in the world. Its content is shaped, not by abstract principles, but by the present. Discipleship calls for a critical evaluation of personal, corporate, and even national narratives that compete with God's vision for the world in light of God's narrative. The four NT **Gospels** serve as models of discipleship materials constructed around dominant context-specific narratives and offer four retellings of God's world-healing story.

Means

Beside God in Christ as the primordial agent of discipleship, the collaborative nature of discipling invites would-be disciples of Christ to self-identify as divinely empowered human agents, called and co-missioned to work with God (Matt. 28:18; John 20:22; Acts 1:8). They, with ongoing reorientation of identity (Gk., *katartizō*; Luke 6:40), and various degrees of personal faith and trust ("some doubted" [Matt. 28:17, NRSV]) in the context of corporate worship, use divinely delegated authority to *disciple* all people, everywhere. Through them, the triune God *disciples* people away from self-enclosed individualism and into God's **image**-bearing persons, always open to God and others and committed to restoring God's **creation**. Such discipleship is sustained by **works** of piety, works of **mercy**, and prophetic actions, which address public ills or injustices. To *disciple* across cultures requires critically integrating unusual rituals meant to shape people as means of God's **grace** to fulfill the discipleship task.

See also Belief/Believe; Call of God; Corporate Responsibility; Evil; Incarnation; Sin.

Resources

Dunn, James D. G. *Jesus' Call to Discipleship*. Cambridge, UK: Cambridge University Press, 1992.
Houston, James M. *The Disciple: Following the True Mentor*. Colorado Springs: David C. Cook, 2007.
Kaiser, Walter C. "למד." Page 480 of vol. 1 in *TWOT*.
Moon, W. Jay. "Using Rituals to Disciple Oral Learners: Part 1." *Orality Journal: The Word Became Fresh* 2, no. 1 (2013): 43-63.
Moore, Mark E. *Kenotic Politics: The Reconfiguration of Power in Jesus' Political Praxis*. London: Bloomsbury T and T Clark, 2013.
Müller, Dietrich. "μαθητής." Pages 483-90 in vol. 1 of *NIDNTT*.
Runyon, Theodore. *The New Creation: John Wesley's Theology Today*. Nashville: Abingdon, 1998.

SEGBEGNON MATHIEU GNONHOSSOU, DMIN

DIVINATION

Divination is the human endeavor to attain knowledge of the future and of the divine will. It can be distinguished from magic and sorcery, which attempt to manipulate divine powers.

Divination was commonly practiced throughout the ANE in biblical times. Practitioners of divination attempted to attain divine knowledge through humanly initiated rituals or through the observation of naturally occurring phenomena. Rituals initiated by a diviner included such acts as shooting arrows; casting lots; mixing liquids such as wine, oil, or water; and communicating with the dead (necromancy). Natural phenomena observed by a diviner included bodily organs of animals, astral occurrences, weather patterns, and the flight of birds. The prophet Ezekiel describes the Babylonian king's use of various techniques of divination, including the selection of arrows, the consultation of household gods (Hebr., *těrāpîm*), and the examination of liver markings (Ezek. 21:21).

While practices of divination sought divine knowledge through humanly initiated rituals or through human observation of natural phenomena, knowledge of the divine will or of the future could also come directly from the deity through individuals recognized by members of the community as having the authority to speak on behalf of the deity. These inspired individuals included the oracles of ancient Greece, the seers of the ANE, the **prophets** of ancient Israel, and the apocalyptic visionaries of early Judaism and early Christianity. Forms of divine communication varied from visions to signs to dreams.

In light of the widespread practice of divination throughout the ANE, the presence of divination in the Bible is perhaps to be expected. Various OT texts assume the presence of practitioners of divination without making a critique of or **judgment** against them.

For example, the narrative of Balaam (Num. 22–23) depicts payment to Balaam by the Moabites and Midians for his divining services against the Israelites (22:7). Balaam concluded that there can be "no divination against Israel" (23:23, NRSV). However, the rationale given by Balaam was not the futile or evil nature of divination but rather Yahweh's blessing upon Israel.

The prophet Ezekiel denounced those prophets of Israel who articulated false visions and carried out deceptive divinations (Ezek. 13:6, 9, 23; see also Jer. 14:14). Ezekiel did not address the ineffectiveness or the wicked nature of their divining practices. Rather, the prophet critiqued the deceptive report that these prophets and diviners gave. Ezekiel's conclusion was that these persons declare, "'Says the LORD,' when the LORD has not sent them" (Ezek. 13:6).

Old Testament texts assume the priestly practice of the Urim and Thummim (Num. 27:21; Deut. 33:8; 1 Sam. 14:41-42). This ritual sought to discover the will of Yahweh through the casting of lots. The precise form of the ritual is not clear. The priest may have drawn one of the two lots from a pouch, or he may have cast both lots to the ground to arrive at an answer. The texts do not provide a critique of the act. They simply assume that the ancient Israelite priests carried out this act in order to receive a divine answer.

Likewise, in the narrative of Jonah, non-Israelites discovered by casting lots that Jonah was responsible for the storm that had arisen on the sea (1:7).

The early Christian community continued the practice of casting lots. After the disciples prayed that the Lord would reveal to them whom he had chosen as Judas's replacement, they proceeded to cast lots in the selection of Matthias (Acts 1:23-26).

Biblical narratives in which divine knowledge came through the observation of natural phenomena typically include neither positive nor negative evaluations.

Initiated by Yahweh, the miraculous budding of Aaron's staff confirmed Yahweh's selection of Aaron and the Levites for priestly service (Num. 17). However, this event appears as a one-time occurrence in ancient Israel rather than as a recurrent divining ritual.

Gideon's desire to confirm God's promise of deliverance first prompted Gideon to request dew on the fleece and subsequently moved him to request dew on the ground surrounding the dry fleece (Judg. 6:36-40). Although the narrative depicts Gideon's request without positive or negative evaluation, the request should be read alongside other indications of Gideon's fear and doubt. Nevertheless, Yahweh participated in Gideon's attempt to gain divine confirmation.

While certain biblical narratives depict diviners and divination without critique or judgment, the Scriptures do contain direct prohibitions against divination, particularly as Israel's neighbors practiced it. Both Deuteronomic and Priestly legislation adamantly prohibited the practice (Deut. 18:9-14; Lev. 19:26, 31; 20:6, 27).

While the text does not make a judgment about Saul's engagement in necromancy through the medium at Endor (1 Sam. 28:3-25), the reader should evaluate this narrative in light of the Deuteronomic prohibition: "No one shall be found among you . . . who consults ghosts or spirits, or who seeks oracles from the dead. For whoever does these things is abhorrent to the LORD" (Deut. 18:10-12, NRSV).

Prophetic texts are consistent in their condemnation of practitioners of divination alongside sorcerers, fortune-tellers, and false prophets (see Isa. 2:6; 3:2-3; Jer. 27:9; 29:8; Ezek. 13:23). Hosea depicts the people's search for a divine word from a piece of wood or from a divining rod as a rebellious act of prostitution (Hos. 4:12). The Deuteronomistic Historian places divination alongside idolatry, worship of the heavenly host, and child sacrifice in explaining the reason for Israel's fall (2 Kings 17:16-18).

Although the Bible presents incidents in which the writers assume various practices of divination without critique or judgment, it consistently understands the divine will to be revealed primarily through **Torah** and through the word of prophets called by Yahweh. The admonitions against divination function to exalt the role of inspired prophets as the ultimate source of knowing Yahweh's intentions for the future and his will for the world.

See also Deuteronomic Theology.

TIMOTHY M. GREEN, PHD

Ee

ELECTION

The concept of election is derived from the Greek verb *eklegomai*. In the Septuagint this verb is predominantly used to translate the Hebrew verb *bḥr*. Both verbs can refer to human choice in profane (1 Sam. 17:40; Luke 14:7) and sacred settings (Josh. 24:15; Acts 6:5) but are most frequently used for a deliberate choice of God. Even though other words are used as well—such as the Hebrew *lqh*, "to take" (Gen. 24:7), and the Greek *proginōskō*, "to fore-know" (Rom. 11:2)—*bḥr* and *eklegomai* are the theological terms expressing the concept of election.

The OT theology of election is most fully articulated in Deuteronomy. Out of all the peoples, God had chosen Israel as his own possession to be his **holy** people (7:6). This election was the result of God's **love** and did not rest on any human quality (vv. 7-8). The emphasis is not on the privileged status of the people, but election solicits a response of **obedience** to God (10:12-19) in order to be a witness to the other peoples (4:5-8).

The concern was that the young nation should not imitate the surrounding culture but be aware of its destiny as God's unique agent. The people were urged to keep their worship pure by gathering in one place chosen by God as the place where he would dwell among his people (twenty-one references in Deut.). This gave **Jerusalem** and the temple their prominent places, as reflected in the songs of Zion in the Psalms.

The preexilic **prophets** did not stress the concept of God's election. Their aim was to awaken the people from a false hope of an election theology severed from obedience to God (Jer. 7; Amos 9:1-10; Mic. 3). In the book of Kings, one can sense the agony over David's descendants, who did **evil** in the sight of the Lord. Even though God had promised that David's house would last forever (2 Sam. 7), toward the end of the story in Kings, rejection ("to reject" [Hebr., *m's*]) is used rather than election (2 Kings 17:19-20; 23:27; 24:20).

The downfall of Israel and Judah and the destruction of the temple caused a theological crisis. The people felt humiliated and rejected by God (Ps. 89:49 [50 HB]; Lam. 3:45; 5:22). In the midst of the crisis, Jeremiah proclaimed that God would not exercise a full rejection (Jer. 33:23-26), and Isaiah spoke of a re-election in the future (Isa. 14:1), implying that God would temporarily abandon his people.

Deutero-Isaiah used election terminology to bring new **hope** to the exiles. God had not rejected his people (Isa. 41:8-13) and was at work doing something new (43:18-19) through his anointed one, the Persian ruler Cyrus (45:1-7).

Election does not exclude a universalist view of God as ruler over all his **creation**. The figure of the king is submerged into the "servant" (Hebr., *'ebed*), who represents the true people of God and who fulfills his task through **suffering** (Isa. 53). Being elected implies not only obedience but suffering as well.

Remarkable in various postexilic writings is the use of the plural, the "chosen ones" (e.g., Pss. 105:43; 106:5; Isa. 65:9, 22; see NRSV). Due to the rebellious nature of the collective, faithful servants caused a division among God's people and challenged a deterministic understanding of election. This anticipated the message of John the Baptist, who challenged the sons of Abraham to "bear fruits" (Luke 3:8, NRSV).

In the **Gospels** Jesus is described as God's chosen one, bringing the gospel of God (Mark 1:14-15), and as the one who chooses. Matthew presented Jesus as the new Israel (2:15 [Hos. 11:1]). Luke described Jesus as God's chosen one (9:35; 23:35). John stressed that Jesus himself chose his disciples (6:70; 13:18; 15:16, 19).

The words "many are called, but few are chosen" (Matt. 22:14, NRSV) are the conclusion of the three preceding parables (21:28–22:13). In these, the disobedience of the son, the refusal of the vine growers to pay the proceeds, and the unwillingness to accept the invitation to the wedding feast refer to the rejection of Jesus by the leaders of Israel. Therefore, sinners from within Israel, and Gentiles from outside, will be invited. Similar to the OT prophets, Jesus also acknowledged that disobedience causes division among the elect.

The elect is not a predetermined group of people. Jesus made this clear in his apocalyptic sermon, where he warned his followers that in the end of the age, many will fall away (Matt. 24:24; Mark 13:22). And unless those days were cut short, none of the elect would endure (Matt. 24:22; Mark 13:20). The elect are both challenged to remain faithful in order not to fall away and made aware of their dependence on God's **grace**.

The new community chosen by God is characterized by Jesus. As Jesus was rejected, so God has chosen the weak and despised, the foolishness and base things, to become God's **wisdom** and power (1 Cor. 1:18-31). James stated that God has chosen the **poor** to be heirs of the **kingdom** (James 2:5). Peter used OT election theology (1 Pet. 2:4-10) to stress the fragile status of the followers of Christ, who are scattered aliens (1:1). Being among God's elect means a call to be "holy and blameless" (Eph. 1:4, NRSV) and to put on love (Col. 3:12-14). The elect are the humble servants, with no room for arrogance.

Election needs to be distinguished from predestination, which is related to God's salvation and the first of those who faithfully respond to God. As Paul made clear in Romans 8:28-39, God predestined the way of salvation from calling till glorification, and nothing can separate God's elect from the love of God. Yet this does not keep Paul from the admonition to present ourselves as instruments of **righteousness** to God (Rom. 6:12-14). The elect are always encouraged to walk according to their calling (Eph. 4:1).

A final question remains. Has God rejected Israel? Paul addressed this question in Romans 9–11. As the gospel reached the Gentiles through the disobedience of Israel, now the Gentiles are God's agents to show **mercy** to Israel (11:31), for God will show mercy to all in their disobedient state (v. 32). Paul called this a mystery (v. 25). This also applies to the whole topic of election, for we will never fully understand God's grace but will never cease to be thankful for it.

See also Call of God; Humility.

ANTONIE HOLLEMAN, DRS

ESCHATOLOGY

Eschatology is the study of the end of all time. Rooted in a biblical context, eschatology points to the culmination of history, the return of Christ, and the final **judgment**. A Christian eschatology necessarily encompasses discussion of the **resurrection** of the dead and the **hope** of eternal life. Here eschatology is closely related to apocalypticism, which is a belief in a set of expectations related to the end of time, including a cosmic battle between good and **evil**.

Though most religions espouse some form of end-time doctrine, Christian eschatology has both particular and universal elements and is derived predominantly from the interpretation of apocalyptic texts. While apocalyptic literature is historically a Judeo-Christian response to eras of intense persecution, the most critical of these texts is Revelation, or literally from the Greek, the "Apocalypse of John." Within the pages of the Apocalypse, epic images of punishment for the wicked (Rev. 6:1–8:11, 13; 12–18), the vindication of the **righteous** (Rev. 6:9-11), and prophetic metaphors rolled out in the form of imperial edicts have offered Christendom ample fodder for the proclamation and interpretation of the messianic return, a potential millennial reign, and the culmination of history.

Because apocalyptic writings and eschatological hope emerge from a time of persecution, the material is best understood in the context of its conception. Apart from a contextual understanding of the texts, persons easily misappropriate expectations and the intent of the literature altogether. Early Jewish apocalyptic texts began to emerge in the second century BCE as a result of perceived persecution from the Seleucid king Antiochus IV. Apocryphal books 1 and 2 Maccabees record the Jewish perspective and national history of Antiochus forcing Jews to give up their holy writings, break their purity vows, and bow down to the current king, thus transgressing the laws of the fathers.

The historical crisis and the years and terrors of persecution that followed informed the writing of Jewish apocalyptic texts and Qumran material. This material then, along with **wisdom** literature, provides the surface on which the NT is drawn. In the NT we see the longed for and promised **Messiah** take on the eschatological hopes of the warrior king who was prophesized and who will push back the Gentile oppressors, restore Israel, and set all things right again. When Jesus's life took a different path and he was murdered as an enemy of the state, early Jesus followers interpreted Jesus's teachings to invoke hope of a second coming. Canonically speaking, the transference of this hope begins with Paul and his letters to the church at Thessalonica.

In 1 Thessalonians, the earliest writing of the NT canon, Paul taught that Christ will return by the command of God, accompanied by the archangel's call and the sound of the trumpet. Those who are "in Christ" and have already died will rise first, and those who are left will then be gathered up (4:16-17, NRSV). Those who have not yet died "will be caught up in the clouds . . . to meet the Lord" in the sky, where they will live with him forever (v. 17, NRSV). Believers are urged to remain vigilant as the return of Christ will come as a "thief in the night" (5:1-2, NRSV). Written around 51 CE, this is the emergence of the eschatological hope associated with the return of Christ. So far as we can tell from his writings, Paul envisioned that the return of Christ would happen in his own lifetime.

Other NT writers followed Paul's example until in the late first century when Christians in the seven cities named in Revelation were being persecuted for their faith (2–3). Thus persecutions gave rise to the writing of Revelation and later apocalyptic documents such as the *Shepherd of Hermas* and the *Apocalypse of Peter*. From the time of those early Christians until now, believers have understood themselves to be living in the last days and have lived in anticipation of the return of the Messiah.

What we might miss in reading the Revelation and other apocalyptic texts is the hope they are meant to convey. Although Revelation was written for those who **suffer**, particularly on account of the witness (Gk., *martureō*) of their **faith**, readers often find themselves erroneously attempting to work out formulas and decipher numbers. Instead, Revelation offers us a multivalent expression of an apocalyptic vision. In each of John's images exist layers of references to ancient Hebrew texts, descriptions of the contemporary world of the first century, and images of cosmic celestial beings. It is clear, however, that the faithful and true witness (22:6) intended to impart to John, who was then to share with the world, the message that God would set all things right in the end.

Eschatology also encompasses a future-looking expectation for a final battle. In John's vision this battle takes place on *Har Měgiddô*, which translated from Hebrew means the "Mountain of Megiddo" and is known in most English translations as "Armageddon." The centuries-old Mountain of Megiddo had seen many horrific battles prior to the time of the writing of Revelation and would see many thereafter in ages to come.

Megiddo is a high point located in the Jezreel valley, with the plains of Galilee to the north and Mount Carmel to the south. It is on this mountain that the oldest battle recorded in history took place between Syria and Egypt's Pharaoh Thutmosis III (ca. 1469 BCE). It was on Megiddo that King Josiah was killed in ca. 609 BCE (2 Kings 23:29; 2 Chron. 35:20-24). In 1929 an excavation of Megiddo unearthed a stela commemorating Shishak's conquest of the city during his reign (ca. 945–923 BCE). To date, there have been at Megiddo over thirty major battles across four thousand years, ranging from Egyptians and Israelites to Crusaders and Mongols, and led by some of the world's most illustrative conquerors, such as Saladin, Napoléon, and Allenby. Understanding the turbulent history of Megiddo offers context for John's vision of the final battle to be played out on the war-torn, storied mound.

Central to the eschatological hope of Revelation, often missed in reading and interpreting the text, is the notion of the redemption of all things. The Scripture reveals that the old world will be made new. It is not that the faithful are moved to another world as much as made new in this new redeemed world. This redeemed, new heaven and earth of the final chapters of Revelation look quite like the paradise of Eden (21:1–22:5). It is, then, a return to the garden and a restoration of what was lost—that is, innocence, purity, and communion with God. It is the continued day-and-night worship of the slaughtered Lamb, and it is the song of the ones who have overcome. It is important to note, within the context of the Apocalypse, that those who have overcome—the ones who have trampled the head of the beast, the ones for whom Satan is bound—have passed through the fires of persecution; they have died in the name of Christ.

In simple form, the study of the end times is essentially a longing for **justice**. Inherent in the human experience is a deep and primitive need to know that in the end we will reap what we have sown, that the amoral, corrupt, and oppressive powers of this world will not always reign. It is a **belief** that a day is coming, an hour of reckoning, when what was lost will be restored, when what has died will live, and when what was wrong will be made right.

See also Demonic/Devil; Fall, The; Parousia; Resurrection; Torah (Law, Instruction).

Resources

Cline, Eric. *The Battles of Armageddon: Megiddo and the Jezreel Valley from the Bronze to the Nuclear Age.* Ann Arbor, MI: University of Michigan Press, 2002.

Hansen, David G. "Megiddo, the Place of Battles." Associates for Biblical Research. November 5, 2014. http://www.biblearchaeology.org/post/2014/11/05/Megiddo-The -Place-of-Battles.aspx#Article.

KIMBERLY S. MAJESKI, DMIN

EVIL

The theme of evil pervades the Bible from Genesis 3 to Revelation 22. Among other things, Scripture tells the story of God and humanity's encounters with evil and their responses to it. This article explores questions about the meaning and origin of evil from a biblical-theological perspective. In the process, we shall also address the existence of different kinds of evil.

The biblical words translated into English as "evil" carry several nuances. The relevant terms in Hebrew (*ra'*, *rā'â*, and *rōa'*) and Greek (*kakia, kakos, ponēria,* and *ponēros*) encompass what English speakers typically mean by the words "evil" or "wicked." However, they also denote more benign circumstances that are simply uncomfortable, inconvenient, or displeasing. Thus scholars often translate them idiomatically into English with words like "bad" and "harmful."

For example, these words can describe a displeasing wife (Exod. 21:8), Jonah's discomfort (Jon. 4:6), severe physical defects (Deut. 15:21; Matt. 6:23), and rotten or bad fruit (Jer. 24:2-3; Matt. 7:17-18). The word group can also apply to a person or entity's character. Thus the **devil** and demons are called "evil" (Luke 7:21; 1 John 2:13-14). On evil people, see Matthew 5:39 and Revelation 2:2.

Occasionally, the Bible refers to God's actions as evil (Amos 3:6). For instance, Exodus 32:14 says God "relented from the evil he had proposed to do to his people" (AT). English translations of Jeremiah 18:8 obscure a similar idea. Literally, the Hebrew of that verse says, "If that nation turns from its evil, I will relent from the evil I intended to bring on it" (AT). Such texts are startling and are easily misconstrued to portray God as a maniacal dictator. However, these passages communicate a human perception of God's actions, not a moral evaluation of God's behavior.

Biblical theology is primarily concerned with two kinds of evil. Moral evil refers to a person's or agent's actions that are sinful and opposed to God's will (e.g., the Holocaust). Natural evil pertains to natural disasters for which no individual is responsible (e.g., an Ebola outbreak). According to John Wesley, both types of evil originated in the **fall** (1984–2015, 2:401).

The big question is, From where does evil come? The Bible mentions several sources of both moral and natural evil. Sometimes, what we perceive as evil can be God's punishment, as was the case with the flood, the destruction of **Jerusalem**, and the untimely deaths of Ananias and Sapphira (Gen. 6–9; 2 Kings 21:10-15; Acts 5:1-11). Other times, God might send evil as a test or without any explanation at all, as Job discovered. In all of these examples, evil is best understood as something displeasing or uncomfortable to humans, not as a moral transgression on God's part, since the Bible does not characterize God in this way. God delivers from evil; he does not generate it (Gal. 1:4; 2 Thess. 3:2-4; 2 Tim. 4:18; James 1:13). Thus "the evil one" is Scripture's antithesis to God (1 John 5:19).

The Bible occasionally associates a person's evil actions with **demonic** possession. However, it does not teach that such possession is an excuse for moral irresponsibility; "the devil made me do it" is never an acceptable defense. When faced with the extent and intensity of evil throughout history, we should not dismiss the possibility of spiritual forces working in conjunction with human **free will**. The brutalities of the Crusades, the Holocaust, and present-day jihadist movements discourage assumptions that use demonic possession as a defense for moral irresponsibility.

Most frequently, moral evil originates within a person who chooses to act contrary to God's will. Jesus said it best in Mark 7:21-23: "For it is from within, out of a person's heart, that evil thoughts come—sexual immorality, theft, murder, adultery, greed, malice, deceit, lewdness, envy, slander, arrogance and folly. All these evils come from inside and defile a person" (NIV). Likewise, Paul identified a drive within himself that acts contrary to God's will (Rom. 7:21-24). Wesleyans sense the dire implications of this predicament and point out that Jesus offers freedom from such bondage. Just two verses later, Paul speaks of there being "no condemnation for those who are in Christ," since the Spirit frees us "from the law of **sin** and death" (8:1-2, NIV).

We should mention that this does not guarantee freedom from the effects of evil. Christians live in a fallen world and experience evil through no fault of their own. Esther provides a good example of such **suffering**. Even though Jews living under the Persian Empire had done nothing to deserve it, they were slated for execution because of Haman's grudge with Mordecai. Likewise, Jesus and his followers died in the NT because of the sins of others.

The potential for such evil exists because God gave humans free will, which is a necessary component of a genuinely loving relationship. God endued people with free will for the greater good of providing the opportunity to choose him. However, this also created a potential for evil. As Wesley said,

"Where there is no liberty, there can be no moral good or evil" (1984–2015, 2:475). Humanity's ability to refuse God creates the possibility for moral evil.

But how do we explain natural evil? Why would a good God create a world in which tornadoes tear houses from their foundations, tsunamis inundate cities, and plagues rob children of their parents? How does biblical theology explain seemingly random events such as Paul's shipwreck, Hezekiah's illness, and Naaman's leprosy? One explanation could be that the earth became cursed when sin entered the world (Gen. 3:17; Rom. 8:19-22). Although it is a plausible option, this reasoning carries difficult assumptions about the prefallen world. Were there only gentle breezes in Eden and did bacteria have no ill effects when consumed? Answering in the affirmative requires one to say the very laws of nature changed with the fall in Genesis 3, but this is more than the Bible itself says.

Another way to resolve the problem is to reconsider the phrasing of Genesis 1, where, as Terence Fretheim points out, **creation** is called "good, not perfect" (2010, 11-17). This is not to insinuate that God made a faulty world but rather that creation was made in such a way that it could grow and mature; it was in need of cultivation (Gen. 1:26-29; 2:5). Creation was designed to mature, but what happens when the creation of fire, which is good, grows uncontrollably? It inevitably deprives other parts of creation of their goodness—this is natural evil.

Perhaps God's intent was to create the world in such a way that it could grow in its relationship to God, just as humans do. Likewise, creation seems capable of failing to reach that goal, especially when humans are irresponsible stewards. As was the case with moral evil, natural evil is a failure to reach the highest potential intended by God.

The story of Job addresses natural and moral evil. From his perspective, Job experienced both types. Job's friends explained his problem in terms of Deuteronomy's theology: Job suffered because he had done something wrong, but Job and the reader know this is incorrect. Job insisted he had done nothing wrong, did not deserve his suffering, and called on God to judge him. At the end of the story, God refused to answer Job's questions and reminded Job of his limited knowledge and understanding.

One of the more troubling aspects of Job is the book's refusal to say why God allowed Job's suffering. This also mirrors the finite understanding of human experience, because it encourages us to trust in the infinite God who made the universe. Christians recognize that we live in a fallen world, one marred by sin that inhibits our ability to live in right relationship with God. That ability was hindered in the fall. Wesley pointed out that Adam's first sensation after his sin was a painful **fear**; the loving relationship had been broken (1984–2015, 2:403).

The ultimate solution to the problem of evil, though, is found not in its source but in the God who became **incarnate**. The purpose of Jesus's life, death, and **resurrection** was not only that God could suffer alongside us, and so become a high priest able "to empathize with our weaknesses" (Heb. 4:15, NIV) but also that, in the Word incarnate, "God was reconciling the world to himself" (2 Cor. 5:19, NIV). Wesleyans recognize God's act on our behalf and take seriously the ability of Jesus to free from sin those who are in Christ. The evil of the broken relationship can be healed.

See also Deuteronomic Theology; Forgiveness, The Art and Necessity of; Reconciliation.

Resources

Fretheim, Terence E. *Creation Untamed: The Bible, God, and Natural Disasters*. Grand Rapids: Baker Academic, 2010.

Wesley, John. *The Bicentennial Edition of the Works of John Wesley*. Edited by Frank Baker et al. 27 vols. Nashville: Abingdon, 1984–2015.

P. BEN BOECKEL, PHD

Ff

FAITH

The popular statement "Faith is believing what you know isn't true" demonstrates a relationship between faith and knowledge but betrays an understanding of knowledge that is limited to verifiable facts. In such a case, faith is necessary only because of the lack of facts. Facts, discoveries, experiment proofs, and accumulated experiences may be "the building blocks for the structure of our society," but they do not encompass all sources of knowledge (Baly and Rhodes 1984, 3). A mature thinker is thoroughly aware that certain features of the world cannot be reduced to facts. Faith is as important to scientific study (through models, interpretations, etc.) as it is to religious understanding. In both cases, faith is based on prior knowledge gained through one or more means.

Biblical Language of Faith

The Hebrew word group built on the root 'mn has a range of meaning relating to agreement with one's prior knowledge. The verb "believe," the noun "faithfulness" (translated rarely as "faith"), and the liturgical formula "amen"—all affirm that the object of faith agrees with the reality of the situation and what is spoken about it. For instance, one's prior knowledge of God's actions and words builds trust in God's character and word. The result is not just agreement but faithfulness. In Deuteronomy 32:20, "children in whom is no faith" (KJV) are people without trust or commitment. Jesus demonstrated this same sense when he said of a Roman centurion, "In no one in Israel have I found such faith" (Matt. 8:10, NRSV).

In the NT, the *pist* word group has a broad semantic range. The Greek noun is built on the "reliability of the one trusted"; the adjective carries the sense of "worthy of trust"; and the verb is basically that of "trust," especially in the passive voice, where it means "to be entrusted with" something (Taylor 2000, 488). In later texts, its uses include "the faith" as the content of the kerygma (1 Tim. 5:8; Jude v. 3), a body of teaching to be trusted and to which one is committed. In both Testaments, the heart of the concept is a relationship between God and God's people, which produces belief, **obedience**, trust, and **hope**.

Faith as Relationship

Abraham's servant was the first to declare the faithfulness of God, during his search for Isaac's wife (Gen. 24:27). In the OT, faith begins with the faithfulness and trustworthiness of God, whose continuous actions in favor of Israel have shown God to be reliable. It is interesting to note that in Genesis 26:5 Abraham is not described as a believer but as one who obeyed God's voice. Thus the one with faith is also a faithful one. Faith or faithfulness is described by relational metaphors: **covenant**, **marriage**, friendship, parenthood, and so on. In all such relationships, faith or faithfulness is reciprocal. The relationship between God and human beings is the essential premise of faith in both Testaments. The OT and Jesus are both clear, however, that this relationship is initiated by God and not by human beings.

Brevard Childs calls the texts that preserve the record of God's revelatory events "witnesses," which at the same time record the events and preserve the faith relationship between God and God's people (1992, 91-92). During the intertestamental period, as these textual witnesses were canonized, faithfulness was transformed from being committed to God relationally to trusting in one's obedience to the **law** to ensure a share in the promised future. It is not surprising, therefore, to see how Jewish leaders could criticize Jesus for his approach to the law or why the inclusion of Gentile Christians was such an important issue.

Pist Word Group

As witnessed by the NT, the kerygma of the early church saw the life, death, and **resurrection** of Jesus as a new revelatory encounter between God and God's people. Through the *pist* vocabulary, the NT reawakened the whole concept of relationship with God as the core of faith. Faith now meant both that one was in agreement with the kerygma's interpretation of the event ("belief that . . .") and that one was called to full relationship with God through the risen Jesus, now Lord ("believe in . . ."). Faith is based on prior knowledge, but this faith in Jesus adds to one's knowledge, through personal acquaintance with the risen Jesus. This relationship results in reciprocal faithfulness, Jesus having proven himself faithful.

Conclusion

Faith, then, is putting one's trust in the One who is worthy of trust.

Resources

Baly, Denis, and Royal Rhodes. *The Faith of Christians: An Introduction to Basic Beliefs.* Philadelphia: Fortress Press, 1984.

Bultmann, Rudolf. "πιστεύω κτλ." Pages 174-228 in vol. 6 of *TDNT*.

Childs, Brevard S. *Biblical Theology of the Old and New Testaments: Theological Reflection on the Christian Bible*. Minneapolis: Fortress Press, 1992.

Purkiser, W. T., Richard S. Taylor, and Willard H. Taylor. *God, Man, and Salvation: A Biblical Theology*. Kansas City: Beacon Hill Press of Kansas City, 1977.

Taylor, Stephen. "Faith, faithfulness." Pages 488-89 in *New Dictionary of Biblical Theology*. Downers Grove, IL: InterVarsity Press, 2000.

Wolpe, David J. *Why Faith Matters*. New York: HarperCollins, 2008.

RUSSELL LOVETT, PHD

FALL, THE

Genesis 2 and 3 describe the creation of Adam and Eve, their garden setting and their tasks, the prohibition God gave them, and their failure to keep it. The account is generally called the fall, a designation never used in the Bible.

The Genesis Account

God planted a garden in Eden and gave "the man" (Hebr., *hāʾādām*) the responsibility of caring for it. Such gardens were known to accompany palaces and temples in the ANE. Two exceptional trees were in the garden, one that conveyed the knowledge of good and **evil** and the other immortality. God forbade the man to eat from the first. Then God formed a woman to be a **helper** like the man. Later the man named her Eve, meaning "living or life" (Gen. 3:20, AT).

A snake, one of the wild animals, asked the woman if they were prohibited from eating the fruit of the trees. The man was with her at the time (v. 6), but he never speaks. In the early stories of the OT, like other literature of the ANE, conversations are between two persons only (cf. book of Job). The snake enticed them to eat of the fruit of the Tree of Knowledge by stating that they would become wise and be like God (v. 5).

The target audience of the story was Israel, a strongly patriarchal culture. In such a culture, if a husband commanded his wife to do something inappropriate, he was responsible for the action and she only secondarily. To make the wife fully responsible, Eve had to decide on the action independently, and then her husband. Husbands were always responsible for their actions. Thus when God confronted the three, including the snake, each was held accountable.

After condemning them, God drove the man out of the garden, thereby denying him access to the Tree of Immortality. God had stated that if the man ate of the Tree of Knowledge, he would die (2:17); clearly he did not die immediately. Some suggest he died spiritually because his close relationship with God was marred by **sin**. In another sense he also died by being barred from the Tree of Immortality. Being created mortal, he thus continued to be subject to the normal processes of aging and death.

In the first five chapters of Genesis, the non-articular Hebrew noun *'ādām* appears nine times and the articular noun *hā'ādām* twenty-five times. In 1:26 God decided to create a "human" (*'ādām*), so he created (v. 27) "the human" (*hā'ādām*), both male and female. In chapters 2–4 he is referred to as *hā'ādām*, "the man," twenty-four times (2:5 reads "no man," AT). Not until chapter 5 is he referred to by the proper name "Adam" (*'ādām*) (vv. 1 [2x], 2-3, 5). After the notice of Adam's death, he is rarely mentioned in the OT. Further, the OT never blames either Adam or Eve for the transmission of death or sin. It is simply accepted that people both sin and die.

Later Interpretations

Later Jewish traditions blamed Adam and Eve for passing on the curse of death to all humanity (Sir. 25:24; Wis. 2:24; *2 Bar.* 48:42-43). This curse is tied to their disobedience (Sir. 25:24; *L.A.B.* 13:8). These traditions viewed Adam and Eve as historical persons whose sin passed down to their descendants the curse of death.

New Testament Interpretations

Other than genealogical mentions by Luke (3:38) and Jude (v. 14), Paul is the only writer in the NT who refers to Adam by name. In 1 Corinthians 15:22 Paul contrasts Adam and Christ. Apart from Christ all persons die, but in him all are made alive. Verses 44-45 contrast their bodies; Adam had a natural body, and Christ a resurrected spiritual body. Paul compared the two patterns to demonstrate the overwhelming superiority of Christ. Paul also contrasts them in Romans 5. Like Adam, all persons have sinned (v. 12) and thus are condemned; yet Christ through his death brings an abundant gift of grace to many (v. 15). In both Corinthians and Romans, Adam represents death, while Christ brings life.

In 1 Timothy 2:14 Paul states that Eve, not Adam, was deceived by the snake. Paul ignored the statement that Adam was with Eve (Gen. 3:6), and followed an intertestamental tradition that the devil deceived Eve but not Adam (*2 En.* 31:5).

In summary, Paul contrasted Adam and Christ as archetypes or representative persons because one brought death and the other life. What God accomplished in Christ was vastly superior to that of Adam. As a first-century Jew, Paul was influenced by the Jewish traditions about Adam and Eve. However, he used those traditions to illustrate the superiority of Christ over Adam.

Science and New Interpretations

Recent scientific findings about the emergence and genetic history of the human race have called into question the historicity of Adam and Eve. The diversity in our genetic code indicates that we are derived not just from two individuals but from a group of several thousand who lived about fifty thousand years ago. How does this affect our interpretations of Genesis 2 and 3?

There are at least three approaches to understanding the text. One approach rejects or reinterprets all findings of science that suggest the earth and the human race are older than six thousand to ten thousand years old. This view claims the Genesis account of creation is historically accurate and that Adam and Eve were historical individuals.

Other interpretations accept the findings of science and suggest that early in the development of the human race, God chose a couple to represent the entire race. Adam may have been the leader or chief of the closely knit human tribe, and Eve his wife. They were placed in the garden to tend it and to mediate between God and the other people. Their failure to follow God's directions brought about their expulsion from the garden and thus denied them and all humans access to the Tree of Immortality.

Another approach suggests the inspired writer drew upon common ANE cultural understandings as well as early Israelite traditions concerning the creation of the earth and of humanity. The idyllic setting has an animal that can talk and trees with miraculous powers. The account conveys theological importance, describing both humanity's sinfulness and God's continuing care for humanity (3:21). The original pair have symbolic names: Adam (5:1), meaning "man" or "human," and Eve (3:20), meaning "life" or "living." In Genesis 2–4, the male is referred to twenty-four times simply as "the man." The indefiniteness indicates that the story is more about humanity than a specific individual. This view sees the account as more parabolic than historical.

Theological Significance

God desires an intimate relationship (Gen. 3:8) with human beings, whom he created in his own image (1:26-28). The restrictions he provides are for their own protection (2:17). Yet each man is Adam and each woman is Eve, because each of us has yielded to the temptation to grasp at being his or her own god. The categories of rebellion (sin) vary from acts of violence to deception to self-glorification. We have all sinned, but through Jesus the **Messiah**, God has graciously opened the doors of **forgiveness** and **reconciliation** and thereby given us access once again to eternal life.

See also Cosmology; Creation; Temptation/Test.

Resources

Giberson, Karl W., and Francis S. Collins. *The Language of Science and Faith*. Downers Grove, IL: InterVarsity Press, 2011.

Lamoureux, Denis O., John H. Walton, C. John Collins, William D. Barrick, Gregory A. Boyd, and Philip G. Ryken. *Four Views on the Historical Adam*. Edited by Matthew Barrett, Ardel B. Caneday, and Stanley N. Gundry. Grand Rapids: Zondervan, 2013.

Walton, John H. *The Lost World of Adam and Eve*. Downers Grove, IL: InterVarsity Press, 2015.

ROBERT D. BRANSON, PHD

FASTING

"Fasting" (Gk., *nēsteia*), willingly keeping oneself from particular comforts such as food, demonstrates concern and petition. While abstaining from food may also be a way of purifying the body of toxins, primarily, however, fasting is a means for calling upon God for help. It enables both the individual and community to draw closer to God.

Fasting by Israel was often accompanied by prayer during significant rituals that were to be strictly observed (Lev. 16:29-30; Num. 29:7). When facing a difficult situation, the motivating factor for proclaiming a fast was to move God to show favor to Israel. Fasting was also often observed in times of individual distress (1 Sam. 20:34; 2 Sam. 1:12; Neh. 1:4; Dan. 6:18).

Christian fasting grew from biblical descriptions, often related to union with Christ as emphasized in the **gospel. Faith, hope,** and charity flow from gospel teaching on fasting. The true attitude of fasting is judged by its outcomes. Wimmer notes that fasting has the "ability to foster union with Christian faith, hope and **love**" and thus "to prepare us for eternal life" (1982, 23-25).

In the NT, fasting is presented as having spiritual importance in the life and teaching of Jesus Christ (Matt. 4:1-4; 6:16-18; Luke 4:1-4). Jesus's forty days of fasting mark him as the messianic figure, the promised **prophet** like Moses (Deut. 18:14-18). Jesus's teaching in the **Sermon on the Mount** highlights the nature of true **righteousness** and humility as opposed to hypocrisy.

Jesus taught that fasting is included with almsgiving and prayer as acts of **righteousness** and promised that such righteous acts would be rewarded (Matt. 6:16-18). Fasting based on confidence in the unseen God's reward reflects faith in and **obedience** to the One whose directions are to be observed.

In the early Christian community, fasting played a vital role. The path to conversion for Saul (later called Paul) included fasting. In his fasting for three days, he was truly humbled (Acts 9:9). His fasting ended with his reception of the **Holy Spirit** and baptism. Fasting for early Christians bore witness to their inward spiritual hunger and their longing for Jesus. In today's church, fasting must demonstrate this same desire for God's presence.

While fasting **remembers** God and his presence, in and of itself, fasting has no merit unless it is given spiritual meaning. The scribes and Pharisees often fasted as acts of righteousness. In the Sermon on the Mount, Jesus stated that "unless your righteousness exceeds that of the scribes and Pharisees, you will never enter the **kingdom of heaven**" (Matt. 5:20, NRSV). Fasting is important because it is one of the spiritual disciplines that bring us closer to God.

Resource

Wimmer, Joseph F. *Fasting in the New Testament: A Study in Biblical Theology.* Mahwah, NJ: Paulist Press, 1982.

SIMON JOTHI, BD, MA

FEAR OF THE LORD/GOD

The human response of fear in the Old and New Testaments has a range of overwhelming terror, on the one hand, and respectful awe, on the other hand. There are more than a dozen Hebrew roots that signify a concept of fear in the OT and almost a dozen Greek words that connote some concept of fear in the NT. In the OT, "fear" (*yr'/yārē'*) takes as its object "Lord" (*Yahweh*), which is the **covenant** name for God, or the more generic divine name for God (*'ĕlōhîm*) in more than three hundred instances. The phrasing "fear" (*phobeomai/phobos*) of the "Lord" (*kyrios*) or "God" (*theos*) is less frequent in the NT, but most of the same nuances in the OT are found in the NT, along with some different ones.

In those instances where the fear of the Lord refers to human terror or crippling fright before the Divine, the impetus may be caused by overt sinful behavior in the presence of divine power (Gen. 3:10), the **holy**-other character of the Lord (Exod. 3:6; Matt. 17:6-7; Luke 5:8-10), the sheer raw power of the Lord (Exod. 20:18-21; Deut. 5:5; Matt. 14:26), or the main apparatus that symbolized the Lord's presence, the ark of the covenant (2 Sam. 6:9). The lengthy acrostic *tôrâ* poem of Psalm 119 epitomizes well this terror as "my flesh trembles for fear of you, and I am afraid because of your judgments" (v. 120, AT).

On the other hand, exhibiting the fear of the Lord often signaled proper reverence and genuine worship for the true God of Israel in the OT (Exod. 1:17) and for the Lord Jesus Christ in the NT (Heb. 12:28). In the book of Deuteronomy (chs. 5–11), **love** of God and fear of God are discussed together within the first thorough attempt to define how Israel was to properly relate to the Lord God through the standards of a new covenant. The love of the Lord exhibited by a worshipper dispels terror, and the fear of the Lord hinders irreverent, presumptuous familiarity (6:1-9; 10:12-13). Compare this notion with that of the writer of 1 John, who argued that perfect love for God and a fear driven by divine punishment are incompatible (4:18).

In the advent text of Isaiah 11:1-10, the source of a reverent fear of the Lord is denoted as the spirit of the Lord (v. 2). Rather than something to be eschewed, the fear of the Lord is delightful to the person of God (v. 3; cf. Matt. 28:8). In essence, the fear of the Lord in the Isaianic text is a form of proper piety. Relatedly, in Psalm 119, the fear of the Lord also repeatedly signifies pious behavior but specifically a behavior of *tôrâ* **obedience**: "I am a friend of all those who fear you, of those who keep your precepts" (v. 63, AT; cf. Eccles. 12:13; Sir. 2:15-17).

In the NT, a new category of worshipper, a Godfearer, had emerged during the late Second Temple period. These Gentile people adopted various beliefs of Judaism arising from the Hebrew Scriptures, particularly monotheism, without becoming total converts (Acts 10:2; 16:14). The primary barrier to full conversion was circumcision.

Perhaps one of the most recognizable aspects of the fear of the Lord in Scripture is that it signals the beginning of **wisdom**. The sages and scribes of the book of Proverbs and other wisdom literature communicated this facet of the phrase explicitly (Prov. 1:7; 9:10; 15:33; Ps. 111:10; Job 28:28; Sir. 1:14, 16). In Proverbs, the fear of the Lord is crucial in the acquisition of knowledge (9:10), turning away from **evil** (3:7), expressing **humility** (22:4), obtaining a long life (10:27), and procuring riches, **honor**, and life (22:4). This phrasing in Proverbs suggests reverence and awe that emanate knowledge and obedience, which further lead to more reverence and awe.

See also Sin; Wrath of God.

Resources

Arnold, Bill T. "The Love-Fear Antinomy in Deuteronomy 5–11." *VT* 61, no. 4 (2011): 551-69.

Castelo, Daniel. "The Fear of the Lord as Theological Method." *JTI* 2, no. 1 (2008): 147-60.

Goldingay, John. "Revering Yhwh." Pages 75-99 in *Israel's Life*. Vol. 3 of *Old Testament Theology*. Downers Grove, IL: IVP Academic, 2009.

MICHAEL D. MATLOCK, PHD

FEMINIST HERMENEUTICS

The term "feminist hermeneutics" encompasses several interpretive approaches that focus on gender and gender relations, with special attention to women's experiences. While feminism is a movement both in and outside of the church, in theological contexts feminist hermeneutics refers to an approach to Scripture or theology that critiques any oppressive patriarchal bias and emphasizes the experiences and voices of the marginalized, particularly **women**, in social, economic, political, and religious spheres. Feminist hermeneutics values interpretations that highlight the transformation of societal structures and relationships into the liberating reign of God.

While the term "feminism" has been used to describe women's rights movements in Western cultures since the late nineteenth century, many trace the advent of feminist biblical hermeneutics to the women's movements of the 1960s. While accurate for biblical scholarship, this neglects earlier women and men who interpreted Scripture for liberating purposes within the **church**. Margaret Fell, a Quaker, wrote an account in 1666 advocating that women have the right to hold any leadership positon in the church because women and men are equal in Christ. This was followed by John Wesley, who allowed that women who received **the call of God** on their lives could testify and pray. This claim was emphasized in nineteenth-century revivals and the broader Wesleyan-**holiness** tradition that stressed the role of the **Holy Spirit** over ordination, supporting the work of Phoebe Palmer, Amanda Smith, Maria Woodworth-Etter, and Aimee Semple McPherson (Leclerc 2004). In the male-dominated field of biblical interpretation in the 1970s and 1980s, trailblazers Elisabeth Schüssler Fiorenza and Phyllis Trible highlighted not only women's experience as readers of Scripture in the present but also the roles of women in Israel and the early church. Using the tools of historical criticism paired with the commitments of liberation theology, these scholars primarily follow a three-step method of deconstructing the patriarchal assumptions of the text (known as applying a "hermeneutic of suspicion"), critically assessing the text and its historical context, and then reconstructing the life-giving potential of the text for all people.

Feminist hermeneutics in biblical scholarship, particularly in the United States, has often been criticized for normalizing the experiences of middle-class North American white women instead of focusing on the needs of all people. The global enterprise of feminist hermeneutics ensures the distinctiveness of each reader's perspective rather than assuming a false universal. This also means that other identity markers, such as race, class, and (dis)ability, must be considered as they intersect with gender and produce both privilege and marginalization. Though all women experience sexism, not all women experience sexism the same way. Operating as part of, alongside, or in challenge to white feminists are, among others, black feminists, womanists, Latina/*mujerista* interpreters, Asian feminists, and specifically *minjung* interpreters from Korea, signaling the intersectionality of contexts and how they affect biblical interpretation.

Feminists' approaches to Scripture are as diverse as the feminist interpreters themselves. The spectrum of feminist interpretation includes those who desire to revitalize Scripture, those who desire to revise Scripture or its interpretations, and those who desire to move beyond Scripture. Because this last category primarily concerns theologians (e.g., Mary Daly and Daphne Hampson) and is less relevant for scriptural interpretation, the following focuses on revitalization and revision.

Those who want to revitalize Scripture are generally concerned with the harm that can be done to current readers by interpretations of various Scripture passages (e.g., Eph. 5:22). This branch of hermeneutics seeks to develop new interpretations of problematic texts that bring life to women's experiences. For example, wives' submission to their husbands in Ephesians 5 is held up as companionship and mutual submission, required of both spouses (v. 21).

Revisionist interpretations of Scripture strive against Scripture's patriarchal context to amplify its salvific claims. Some interpreters minimize the damage that problematic passages can do (e.g., 1 Cor. 14:34-35; 1 Tim. 2:8-15) by limiting their meaning to the original recipients. Instead, readers emphasize the broader narrative about women and men illustrated in

Scripture, from equality in Genesis 1:27; to God's work through women (e.g., Hagar, Shiphrah, Puah, Miriam, Deborah, Jephthah's daughter, Ruth, Huldah, Mary, Mary Magdalene, Priscilla, Phoebe, and Junia); and to pivotal texts in Scripture such as the Spirit's descent on all people, regardless of age or gender, at Pentecost (Acts 2), or the equality bestowed in baptism (Gal. 3:27-28). These larger themes and examples within Scripture are given more credence than the localized restrictions placed on women in some early church contexts. This approach does not suggest that cultural patriarchy can be separated from theological claims but rather implies that although Scripture was written in a patriarchal context, it reaches beyond such oppression.

Other revisionist interpreters similarly discount the power of passages that minimize women's experience, but these interpreters do so primarily because of an ideology of **justice** stemming from liberation theology. Like Schüssler Fiorenza, these readers are more likely to seek historical models for redemptive action (e.g., female leadership in the early church). Through the method of deconstructing the text, these interpreters find something innate to the text that is liberating to women and therefore not bound to cultural patriarchy.

Feminist hermeneutics has contributed to biblical interpretation over the last decades in many positive ways: highlighting the importance of women's diverse and intersectional experience as readers and as leaders, accentuating the often unrecognized role of gender and gender identity within the text and within interpretations, underlining (along with liberation hermeneutics) the importance of readers' preunderstanding, and working to align the church with the justice-seeking reign of God.

See also Matriarchs; Women in the Old Testament; Women Leaders; Women's Roles in the Church.

Resources

Leclerc, Diane. "Wesleyan-Holiness-Feminist Hermeneutics: A Historical Rendering with Contemporary Considerations." Pages 217-41 in *Reading the Bible in Wesleyan Ways: Some Constructive Proposals*. Edited by Barry L. Callen and Richard P. Thompson. Kansas City: Beacon Hill Press of Kansas City, 2004.

Schüssler Fiorenza, Elisabeth. *Changing Horizons: Explorations in Feminist Interpretation*. Minneapolis: Fortress Press, 2013.

Thiselton, Anthony C. *Hermeneutics: An Introduction*. Grand Rapids: Eerdmans, 2009.

Trible, Phyllis. *Texts of Terror: Literary-Feminist Readings of Biblical Narratives*. Overtures to Biblical Theology 13. Philadelphia: Fortress Press, 1984.

LAURA SWEAT HOLMES, PHD

FESTIVALS

God intended life for the OT believer to be filled with communal celebration. Multiple times throughout the year Yahweh commanded his people to gather for a sumptuous meal, to **rest** from their labors, and to worship.

The people also gathered to reflect on Yahweh's work among them. In some festivals, they focused more on God's past help, such as delivering them from Egypt and providing for them in the **wilderness**. At other festivals they considered God's present and future provision, particularly through the harvest. Each festival also allowed them to reflect on Yahweh's lordship over Israel.

The Christians of the NT period continued to observe the old festivals but almost immediately began to understand their deeper significance in the light of Christ. What remained the same for the NT believers was a profound sense of communal joy, food, worship, and reflection.

Festivals of the Old Testament

The "big three" OT festivals were Passover and Unleavened Bread, Weeks (or Pentecost), and Tabernacles. These were occasions of pilgrimage to **Jerusalem** (the Hebrew term for pilgrimage is the source of the Arabic term *hajj*), the first two in the spring and the third in the fall.

Passover and the Festival of Unleavened Bread were actually two events that quickly came to be regarded together. Passover marked the beginning of the Jewish ceremonial year in the month of Nisan (March–April), a day established to celebrate when God "passed over" the Israelites but decimated the Egyptians. This day was followed immediately by a seven-day festival to celebrate the barley harvest (Exod. 12–13; 23:14-17; 34:18, 25; Lev. 23:5-14; Num. 9:1-14; 28:16-25; Deut. 16:1-8, 16-17; Josh. 5:10-12; 1 Kings 9:25; 2 Kings 23:21-23; 2 Chron. 8:12-13; 30; 35:1-19; Ezra 6:19-22; Ezek. 45:21-25).

Fifty days after Passover, in the month of Sivan (May–June), the Israelites celebrated the wheat harvest at what is variously known as Pentecost, the Feast of Weeks, the Feast of Harvest, or the Day of Firstfruits (Exod. 23:16*a*; 34:22*a*; Lev. 23:15-22; Num. 28:26-31; Deut. 16:9-12).

The third pilgrimage festival, Tabernacles (Booths) or Ingathering, was regarded as the most important annual festival (Exod. 23:16*b*; 34:22*b*; Lev. 23:33-36, 39-43; Num. 29:12-38; Deut. 16:13-15; Neh. 8:13-18; Ezek. 45:25; Zech. 14:16-19). In several passages, it is referred to simply as "the feast" (1 Kings 8:2, 65; 12:32; 2 Chron. 5:3; Isa. 30:29; Ezek. 45:25). It was held from the fifteenth to the twenty-first of the seventh month (Tishri, September–October) and involved living in temporary shelters. The main purpose of the festival was to commemorate Israel's sojourn in the wilderness, but it also celebrated the fruit harvest.

Earlier that month, the Israelites celebrated the Festival of Trumpets, better known as Rosh Hashanah (lit., "the head of the year") (Lev. 23:23-25; Num. 10:10; 29:1-6). It marked the beginning of the civil and agricultural year but, more important, marked the beginning of preparations for the most **holy** of Israelite holy days, which occurred on the tenth day of Tishri. On Yom Kippur, the Day of Atonement, the Israelites were to "afflict themselves"—that is, refrain from food, drink, and sexual activity. The only annual fast prescribed in the Mosaic **law**, Yom Kippur was also marked by rest and elaborate purification rituals (Lev. 16; 23:26-32; Num. 29:7-11).

Festivals added after Moses's time included Purim in February or March (Esther 9:18-32) and the Feast of the Dedication (or Hanukkah) in December (1 Macc. 4:36-59; 2 Macc. 1:9, 18; 10:5-8; John 10:22).

Festivals of the New Testament

As the NT opens, one sees that the festivals of the OT continued to be observed. Every year Mary and Joseph took their son to the temple in Jerusalem for Passover (Luke 2:41); Jesus regularly made the same trip for the same reason as an adult (Matt. 26:17-30; Mark 14:1-26; John 2:13-23; 11:55). Nor was this the only festival he frequented (John 7; 10:22).

Even after the death, **resurrection**, and ascension of Christ, his followers did not immediately abandon the old festivals. Paul spoke of himself being "under the law," likely including the laws that mandate festivals, when among those "under the law" (1 Cor. 9:20, NRSV). At one point he hurried to Jerusalem, hoping to make it by Pentecost (Acts 20:16).

At the same time, one notices two changes in how these festivals were understood by NT believers. First, they came to be regarded more symbolically. Paul encouraged the Corinthian believers to "celebrate the [Passover] festival, not with the old yeast, the yeast of malice and evil, but with the unleavened bread of sincerity and truth" (1 Cor. 5:8, NRSV; cf. Rom. 3:24-26; 8:23; 11:16; 1 Cor. 15:20-23). This shift is even more pronounced in Hebrews (8–10; 11:28).

Second, some early Christian writers expressed caution about the practices of Judaism, including the festivals. In addition to the concerns expressed by the author of Hebrews (9:10-14), Paul warned his churches not to mistake the shadow for the reality (Rom. 14:5-22; Col. 2:17). For the early Christians, the reality toward which the festivals and other elements of the Jewish law were pointing was Christ. Since his coming, every aspect of the law needed to be understood differently (Col. 2:13-17). These changes were further facilitated by the increasing influx of Gentiles into the **church**, heightening Jewish-Gentile tensions, and the destruction of the Jewish temple in AD 70.

Although the observance of Jewish festivals declined among Christians, Christians continued to experience what those festivals were meant to accomplish in other ways. During the NT period, they celebrated God's work among them and acknowledged his sovereignty on the Lord's Day, the first day of the week, on which Christ rose from the dead. This was a time of worship and a shared meal.

Conclusion

Most branches of Christendom have long recognized the importance of setting aside **sacred times** for communal celebration. In recent years, evangelical Christians seem to be catching on. Churches that once observed special celebrations only at Christmas and Easter are now attending to Advent, Lent, Pentecost, even Maundy Thursday. This trend is helpful in communicating God's desire for his people to contemplate his intervention into history, celebrate his ordinary and extraordinary gifts, and recognize his lordship. Most importantly, such festivals allow God's people to reflect on the centrality of Christ to all time.

Resources

Milgrom, Jacob. *Leviticus: A Book of Ritual and Ethics*. A Continental Commentary. Minneapolis: Augsburg Fortress, 2004.

Miller, Patrick D. *The Religion of Ancient Israel*. Library of Ancient Israel. Louisville, KY: Westminster John Knox Press, 2000.

Ross, Allen P. *Recalling the Hope of Glory: Biblical Worship from the Garden to the New Creation*. Grand Rapids: Kregel, 2006.

Wenham, Gordon J. *The Book of Leviticus*. NICOT. Grand Rapids: Eerdmans, 1979.

STEPHEN J. LENNOX, PHD

FORGIVENESS, THE ART AND NECESSITY OF

The NT primarily uses two Greek words that inform us about God's gracious decision to offer forgiveness to us and about his command that we forgive others. First, the verb *charizomai* refers to someone freely showing favor ("**grace**" [*charis*]) to another by canceling a debt or pardoning an offense. Thus God demonstrates his grace by offering forgiveness to us because of the atoning **sacrifice** Jesus made on the cross. Second, NT writers used the verb *aphiēmi* to refer to a "release," "pardon," or "cancellation" of a legal, moral, or legitimate debt or obligation that someone owes for a wrong committed.

God's gracious forgiveness, however, is not automatic, nor is it forced on those who do not want to receive it. To sinners who believe in Jesus as their Lord and **Savior**, genuinely confess their **sins**, and repent from their **evil** ways, God graciously grants forgiveness. God does not automatically release us from the earthly consequences of our sins, but he does, in Christ, pardon us from the guilt we should incur on **judgment** day for the sins we have committed.

It is important to understand that sins are committed principally against God and secondarily against humans (Gen. 20:6; 39:9; 1 Sam. 2:25; 7:6; 12:23; Ps. 51:4 [6 HB]; Acts 5:3-4). Otherwise, on what basis could God forgive some wrong, if it was not done to him? This is why God is the only one who can forgive sins, ultimately (Mark 2:7). Humans may be the ones wronged on earth by sinful actions, but the sin itself is committed against God. Humans are only the channels through which the sin is done. Thus we can say one person "sins against" another, but only in the sense that one human being has sinned against God by doing a sinful act to another person.

God has graciously forgiven us in Christ; therefore, God expects us to forgive (Matt. 6:14-15; Eph. 4:32; Col. 3:13). As in other areas of a Christian's life, God's commands for us to forgive others are for our own good; namely, forgiveness allows us to begin a process of healing from the harm. By practicing forgiveness, our minds and hearts can find freedom from frequent, intrusive thoughts of retaliation, anger, and bitterness. Forgiving others helps us not to focus on the emotional pain of the sin and helps us not to brood over the debt or hold in contempt the person who owes the debt.

Forgiveness may become a unilateral process for Christians when the other person refuses to cooperate, is unwilling to confess, does not ask to be forgiven, or is unaware of our willingness to forgive. However, we are not to set conditions before forgiving others, such as saying, "I'll forgive if . . . " or "I'll forgive when . . ." or "I'll forgive you just this once." Forgiveness when requested is not an option (Matt. 18:21-22). When we pray the Lord's Prayer, we're asking God to forgive us "as we also have forgiven" (6:12, NIV).

However, genuine **confession** and **repentance** are required if the wrongdoer wants to receive forgiveness and live a cleansed life (1 John 1:9; cf. 1 Sam. 15; 2 Sam. 12). When others who sin against us refuse to repent, we may respond as did Jesus on the cross (Luke 23:34). We give to God the offense. If in the future they repent, he may forgive them.

When we sin, we should not try to shift the blame. Our confessions must be genuine and show that we have taken full responsibility for our offense and that we will do our best to make things right. Since we remember failures, often the difficult part is forgiving ourselves, even if we have received forgiveness from God and the injured party.

Because humans do not forget, being able to release an offense completely may take time and considerable effort. While we begin the process of forgiveness by making a conscious decision to forgive the wrongdoer, the hurt, pain, and **suffering** we have experienced may continue to be felt. Wrong actions cannot be undone, but they can be forgiven.

The sooner the decision to forgive is made, the sooner the healing process can begin. When we learn to forgive ordinary and everyday grievances quickly, we can more easily forgive more significant ones. Forgiveness does not necessarily mean we will be reconciled with the other person. It is, however, a necessary first step toward **reconciliation**.

BRAD FIPPS, PHD

FREE WILL

The Bible affirms that God is the creator and sustainer of all. The Bible also talks clearly about human choices to fulfill or to reject God's purposes. But theological and philosophical questions arise about the relationship between God's control as Creator and Sustainer and human freedom. How can God control and how can people simultaneously experience freedom? This question has puzzled readers of the Bible from biblical times to the present. God's control seems to leave no room for freedom. Also human responsibility appears to disappear if humans can only do what God determines.

Multiple biblical passages are cited in support of divine control. Examples of passages supporting divine control appear throughout the OT. God allowed Pharaoh to live in order to display God's power (Exod. 9:16). Josiah was named before his birth (1 Kings 13:1-2). Job acknowledged that "no purpose of [God's] can be thwarted" (Job 42:2, NIV).

The NT also affirms God's sovereignty. For example, in Acts 2:23, Peter says that God handed Jesus over to the Jewish leaders according to God's "plan and foreknowledge" (NIV). Romans 8:28-30 says that God foreknew those who were **predestined** to conform to the image of the Son. Philippians 2:12-13 affirms that God is at work in people enabling them both to will and to work for God's pleasure.

On the other hand, numerous biblical materials refer to human freedom, beginning in the OT with Genesis 2:15-17 and 3:6-7, which show that Eve and Adam chose to disobey God's command. The promises and blessings recorded in Leviticus 26:3-46 and God's call to Israel in Deuteronomy 30 affirm that the **covenant** involves people making choices to obey or disobey God's commandments. Although the clay of the potter in Jeremiah 18:1-12 is often understood to communicate God's control, God's control comes in response to Israel's decision. If Israel turned from its **evil**, God would not bring evil on the nation. Likewise, if a nation that is blessed chooses evil, it will experience disaster. When Nineveh repented, God did not bring calamity upon the city (Jon. 3:10).

Examples of the importance of personal decisions appear in the NT with the story of the prodigal son (Luke 15:11-32) and in Paul's description of people rejecting knowledge of God and God giving up the ungodly (Rom. 1:20-28). James rejected the position that **temptation** comes from God, indicating that while God enables the believer to resist temptation, God does not cause temptation and thus does not control all that happens to a person (1:13).

Confronted with biblical materials affirming both God's control and human choice, theological interpretations developed in order to understand how both can be affirmed. In one way or another, each of these options seeks to maintain the beliefs both that God is in control and that humans make free decisions. In contemporary theology, three options dominate. One option is to affirm that God's control is absolute but that humans are free. Another option is that the relationship between God's control and human freedom is a mystery. The third option is that humans are free and that God brings good out of human decisions.

The first option is called compatibilism because God's control is compatible with human choice. Human freedom is a matter of internal decisions unaffected by external control. God's influence shapes the person so that he or she seeks to do what God wants done instead of God forcing the person to do what God seeks. Some compatibilists explain God's control as the result of God's knowledge of all future possibilities. Instead of forcing a person to do a specific act, God uses knowledge of future possibilities to establish the conditions that will lead to the person choosing the act that fulfills God's purposes. This understanding of freedom has often been called freedom of spontaneity and is held by Calvinism.

Explaining the relation between God's control and human freedom through mystery appeals to the difference between God and humans. Because of that difference, humans are unable to understand how God's control is consistent with human experiences of freely choosing.

In a libertarian understanding, freedom involves choice among alternatives. From a libertarian perspective, freedom exists because of God's self-limitation, God's **creation** of free creatures, or God's prevenient **grace**. God's control is maintained through God's response to the decisions that humans make. God's response establishes the next set of conditions to which humans respond with another choice. This has been called freedom of indeterminacy.

Each of these three options faces difficulties. Compatibilism's substitution of internal causation for external causation still involves causation different from the individual's choice. God's internal control does not allow for any significant contribution to God's purposes by humans because each decision carries out God's plan for accomplishing God's purposes. Also, responsibility for human choices ultimately returns to God's actions either through influence within the person or influence upon the conditions leading to the person's internal decision.

Mystery as a way of understanding the relation between divine choice and human choice separates divine choice and human choice, making it difficult again for humans to cooperate with God's purposes. If God is so radically different from humans that it is impossible to understand God's actions and purposes, humans cannot understand enough to choose either for or against God's purposes.

Libertarian understandings of human freedom have no way of accounting for the specific choices that people make. Freedom of the will means the will has no prior cause. Each choice is basically arbitrary, making any consistency in actions problematic.

Theologically, the various forms of Arminianism hold to libertarian understandings of human freedom. John Wesley utilized the concept of prevenient grace, God's grace enabling each person to choose for or against God, to maintain the necessity of God's action in salvation.

Resource

Basinger, David, and Randall Basinger, eds. *Predestination and Free Will*. Downers Grove, IL: IVP Academic, 1986.

JOHN CULP, PHD

Gg

GIFTS OF THE SPIRIT

Two different Greek words are translated as spiritual gifts. The first word is *pneumatika*, a cognate of *pneuma*, which means "spirit." The second is *charismata*, a cognate of *charis*, which mean "**grace**." Taken together, the two words indicate that spiritual gifts are endowments of the Spirit and grace of God.

The most detailed discussion of spiritual gifts occurs in Paul's writings, particularly Romans 12:3-13; 1 Corinthians 12–14; and Ephesians 4:8-13. There is also a brief reference to spiritual gifts in 1 Peter 4:10-11. The material in 1 Corinthians is the most detailed and sustained treatment of spiritual gifts.

Paul's frequent use of *charismata* in 1 Corinthians 12–14 indicates his preference for it over *pneumatika* as a designation for spiritual gifts. The term *pneumatika* may conceivably be taken to mean natural talents originating in the human spirit. On the other hand, *charismata* clearly indicates that the gifts are bestowed by the grace of God.

In 1 Corinthians 12:4-6 Paul differentiates between gifts, ministries, and activities, and these three are coupled with **Spirit**, Lord, and God respectively. One cannot make a tight connection between a particular endowment and a person of the triune God. Precise formulation of the doctrine of the Trinity came about several centuries after Paul.

Paul lists spiritual gifts in a variety of ways. His lists are illustrative and flexible rather than exhaustive, as demonstrated by placing them side by side as follows:

Romans 12:6-8	1 Cor. 12:8-10, 28-30	Ephesians 4:11
prophecy	utterance of **wisdom**	apostles
ministry	utterance of knowledge	**prophets**
teaching	**faith**	evangelists
exhortation	gifts of healing	pastors
generosity in giving	working of miracles	teachers

diligent leadership	prophecy
cheerful **compassion**	discernment of spirits
	tongues
	interpretation of tongues
	apostles
	prophets
	teachers
	deeds of power
	healing
	assistance
	leadership

The gifts of the Spirit include not only the more dramatic and miraculous variety, which the Corinthian Christians apparently sought after, but also such activities as servanthood, administration, pastoring, and teaching. This shows that Paul intended to correct some ill-conceived notions about spiritual gifts among the Corinthians.

Although spiritual gifts are varied and are endowed by the Spirit, Paul does urge the Corinthians to seek a particular gift over another, depending on the context and circumstances. For example, Paul argued that in the context of Christian assembly, prophecy is a more useful gift than speaking in tongues (1 Cor. 14:1-19). When the **church** has gathered for worship, any kind of speaking must be for the purpose of communicating a message from God in intelligible language to those gathered. Speaking in tongues is fine in private prayer when no one is listening except God. But if a person speaks in tongues in a gathered assembly, he or she must pray for the power to interpret (v. 13). If there is no interpretation, that person must not speak in tongues publicly (v. 28).

When the church has gathered for worship, speakers who utter a Spirit-inspired message, prayer, or blessing must engage their own minds as well as the minds of the hearers (vv. 13-19). Effective communication in a **communal** context must engage the intellect of the speaker as well as that of the hearer.

The purpose of spiritual gifts in the church is not for personal benefit or exaltation but for mutual edification and instruction. For this reason Paul urged the Corinthians to aspire for the gift of prophecy rather than tongues (vv. 1-3) because a prophetic word brings understanding and encouragement to the entire congregation.

The exercise of spiritual gifts in the church not only must be for the benefit of others but also must be well ordered. When someone in the congregation receives an inspired message from the Spirit, he or she must wait until the previous person has finished speaking. The whole congregation cannot speak at the same time and create a chaotic, unintelligible cacophony. Furthermore, only two or three persons may speak in a worship gathering. This means that a person is responsible for exerting some control over how and when an inspired message is delivered to the congregation. At the same time, members of the congregation listening to an inspired speaker have an active role to play, namely, to weigh (*diakrinetōsan*) what is said (v. 29). The verb *diakrinō* means to "make a distinction," "judge correctly," and "render a decision." A speaker claiming to bring a Spirit-inspired prophetic message must still submit to the authority of other prophets in the congregation (vv. 29-32).

Since all spiritual gifts are necessary for the well-being of the church, no gift must be despised or unduly elevated. In this regard, Paul uses the analogy of the human body. One member of the body cannot regard other members as useless. Just as all members are needed for the proper functioning of the human body (12:14-26), so also with the church. Diversity of gifts and unity of spirit are equally indispensable. Accordingly, right in the middle of his spiritual-gifts discussion, Paul devotes an entire chapter (ch. 13) to the necessity of **love** in the Christian community.

The various lists of spiritual gifts indicate that administrative, pastoral, and teaching offices are also gifts of the Spirit. When the church ordains, elects, or appoints persons to certain ministries and offices, it must do so with the understanding that its role is to recognize, confirm, and give its blessing to such persons who have demonstrated the gifts and graces bestowed on them by the Spirit of God. Paul did not distinguish between a so-called charismatic person and one who fills an ecclesiastical office. All in the church are charismatic in that the gifts of the Spirit are given by grace in various ways for the benefit of the entire church.

See also Witness of the Spirit.

Resources

Fee, Gordon D. *The First Epistle to the Corinthians*. NICNT. Grand Rapids: Eerdmans, 1987.

Hays, Richard B. *First Corinthians*. IBC. Louisville, KY: Westminster John Knox Press, 1997.

Martin, Ralph P. "Gifts, Spiritual." Pages 1015-18 in vol. 2 of *ABD*.

JIRAIR S. TASHJIAN, PHD

GLORY

When Isaiah saw a vision of God seated on the heavenly throne, the heavenly hosts proclaimed that the "whole earth is full of his glory" (Isa. 6:3, NRSV). Throughout the Bible, glory is experienced in divine encounters with God, and this divine glory is a defining theme for **Jesus's ministry**. Jesus, himself, is called the "glory to your people Israel" (Luke 2:32). Glory has been shared between the Father and Son since before **creation** (John 1:14, 17:4-5), and this shared glory in the Trinity is a symbol for Christian unity (17:22-24).

While in English, glory may convey a sense of awe or **victory**, the primary meaning of the Hebrew word for glory (*kābôd*) is "heaviness" or "abundance." God's hand is "heavy" in **judgment** (1 Sam. 5:11), which corresponds to the Son of Man coming in glory to judge humanity (Matt. 16:27; 24:30; Mark 13:26). When Peter, James, and John were present at Jesus's transfiguration, there was a play on this meaning: "Peter and his companions were weighed down with sleep; but . . . they saw his glory" (Luke 9:32, NRSV). Similarly, before Moses had an encounter with God, he asked God to show him his glory (Exod. 33:18).

Glory was also revealed in God's actions and was, in some cases, the agency of miracles. God's glory thundered over waters (Ps. 29:3). Jesus's first **miracle** was a display of glory (John 2:11). Jesus, himself, was raised from the dead by the glory of God (Rom. 6:4).

John Wesley and subsequent holiness writers also used the term "glory" regularly in two different ways, but both Wesley and the holiness writers associated it with a divine encounter with God. Along with early Christian writers, glory was tied to salvation, particularly with the concept of "bringing . . . to glory" (Heb. 2:10, NRSV). Second, the phrase "enter into . . . glory" was used commonly to mean a divine encounter or being admitted into heaven (Luke 24:26, NRSV; cf. 1 Pet. 5:10), the place where God's glory is its light (Rev. 21:22-27). In contrast, hell is absent the presence of God and his glory (2 Thess. 1:9). Holiness writers also depicted saints as having a similar visionary experience to that of Stephen, seeing the glory of God and being admitted into his presence (Acts 7:55).

Throughout Scripture, the "heavy" glory of God describes the human experience of a divine encounter, whether it resulted in judgment or miracles. It is the same glory into which believers ultimately **hope** to enter in order to find their homes in the presence of God.

See also Afterlife; Resurrection.

Resources

Lewis, C. S. "The Weight of Glory." Pages 24-46 in *The Weight of Glory: And Other Addresses*. San Francisco: HarperSanFrancisco, 2001.

Wesley, John. "The Way to the Kingdom." Pages 123-32 in *John Wesley's Sermons: An Anthology*. Edited by Albert C. Outler and Richard P. Heitzenrater. Nashville: Abingdon Press, 1991.

SCOTT A. WILLIAMS, MA

GODLINESS/GODLY (*ḥāsîd, eusebeia*)

In the OT, the root word for "godly" derives from the Hebrew *ḥāsîd*, meaning "the pious, faithful," and indicates principally the faithfulness of believers. It is often translated with the English words "**saints**," "godly," "merciful," "faithful," "kind," "**holy**," and "devout." Twenty-four of the thirty-two occurrences are in the Psalms and depict the godly or saints as objects of God's special, providential care (4:3 [4 HB]; 12:1 [2 HB]; 37:28), as worshippers (52:9 [11 HB]; 132:16; 145:10), or as those being exhorted to worship (30:4 [5 HB]; 31:23 [24 HB]; 32:6). In **wisdom** literature, the lifestyle of the godly is contrasted frequently with that of the ungodly. In the OT, "godly" describes the character of those who demonstrate their **faith** through faithfulness to God.

A single family of Greek words accounts for the majority of appearances of the English words "godliness," "godly," or "piety" in the NT. The Greek root is *sebō*, "to show reverence for," and includes the idea of reverence for the gods or God, for others, and for society and governments. The Greek *eusebeia* and related terms have been translated variously as "godliness," "godly," "piety," "devout," and "religion." Responding to the crowd's astonishment at their healing the lame man, Peter and John deny any inherent "piety" as the source of the **miracle** (Acts 3:12) but stress that the man was made whole "by **faith** in the name of Jesus" (v. 16, NIV).

The term appears most frequently in the Pastoral Letters, with fourteen of nineteen occurrences. Paul challenged the two young pastors, Timothy and Titus, to bring order to their churches and provided them with instructions for their own lives and ministries. The strange teachings of Paul's opponents were to be avoided (2 Tim. 3:5) and counteracted with "godly" teaching (1 Tim. 6:3) or training in godliness (2:2; 4:7-8; 6:5-6; Titus 2:12). Despite one reference to godliness as the whole of Christian religion (1 Tim. 3:16), the majority of references are exhortations that underscore the expectation of ethical living on the part of Christians. Readers are encouraged to pursue godliness (6:11) and to consider virtues related to it, including a "peaceful and quiet" life (2:2, NIV), duty to family (5:4), "contentment" (6:5-6, NIV), and "knowledge of the truth" (Titus 1:1, NIV). However, godly living comes at a cost, for "everyone who wants to live a godly life in Christ Jesus will be persecuted" (2 Tim. 3:12, NIV).

The Petrine letters have the remaining five occurrences of the term. Like Paul, Peter associated godliness with other virtues (2 Pet. 1:6-7); he also echoed the OT theme of divine, providential care over the godly (2:9). Peter also stressed divine empowerment for godly living: "His divine power has given us everything we need for a godly life" (1:3, NIV).

See also Biblical Ethics; Providence of God; Suffering.

Resources

Fiedler, Peter. "εὐσέβεια." Pages 84-85 in vol. 2 of *EDNT*.
Foerster, Werner. "εὐσέβεια." Pages 168-96 in vol. 7 of *TDNT*.
Mundle, W. "Godliness, Piety." Pages 90-91 in vol. 2 of *NIDNTT*.

J. RUSSELL FRAZIER, PHD

GOSPEL

"Gospel" derives from a combination of the Middle English words "god" (good) and "spell" (announcement). This is an excellent translation of the Greek noun *euangelion* (good news) and the verb form *euangelizō* (evangelize), which joins the prefix *eu* (good) and the noun *angelia* (message). The following survey will explore the use and meaning of gospel and evangelize in the Hellenistic-Roman world and in the Testaments of the Bible before summarizing key themes that characterize the gospel in Scripture.

Hellenistic-Roman World

Both the noun and verb forms refer to announcements of military victories, which were frequently accompanied by **festivals** and **sacrifices** (Xenophon, *Hell.* 1.6.37; Plutarch, *Reg. imp. apophth.* 35). The plural *euangelia* appears in inscriptions celebrating the birth of Augustus as a "**savior**" who caused a new wave of "glad tidings" across the empire. However, many instances of "good news" are paradoxical. Good news can be mistaken (Appian, *Bell. civ.* 3.13.93) or faked (Xenophon, *Hell.* 4.3.14). Good news can be premature (Plutarch, *Phoc.* 23) or entail a tragic death (Appian, *Bell. civ.* 4.4.20; Josephus, *Ant.* 7.245).

Old Testament

In the Septuagint, forms of the Greek term translate the Hebrew root *bśr*. The noun *euangelion* (2 Sam. 4:10) and verb *euangelizō* (Ps. 68:11-12 [12-13 HB; LXX 67:12-13]) both refer to military victories. However, tragic twists appear as well (1 Sam. 31:9 at the death of Saul and 2 Sam. 18:19-20 at the death of Absalom). Several OT uses of the verb refer to poets and **prophets** announcing that God will bring salvation and **peace** to Israel, particularly to the exiled and oppressed (Ps. 40:9 [10 HB; LXX 39:10]; Isa. 52:7; Joel 2:32 [LXX 3:5]; Nah. 1:15 [LXX 2:1]).

New Testament

Luke uses the verb throughout the Third Gospel and Acts (25x, but the noun only 2x). The births of John and Jesus are announced as good news by angels (Luke 1:19 and 2:10; cf. Augustus's birth noted above). In Luke 4:18-19, Jesus cites Isaiah 61:1, declaring that he has been anointed "to preach good news to the **poor**" (cf. Matt. 11:5 and Luke 7:22, AT). Jesus's ongoing proclamation of the kingdom (Luke 4:43) includes this proclamation of freedom and restoration as enacted in the defeat of satanic powers (vv. 31-37) and the healing of diseases (vv. 38-41).

Matthew and Mark, along with Luke, characterize Jesus's message as the proclamation of the "good news of the **kingdom of God**" (Matt. 4:23; Mark 1:15, AT; neither the verb *euangelizō* nor the noun *euangelion* appear in John), especially as an eschatological reality (Matt. 4:15-17; Mark 1:14-15; Luke 16:16). The good news of the kingdom in the Gospels is paired with healings and exorcisms performed by Jesus (Matt. 9:35; Mark 16:15-18; Luke 8:1-2) and his apostles (Matt. 10:7-8; Luke 9:2). The proclamation of this good news also has a tragic twist, for it entails sacrifice (Mark 8:35; 10:29) and rejection (Matt. 10:14; Luke 10:10).

Acts shifts the content of this good news, for the message of the apostles is primarily good news *about* Jesus the **Messiah** (5:42; 11:20; 17:18). In Acts, Luke often used the verb "evangelize" (8:40; 14:7; 16:10) to refer to the apostles' message about the salvation offered in Jesus's name (4:12; 16:17-18). Yet Acts retains other aspects of the gospel as well. Philip "proclaimed the good news of the kingdom of God and the name of Jesus" (8:12, NIV), and Peter preached about **peace** available through Jesus Christ (10:36). In his inaugural sermon in Acts, Paul summarized the proclamation of the gospel as the fulfillment of God's promises to Israel in the **resurrection** of Jesus (13:32-33).

Paul used "gospel" and "evangelize" frequently (*euangelion* 19x and *euangelizō* 61x) and had become so connected to his proclamation of the gospel that he sometimes employed the noun as a synonym for "ministry" (1 Cor. 9:14; 2 Cor. 8:18; Phil. 4:3). Paul referred to the "gospel of God," probably indicating that God is the source of this good news (Rom. 1:1; Gal. 1:11; 1 Thess. 2:8-9). More specifically, Paul said that the content of "my" gospel (Rom. 2:16; 2 Tim. 2:8) is good news *about* the Christ (1 Cor. 9:12; 2 Cor. 2:12; Gal. 1:7). Paul's summary of the gospel stressed the fulfillment of God's promises through the death and resurrection of Christ (1 Cor. 15:1-4), which brings salvation (Rom. 1:16), inclusion in the people of God (Eph. 3:6), and **hope** (Col. 1:23). Paul also vigorously contended for the gospel in two ways: that the truth of the gospel of Christ be preserved (2 Cor. 11:4; Gal. 1:8-9) and that believers live their lives in accordance with the gospel (2 Cor. 9:13; Gal. 2:14; Phil. 1:27).

Conclusion

Even with the diverse and contextualized uses of the various forms of gospel and evangelize in the Bible, a few key themes stand out. First, this is truly good news for people, offering salvation, **peace**, and **forgiveness** (Ps. 40:9 [10 HB; LXX 39:10]; Luke 4:18-19; Rom. 1:16). Second, it is a message about God's kingdom (Matt. 24:14; Mark 1:14-15), but more importantly, God is the source of this good news (Rom. 1:1; Gal. 1:8-9). Third, it is good news about Jesus Christ and the benefits available through him (Acts 8:35; Rom. 1:8-14; Eph. 3:8), with the tragic twist that this good news includes the unjust execution of Jesus (Acts 10:36-39; 1 Cor. 15:2-3). Fourth, this gospel calls for a response from human beings, including **repentance** (Mark 1:14-15; Rev. 14:6-7), **belief** (Acts 15:7; Rom. 1:16), and **obedience** (2 Cor. 9:13; Phil. 1:27). Fifth and finally, this gospel is the eschatological fulfillment of the promises to Israel that announces a new era of salvation (Mark 1:14-15; Luke 4:17-21; Gal. 1:11; 1 Pet. 1:11-12).

See also Demonic/Devil; Eschatology; Incarnation.

Resources

Jervis, L. Ann, and Peter Richardson, eds. *Gospel in Paul: Studies on Corinthians, Galatians and Romans for Richard N. Longenecker.* JSNTSup 108. Sheffield, UK: Sheffield Academic Press, 1994.

Stanton, Graham N. *Jesus and Gospel.* Cambridge, UK: Cambridge University Press, 2004.

Stuhlmacher, Peter, ed. *The Gospel and the Gospels.* Grand Rapids: Eerdmans, 1991.

BART B. BRUEHLER, PHD

GOSPEL OF JOHN, THEOLOGY OF

The theology of the Gospel of John is preeminently a Christology. In this sense it is focused, but as will become clear, it is also sweeping and magisterial. As a starting point, we will unpack the prologue (1:1-18), since it is the introduction to and the road map through this theological masterpiece. It reveals the mission of the Logos: *(a)* to enlighten the blind, *(b)* to give life to the lifeless, *(c)* to unveil the invisible Father, and *(d)* to take back the world (a redemptive invasion).

The Prologue

This poetic prologue of eighteen verses would have prompted different thoughts for different people groups in the first-century Hellenistic world. Though it introduces Jesus as a historical person (finally named in 1:17), the terms describing him suggest a variety of significant ideas including God, Creator, Truth, Light, Reason, **Torah**, **Wisdom**, **Messiah**, and Son. Though they describe a man named Jesus (v. 17), the opening descriptors of "**word**," "life," and "light" (Gk., *logos, zōē,* and *phōs*) are masculine, feminine, and neuter respectively, encompassing all genders. We cannot speak of the gender of God. God transcends gender, though in the incarnation one is acquired.

These theological realities made this Gospel a multicultural and multiethnic communication phenomenon, casting its light upon readers be they Jewish, Greek, Roman, Stoic, Cynic, Platonic, Gnostic, or members of some other group. It continues to do this today.

From the beginning, it is clear that the subject of the narrative transcends the historical. The words used in the opening five verses echo the opening five verses of Genesis ("beginning," "word," "**creation**," "light," "darkness," "life"). But while Genesis refers to the physical universe, John refers to the moral universe. "Light" does not refer to sunlight, and "darkness" does not refer to the absence of light; instead, these terms refer to the spiritual domains of good and evil. Here, as so often in this Gospel, the meaning intended is a metaphorical leap from the physical. So sight refers to spiritual comprehension, and blindness refers to living in spiritual darkness (ch. 9, we are all born blind). Birth refers to a spiritual beginning (ch. 3, we are all in need of another birth). Thirst and hunger refer to appetites of the soul (chs. 4, 6). Restoration to biological life refers to eternal life and **resurrection** (ch. 11).

From this opening, we are tutored in an important way to read the story. History is only a starting point. Our experience of the physical is a preunderstanding used to communicate dimensions of the spiritual. Our experience of corporeal life is the asset used to explain and understand the significance of Jesus.

This is theology in its most simple yet profound form. If in the Synoptics Jesus's parables were metaphors of the reign or **kingdom of God**, in this Gospel it is Jesus himself; he is the parable of the kingdom.

Light versus Darkness

While John is fond of dualistic language where opposites are set off against each other (above vs. below; spirit vs. flesh; truth vs. lie; life vs. death), with darkness and light we are introduced to a dualism involving a cosmic war. Jesus is portrayed as coming from the world of light into the *kosmos*, the "world" created by the Logos, but also the place now ruled by darkness (12:35; 14:30; 16:11). The prologue says "he came to his own ['things," *ta idia* (neuter)], yet his own ["people," *hoi idioi* (masculine)] did not receive him" (1:11, AT). Here is the tragedy and the dilemma. The Logos entered the *kosmos*, made by him, but the *kosmos* neither recognized nor received him (v. 10). So the Logos invades the dark *kosmos*, and the reader anticipates the animosity of the darkness and the hostility of the *kosmos* to the light.

Here is the context for the mission of the Logos: "to make known" (*exēgeisthai*) God (v. 18); "to enlighten" (*phōtizein*) all people (v. 9); to engage with evil and "to expel" (*ekballein*—from the early Christian language of exorcism) the "ruler of this world" (12:31, AT); and to restore creation. Here also is the context for the exclamation of Jesus on the cross, "It is finished" (19:30, AT; *telein*, an echo of Gen. 2:1, *suntelein* [LXX]). From the very beginning of the biblical story, this mission and this outcome are anticipated.

It is explained: "And the light shines [*phainein*] in the darkness, and the darkness does not overcome [*katalambanein*] it" (John 1:5, AT). These three—"light," "darkness," and "overcome"—recur also in 12:35: "For yet a little while the light will be among you; walk in the light that you have so that the darkness does not overcome [*katalambanein*] you" (AT). As night flees with the rising of the sun, so does darkness flee from the presence of the light.

This engagement is the hub of almost every theological topic of this Gospel (v. 46). Enlightenment is illustrated by the central **miracle** of this Gospel (ch. 9, the man born blind); spiritual birth, by the dialogue with Nicodemus (ch. 3); and eternal life, by the cataclysmic raising of Lazarus from the grave (ch. 11).

So, too, is the inability of darkness to overcome light illustrated by the story of the woman "caught" in adultery (8:1-11). Not only did the woman who was "overcome [*katalambanein*; vv. 3-4] by evil" get rescued by Jesus (the Light), but so also did her accusers, who had themselves been overcome by evil. This pericope is followed immediately by Jesus's words, "I am the light of the world. Those who follow me shall not walk in darkness but shall possess the light [*phōs*] of life [*zōē*]" (v. 12, AT). But the rescue was done with gentleness and great personal risk to Jesus. So **love**, even here, shows itself to be **sacrificial**.

The readers are guaranteed only one safe place in the world, "following" Jesus, "abiding" in him, walking in the light provided by his teaching and presence, as a branch abides or lives because it is connected to the vine (ch. 15). But the path of this safety is most unexpected in our world, for it was through folly that **wisdom** expelled folly, through servanthood that leadership showed strength (13:1-20), through crucifixion that the **glory** of God was "raised up" (*hupsoō*; 3:14; 8:28; 12:32, 34), and through **love** that the power of God overpowers hate (note the emphasis on the command of love: 14:15, 21; 15:10).

Reading from a Greek Perspective

Besides the insight gained from reading the prologue through the lens of the creation story, insight is gained from reading it as a Greek. According to the "Myth of the Cave" in Plato's *Republic* (bk. 7), enlightenment is experienced when one escapes from the dark world of "the cave" and journeys to the world of light, outside the cave. Such a one then feels compelled to reenter the cave and enlighten those still living in darkness about the shadowy, temporal, deceptive dark world where they live, enchained by lies. It is not difficult to see in John that the messenger who comes from the world of light to enlighten is Jesus. The Christian alteration of this well-known story is that Jesus is a Being who not only came from the domain of light but is the Light. This eternal, unchanging Being actually became a part of the world of Becoming by "becoming flesh." This would have been considered impossible to Plato, since the domain of eternal, unchanging Being and the created world of temporal, always-changing Becoming can never mix (see Plato, *Tim.*). But in Christianity they do; in John this impossibility is asserted. This is the incarnation, and understanding this will give readers today some insight into the intense Christological controversies of the early centuries of Christianity.

There are other parts of John's narrative that hold similar irony when read through Greco-Roman eyes. For example, for Jesus to turn water to wine (ch. 2) was mimicry of the signature miracle of Dionysus, the Olympian Greek god of wine, who turned water to wine for humans. The Dionysian cult, ancient and widespread, was an active mystery religion in the first century. Celebrants of this cult even "ate the flesh" of the god in ritual (cf. ch. 6). A comparison would most certainly be made to Jesus.

The Greeks would also have been comparing Jesus to Asclepius, a centuries-old Greek god of healing who had widespread temples in the first century. Asclepius was granted permission by Zeus to heal ailing mortals, but he was forbidden to raise the dead to life. The account of the raising of Lazarus would have led clearly to a bold comparison of Jesus and Asclepius.

In subtle and simple ways, the evangelist has written a narrative with wide appeal. One last well-known example is the confession of Thomas to Jesus: "My Lord and my God!" (20:28, AT). Thomas's words echo the **confession** required by the Roman emperor Domitian (AD 81-96), giving not only a clue to the date of this Gospel but another vista of the powerful message of this book in that first-century culture. Faithful Christians said these words to Jesus, not the emperor, but at the cost of their lives.

To return to Plato, one might say that John continued his exposition of the Logos as the Form, leaving all other worldly analogues as shadows in the cave.

Jesus the "I Am"

The divine profile of Jesus in John is painted with broad, bold brushstrokes; the danger is to underplay them. The purpose of the Logos becoming flesh was to reveal truth about the invisible God, so we are invited to look through the Gospel toward this end. There are at least a couple more facets of the profile worth enhancing.

While in the Synoptics Jesus speaks often about the kingdom (or reign) of God, yet very little about himself, the inverse is true in John. The phrase "I Am" (*ego eimi*—the verb "to be" [*einai*] with an emphatic first-person pronoun) occurs over forty times in John (cf. three times in **Mark**: 6:50; 13:6; 14:62). Sometimes the "I Am" occurs with a predicate such as "I Am the bread of life" (John 6:35, 48, AT), "the light of the world" (8:12; 9:5, AT), "the gate for the sheep" (10:7, AT), "the good shepherd" (10:11, 14, AT), "the **resurrection** and the life" (11:25, AT), and so on. These statements emphasize some relational existential advantage of knowing Jesus, and they all meet some urgent need that we have as human beings in a dark, hostile world.

Sometimes the "I Am" occurs in a simple absolute form as when "Jesus said to them, 'Truly, truly, I say to you, before Abraham was born, I am'" (8:58, NASB). A few occurrences are remarkable, such as in Gethsemane. When the arresting party asked Jesus if he was Jesus the Nazarene, he answered "I Am," and "When Jesus said to them 'I Am,' they stepped back and fell to the ground" (18:4-6, AT). It is hard to avoid the conclusion that what is intended by *ego eimi* is the divine name (cf. Exod. 3:14-15) and that Jesus was claiming it for himself.

See also Gospel of Mark, Theology of; Gospel of Matthew, Theology of; Luke-Acts, Theology of.

Resources

Ferguson, Everett. *Backgrounds of Early Christianity.* 3rd ed. Grand Rapids: Eerdmans, 2003.

Keener, Craig. *The Gospel of John: A Commentary.* Grand Rapids: Baker Academic, 2010.

C. MICHAEL ROBBINS, PHD

GOSPEL OF MARK, THEOLOGY OF

Mark's Gospel addresses the question of Jesus's identity. This is explored through **titles** given him as well as his words and deeds. The implications of a positive response to Jesus are also of particular concern.

Various titles for Jesus appear in Mark's Gospel: Christ, Son of David, Son of Mary, Lord, Rabbi, Teacher, Prophet, Son of Man, and Son of God. Of key importance is Mark's identification of Jesus as "Christ, the Son of God" (1:1, NRSV). Another significant title is "Son of Man" (2:10, NRSV). Some scholars argue that Jesus as the Christ and Son of God may only be understood through Jesus's work as Son of Man. Taken together these three designations indicate Mark's essential understanding of Jesus.

The title "Christ" in the NT and its OT equivalent "**Messiah**" derive from the Hebrew word *māšîaḥ* meaning "anointed one." The term referred to one set apart for God by anointing with oil. In the OT, *māšîaḥ* was used of priests (Lev. 4:3), **prophets** (1 Kings 19:16), and kings (1 Sam. 24:6).

In Israel, a hope arose for the advent of a Messiah associated with Israel's second king, largely based on the oracle of Nathan to David in 2 Samuel 7:12-16. David was promised that God would raise his offspring and establish the throne of his **kingdom** forever. Old Testament references concerning the continuation of the Davidic dynasty are widespread (2 Chron. 6:16; Ps. 89:3-4 [4-5 HB]; Isa. 11:1-9; Jer. 23:5-6; Ezek. 34:23-24). Outside the Hebrew canon, in the first century BC this hope was vividly expressed in Psalms of Solomon 17:21-46, one of the most thorough accounts of messianic expectations in the pre-Christian century.

In Mark's Gospel, Davidic descent as the anointed one is identified with Jesus. While in the district of Caesarea Philippi, Jesus asked his disciples, "Who do people say that I am?" (8:27, NRSV). While some saw Jesus as John the Baptist, Elijah, or one of the prophets, Peter declared Jesus as the Christ (v. 29). While traveling to **Jerusalem**, a blind beggar recognized Jesus as the Son of David, a title Jesus did not deny (10:47-48). Standing before the Sanhedrin, Jesus was questioned by the high priest: "'Are you the Messiah, the Son of the Blessed One?' Jesus said, 'I am; and "you will see the Son of Man seated at the right hand of the Power," and "coming with the clouds of heaven"'" (14:61-62, NRSV).

Mark provides affirmation of Jesus as the Christ, as well as titles associated with the explication of how this messiahship was revealed—namely, through his roles as Son of God (the Blessed One) and Son of Man.

Scholars have long recognized that the title "Son of God" was not foreign to the ancient world. Pharaohs of Egypt were considered "sons of God" and recognized as exhibiting divine rule. At times, rulers in the Hellenistic and Roman worlds were referenced in like manner. Rome was well known for its emperor cult. Son of God, associated with the idea of a "divine man" (Gk., *theios anēr*), was aligned with concepts of divine favor, adoption, and power. Some derived Jesus's sonship from this idea. More recent scholarship, however, has questioned "divine man" as being a fixed concept in the Hellenistic world.

In the OT, sonship was closely linked with **obedience**. Davidic kings were called sons of God as faithful servants of God and representatives of God to the people (2 Sam. 7:14-17; 1 Chron. 17:11-15). The people of Israel also were referenced collectively as sons or children of God (Deut. 14:1; Isa. 1:2).

Whether or not Jesus as the Son of God (Mark 1:1) was a part of the original Markan text is questioned. In some manuscripts, the phrase "of God" does not appear. While this precise designation for Jesus does not appear elsewhere, arguably equivalent titles are found—namely, "my Son, the Beloved" (1:11, NRSV), "Son of the Most High God" (5:7, NRSV), "the Son of the Blessed One" (14:61, NRSV), and "God's Son" (15:39, NRSV). While the OT concept of obedience is associated with Mark's usages, an expanded understanding concerning Jesus is evidenced. Mark did not regard him simply as an individual who experienced God's favor and adoption as a king in the line of David.

At Jesus's baptism, a heavenly voice declared: "You are my Son, the Beloved, with you I am well pleased" (1:11, NRSV). The primary question concerns how Jesus is to be understood as Son of God. Generally, scholars recognize that this text has as its background, singly or jointly, Genesis 22:1-2, Psalm 2:7, and Isaiah 42:1.

Jesus's sonship may be understood as being obedient to God. Genesis 22:1-2 recounts God's testing of Abraham in asking for his son Isaac's life as a burnt offering. Like Isaac, Jesus was a son to be sacrificed, although in the Genesis account, the sacrifice was ultimately provided by God. Such was not the case for Jesus. Jesus willingly accepted the path God had chosen in giving his life as a "ransom for many" (Mark 10:45, NRSV). Contrary to Jewish beliefs about the Messiah, Jesus indicated the path set forth for him involved great **suffering**, rejection by religious leaders, death, and then **resurrection** (8:31; 9:31; 10:33-34).

Jesus's sonship may also be understood as being a king in the line of David. At Jesus's baptism (1:11), a voice from heaven cited Psalm 2:7, a text associating sonship with God's chosen king. Jesus responded positively to the question of the high priest whether he was the "Messiah, the Son of the Blessed One" (Mark 14:61, NRSV). The religious leaders at the foot of the cross taunted Jesus with the words: "Let the Messiah, the King of Israel, come down from the cross now, so that we may see and **believe**" (15:32, NRSV). These words of ridicule become an explicit confession of **faith** by a Roman centurion. Upon witnessing Jesus's death, he declared, "Truly this man was God's Son!" (v. 39, NRSV).

If Isaiah 42:1 underlies Mark 1:11, Jesus's sonship may also be understood as being a faithful servant of God on whom God's Spirit had been placed: "Here is my servant, whom I uphold, my chosen, in whom my soul delights; I have put my spirit upon him" (Isa. 42:1, NRSV). In Mark 1:10, the Spirit descended like a dove on Jesus.

In the four canonical gospels, "the Son of Man" (Gk., *ho huios tou anthrōpou*) is the primary self-designation used by Jesus (Mark 2:10; Matt. 8:20; Luke 17:24; John 3:13-15). Two prominent theories involve the origin and meaning of this title. Since Jesus's primary language was Aramaic, the phrase he would have used was *bar nasha*. This phrase meant "a person," "a human being," or "son of humanity."

Another theory concerning Son of Man sayings involves Daniel 7:13-14, where the Son of Man is depicted as "coming with the clouds of heaven," presented before the "Ancient One," and given "dominion and glory and kingship that all peoples, nations, and languages should serve him" (NRSV). Scholars generally recognize that this imagery in Daniel may not relate to a messianic or divine figure, but perhaps to Israel as God's servant. Clear verbal links, however, exist between the Son of Man of Daniel and Jesus in the Markan narrative (8:38; 13:26; 14:62). Mark appears to link these two figures, as Jesus filled the figure from Daniel with new meaning.

Jesus as the Son of Man appears throughout Mark's Gospel (2:10; 8:31; 9:9; 10:33; 13:26; 14:21). As human, he followed God's path of suffering and rejection on the way to the cross (8:31; 9:12, 31; 10:33-34, 45; 14:21, 41). As divine, the Son of Man "has authority on earth to **forgive** sins" (2:10, NRSV), "is lord . . . of the sabbath" (v. 28, NRSV), will be raised from the dead (8:31; 9:31; 10:34), will come "in the glory of his Father with the holy angels" (8:38, NRSV), and will be seen sitting "at the right hand of the Power" (14:62, NRSV).

In Mark 14:61-62, Jesus appears as Christ (Messiah), Son of God (Blessed One), and Son of Man. Mark's initial declaration of Jesus as the "Christ, the Son of God" (1:1, NRSV) was affirmed in Jesus's work as Son of Man. Jesus's identity is inextricably linked with what he accomplished on the cross.

The cross was central not only for Jesus's mission but also for his followers. They also must take up their crosses (8:34). **Discipleship** involves suffering. The Twelve lacked comprehension concerning this, as well as other aspects of Jesus's teachings (4:13; 6:51-52; 8:17-18, 33).

Questions abound concerning what is deemed the "Messianic secret" in Mark, situations where Jesus commanded his identity and mighty deeds not be disclosed (1:25, 34; 7:36; 8:30). Scholars evidence no consensus for this secrecy. Whatever the precise reason, this admonition focused attention upon the nature of Jesus's messiahship and thereby upon the nature of Christian discipleship. As Christ had to suffer on his way to resurrection, so those who follow him must suffer as well.

LARRY MURPHY, PHD

GOSPEL OF MATTHEW, THEOLOGY OF

The primary subject of Matthew's Gospel is the story of **Jesus**; its primary purpose is to give instruction on **discipleship**. Accordingly, the theology of this Gospel focuses on Jesus Christ and discipleship. Under these two broader rubrics, we will discuss other significant aspects of Matthew's theology, such as **the church** (ecclesiology), **mission** (missiology and evangelization), the **kingdom of heaven/God** (eschatology), and the history of God's work of **redemption** through Israel culminating in God's activity in Jesus (salvation history).

Christology

Matthew communicates his understanding of Jesus through his composition of the Gospel, his description of Jesus's activity, and the **titles** that he and the persons presented in the narrative use for Jesus.

Matthew seems to construct his Gospel according to a three-part schema, with the major turning points at 4:17 and 16:21 (Kingsbury 1975, 1988; Bauer 1988). These verses are parallel, each beginning with the phrase "From that time Jesus began to . . ." (RSV).

In 1:1–4:16 Matthew gives the background for the story of Jesus **Messiah**, Son of God; everything recorded here precedes the beginning of Jesus's ministry in 4:17. In 4:17–16:20 Matthew sets forth the proclamation of Jesus Messiah, Son of God, to Israel; and in 16:21–28:20 he presents the passion and **resurrection** of Jesus, Messiah, Son of God. Each of these three divisions reaches a climax in the declaration that Jesus is the Son of God.

The climax of the first major division comes at 3:17 with the declaration from God that Jesus is his Son. In the temptation narrative that follows, the **devil** draws on God's declaration about Jesus and accordingly tempts Jesus in his capacity as Son of God (4:3, 6).

The climax of the second major division comes at 16:13-20 with the **confession** from Peter, arguably speaking on behalf of the circle of disciples (cf. 14:33; 16:13-16), that "You are the Christ, the Son of the living God" (16:16, RSV).

The initial climax of the third major division comes at 27:54, where the centurion and those with him declare, "Truly this was the Son of God" (RSV). The final climax to the third major division is the missionary commissioning, where Jesus himself commands his disciples to baptize "in the name of the Father and of the Son and of the Holy Spirit" (28:19, RSV). These structural considerations suggest that Matthew wished to present Jesus primarily as Son of God.

For Matthew, Jesus is Son of God as the one who has his origin in God by virtue of the virgin conception by the **Holy Spirit** (1:18-25) and thus has a unique, intimate relationship with God as Father. Indeed, only the Father knows the Son, and only the Son knows the Father and can reveal the Father (11:27). In addition, as Son, Jesus knows the Father's will and thus reveals God's will that lies behind the letter and the **law** and in this sense fulfills the law (5:17-48; 7:28-29).

But Matthew emphasizes that Jesus is God's Son as the one who perfectly obeyed the will of his Father (3:17; cf. 3:13-15). Israel, also named as God's Son (2:15), repeatedly yielded to **temptation** and fell into disobedience during forty years of wilderness wanderings (Deut. 6–8). In contrast to Israel, Jesus, God's Son, refused to yield to the devil's temptations during forty days and forty nights in the **wilderness**, remaining obedient to God's will. That Jesus was condemned to death by the high priest, scribes, and elders (the Sanhedrin) on the charge that he claimed to be the Son of God (Matt. 26:63-67) and that three times within the crucifixion scene Jesus is said to be Son of God (27:40, 43, 54) suggest that Jesus died as Son of God. The crucifixion was Jesus's last and greatest temptation; indeed, the mockeries around the cross echoed Satan's temptation of 4:1-10 (see esp. vv. 3, 6; cf. 27:40). The cross was the ultimate expression of Jesus's perfect **obedience**, an enactment of Jesus's prayer in Gethsemane, where he submitted his will totally to God (26:42).

As God's Son, Jesus shared the work of the Father. In 1:18-25 the angel of the Lord instructed Joseph to name the child "Jesus," which is the shortened form of "Joshua," meaning "Yahweh saves." Yahweh brings salvation to his people through his Son, who is "Emmanuel" or "God with us" (1:23, RSV; cf. 28:20). At the cross, Jesus died as the Son of God, overcoming the ultimate temptation to save himself by coming down from the cross. At the cross, he became the atoning **sacrifice** for **sin**, pouring out his blood for the **forgiveness** of sins (26:28) and giving "his life as a ransom" (20:28, RSV).

In Matthew's Gospel Jesus is also the "son of Abraham" (1:1-17, RSV), indicating that Jesus fulfilled God's promise that in Abraham's son (or "seed") all the nations of the earth would be blessed (Gen. 12:3; 22:18). This role relates to Matthew's concern to show that, through Jesus, God is bringing Gentiles to the worship of God and incorporating them into God's people (2:1-12; 4:12-16; 12:21; 21:43), a theme that comes to full expression in the commission to make disciples of "all nations" (28:19, RSV).

Matthew also emphasizes that Jesus is Son of David. This title appears more often in Matthew than in all the rest of the NT. Matthew links Son of David to Jesus's healing activity; repeatedly persons in need of healing cry out to Jesus as Son of David, and in that capacity Jesus heals them (9:27; 15:22; 20:30). Jesus is thus King in the line of David (1:1-17; 2:1-12), who is the agent of God's rule over God's people and ultimately over the entire earth (28:18). He expressed this rule and authority through humbly attending to the needs of the **poor** and **suffering** and through subverting typical human conceptions of power by giving his life on behalf of his people. Jesus died not only as Son of God but also as King (20:28; 27:11-14, 29, 37, 42).

As Son of David, or King in the line of David, Jesus announced, embodied, and established God's kingdom. Matthew typically speaks of the "kingdom of heaven," employing this phrase, which appears nowhere else in the NT, thirty-three times. This phrase is synonymous with "kingdom of God," which is employed four times in the Gospel. As Pennington (2009) has argued, one reason Matthew used "kingdom of heaven" was to emphasize the great transcendent difference between God's kingdom, or rule, and typical human ways of thinking about reality and power. Repeatedly throughout Matthew's Gospel the kingdom of God challenges human ways of thinking and evaluating. Moreover, the kingdom that Jesus established is both present and future. The kingdom has already come in the ministry of Jesus (e.g., 12:28), but it awaits its full appearance, which will take place only at the end with the second coming (**parousia**) of Christ (13:43; 25:34).

Finally, Matthew presents Jesus as the Messiah, or the Christ. Matthew sets forth the meaning of Jesus as Messiah already in the genealogy (1:1-17), where Matthew indicates that Jesus brings the history of God's dealings with his people Israel (salvation history) to its climax and fulfillment in the birth of Jesus, "who is called Christ" (1:16, RSV). The salvation history that precedes the Christ can be divided into three periods of fourteen generations (1:17), suggesting careful divine planning toward the fulfillment of salvation history in Jesus. The repetition of fulfillment quotations (1:22; 2:15, 17, 23; 4:14; 8:17; 12:17; 13:35; 21:4; 26:56; 27:9; cf. 5:17; 26:54) develops the notion set forth in the genealogy that Jesus brings to realization all God was doing in the preceding period; even individual events and OT passages find their fulfillment in Jesus as the Christ.

Discipleship
Closely related to the Christology of Matthew is **discipleship**, because discipleship stems from Jesus and involves a holistic commitment to Jesus's person (4:18-22; 11:28-30; 16:21) and teachings (note the role of the five great speeches, or blocks of teaching: chs. 5–7, 10, 13, 18, 24–25). Matthew indicates the importance of discipleship by presenting Jesus's first specific act of ministry as the calling of disciples (4:18-22).

In this Gospel, the appropriate response to Jesus's proclamation of the kingdom is **repentance** (4:17; cf. 3:2; 11:20). Repentance involves the reorientation of one's whole life, beginning with one's thinking, around the one ultimate reality: God is establishing the end-time rule of salvation and **judgment** in Jesus. Such repentance is not a single event in a person's life but is a constant, lifelong process. At each new point where the kingdom challenges accepted ways of thinking and behavior, persons are called upon to repent. And repentance takes concrete form in discipleship (note that the call to repentance in 4:17 is immediately followed by the calling of the first two sets of brothers to discipleship in 4:18-22).

According to Matthew, discipleship is initiated by Jesus. In 4:18-22 the two sets of brothers did not decide to become disciples and approach Jesus. On the contrary, Jesus approached them and called them. This is also the way Jesus called Matthew (9:9), the only other account in this Gospel of a person embarking upon discipleship. (In Matthew's Gospel, only the Twelve are explicitly called disciples, although the verb "make disciples" is used to describe those who will be discipled by the disciples [28:19, RSV].) This procedure does not indicate a kind of limited **election**, so that only a few pre-selected persons can become disciples, for later in the Gospel Jesus calls all persons to discipleship (11:28-30). But this initiation of discipleship by Jesus alerts us that discipleship is a matter of **grace** and **faith**, placing confidence in the Christ who calls.

Moreover, discipleship involves submission to Jesus's authority, for Jesus appeared unexpectedly on the scene, uttered the radical command to "follow" him, and the brothers responded "immediately" (4:19-20, 22, RSV). The theme of Jesus's authority is prominent throughout Matthew (e.g., 7:28-29; 9:6; 21:23-27; 28:18), and it includes both the power to act (capability) and the right to act (prerogative). It thus indicates that discipleship means fully embracing the reality that God has given to Jesus legitimate capability to effect ultimate, real change.

In addition, discipleship involves profound cost, for Simon and Andrew were required to abandon the security of vocation ("nets" [4:20, RSV]), and James and John abandoned the security of property ("boat" [v. 22, RSV]) and family ("father" [v. 22, RSV]). One can know God as Father in discipleship (5:45, 48; 6:1, 4, 6, 8-9, 14, 18, 26, 32; 7:11) only by rejecting the ultimate claims of family relationships (8:21-22; 10:37). Yet discipleship is sufficiently broad that when family responsibilities are taken up and made part of discipleship, these responsibilities are intensified (15:1-9; 19:3-8).

Furthermore, discipleship involves **mission**, for Jesus connected the call to discipleship with the promise to make these disciples fishers of people (4:19). When Jesus said that he would make them fishers of people, he suggested that he would enable disciples to perform this mission, both by instruction (10:1-42) and empowerment through his presence (28:20).

Finally, discipleship involves the creation of a **community** around Jesus, for in 4:18-22 Jesus called two sets of brothers, and throughout Matthew there is constant attention to the demands of Christian community (18:1-35) and indeed to the establishment of the church, which Jesus himself builds (16:18-19).

Resources

Bauer, David R. *The Structure of Matthew's Gospel: A Study in Literary Design.* JSNTSup 31. Sheffield, UK: Almond Press, 1988.

France, R. T. *Matthew: Evangelist and Teacher.* Grand Rapids: Zondervan, 1989.

Kingsbury, Jack Dean. *Matthew: Structure, Christology, Kingdom.* Philadelphia: Fortress Press, 1975.

———. *Matthew as Story.* 2nd ed. Philadelphia: Fortress Press, 1988.

Pennington, Jonathan. *Heaven and Earth in the Gospel of Matthew.* Grand Rapids: Baker Academic, 2009.

DAVID R. BAUER, PHD

GRACE (*ḥēn, charis*)

The abstract noun "grace" describes an intangible attitude of uncoerced generosity or activity of freely giving help to the undeserving. In Scripture, its meaning overlaps with that of "**mercy**," "**love**," "kindness," and "forgiving." These terms describe God's self-revealed character throughout the OT (Exod. 34:6-7). God's initiative, not human merit, is the one necessary and sufficient prerequisite for salvation.

The Hebrew roots *ḥnn* (gracious) and *ḥsd* (love) most often communicate the OT concept of grace. *Ḥnn* describes the **compassion**, condescension, protection, or favor shown by a superior to an inferior. The Aaronic blessing of Numbers 6:24-26 closely associates Yahweh's grace with his personal presence and gift of **peace**—total well-being.

Ḥsd emphasizes the extraordinary loyalty, favor, and loving-kindness that arise out of a **covenant** relationship. But it describes free and spontaneous acts of assistance, beyond the demands of duty, community, religion, or ethnicity (Ruth 1:8; 2:20). Because God initiated the covenant with Israel, even it is an act of grace.

Charis, in Classical Greek, described the beauty, charm, and attractiveness that prompted the favor, generosity, and assistance of another. During the later Hellenistic period, it came also to refer to the gratitude one felt toward such a benefactor. The LXX invested the term with unprecedented theological force by using it to translate the Hebrew terms *ḥēn* and sometimes *ḥesed* (more often *eleos*, "mercy").

Of the 155 appearances of *charis* in the Greek NT, nearly two-thirds (100) are in Paul's letters. He typically followed the religious usage of contemporary Greek-speaking Jews (Wis. 3:9; 4:14-15; *1 En.* 5:4-8; 99:13), who used grace to describe the present experience of end-times salvation.

Grace characterizes God's saving activity as generous, undeserved, and unexpected. The NT sometimes personifies grace, treating it as a person or power, acting independently of God (Acts 4:33; 11:23; Rom. 5:20-21; 6:1, 14; Eph. 3:8; 4:7; Titus 2:11-12). But even in such instances, grace clearly refers to God's activity of freely saving sinners and empowering them to live transformed lives "in this present age" (Titus 2:12, AT). Ultimately, the **gospel** is the proclamation of the good news of God's grace, embodied in the person of Jesus Christ (John 1:14-17; Rom. 5:21; 1 Cor. 1:4).

Grace is the undeserved gift of God expressed as "power" in two senses. It is the divine empowering of sinners to be and do what honors God. And it is the power of God that would rule in the lives of its recipients. He enables those who live under his sovereignty to obey him (Rom. 6:13-14). Sinners did not merit salvation and were unable to save themselves. Grace alone makes salvation available. But grace is a demand as well as a **gift**. Grace calls upon regenerated people to live new lives.

God's grace is demonstrated in action "in his kindness [*chrēstotēti*: "graciousness," "generosity," "goodness"] to us in Christ Jesus" (Eph. 2:7, AT). His gift of Christ—from the **incarnation** to the cross—was an act of unprecedented generosity, an embodiment of immeasurable and inexhaustible grace (2 Cor. 8:9; Eph. 1:6-7). God actively expressed his kindness because of his great love for undeserving sinners (Eph. 2:1-10).

The cross is the supreme historical demonstration of the extent to which God's **love** and grace would go to save fallen humanity (Rom. 5:1-11). If God would give his Son for us, there is nothing he would not give (Rom. 8:32; 1 Cor. 3:21-23). In Christ's death, God extends his generous offer of salvation to the unworthy.

Grace is not only God's kind decision to give us what we don't deserve but also the effective *source* of salvation. **Faith**, the necessary *means* by which grace is received (Rom. 3:22, 25-26; Gal. 2:16), is the human response. Faith gives God permission to do what he alone can. It is receptivity to grace. It is not merely a onetime act that enables us to become Christians; grace empowers us to express our gratitude in God-honoring ways in a lifetime of faithfulness, a sustained relationship with God (Rom. 5:2).

The ultimate purpose of grace is not so we can "get saved." Nor is the purpose of salvation by grace to prevent us from boasting, although it does undermine human pride. Humans can take no credit for their acceptance with God or changed lives (Rom. 4:4-5; 5:11; 1 Cor. 4:7). The *purpose* of grace is so that redeemed sinners can "do good **works**" (Eph. 2:10, AT; Rom. 2:7; 2 Cor. 9:8; 2 Thess. 2:17).

Paul's apostolic labors and the various ministries of all believers were expressions of God's grace (Rom. 1:5; Gal. 1:15; Eph. 3:2-13). Grace is the incredible privilege of working for Christ in the power of the Spirit. Christians not only are recipients of grace but also mediate grace to others (1 Cor. 12:14-31; 1 Pet. 4:10-11).

Our old lives, weaknesses, and unworthiness only highlight the incredible grace of God (Eph. 3:7-8; 1 Tim. 1:15-17). No one earns God's favor, and no one alone possesses all the gifts necessary for the proper functioning of Christ's **church**. Yet Christ gives everyone some essential grace gift (1 Cor. 12:7-26; Eph. 4:11-16).

The Greek word *charis* in the NT era was a part of the vocabulary of the **patronage system**. In this cultural context Paul's readers understood that God expected them not only to receive their divine Patron's extraordinary gifts but to use them to bring **honor** to him (2 Cor. 5:15). Since Christ graciously gave his life to save them, gratitude meant giving their lives in his service. We misunderstand grace if we take grace to mean we are free from any obligation to respond to God's outlandish gift.

The free gift of salvation was uncoerced by any human act (Rom. 11:35). But this does not free us from the obligation to reciprocate. God's freely given favor is to be met with *charis* ("gratitude," "thanks"). We can never repay God for his grace, but we demonstrate we are grateful for it by living lives of loving service, imitating the model of Christ (Eph. 4:32–5:2).

Some Reformed Protestants take issue with the necessary correlation between grace and responsibility. But it is entirely at home in the Catholic, Orthodox, and Wesleyan-holiness traditions. **Justification** must find expression in the life of **sanctification**. Saving grace can be received in vain (2 Cor. 6:1), nullified (Gal. 2:21), or forfeited (5:4). Grace is not so irresistible that our salvation is eternally secure. Grace does not give us a license to **sin** (Rom. 6:1-4, 14-15). Instead, it frees us to enjoy a new quality of life—**obedience**, the life of **holiness** (vv. 15-22).

Grace not only refers to the mercy of God that makes salvation possible (Eph. 2:8) but sometimes serves as an equivalent to **spiritual gifts** (*dōreas* [4:7] and *domata* [v. 8]; or *charismata* [Rom. 12:6; 1 Cor. 12:4-11, 31]). Grace enables believers to contribute to the upbuilding and unity of the church. It is the God-given calling and empowerment that equips both apostles and ordinary believers to minister effectively (Rom. 12:3; 1 Cor. 1:4-7; Eph. 3:2; 4:11-13).

Within the church, edifying words "give grace to those who hear" (Eph. 4:29, NRSV). Godlike mutual **forgiveness** entails extending to others the same grace we have received from God. In Ephesians 4:32, the Greek verb *charizomai* (forgive) has the same Greek root as the noun grace.

The terminology of grace is infrequent in the Gospels, but the concept is clearly present in narrative form. Throughout his ministry, Jesus reached out to sinners, the marginalized, and the unworthy with acceptance, forgiveness, and healing. For example, Matthew 4:17 clearly assumes the theological priority of grace ("the **kingdom of heaven** has come near" [AT]) to the human response ("Repent" [AT]). The paradigmatic stories of the call of the first disciples that follow in verses 18-22 illustrate the point: Jesus takes the initiative, meets disciples where they are, invites them to abandon their old lives, and urges them to become his followers. This narrative provides the setting for the **Sermon on the Mount**, which presumes a target audience of disciples (5:1-2)—people who have already responded to Jesus's call to **repentance**. It is not a prescription for how one becomes a disciple but an idealized description of the graced life of **discipleship**.

Resources

Conzelmann, Hans, and Walter Zimmerli. "χαίρω κτλ." Pages 359-415 in vol. 9 of *TDNT*.
deSilva, David A. *Transformation: The Heart of Paul's Gospel*. Snapshots. Bellingham, WA: Lexham Press, 2014.
Esser, H. H. "Grace, Spiritual Gifts." Pages 115-23 in vol. 2 of *NIDNTT*.
Green, Joel B. "Grace." Pages 534-27 in *New Dictionary of Biblical Theology*. Downers Grove, IL: InterVarsity Press, 2000.
Spicq, Ceslas. *TLNT*.
Stoebe, H. J. "חֶסֶד *ḥesed* kindness." Pages 449-64 in *TLOT*.

GEORGE LYONS, PHD

Hh

HATE (*śānē'*, *miseō*)

When the Hebrew word for "hate" (*śānē'*) appears in an emotional context, the normal meaning is that one has a settled animosity or dislike for someone or something. The Greek word for "hate" (*miseō*) also generally carries this same semantic value. However, another meaning arises out of the ANE culture. Treaties, or **covenants**, were made by sovereign kings with subordinate rulers, and occasionally between equals. Those who kept the covenants were said to **love** the king. Those who broke the covenant, or who did not have a covenant with the king, were designated as those who hated the king. Some emotional value could have been implied, but the words primarily indicated that the covenant was either kept or breached.

This usage of the Hebrew word *śānē'* is found in a number of covenantal passages. In the Ten Commandments, perhaps the best example, those who broke the commandments by making idols were said to hate God, but those who did not, "to love" (*'āhab*) God (Exod. 20:5-6; Deut. 5:9-10).

Understanding the covenantal use of the words "hate" and "love" illuminates the difficult text of Malachi 1:2-3: "I have loved Jacob, but Esau I have hated" (NIV). Jacob, or Israel, was in covenant relationship with God, but Esau, or Edom, had no such covenant. Therefore, Jacob's descendants were preserved, but Esau's were not. The two words do not have to appear together for *śānē'* to have this covenantal meaning (see Deut. 32:41; 2 Sam. 19:6; 22:41; Pss. 21:8 [9 HB]; 45:7 [8 HB]; 89:23 [24 HB]; Mic. 3:2).

In the context of marital covenants, *śānē'* can mean "to divorce" a spouse. When Samson returned to claim his wife (Judg. 15:1-2), his father-in-law refused, saying that he thought Samson hated, that is, divorced her (see Deut. 22:13, 16; 24:3; Prov. 30:23). Even God said he divorced his people (Jer. 12:8).

The term *śānē'* can also indicate preference. Jacob loved Rachel more than Leah, but when "Yahweh saw that Leah was hated [loved less], he opened her womb" (Gen. 29:30-31, AT). Obviously Jacob did not refuse Leah her sexual rights, for she bore him six sons and a daughter (vv. 32-35; 30:17-21). He also would have given her food and clothing and taken care of her as a wife. Yet his first love was always for Rachel.

There are in the NT a few texts where "hate" (*miseō*) and "love" (*agapaō*) indicate a kept or broken allegiance. Jesus stated that a person could not serve two masters, God and money, but would eventually betray one to be loyal to the other (Matt. 6:24; Luke 16:13). In John 15:18-25, *miseō* appears eight times. Certainly there are emotional overtones, but the main thrust is that no allegiance existed between Jesus and those who rejected Jesus's words. In spite of their claims, Jesus's enemies had broken their relationship with the Father and thus hated him.

Like many other words, "hate" has a variety of meanings in both Hebrew and Greek, each determined by its context. While it often is understood as an emotional term, it may also indicate actions, such as a failure to keep the covenant or to maintain loyalty to God. If a person professes to love God but fails to keep covenant or do what Jesus requires, that person actually hates God—that is, has a broken relationship with him.

See also Covenant.

Resources

Branson, Robert D. "The Polyvalent שׂנא: An Emotional, Performative, and Covenantal Term." *Biblical Research* 52 (2007): 5-15.
Moran, William L. "The Ancient Near Eastern Background of the Love of God in Deuteronomy." *CBQ* 25 (1963): 77-87.

ROBERT D. BRANSON, PHD

HEBREWS, THEOLOGY OF

Hebrews begins by identifying God as one who communicates with humanity. In OT times God spoke in a piecemeal and diverse manner; in these "last days" God's complete and final revelation is found in his Son (1:1-2, NIV).

By placing many OT citations in the mouth of God, Hebrews intimates that God speaks through the Scriptures. Moreover, the author repeatedly warns his readers to heed the speaking God; there are dire consequences for ignoring him (2:1-4; 4:2, 7; 12:25). The **word of God** is living and powerful (4:12).

God is the creator who fashioned the world by his word (11:3) through the agency of his Son (1:2). He is the source (2:10) and builder of all things (3:4). "On the seventh day [he] rested from all his works" (4:4, NIV; v. 10).

God's primary relationship is as Father to Jesus, whom he has begotten (1:5; 5:5). As Father, God appoints Jesus as high priest (5:6, 10) and "heir of all things" (1:2, NIV).

God also relates to human beings as a father who disciplines his children (12:5-10). In turn, human beings relate to God as his children and to Jesus, to whom they are entrusted, as a brother (2:11-14).

God is the judge of all people (10:30; 12:23). He was angry with the exodus generation for their disobedience and unbelief and did not allow them to enter into his rest (3:7-19).

God will inflict vengeance on anyone who rejects his Son and the salvation that he offers (10:26-30). Hebrews warns that "God is a consuming fire" (12:29, NIV). No creature can hide from God's sight; all people lay exposed and vulnerable before the all-seeing eyes of God (4:13). **Judgment** for human beings is as certain as death (9:27).

On the other hand, God is a rewarder of those who seek him (11:6), and he keeps his promises (6:12-18; 10:23). God remembers those who work and demonstrate love toward his name (6:10), and he is pleased with those who exhibit **faith** (11:5-6) and who do good and share (13:16). God is the **helper** of human beings and will never forsake them (vv. 5-6). He equips them with every good thing to do his will (v. 21) and will bring them to **glory** (2:10).

Hebrews highlights numerous attributes of God. There is no being greater than God (6:13). God's throne is symbolic of his sovereignty (4:16; 8:1; 12:2). He is a living God (3:12; 9:14; 10:31; 12:22) who is characterized by majesty (1:3), omniscience (4:13), invisibility (11:27), **grace** (2:9), **mercy** (4:16), **justice** (6:10), truth (6:18), faithfulness (10:23), **love** (12:6), **holiness** (12:10), and **peace** (13:20).

Jesus Christ is God's Son (1:2) and "firstborn" (1:6, NIV). Hebrews points to Jesus's divinity. Jesus is called God (1:8-9) and "Lord" (Gk., *kyrios*; 7:14; 13:20), a designation that is also used of God (7:21; 10:16). Jesus shares the same nature as God: he "is the radiance [or reflection] of God's glory and the exact [imprint] of [God's] being" (1:3, NIV). His nature is eternal and immutable (1:10-12; 13:8). Jesus played a role in the **creation** of the heavens and the earth (1:2, 10), and he sustains everything "by his powerful word" (1:3, NIV). He shares in God's sovereign rule (1:3; 8:1).

Jesus is superior to the angels, having inherited a greater name than them (1:4). God never identifies angels as sons (v. 5), nor are they ever invited to share God's rule (v. 13). The angels are worshipping beings, while Jesus is the object of worship (v. 6). The angels are created, mutable beings who serve others (v. 14). God's revelation spoken through Jesus is superior to the revelation spoken through angels (2:2-4).

Much of the significance of Jesus revolves around the salvation of humanity. Hebrews calls Jesus the "author" (the Gk. *archēgos* is also translated as "captain" and "pioneer") of salvation (2:10) and of faith (12:2), as well as the "perfecter of faith" (v. 2, NIV). Jesus is also the "source of eternal salvation for all who obey him" (5:9, NIV).

Jesus was temporarily "made lower than the angels" (2:9, NIV). In obedience to his Father's will, Jesus received a body prepared for him by God (10:5, 9). He was made like other human beings (2:17), sharing "flesh and blood" with them (v. 14, NIV). He was tempted in "all things" yet remained without sin (4:15, AT). Jesus experienced suffering and death (2:9-10). He learned **obedience** from his **sufferings** (5:8), and he was perfected for his role as high priest and the source of salvation (vv. 8-10).

Jesus was appointed by God as high priest according to the "order of Melchizedek" (v. 6, NIV), not as part of the Levitical priesthood (7:14). The Levitical priests had effectively tithed through Abraham to Melchizedek and were blessed by him (vv. 4-10). Melchizedek, however, being a king and a priest (v. 2) combined both roles, as Hebrews implies did Jesus (vv. 15-17). Thus in several ways Jesus's priesthood is superior to the Levitical priesthood. First, since Jesus was without sin (vv. 26-27), he was not obligated to offer sacrifices on his own behalf, as the Levitical priests, who were beset with weaknesses and sins, were (5:2-3). Second, the Levitical priesthood was based on lineage (7:13-14), but Jesus's priesthood is based on the "power of an indestructible life" (v. 16, NIV). Third, the Levitical priesthood lacked continuity since its priests were subjected to mortality (v. 23); Jesus holds his priesthood permanently (v. 24). Fourth, unlike the Levitical priesthood, Jesus's priesthood is confirmed with a divine oath (vv. 20-21). Fifth, the Levitical priests served in an earthly sanctuary (8:4-5), while Jesus ministered in a heavenly sanctuary made by God (9:24).

Jesus offered himself as the perfect sacrifice. His sacrifice was superior to animal sacrifices for a number of reasons. First, animal sacrifices could only cleanse the flesh (v. 13) and were incapable of removing sins (10:4, 11); Jesus's blood was efficacious for cleansing the **conscience** and "obtaining eternal redemption" (9:12-14, NIV). Second, Jesus offered himself willingly (10:9-10). Third, Jesus's sacrifice is a once-for-all, permanent sacrifice; it does not have to be repeated (7:27).

Jesus is also the "guarantor" (v. 22, NIV) and "mediator" of a new and better **covenant** (8:6, NIV). Under the old covenant, neither the law (7:19) nor the Levitical priesthood (v. 11) nor "gifts and sacrifices" (9:9, NIV) could perfect the believer. The new covenant is superior to the old covenant because it is based on better promises: believers receive an internalized law, knowledge of God, forgiveness of sins (8:8-12), and an "eternal inheritance" (9:15, NIV).

God raised Jesus from the dead (13:20). Jesus entered into heaven, where he conducts his ministry in the heavenly sanctuary (9:11-12). He sits at the right hand of God (1:3), where he is "crowned with glory and **honor**" (2:9, NIV) and is victorious over all his enemies (10:13).

Hebrews highlights numerous salvific benefits that Jesus accomplishes for humanity. He gives help to humanity (2:16), sympathizes with their weaknesses (4:15), aids those who are tempted (2:18), and intercedes for them (7:25). He purifies (1:3), removes (9:26), bears (v. 28), and atones for (2:17) sins and cleanses consciences (9:14). Jesus perfects (10:14), sanctifies (13:12), redeems (9:12), and saves forever (7:25). He renders ineffective the **devil**'s power over death and frees humanity from the fear of death (2:14-15). He enables human beings to approach God's throne with confidence (4:16). Hebrews anticipates the imminent return of Jesus to complete the salvation of his followers (9:28; 10:37).

Hebrews repeatedly warns the audience to avoid apostasy (2:1-3; 3:7-19; 6:4-8; 10:26-30; 12:15-17) but to be diligent and to persevere in their faith lest they forfeit their opportunity for salvation (3:6, 14; 4:11, 14; 6:1, 11-12; 10:23-25, 35-39; 12:1-3). Hebrews defines faith as the certainty of **belief** in the future, unseen reality of the spiritual world (11:1).

Hebrews uses various images to describe the future heavenly realm. First, it is the place of God's **rest**, which remains available for believers to enter (4:1-11). Second, it is a heavenly tabernacle or sanctuary, made by God (9:11-12). Believers have the **hope** of entering into this "holy place" through the "veil" because Jesus entered as a "forerunner" who inaugurated the way of entry through the sacrifice of himself (6:19-20; 10:19-20, AT). Third, it is described as a heavenly city (11:16), which is populated by an assembly of divine and heavenly beings (12:22-24).

See also Jerusalem; Resurrection; Sacrificial System; Sanctification.

BRIAN C. SMALL, PHD

HELPER (*ʿēzer*)

After placing Adam in the garden, God discerned that it was not good for him to be alone. This is a startling concession in the light of God's having proclaimed each stage of **creation** "good" (Gen. 1, NIV). Immediately God proceeded to correct this deficiency by making a "helper" (Hebr., *ʿēzer*) for Adam (2:18, NIV). This English word is problematic because for many it implies a person having a lower social standing. But that is not the case with the Hebrew term. In the OT God is often praised as the helper of the devout (e.g., Pss. 10:14; 22:19 [20 HB]; 33:20; 70:5 [6 HB]; cf. 40:13 [14 HB], 17 [18 HB]; 94:17; 146:5) and of Israel (Deut. 33:7, 29; Ps. 115:9-11). But in English "helper" is never used for a king or a president. Thus a more accurate English rendering of the Hebrew term is "companion."

Several details in the context (Gen. 2:18-25) substantiate that God's desire was to provide Adam one who was on a par with him: (1) "Alone" conveys that the man needed a companion, not a servant (v. 18, NIV). (2) Adam was unable to find a "suitable [companion]" among the animals (v. 20, NIV).

"Suitable" (Hebr., *negdô*) restricts the sense of *'ēzer* to one who is "fitting," "matching," "complementary." The *'ēzer* must have the same essence as the man's and also possess qualities and skills that complement his so that in living together they would contribute to each other's identity, well-being, and growth. (3) When God presented the *'ēzer* to Adam, he jubilantly declared, "This is now bone of my bones and flesh of my flesh" (v. 23*b*, NIV). With this exclamation, he acknowledged that the **woman** was truly a companion, one who was on a par with him. (4) His excitement indicates that he anticipated having a deep, reciprocating relationship with her that would greatly enrich their lives.

See also Creation; Fall, The; Rest.

Resources
Sarna, Nahum M. *Genesis*. JPSTC. Philadelphia: Jewish Publication Society, 1989.
Wenham, Gordon J. *Genesis 1–15*. WBC, vol. 1. Waco, TX: Word Books, 1987.

JOHN E. HARTLEY, PHD

HOLINESS (*qdš, hagios*)*

"Holy" (OT Hebr. *qdš* and NT Gk. *hagios*) and its cognates, including "holiness," occur over 850 times in Scripture, but even this vast number belies its importance. Holiness is never defined in Scripture. Rather, its essence is inferred from the story of God's interaction with Israel; displayed in the **Messiah**, who is the Holy One of God, God with us; lauded in the worship of God's people; and to be lived out in their lives. It undergirds the whole story of God and his people from creation to consummation, where the **holy** God makes all things new and lives in the midst of his holy people in the holy place.

Holiness and the Story of God

God is holy. It is the intrinsic character of God, who alone is holy in essence. All other objects, **times**, places, and beings are holy only in relationship to God. The notion evokes images of otherness, transcendence, and mystery. Cognate ideas also attach to it: purity, separateness from **sin**, life, **glory**, light, radiance, perfection, **sanctification**.

God's transcendence over the created order and hostility to all that goes against **peace** imply that God's holiness cannot tolerate impurity or sinfulness. Understood in this way, any approach to God must be with "clean hands and a pure heart" (Ps. 24:3-4, NIV). This is at the heart of the pentateuchal emphasis on purity. These purity regulations are graciously given to enable

---

*Portions of this article have been published previously as Kent Brower, "Holiness," in *Dictionary of Scripture and Ethics* (Grand Rapids: Baker Academic, a division of Baker Publishing Group, 2011), 361-64. Used by permission.

God's people to dwell in the presence of this holy, dangerous, but loving God (see Lev. 10:1-2).

Holiness requires purity, but holiness and purity are not identical. The antonym of "holy" is "profane"; the antonym of "pure" (**clean**) is "impure" (**unclean**). A profane person, object, or place could be either pure or impure (clean or unclean). Similarly, a pure (clean) person, object, or place could be holy or profane. But a person, object, or place cannot be impure and holy.

Separation from the unclean becomes a primary means of averting danger. But concentration on separation, danger, and purity can lead to legalism. It risks missing the dynamic graciousness of God's holiness. It may also lead to seeing God's holiness as austere and demanding. Holiness then becomes associated with ritual and rule keeping, reading the "**fear of the Lord**" in punitive terms.

But this is only part of the picture. Scripture read canonically points to the triune character of God. God is Being-in-Communion—the Holy Trinity—existing in the lively dynamic of unending holy **love**, so that the holiness of God is clearly manifest in this love relationship. God's love emanates from his holiness and is inseparable from it.

"Holiness" is thus a relational term centered on love. Human holiness is always derived and dependent upon being in relationship with the holy God. This reality emerges in the reading of the underlying narrative of God's purposes. It runs implicitly through Scripture but has direct expression in Leviticus 19:2 and in 1 Peter 1:14-15; 2:9-10. It starts with the canonical shape of the Pentateuch, formed as a chiasmus with the Holiness Code (Lev. 19–26) at its center. Then, in what Jonathan Sacks calls "one of the most remarkable of all religious ideals," God calls Israel to be holy because God is holy. Humans, created in God's image (Gen. 1:27), are called to act in God's ways (n.d.). The description of what that image is like comes to summary expression in the call to be holy as God is holy. The epicenter of this call is love—the love of neighbor and alien (Lev. 19:18, 34) and the love of God in the Shema (Deut. 6:4-5).

Within Scripture, God reveals himself as holy. The story of God's rescue, **redemption**, restoration, and renewal of all **creation**, including humans, is all an expression of God's holy love. Indeed, the first and, therefore, critical disclosure of God's name as Yahweh to Moses (Exod. 3:15) makes the place holy by God's very presence. "It is the very character of YHWH as holy, as compassionate, as deliverer that is in view" (Robson 2011, 133). Crucially, this revelation is within the context of the rescue of Israel; God's compassion manifests his holiness. Isaiah frequently uses the phrase "Holy One of Israel" to disclose who Yahweh is. This binding of Yahweh to Israel is also crucial. Yahweh lives in the midst of Israel, exercising **justice** and **righteousness** and expecting the same from his holy people. As God dwells in the midst of his people, his very presence is transforming them (see Isa. 57:15). They are to reflect who God is, embodying the way in which God manifests his holiness in righteousness, **compassion**, tender loving care and justice (Mic. 6:8). His holiness is also displayed in his saving activity (see Isa. 52:10). His "righteousness" (*şĕdāqâ*), "justice" (*mišpāṭ*), and "loving-kindness and tender **mercy**" (*ḥesed*) are predicated upon his identity (see Jer. 9:23-24). In a remarkable statement, God's self-revelation is a disclosure of his holiness in saving love (see Hos. 11:9) rather than **wrath** because he is the Holy One.

Israel as the Holy People of God

Right from Adam's disastrous choice to assert independence from God, God has called people to be on his rescue mission. The story begins in earnest with Abraham (Gen. 12:1-3), who was called to walk before God and be blameless (17:1-2); it continues with the deliverance of Israel from Egyptian oppression. From this downtrodden people, God created "a kingdom of priests and a holy nation" (Exod. 19:6, NIV) to model and embody God's holiness amongst the nations. Because Israel was God's own possession, it was to be holy as God is holy (Lev. 19:2) in imitation of God. The Holiness Code (chs. 19–26) gives details of how this call to holiness is "democratised" (Sacks, n.d.) in the community.

Much of this has to do with boundaries between profane and sacred, boundaries between clean and unclean, separation from idolatry, and limitations of sexual relationships. God led them and dwelt in their midst, symbolized by the pillar of cloud by day and fire by night. The people were arranged in concentric circles around the tabernacle containing the holy of holies. During the monarchy, the temple was the dwelling place of Yahweh. In turn, Israel was called to exclusive worship of God, but little attention was given to personal piety. Rather, Israel was addressed as a people living in community with communal practices of holy living summarized in the command "Love your neighbor as yourself" (Lev. 19:18, NIV).

Scripture details Israel's failing in its calling. Because God's holiness and righteousness are inextricably intertwined, his holy people were to act righteously (see Isa. 5:7, 16). But holiness became synonymous with separation as an end in itself, centered on ritual and performance. Israel began to see its election as a right based upon God's irrevocable promises to David (2 Sam. 7:14-16), while ignoring their conditionality so clearly set out in **Torah** (Deut. 28–30). So Israel did not maintain its exclusive fidelity to Yahweh; instead, it embraced idolatry. It forgot its past (6:21; 7:6-8; 10:18-19) and did not care for the alien, the **poor**, and the dispossessed. Instead, it trampled the poor in the dust and robbed widows and orphans (Amos 2:6-8; 4:1; 5:10-12, 23-24), clearly a breach of God's holiness (4:2). Prophets warned against **covenant** faithlessness, but Israel did not heed. It failed to proclaim the name of Yahweh in the nations; rather, its sins were the same as the surrounding nations (Amos 1–2), so that the curses of Deuteronomy were realized in exile (28:15-68) and the holy name of God was profaned in all the earth (Ezek. 36:20). But God rescued them from exile in a display of his holiness before the nations (v. 32). In sum, Israel began to view holiness as exclusivity and separation, rather than service; it no longer modeled God's love and justice.

The return from exile brought a renewed concern for holiness. The reforms of Nehemiah confirmed "separation" as the denotation of holiness. Boundaries between Israel and the Gentiles that were seriously eroded during the monarchical period and the exile needed to be reestablished in line with priestly ideals of the Torah. In an agenda-setting concentration on ethnicity as the defining identification of who is included in God's holy people, the returnees even divorced their foreign wives (Ezra 10). Ethnic purity as separation from surrounding nations became crucial in later self-identity through heightened attention to boundary markers.

The return from exile was not as glorious as promised. The promised circumcision of the heart (Deut. 30:6), the new covenant (Jer. 31:31-34), and the Spirit within (Ezek. 36:26-27) became foundational for restoration eschatology. With the exception of the period following the Maccabean revolt, Israel never returned to the idealized picture of David's reign. Questions about how the holy God could once again dwell among his people remained. So holiness movements arose.

The Messiah and the People of God

Jesus, John, the Pharisees, and the Qumran community shared this desire for renewal of the holy people of God. The Pharisees believed that holiness demanded separation within society and sought to maintain and extend pockets of priestly purity so that the whole people would be a kingdom of priests. The Qumran community considered the temple hopelessly corrupt and looked for a new temple. So they withdrew from society to live a life as God's righteous remnant, making atonement for the land and people (1QS 8:10). Strict obedience to the Torah as God's command had to be initiated. Nevertheless outward obedience had to be matched by inward holiness for the men of perfection (see 1QS 8:1-14).

Jesus and John before him were in this reforming tradition. But the story of the holy God's redeeming interaction with the created order came into focus through the life, death, **resurrection,** and ascension of Jesus. His story overlays the story of Israel and illuminates it as God's way of bringing blessing to all. The long-awaited day has dawned.

Jesus was recreating the holy people, centered on him, "the Holy One of God" (Mark 1:24; John 6:69, NIV). In a scene reminiscent of Exodus 24, Jesus called, named, and commissioned the apostles to be with him (Mark 3:13-19). This reshaped remnant, no longer to be defined by blood ties, was doing the will of God (vv. 31-35), pressing back to the foundations of loving God with the whole heart and the neighbor as oneself (12:28-34; Matt. 22:36-40; Luke 10:27-28). This holiness was contagious, seen most clearly in Jesus's hospitable dining with sinners, exorcisms, and healings. Boundaries were breached; people were transformed and restored to the community.

The Fourth Gospel takes this hospitality theme even further. The disciples of Jesus, then and now, are invited to share, through mutual indwelling, in the very life of the Holy Trinity (John 17:20-23; see 2 Pet. 1:4). The hospitality of God in welcoming people into this relationship is to be mirrored in their lives of hospitality in community. Followers of the Messiah were sent into the world just as Jesus had been sent (John 20:19-23).

Jesus redefined holiness as compassion, transformation, and mission, not separation. The purity that matters is the pure-in-heart, motivational center of people who are participating in the Messiah and are aligned with the will of God. The pure in heart love as God loves the world. Its primary external expression is faithful, single-minded, and wholehearted love of God and our neighbors—and the "aliens" in our midst—as we love ourselves (Lev. 19:34). It is God reflecting: faithful, generous, compassionate, welcoming, redemptive, transformative, missional, holy love.

Become Who You Are in Christ by the Spirit

Paul tied holiness intimately with participation in the death, resurrection, and mission of the Messiah, who is the embodiment of God's salvific purposes. Those who are reconciled to God in Christ are saints, a reconfiguring of the people of God around the crucified and risen Messiah. Believers are holy "in Christ" because Christ is holy. They are also called to imitate Christ.

Those who are in Christ, located in various places, are God's holy people, both personally and communally. Their status is wholly dependent upon the fact that they have been brought into a right relationship with God. They have peace with God because they have been baptized into the Messiah's death, have put to death the old way of being in Adam because they have been crucified with Christ, and have been raised to newness of life. "God's love has been poured out" in their "hearts through the **Holy Spirit**" (Rom. 5:5, NIV; see chs. 5–6). Love is the hallmark of God's holy people, simply because God is love, and those who abide in love abide in God, and God abides in them. The consequence is that as he is, so are we in this world (1 John 4:16-17).

The early followers of the Jewish Messiah, some Jews but predominately Gentiles, were no longer divided on ethnic grounds but became one new people in Christ (Eph. 2:11-22) who embodied the **call of God** to Israel. They were to be agents of God's reconciliation in the world (2 Cor. 5:18-21) as Israel was called to be, saints in both communal and personal terms, with an identity solely determined by being in Christ. The scriptural continuity of God's call of a holy people is implicit in Romans 12:1-2; 13:10; 15:15-18.

They were a "walking temple," both personally (1 Cor. 6:19) and corporately (3:16), in whom the Holy God dwelt through his Spirit, purifying "their hearts by faith" (Acts 15:8-9, NIV).

This statement of identity has attached to it the imperative of living as God's holy people. They were on the mission of the holy God by discerning the will of God through the mind of Christ, embodying and proclaiming the gospel and representing the holy God; they were imitating God in his holiness demonstrated in loving community and in righteousness, justice, and mercy in the world that God loves. As they walked according to the Spirit in the Spirit-enabled obedience of the children of God, they resisted the "works of the flesh" (Gal. 5:19, KJV), putting to death the "deeds of the body" (Rom. 8:13, KJV), those community-destroying and self-centered actions and attitudes that fail to reflect the cruciform mission of God. And in this process of being led by the Spirit and perceiving the **image of God**, believers were being transformed "from glory to glory" as they gazed upon the image of the invisible God (2 Cor. 3:18, KJV).

On this journey, failure could occur. But the gracious provision of the holy God through Christ is that God's people might be cleansed from all sin and be restored to the community of **faith** (1 John 1:5–2:2; Gal. 6:1-2; Heb. 12:12-14). The goal lies before (Phil. 3:12-14; see Heb. 13:14), when God's good purposes are finally accomplished. First John 3:2 captures this "already, but not yet" understanding of human holiness: "We are God's children now; what we will be has not yet been revealed. What we do know is this: when he is revealed, we will be like him, for we will see him as he is" (NRSV).

See also Communal Holiness; Incarnation; Progressive Revelation.

Resources

Barton, Stephen C., ed. *Holiness Past and Present*. London: T and T Clark, 2003.

Blomberg, Craig L. *Contagious Holiness: Jesus' Meals with Sinners*. Downers Grove, IL: IVP Academic, 2005.

Brower, Kent. *Holiness in the Gospels*. Kansas City: Beacon Hill Press of Kansas City, 2005.

———. *Living as God's Holy People: Holiness and Community in Paul*. Carlisle, UK: Paternoster, 2010.

Brower, Kent, and Andy Johnson, eds. *Holiness and Ecclesiology in the New Testament*. Grand Rapids: Eerdmans, 2007.

Gorman, Michael J. *Becoming the Gospel: Paul, Participation, and Mission*. Grand Rapids: Eerdmans, 2015.

Johnson, Andy. *Holiness and the Mission Dei*. Eugene, OR: Cascade Books, 2016.

Robson, James E. "Forgotten Dimensions of Holiness." *Horizons in Biblical Theology* 33, no. 2 (2011): 121-46.

Sacks, Jonathan. "Leviticus: The Democratisation of Holiness." n.d. Rabbisacks.org. Accessed December 28, 2016. http://www.rabbisacks.org/wp-content/uploads/2015/02/CCVayikraPreview.pdf.

KENT BROWER, PHD

HOLY SPIRIT

The presentation of the Holy Spirit in the OT is the foundation for the portrayal of the Spirit in the NT. The OT associates the Spirit of God with God's presence, power, and provision. The NT offers a specific fulfillment of these themes by connecting the Holy Spirit to the life, ministry, and **gospel** of Jesus Christ.

The Hebrew word *rûaḥ* can be rendered "spirit," "wind," and "breath," with context often serving as a significant factor in the translation. The *rûaḥ* of God is sometimes described as an agent of God, either natural (such as wind) or supernatural (a spirit). It is often helpful to consider ways in which both connotations fit the context.

A reference to the *rûaḥ* of God can indicate Yahweh himself (e.g., Isa. 63:10), as well as an inner part of Yahweh (see the comparison of God as "a wife forsaken and grieved in spirit" in 54:6 [NRSV]). As an inner part of God, *rûaḥ* can sometimes be translated "will" (e.g., 30:1) and "patience" (Mic. 2:7).

To describe God's *rûaḥ* as "holy" (*qādōš*) points to the divine quality of his Spirit. While the phrase "holy spirit" (*rûaḥ qādōš*) appears only three times in the OT (once in Ps. 51:11 [13 HB] and twice in Isa. 63:10-11), the theme of God's Spirit runs throughout. The construct phrases "spirit of God" (*rûaḥ 'ĕlōhîm*) and "spirit of Yahweh" (*rûaḥ yhwh*) are found in multiple passages, and many passages speak of *rûaḥ* in relation to God in various ways.

Yahweh's *rûaḥ* can indicate his presence. For example, the psalmist uses the term "your spirit" as a parallel to "your presence" in Psalm 139:7-8. Similarly, the Davidic prayer of **repentance** found in Psalm 51 requests that God not take away his presence or his "holy spirit" (*rûaḥ qādōš*) (Ps. 51:11 [13 HB]). In Haggai, Yahweh encourages the remnant of his people and their leaders that he is present, saying that his *rûaḥ* abides with them so that they should not fear (2:1-5).

God's *rûaḥ* is often connected to God's role as Creator and as Redeemer. Yahweh is described as sending forth his *rûaḥ* in his act of **creation** (Ps. 104:30). God's power over chaos is demonstrated when his *rûaḥ* hovers over the waters in Genesis 1:2, and when God sends a *rûaḥ* to quell the flood in Genesis 8:1. Yahweh uses a *rûaḥ* to bring locusts against Egypt and then to remove them (Exod. 10:13, 19). He also uses a *rûaḥ* to divide the Red (or Reed) Sea, allowing the Israelites to pass through the waters on dry ground (14:21-22). The psalmist celebrates God's powerful creative and redemptive acts, including those achieved by "the blast of the [*rûaḥ*] of your nostrils" (Ps. 18:15 [16 HB], NRSV).

Yahweh's *rûaḥ* can also serve as an agent for God. This can involve transportation (e.g., 1 Kings 18:12) or provision of food (Num. 11:31). A *rûaḥ* can be an agent of God's **judgment**, especially against kings and Yahweh's adversaries, but also against Yahweh's own people (Hos. 13:15).

Yahweh can send his *rûaḥ* to perform certain tasks, both with Israelites (Exod. 31:1-11) and non-Israelites (Num. 24:2-9). Closely connected to **wisdom** and right judgment (Gen. 41:38-39; Isa. 11:2), God's *rûaḥ* enables leaders to serve the people of God. Moses, Joshua, Othniel, Gideon, Jephthah, and Samson are each empowered by the *rûaḥ yhwh* to serve Israel. God's *rûaḥ* also empowers kings such as Saul (1 Sam. 10:6; 11:6) and David (1 Sam. 16:13-14). The *rûaḥ* of God can also come upon people (Num. 11:16-17) to lead (serve) and his "chosen" servant to "bring forth **justice** to the nations" (Isa. 42:1, NRSV).

Many passages associate the *rûaḥ* of God with prophecy. When Yahweh takes some of the *rûaḥ* from Moses and places it upon the seventy elders of Israel, they prophesy (Num. 11:24-25). The *rûaḥ* of Yahweh sends Saul into a "prophetic frenzy" along with the **prophets** (1 Sam. 10:6, NRSV). The *rûaḥ* of God speaks through King David (2 Sam. 23:2) and gives prophets messages to kings and to the people (e.g., Ezek. 11:5-12).

After God's people go into exile, Yahweh tells them that he will give them a new heart and a new *rûaḥ* that will enable them to follow his statutes and ordinances (cf. Ezek. 36:22-32; 37:11-14). Yahweh says that he will pour out his *rûaḥ* on the descendants of his servant Israel (Isa. 44:1-3) and speaks of his *rûaḥ* being upon them as his **covenant** with them (59:21). Yahweh says that he will pour out his Spirit on all people, regardless of gender, age, or economic position (Joel 2:28-29). According to Yahweh, it is "not by might, nor by power, but by my [*rûaḥ*]" (Zech. 4:6, NRSV).

The NT refers frequently to the Holy Spirit, sometimes with *pneuma* (Gk., "spirit") along with *hagios* (Gk., "holy"), but often simply with *pneuma*. As in the case of *rûaḥ*, *pneuma* can also refer to wind, although this usage of *pneuma* is rare. As in the OT, the NT can speak of the Holy Spirit as a part of God and as an agent of God. Other references emphasize the divine connection of the Spirit, such as "Spirit of God" (Matt. 12:28, NRSV), "Spirit of the Lord" (Acts 8:39, NRSV), "Spirit of Jesus" (16:7, NRSV), "Spirit of Christ" (1 Pet. 1:11, NRSV), "the Spirit of the living God" (2 Cor. 3:3, NRSV), "the spirit of **glory**" (1 Pet. 4:14, NRSV), and "the Spirit of truth" (John 14:17, NRSV). Frequently described as a gift from God to his people, the Holy Spirit is irrevocably tied to the proclamation of the gospel of Jesus Christ and works to empower God's people to live for him as they testify about Jesus to the world.

The Holy Spirit plays an integral role in Jesus's life and ministry, starting with his conception (Matt. 1:18-20; Luke 1:35). The Spirit also fills John, who later will testify about Jesus, while John is in the womb (Luke 1:15). The Holy Spirit testifies to the significance of Jesus before his birth (vv. 39-

45) and shortly after his birth (2:25-26). After Jesus is baptized, the Spirit descends upon him like a dove, and a voice from heaven reveals his identity as the Son of God (Mark 1:10-11). The Spirit leads and empowers Jesus throughout his ministry (Matt. 12:17-18; Acts 10:38).

Jesus also teaches his disciples about the Holy Spirit, whom he describes as a **helper** and teacher. According to Jesus, the Holy Spirit will remind them of what he has said and guide them in all truth (John 14:25-27). The Spirit will also work in the world (16:8) and will give believers words to speak to the authorities (Mark 13:9-11). When the Pharisees attribute Jesus's power to Satan, Jesus attributes his actions to the Spirit of God and tells them that there is no **forgiveness** for those who speak against the Holy Spirit (3:22-30). The offering made by Jesus on the cross is accomplished through the Holy Spirit (Heb. 9:13-14).

After the death and **resurrection** of Jesus, the Holy Spirit empowers believers to testify about Jesus to the world. On the day of Pentecost, the Holy Spirit "filled" believers, enabling them to testify about Jesus in other languages (Acts 2). This event is described as a fulfillment of Joel 2:28-29, and it also fulfilled words spoken by John (Mark 1:8) and by Jesus (Acts 1:8). Individuals and groups are said to be "filled" by the Holy Spirit, including Peter, Stephen, Barnabas, Paul, and the disciples (13:52). The Spirit enables people to speak boldly and with power (4:31; 13:8-12). The Spirit leads believers where to go (8:29; 13:4; 16:6-8) and can provide supernatural transportation (8:39-40). The proclamation of the crucifixion of Jesus is not a matter of human words or wisdom, but a "demonstration of the Spirit" and God's power (1 Cor. 2:1-5, NRSV; 1 Thess. 1:5).

While the mission of the Holy Spirit is consistent throughout the NT, God is described as giving the Spirit in a variety of ways. For example, the Holy Spirit comes on the disciples when Jesus breathes on them (John 20:21-23). At Pentecost, the coming of the Spirit is accompanied by a sound like the rush of wind and by what appear to be tongues of fire (Acts 2:2-4). The giving of the Spirit is frequently connected with baptism and with the laying on of hands, but without a uniform method or sequence. The Spirit is not limited by these means and can simply fall upon hearers of the **word of God** (10:44-48). As a gift freely given by God (Luke 11:9-13), the Holy Spirit cannot be obtained by money (Acts 8:18-20) or by works (Gal. 3:2). The Spirit is a gift for Gentiles as well as Jews (Acts 15:8-9).

The Holy Spirit not only equips believers to give their testimony about God but also enables them to live out their relationship with God. The Spirit lives inside believers (2 Tim. 1:14; 1 Cor. 6:19-20) as a sign of their adoption as God's children and a guarantee of the life to come (Gal. 4:1-7; 2 Cor. 5:4-5). God's Spirit also facilitates communication with God. Believers are to "pray in the Spirit at all times" and in all situations (Eph. 6:18, NRSV), with the Spirit serving as an intercessor (Rom. 8:26-27). Churches are to live by the Spirit instead of for the flesh (Gal. 5:16-21; Rom. 8:5-8) and to yield the fruit of the Spirit: "love, joy, peace, patience, kindness, generosity, faithfulness, gentleness, and self-control" (Gal. 5:22-23, NRSV). Believers abide in God, and God abides in them by the Spirit, and this leads to a life of love (1 John 4:7-16).

The Spirit also works to strengthen believers' relationships with each other in unity (Eph. 4:1-6). The Spirit calls some to be leaders (Acts 13:1-4; 20:28) and gives all believers a variety of gifts for the benefit of all and to build up the church (1 Cor. 12:7; 14:1-5). Such gifts include wisdom, knowledge, faith, healing, working of miracles, prophecy, discernment, tongues, and the interpretation of tongues (12:8-11). While there are different gifts, the members of the body of Christ all share the same Spirit (vv. 12-13). The test for whether someone is speaking in accordance with the Holy Spirit involves what they say about Jesus (vv. 1-3; 1 John 4:1-6), and those who are devoid of the Spirit cause division (Jude v. 19). Living in ways that do not build up the church grieves the Holy Spirit (Eph. 4:25-32) and can even enrage the "Spirit of grace" (Heb. 10:29, NRSV). Believers can also "rekindle" the gift of God's Spirit (2 Tim. 1:6-7, NRSV).

The NT affirms the work of the Holy Spirit in connection with the proclamation of Jesus Christ in the past (Mark 12:35-36; 1 Pet. 1:10-12) and the present (Heb. 10:15-18; Rev. 3:6). The Holy Spirit reveals the mysteries of God (1 Cor. 2:6-16) and brings freedom (2 Cor. 3:17), sanctification (2 Thess. 2:13; 1 Pet. 1:1-2), comfort (Acts 9:31), joy during suffering (1 Pet. 4:13-14; 1 Thess. 1:6-7), and eternal life (Gal. 6:7-8).

See also Communal Holiness; Holiness.

STEVEN T. MANN, PHD

HOLY WARFARE

"Holy warfare" refers to warfare either initiated by God or supported by God for his covenantal people.

The first examples can be found in the books of Exodus and Joshua. In Exodus 14, God fought for his covenantal people Israel, destroying the army of Pharaoh. In Exodus 17:8-15, when Amalek attacked Israel, Israel had to mount a defensive holy war. The conquest of the promised land, under the leadership of Joshua, was accomplished by holy warfare (Josh. 5–12).

A key feature of holy warfare was obedience to God—listening to God and doing what he said. Sometimes God spoke directly to the military leader (Exod. 14; 1 Sam. 23:2); other times, through intermediaries such as prophets or priests (2 Kings 19:5-7).

Ultimately, it was God who gave the victory, such as the destruction of Pharaoh's army, the guidance given for the attack of Jericho (Josh. 6), Gideon's victory with only three hundred warriors (Judg. 7–8), and the failure of Sennacherib's army before Jerusalem (2 Kings 18–19).

When the covenantal people of Israel were unfaithful, even if it was a single person like Achan (Josh. 7), the Lord might refuse to guide Israel to victory; the warfare was no more holy. When the people of Israel refused to obey God's commands, yet tried to force him to fight for them by bringing the ark of the **covenant** into battle (1 Sam. 4:1-11), it did not lead to victory but to defeat and shame.

The description of holy warfare found in Deuteronomy 20 highlights the importance of faithfulness and **obedience** to God.

The divine command "to devote for destruction" (Hebr., *hāram*) whole cities or peoples (e.g., Deut. 20:16-18) is difficult for modern readers to accept. Gerhard von Rad argues rather unconvincingly for a defensive action (1991, 65). Heiser offers an interesting approach (2015, 202-5). He argues that the descendants of the rebellious sons of God (Gen. 6:1-4), the Nephilim, also linked to the Anakim and Rephaim, were part of the people whom God commanded Israel to destroy. Ultimately, if we believe that God gives life, this implies that he also has the right to take life. He is the final judge, not us, whether we understand his actions or not.

In the Bible, holy warfare's impact on persons was the consequence of their attitude toward God. If the person or people were faithful to God, they would be delivered from enemies. If they were unfaithful, they would be defeated by enemies—even by unholy enemies. This is what happened in 2 Kings 25:1-21, when the remnant of Judah was defeated by Nebuchadnezzar, which was the fulfillment of the prophecies of Jeremiah.

While the theme of holy warfare was used for the conquest of the promised land, it is much less visible after the exile of 586 BC. It reappears indirectly in the theme of the Day of the Lord, when God will vindicate the faithful and destroy the unrighteous (Joel 2:1-11). Yet in the context of the Day of the Lord, humans seem to have no part in this holy warfare. It will be an act of God and his angels.

In the NT the theme of holy warfare is refocused toward a holy spiritual warfare. Many Jews expected the coming **Messiah** to lead Israel to a holy war against the colonial power of Rome. Yet Jesus emphasized carrying the cross, the absolute opposite of physical warfare. In Jesus's teaching, we do find the key element of holy warfare—obedience to God. However, no longer does the context of warfare of nation against nation exist. The fight concerns our obedience to God and the rejection of the devil's temptations, as exemplified in Jesus's forty days in the desert (Matt. 4:1-11). Thus a reorientation of the concept of holy warfare becomes established with the proclamation of the gospel to all nations.

Paul provided for us a description of spiritual warfare. Our armor is spiritual, and our fighting is against evil spirits, not against flesh and blood (Eph. 6:10-19). This evolution of holy warfare finds its climax in the final cosmic battle. The forces of **evil**, led by the **devil**, will be defeated by the Lamb of God, who is accompanied by his people who have been faithful to the end. The faithful will not be those who have slain others, but they who have been faithful to God, even to martyrdom (Rev. 7:13-17).

The book of Revelation portrays the final victory of God and his covenantal people against evil, of **holiness** against idolatry and impurity, of love against hatred and destruction (16–21).

Resources

Heiser, Michael S. *The Unseen Realm: Recovering the Supernatural Worldview of the Bible.* Bellingham, WA: Lexham Press, 2015.

Rad, Gerhard von. *Holy War in Ancient Israel.* Göttingen, DE: Vandenhoeck, 1991.

STÉPHANE TIBI, MDIV

HONOR-SHAME CULTURE

What modern biblical scholarship has conveniently labeled "honor-shame" refers to an ANE and Mediterranean societal dynamic that was an important part of the cultural background of the biblical texts. In the cultures of the OT and NT worlds, the social status a person possessed in the eyes of people whose opinions were considered important, and how that status could increase and decrease, was of major significance. The potential for increased or decreased honor and shame in the view of other people often regulated how people communicated with and acted toward those of inferior, equal, and superior social position. An awareness of this fundamental cultural dynamic will aid the biblical interpreter in a clearer understanding of how OT and NT texts were received in their earliest settings.

The Hebrew word *kābēd* in the OT and the Greek verb *timaō* in the NT are the terms most often translated "honor" in English Bibles. The Hebrew consonant root *kbd* appears about 200 times in the OT and can carry a literal, nontheological meaning of "weight," "impressiveness," "magnificence," or "respect" (Holladay 1988, 151). To honor another was to act toward that one in keeping with his or her social "weight" by respecting and esteeming him or her. In the NT the Greek verb *timaō* occurs 21 times and, depending on the context, can be translated "set a price on," "honor," or "revere" (Trenchard 1998, 110). *Kābēd* and *timaō* are employed throughout both Testaments to refer to honor given either to God or to another human being.

The terms in the original biblical languages typically standing behind the word "shame" are the Hebrew verb *bôš* and the Greek verbs *epaischynomai* and *kataischynō*. Throughout the OT the Hebrew verb *bôš* is used 105 times, most often in the **Wisdom** literature and the Major **Prophets**, carrying meanings such as "be ashamed of," "behave shamefully," "stand ashamed," or "come to ruin" (Holladay 1988, 36). In the NT, the verb *epaischynomai* occurs 11 times and the verb *kataischynō* 13 times. These words carry the meanings of "to be ashamed," "to dishonor," or "to be disappointed" (Trenchard 1998, 9).

Although lexicology is important, the background dynamic of "honor" and "shame" in biblical texts is by no means limited to the appearance of these terms. The honor-shame dynamic looms large in the background of biblical accounts even when these words are not present. More important than terminology is an understanding of how both honor and shame could be gained and lost.

Biblical scholars who have devoted significant attention to the honor-shame dynamic have generally agreed that in biblical cultures honor could be possessed or attained in two basic ways.

On the one hand, *ascribed* honor related directly to such things as a person's birth into a prominent family, socioeconomic status, gender, ethnicity, age, and physical appearance (i.e., height, grooming, etc.). To some extent the expectation of how much honor a person could hope to accumulate in a lifetime was dictated by these factors, most of which were completely beyond that person's control.

On the other hand, *acquired* honor related to social dynamics that a person could become skilled in no matter what level of ascribed honor he or she possessed. This second type of honor has to do with such things as a person's social **grace**, pleasant or endearing disposition, virtuous character, religious devotion, and/or courage in the face of a challenge.

In short, "One's basic honor level, usually termed *ascribed* honor, is inherited from the family at birth. . . . By contrast, honor conferred on the basis of virtuous deeds is called *acquired* honor" (Moxnes 1996, 20).

The concept of shame in biblical cultures was understood both negatively and positively. The public loss of either ascribed or acquired honor resulted in negative shame.

However, shame, in a sense, was a positive attribute because it had to do with a socially acceptable and expected measure of sensitivity essential to the honor of the individual or that person's social relationships. A person who lacked this positive, socially expected type of shame was considered to be "shameless" or to "have no shame." Biblical examples of this type of "shameless" person include "the unrighteous" who "know no shame" (Zeph. 3:5, NIV) and those who "live as enemies of the cross of Christ" whose "glory is in their shame" (Phil. 3:18-19, NIV).

General examples of social realms in which the honor-shame dynamic was especially significant in biblical culture include the parent-child relationship, the slave-master relationship, **poverty**, and sexuality.

Both the OT and the NT affirm that children are to give honor to both their father and their mother (e.g., Exod. 20:12; Matt. 15:4).

Though **slavery** in the ancient world was not always a dishonorable state for the slave, it often was the undesirable fate forced upon those captured in war or economically crippled by insurmountable financial debt. For those suffering such misfortunes, entering into the realm of slavery—while perhaps saving them economically or even physically—resulted in a loss of honor and an increase in shame.

While a life of poverty could be entered into intentionally as a path to everlasting well-being (this seems to be the view of Jesus in Luke 12:33-34), it was generally viewed unfavorably as a dishonorable estate. Decreased economic status resulted in decreased honor and increased shame.

Economic honor was important, but sexual honor was even more important, especially for women. The sexual honor of males was somewhat flexible, but the sexual honor of females was fixed. If sexual dishonor came to a woman, not only could she not reacquire her lost honor but she also brought shame and disgrace on her and her family.

An awareness of the cultural dynamic of honor and shame may illuminate a number of biblical texts for the interpreter.

In the OT, for example, King Saul expressed a lingering concern for honor when he pleaded with Samuel to honor him before the elders of Israel after his defeat of the Amalekites—even after Samuel made it clear that the Lord had rejected Saul as king (1 Sam. 15:30).

Another OT example occurs in Ps. 31:17 [18 HB], where David's prayer—that the Lord allow the wicked but not allow him to be put to shame—may be taken as representative of the basic OT perspective on shame, as altogether undesirable for the godly and altogether deserving for the ungodly.

Additional OT texts indicate that shame could come on those who refuse to trust in God and walk in **obedience** (Ezek. 7:18), disregard discipline and correction (Prov. 13:18; 29:15; see NKJV), answer before listening (18:13), have children who mistreat them (19:26), and hastily bring their neighbor to court (25:8).

Honor-and-shame language abounds throughout the NT as well.

Breaking with conventional wisdom, Jesus instructed his disciples to take the lowest seats at a wedding feast rather than the places of honor. Such action would spare disciples the humiliation of having to move from high places to low places and would put them in positions to be honored in the presence of all the other guests (Luke 14:10-11).

In Romans, Paul insisted that believers are to honor one another above themselves and to give everyone what they owe them, including honor (12:10; 13:7). In the Pastoral Epistles, widows in need were to be given honor, and slaves were to consider their masters worthy of all honor (1 Tim. 5:3; 6:1).

Peter indicated that trials have come to some believers so that the proven genuineness of their **faith** may result in honor when Christ is revealed (1 Pet. 1:7).

According to Jesus, his heavenly Father "has entrusted all **judgment** to the Son, that all may honor the Son just as they honor the Father" (John 5:22-23, NIV), but when the Son of Man "comes in his Father's **glory** and with the holy angels," he will be ashamed of anyone who is ashamed of Jesus (Mark 8:38, NIV; Luke 9:26). "Jesus is not ashamed to call [those who are made **holy**] brothers and sisters" (Heb. 2:11, NIV).

Paul was not ashamed of the **gospel** (Rom. 1:16), and he recognized that God gave wicked humanity over to shameful lusts, evidenced by how "men committed shameful acts with other men, and received in themselves the due penalty for their error" (v. 27, NIV). While in chains and awaiting a final outcome, Paul hoped and expected that he would not be ashamed in any way but would have "sufficient courage" (Phil. 1:20, NIV). Three times the NT writers note that the one who trusts in the Lord "will never be put to shame" (Rom. 9:33; 10:11; 1 Pet. 2:6, NIV).

In some NT texts it is clear that the potential for loss of honor and increased shame is to serve as an impetus toward **godliness**. Paul's Corinthian correspondence is especially filled with urgings to avoid shame for the Corinthians' own benefit, for Paul's benefit, and for the benefit of the gospel. Paul represented "shame" as part of his reason for confronting the Corinthians about taking lawsuits among believers before public courts (1 Cor. 6:5) and later implored them, "Come back to your senses as you ought, and stop sinning; for there are some who are ignorant of God—I say this to your shame" (15:34, NIV). Paul and his gospel coworkers "have renounced secret and shameful ways" (2 Cor. 4:2, NIV), and with respect to the collection for the Lord's people, Paul warned them not to be found unprepared so that he would not "be ashamed of having been so confident" in them (9:4, NIV).

In 2 Thessalonians Paul instructed his audience not to associate with anyone who refused to obey the instructions given in the Epistle in order that that person might feel ashamed (3:14). He exhorted Titus to show **integrity**, seriousness, and "soundness of speech that cannot be condemned, so that those who oppose you may be ashamed" (Titus 2:8, NIV). So also Peter instructed his audience to always be prepared to give an answer for the **hope** that they had but to do this "with gentleness and respect . . . so that those who speak maliciously against your good behavior in Christ may be ashamed of their slander" (1 Pet. 3:15-16, NIV).

Perhaps the most remarkable observation about the honor-and-shame dynamic in the NT is that in some places what is socially expected appears to have been turned on its head. With reference to the message of the cross, the preaching of Christ crucified, and the lack of influence and nobility of the Corinthians when God called them, Paul wrote that "God chose the foolish things of the world to shame the wise; God chose the weak things of the world to shame the strong" (1 Cor. 1:27, NIV). Timothy was admonished to "not be ashamed of the testimony about [the] Lord" or of Paul as a prisoner, but to join Paul "in **suffering** for the gospel" (2 Tim. 1:8, NIV). Paul's suffering was "no cause for shame," because of Paul's knowledge and eschatological conviction about Christ (v. 12, NIV). Most remarkable of all, according to the author of Hebrews, Jesus "for the joy set before him . . . endured the cross, scorning its shame" (12:2, NIV).

See also Eschatology; Women in the Old Testament; Women's Roles in the Church.

Resources

Holladay, William L., ed. *A Concise Hebrew and Aramaic Lexicon of the Old Testament.* Grand Rapids: Eerdmans, 1988.

Moxnes, Halvor. "Honor and Shame." Pages 19-40 in *The Social Sciences and New Testament Interpretation.* Edited by Richard L. Rohrbaugh. Grand Rapids: Baker Academic, 1996.

Trenchard, Warren C. *Complete Vocabulary Guide to the Greek New Testament.* Rev. ed. Grand Rapids: Zondervan, 1998.

RYAN K. GIFFIN, MATS

HOPE (*elpis*)

"Hope" is a hugely significant word in Wesleyan theology. Albert Outler made the oft-quoted statement about Wesley's "optimism of **grace** rather than of nature" (1985, 500). This hope or optimism is not based on what human beings can achieve but on God's promises throughout the Old and New Testaments, on the death and resurrection of Jesus Christ, and on the reality of the continued work of the **Holy Spirit** in the lives of believers. So how did this concept of Wesleyan hope develop and what is its biblical basis?

There are at least twelve different words in the Hebrew Bible that are translated "hope" in different contexts. Hope as the expectation of or the waiting for something good is a strong theme in these key words. This certainly makes sense when we think of the expectations of the Israelite people for the fulfillment of God's promises and the arrival of the **Messiah**. One word in this group (*miqweh*) also has the meaning of "a gathering of waters" (pool or fountain) or "a congregation," which colors the meaning with the hope that comes within and for the community. Israel's hope was not individualistic, but for the whole community. Rabbinic Judaism later (in the sixth century CE) also affirmed the Judaic communal nature of hope, which depends on the relationship of God's people to God and their keeping of the **covenant**.

Among the Hebrew words translated into English as "hope," another theme is that of trust and confidence. This indicates that hope is not just a communal wish for things to be better in the future but a trust that God will do what God has promised. To have confidence in someone indicates a history of relationship that has been consistent and predictable. This is the kind of relationship the Jewish people had with their God and the kind of relationship that continues on into the first-century Christian understanding of God.

The last theme emerging from the Hebrew words for "hope" is not as easy to describe; this kind of hope is not passive but requires work, even pain and grief, and sometimes the exploring of a relationship. This makes sense in the context of the covenant that the Jewish people had with their God. In accord with God's consistency, there were consequences that resulted in pain and grief when God's people did not fulfill the requirements of the covenant. But this consistency was also the source of the hope that God would do what God had promised.

As we move into the NT, we find that Greek has only the verb and noun for "hope" (*elpizō* or *elpis*), and they encompasses all of the themes we found in the Hebrew. While "hope" is an important word in the Christian Scriptures, it was not so for the ancient Greeks and Romans. For Plato, human beings determined what they hoped for. Hope was based on what humans could do for themselves. Sophocles thought hope was really just for someone in a difficult situation, and he or she could be easily deceived by hope. Stoicism, the philosophy of the common people in the first century CE, had no interest in hope, since Stoics dealt with life by resorting to fatalism—that is, "What will be will be." The only thing one could do was control one's attitude about life. (For a more in-depth discussion on the Greco-Roman view of hope, see Bultmann and Rengstorf.) This background on the Greco-Roman view of hope broadens our understanding of what Paul says in 1 Thessalonians 4:13. Paul was not referring just to the hope of **resurrection** but to the difference between living life as a Stoic pagan and living life as a hope-filled Christian.

Significantly, the **Gospels** do not record Jesus using the word "hope" in his teaching. Some suggest that Jesus did not want to confuse his hearers with hope for the future, because he was the promised Messiah, the one for whom the Jews had hoped, waited, and worked. This implies that when we are with Christ, there will be no need of hope. That is why Paul says, "And now these three remain: faith, hope and love. But the greatest of these is love" (1 Cor. 13:13, NIV). **Faith** and hope are necessary only here on earth. **Love** is forever.

But the idea of Christian hope is often found in Paul's letters, which were written after Jesus's ascension. Paul refers to Jesus as "our hope" in 1 Timothy 1:1 (NIV) and implies this at least six more times in his writings. We also find Scripture verses in 1 John 3:2-3 and Hebrews 6:11 reminding us that Jesus is our hope. In the Pauline and General Letters, we find hope referred to at least sixty-seven times, indicating that for the fledgling Christian **church**, hope was the fertile ground on which God's **kingdom** would increase here on earth.

See also Grace; Mercy.
Resources
Bultmann, Rudolf, and Karl Heinrich Rengstorf. "ἐλπίς, ἐλπίζω." Pages 517-33 in vol. 2 of *TDNT*.
Outler, Albert C., ed. *Sermons II*. Vol. 2 of *The Bicentennial Edition of the Works of John Wesley*. Nashville: Abingdon Press, 1985.

C. JEANNE ORJALA SERRÃO, PHD

HOUSEHOLD CODES

The phrase "household codes" is derived from the German *Haustafeln* (tables of household rules), a technical term derived from Luther's commentaries on Ephesians and Colossians to designate the duties of various members within the household. Household codes were used widely in the moral instructions of ancient times to convey the proper or ideal management of an individual's relationships at home or in society. Such codes can be found in Greek ethics, philosophical traditions, Hellenistic Judaism, and early Christian writings. Most scholars agree that the discussion of household codes can be traced back to Aristotle in the fourth century BC. Aristotle (*Pol.* I.1253b, 1-14) described three social-relationship pairs—master-slave, husband-wife, father-children—in which one group in each pair is naturally subordinate to the other. The Aristotelian social structure of these three pairs was assimilated into other ancient moral writings, including those of Hellenistic Judaism. Direct literary dependence of the Christian adaptation of the *Haustafeln* cannot be traced to Hellenistic Judaism, but it is most likely that these Jews brought many of these ideas and materials with them when they became Christians.

The earliest Christian household codes are found in Ephesians 5:21–6:9, Colossians 3:18–4:1, and 1 Peter 2:13–3:7. Some scholars include 1 Timothy 3:2-12; 5:1–6:2; Titus 2:1-10; and 3:1-2 among the household codes, but they fit more appropriately into a "congregational code" (Ger., *Gemeindetafeln*), which outlines the behaviors and responsibilities of groups within the **church**. First Peter includes a household code (2:13–3:7) and a congregational code (5:1-5) in two separate places, indicating that these codes should probably be treated separately. The three social pairs of master-slave, husband-wife, and father-children appear in the ethical instructions of Ephesians and Colossians. First Peter deals with the pair husband-wife and discusses the role of slaves but omits any reference to masters or father-children.

History

Significantly, the household codes appear only in the later (so-called deuteropauline) writings and not in the earlier writings of Paul. Most scholars consider the household codes to be a corrective to the early church's eschatological enthusiasm, which viewed the present structures of this world to be "passing away" (1 Cor. 7:31, NIV). Paul's declaration in Galatians

3:28—"There is neither Jew nor Greek, neither slave nor free, nor is there male and female, for you are all one in Christ Jesus" (NIV)—represented a significant challenge to the social conventions of the first century. Egalitarian perspectives toward **women** and slaves proliferated within the fertile "freedom in Christ" ideology of the young movement (5:1; 1 Cor. 12:13), creating friction and social unrest.

The household codes provided Christians a new social code for continued life within a society that was increasingly suspicious and antagonistic toward them. The household codes represented an accommodation of the new spiritual reality of the Christian to the social realities of the prevailing culture. This accommodation, however, did not simply conform to and promote the existing hierarchy of men and masters over women and slaves, even though the codes have often been interpreted in this way. Rather, the codes criticized and corrected the prevailing culture, even as they provided instructions for Christians to assimilate and function within the often unfair hierarchy of the times.

Theological Implications

Most scholars assume the Colossian code is the earliest, but the Petrine code could be just as early and does not display any literary dependence upon the Colossian code. The Colossian code is strikingly similar to those of Jewish and Stoic sources, but it Christianizes the code by repeatedly relating it in some way to the rule of the Lord (Col. 3:18, 20, 22-24; 4:1). The Ephesian code, which is dependent upon Colossians, and the Petrine code provide a deeper Christological foundation in their instructions. First Peter exhorts slaves to follow the example of Christ in their endurance of unjust **suffering** (2:21). Ephesians expands the code in Colossians by providing an explicitly Christian motivation, especially visible in the parallel between the relationships of husband-wife and Christ-church (Eph. 5:22-33).

The household codes have often been criticized for their perceived subjection of women and promotion of **slavery**. Moreover, the instructions to women and slaves are significantly longer than the corresponding instructions to men and masters. This is undoubtedly due to the greater number of women and slaves in the earliest churches.

The codes are instructions for believers within a particular cultural situation (patriarchal hierarchy) in the first century. They do not claim to be timeless rules for every **time** and place. Moreover, even as they call Christians to live within the framework of existing social orders, the Christian codes possess a critical assessment of the prevailing hierarchy. For instance, they call believers to live in mutuality, not merely hierarchy (Eph. 5:21). They reject the social tradition that a wife must fear her husband and worship only his gods. Instead, 1 Peter exhorts wives to maintain their Christian **faith** and not be intimidated by their husbands (3:1-6). Indeed, husbands are instructed that their prayers will be hindered if they are inconsiderate and disrespectful toward their wives (v. 7), and husbands are called to love and give themselves for their wives as Christ loved and gave himself for the church (Eph. 5:25-33). Whereas Aristotle argued that tyranny is the basis of a proper relationship between slave and master, the Christian codes promote justice, calling masters to treat slaves with "justice and fairness" (Col. 4:1, NASB) and reminding slaves that God judges all justly (1 Pet. 2:19-20). Finally, the motivation for Christians to submit to the prevailing hierarchy is for the sake of the mission of the church. Through believers' submissive and exemplary lives, others may be won over to the faith (v. 12; 3:1, 15-16).

See also Matriarchs; Women in the Old Testament; Women's Roles in the Church.

Resources

Balch, David L. *Let Wives Be Submissive: The Domestic Code in 1 Peter.* SBLMS 26. Chico, CA: Scholars Press, 1981.

Boring, M. Eugene. "Christian Existence and Conduct in the Given Structures of Society." Pages 102-28 in *1 Peter.* ANTC. Nashville: Abingdon Press, 1999.

Bruce, F. F. *The Epistles to the Colossians, to Philemon, and to the Ephesians.* NICNT. Grand Rapids: Eerdmans, 1984.

Powers, Daniel G. *1 and 2 Peter / Jude.* NBBC. Kansas City: Beacon Hill Press of Kansas City, 2010.

DANIEL G. POWERS, PHD

HUMILITY

Humility is a selfless attitude and behavior. It originates with a profound sense of creaturely dependence upon God. It reveals itself positively in multiple but closely related expressions, such as repentance and penitence for sins, obedience to God and service in his name, deference to others, a gentle nonvindictive demeanor, the practice of love and mercy, and a dedication to social justice. Expressed negatively, humility is the absence of pride and arrogance, denial of self-interest, indifference to fame, rejection of despotism, and the refusal of both hereditary distinctions and social rankings based on race, class, and gender.

In the Hebrew of the OT, the most common verbal indications of humility are *kāna'* and *šāpēl*, but only in their volitional-reflexive sense (to humble oneself). These and other verbs with a semantically similar range also have an impositional-causative sense (to humiliate). There is also a punitive-retributional sense (to humiliate). This is when God acts in response to arrogant oppressors to "bring them low" (Isa. 2:11, AT).

The most common Hebrew substantive indications of humility are *'ānî* and *'ānāw* but only in their subjective case (the humble). In the objective case, the terms take on more nuanced meanings depending on their situations, such as "the afflicted," "the oppressed," "the lowly," "the meek," and "the humiliated." In these objective cases, the referents become more of a social category than a religious type.

In the Greek of the NT, the volitional-reflexive sense of the verb *tapeinoō* is dominant: "Whoever humbles himself shall be exalted" (Matt. 23:12, NASB). In this same sense, Jesus "humbled himself, and became obedient unto death" (Phil. 2:8, KJV). The most common Greek substantive indications of humility are *tapeinos* and *tapeinophrosunē*, which are usually objects of the verb. In these cases, the faithful are urged to "put on" (Col. 3:12, NASB) or "clothe" themselves with (1 Pet. 5:5, NASB) humility.

Other lessons in humility appear in both Testaments even when the specific terms for it do not appear. Moses was the model of humility because of his **obedience** to God and self-abnegation (Exod. 4:10; Num. 12:3). However, it is obedience that especially becomes the hallmark of humility in the preaching of the **prophets** (Isa. 1:19; Jer. 7:23-24). Using a child as an example, Jesus placed more emphasis upon humility as an inward disposition or trait of the spirit (Matt. 18:4). For Jesus, humility meant a relationship of trust in and dependency upon God. For Paul, the humility required for membership in the family of God replaced the hierarchy that characterized the *paterfamilias* (Lat., "father of a family" or "dominant father") and **patron-**client systems of the Roman Empire. In the family of God, hierarchical relationships between Jew and Greek, between slave and free, and between male and female are removed in Christ (Gal. 3:28). Both Jesus and Paul saw humility as obedient behavior before God as expressed in the OT, but they also saw it as an inner quality posited by the **Holy Spirit**, a quality in which that behavior was grounded (Matt. 5:3; Rom. 12:16).

See also Slavery.

KENNETH L. WATERS SR., PHD

Ii

IDOLATRY

A biblical theology of worship provides a framework for defining and understanding idolatry. In such a theological reading of the Bible, four recurring themes emerge concerning how a follower of God can avoid idolatrous worship. Observance of these four core principles is central to worship that is acceptable and pleasing to God—namely, worship that keeps one from idolatry.

First, idolatry is avoided by establishing worship of the *right God*. Worship of any god other than the one true and living God is idolatry. Among the many false deities worshipped in the biblical accounts, Baal stands most prominent (e.g., Num. 25:1-5; Judg. 6:25-32; 1 Kings 18:16-40). We know of Baal also from extrabiblical texts, such as those from Ugarit. As the storm god, Baal would have played an important role in an agrarian society, being viewed as a strategic god for one's survival and prosperity. Other false gods mentioned and worshipped throughout the biblical narrative include Asherah, Molech, Aphrodite, and Zeus.

The Bible not only makes sure to identify the wrong gods but also clearly names the right God. In Exodus, at the burning bush, God makes known to Moses his name—"I AM" (3:14, NIV), which in Hebrew is closely associated with God's personal name Yahweh (represented as "LORD" in most English versions). This is the same God who came to Abraham, Isaac, and Jacob (v. 15); who is revealed in Jesus Christ (John 1); and who is manifested in the presence, power, and **work** of the **Holy Spirit** (Acts 2:1-39). This God is also the God who faithfully seeks out and desires relationship with all humanity, for he is the covenantal God (Gen. 15). The worship of any god other than Yahweh would be worship defined biblically as idolatrous.

The second way to avoid idolatry is to worship the one true God *exclusively*. The call to the exclusive worship of Yahweh (Deut. 6:4-5) is a central biblical theme. Jesus declared that the Greatest Commandment included the worship of the Lord in exclusivity and with one's full being (Mark 12:29-30). When early believers questioned whether there were two gods—one for the Jews and one for the Gentiles—Paul was quick to declare that there was only one true God (Rom. 3:29-30). Throughout the biblical world, polytheism was the norm. Thus the biblical demand for exclusivity in worship was countercultural, and it set the followers of Yahweh apart from those around them. It was not sufficient to worship Yahweh as one's supreme god while still recognizing and worshipping other deities (henotheism), for this, too, was idolatry (Josh. 24:15). Instead, humanity has been called to an exclusive relationship with Yahweh.

The third tenant of right worship that leads away from idolatry is demonstrating the *proper spirit* in the worship of God. A true or right spirit involves approaching God with both **humility** and reverence (Prov. 21:27; Amos 5:21-24; 1 Cor. 11:17-32), confessing one's sins (Lev. 5:5; 16:21), and making restitution for one's offenses to God and people (Num. 5:6-7). Followers of God must surrender their pride and respond to their covenantal relationship with God by loving him in exclusivity and by loving their neighbors as themselves (Mark 12:30-31). Biblical worship is worship that comes out of an obedient heart in a spirit of humility, reverence, and **love**. Otherwise, worship is rebellious and arrogant, attitudes equated with "the **sin** of **divination**" and the "the **evil** of idolatry" (1 Sam. 15:22-23, NIV). God calls us as worshippers beyond the ritual act (see below) to **obedience** of the heart.

Finally, to avoid idolatry one must shun *false ritual practice*. One of the most common false rituals is the creation of a physical representation of a god—usually our first and primary definition of idolatry. Physical idols are prohibited in the Ten Commandments (Exod. 20:3-4; Deut. 5:7-8) because they are a creation of humanity and thus without power or life (Ps. 115:4-8; Isa. 44:9-20; Jer. 10:8-10). Biblical examples of physical representations of a god include the household gods that Rachel took from her father Laban (Gen. 31:30-34) and the calf idols that were fashioned at Sinai, Dan, and Bethel (Exod. 32:2-4; 1 Kings 12:28-30). The archaeological record has also yielded evidence of idols. For example, at Ashkelon, a small (4-by-4½-inch) bronze bull with an accompanying ceramic shrine was found outside of the city gates and is thought to date to the Middle Bronze Age (ca. 1750–ca. 1550 BC) (Stager, 106). Similarly, on top of a hill four miles east of Dothan and north of **Jerusalem**, a bull idol was found in an Iron Age (ca. 1200–ca. 1001 BC) open-air cult site (Mazar 1992, 350-52).

Although the **church** often limits the definition of idolatry to false ritual practice, idolatry can also stem from the worship of the wrong god, from the failure to worship the right God exclusively, and from the worship of the right God with the wrong spirit. If the church only focuses on right religious practice, such as not creating physical representations of deities, then it runs the risk of forgetting that true worship must also reflect a singular focus on God (Father, Son, and Holy Spirit), with each worshipper wholly engaged with this covenantal God through a fully surrendered heart, mind, and soul.

See also Covenant; Love; Names of God.

Resources

Block, Daniel I. *For the Glory of God: Recovering a Biblical Theology of Worship*. Grand Rapids: Baker Academic, 2014.

Mazar, Amihai. *Archaeology of the Land of the Bible: 10,000–586 BCE*. New York: Doubleday, 1992.

Stager, Lawrence E. "Ashkelon." Pages 103–12 in vol. 1 of *NEAEHL*.

BRIAN T. BERNIUS, PHD

IMAGE OF GOD

The radical and significant concept that humanity is created in the "image of God" (Lat., *imago Dei*) is addressed limitedly in the biblical text. This idea, stated in Genesis 1:26-27, occurs again in the OT only in Genesis 9:6 (see 5:1-2, which also speaks of God's "likeness"). From these texts, the following widely accepted assertions can be made:

1. Humanity's creation in the image of God differentiates human beings from the rest of God's **creation**. Although animals share some properties with humans, including being filled with the breath of life (Gen. 2:7; 7:22) and being living "being[s]" (Hebr., *nepeš*; traditionally translated "soul" [KJV] in 2:7, but "creature" in 1:20, 24 [KJV]), only humankind is created "in [the] image, according to [the] likeness" (v. 26, NRSV). This differentiation seems most clearly expressed in humanity's distinctive relationship with God.

2. The divine image is bestowed upon all humanity. This point is stressed both in the all-encompassing phrase "male and female" in Genesis 1:27 and 5:2 and in the plurality of the verb "rule" in 1:26, whose placement following the phrase "Let us make *ādām*" validates the understanding of that grammatically singular noun as the collective "humankind" (NRSV; see also 5:2; 6:1; Isa. 2:20; 31:3).

3. The image of God imparts an inherent dignity and sanctity to all human life. Seen in several ways in Genesis 1–2, particularly in the exclusive commands to subdue and rule, it is affirmed most specifically in 9:6, which explicitly bases its prohibition against the shedding of human blood on humanity's being created in the image of God.

In the NT, James 3:9 also emphasizes the dignity of humanity based upon creation in the divine image. Generally, however, the NT engagement with the concept of the *imago Dei* centers around two considerations: (1) Christ as *the* image of God and (2) the transformation of humanity into the divine image.

Christ, as the fully human **incarnation** of God, perfectly displays the image that humanity was created to bear (2 Cor. 4:4; Col. 1:15; Heb. 1:3). For the rest of humanity, however, it is those who experience true relationship with Christ who are changed into his image (Rom. 8:29; 2 Cor. 3:18; Col. 3:10; cf. Eph. 4:17-24).

This raises the question about the status of the image of God in fallen humanity. The biblical evidence suggests that the divine image is, to some extent, retained in humanity (thus the perpetual command against murder), though corrupted. In the NT, it becomes clear that the truest reflection of the image of God within humanity transpires by transformation into the image that is Christ. Ultimately, "We learn from Jesus what it is to be human" (Marshall 2001, 55).

Through many scholarly attempts to define precisely what the image is, the following three broad categories have emerged, each having nuanced variations and without mutual exclusivity: (1) The image is the capacity of humans for relationship with both God and one another, reflecting the relational nature of God himself. (2) Humanity's function as God's representative in creation defines the image (humanity not *in* the image, but *as* the image). (3) Humans possess one or more qualities or properties that resemble God, whether that be a natural property (reason, will, etc.) or a moral property (**love**, "**righteousness** and true **holiness**" [Eph. 4:24, KJV]).

Wesley's threefold elucidation of God's political, natural, and moral image (with emphasis on the moral) incorporates the latter two views, though understanding the moral image as derived from our ongoing relationship with God rather than as a capacity we possess (1985, sec. 1, para. 1). It is, therefore, necessary to be re-created into this image through our sanctifying experience with God for the purpose of "imaging" or reflecting God to the fallen world.

See also Biblical Ethics; Fall, The; Sanctification; Sin.

Resources
Clines, D. J. A. "The Image of God in Man." *TynBul* 19 (1968): 53-103.
Marshall, I. Howard. "Being Human: Made in the Image of God." *Stone-Campbell Journal* 4, no. 1 (Spring 2001): 47-67.
Middleton, J. Richard. *The Liberating Image: The Imago Dei in Genesis 1.* Grand Rapids: Brazos Press, 2005.
Runyon, Theodore. *The New Creation: John Wesley's Theology Today.* Nashville: Abingdon Press, 1998.
Wesley, John. "The Image of God." Sermon 141. Pages 290-303 in vol. 4 of *The Bicentennial Edition of the Works of John Wesley.* Edited by Albert C. Outler. Nashville: Abingdon Press, 1987.
———. "The New Birth." Sermon 45. Pages 186-201 in vol. 2 of *The Bicentennial Edition of the Works of John Wesley.* Edited by Albert C. Outler. Nashville: Abingdon Press, 1985.

ELAINE A. BERNIUS, PHD

INCARNATION

The word "incarnation" derives from the Latin term *incarnatio* and means "enfleshed." Within Christian literature, it refers to the coming together of the divine nature and human nature in the person of Jesus Christ.

While this doctrine as we know it today is fully articulated in the creedal statements of the fourth and fifth centuries CE, most of the biblical texts only hint at this future development. This implicitness is partly because Greek (i.e., NT) lacks a word for "incarnation" and because only a handful of biblical passages clearly give expression to Jesus's preexistence. Only as the early **church** arrived at the affirmation about Jesus's divine preexistent nature could that understanding be joined with the affirmation about his humanity to articulate the mystery that the divine preexistent One became, in the flesh, the human being named Jesus.

All biblical writers affirm that Jesus had a special relationship with the divine. For the Synoptic Gospels, Jesus is the divine Son, as expressed in the title "Son of God" (Matt. 4:3; Mark 1:1; Luke 1:35). However, none of these Gospels ground this relationship in Jesus's divine preexistence. Instead, Jesus is first identified as God's Son at his baptism (Mark 1:9-11) or at his conception (Luke 1:26-38 and Matt. 1:18-25). For these **Gospel** writers, Jesus is a messenger of God like Moses and Elijah (Matt. 17:3; Mark 9:4; Luke 9:30). On the other hand, Jesus is the only messenger that God himself identifies as his Son (Matt. 17:5; Mark 9:7; Luke 9:35).

Though all biblical writers affirm that Jesus is God's Son, this title does not necessarily lend itself to the notion of incarnation. Something more is needed, which both Matthew and Luke do add to their depictions of Jesus. At key points in these Gospels, the disciples worshipped Jesus (Matt. 14:33; 28:9, 17; Luke 24:52), an act that should be reserved for God alone.

Thus for Matthew and Luke, as they describe certain encounters between Jesus and his disciples, especially **resurrection** appearances, they depict the disciples as responding to Jesus as if they were encountering God himself. To be sure, readers of Matthew's Gospel are not surprised about this response, as this intimate connection between Jesus and God is already alluded to in the birth narrative. There the angel of the Lord announced that Jesus would be called "'Emmanuel,' which means 'God with us'" (1:23, NRSV). So while these Gospel writers may not argue for incarnation directly, they do allude to a deeper connection between God and Jesus than is found in the title "Son of God" alone.

Another biblical text articulates this deeper connection between God and Jesus as well. In the book of Revelation, because of Jesus's death and resurrection, Jesus is the sacrificed Lamb that is elevated to the throne upon which God sits (ch. 5). From that point forward in Revelation, those in heaven worship at one and the same time both the One on the throne (God) and the Lamb (vv. 6, 13; 7:9-10, 17; 22:1, 3). In essence, for Revelation and the Gospels of Matthew and Luke, an encounter with Jesus, especially as the resurrected One, is an encounter with God. Because this is so, the resurrected Christ is worthy of the same worship that God deserves.

Beyond these affirmations that Jesus has a special relationship with God, however, none of the texts explored so far would necessarily lead to a doctrine of incarnation. It is only with Paul that we find texts that make a clear connection with Jesus's divine status and his preexistence. Two texts stand out in this regard: Philippians 2:6-11 and Colossians 1:15-20.

In Philippians 2:6-11, Paul cites what is likely an early Christ hymn. In context, the hymn describes three distinct stages that Jesus went through. The first can be interpreted as a preexistence in which "he was in the *form* of God" (v. 6, NRSV, emphasis added). Whatever that was, in the second stage, he emptied himself of that form and took on human form and lived a life as a servant until his death (vv. 7-8). Then in the third stage, God exalted Jesus as Lord of all (vv. 9-11). While this hymn may be referring to Jesus's preexistence, more striking are the reasons why Jesus should be understood as Lord of all. Jesus is not Lord because of his preexistence, but instead, he is Lord of all because he faithfully "humbled himself" and was "obedient to the point of death—even death on a cross (v. 8, NRSV). Thus these verses ground Jesus's exalted status as the divine Son in his death and resurrection (see also Rom. 1:4, NIV, where Jesus is "appointed the Son of God in power by his resurrection from the dead").

Jesus's preexistence is clearly stated in Colossians 1:15-20. This, too, is a Christ hymn in praise of the exalted Christ. In these verses, references to Jesus's preexistence parallel the kinds of claims made for preexistent **Wisdom** that are found in the OT wisdom tradition (Prov. 8:22, 25; Sir. 24:9; Wis. 7:26). In this tradition, Wisdom is evident in **creation** itself, forms the foundation that makes creation possible, and is the agent through which God reveals himself to his creation. These claims are transferred to Jesus in the Colossians hymn: he is the "image of the invisible God, the firstborn over all creation" (1:15, NIV). Thus, not only does the resurrected Christ fulfill all that is believed about God's divine Wisdom, but only in Jesus are we able to truly see God and what he is like (see also v. 19 and 2:9; along similar lines is Heb. 1:1-14).

With Colossians 1:15-20, we have a clear affirmation of Jesus's preexistence; yet the focus of this passage is not on this affirmation. Like Philippians 2:6-11, it is Jesus's exalted status as the resurrected Christ that is the focus of the Colossians hymn (cf. 1:20, 22). Paul is not as interested in affirming Jesus's preexistence as he is in arguing that the resurrected One is the true fulfillment of all previous conversations about divine Wisdom (see Dunn 1996, 194-96).

With the Johannine writings, we get language that ties more closely to the doctrinal teaching of incarnation in the fourth-and-fifth-century creeds. In the prologue of John's Gospel (1:1-18), John affirms that the preexistent Logos became the person Jesus Christ. More specifically, the Logos preexisted from the beginning, was with God, and can even be called God (vv. 1-3; see also 6:62; 8:38). This Logos then descended from heaven (3:13; 6:33) and lived among us as a real flesh and blood human being named Jesus (1:14; 1 John 4:2-3). Then once his ministry was completed on earth, he returned back to his place with God (John 13:1-3; 20:17). Thus, with John's theology, we have the biblical description of Jesus that conforms the closest to the doctrine of incarnation as articulated in the creeds of the early church.

See also Humility; Image of God; Obedience.

Resources

Dunn, James D. G. *Christology in the Making: A New Testament Inquiry into the Origins of the Doctrine of the Incarnation.* 2nd ed. Grand Rapids: Eerdmans, 1996.

Keck, Leander E. *Why Christ Matters: Toward a New Testament Christology.* Waco, TX: Baylor University Press, 2015.

WILLIAM H. MALAS JR., PHD

INDIAN HERMENEUTICS

Beginning of the Indian Tradition of Biblical Interpretation

Nobel Prize winner Amartya Sen, in the book *The Argumentative Indian* (2006), has argued convincingly that from ancient times India has had a tradition of public debate and intellectual pluralism. This debate encompassed (1) the interpretation of reality, (2) the interpretation of religious texts, and (3) the interpretation of cultural norms. Foundational to interpretation is the system of logic that was developed over the centuries. Ancient Indian philosophers as early as the sixth century BC have been compiling various principles of interpretation that were circulating in oral tradition and practices. The Indian system of logic that was developed is substantially different from the Western system of logic.

Historically, hermeneutical exercises can be traced to efforts to appropriate the Vedas to guide daily life. Vedas, the foundational texts of Vedic Hinduism, were developed as early as the third century BC. Sabara around the fifth or sixth century AD produced a major commentary on the Vedas. He employed the Mimamsa school of Vedic interpretation. The main inquiry was to find out the rules of righteous living (dharma) and the rules for the rituals. The text called the Mimamsa Sutra codified the basic rules of Vedic interpretation.

Buddhism emerged on the world scene six centuries before Christianity. Buddhist literature is comprised of the words spoken by Buddha and other Buddhists or "enlightened souls." The main goal of Buddhist hermeneutics is to elucidate spiritual principles and practices useful for reaching enlightenment (nirvana).

Indian Christianity has been the product of Western missionary efforts, except for the small communities of Christians in the Kerala State, which is in the southwestern corner of India. These Christian communities trace their history back to AD 52 with the arrival of the apostle Thomas. They have followed Orthodox liturgical traditions but have not engaged in analytical biblical study and thus have not contributed much to the advancement of hermeneutical methods. The Syriac Bible has been used for reading, and the churches have sung songs in Syriac. However, even priests have not been sufficiently proficient in the Syriac language to interpret the biblical texts. Their liturgy has been limited to reading and chanting. The first translation of the Peshitta (the Syriac Bible) into Malayalam (the language of Kerala) was completed only in 1811, and only three hundred copies were printed for use in churches. The Catholic Church arrived in India at the beginning of the sixteenth century, but its contribution to Indian biblical interpretation has also been insignificant.

The spread of Christianity in India was primarily the result of Western missionary efforts. Because Western missionaries interpreted the Bible for new Christians, the common worship practice of an Indian Christian congregation does not differ very much from that of a Western congregation. However, instruction by the Western missions has been a major contribution to the development of Indian biblical interpretation.

Orientalism and Its Impact on Indian Hermeneutics

The British East India Company and other Europeans arrived in India primarily for trade. However, their impact was far more widespread than simply economics. Along with traders, scholars and missionaries from all over Europe also arrived in India and significantly impacted India's culture, traditions, and politics. They ventured into the study of Sanskrit, hitherto the language of the priestly class and scholars, and translated religious treaties, including the Vedas, into their European languages.

Thus European scholars, later known as Orientalists, helped in the revival and popularization of India's ancient religious, cultural, and philosophical traditions, which were inaccessible to the Indians who did not know Sanskrit. It was a language only of the educated people—that is, the upper castes. Thus a social change to accessing knowledge occurred. As Sanskrit texts were translated into European languages, the Orientalists redrew the intellectual map of India. Their work was not limited to Sanskrit but spread to other regional languages as well. The missionaries produced dictionaries and wrote grammars for the major regional languages of India. They also published books, newspapers, and magazines in these languages. India thus experienced a literary revival through the work of the European scholars.

Besides the literary impact of the Europeans was yet another unforeseen effect. Orientalism helped to challenge the negative attitude of the European rulers toward India and at the same time made Indians proud of their own heritage.

The Work of Indian Scholars and Religious Leaders

The availability of the ancient literary traditions in European and Indian languages greatly influenced the new converts to Christianity. One notable example was Krishna Mohan Banerjea (1813-85), who argued that Christianity was the fulfillment of the ancient Indian Vedas. The Vedas were viewed as preparation for the NT just as the OT was viewed by some as preparation for Jewish believers and the Septuagint as preparation for Gentiles. Being a prolific writer, he argued that the Vedas foresaw the advent of Christ. Banerjea and those who shared similar views of Hindu and Christian scriptures paved the way for interpreting the Bible in the light of Hindu scriptures and Brahminical philosophical traditions, approaches usually described as comparative hermeneutics. Examples of these comparative hermeneutical approaches are found in the works of Robin Boyd, T. M. Manickam, Swami Abhishiktananda, and M. A. Amaladoss.

However, another trend that was related, but differed considerably, also emerged. Instead of comparing the Hindu traditions with those of Christianity, various Indian or Hindu interpretive tools were used to read the Bible itself. This was a total rejection of the historical-critical methods that the Protestant missionaries taught their Indian coverts and which were prevalent in the churches. Two main figures in this area came from the Syrian Orthodox tradition. Paul Gregorios, who was the principal of the Orthodox Seminary in Kerala, proposed that the interpretive rules employed by the Indian philosophical schools such as Nyaya, Vaisesika, and Samkhya could be used for biblical interpretation. A second figure was K. P. Aleaz (1991), who proposed that the Lakshana method is a useful interpretive tool.

Another remarkable Hindu convert to Christianity is Sister Vandana, a Catholic nun. She brought with her the widely accepted Hindu interpretive practice of the Dhvani method as a means of interpreting the NT.

This trend was not limited to Christian scholars from European Christian traditions but also included those who belonged to missionary churches. For example, Thomas Manickam proposed that three other Indian interpretive traditions were useful in understanding the Bible, the Mimamsa, Vyankarana, and the Vedanta methods. The German scholar Martin Kampchen and Indian artist Jyoti Sahi used the Indian interpretive method of *rasa* and represented their interpretation of Psalms through paintings.

Brahminical or Sanskritic modes were not the only modes of interpretation that were available. The Puranas—that is, the great epics—also played important roles in the religious formation of Indian minds. These are stories told of great heroes who were deified in Sanskrit literature. Various recensions and adaptations of Sanskrit Puranas were available in many regional languages.

The bhakti movements came into existence during the seventh century, beginning in southern India and spreading into northern India. *Bhakti* (devotion) means expressing devotion to a "chosen god" (*ishta devata*) from the 3.3 billion strong Hindu pantheons. This was partly a reaction to the domination of Sanskrit, the language of the scholar of religions, and also partly a rejection of philosophizing religious thought. This reaction is seen by many scholars as part of the anti-Sanskritization of Indian religious culture. India is home to forty-plus fully developed languages that have rich heritages of secular and sacred literature. The leaders of these different bhakti movements in the regional languages (or bhakti saints), most of whom were originally ballad singers, were actually interpreters. They produced devotional literature in their own languages by retelling the stories in the form of songs and hymns. Tukaram in Marathi, the Alvars in Tamil, and Kabir in Punjabi are some examples of the leaders of these bhakti movements and their respective languages.

Many Christian interpreters also adopted these methods by composing songs, hymns, stories, and epics similar to those of the bhakti movements. Sadhu Sundar Singh, a Punjabi evangelist, used stories from Indian traditions to retell the biblical narratives. Vaman Tilak of Maharashtra produced a Christian Purana (epic) in Marathi that resembles *Ramayana*, the life of the god Rama. One notable aspect of Tilak is that he was a Hindu bhakti poet who wrote hymns about Jesus before his conversion. Later in his life, he reflected that he came to Jesus Christ "over the bridge of Bhakti." Other practitioners of vernacular or nativist hermeneutics are Iyadurai Bhagavatar, H. A. Krishna Pillai, and A. J. Appasamy (all in the Tamil language) and K. V. Simon (in Malayalam).

Modern Hermeneutical Approaches

Various modern hermeneutical approaches have been adopted by Christian scholars in India. These fall generally in the class of reader-centered hermeneutical approaches. Reading from the margins is a common method in Christian academia. Examples include subaltern, postcolonial, feminist, and ecocritical readings.

Though methodologically these approaches share most of the same features wherever they are used in the world, some of them have specific relevance to India. One of them is *dalit* hermeneutics. Dalit readings of the Bible have been significantly popular for over a decade. The word *dalit* refers to those people who are the lowest in the Hindu caste system, the untouchables. Another group is the Adivasi, a tribal people who first settled the central part of India. One of their main concerns is land rights, particularly the destruction of forests due to commercial forestry and the encroachment of agriculture. Adivasi theologians are focusing their theological energy on these issues and trying to read the Bible from Adivasi perspectives. Reading Scripture from the perspectives of both the tribal Adivasi and the Hindu dalits is gaining popularity among Christian scholars, since a significant number of Indian Christians are dalits and Adivasi.

Deconstruction hermeneutics is another Western approach that some theologians have adopted. This includes feminist or womanist readings of the Bible in India. The assumption in this approach is that the Bible is a construct of patriarchy.

See also Feminist Hermeneutics.

Resources

Aleaz, Kalarikkal P. *The Role of Pramanas in Hindu-Christian Epistemology.* Calcutta: Pun-thi-Pustak, 1991.
Gregorios, Paul. "Hermeneutics in India Today in the Light of the World Debate." *IJT* 28 (1979): 1-14.
Raja, R. J. "Seeking God, Sought by God: A Dhvani-Reading of the Episode of Zacchaeus (Luke 19:10)." *Jeev* 25 (1995): 139-45.
Sen, Amartya. *The Argumentative Indian: Writings on Indian History, Culture and Identity.* London: Penguin Books, 2006.
Soares-Prabhu, George M. "And There Was a Great Calm: A 'Dhvani' Reading of the Still-ing of the Storm (Mark 4:35-41)." *BiBh* 5, no. 1 (1979): 295-308.

PAULSON PULIKOTTIL, PHD

INHERITANCE

The concept of inheritance was ubiquitous throughout the ANE, and there is nothing inherently theological about it. However, at critical points Scripture theologizes the concept, rendering it a theological concept rooted in the thought world of the ANE. The concept is largely expressed by the Hebrew verbs *nāḥal* (to take possession) and *yāraš* (to inherit) as well as the Greek verbs *klēroō* (to appoint by lot) and *klēronomeō* (to inherit) and the nouns *klēros* (lot), *klēronomos* (heir), and *klēronomia* (inheritance).

Secular Dimension

Inheritance can refer to the passing on of goods and possessions according to patrilineal expectations (Gen. 48:6; Matt. 21:38; Mark 12:7; Luke 12:13; 20:14). For example, land may be passed from generation to generation (1 Kings 21), as well as slaves, people, homes, and wealth (Lev. 25:46; Ruth 4:5; Prov. 19:14). Ostensibly, abstract qualities are also inheritable based on one's quality of life (Prov. 3:35; 11:29; Eccles. 7:11). Yet Genesis 21:10, Judges 11:2, and Ruth 4:1-10 reveal that the process could be subjected to coercion based on personal preference and/or social stigma. It could, however, be hindered by biological phenomenon (Num. 27:1-11).

Theological Dimension

The implications of God's covenant are at the core of the theologizing of inheritance. Thus the Pentateuch anticipates Israel's inheritance of the promised land, which becomes the dominant manifestation associated with the concept through the OT. Inheritance can refer to the promised land in toto (Deut. 26:1) as well as specific tribal allotments (Num. 32; Josh. 13–21). Notably, the inheritance-as-promised-land concept is largely abandoned throughout the rest of the Historical Books with exception of a few passages that exhibit a postexilic context (1 Kings 8:36; 1 Chron. 16:18; 28:8; 2 Chron. 6:27; 20:11; Ezra 9:12). In Ezekiel and Isaiah the inheritance of the land manifests an eschatological nuance (Isa. 57:13; Ezek. 47–48), and in Psalm 37, the inheritance of the land is linked to personal integrity and general morality.

Inheritance is also relational. Israel is spoken of as God's inheritance. For example, Moses appeals to this relationship when interceding for the nation at Sinai (Exod. 34:9), and Jeremiah uses it as a pillar for emphasizing God's creative power against the worthlessness of idols (Jer. 10:16; 51:19). Zechariah anticipates the Lord once again inheriting Judah, which alongside the choice of Jerusalem will culminate with the nation's redemption from exile (Zech. 2:12). On the other hand, the Lord is the inheritance of the Levites and priests because they were not entitled to a geographic inheritance (Deut. 10:9; 18:2; Ezek. 44:28).

More generically, 2 Kings 2:9 attests that spiritual power can be inherited as well as social honor (1 Sam. 2:8), both of which can be understood as the sign of the Lord's empowerment and sovereign provision. However, the OT also suggests that inheritance is not unqualified. Joshua 14:9 recounts that Caleb's personal inheritance was substantiated in his faithfulness. Jeremiah associates Judah's idolatry with the pollution of the land and subsequent judgment (Jer. 16:14-18), and Lamentations 5:2 mourns the forfeiture of Israel's land as it recounts the destruction of Jerusalem. Most pervasively, Deuteronomy and its Deuteronomic ideology, which inform much of the OT, dictate that covenantal disobedience will result in the forfeiture of the inherited land.

In the NT, inheritance is associated with eternal life (Matt. 19:29; Mark 10:17; Luke 10:25). Similar also to inheritance in the OT, inheritance in the NT is qualified. It is contingent upon faith in the work of Jesus Christ (Acts 20:32; Rom. 4:13; Gal. 3:14; Eph. 1:3-14; Col. 3:24), and immorality will result in disqualification (1 Cor. 6:9-10; Gal. 5:21; Eph. 5:5).

Conclusions

The OT recognizes the secular dimension of inheritance, but ultimately accentuates the theological dimension. Throughout Scripture, inheritance describes foundational realities about God's relationship with his people, and so the theologizing of this secular concept ostensibly stems from a need to articulate efficiently the implications of the covenant. In the NT, the theologizing of inheritance is advanced in response to Christ. Spiritual realities, such as eternal life and inclusion in the **kingdom of God**, are inherited upon the condition of faith and a transformed life. Yet most fundamentally, inheritance throughout Scripture testifies to the God who reveals himself to his people in familiar terms in order to foster a relationship and bring about transformation.

See also Completeness/Integrity; Eschatology; Obedience.

Resources

Chambers, Chad. "Inheritance." In *LBD.*
King, Philip J., and Lawrence E. Stager. *Life in Biblical Israel.* Library of Ancient Israel. Louisville, KY: Westminster John Knox Press, 2001.
Silva, Moisés. "Inheritance." Pages 1035-37 in *BEB.*
Vaux, Roland de. *Ancient Israel: Its Life and Institutions.* Translated by John McHugh. Grand Rapids: Eerdmans, 1997.

DAVID B. SCHREINER, PHD

INSPIRATION OF SCRIPTURE, WESLEYAN UNDERSTANDING OF

The doctrine of biblical inspiration is of crucial importance. There is a direct relationship between the way we understand the inspiration and authority of Scripture and the normative development of our faith and Christian life.

The participation of the Holy Spirit gives a unique and singular character to Scripture as the **Word of God** that distinguishes it from any other type of literature. This radically differentiates it from the generic and common use of the term "inspiration" in reference to other types of literature, art, or music.

God has taken the initiative of revealing himself to us. Inspiration is the supernatural interaction of his Spirit with chosen persons for the purpose of guiding them to express his will through the biblical writings.

Many passages in both the OT and NT attest to the inspiration of Scripture. Two passages in the NT particularly illustrate the claim of Scripture's inspiration.

Second Timothy 3:16 affirms, "All Scripture is God-breathed and is useful for teaching, rebuking, correcting and training in **righteousness**" (NIV). The translation "God-breathed" or "inspired by God" (NRSV) comes from the Greek *theopneustos*—*theos*, "God," and *pneō*, "breathe" or "blow out of"—thus "God breathed." Scripture was produced by "God breathing," "God blowing," or "God gently blowing." The implication of this statement is that Scripture is given by divine authorship. This essential and exclusive quality grants the Bible authority to fulfill its purpose as a guide for the full development of the believer, "so that the servant of God may be thoroughly equipped for every good **work**" (v. 17, NIV).

Second Peter 1:21 affirms, "Prophecy never had its origin in the human will, but **prophets**, though human, spoke from God as they were carried along by the **Holy Spirit**" (NIV). This verse attributes the origin of Scripture to the initiative and participation of the Spirit. The prophets did not take the initiative themselves. Rather, they were inspired supernaturally for the proclamation of the prophetic discourse in the OT, just as others were so inspired for the writing of all the canonical books of the Bible (cf. 1 Cor. 2:13; 1 Thess. 2:13).

We do not find in the Bible details relating to how the Spirit inspired the biblical writers to transmit their message. Although Christians generally agree that the Bible is a divine and human word, a polemical and controversial atmosphere has risen concerning the participation and interaction of each of these two factors in the process of inspiration. Because of that, several theories have been generated to try to explain that relationship.

The *mechanical* or *dictated theory* emphasizes divine action over human participation. It proposes that God dictated word for word each book of the Bible. The biblical writers became mere secretaries or scribes that recorded the will of God under the instruction of the Spirit but without any active participation. However, the Scriptures themselves give sufficient evidence that God respected the individual literary styles, backgrounds, and experiences of the human writers.

The *intuition* or *natural inspiration theory* underscores human participation over divine intervention, denying the supernatural dimension of the process. This view equates Scripture to an outstanding literary work, but of human authorship only.

To the writers' human capacity, the *illumination theory* adds their spiritual and mental training for receiving the message from God. There is a subtle but important difference between the inspiration of other human writers and the production by the biblical writers. However, according to this theory, the divine supernatural element remains relegated to a secondary level, underscoring the human instrumentality.

The *verbal inspiration theory* maintains that divine action through the Spirit was sufficient to assure that what God wanted written finally would be registered in Scripture without alteration, regardless of the styles, backgrounds, and personalities of the writers. Divine participation was not limited to the contents of the message but transcended the free choice of the specific words of the writers found in the sacred text.

The *plenary inspiration theory* proposes that *each part* of the Bible is equally inspired by God by means of his Spirit. All of the human writers, however, were clearly grounded in their specific cultural and historical contexts. This view affirms that the sacred text itself gives testimony to the individual contributions of its writers, which are exhibited in the writers' literary styles, vocabularies, and temperaments. Even the subjects broached coincide with the biblical writers' personality profiles, training, and experiences; compare, for example, the books written by Paul and John. In such a synergistic process the divine or supernatural factor and the human factor maintained a healthy harmony.

Summary

God, by means of the Spirit, supernaturally and uniquely inspired faithful and consecrated servants, the biblical writers, to record his will in the Old and New Testaments. It is fundamental to affirm that the Word of God revealed by his Spirit contains everything necessary to attain salvation. The Bible as the Word of God has the authority to set the norms for what we believe (our doctrine) and the way we should live (our ethics).

The purpose of Scripture is not scientific, but redemptive. It does not intend to resolve all the historical, critical-literary, or geographic questions that can be asked. Rather it seeks to communicate the original plan of God that believers may live in righteousness and **holiness** (2 Tim. 3:17; cf. 1 Thess. 5:23-24).

The Word of God has a practical purpose for the lives of believers. Because of our human limitations, we cannot understand with unequivocal precision the mysteries of God surrounding the levels of the divine and human elements in inspiration. Nonetheless, we should not let that affect our **faith** and subtract from the authority of the sacred text. As Wesleyans, we affirm and believe that Scripture is an authorized and unique rule of faith on which we build our theology, our history, and our style of life as people of God.

See also Biblical Ethics; Free Will.

Resources

Dunning, H. Ray. *Gracia, Fe y Santidad.* Edición en CD. Kansas City: Casa Nazarena de Publicaciones, 2018. Originally published as *Grace, Faith, and Holiness* (Kansas City: Beacon Hill Press of Kansas City, 1988).

Martínez, José M. *Hermenéutica Bíblica.* Terrassa, Barcelona: Editorial CLIE, 1984.

Purkiser, W. T., ed. *Explorando nuestra fe Cristiana.* Kansas City: Casa Nazarena de Publicaciones, 1988. Originally published as *Exploring Our Christian Faith* (Kansas City: Beacon Hill Press of Kansas City, 1978).

Taylor, Richard S. *Autoridad Bíblica y la fe Cristiana.* Kansas City: Casa Nazarena de Publicaciones, 1985. Originally published as *Biblical Authority and Christian Faith* (Kansas City: Beacon Hill Press of Kansas City, 1980).

———, ed. *Diccionario Teológico Beacon.* Kansas City: Casa Nazarena de Publicaciones, 1994. Originally published as *Beacon Dictionary of Theology* (Kansas City: Beacon Hill Press of Kansas City, 1983).

Wiley, H. Orton, and Paul T. Culbertson. *Introducción a la Teología Cristiana*. Kansas City: Casa Nazarena de Publicaciones, 1982. Originally published as *Introduction to Christian Theology* (Kansas City: Beacon Hill Press, 1946).

Williams, Colin W. *La teología de Juan Wesley: Una investigación histórica*. San José, CR: Ediciones Sebila, 1989. Originally published as *John Wesley's Theology Today* (Nashville: Abingdon Press, 1960).

JORGE L. JULCA, DMIN

INTERTEXTUALITY, HERMENEUTICS OF

Rise of Intertextuality

The term "intertertextuality" (Fr., *intertextualité*) goes back to Julia Kristeva, a literary critic who first formulated the term in 1969. Kristeva credited Mikhail Bakhtin with introducing this concept into literary theory, but she was first to give a systematized description of the phenomenon.

"Intertextuality" means "between texts." By "text" Kristeva meant all kinds of cultural, historical, and social interrelationships. Intertextuality assumes that every text consists of other texts and that those also consist of other texts and so on. Barthes has described it through a metaphor of "weaving" (1977, 145). Every text is woven out of the threads of countless other texts.

The concept of intertextuality assumes that the texts have relationships between each other. Some literary critics insist that there is always a power play between texts, every text seeking to replace the previous texts; it is a conflict of surfaces where different authorial intentions, semiotic systems, and ideologies compete. Others suggest that conflict as the primary relationship between texts is too limiting. Texts can have many possible relationships. Baxandall lists over forty different kinds of relationships that texts may have (1985, 58-59).

The idea of conflict may be attractive in a postmodern context, but when speaking of ancient texts, one should not assume that the new always battles the old. For ancient authors the goal may have been to mimic rather than dethrone the old text.

Whatever the relationship, there is dependence between old and new texts that can range from shared words, sounds, or terms to an explicit citation. All texts are inseparable from other texts. No text is autonomous, but every text is an *intertext*.

Kristeva proposed a dialogue between texts. When texts are brought into a dialogue, the ideas of truth and meaning become decentralized. There can no longer be one authorially intended meaning that can be discovered from the text. The intertextual method in its original poststructuralist framework is very reader oriented. It suggests that the text by itself does not "have meaning," but meaning is assigned to the text by a reader. A reader is also an interpreter and full of "texts." Each reader is different, and different readers produce different readings.

Intertextuality in Biblical Studies

Since the 1980s the term "intertextuality" has been increasingly used among biblical scholars, and almost every book of the canon has been subjected to some form of intertextual analysis. However, much of Kristeva's original concept was abandoned in this cross-disciplinary move, resulting in considerable methodological confusion.

Intertextuality and Source Criticism. Intertextuality found its way into biblical studies through source criticism. Hatina claims that biblical scholars are in fact doing source-influence studies under a new fashionable label "intertextuality" (1999, 42). The distinctions between intertextuality and source criticism clearly need clarification.

The two methods are similar in determining that texts consist of other texts, but they have different focuses. Source criticism focuses on the redactors' intentions and the ways traditions are edited. It asks, Which source text has been used? What has happened to the source text in the process of transmission? It is an author-oriented approach to interpretation and belongs to the historical-critical method.

Intertextuality, in contrast, asks, What is the relationship between the old and new texts? What happens to that old text in its new context? How are both texts changed when placed into a canonical dialogue? How is the new allowing us to see the old in a new light? It is a reader-oriented method.

Biblical Studies and Authorial Intention

In the context of biblical studies, some features of the original intertextuality have been abandoned. First, the "text" is understood in a more limited way as "literary text," and study involves examining how two or more literary texts relate and produce new meanings. Second, the literary texts are typically chosen from within the canon of Scripture. The canon naturally lends itself to intertextual analysis because NT writers frequently used the OT.

Third, most scholars maintain that texts "have a meaning" or at least a limited range of meanings, leading to a discussion of authorial intention. In and through Scripture the Divine Author is speaking through human voices, but always with authority. The reader is therefore held accountable to the Author. Yet whenever the Bible is read as Scripture, it is expected that biblical texts "speak" to all people in all circumstances, resulting in multiple meanings.

The authorial decision to use a previous text matters, but so does the reader's ability to acknowledge the intertextual relationship and place the two texts into dialogue.

Intertextual reading relies on the reader's competency and creativity in ascribing meaning to a text. There is a continued discussion about the range of hermeneutical freedom ascribed to a reader, for clearly the NT authors took some liberty with the OT texts. In general, however, biblical scholars reject the poststructuralist position that "kills the author."

Application of Intertextuality

Richard B. Hays differentiated between the terms "quotation," "allusion," and "echo." "Quotation" refers to an intertextual reference with an explicit quotation formula. "Allusion" and "echo" are terms to mark the different degrees of certainty that what we are dealing with is an intertextual reference in a particular text where there is no explicit quotation formula by the author. "Allusion" is a term for a more obvious intertextual reference; "echo," for a subtler one (1989, 21).

Hays proposed seven criteria for testing a claim for an intertextual echo: *availability* (whether the source was available to the author), *volume* (the degree of explicit repetition of words and syntactical patterns in the text), *recurrence* (how often the author alludes to the same Scripture elsewhere), *thematic coherence* (does the echo fit the argument), *historical plausibility* (whether the author could have intended this effect and whether his readers could have possibly understood it), *history of interpretation* (whether other interpreters have heard the same echoes), and *satisfaction* (whether the proposed reading makes sense or not). The strongest claim for intertextuality is made when "it can credibly be demonstrated that [the intertextuality occurs] within the literary structure of the text and that [it] can plausibly be ascribed to the intention of the author and the competence of the original readers" (1989, 28).

Intertextuality should entail looking not only for similar wording but also literary templates, narrative patterns, and themes. For example, while the similarities of wording between Genesis 1–3 and Revelation 21–22 are few (Tree of Life in Gen. 2:9; 3:24; Rev. 22:2, 14), there are significant parallels between these texts at the level of narrative components such as characters, setting, and plot.

Intertextuality challenges readers to hear Scripture within Scripture. One must, however, avoid excessive parallelomania. Authorial intentionality and historical plausibility of suggested parallels must always be carefully considered. Intertextual reading is best practiced alongside historical-critical methods and *intratextual* study of language and grammar.

How intertextuality is applied depends largely on the different aims that biblical scholars have. A few maintain closer similarity with Kristeva's concept. For example, Tina Pippin uses theories of intertextuality when discussing depictions of Jezebel in 2 Kings 9 and Revelation 2, showing how the biblical image has impacted American cultural history (1999, 32-33). Such is a decidedly experimental reading, not concerned with authorial intentionality.

Intertextuality as generally practiced within biblical studies shares much in common with inner-biblical exegesis, synchronic reading, and midrash. Biblical authors encourage intertextual readings (e.g., Luke 24:25-27 and John 5:46). The intertextual method borrowed from the literary field provides terminology and a methodological framework for the art and science of biblical interpretation.

See also Reader-Response Hermeneutics.

Resources

Barthes, Roland. "The Death of the Author." In *Image Music Text*. Translated by S. Heath. New York: Hill and Wang, 1977.

Baxandall, Michael. *Patterns of Intention: On the Historical Explanation of Pictures*. New Haven, CT: Yale University Press, 1985.

Hatina, Thomas R. "Intertextuality and Historical Criticism in New Testament Studies: Is There a Relationship?" *BibInt* 7, no. 1 (1999): 28-43.

Hays, Richard B. *Echoes of Scripture in the Letters of Paul*. New Haven, CT: Yale University Press, 1989.

Hays, Richard B., and Joel B. Green. "The Use of the Old Testament by New Testament Writers." Pages 222-38 in *Hearing the New Testament: Strategies for Interpretation*. Edited by Joel B. Green. Grand Rapids: Eerdmans, 1995.

Kristeva, Julia. *Sēmeiōtikē: Recherches pour une sémanalyse*. Paris: Éditions du Seuil, 1969.

Miscall, Peter D. "Isaiah: New Heavens, New Earth, New Book." Pages 41-56 in *Reading between Texts: Intertextuality and the Hebrew Bible*. Edited by D. N. Fewell. Louisville, KY: Westminster John Knox Press, 1992.

Moyise, Steve. "Intertextuality and Historical Approaches to the Use of Scripture in the New Testament." Pages 23-32 in *Reading the Bible Intertextually*. Edited by Richard B. Hays, Stefan Alkier, and Leroy A. Huizenga. Waco, TX: Baylor University Press, 2009.

Pippin, Tina. "Jezebel Revamped." Pages 32-42 in *Apocalyptic Bodies: The Biblical End of the World in Text and Image*. London: Routledge, 1999.

Sanders, James A. "Intertextuality and Dialogue." *BTB* 29 (Spring 1999): 35-44.

Tõniste, Külli. *The Ending of the Canon: A Canonical and Intertextual Reading of Revelation 21–22*. London: Bloomsbury, 2016.

Vorster, Willem S. "Intertextuality and Redaktionsgeschichte." Pages 15-26 in *Intertextuality in Biblical Writings: Essays in Honour of Bas van Iersel*. Edited by S. Draisma. Kampen, NL: Uitgeversmaatschappij J. H. Kok, 1989.

Wolde, Ellen van. "Trendy Intertextuality?" Pages 43-49 in *Intertextuality in Biblical Writings*.

KÜLLI TÕNISTE, PHD

ISAIAH, THEOLOGY OF

The book of Isaiah begins with the announcement "The vision which Isaiah the son of Amoz saw" during the times of four Judean kings, the last of whom was Hezekiah (1:1, AT). This statement intends to apply the "vision" to all sixty-six chapters. Yet Isaiah's ministry to Judah and **Jerusalem** continues only through chapters 1–39. It concludes with Isaiah's final prophetic word to King Hezekiah, that there would come a future Babylonian deportation of Judeans into exile (39:6-7). Chapters 40–66 speak encouragement to God's people in exile, of rescue from exile and resettlement in Jerusalem and Judea. They speak of God extending his salvation to peoples worldwide. The theological center of the book of Isaiah is Isaiah's view of God, who is absolutely different from all deities worshipped by Israel's ANE neighbors. The "vision" is also the vision that God has for his people, both then and in the future.

The pivotal passage of the book of Isaiah is Isaiah's unanticipated encounter with God in the Jerusalem temple (6:1-13). There he saw God as the "Sovereign" (Hebr., *'ǎdōnāy*; v. 1, AT), "the King" (Hebr., *hammelek*; v. 5, AT) of the whole universe, and as "Yahweh of Armies" (Hebr., *yhwh ṣĕbā'ôt*; v. 5, AT), who commanded the armies of both heaven and earth. In that temple encounter, Isaiah witnessed divine beings (seraphim) continually calling out, "Holy, Holy, Holy is Yahweh of Armies" (v. 3, AT). From this, Isaiah came to see God's **holiness** so absolutely in contrast to his and his people's uncleanness (v. 5), that he could only cry out, "Woe to me" (v. 5, AT). God's response was to graciously remove Isaiah's iniquity and forgive his **sin** through the symbolic act of touching his lips with a fiery coal (v. 7). This act is later echoed in God's end-of-exile removal of Jerusalem's iniquity and sins (40:2). It may be from Isaiah's temple experience that the title "the **Holy** One of Israel" (Hebr., *qĕdôš yiśrā'ēl*) came to be ascribed to Yahweh twenty-eight times throughout the book of Isaiah—twelve in chapters 1–39 (the first in 1:4) and sixteen in chapters 40–66 (the last in 60:14).

In interplay with the title "the Holy One of Israel," the canonical text gives theological significance to the term "know" (from Hebr. *yd'*). In the early chapters, Yahweh's "children" (Hebr., *bānîm*; 1:2, 4, AT) have "abandoned," "despised," "turned away" (v. 4, NASB), and "rejected" (5:24, NASB) Yahweh. Thus they cease to "know" him (1:3, NASB). A consequence of the people's not knowing Yahweh would be the devastation of Zion and the **land** of Judah by Judah's enemies (Hebr., *zārîm* [strangers]; vv. 7-9).

In the concluding chapters, however, a "Redeemer" (Hebr., *gō'ēl*; 59:20, AT) will come to a **repentant** Zion. Then, having been "[re-] beautified" (60:9, AT), Jerusalem will become a magnet to all her past enemies (vv. 3, 10, 14), who will stream to Zion "because of the name of Yahweh" (Hebr., *lĕšēm yhwh*; v. 9, AT). They will call Jerusalem "the city of [Yahweh], / The Zion of the Holy One of Israel" (v. 14, NASB). When coming, they will bring with them Israel's dispersed offspring (vv. 4, 9). The inhabitants of Zion will then "know" Yahweh anew as "**Savior**" and "Redeemer" (v. 16, NASB).

A central theological theme of Isaiah is salvation, both physical and spiritual, especially in chapters 40–55. This section opens with God's clarion command to his **prophet** to pronounce **forgiveness** to Jerusalem for her past sins (40:1-2). He would also announce to Jerusalem-Zion and Judah's cities (v. 9), using a shepherd-sheep metaphor (v. 11), that "Sovereign Yahweh" (v. 10, AT) would soon come, bringing with him the Judean exiles from Babylon. The section closes with Yahweh's exultant "word" to the exiles still languishing in Babylon: "You will go out with joy" (55:11-12, NASB). Language extolling God rings out between these opening and closing words of exultation.

God is extolled for his creatorship and authority over nations, idols, and all rulers (40:12-31). Here is an essential theological issue, not only for Judah's exiles but for God's people of all times. One must choose to **believe** that God is sufficiently powerful to extricate the exiles from Babylonian power and deliver them safely to their homeland. In like manner he can deliver his people now from seemingly impossible situations of hopelessness. It is in this theological context that Yahweh, the Redeemer, is extolled for his power over King Cyrus of Persia, even using him, postexile, to rebuild Yahweh's beloved Jerusalem and its temple (44:24-28).

God is extolled for his ability to carry out what he says he will do. Isaiah insists on this consistency in the scenes in which God and the deities of the nations are challenging one another over who is truly God (41:1-5, 21-29; 43:8-15; 44:6-8; 45:20-25). Since God had proven his word in the past to be consistent with its outcome, his people could trust that his present promise of salvation from exile would indeed come to pass.

Chapters 52–53 speak of spiritual salvation. Someone whom God calls "My Servant" (Hebr., ʿabdî; 52:13; 53:11, NASB) will take upon himself "our griefs," "our sorrows," "our iniquities," and "the sin of many"—that is, of all humankind (53:4-6, 12, NASB). Through his voluntary death, "Like a lamb that is led to slaughter" (v. 7, NASB), and because he himself is to be "numbered with the transgressors" (Hebr., pōšěʿîm), "transgressors" who will be justified (vv. 11-12, NASB). When looking back through the lens of NT interpreters, the Isaian Servant's person and mission were understood to have been fulfilled in Jesus the **Christ** or **Messiah**. This is expressly how Philip interpreted this Isaian passage to the Ethiopian queen's court official, resulting in his baptism (Acts 8:26-38).

An essential theological concept for which God is extolled is his uniqueness—for his claim to being "the first" and "the last" (Isa. 44:6; 48:12 NASB). There is no other deity who can claim to be truly God (vv. 6, 8; 45:5-6, 21; 46:4; 48:12). According to the ANE myths, all others who claimed the status of deity (e.g., Marduk, Bel, and Nebo) began through some means of **creation** and were subject to extinction through death. The Isaian conviction is that Israel's God existed before he brought time into existence and will continue to exist after he abolishes time (Ps. 90:2).

The title "Adonai" (Hebr., ʾădōnāy), or "Sovereign," occurs fifty-seven times throughout the book of Isaiah, signifying God's sovereignty over all empires, kings, kingdoms, and people. It is the Sovereign whom Isaiah saw in his temple vision and who then sent Isaiah out newly commissioned (6:1, 11). It is the Sovereign who both used Assyria to punish Israel and Judah and then brought punishment upon the arrogant king of Assyria (8:7; 10:12). The

Sovereign's punishment fell upon individuals, such as Judah's royal steward Shebna, who in arrogance gave more importance to himself and his family than was warranted (22:15-21). It is the Sovereign who "will swallow up death for all time" and "wipe tears away from all faces" (25:8, NASB). Paul and John echo both these concepts in the contexts of resurrection and God's coming to dwell again with his people (1 Cor. 15:54; Rev. 21:4).

The expression "an oracle of Sovereign Yahweh" (Hebr., *nĕ'um 'ădōnāy yhwh*) occurs three times in the book of Isaiah. The first, 1:24, occurs in the context of the Sovereign's contention with Jerusalem's "rulers," who were withholding "**justice**" and "**righteousness**" from those who lived on the fringes of society, the "widow" and "orphan" (vv. 21-23, NASB). The Sovereign promises that in a future day he will "restore" to Jerusalem "judges" and "counselors" who will dispense "justice" and "righteousness" (vv. 26-27). The second, 3:15, occurs in the context of the Sovereign's contention with the "elders and princes" of Jerusalem and Judah (v. 14, NASB). These leaders are accused of plundering and crushing "the poor" (vv. 14-15, NASB), again society's fringe people. The third, 56:8, occurs contextually following Yahweh's call to the exiles to accept his pardon (55:7) and to "go out with joy" (v. 12, NASB) from Babylon.

Having gathered his people out of exile and resettled them in Jerusalem and Judea, Yahweh then commands that doing "justice" and "righteousness" (56:1, NASB) was the way life was now to be lived! Why? Because more of Yahweh's "salvation" and "righteousness" (v. 1, NASB) were about to be extended to those people considered on the fringes of Judean society: foreigners and eunuchs (vv. 3-6), persons forbidden inclusion in the Israelite assembly (Deut. 23:1-8). It is the prerogative of "Sovereign Yahweh" (Hebr., *'ădōnāy yhwh*; Isa. 56:8, AT), however, to include among those to whom he extends his "salvation" (v. 1, NASB) all "who join themselves to [Yahweh]" (v. 6, NASB).

See also Call of God; Idolatry; Poor/Poverty; Word of God/Yahweh, The.

Resources
Oswalt, John N. *The Book of Isaiah, Chapters 1-39*. NICOT. Grand Rapids: Eerdmans, 1986.
———. *The Book of Isaiah, Chapters 40-66*. NICOT. Grand Rapids: Eerdmans, 1998.

BARRY L. ROSS, PHD

Jj

JEREMIAH, THEOLOGY OF

The book of Jeremiah gives a theological rationale for the destruction of **Jerusalem** by Babylon in 586 BC; the book also gives **hope** for the nation's return from its exile and its rebuilding in the promised land. The book accomplishes its theological task by linking contemporary events with God's purposive actions in history. In so doing, the prophet makes the theological claim that Yahweh, the God of Israel, is the Sovereign Lord of history. The book lacks a systematic expansion of this; however, we find it clearly expressed where the prophet speaks of **creation**, God's **covenant** with Israel, his relationship to the nations, his sovereign freedom, Israel's **sin** and God's **judgment**, Israel's restoration, and the power of **God's word**.

Contemporary scholars find evidence of the influence of Hosea and Deuteronomy on Jeremiah's theological thinking. Most recent scholars hold that the long, extended prose sermons in the book in their final form are the work of Deuteronomistic editors.

God the Creator

Jeremiah's claim of the sovereign lordship of God is linked to his understanding of God as the incomparable creator of the earth and the heavens (10:10; 51:15). Jeremiah's frequent use of the epithet "Yahweh of Hosts" (Hebr., *yhwh ṣĕbā'ôt*) (82x) shows his firm **belief** that the sovereignty and dominion of Yahweh the Creator extends over all forces and powers, both in heaven and on earth.

The Creator, the living and true God, is the source of life, life that no idols have the capacity to give (2:13). This incomparable "God of all flesh" (32:27, NRSV) is an all-powerful God; there is nothing too difficult for him (vv. 17, 27). Though the creator God is near to his creation, he is also far off; he fills the heavens and the earth, but he is in contact with every part of creation (23:23-24). Nothing in creation is hidden from him, and nothing in creation is outside of his sovereignty.

God's Covenant Relationship with Israel

Jeremiah emphasizes the sovereign God's covenant relationship with Israel, his "bride," a people "**holy**" to God (2:2-3, NRSV). God is Israel's "Father" (3:19, NRSV), and the shepherd who gathers his flock (23:3). God's covenant with Israel is clear in the portrayal of God as "your God" and Israel as "my people" (see variations of the covenant formula "You will be my people and I will be your God" in 30:22; 31:1; 32:38). God's covenant with Israel is eternal; it is the basis for Israel's hope in its continued existence as a people in the world (31:35-37). God promised not to reject Israel; this promise is grounded solely on God's faithfulness to the covenant with Israel's ancestors Abraham, Isaac, and Jacob (vv. 36-37). He offers a new covenant to the people who have broken their covenant with him (vv. 31-34).

God and the Nations in the World

The sovereign Creator of the universe, who has a special relationship with Israel, is also the sovereign God of the nations. He summons the kingdoms of the north to come and set up their thrones in Jerusalem (1:15). More specifically, he intends to bring the king of Babylon against Judah (20:4); the mighty king of the great empire will serve God as his servant, a vassal who is not free to act on his will or freedom (25:9). God determines and directs the destiny of the nations and uses them as agents of his sovereign plans and purposes (see chs. 27–29, 46–51). Babylon's destruction, accomplished by kings of the Medes, was Yahweh's "purposes against Babylon" (51:29, NRSV). Moreover, it was part of Yahweh's plan to restore the exiles of Israel to their homeland.

God's Sovereign Freedom

Jeremiah held God's sovereignty and his freedom in proper balance. God who determines the course of history is also open to changing his plans and purposes; he indeed changes his mind according to human response. The decisions he makes are not inflexible and final. In 18:1-12, using the image of a potter, God makes known his freedom to determine the destiny of nations and his freedom to change his plans. He declares the uprooting and destruction of nations but changes his mind when a nation repents of its **evil**. In the same way, he declares the building and planting of nations but changes his mind when the nation to which this word is spoken does evil in his sight. Jeremiah 18:1-12 is an excellent example of human freedom responding either positively or negatively to God's plans and purposes (see also 2:20; 6:16-17; 11:8; 13:11; 18:12; 22:21; 26:3; 36:3). He has chosen Babylon as the instrument of his judgment, but by calling Judah to submit to the yoke of Babylon, he gave the nation the opportunity to live (ch. 27). Ultimately, God's word of judgment on Judah became a reality, not because it was an unalterable decree, but precisely because Judah refused to give heed to God's repeated calls to repent and return to him.

Israel's Sin and God's Judgment

God's actions in history, according to Jeremiah, served, first and foremost, the purpose of bringing his harsh judgment on Judah. God announced his plan "to uproot and tear down, to destroy and overthrow" (1:10, NIV), to make the **land** and the city of Jerusalem desolate, because the people had rejected his *tôrâ* —his gracious instructions for faithful covenant living (6:19; 7:24; 8:9). The sin of Judah was deeply ingrained in the heart of the nation (17:1; see also 5:23; 9:26; 17:9). Judah rejected God and his appointed watchmen (6:16-17; see also 11:8; 13:11; 22:21). Jeremiah held the spiritual and political leaders of the covenant nation responsible for the impending death of the nation (5:12-14; 14:13-16; 21:1–22:30; 23:9-40). The prophet gave clear warning to Judah that the Babylonian invasion was Yahweh's punishment for its continued resistance to Yahweh's will (see chs. 27–28, 34, 37–38). The narratives in chapters 39–40 show that destruction of Judah and Jerusalem indeed happened.

Israel's Restoration

Jeremiah made clear that judgment was not God's final word to his people; beyond the days of uprooting and tearing down lie days of building and planting (1:10). The letter to the exiles of 597 BC conveyed Yahweh's plan to bring them back to their homeland (29:10-14). Like a shepherd, Yahweh would keep Israel his flock and lead them to their homeland (31:8-14; 32:37; 50:19). Yahweh would restore the fortunes of Israel (30:3, 18; 32:42-44; 33:7). God would set over his people faithful shepherds who would diligently administer justice and righteousness in the land (see 3:15; 23:1-9; 30:9; 33:15). Jeremiah's purchase of the land while he was in prison was the most incredible and outrageous display of **hope** in the return of normal life in the land (ch. 32).

Jeremiah also proclaimed God's healing of his people who had refused to come to him, their physician (30:12-17; 33:6; see 8:22). God would forgive and pardon the nation and cleanse it from its sin and guilt (33:8; 50:20). He would enter into a new covenant with the restored, forgiven, and cleansed nation; the laws of the new covenant would be written on the heart of individuals (31:31-34). The new covenant also promised Yahweh's forgiveness of Israel; he would remember Israel's sin no more (v. 34). In the restored community, all would know Yahweh and all would enjoy the gift of the singleness of heart to live in **obedience** and **fear of Yahweh** (v. 34; 32:39-40). Moreover, the covenant with Israel would be an eternal covenant (32:40).

God's Sovereign Word

The book, from beginning to end, shows how God's sovereign word was at work in Judah's national life, including the life of the prophet, as well as in the international scene. It was this sovereign word that called and appointed Jeremiah to be a prophet to the nations (1:4-10). **God's word** has power (vv. 9-10). The prophet himself experienced the destructive power of the word on those who resisted him; he says, "His word is in my heart like a fire, / a fire shut up in my bones" (20:9, NIV). Priests, prophets, people, kings, royal family, the temple worship, nations in the world—all came under the judgment of the word (2:4-13; 5:30-31; 7:1-15; 8:8-12; 20:1-6; 21:1–22:30; 25:1-38). Rejection of the word meant tragic consequences (see chs. 39–41). However, the word also brought about restoration and rebuilding, healing, covenant renewal, faithful **leadership**, and secure life in the land. The divine word, graciously spoken, was thus the hope of the nation under judgment (see chs. 30–33).

The book acknowledges that God's word was often distorted and contradicted by false prophets who claimed to have their authority from God to deliver the word. False prophets derived words from the visions of their hearts and delivered falsehoods; however, the people loved to hear those words that offered them **peace** and well-being. They rejected and ridiculed the true words of God spoken by the true prophet. God's sovereign word ultimately triumphed and revealed the falsity of words spoken in his name by false prophets (6:13-15; 14:13-16; 23:9-40; 28:1-17).

Finally, Yahweh's sovereign word cannot be silenced or destroyed. King Jehoiakim tried to silence Yahweh's word by burning the scroll of Jeremiah (see ch. 36). The survival of the book and its placement in the Hebrew Scriptures is a remarkable testimony to the power of Yahweh's sovereign word.

ALEX VARUGHESE, PHD

JERUSALEM

Jerusalem functioned as the political and religious capital of the people of Israel throughout the Old, Intertestamental, and New Testament periods. The name "Jerusalem" (Hebr., yĕrûšālayim; Gk., Iepousalēm) is derived from two Semitic words meaning "foundation of **peace**." Originally a Canaanite city, its name is attested as early as the nineteenth and eighteenth centuries BCE in the Egyptian Execration Texts and in the fourteenth-century BCE Amarna Letters. Jerusalem also figured prominently in the annals of the Assyrian king Sennacherib, which date to biblical times (eighth century BCE).

Throughout the OT, Jerusalem is identified by various names. It was known simply as Salem (Hebr., šālēm) in the Abrahamic traditions (Gen. 14:18). In premonarchical narratives the city is called Jebus and was inhabited by a people known as the Jebusites (Judg. 1:21; 19:10-11; 2 Sam. 5:6), a subgroup of various peoples generally labeled "Canaanite" (Gen. 10:15-18; Josh. 3:10). In other texts, Jerusalem is associated with Moriah, the location where God called Abraham to sacrifice Isaac (Gen. 22:2), as well as the site where Solomon constructed the temple complex (2 Chron. 3:1).

Although the city appears in premonarchical accounts, it did not come under Israelite control or attain political and religious significance for the nation of Israel until the time of David. After he was anointed king over the Israelite tribes (2 Sam. 5:1-5), David and his warriors captured Jebus and established it as the capital city of the newly formed united monarchy (vv. 6-10). With this conquest complete, Jerusalem came to be known as the "city of David" (v. 9; 1 Chron. 11:7, NASB). The city of David occupied only a portion of Jerusalem, but the title was used as a synonym for the city as a whole.

The name "Zion" also became equated with the city of David and the city of Jerusalem. The term does not appear often in narrative contexts but is used frequently in poetic and figurative language (Ps. 87:2; Isa. 60:14; Heb. 12:22; Rev. 14:1). At other times, the terms "daughter of Zion" or "virgin daughter of Zion" were applied in a broad sense to describe Jerusalem (Ps. 9:14 [15 HB], NASB) or the people of Israel (2 Kings 19:21, NASB).

David's decision to establish Jerusalem as the capital of Israel changed the nature and status of the city profoundly. Zion served not only as the political hub of David's kingdom but more importantly as the epicenter for the religious life of the king and the people. In a highly symbolic gesture, one of David's first official acts as king was to transport the ark of the covenant to Jerusalem (2 Sam. 6:1-19). This move showed deference to the northern tribes, for whom the ark was an important religious object, but it also demonstrated that the holy presence of God, which rested on the outstretched wings of the cherubim (Ps. 80:1 [2 HB]; Isa. 37:16), would dwell in the heart of the nation. God's presence took up more permanent residence in Jerusalem when the ark was deposited in the temple Solomon constructed (1 Kings 8:1-21). The text speaks of God being "enthroned in Zion" (Ps. 9:11 [12 HB], NIV), with the temple serving as God's "dwelling place" (76:2 [3 HB], NIV), and Zion as the location where God's name took up residence (Isa. 18:7).

With these developments, a unique theological relationship grew between God, the Davidic king, and the city of Jerusalem-Zion. The king enjoyed the special status as the adopted son of God (Ps. 2:7), who ruled on behalf of God to ensure justice and righteousness in Israel's community (72:1-4). Zion was the holy city where God reigned with his servant, the king. Consequently, the city and people could expect special succor and protection from God in times of calamity or distress (a concept known as Zion theology). This theological notion proved true when God protected the city from the Israelite-Syrian threat during the reign of King Ahaz (2 Kings 16;

Isa.7:1-16), and again in the days of King Hezekiah, when God rescued Jerusalem miraculously from the powerful army of the Assyrian king Sennacherib (2 Kings 19; Isa.37:14-38).

Over time, however, the people grew complacent, falsely believing God would always protect the city, whether they abided by God's **covenant** standards or not. The prophet Jeremiah strenuously confronted this erroneous assumption in his famous temple sermon, stating that the city and the people were not immune from destruction if they did not amend their ways (Jer. 7:1-15). The inhabitants did not heed Jeremiah's warnings, and God allowed the Babylonians to capture the city (586 BCE), burn down the temple, and deport the Davidic king to Mesopotamia (2 Kings 25; Jer. 39). Zion's capture by a foreign army and the subsequent Babylonian exile created a profound existential crisis that prompted serious theological questions in the minds of the people about the **justice** and fairness of God (Ps. 44), the reasons the catastrophe took place, and what their relationship with God would be like going forward (Deut. 30:1-10; 1 Kings 8:33-53; Isa. 40–55).

Roughly fifty years after the destruction of the city, King Cyrus of Persia defeated the Babylonian armies (539 BCE) and permitted the Jewish captives to return to Jerusalem (2 Chron. 36:22-23; Ezra 1:4) and rebuild the temple. Under the leadership of Zerubbabel (Ezra 2:2; 3:2) and the encouragement of the prophets Haggai (Hag. 1:1-8) and Zechariah (Zech. 1–8), the people completed the temple in 515 BCE. Under the direction of Nehemiah (445 BCE), the city walls were repaired (Neh. 2–6; 12:27-43). With the temple and city restored, Jerusalem served as the religious capital of Judea throughout the postexilic and intertestamental periods.

Jerusalem occupied an important place in the life of Jesus. During his ministry (John 2, 5, 7–10, 11–19), Jesus journeyed to Jerusalem to celebrate important religious holidays such as Passover, the Festival of Booths, and the Festival of Dedication (Hanukkah). The significant events of Holy Week took place in Jerusalem: Jesus's ride into the city (Matt. 21:1-11), the cleansing of the temple (vv. 12-17), the last supper with his disciples (Luke 22:7-23), his arrest and trial before Pilate (John 18:28-40), and his crucifixion (Mark 15:21-32).

After Jesus's **resurrection**, he instructed his disciples to remain in Jerusalem until the advent of the **Holy Spirit** (Acts 1:4). The church age was inaugurated in Jerusalem when the Holy Spirit descended upon believers during Pentecost and the first Christian community was formed (ch. 2).

As the **church** expanded into Gentile regions through missionary efforts, leaders of the church convened in Jerusalem (ca. 48-49 CE) to decide whether certain rituals of Judaism were necessary for Gentile converts to keep (15:1-21). About a decade later (58 CE), Paul returned to Jerusalem after his third missionary journey to worship at the temple (21:17-26).

This action led to his arrest and subsequent imprisonment in Rome (28:11-31). Shortly after Paul's martyrdom (ca. 64-65 CE), Jewish rebels revolted against Rome (66-70 CE). Led by the future emperor Titus, the Roman army captured and destroyed Jerusalem and the temple (70 CE).

Despite the tragedies of 586 BCE and 70 CE, biblical writers envisioned a hopeful future for the city in God's eschatological plan of redemption. God indicated through the **prophets** that a future deliverer-redeemer would come forth from Zion (Isa. 59:20; Rom. 11:26). From Zion God's instruction would go forth to all the nations (Mic. 4:1-4). There the Lord would rule forever (v. 7). The future redemptive role of Jerusalem is especially apparent in John's apocalyptic visions in Revelation. The "new Jerusalem" would descend out of heaven as the eternal dwelling place for those who belong to Christ (ch. 21).

See also Festivals; Names of God; Sacred Space; Sacred Times.

Resources

Batto, Bernard F., and Kathryn L. Roberts, eds. *David and Zion: Biblical Studies in Honor of J. J. M. Roberts*. Winona Lake, IN: Eisenbrauns, 2004.

Levenson, Jon D. *Sinai and Zion: An Entry into the Jewish Bible*. Minneapolis: Winston Press, 1985.

Routledge, Robin. *Old Testament Theology: A Thematic Approach*. Downers Grove, IL: IVP Academic, 2008.

KEVIN MELLISH, PHD

JESUS AND THE LAW

The **Gospels** depict Jesus not only as the perfect example of living according to God's law but also as the crucial interpreter of God's law.

As a first-century Jew, the majority of Jesus's interactions were with common people who were descendants of Abraham, just as he was. Jesus's teaching and ministry were punctuated by noteworthy interactions, often adversarial, with representatives from two of the three major competing sects of Judaism in his day, the Pharisees and the Sadducees. These sects distinguished themselves by how they applied the scriptural law.

Evaluating his teaching and the major points of contention with his fellow Jews, we can say with confidence that Jesus lived as a Jew seeking to observe the law *(tôrâ)*. As a teacher, he was concerned with providing his community of followers with the best way to implement God's law in their daily lives (equivalent to oral law). Jesus's debates and disagreements with his fellow Jews underscored the importance of the law.

One of the complicating features of determining Jesus's position on the law is that our stories of Jesus are found in four Gospels, each of which presents him through a different lens. "No two gospels are identical in their approach to Jesus' attitude towards the Law" (Loader 1997, 509).

Jesus's clearest statement on his particular perspective on the law is found in his **Sermon on the Mount** (Matt. 5:17-18). There we find Matthew's first use of *nomos*, "law," the Greek translation of the Hebrew word *tôrâ*. Jesus asserted that his coming was neither to destroy the law (v. 17) nor to alter it in the slightest (v. 18). Instead of reducing or undermining the law, Jesus insisted that he came to fulfill it (Gk., *plēroō*). He redoubled this point by dictating that one's **righteousness** must exceed that of the scribes and Pharisees—careful keepers of the law—in order to enter the **kingdom of heaven** (v. 20).

After Jesus's emphatic statement of commitment to preserving and fulfilling the law, the next section of teaching in the Sermon on the Mount represents an amplification of the law. Each instruction begins with some version of the formula "You have heard that it was said . . . But I tell you . . ." (vv. 21-22, 27-28, 31-32, 33-34, 38-39, 43-44, NIV). Instead of undercutting the law's instructions on murder, adultery, divorce, oaths, or retribution, Jesus intensified the demands on his followers. For example, instead of forbidding merely the act of murder (v. 21), Jesus identified anger and name-calling as making one liable to **judgment** (v. 22). In each instance, Jesus provided examples that illustrate the potential applications of his amplified laws—such as turning the other cheek and going the extra mile (vv. 39, 41)—each one challenging.

While Jesus's statements about his position on the law are clear within Matthew's Gospel, his interpretation of the law is much more complex in particular situations. Instead of citing precedent for his interpretations, he spoke as the authoritative interpreter of the law.

For instance, many of Jesus's debates with his fellow Jews began with their insistence that Jesus was breaking the law. Most often, they accused him of violating Sabbath laws by healing on the day reserved for rest. Each Gospel recounts at least one controversy that Jesus sparked by restoring people to health on the Sabbath.

One such instance in which Jesus healed a man with a withered hand, under the scrutiny of scribes and Pharisees, is repeated in three Gospels (Matt. 12:10-13; Mark 3:1-4; Luke 6:6-10). In Jesus's opinion, healing acts did not qualify as work but instead as doing good (Matt. 12:12; Mark 3:4; Luke 6:9).

In another instance, the Pharisees questioned Jesus about his disciples' breach of laws pertaining to working on the Sabbath, holding the teacher responsible for his students' actions (Matt. 12:1-2; Mark 2:24; Luke 6:2).

Luke and John further emphasized this conflict over Sabbath healing, citing several further occasions of healing and conflict (Luke 13:10-17; 14:1-6; John 5:1-16; 9:14-16). Jesus maintained that Sabbath laws do not exist in isolation: "The sabbath was made for humankind, and not humankind for the sabbath" (Mark 2:27, NRSV). That is, according to Jesus, the purpose of the commanded Sabbath rest (see Exod. 20:8-11; Deut. 5:15) is meant to benefit people rather than be a goal in and of itself.

Further, Jesus declared that "the Son of Man is Lord of the Sabbath" (Matt. 12:8; Mark 2:28; Luke 6:5, NIV). This statement of sovereignty is a further equation of Jesus with the ultimate Lawgiver, God. Jesus enacted authority in applying laws to human need (the "humane focus of Jesus' application of Torah" [Loader 1997, 520]).

Beyond the Sermon on the Mount, there were some situations in which Jesus's instructions served to make the law more stringent and others that diminished or nullified the law. In the former category, Jesus's guidelines on divorce (Matt. 19:3-12; Mark 10:2-12; Luke 16:18) were more rigid than Moses's (Deut. 24:1-4), as Jesus himself stated (Mark 10:5).

In the latter category of Jesus's diminishing of the law, Mark 7:14-23 includes Jesus's teaching on what makes a person clean or unclean. Mark further interjected a comment that implies a rejection of kosher food laws: "In saying this, Jesus declared all foods clean" (v. 19). It seems more likely that Mark saw a diminishing of food laws as an eventual outcome of Jesus's focus on the intention of the person rather than that Jesus himself canceled out the law's provisions. In fact, Peter's statement in Acts 10:14 makes clear that Jesus's disciples continued to follow the law's guidelines on **clean** and **unclean** foods even after Jesus's **resurrection** and ascension and the coming of the **Holy Spirit** at Pentecost.

Another diminishment of the law can be found in John's Gospel, in which Jesus seemed to distance himself from the law. He called it "your Law" when addressing his opponents (8:17; 10:34, NIV) or "their Law" when talking to his disciples about those who will persecute them (15:25, NIV).

Despite presenting an uneven portrait of Jesus's relationship to the law, the precedent and relevance of the OT is presumed in all four Gospels. Jewish holidays, cleansing practices, cultural mores, and stories constituted the backdrop for Jesus's ministry. In his teaching, Jesus also referred to "the Law and the Prophets" as likely shorthand for all of Israel's Scriptures (Matt. 5:17; 7:12; 11:13; 22:40; Luke 16:16; 24:44, NIV).

In each of these instances, Jesus assumed the ongoing authority of the Law and the Prophets for his followers. In John 1:45, Philip found Nathanael and told him that they had found the one foretold by Moses in the Law and the **Prophets**: "Jesus of Nazareth" (NIV). Thus Jesus both confirmed the authority of the Law and the Prophets and was confirmed by them as well.

When asked, "Which is the greatest commandment in the Law?" (Matt. 22:36, NIV), Jesus gave a twofold answer, quoting from Scriptures that require **love** of God and neighbor (vv. 35-40; Mark 12:28-34; see Lev. 19:18; Deut. 6:4-5). As Matthew tells the story, Jesus went on to say that these two commandments do not merely stand out from all the others but instead encompass them: "All the Law and the Prophets hang on these two command-ments" (Matt. 22:40, NIV).

A crucial legal concept in the OT is that of **covenant** (Hebr., *běrît*; Gk., *diathēkē*). The Israelites' obligation to the law given by God came because of a special relationship to God, secured by a covenant (Exod. 24:3-8). Jesus used covenantal language and connected it to his own blood (Matt. 26:28; Mark 14:24; Luke 22:20). Thus it is not only Jesus's life that shapes his fol-lowers' perspectives on how to live according to the law but also his death. It is Jesus's death that demonstrates the extent of the love that sums up the commandments (John 15:13; Rom. 5:8; 1 John 3:16; 4:10-11).

See also Festivals; Rest.

Resource

Loader, William R. G. *Jesus' Attitude towards the Law: A Study of the Gospels.* WUNT 2.97. Tübingen, DEU: Mohr Siebeck, 1997.

KARA J. LYONS-PARDUE, PHD

JESUS'S MINISTRY

In his public career Jesus personified ministry, and his humble, self-denying service is the norm and pattern for ministry today. The Greek word for min-istry (*diakonia*) literally means "waiting at table"; in the NT it came to mean the giving of service in **love**. Jesus's reinterpretation of the Messiah's actions and status as *diakonia* shocked and disturbed the Jews of his time. In fact, the idea of servant ministry continues to confuse and distress Jesus's disciples who are called to emulate him.

The Character of Jesus's Ministry

Jesus declared that he "did not come to be served, but to serve, and to give his life as a ransom for many" (Matt. 20:28, NIV). He said that he came to preach (Mark 1:38); he showed **compassion** and empathy for people (Matt. 9:36; Mark 1:41). When he healed the paralytic, Jesus demonstrated his authority to forgive **sins** for spiritual healing as well as physical healing (Mark 2:1-12; see also Matt. 9:6-8; Luke 5:24-25). He also demonstrated his authority over the **law**, the Sabbath, and the temple (Matt. 12:6; 21:23; Mark 11:27-28; Luke 20:2-8). Yet throughout his ministry Jesus's authority was questioned (cf. Matt. 7:28-29; Mark 1:27).

Although the crowds and the religious establishment did not recognize Jesus's authority, some outsiders did. The centurion who asked for Jesus's help for his paralyzed servant recognized Jesus's authority to make things happen at his command (Matt. 8:8-9). Jesus also conferred authority and responsibility on his disciples (Matt. 10:1; Luke 10:17, 19), and we share in that privilege.

Jesus revealed the character of God through his ministry; he was fully divine. But he was also fully human. He suffered the full range of **temptations** (Heb. 4:15) and emotions. He cried (John 11:33-38; Luke 19:41-44); he felt anger (Matt. 21:12; Mark 3:5; 11:15-17), pain (John 11:33-38), abandonment (Matt. 26:36-46; Mark 14:32-34; 15:34; Luke 22:40-46), grief (Matt. 26:38), and compassion (Matt. 14:14; Mark 1:41; Luke 7:13), as do all his followers in ministry.

Jesus's ministry was relational. He often addressed people by name, even awarding them a symbolic name. When he called Simon, son of Jonah, *Petros* (Gk., "rock"), Jesus declared this rock as the foundation of the **church** (Matt. 16:18). Other symbolic names included James and John as the "sons of thunder" (Mark 3:17, NIV). Jesus also offered relationship through his use of titles. He tenderly called the paralytic "son" (2:5, NIV) and the woman with issue of blood "daughter" (5:34, NIV). His physical touch also communicated intimacy. Contrary to the religious and cultural sensitivities of the time, Jesus touched the leper (1:41), Jairus's daughter (5:41), sick people in Nazareth (6:5), and the blind (Matt. 20:34; Mark 8:23). Jesus's approachability was evident, giving Greeks the temerity to seek an audience with him (John 12:20-22). Although the disciples did not understand, Jesus encouraged children to come to him (Matt. 19:13; Mark 10:14).

He who will be the judge of all was nonjudgmental, a friend to sinners (Matt. 11:19; Luke 7:34; 15:2). He responded to the needs of the people. He was sensitive to the woman who touched him in a crowd (Mark 5:24-34), told the truth to the wealthy young man (Matt. 19:16-22; Mark 10:17-22; Luke 18:18-23), questioned the man by the Bethesda pool (John 5:6-7), and discussed theology with the woman at the well (4:7-26).

Yet Jesus was not a mild man, as portrayed in some Sunday school stories. He was direct: he moved to the heart of a problem and confronted the issues. Examples include his challenge to the religious establishment (Matt. 23), the sons of Zebedee (Mark 10:35-40), Peter (8:33; 14:30, 37; John 21:15-17), and the disciples (Matt. 17:17; 19:14; Mark 4:40). He had no patience for those who would deter him from his goal, including his family (Matt. 12:46-50) and closest friends (16:23-24; Mark 8:33). He warned that his coming meant division and **judgment** as well as salvation: the wheat will be separated from the chaff (Matt. 3:12); family members will betray each other (10:21-22); and those who are not ready will be shut out (25:1-13; Luke 12:44-50).

Quests for the "Historical Jesus"

The Gospels are the primary documents for Jesus's ministry, although they are more theological than biographical. Since the eighteenth century, groups of scholars have tried to apply a variety of historical-critical methods to uncover the "historical Jesus." The first phase, which began in 1778, ended when Albert Schweitzer criticized the methodology in 1903. The result was to drive a wedge between the Jesus of history and the "Christ of faith." A "no quest" period (1903-53) was followed by a second quest, which employed different research criteria and gave rise to the Jesus Seminar. A third-quest label was applied to a group of scholars working independently in the 1980s.

While the quests asserted the historicity of Jesus, as well as a broad outline of his life, their portraits of Jesus varied widely from each other as well as from the Gospels. Looking more like a reflection of each author's agenda than "scientific" findings, Jesus was variously portrayed as a revolutionary who tried and failed, an apocalyptic prophet, or a great teacher and philosopher.

In our considered opinion, it is more helpful to concentrate on the canonical accounts and accept that their contents and purposes reveal God through the life and ministry of Jesus Christ.

Portrayals of Jesus's Ministry: The Synoptics and John

According to the Synoptics (Matthew, Mark, and Luke), Jesus's ministry began with his baptism by his cousin John near the Jordan River (Matt. 3:13-17; Mark 1:9; Luke 3:21). In this public act Jesus showed his **humility** (Matt. 3:14-15). The voice from heaven (Matt. 3:17; Mark 1:11; Luke 3:22) affirmed the baptism and revealed Jesus's divine-human personhood as well as God's approval of him.

Immediately following his baptism, the **Spirit** led Jesus into the Judean desert for forty days of **fasting**. Matthew and Luke emphasize Jesus's humanity by adding the understatement that, at the end of the forty days, Jesus was hungry. It was then that Satan came to "tempt" or "test" (Gk., *peirasmos*) him. Mark's sparse account (1:12-13) is expanded by Matthew (4:1-11) and Luke (4:1-13), which record the conversations between Jesus and the **devil**. The challenges recall Israel's testing in the wilderness and foreshadow Jesus's even greater trials. Satan's lies and Jesus's **integrity** as he countered the temptations with Scripture provide a model for Jesus's followers. The three specific temptations affirm Jesus's ministry and reinterpret false contemporary expectations of the **Messiah**. The narrative affirms the radical combination of Jesus's God-human ministry.

The fact that theological truth rather than historical precision is the focus of the Gospels is evidenced by the difficulty in pinpointing the exact historical beginning date and sequence of Jesus's ministry. Jesus began his ministry when he was "about thirty years old" (Luke 3:23, NIV). A comparison of biblical historical references (vv. 1-2; John 2:13-20; Acts 10:37-38) and external evidence (the dates of Tiberius's reign; the temple's reconstruction by Herod; the **marriage** of Herod Antipas to Herodias [see Matt. 14:4; Mark 6:18]) places the probable date at AD 27-29.

Whatever the precise historical dating might be, the Synoptic Gospels present a similar time line of Jesus's life. They emphasize his preaching (Gk., *kēryssō*; Matt. 4:17, 23), teaching (Gk., *didaskō*; v. 23; 5:2; 9:35), and miraculous activity (Gk., *therapeuō* [4:23; 8:16]; Gk., *sōzō* [9:21-22; Luke 8:36]). Within the context of Jesus's identity as the unique Son of God and **Savior** of the world, the account of Jesus's ministry and acceptance by the people is juxtaposed with that of a growing hostility from the Jewish religious establishment. Approximately one-third of the content of the Synoptics focuses on Jesus's ministry; then the pace slows significantly to concentrate on the final week of Jesus's life (his death and **resurrection**). In Acts 10:37-38, Peter succinctly summarized Jesus's ministry as "doing good and healing" those "under the power of the devil" (NIV).

John's **Gospel** provides a different time line, where Jesus teaches in discourses rather than parables and where miracles are interpreted as "signs" (Gk., *sēmeia*). According to the Synoptics, after his baptism and **temptation** in the **wilderness**, Jesus returned to Galilee. There he began his ministry by proclaiming the arrival of the **kingdom of God** and urging people to repent and **believe** the gospel (Mark 1:14-15). John's Gospel records three trips to **Jerusalem** for Passover; there may have been more (see 21:25).

In the Synoptics Jesus began his ministry in the northern area of Galilee and moved south to Judea, eventually arriving in Jerusalem for Passion Week. The emphasis on this single Easter-centered Passover suggests that the trajectory of Jesus's ministry moved steadfastly toward the cross. This north-to-south geographical theology is further heightened by Peter's declaration that Jesus is the Messiah (Matt. 16:16; Mark 8:29; Luke 9:20) in northern Galilee. After this climactic event, according to the Synoptics, Jesus determinedly "set out for Jerusalem" (Luke 9:51, NIV). Jesus moved from the high point of Peter's declaration in the far north of Israel to his death in Jerusalem in Judea amid growing opposition. As he traveled southward, Jesus repeatedly forewarned his disciples of his death (Matt. 16:21-22; 17:22-23; 20:17-19; Mark 8:31-38; 9:30-32; Luke 9:22-25). Although John's time line is different, he also includes Jesus's statement of the necessity of his death (12:20-26).

John's rather different portrait of Jesus's gospel begins with a prologue that introduces Jesus as the preincarnate **Word of God**. This high Christology is developed throughout John as titles such as "Only Begotten" (Gk., *monogenēs*) are added to the Synoptic titles. In addition, Jesus reveals himself through the "I Am" (Gk., *egō eimi*) sayings (see below).

Jesus's Ministry as Preacher-Teacher

Jesus was widely recognized as a great preacher-teacher. He called people to repent of their sins and to devote themselves completely to God. He taught people to follow the **law**, which he reinterpreted from the rabbis' perversion of it. He practiced a peripatetic style of teaching that dates back to Aristotle and was practiced by first-century rabbis. His teaching, as he walked through the countryside of Israel, was effective: large crowds gathered to listen to this rabbi who healed both the body and the soul.

Introductory summary statements in the Synoptics (e.g., Luke 4:14-15) tell of the acclaim Jesus received in the beginning of his ministry. This adulation quickly changed when he attended the synagogue in his hometown of Nazareth. There he read Isaiah 61:1-2 and announced that he was the fulfillment of the **prophecy**. The crowd was amazed but rejected Jesus when they realized the significance of his words (Luke 4:16-30; see Matt. 13:53-58; Mark 6:1-6). This motif of amazement and rejection continued throughout Jesus's ministry.

The most well-known and most often-quoted example of Jesus's preaching is the **Sermon on the Mount** (Matt. 5–7). Luke includes most of the teachings scattered throughout his Gospel. Some are collected with modification in the Sermon on the Plain (Luke 6:17-49). It may be that memories of the teachings differed or that Jesus spoke more than once on the same subject with different emphases.

The Sermon on the Mount, which begins with the memorable Beatitudes, is full of lively word pictures. It also includes commandments, exhortations, propositional statements, theological arguments, and warnings. The Sermon on the Mount calls disciples to live out Christlike lives, to live authentically in both their public and private lives.

The parable (Gk., *parabolē*) is one of the most striking of Jesus's teaching genres in the Synoptics. These deceptively simple word pictures convey profound spiritual lessons. Many of Matthew's kingdom parables have an eschatological perspective. Mark's parables illustrate the power and rule of God. Luke's unique parables focus on **repentance** and salvation. Jesus's parables are clear and simple, making the message accessible and calling listeners to repentance and **faith**. They arouse interest and are easily memorable, yet their riddle-like format often shocked and challenged Jesus's first-century audience. The hearers included the disciples, the crowds following Jesus, and those who opposed him. The chief priests and elders surely saw themselves in the parables of the two sons, the tenants, and the wedding banquet. In response to questions about his use of parables after Jesus had told the parable of the soils, Jesus quoted Isaiah 6:9-10, explaining that parables accomplish their tasks for those who are willing to hear but that those who oppose and reject Christ can neither comprehend their truth nor understand Jesus (Matt. 13:10–17; Mark 4:10–12; Luke 8:9–10).

Although the message of Jesus's teaching in John is the same as the Synoptics, the form is quite different. Instead of short, pithy sayings and stories using similes, Jesus gives a number of lengthy discourses. Most of chapter 10 consists of the discourse on the Good Shepherd, and chapters 14–17 constitute the farewell discourses. The discourses contain metaphors and other symbolic language that are often difficult to follow. They speak about living a life of faith in difficult circumstances and probably reflect the church-synagogue debates at the time when John's Gospel was written (i.e., the last decade of the first century).

One of the most striking ways Jesus communicates in John is his "I Am" (*egō eimi*) sayings that recall God's self-identification to Moses (Exod. 3:14). Seven have predicate nominatives explaining facets of Jesus's person and work: John 6:35, 48, "the bread of life"; 8:12 and 9:5, "the light of the world"; 10:9, "the gate"; v. 11, "the good shepherd"; 11:25, "the resurrection and the life"; 14:6, "the way and the truth and the life"; and 15:1, "the true vine" (NIV).

The **kingdom of God** is the central theme of Jesus's teaching and the foundational message of the **church**. The Gospels refer extensively to the term (4x in Matt., 14x in Mark, 31x in Luke, and 1x in John). Because of the Jewish ban on using the name "God," Matthew more often (31x) uses "kingdom of heaven." Mark explains that Jesus preached the gospel (good news) of the kingdom of God and urged people to repent and believe in the gospel (1:15; see also Matt. 4:17; Luke 8:1). Jesus inaugurated the kingdom through his **incarnation**. His life, death, and **resurrection** enabled his follow-ers to live lives under his reign, and that is the good news he proclaimed. But this kingdom is not yet consummated. Jesus called people to love God and others (Matt. 22:36-38; see Mark 12:28-30; Luke 10:25-28) until he returns to bring heaven to earth. After training his twelve disciples, Jesus sent them out to preach the kingdom of God and heal the sick (Luke 9:2).

After his crucifixion and resurrection, Jesus appeared before the dis-ciples and continued teaching about the kingdom of God (Acts 1:3). He trained his disciples to proclaim the message, and that is the task of the church until Christ's return. We are to live into the kingdom sharing the good news through the Spirit's empowerment.

Jesus's Miracles and "Signs"

Jesus's miracles demonstrated his power and authority over the earthly realm. His ministry included many individual miracle stories as well as nu-merous summary statements of his healing the sick, casting out **demons**, and performing signs and wonders (see Matt. 4:23-25; 9:35; Mark 1:32-34). Al-though the miracles can be divided in a variety of ways, there are two broad categories: nature and healing.

Nature miracles are varied and serve as enacted parables to teach a va-riety of lessons, including Jesus's power, trust, and priorities. The miracles are also varied in content and context: calming the storm (Matt. 8:23-27; Mark 4:37-41; Luke 8:22-25), walking on water (Matt. 14:25; Mark 6:48-51), the withered fig tree (Matt. 21:18-22; Mark 11:12-14, 20-21), coin in fish's mouth (Matt. 17:24-27), and miraculous catches of fish (Luke 5:1-11; John 21:1-11). A subset of nature miracles are abundance miracles, which serve similar functions. They include changing water into wine (John 2:1-11), the feeding of five thousand (Matt. 14:15-21; Mark 6:35-44; Luke 9:12-17; John 6:5-13), and the feeding of four thousand (Matt. 15:32-38; Mark 8:1-9).

The Gospels record three instances of Jesus's raising people from the dead: Jairus's daughter (Matt. 9:18-26; Mark 5:31-43; Luke 8:40-56), a widow's son at Nain (Luke 7:11-17), and Lazarus (John 11:1-44). Each not only shows Jesus's **compassion** but also incorporates a more nuanced message in its context.

Individual healing miracles abound (thirty to forty, depending on how they are categorized). They emphasize Jesus's healing power, but as with the other miracles, each showcases a profound lesson. An obvious example is when Jesus both heals and forgives a paralytic (Matt. 9:1-8; Mark 2:1-12; Luke 5:17-26). Often Jesus told recipients of healing that it was their **faith** that had healed them, so the main focus was not on Jesus's power to heal. Bartimaeus was told that his faith had healed him (Mark 10:46-52; see also Matt. 9:27-30; Luke 18:35-43).

Mark, the briefest of the Gospels, devotes the most space to healing miracles, usually giving the recipients a voice. A frequent motif is that the people ask Jesus to heal them and tell Jesus that they believe in his power to heal (e.g., Matt. 8:2; Mark 1:40; Luke 5:12). Sometimes, attention to the details of the physical ailments emphasizes the **suffering** of the individuals. The suffering of the woman with the issue of blood (Matt. 9:20-22; Mark 5:25-34; Luke 8:43-48) is very clear. Jesus sometimes uses folk remedies to gain the confidence of the sufferer. In one such case Jesus told a man born blind to "wash in the pool of Siloam" (John 9:7, NIV). John uniquely emphasizes the significance or purpose of Jesus's miracles. John highlights only a few miracles, which he labels "signs" (*sēmeia*). These signs, like the miracles of the Synoptics, do more than illustrate Jesus's power; they give evidence of who Jesus is as well as his purpose on earth.

See also Forgiveness, The Art and Necessity of; Holy Spirit.

CAROL ROTZ, DLITT ET PHIL

JESUS'S VICTORY OVER SIN AND DEATH

The crucifixion of Jesus gave all the appearances of the defeat of **righteousness** and the triumph of **evil**, yet the early **church** constantly emphasized that through his death on the cross Jesus triumphed over the powers of evil (Col. 2:15). The Bible does not give us a "theory of the atonement" but rather gives us a series of images that are found throughout the OT and that find completion in the NT as they relate to Christ and his cross.

Sacrifice of Atonement

In many cultures around the world, people **believe** that restoring broken relationships requires the giving of a gift. The bigger the wrong, the bigger the gift or sacrifice required. The greater the person or deity offended, the greater the gift needed.

God's **love** for humanity and all of **creation** is strong and intense. Consequently God's intense reaction to all that is evil and destructive of what he has made can only be described as **wrath**. In order for relationships to be restored, the wrath must be appeased.

God in his **grace** "presented Christ as a sacrifice of atonement" (Rom. 3:25, NIV) so that we may be put right with God. Motivated by **love**, Jesus gave himself as an atoning **sacrifice** to reconcile us to God. "God took his own loving initiative to appease his own righteous anger by bearing it his own self in his own Son when he took our place and died for us" (Stott 1986, 174).

Redemption

The imagery of sacrifice came from the temple. The imagery of **redemption** came from the **slave** market. We as sinners are held in captivity, and only a ransom can set us free. That ransom is nothing less than the **Messiah**'s own life. Jesus said the Son of Man came to "give his life as a ransom for many" (Mark 10:45, NIV).

Justification

Justification refers to our being forgiven and restored to a righteous standing before God. This follows logically from the previous two points. Because the sacrifice of atonement has been made and we have been redeemed by the blood of Jesus, we can now be forgiven and declared righteous by God.

Reconciliation

Justification refers to our legal standing before our judge in the court. **Reconciliation** refers to our personal relationship with our heavenly Father. Closely associated with this is the concept of adoption, which refers to our becoming children of God. As a result, we have access to God and "may approach God with freedom and confidence" (Eph. 3:12, NIV).

Jesus came to give his life as a sacrificial atonement to redeem, justify, and reconcile us to God. Peter declares that the work of Jesus on the cross was made possible because of Jesus's sinless life: "You were redeemed . . . with the precious blood of Christ, a lamb without blemish or defect" (1 Pet. 1:18-19, NIV).

Jesus's Path to Victory

The **Gospels** show Jesus deliberately and consciously moving toward the cross. When Peter tried to dissuade him from this direction, Jesus turned abruptly to Peter and said, "Get behind me, Satan" (Matt. 16:23, NIV).

The Gospels give us no description of the crucifixion, but they do describe in detail the events leading up to it. Jesus was weakened physically by the flogging. He was hurt emotionally and psychologically by the betrayal, denial, and desertion of his disciples and the rejection of the people and the religious leaders. He was publicly humiliated by spitting, mocking, and nakedness.

During his crucifixion Jesus was mocked and tempted by the chief priests, teachers of the **law**, elders, bystanders, soldiers, and criminals (27:39-44) as they said, "Save yourself! Come down from the cross" (v. 40, NIV). However, Jesus was obedient unto death and in so doing took upon himself the sins of the world, vanquishing the forces of the tempter. His self-giving love conquered evil with good. He overcame pride with **humility**, arrogance with meekness, and selfishness by laying down his life as a sacrifice for others. Jesus was obedient unto death, and by his **obedience**, love, and meekness, he won a great moral and spiritual victory.

John Wesley wrote, "Satan brought in **sin**, and sin brought forth death. And Christ, when he of old engaged with these enemies, first conquered Satan, then sin, in his death; and, lastly, death, in his **resurrection**" ([1755] 1981, comment on 1 Cor. 15:26).

Jesus's Victory

When Jesus, the Author of Life, entered the world of the dead, the cosmos changed forever. The "earth shook," "tombs broke open" (Matt. 27:51-52, NIV), and dead people came to life (vv. 52-53). Death could not hold Jesus because it had no power over him (Acts 2:24).

The OT pictured death as a black hole into which people went but never returned. After the death and resurrection of Jesus, the concept of death was changed forever. Now it is described as sleeping, implying that it is temporary until Christ returns (1 Thess. 4:13-17).

The NT emphasizes the resurrection from the dead. Our baptism is a visible declaration of our **faith** in Jesus's death and resurrection. Through it we experience death to sin and the beginning of a new life in Christ (Rom. 6:2-10).

By his perfect obedience, which led to death on the cross, Jesus defeated Satan and provided atonement for **sin**. The victory over sin, death, and the **devil** was won at the cross. The resurrection vindicated that this Jesus who died on the cross was the Son of God and that his sin-bearing death had been effective for the **forgiveness** of sins and our reconciliation with God.

Resources

Stott, John. *The Cross of Christ*. Leicester, UK: Inter-Varsity Press, 1986.

Wesley, John. *Explanatory Notes upon the New Testament*. 1755. Reprinted in 2 vols. Kansas City: Beacon Hill Press of Kansas City, 1981.

NEVILLE BARTLE, DMISS

JUDGMENT

A word in any language gets its meaning when it is used in a phrase or sentence within a specific context. The word "judgment," either in its nominal (Hebr., *mišpāṭ*; Gk., *krisis* or *kriseōs*) or its verbal form (Hebr., *šāpaṭ*; Gk., *krinō*), expresses different senses when used within different contexts in the Bible. It expresses the legal act of a judge, a **law**giver, or a governor who decides on controversies between people, condemning the wrongdoer and exonerating the innocent. The judgment is done in reference to the law, which can be domestic, civil, political, or religious. The one judging sits, hears a case, and renders a proper verdict (Deut. 1:16) or defends the right of a defendant.

In the OT, not only did God pronounce judgment, but he also enlisted human beings to act as judges. Moses with his assistants (Exod. 18:13, 24-25), as well as judges (Judg. 4:4-5) and kings (1 Kings 3:16-28), rendered judgment.

As the Just Judge, God in his sovereignty judges justly the whole earth (Gen. 18:25). The major **prophets** proclaimed God's judgment against the nations that surrounded Israel, including Egypt (Isa. 19–20; Jer. 46; Ezek. 29–32), Moab (Isa. 15–16; Jer. 48:1-22; Ezek. 25:8-11), Tyre (Isa. 23; Ezek. 26–28), and Babylon (Isa. 21; Jer. 50–51). God did not spare even his own people when they broke the **covenant** by worshipping other gods, corrupting **justice**, and exploiting the **poor**. Judgment fell first on Israel when Sargon II of Assyria in 721 BC breached the walls of Samaria, defeated the Israelite army, and deported the survivors (2 Kings 17:6-17). Judah survived another 130 years until Nebuchadnezzar of Babylon in 586 BC took **Jerusalem**; burned the city, including the temple; and deported all the people except the poorest of the land (25:1-12). However, God is just, even in his judgment. The prophet of the exile proclaimed that God had not forgotten his people. Their exile would end, and they would return to Jerusalem (Isa. 54:1-15). The God of Israel used Cyrus the Persian to conquer Babylon (45:1-4) and in 538 BC proclaim the people's release. The exiles were free to return to Jerusalem (Ezra 1:1-4).

In the Greek NT, like the LXX, the verb *krinō* has a wide range of meanings: "think," "evaluate" (Rom. 14:5; Acts 13:46), "criticize" (Matt. 7:1; James 4:11), "resolve," "determine" or "decide" (Acts 16:4), "condemn," "administer **justice**," or "punish" (2 Thess. 2:12). In Luke 22:30, it has the sense of "ruling" or "governing."

"Judgment" can express a reward or a punishment, making a decision, ruling or governing. When it refers to the "judgment day," the "day of the Lord," the "judgment seat," it is final (2 Cor. 5:10). While it may refer to how God has judged his people in the past, God also judges what humanity is doing presently: polluting the earth, committing genocide, bombing innocent people in terror attacks, and committing all sorts of gender-based violence.

Though the judgment has been carried out by God in the past and in the present, there will come a final judgment day, fixed by God. All will be judged by God through his Son, Jesus, the "Light [who] has come into the world" (John 3:19, NIV), for the responsibility of this judgment has been given to the Son (5:22). The judgment will be done according to what is written in the books, including "the book of life" (Rev. 20:12, NIV). This final judgment will result in the reward of eternal life for those who will have lived responsibly according to the law of God (21:1-4) and in the condemnation of damnation in fire for those who will have refused the salvation offered to all by God through the Son (20:15). This judgment will be just to the point that, according to Henry C. Thiessen (1999, 431), no one will complain or will have a reason to complain.

See also Eschatology.

Resources

Strong, James. Pages 642, 1199 in *The New Strong's Expanded Dictionary of Bible Words.* Nashville: Thomas Nelson, 2001.

Thiessen, Henry C. *Guide de doctrine biblique: Fondement d'une vie nouvelle.* Lennoxville, QC: Paroles de vie, 1999.

AGNÈS UWIMANA IBANDA, MA

JUSTICE, NEW TESTAMENT

The justice of God in the NT is a particular expression of God's overall approach to the human race since **creation: reconciliation** and unstinting **love**. Because God created humans in and for love, God treats people justly (with **righteousness**). The Greek stem *dik* lends itself to being translated as "right," "righteous," or "righteousness," as well as "just" and "justice." Thus the "righteousness of God" could be rendered the "justice of God." Jesus is called the "Righteous ["Just," *dikaios*] One" (Acts 3:14; 7:52; 22:14, NIV).

God's justice includes God's impartiality in salvation. Both Jew and Gentile are welcomed (Rom. 1:16-17). Also, John 3 affirms that God's love extends to the entire world.

In Luke 18:1-8 Jesus depicted God's justice in contrast to the way humans sometimes dispense justice. The unrighteous judge first refused to give the widow her just claim. After the widow pled often with him, the judge finally gave in, fearing that she might attack him. However, God, unlike the unjust judge, cares for us and will hear our prayers and grant us justice without such long delay. God is just; God is our loving Father.

God demonstrates what is known as restorative justice by taking up the cause of those who are being treated unjustly by others. God not only extends proper treatment to those who are oppressed but also responds to the perpetrators of injustice through the corrective punishment of **sin**. God's laws call for the just treatment of one another and the proper treatment of God—namely, **repentance** and worship. Even God's enacting of justice in **judgment**, however, should be understood in the framework of shalom— namely, God working for the reconciliation and restoration of his creation.

Old Testament Background

In the Hebrew Scriptures, people are called on to refrain from stealing, withholding wages, lying, and killing. Instead, they are to treat others with respect. The people of God are to go beyond refraining from harm; they are to love one another. The just treatment of the other is part of loving one's neighbor as oneself (Lev. 19:18*b*). Loving one's neighbor functions as the summation of ethical instruction (Wolterstorff 2011, 83).

God's people are also called on to right the wrongs of injustice, which too often cause **suffering**, to restore justice to those to whom it has been denied. The **prophet** Isaiah's call for justice includes rescuing the oppressed, defending the orphan, and pleading "the case of the widow" (Isa. 1:17, NIV). God's people must take up the cause of the oppressed and protect the rights of the vulnerable, particularly the widows, the orphans, the **poor**, and the foreigners (Exod. 22:22; 23:9). This falls under the framework of loving one's neighbor. Those who love their neighbors will defend them against unjust treatment. The Israelites were called to lift the burden of the oppressed, be-cause God had acted to rescue them from slavery in Egypt. God is righteous and just, so God's people should be righteous and just.

New Testament Teachings

1. *Restorative Justice.* Some models of the atonement in the NT pick up the theme of restorative justice. One of the few times Jesus indicated what his death would mean, he used a metaphor of buying back the enslaved (Mark 10:45). Similarly, God loosing those suffering under the bondage of sin appears again in the claim that the ones set free by the Son "will be free indeed" (John 8:36, NIV). God is pictured as freeing the enslaved, relieving the oppressed.

Another set of images of salvation that point to God's efforts at restor-ative justice are the distance metaphors: once we were far off, strangers, but now are brought near (Eph. 2:11-22). Through Christ "those who were near" and "[those] who were far off" "have access in one Spirit to the Father" (vv. 17-18, NRSV). We were weak, we were sinners, and we were enemies of God, but Jesus came into the world to draw us near (Rom. 5). God orches-trated reconciliation through the death of Jesus (see 2 Cor. 5:19). God spans the breach between God and human beings through his love.

Sacrifice is another image of restorative justice, not a sacrifice that ap-peases God, but one that serves to expiate, or remove sin's stain and bondage through God's **grace**. By accepting the death on the cross, Jesus provided justification for those who have **faith** (Rom. 5:1-2, 9-21). Paul uses courtroom imagery in which the punishment borne by Jesus is a demonstration of love rather than a satisfaction of punishment. It is a rescue rather than a payment. Jesus took on our suffering, even the sense of being abandoned by God (Matt. 27:46; cf. Ps. 22:1 [2 HB]), out of a love and desire for renewed relationship.

The atonement itself is the expression of God's redemptive power breaking into the human race in order to restore relationship. Rather than a legal imputation of guilt, the cross is part of the larger picture of the **incarnation** and life of Christ: a demonstration of Christ's solidarity and identification with broken humanity. It is an expression of God's justice, as God intervenes to end alienation and to restore relationship.

2. *Corrective Justice.* Corrective justice is the other side of this coin. God takes up the cause of the oppressed, vindicating them by punishing the perpetrator. The punishment is not to satisfy God's anger or an arbitrary standard of **holiness** but to help the oppressors see the error of their ways. Even in judgment, God's own activity revolves around restoration. The **prophets** warned of impending **judgment**, including punishment for sins, but always in the context of redemption. They predicted the incursion of foreign armies, with the ultimate aim of turning the people of God from their sins and fostering renewed relationship with God. "Exile" was not the last word, but "return."

Paul took a similar approach (though on a smaller scale) in advocating redemptive shunning—that is, putting people out of the fellowship so they can see the error of their ways and be reconciled (1 Tim. 1:20). Justice includes setting things right.

Jesus's warnings about judgment serve the purpose of pulling people in so they can receive redemption. He spoke to his critics in parables and warnings, not out of a sense of gleeful retribution, but with the intent of drawing them into **belief** and **repentance**. Jesus did not come to condemn but to draw people into salvation. Yet he also claimed that God gave him authority to pass judgment and establish justice (John 5:2-30).

The theme of judgment, especially in the apocalyptic sermons of Jesus and the visionary material in Revelation (19:11-16), points to the conquest of **evil** by God. Ultimately, the Son of God, also depicted as the Lamb of God, will subdue the forces of evil that maim and destroy. In the final victory, Jesus, having established a reign of **peace** and justice, will be enthroned. All tears, and all cause for tears, will be wiped away (21:3-4).

God has also delegated authority to humans to administer justice (Rom. 13:1-7). Rulers are to enforce laws for the functioning of society and the right treatment of others. Jesus made an oblique statement about Pilate's authority. He had no power over Jesus, except that it was given by God (John 19:11).

3. *Jesus Enacted Justice.* Jesus enacted both restorative and corrective forms of justice. If justice is treating people as they deserve, giving all people the respect that their creation warrants, then Jesus demonstrated God's enacted justice. Jesus rejected the culturally sanctioned ill treatment of various low-status people. He welcomed **women** to his circle of disciples (Luke 8:1-3) and endorsed Mary's choice to listen at his feet (10:38-42). He included some of the most despised men into his group of followers: tax collectors Matthew and Zacchaeus. He interacted with the ceremonially unclean (bleeding women, lepers, and the dead) and socially marginal (Samaritans, children, beggars, and prostitutes). He transgressed social boundaries with the apparent intent of critiquing injustice. In acting this way, Jesus reinforced the law's requirement that people should treat one another justly, thus living out the commandment to love one's neighbor. Furthermore, Jesus sometimes predicated admission into eternal life on the treatment of the other (see Matt. 25 and Luke 16).

Economic justice, a requirement of the people of God in the OT, is reiterated in the teaching of Jesus. The rich should host not just the wealthy but also "the poor, the crippled, the lame, the blind," those who were socially marginalized (Luke 14:12-14, NIV).

Jesus also symbolically enacted the corrective justice of God. The cursing of the fig tree (Mark 11:12-21) and the cleansing of the temple (Matt. 21:12-13) foreshadow the more complete judgment Jesus will exercise at the consummation of his kingdom (Rev. 20:11-15).

It is not just the Gospels that highlight the theme of economic justice as an expression of Christian piety. Luke describes how the nascent believing community shared all things (Acts 4:32-37). Paul urged the Gentile churches to prepare a large offering for the famine relief of the church in Jerusalem (1 Cor. 16:1-4; 2 Cor. 8:1–9:5). Paul also touched on this theme in his description of the Jerusalem Council (Gal. 2:1-9). The one thing the leaders in Jerusalem asked Paul and his fellow missionaries to do was to "remember the poor, which was actually what I was eager to do" (v. 10, NRSV). In this regard, Paul agreed with James that it is a Christian duty (privilege) to care for the poor around us (James 2:14-17) and thus reflect the justice of God.

Resource
Wolterstorff, Nicholas. *Justice in Love.* Grand Rapids: Eerdmans, 2011.

KRISTINA LACELLE-PETERSON, PHD

JUSTICE, OLD TESTAMENT

Justice is a significant theological concept in the Bible. It is central to the **covenant** between God and humanity. It defines the character for proper relationship by establishing the attitudes, actions, and regulations necessary to create *šālôm* (Hebr., "wholeness" or **"peace"**) in **creation**.

The Hebrew root *šāpaṭ* (judge) and its cognates *mišpāṭ* (justice) and *mišpāṭîm* (judgments) occur over six hundred times in the OT, highlighting the importance of this concept. Many of the occurrences of justice take place alongside two other important concepts: **"righteousness"** (*ṣĕdāqâ*) and "steadfast **love**" (*ḥesed*). This triad of right action, covenantal love, and judgment form a basis for understanding how Israel thought about its relationship with God and God's action in the world.

One of Israel's primary theological claims was that YHWH is "gracious," "merciful," "slow to anger," and "abounding in steadfast love" but also punishing the wicked "to the third and the fourth generation" (Exod. 34:5-7, NRSV). Thus justice is the lived expression of a covenantal relationship with God. It is based on God's righteous nature and **mercy** toward humanity. Yet it does not allow that which is opposed to God's purposes, also known as injustice (Hebr., *'āwel*), to continue to exploit and disrupt creation.

This article explores this understanding of justice in the OT as it relates to Israel's understanding of God's character of justice and humanity's responsibility to work with God for justice in creation.

God and Justice in the Old Testament

Israel believed that one of the main characteristics of its God, YHWH, is justice. The psalmist declares that YHWH is the true God because the Holy One judges rightly and takes care of the **poor** and needy (Ps. 82:3-4). Justice was simply part of what makes YHWH the true God and differentiates him from idols. Israel believed that God is just and that God's justice includes creating conditions that allow for the flourishing of humanity, especially those on the margins of society.

Other psalms proclaim justice as an essential part of God's character. "Righteousness and justice are the foundation of [God's] throne" (89:14 [15 HB], NRSV), and YHWH judges the cause of the righteous against the wicked and ungodly (43:1 [2 HB]).

In the book of Job, Elihu, the young spokesperson, argued that the Almighty is awesome in "power and justice," with "abundant righteousness" that will not be violated (37:23, NRSV).

The **prophets** also attested to this characteristic of God. When Micah asked rhetorically what God desires of humanity, the response was that humans are "to do justice, . . . to love kindness, and to walk humbly with your God" (Mic. 6:8, NRSV). What God desired of Israel was that it would learn to "seek justice" (Isa. 1:17, NRSV).

In Exodus YHWH is described as the mighty God who would deliver the Hebrew slaves "with mighty acts of judgment" (6:6, NRSV) against Pharaoh, who had set himself up as a cruel and unjust god. Moses, speaking for God, declares, "My ordinances [*mišpāṭay*] you will keep [because I am your God and I am holy]" (Lev. 18:4, AT).

The connection of God's **holiness** and just ordinances as **justification** for Israel's **obedience** is particularly important in the legal codes of the OT. Israel understood that YHWH is the "Lord of lords" (Deut. 10:17, NRSV) and acts justly by not taking bribes and by looking out for the widow, orphan, and sojourner (vv. 17-18).

These last three people groups were especially important to God. A number of texts include either all three or some selection of them for special mention in how God takes notice and treats them in ways that ensure their flourishing (Exod. 22:21; Ps. 146:9; Jer. 22:3). The people of Israel connected God's character with the justification for their obedience, giving special attention to care for the most vulnerable in creation. Additionally, there was a consistent reminder for the Israelites that they were once a part of the most vulnerable and therefore must always be committed to imitating their God's commitment to care for and ensure that those on the margins of society have the opportunity to flourish.

Humanity and Justice in the Old Testament

Because Israel's witness to God's character is particularly centered on YHWH's commitment to justice, much of the OT also includes texts that call humanity into the struggle for justice in creation. Israel understood God's creation of the world as a place of order and well-being (Gen. 1–2). Right relationships and the caretaking of creation create the conditions in which all are able to flourish. Unfortunately, humanity quickly and repeatedly has chosen the opposite of flourishing.

The first eleven chapters of Genesis weave a narrative of brokenness that lead to God's choice of a particular family in hope of restoring the initial blessings. God's entrance into a covenantal relationship with Abraham and Sarah includes the specific injunction that "in you all families of the earth will bless themselves" (12:3, AT).

1. *Abraham and God's Justice.* In the course of Abraham and Sarah's journey, the reader is constantly asking, How are the relationships displayed leading to blessing? One poignant example was when Abraham and God were discussing the fate of Sodom and Gomorrah, two cities whose injustice had come before God. God decided to tell Abraham what was going to be done to the two cities, because God had chosen him "to keep the way of the Lord by doing righteousness and justice" (Gen. 18:19, NRSV). Abraham responded by questioning God about what was to be done to the two cities: "Far be it from you! The judge of all the earth will not do justice!" (v. 25, AT).

This rich dialogue between Abraham and God highlights the importance of justice and injustice in the relationship between humanity and the Divine. To believe that justice is only a matter of obeying certain guidelines or that injustice is only a matter of choosing what consequences to mete out misses the nuances of Israel's testimony.

This dialogue illustrates the depths that Israel should go to explore the covenantal relationship between YHWH and humanity in order to create the conditions for the flourishing of all creation. God was engaged in an honest relationship with humanity, working to ensure that injustice would not go unnoticed.

One of the reasons the two cities were destroyed was their lack of hospitality and justice for the sojourner, "the poor and the needy" (Ezek. 16:49, NRSV). Thus Abraham and Sarah represent a significant narrative tradition in the OT about what it means to be human and live in covenant relationship with this God of justice.

2. *Justice and the Covenant.* Another narrative example of God's concern for justice is illustrated when God called Moses to help liberate the Hebrew slaves from Pharaoh's grasp and take them to Mount Sinai. There God commanded Moses to write on tablets a new covenant, which would set the guidelines for the covenant community. This covenant with its commandments was intended to enable the people to become a holy community among the nations so that God's just purposes might be fulfilled (Exod. 19:6).

The commandments also found in Leviticus and Deuteronomy made clear that they were intended to create the conditions for human flourishing and *šālôm* in creation. Israel was not to render unjust judgments but to be impartial in their cases (Lev. 19:15). Sojourners in Israel's midst could participate in the Passover if they desired, in effect allowing foreigners to become Israelites (Num. 9:14). Moses established cities of refuge to which persons who accidently killed another might flee (Deut. 4:41-43). These cities represent an attempt to extend the justice system to difficult cases and stop the cycle of violence that was prevalent in the ANE.

3. *Israel's Living Out Justice.* In the eras of the conquest, the judges, and the kings, God raised up leaders who would do justice and lead according to his character. The book of Joshua highlights Israel's journey into the land and its struggle to remain faithful to YHWH. The book ends, though, with Joshua at Shechem establishing a covenant with the people, together with statutes and justice (24:25).

In the book of Judges, God raised up charismatic leaders to deliver the Israelites. Because they had sinned God allowed them to be oppressed by foreign nations. Judges such as Othniel, Ehud, and Deborah were faithful in both delivering and judging Israel. However, toward the end of the book, the cycle of sin spun more out of control and Israel was forced to face the consequences of their injustice. In one of the most horrific narratives, a Levite allowed his concubine to be sexually abused and killed (ch. 19). This injustice sparked a war that decimated Israel. The book ends with an ominous phrase that highlights the depths of human deprivation: "At that time, there was no king in Israel and everyone did what was right in their own eyes" (21:25, AT).

This phrasing highlights the complete opposite of the covenant in which God desires Israel to live, the complete opposite of human flourishing and wholeness in creation.

In the books of Samuel and Kings, God raised up new leaders who in varying levels of success and failure sought to imitate God's call for justice. David was one of the high marks with regard to justice. Though he was certainly flawed, 2 Samuel 8:15 states that David was a king who reigned in righteousness and justice. David's son Solomon prayed for understanding to judge rightly (1 Kings 3:9). Though Solomon was also a king who had many flaws, the queen of Sheba praised him as one whom God had established "to maintain justice and righteousness" (10:9, NIV).

The **prophet** Isaiah later voiced Israel's deep desire for a leader who would follow God's way as did David. The prophet spoke of a ruler in that line who would rule with endless peace because his throne would be established in justice and righteousness (Isa. 9:6-7).

Most kings, however, failed at this ideal. After Solomon died, the kingdom split into Israel and Judah. Israel was eventually destroyed (721 BC) due to its ruler's inability to faithfully lead the people in proper worship and the practice of justice (2 Kings 17). Amos castigated the elite of Samaria for their lack of care for the poor and the needy. They continued to eat and drink while the poor were dying (Amos 4:1-4).

Judah's demise (586 BC) is framed in Judah's refusal to turn from false gods (2 Kings 21) and its lack of keeping the judgments of YHWH (23:26). The nation went into exile because the people and their leaders failed to be the people God had called them to be. After their return from the exile (539 BC), the prophets continued to call on the people to live justly and to work to create a new reality where wholeness was possible for all (Isa. 58; Zech. 7:9; 8:16).

The OT witnesses that Israel was called by a just God to be a people oriented toward and engaged in actions that create places for all people to flourish and live in the type of community God originally intended. These actions and attitudes were what made up justice in the OT.

See also Idolatry; Justice, New Testament.

Resources

Dempsey, Carol J. *Justice: A Biblical Perspective*. St. Louis: Chalice Press, 2008.

Houston, Walter J. *Contending for Justice: Ideologies and Theologies of Social Justice in the Old Testament*. New York: T and T Clark, 2006.

Lupton, Robert D. *Compassion, Justice and the Christian Life: Rethinking Ministry to the Poor*. Ventura, CA: Regal Books, 2007.

McCann, J. Clinton, Jr. "The Single Most Important Text in the Entire Bible: Toward a Theology of the Psalms." Pages 63-75 in *Soundings in the Theology of the Psalms: Perspectives and Methods in Contemporary Scholarship*. Edited by Rolf A. Jacobson. Minneapolis: Fortress Press, 2011.

Pleins, J. David, ed. *The Social Visions of the Hebrew Bible: A Theological Introduction.* Louisville, KY: Westminster John Knox Press, 2001.

Reventlow, Henning Graf, and Yair Hoffman, eds. *Justice and Righteousness: Biblical Themes and Their Influence.* JSOTSup 137. Sheffield, UK: Sheffield Academic Press, 1992.

STEPHEN RILEY, PHD

JUSTIFICATION

Justification describes the act in which persons are set or declared to be in right relation to God. Though it has developed as a key theological concept, the noun "justification" is not common in Scripture. Where the Greek term *dikaiosynē* appears in Paul and elsewhere in the NT, it is usually translated "**righteousness**" or "**justice**." Strictly speaking, "justification" occurs only in Rom. 4:25 and 5:18, translating *dikaiōsis* in the statements that Christ was "delivered over to death for our sins and was raised to life for our justification" (NIV) and that "one man's act of righteousness leads to justification and life for all" (NRSV). In spite of this scarcity, the concept is often claimed to be the central message of Paul's gospel.

The justification of persons is closely tied to the divine character of God, or God's own righteousness. It is also tied to images of the law court, judgment before the bar, and **covenant**, the legal framework for such **judgment**. For God to act righteously or with justice is for God to act in accordance with the covenant, or to be faithful to the covenant. The human demands of the covenant are both vertical and horizontal, the covenant-keeping **love** for God and neighbor. As such, justification has to do with the establishment or restoration of covenant relations. It is also tied to **eschatology**, to future judgment and salvation. In the NT, to be justified is for humans to become or to be declared in the right, in advance of the judgment to come and on the basis of the death of the **Messiah**.

In the OT, the root of justification language is the Hebrew *ṣedeq*. In Genesis 38:1-26, Tamar tricks Judah into fathering her sons but is declared "more in the right" than he (v. 26, NRSV), because Judah failed to fulfill the obligations established by the covenant. In Genesis 15:6, Abraham "believed the LORD; and the LORD reckoned it to him as righteousness" (NRSV). Though explicit legal covenantal language is absent in the latter passage, Paul identified Abraham's standing before God as that normally attributed to those in the Mosaic covenant (Rom. 4:3-8).

Most occurrences of the Hebrew term are in the **Prophets**, Psalms, and **Wisdom** literature, where God watches over righteousness and justice and distributes reward and punishment. The psalmist prays that the king may "judge [God's] people with righteousness, and [his] **poor** with justice" (Ps. 72:2, NRSV), and God's own righteousness is the grounds for invoking covenant promises (31:1 [2 HB]; 71:2). God's *ṣedeq* is associated with other terms related to covenant: *mišpaṭ* (justice), *ḥesed* (God's covenant faithfulness), and *šalôm* (peace). In view are positive communal relationships (right dealings between God, the king, and people), along with well-ordered circumstances. Sometimes justice and righteousness can be far away. During Israel's exile, God's faithfulness was questioned.

The NT's use of the concept follows from Israel's Scripture and tradition. In the Gospels, "Wisdom is vindicated [justified or proved right] by her deeds" (Matt. 11:19, NRSV; Luke 7:35). Humans attempt to justify themselves by seeking to establish their own rightness before others, by seeking human approval (Luke 10:29; 16:15). Matthew evokes the lawcourt context in a reference to the final judgment: "For by your words you will be justified, and by your words you will be condemned" (Matt. 12:37, NRSV). The description of Jesus as "the Righteous One" (Gk., *ho dikaios*; Acts 3:14; 7:52; 22:14) shows a Christological innovation: "For Christ also suffered for **sins** once for all, the righteous for the unrighteous" (1 Pet. 3:18, NRSV). Read with Scripture as the backdrop, Jesus becomes the fulfillment of God's righteousness through his unjust persecution and sacrificial death, **resurrection**, and vindication. The idea that God's deliverance is enacted in and through Jesus's faithfulness in some kind of exchange is more fully developed in Paul's letters.

Paul says that Jesus our Lord "was handed over to death for our trespasses and was raised for our justification [*dikaiōsis*]" (Rom. 4:25, NRSV). Christ is our "righteousness" (1 Cor. 1:30, NRSV). Believers might "become the righteousness of God" (2 Cor. 5:21, NRSV), having been justified (1 Cor. 6:11). It is clear that Christ's death and resurrection are the basis for justification. As Paul was bringing Jew and Gentile together in the new covenant community, it was important that he assert that justification no longer takes place through "works of the law" but through trust in Christ (Gal. 2:15-16, NRSV). Exactly what Paul meant by "works" is still contested. In a former paradigm where Paul was characterized as setting a legalistic Judaism over against a gracious, inclusive Gentile **faith** in Christ, his phrase "works of the law" (*ergōn nomou*) stood for those who sought to earn salvation through (self-)righteousness, or covenant-keeping deeds. More recently, the specific context of Paul's letters has led some to conclude that his emphasis is rather a means to enable Gentile believers to participate in the covenant, without demonstrating the identity markers of Judaism (observing the Sabbath, food laws, and circumcision). Since Abraham was reckoned righteous while still uncircumcised, he is the prime example for the inclusion into God's covenant of uncircumcised Gentiles by faith. For Paul, the promises of Abraham's worldwide family are being fulfilled in the community now gathering in response to the **gospel** of Christ.

God's fidelity to the covenant remains the framework for justification. Paul's shorthand for this is his phrase, the "righteousness of God" (*dikaiosynē theou*). In the NT God is righteous or faithful in the sense that Christ's death is a gift of God's gracious initiative and that Christ demonstrates faithful **obedience** or covenant faithfulness. Traditionally, Paul has been interpreted as claiming that justification is "through faith [or believing] in Jesus Christ" (Gal. 2:16; 3:22; Rom. 3:22, 26, NRSV). Such human believing has been set over against human doing, the faith-works antithesis. However, some suggest a more coherent interpretation is that justification is through the faith (or faithfulness) of Christ. In other words, our justification is not human faith in Christ but Christ's own faithfulness to God. Indeed, Christ's faithful death is claimed to embody the righteousness of God (Rom. 3:22). These approaches do not need to be mutually exclusive, however.

More recently, narrative and transformational approaches to justification have come to the fore. They are narrative because the sacrificial death of Christ is understood as the fulfillment of Scripture, the revelation of God's righteousness through the story of God. They are transformational because they take seriously the language of exchange and the idea of humans becoming the righteousness of God. *Participation* in the life, death, and resurrection of Christ has been highlighted as an important aspect of justification. Justification by "cocrucifixion" (Gk., *systauroō*) has further developed the approach, with the paradigm of Christ's self-emptying at its heart (Phil. 2:5). As believers experience death and resurrection life through the Spirit, they experience justification *and* consecration as a work of the Spirit. In this interpretation, justification is not merely an event, a legal declaration of status that may or may not have moral implications, but a very real participation in the ongoing resurrection life of Christ, including in Christ's **suffering**. In this Spirit-enabled human transformation, the exchange of righteousness makes possible a growth in **holiness** and ultimately Christlikeness or Godlikeness.

See also Holy Spirit.

Resources

Gorman, Michael J. *Inhabiting the Cruciform God: Kenosis, Justification, and Theosis in Paul's Narrative Soteriology.* Grand Rapids: Eerdmans, 2009.
Wright, N. T. *Justification: God's Plan and Paul's Vision.* London: SPCK, 2009.

SARAH WHITTLE, PHD

Kk

KINGDOM OF GOD/HEAVEN

Linguistic Data

The words "kingdom of God" appear 68 or 69 times in the NT (the reading of Matt. 6:33 is textually uncertain). The words "kingdom of heaven" appear 33 times in the Gospel of Matthew. This phrase is likely equivalent in meaning to the "kingdom of God," since it appears in passages in Matthew that are parallel to passages in Mark and/or Luke referring to the kingdom of God. Because Judaism commonly used the circumlocution "heaven" to avoid pronouncing the name of God, the phrase "kingdom of heaven" should be taken as equivalent to "kingdom of God." The word "kingdom" modified by "a," "the," "your," "his," "Father's," and "of his Father" appears 33 times. Of these 134 references, 104 appear in the Synoptic Gospels: 51 in Matthew, 14 in Mark, and 39 in Luke.

The phrases "kingdom of God" and "kingdom of heaven" do not appear in the OT, though "kingdom of the Lord [YHWH]" appears in 1 Chronicles 28:5 and 2 Chronicles 13:8. First Chronicles 17:14 and Psalms 103:19; 145:11, 12-13 reference the kingdom of YHWH by means of the modifiers "my," "his," and "your." Many OT passages describe YHWH as "king" (Hebr., *melek*) or as "reigning" (Hebr., *yimlōk*) over either Israel or all the earth. The concept is sufficiently present that some scholars regard the kingdom of God as a significant theme in the OT. However, because most of the references to the kingdom of God appear in the NT, those references are the focus of this article.

The Greek word used in the Synoptics for kingdom is *basileia*, which refers primarily to the function and act of ruling and only secondarily to the territory or realm in which the ruling takes place. Mid-twentieth-century scholarship traced this distinction between the relational-functional character of kingly rule and the territorial understanding of realm to the Aramaic word for "kingdom" that Jesus was thought to have used (*malkû*) and to the corresponding Hebrew term (*mamlākût*). Present scholarship is disposed to consider Jesus to have been at least bilingual (Aramaic and Greek) and so to make the distinction between function and territory based on usage rather than on original language.

Of the 104 Synoptic references to the kingdom, 89 are on Jesus's lips. Seven appear in narrative descriptions of Jesus's ministry, 5 are responses to or statements about Jesus, 2 describe Joseph of Arimathea, and 1 is a statement by John the Baptist. Thus kingdom references are overwhelmingly centered in the teaching and the descriptions of **Jesus's ministry**.

The most common verb associated with the kingdom is "enter" (Gk., *eiserchomai*), a combination occurring 13 times in the Synoptics, once in John 3:5, and once in Acts 14:22. Matthew 21:31 uses *proagousin eis* (lit., "going before into") for the NIV's "entering ahead." Second Peter 1:11 speaks of "entrance into the eternal kingdom" (*eisodos eis tēn aiōnion basileian*). The NIV translates *eisodos* (entrance) "welcome." Such entry into the kingdom is possible because the kingdom "has come near" (*ēngiken*, perfect tense of *engizō*). This expression appears 5 times in the Synoptics, and Luke 21:31 declares that the kingdom "is near" (the verb *estin* with the cognate adverb *engus*).

Mid-twentieth-century scholar C. H. Dodd argued that *ēngiken*, the perfect tense of "come near," meant "arrived." This interpretation of the "come near" passages was one of the elements supporting his argument for realized **eschatology**, the idea that the kingdom had arrived. More recent scholarship has placed less weight on this interpretation of "come near." Even before one has entered the kingdom, it is possible to not be "far from the kingdom" (Mark 12:34, NIV). It is also possible to "shut the door of the kingdom" (Matt. 23:13, NIV).

The kingdom is also often associated with verbs of speaking such as "proclaiming" (9x in the Synoptics and 3x in Acts), "speaking about" (Luke 9:11; Acts 1:3), "testifying" (Acts 28:23), and "arguing persuasively" (19:8, NIV). Seven times in the Synoptics verbs of eating and/or drinking are associated with the kingdom, though Paul observes in Romans 14:17, "The kingdom of God is not a matter of eating and drinking, but of **righteousness, peace** and joy in the **Holy Spirit**" (NIV). Three times the Synoptics speak of "seeing the kingdom," and three times the NT speaks of "receiving the kingdom." The kingdom is also the object of the verb "inherit" (Matt. 25:34 and 4x in Paul). Matthew 8:12 and James 2:5 refer to the same concept with the phrase "heirs of the kingdom" (NRSV), and Ephesians 5:5 mentions having an "**inheritance** in the kingdom." Twice Jesus commands his followers to "seek" the kingdom with the promise that their other needs will be met (Matt. 6:33; Luke 12:31). The kingdom is never the object of the verb "build."

Seven times the kingdom is the subject of the verb "come." The most familiar instance is the petition of the Lord's Prayer for the kingdom to come (Matt. 6:10; Luke 11:2). Twice Jesus points to his ministry of **demon** exorcism as evidence that the kingdom had come (Matt 12:28; Luke 11:20). Thirteen times the kingdom is the subject of a construction (with the verb *homoioō* or a predicate adjective *homoios*) translated "is like" or "may be compared to/with." This construction appears 10 times in Matthew alone. Six times the kingdom is modified by a possessive form of a pronoun (Matt. 5:3, 10; 19:14; Mark 10:14; Luke 6:20; 18:16) indicating that persons can, in some measure, possess the kingdom. However, failure to produce fruit can lead to the kingdom being taken away and given to others (Matt. 21:43).

Jewish Background

The concentrated usage in the Synoptic Gospels, the emphasis on the coming of the kingdom, and the eschatological contexts of many kingdom references make it obvious that the NT usage flows out of a Jewish (Palestinian) context. The OT is clear that God's kingdom is an everlasting kingdom (Ps. 145:13). This affirmation of faith led Judaism at the time of Jesus in two directions. First, Jews saw God's kingdom as a call to faithful **obedience** to God's sovereign rule. This commitment was often described as taking upon oneself "the yoke of the kingdom."

The second direction was an attempt to reconcile the gap between affirming that God's kingdom is over all and the reality that so much of what happens in the world arises from disobedience to God's kingly rule. Judaism's unique eschatology distinguished between this present **evil** age in which disobedience to God flourished and the age to come characterized by God's sovereign rule over all. The "kingdom of God" became another term by which Jews spoke of the age to come. Part of Jewish piety by the first century was the fervent prayer for that kingdom (and that age) to come. The Kaddish prayer included the petition, "May he [God] establish his kingdom during your life and during your days, and during the life of all the house of Israel, even speedily and at a near time" (Barrett 1987, 206). The close relationship between this line of the Kaddish and the lines of the Lord's Prayer, "Thy kingdom come, Thy will be done in earth, as it is in heaven" (Matt. 6:10, KJV), is often noted.

When Did or Does the Kingdom Come?

The central question of the twentieth-century interpretation of the kingdom was, When did Jesus and the early Christian movement envision the kingdom coming? Dodd's interpretation of *ēngiken* as "has arrived" was neither the only nor even the primary evidence that Jesus believed the kingdom was present in his ministry. Matthew 11:4-15; Luke 7:18-28; and 11:20—all indicate that Jesus saw his healing ministry and his exorcism of demons as evidence the kingdom was present. The "seed" parables, including the seed growing of itself (Mark 4:26-29), the mustard seed (4:30-32), and the wheat and the weeds (Matt. 13:24-30), also point to the present reality of the kingdom. This perspective in Jesus's teaching on the kingdom being present is called, as noted earlier, realized eschatology and is popularly referred to as the "already" kingdom.

It is evident that Jesus regarded the kingdom as future (cf. Matt. 10:23; Mark 9:1; 13:28-29), though that future might be very near. The parables of watchfulness found in Matthew 24:45–25:46 envision a future kingdom for which the followers of Jesus must be prepared. This perspective, most often associated with Albert Schweitzer, has been called either futuristic or consistent eschatology and is popularly referred to as the "not yet" kingdom.

Though some interpreters continue to favor realized eschatology and others futuristic eschatology, most now recognize that the kingdom must in some way be understood to be both present and future. The most common description of this perspective is inaugurated eschatology, and it is popularly referred to as the "already, but not yet" kingdom. In this view, Jesus inaugurated the presence of the kingdom in his own ministry and person but anticipated its consummation in the future. Later NT writers connected the consummation of the kingdom with the second coming of Christ.

The Politics of Jesus

The idea that Jesus intended to establish a Davidic-like kingdom in Jerusalem that would end the rule of the Roman Empire emerged regularly, though not persuasively, in the twentieth century. A century of political revolutionaries found that an attractive model for Jesus. However, the evidence does not support such a claim. The counterview that the kingdom of God is simply a spiritual reality residing in human hearts is not persuasive either.

The rise of postcolonial interpretation and empire criticism at the end of the twentieth century makes it impossible to assume that Jesus's message of the kingdom would have been heard solely as a spiritual message. Given the lack of separation between **church** and state in the ancient world, kingdom language would have had political implications. So far, scholars have not been able to agree on the precise shape of these implications.

This tension between the spiritual and political significance of Jesus's kingdom teaching is especially present in the **ethics** of the kingdom, found in concentrated form in the **Sermon on the Mount** (Matt. 5–7). Structurally, the center and organizing principle of the Sermon on the Mount is the Lord's Prayer (6:9-13), with its petition for God's kingdom to come. That prayer is part of Jesus's teaching on maintaining the motivation for righteousness in one's relationship with God rather than in seeking acclaim for pious actions. The focus is individual spiritual piety. However, interpreters have long debated whether or not the Sermon on the Mount's teachings on nonretaliation (5:38-42) have implications for public policy as well as for personal piety.

The Kingdom Is Centered in Jesus

Christian faith and biblical interpretation suffered significant loss in the centuries when the understanding of the kingdom was separated from its background in Judaism and Jewish eschatology. But a greater loss threatens interpretation of the kingdom today when the kingdom is separated from Jesus himself. The authors of the Synoptic Gospels seem to interchange references to the kingdom and to Jesus. Mark 9:1 and Luke 9:27 speak of followers of Jesus not tasting death "before they see the kingdom of God" (NIV). The parallel passage in Matthew 16:28 states that those disciples "will not taste death before they see the Son of Man coming in his kingdom" (NIV).

In Luke 18:29 Jesus speaks of his followers leaving houses, wives, and other family members for the sake of the kingdom of God. The parallel passage in Mark 10:29 speaks of leaving houses and family members for the sake of Jesus and the gospel. Though not entirely interchangeable, Jesus and the kingdom appear inseparable.

Jesus's primary teaching subject was the kingdom. The activities of his ministry were evidence that the kingdom "has come to you" (Luke 11:20, NRSV). If the kingdom is the sovereign rule of God, it is most clearly seen in the life and teaching of Jesus.

Resource

Barrett, C. K., ed. *The New Testament Background: Selected Documents.* Rev. ed. London: SPCK, 1987.

ROGER L. HAHN, PHD

Ll

LAND, THEOLOGY OF THE

Land is the locus of human habitation and thus the space where a relationship with God happens. While the term "land" often identifies a particular geographical location in the Bible, it also regularly signifies **sacred space** where people experience God and an accompanying sense of belonging and safety.

In the OT, the primary Hebrew terms translated "land" include *'ereṣ, 'ădāmâ,* and *tēbēl.* Biblical writers could use these terms interchangeably, but each connotes something particular. The most common term, *'ereṣ,* typically signifies the earth in distinction from the heavens and the waters, as well as a particular region or political entity. The term *'ădāmâ* most often designates soil or ground. Genesis 2:7 highlights the relationship between humans and land when it relates how God formed humanity (*'ādām*) from "the dust of the ground [*'ădāmâ*]" (NIV). The term *tēbēl* usually connotes the "world" or the entirety of **creation**.

In the LXX and NT, the Greek terms *gē, agros, chōra,* and *kosmos* convey a similar range of meanings found in the OT words. The most common translation for *'ereṣ* and *'ădāmâ* in the LXX is *gē.* In the NT it designates geographical regions and also refers to the arena of human life in general, as well as tillable soil such as a field. This latter meaning is most often expressed with *agros* or *chōra,* though both can designate a larger area such as a country as well. English translations usually render *kosmos* as "world," indicating all of creation. But at times it signifies the particular sphere of human habitation.

The most important theological use of land in the OT occurs in relation to God's **covenant** with Abraham. The background for that usage begins at creation, when God established ownership of the land. According to Genesis 1, God created all that exists and distinguished between sky, waters, and dry ground, calling the latter "land" (*'ereṣ*). As its creator, God owned the land and possessed authority to assign its purpose and caretakers. Thus God placed humans in Eden to "take care of it" (2:15, NIV). Within this space, God might come "walking . . . in the cool of the day" and engage humans in conversation (3:8, NIV). Thus Eden became a special place where humans experienced intimate fellowship with God.

God set up guidelines for living in a place such as Eden. When humans violated God's guidelines, the land suffered a curse along with the rest of creation (vv. 17-19). Later, when the relationship with humans reached extreme dysfunction, God cursed the land with a flood that nearly extinguished humanity (6:6-8).

With this conceptual background, the promise of land forms one of the three essential elements of God's covenant with Abraham. The Pentateuch continually articulates this promise in terms of descendants, relationship, and land (see 17:7). The interrelationship and significance of these elements can be seen in the way they shape the narrative of the Pentateuch. Focus upon descendants in the stories of Genesis gives way to emphasis upon relationship in Exodus–Leviticus before the land becomes the major concern in Numbers–Deuteronomy.

The inseparable connection between these three elements assures that the gift of land cannot be misunderstood as an end in itself. God gifted the land to Abraham's descendants so they could live there in covenant fellowship with God. The primary aim of the promise to Abraham was a committed relationship with God. Possession of land, as well as continuance of descendants within it, signified the existence of this relationship.

God allocated the land of Canaan as an "inheritance" for his people to "possess" (Deut. 15:4, NIV). Such terminology reflects a concept of land tenure maintained throughout the biblical narrative. "Inheritance" (Hebr., *naḥălâ*) did not indicate private ownership but rather referred to the assigned stewardship of land. God remained the landlord, while Israel functioned as caretaker. Therefore, land could not be sold permanently in Israel. God declared, "The land is mine and you reside in my land as foreigners and strangers" (Lev. 25:23, NIV). Inheritance language also affirmed God's father-son relationship with Israel. Israel inherited the land from God as the "firstborn son" (Exod. 4:22-23, NIV; Deut. 8:1-5).

As in Eden, God gave guidelines for a relationship with him within the promised land, the **laws** at Sinai. Moses explained that this was the purpose of these laws and warned that observing them carried significant consequences (Deut. 4:5-14). **Obedience** produced blessing, while disobedience brought on curses that included drought and blight on fields and could even result in loss of the land (ch. 28).

The ways that Israel experienced God's blessings and curses while living in the land guides the plot of the OT historical narrative in Joshua–Esther. This story relates how the land was given, possessed, lost, and restored. As such, Israel's relationship to the land acted as a barometer of its relationship with God. During the days of David and Solomon, God gave the land to his people as a safe place for them to live (2 Sam 7:10) and caused his name to dwell in the **Jerusalem** temple (Deut. 12:5; 1 Kings 8:20-21). Though the Lord could not be restricted to one place on earth, his special presence in Jerusalem made it a sacred space where God's people could encounter their God in unique ways (vv. 27-30).

The complete loss of land in the exile triggered a major theological crisis for Abraham's descendants. It signified a significant breach of Israel's covenant relationship with God. Jeremiah maintained that exile came about because Israel "defiled the land" with **idolatry** and injustice (Jer. 3:2, NIV). In other words, Israel's failure to observe the most basic commandments to **love** the Lord and their neighbor ritually polluted the land, which rendered it unusable for its sacred purpose of fellowship with God. In addition, Israel's father-son relationship with the Lord came into question, for the exile meant that God had forsaken his "house" and abandoned his "inheritance" (12:7-9, NIV).

Within this context, the land also became part of the image of **hope** for Israel's future. Through Israel's **prophets**, God promised to "restore them to the land" following exile (16:15, NIV) in order to "give [them] a new heart and put a new spirit in [them]" (Ezek. 36:26, NIV). This was a fore-taste of the messianic age, when God would create "new heavens and a new earth" and reestablish the relationship with his people as originally designed for Eden (Isa. 65:17-25, NIV). In that day God promised to "plant Israel in their own land, never again to be uprooted from the land I have given them" (Amos 9:15).

The NT clarifies the OT's theology of land and transforms it. Though first-century Judaism maintained hope in reclaiming a tangible piece of real estate for God's people, the teaching of Jesus and the early **church** indicate no interest in a literal fulfillment of that promise. Rather, they emphasize that the arena in which a special relationship with God can happen includes all the earth, not simply a particular portion of it. Jesus declared that the meek would "inherit the earth" (Matt. 5:5, NIV) in agreement with Ps. 37:11. But he defined this inheritance within the context of the Beatitudes as the "**kingdom of heaven**," which is a place where one "will see God" and "be called children of God" (Matt. 5:3-10, NIV). Thus God's promise to Abraham to bless "all peoples on earth" through him (Gen. 12:3, NIV) finds fulfillment when Jesus's disciples take the **gospel** "to the ends of the earth" (Acts 1:8, NIV). The NT, then, confirms the OT assertion that people can live in a committed relationship with God even outside the promised land (see Ezek. 1).

Even more significantly, the NT transforms the OT's theology of **sacred space** by insisting that the locus for a relationship with God happens in Jesus

Christ. Thus Jesus fulfills the role of the promised land in the OT, as he did with other OT institutions and images. The vine metaphor in John 15 provides a striking example of this point. As the vine, Jesus himself rather than the land of Israel becomes the place where believers "dwell" (Gk., *menō*) in order to find spiritual life (v. 5). Paul makes the same point in his letters by suggesting that Christians gain the privileges of land tenure in Christ. They become "heirs together with Israel" (Eph. 3:6, NIV) and, as a result, come to be known as "children of God" (Gal. 3:26-29, NIV; Rom. 8:16-17). Therefore, like those living faithfully in the land in the OT, followers of Jesus are blessed "with every spiritual blessing in Christ" (Eph. 1:3, NIV).

Thus the NT lays no claim to a particular geographical location as its "holy land." Believers find sacred space for living in intimate fellowship with God in Christ Jesus alone.

See also Cosmology; Deuteronomic Theology; Fall, The; Messiah/Christ; Sacred Persons; Sacred Space; Sacred Times.

Resources

Brueggemann, Walter. *The Land: Place as Gift, Promise, and Challenge in Biblical Faith*. 2nd ed. Minneapolis: Augsburg Fortress, 2002.

Burge, G. M. *Jesus and the Land: The New Testament Challenge to "Holy Land" Theology*. Grand Rapids: Baker Academic, 2010.

Wright, C. J. H. *God's People in God's Land: Family, Land, and Property in the Old Testament*. Grand Rapids: Eerdmans, 1990.

JAMES O. EDLIN, PHD

LATIN AMERICAN HERMENEUTICS

The word "hermeneutics" comes from the Greek *hermēneuō*, which means "to interpret, explain, make clear." When referring to the sacred text, the adjective "biblical" is added. As an interpretive science, biblical hermeneutics seeks to discover what a sacred text is saying to us.

Multiplicity of Approaches

When speaking of biblical hermeneutics in Latin America, there is more than one way to approach a sacred text in order to discover what God has to say to his people. There is a close and binding relationship between history and hermeneutics, which implies that just as our theological history has shaped itself, so have the different approaches to the biblical text developed according to their theological traditions.

Thus in Latin American there is a wide spectrum of hermeneutics that ranges from the more conservative and fundamentalist theological positions to the more liberal ones. To honor our diversity and theological traditions, it is more accurate to speak about Latin American hermeneutics in the plural, recognizing the various forms of exegesis. Some of the more current ones include evangelical apologetic reading, dispensationalism, popular reading, political reading, liberation reading, intercultural reading, and community reading. There has also been a recent resurgence by neo-Pentecostalism of allegorical reading, as well as readings from prosperity theologies. Protestant churches—inheritors of the Protestant Reformation—have used and taught historical methods for the hermeneutical task in most of their theological schools and seminaries.

The task of biblical hermeneutics, when it comes to determining an appropriate meaning of the text, is challenging and demanding. Latin American scholars have agreed that their task is more than a one-sided search. To find the meaning of the text in its original sense begins with the study of the original languages. It also includes making the message relevant for the present day. This double contextualization that distinguishes the interpretive task establishes a bridge between the biblical context of the author and the current context of the reader.

The exegetical-hermeneutical task fulfills its purpose by (1) discovering the message that God has for his people, (2) showing its pertinence to modern cultural contexts, and (3) impelling and transforming the missionary activity of the church. The biblical text has a message for the people of God in their concrete contexts with specific socioeconomic, historical, cultural, and religious characteristics. This aspect linked to Latin American theology imprints a pastoral and missiological characteristic that transcends the scholarly approach.

Cultural Influences

Latin America historically has been a continent of contrasts and paradoxes. Wealth exists alongside poverty; the latest technology, alongside illiteracy; democracy, alongside corruption; opulence, alongside misery. The continent has the greatest social gap between rich and **poor**. Globalization, internal and external migrations, new spirituality, evangelical growth, marginalization, ecological crises, moral relativism, white **slave** trafficking, exploitation of minors, social polarization, family violence, child abuse, and teenage mothers compose an ever more common terminology for the Latin American context because they describe its emergent social reality.

In such a diverse and complex Latin American context, the Word has a message to deliver today to the people of God. In this sense, on the way to discovering the meaning of the biblical text, three determinant elements intervene: (1) the eternal message from the Word and its primary meaning for the biblical recipients, (2) the personal perspectives that readers construct throughout their lives by means of varied experiences, and (3) the community as a shaper of social meaning. The interpretive act takes place in the context of the community, and the biblical message only comes to have a deep personal meaning as it grows out of the integral context of that community.

Any hermeneutical approach must not overlook this synergy, given that the reader is part of a particular community and, in a certain sense, is immersed and conditioned by that community. As the **church** carries out its missionary task, it encounters diverse worldviews in the different cultures where it ministers. These worldviews develop historically and culturally and are filters used to interpret all reality, including the Word of God and Christian **faith**. In its missional work, the church must come to understand these worldviews and examine them in the light of the transforming message of the Word so that it can "test everything" and "hold fast to what is good" (1 Thess. 5:21, NRSV). These worldviews allow us to understand aspects of the culture of a given people, and they often demand the redesign of ecclesial practices.

In its search for relevant answers, Latin American hermeneutics has raised these questions: From what cultural point do we interpret a biblical text? Is the hermeneutical process straightforward? Does it start with the historicobiblical context or from an established body of doctrine? Or does it proceed from the presuppositions of the interpreter?

Hermeneutical Circle

In that search, during the 1970s, a different "hermeneutical circle" was introduced by followers of the German NT scholar Rudolf Bultmann and philosopher Martin Heidegger. Latin Americans Juan Luis Segundo, Juan Stam, José Míguez Bonino, and José Severino Croatto stood out. The hermeneutical circle developed from the dynamic tension between the objectivity and subjectivity of the interpretive act. It raises the idea that there can be neither understanding nor interpretation without a prior understanding. The presuppositions lead to an interpretation that must in turn be modified, thus reaching a new interpretation, thus producing a circularity of "precognition-interpretation-modification for a new interpretation" (Stam 2006, 61).

According to Stam, instead of being just a "vicious circle" consisting of the existential subject and its self-understanding, the hermeneutical circle is understood as the dynamic interaction between the reading of the biblical text and the persistence of contemporary reality. The hermeneutical circle is continuous, without having a fixed point of origin, but which situates itself at the center of interpretation for those who emphasize the historical context of the Word as a fixed point of departure.

The hermeneutical circle offers an opportunity to reread the biblical text and rethink life and the church's task in a continuous manner. These rereadings permit the discovery of biblical counsel that is adequate for facing the new challenges that the church encounters along its path and that accompany its pastoral and missionary activity.

Postmodernity and Globalization

Without a doubt, Latin America lives in an era of transition. It is beginning to feel the effects of postmodernity, which is an emerging paradigm possessing a new interpretive proposal of reality. In the past, modernity took its inspiration from the premise that one can change the world through reason. That ideal of progress, however, turned into tragedy with the discovery that the so-desired progress was going against humanity.

The new framework of postmodernity has had an effect on hermeneutical reading within the Latin American context. It has made evident an openness toward the sacred that has led to an ever-growing religious pluralism. In recent decades many Latin American countries have modified their constitutions to recognize the multicultural, multilingual, and multireligious character of their societies.

Historically Latin America has been considered in its majority a Catholic continent. As a result of the search for religious transcendence, multiple religious expressions live together peacefully. These religious expressions include the indigenous religions, Eastern religions, Afro-Brazilian spiritism, and the New Era with its multiple expressions. In such a framework, the path is open to religious individualism. Spirituality turns personal in character, without a center of reference. The validity of the beliefs is legitimized by the experience of the individual.

As a product of globalization, the influence of other theological currents on the interpretation of the biblical text and its dialog with reality has become evident. The teachings of other theologies, mainly those of a neo-Pentecostal or neo-charismatic nature, have influenced to a greater or lesser degree nearly all evangelical denominations.

Hermeneutically, with the influence of these theological currents, the allegorical reading of the Word has sprung up, which becomes evident in a return to the OT and especially to a spiritual and ahistorical interpretation. Likewise, under the presuppositions of prosperity theologies, a hermeneutic has arisen that is slanted more toward a society of consumerism than toward faithfulness to the biblical text, reducing it to existentialist and individualist categories.

Summary

On the way to fulfilling its divine calling to be an agent of God in its mission, the Latin American church throughout its history has been shaping various ways of approaching sacred text. The distinctive aspect of Latin American hermeneutics rests on the proposal of discovering the message of God for his people in a constructive, relevant, and continuous dialog with its specific context for the purpose of addressing the pastoral and missionary activity of the church.

Resources

Escobar, Samuel. "Una nueva manera de hacer teología." In *La fe evangélica y las teologías de la liberación*. El Paso, TX: Casa Bautista de Publicaciones, 1987.

Hansen, Guillermo, ed. *Los caminos inexhauribles de la Palabra*. Buenos Aires: Editorial Distribuidora Lumen, 2000.

Míguez Bonino, José. *Rostros del protestantismo Latinoamericano*. Buenos Aires: Nueva Creación; Grand Rapids: Eerdmans, 1995.

Padilla, René. "La Palabra interpretada: Reflexiones sobre hermenéutica contextual." *Boletín teológico* 1, no. 1 (January–March 1981): 1-8.

Piedra, Arturo, ed. *Haciendo teología en América Latina*. San José, CR: Sebila, 2006.

Segundo, Juan Luis. "El círculo Hermenéutico." In *Liberación de la Teología*. Buenos Aires: Ediciones Carlos Lohlé, 1975.

Stam, Juan. *Haciendo teología en América Latina*. San José, CR: Sebila, 2006.

———. "Pautas para una hermenéutica evangélica contextual." In *La hermenéutica bíblica desde una óptica liberadora*. Edited by Victorio Araya. San José, CR: Sebila, 1985.

JORGE L. JULCA, DMIN

LEADERSHIP

Over the centuries the Bible has been mined for models and examples of leadership and often drawn upon to support or reject contemporaneous types of leading. However, it seems that the Bible has narratives of leadership that describe more than prescribe the way leadership is to be shaped. The word "leader" or "leadership" is rarely used in itself; instead, a whole range of other terms are drawn upon, from "king" to "shepherd," from "servant" to "teacher." The work of leadership is left for the reader to infer. The primary exception to this is in Mark 10:42-45, where Jesus clearly cautions his disciples against leadership that mirrors that of the Gentiles.

In the Hebrew Scriptures, common positive exemplars are the patriarch Abraham, with a faith-into-the-unknown leadership approach (Gen. 15:1-21); the liberating Moses, with his holy encounter that propelled him into the exodus leadership and lawmaking for the people (Exod. 3, 20); and his wise father-in-law, Jethro (ch. 18), who advised Moses to share the role of leadership among identified others. Further examples include the prophetic Samuel (1 Sam. 7:3-17); the kingly David, commonly cited for his being "after [God's] own heart" (Acts 13:22, NIV; 1 Sam. 16:13); Daniel, a leader of countercultural stature (Dan. 1:20); and later on the **prophets**, who either called to account those allegedly leading the people or demonstrated the way to a new future where the shepherd-leader would enable the whole restoration of Israel. There were some notable **women leaders** also; the lives of Huldah (2 Chron. 34:21-33), Deborah (Judg. 4:4-14), and Esther are sometimes held as models of leadership. There were also less-than-exemplary leaders who were seen as leading God's people astray: Aaron and his golden calf (Exod. 32:1-6), Saul and his descent into madness (1 Sam. 13:13-14), the notorious Ahab and Jezebel (1 Kings 16:31; 2 Kings 9:7), and a series of kings and priestly shepherds who were held to account by the prophets (see Jer. 50:6; Ezek. 34).

In the NT, the prophetic and messianic roles of leaders are noted: from John the Baptist to Jesus and his disciples, sent in their pairs with a message, to Paul and the teams of people he encountered, developed, and released. There are also the famous lists describing the attributes of overseers and establishing a framework for leadership as a matter of character not merely ability. The demands of leaders to make decisions on behalf of people are exposed to scrutiny in the book of Acts, and there are a number of contentious issues raised in the NT that indicate the complexity of leadership. The goal of leadership appears, however, to be internally consistent: to declare Jesus as Lord, lead people into deeper lives of **faith**, and to proclaim and practice Jesus's lordship in community and for the sake of others. The glory given to the Father and empowered by the Spirit in and through Christ is an important aspect of the church's self-understanding, which is essentially triune. The self-giving love of the eternal triune God offers participation in similar self-giving love on the part of the leader within the community of the church. The overarching claim in Scripture about leadership formed by Christ is that it is cruciform, **sacrificial**, and servant-like. The trajectory of NT leadership moves away from status or power exercised for its own sake; however, this trajectory certainly allows room for godly authority based on relationships of **love** climaxing in glorifying the Father (see Eph. 3).

What does the Bible then tell us about leadership in this sweep of people and testament? The divine appointment of leadership is framed by encounters with God that are life transforming. Leadership is for the sake of the people of God and the society around them, and it has a global vision and reach for the sake of the other nations. The role of leadership is profoundly influenced both for good or ill by the context in which that leadership is exercised. God's call to lead is deeply personal but is also affirmed by seasoned leaders and followers.

Leaders can mishear and mislead God's people, and so the guardianship of leaders and their actions and behavior is vital. In current parlance, accountability matters. Since the role of the leader is fragile and leaders are often deeply complex and critically flawed people, this tension is a difficult one; David, for example, was not wholly "good." Leaders pursuing God at one instance can be led astray by love of money, status, or unhealthy personal relationships. In the NT, particularly, it seems that the call to lead is attached to **integrity** and worthiness both of life and in embodied ways within the community. The role of leadership is not necessarily a lifetime role exercised in the same way in all places. There is a sense that leadership is malleable and exercised in contextual ways for the sake of encouraging communities to become Christ centered, worthy of their calling.

A critical element of what it means to lead God's people is declaring both God's **love** and **judgment**. The leaders that are rooted and grounded in the love of God in Christ are also leaders of ordinary and messy communities, and it is clear that leaders of churches can exert influence in both healthy and unhealthy ways. The navigation of leadership that is formed by the **Holy Spirit** and for the people of God is part of the church's role—to identify its leaders and support them, but the church is also to beware of those who are falsely teaching (Acts 20:29-31; 2 Cor. 11:3; 2 Pet. 2:1-2).

In contemporary approaches to leadership, there can be a propensity to emphasize distinctive characteristics in a hierarchical or technical sense, drawing from Scripture (e.g., "Apest" [acronym for "apostles, prophets, evangelists, shepherds, teachers"] models based on Eph. 4:11-12), or to focus on a philosophy of leadership that asserts a strong entrepreneurial personality or acquired techniques of leadership that will help a church grow. Scripture suggests, however, that the church should be somewhat wary of approaches to leadership that consume popular cultural ideas of leadership (whether they be secular, Buddhist, communist, or capitalist) and attempt to map that onto the leadership of churches. The church's theology of leadership should reflect the tone, tenor, and trajectory of Scripture toward a slain Lamb and a worshipping community attentive to the lordship of Christ as the only head of the **church** (Col. 1:18).

See also Call of God; Messiah/Christ.

Resources

Bass, Dorothy, ed. *Practicing Our Faith*. San Francisco: Jossey-Bass, 1997.
Peterson, Eugene. *Working the Angles*. Grand Rapids: Eerdmans, 1987.
Pritchard, John. *Living Faithfully*. London: SPCK, 2013.
Taylor, Barbara Brown. *This Preaching Life*. Boston: Cowley, 1993.

DEIRDRE BROWER-LATZ, PHD

LOVE (ʾāhab, ḥesed, agapaō, phileō)

English translations generally use only one word for love, whereas several words are used in both the Hebrew and Greek texts to express this concept.

In the OT the Hebrew word *ḥesed* is often translated as "steadfast love," especially when God is the agent. It generally refers to a positive attitude or an attitude of approval that someone has toward someone else. God's steadfast love (*ḥesed*) was often invoked by people who expected a positive outcome from a situation (Gen. 24:12, 27; 39:21). In his steadfast love, God led Israel, the people he had rescued (Exod. 15:13). God's actions were characterized by his steadfast love (20:6; Deut. 5:10; 2 Sam. 7:15). This term is particularly important as a descriptor of God's relationship to David and his lineage (1 Kings 3:6; 1 Chron. 17:13). Humans could depend on God's steadfast love (Pss. 33:5; 69:16 [17 HB]), and thus God was praised for his steadfast love (Exod. 34:6-7; Num. 14:18). Not only did God perform *ḥesed* (also translated "kindness" or "loyalty"), but humans are capable of this trait as well (Josh. 2:12-14; Judg. 1:24; 8:35; 2 Sam. 9:7).

By far the most common word describing God's and human love consists of derivatives of the Hebrew word *ʾāhab*, sometimes transliterated *ʾahav*.

Usually, love serves as the basis of **marriage**, friendship, and emotional attachment among human beings, such as Isaac's love for Rebekah (Gen. 24:67), Jacob's love for Rachel (29:18, 20), and Saul's affection for David ("he loved David greatly" [AT]) when he came into his service (1 Sam. 16:21). Similarly, the close bond between David and Saul's son Jonathan is described as love (18:1). In his elegy for Jonathan, David expressed how much more intense was his love for Jonathan than for women (2 Sam. 1:26). Solomon's fondness for foreign women is described as love (1 Kings 11:1).

The word "love" (*ʾāhab*) may simply be used to indicate a preference for something, as in Isaac loving a favorite dish (Gen. 27:9). Both parental love and predilection are seen in Abraham's love for his son Isaac (22:2) and Jacob's for his younger son Joseph (37:3-4).

This favoritism is not too far off from God's own election of Israel (Deut. 4:37; 10:15). God's favor toward Abraham is defined as love when he is called "my loved one" (*ʾōhăbî*; Isa. 41:8, AT). The appointment of the monarchy, especially of David, is seen as an act of love (2 Chron. 9:8; cf. 6:42, which uses the word *ḥesed*). Preference is also expressed as love when the people of Israel manifested their affection for David (1 Sam. 18:16), and God promised not to retire his "steadfast love" (*ḥesed*) from David (2 Sam. 7:15; 1 Chron. 17:13).

Love is both an emotion and a commitment. Throughout the OT one finds many texts exhorting people to look for a proper object of love (*ʾehĕbû ʾet yhwh*, "Love the LORD!" [Ps. 31:23 (24 HB), AT]). "Love truth and peace," instructs Zechariah 8:19 (NIV). Love is also set in antithetical parallelism to hate: "Hate evil, love good" (Amos 5:15, NIV; cf. Ps. 119:163).

In the Bible love is not only an emotional force but also primarily an act of the will that involves making choices and focusing on the object of one's affections. However, human love is imperfect because sometimes it is misdirected, such as when one loves "simple things" (Prov. 1:22, AT) or "vain words" (Ps. 4:2 [3 HB], NRSV). On the other hand, the psalmist was able to obey God's statutes because he loved them greatly (119:167).

Nowhere is choice more evident than in the **wisdom** tradition. There the audience is instructed to love wisdom (Prov. 4:6) because she loves those who love her (8:17). YHWH is said to love *ṣĕdāqâ* and *mišpāṭ*, "**righteousness**" and "**justice**" (Pss. 33:5; 99:4). The Lord hates those who love violence (11:5). What God then requires of his people is to love and serve him with all of the heart and soul (Deut. 10:12).

Love may simply fit a person's particular season in life (Eccles. 3:8) or be a quality of consistent human behavior: "A friend loves at all times" (Prov. 17:17, NIV).

The well-known command to love the neighbor occurs in Leviticus 19:18. Israelites were supposed to treat foreigners as they would one of their own—that is, to love them, because the Israelites had been foreigners in Egypt (v. 34; Deut. 10:19). This was grounded on YHWH's love for the foreigner and the most vulnerable (Deut. 10:18).

Love is prominent in Deuteronomy. Accordingly, YHWH's deliverance of Israel from Egypt was based on his love (7:8). For that reason, Israel was called to love God in return (6:5; 10:12). In fact, an important use of "love" (*'āhab*) occurs in regard to **covenant** observance. Those who keep the terms of the covenant, that is, who keep the commandments are said to "love" God (Exod. 20:6; Deut. 5:10; 7:9; 11:1, 13, 22; 19:9; Josh. 22:5; 1 Kings 3:3). This would in turn result in God's covenant "loyalty" or "steadfast love" (*ḥesed*) and blessings (Deut. 7:9, 13; 30:16). Conversely, those who do not observe the terms of the covenant—that is, do not keep the commandments—are said to "hate" God (Exod. 20:5; Deut. 7:10).

The choice to love is exemplified magnificently by God, who loved Israel despite Israel's repeated unfaithfulness. As a young bride, Israel loved the Lord (Jer. 2:2) but then abandoned these previous affections in favor of foreign gods (vv. 25, 33; Ezek. 16:37). Also, her pursuit of foreign alliances is likened to adulterous love (Ezek. 23:17). Love appears prominently also in Hosea—the great allegory of the adulterous dalliances of Israel with other gods. Hosea was to imitate God in loving the undeserving. He was to show his love for his adulteress wife, as God showed his love for wayward Israel (3:1; 9:1, 10). Hosea also contains some of the most endearing images of love in the Bible: "When Israel was a child, I loved him" (11:1, NRSV), and "I led them with . . . bands of love" (v. 4, NRSV). Despite their disobedience, YHWH promised to love them even so: "I will heal their waywardness and love them freely" (14:4, NIV).

Likewise, Israel was assured of God's love during the exile by the words of Deutero-Isaiah (Isa. 43:4). Moreover, the prophet announced that it was possible for foreigners to "bind themselves to the LORD" in love (56:6, NIV).

Love is also prominent in the Song of Songs. The book uses two words. First, *dôd* ("lust"; its Akkadian cognate *dādu* means "lovemaking") most likely refers to physical love (1:2-4; 5:1; 7:12 [13]). The second word for love, *'āhab*, points to a strong, almost incontrollable, attraction and desire to be with the beloved (2:7; 3:1-3; 8:4, 6-7).

Love is the predominant motif in the NT. Again, different Greek words are often translated into English by the singular word "love." The most significant word is the verb *agapaō* (noun *agapē*, "brotherly love" or "charity"). It denotes a profound attachment and respect (Matt. 5:43-44; 22:37-39).

Agapē is the kind of love that Jesus called his disciples to have for each other (John 13:34-35; 15:12, 17). It is the supreme standard by which Jesus's disciples should live and for showing their commitment to him and his commandments (14:21-24). Jesus put love of God and neighbor front and center of his ethics: "Love your enemies" (Matt. 5:44, NIV; cf. Mark 12:30-31). Accordingly, love is the measure of true discipleship (John 13:35).

Paul often mentioned "love" (*agapē*) as his motivation for missionary activity (Phil. 4:1; 1 Thess. 2:8), and he insisted that love ought to be the rule among churches (Rom. 12:9; Phil. 2:2; 2 Thess. 1:3; Phlm. vv. 5, 7). Paul confessed that "God's love has been poured out into our hearts through the Holy Spirit" (Rom. 5:5, NIV). Moreover, there is continuity between the OT and the NT in God's love for people: "God demonstrates his own love for us in this: While we were still sinners, Christ died for us" (v. 8, NIV). Thus people can be certain that nothing can separate one from God's "love" (*agapē*; 8:35, 39). For Paul, "Love is the fulfillment of the **law**" (13:10, NIV; Gal. 5:14). Love is above any other virtue (1 Cor. 13). Paul also listed love first among the gifts of the Spirit (Gal. 5:22). Against such love there is no argument (Rom. 12:9; 13:8-10; 1 Cor. 13; Gal. 5:6; Eph. 5:2).

In the Johannine literature, love of neighbor is of paramount importance for Christians: "Whoever claims to love God yet hates a brother or sister is a liar. For whoever does not love their brother and sister, whom they have seen, cannot love God, whom they have not seen" (1 John 4:20, NIV; see 2:10; 3:11-23; 4:7-21).

The secondary word for love in the NT is *phileō*, which refers to affection, fondness, or predilection for something (Matt. 6:5; 10:37; Luke 20:46; John 11:3). It is not used to the same extent as *agapē*.

See also Idolatry; Poor/Poverty.

GILBERT LOZANO, PHD

LUKE-ACTS, THEOLOGY OF

The title "Luke-Acts" reflects contemporary scholarly consensus that the Gospel of Luke and the Acts of the Apostles originally comprised a single literary work in two volumes. It is recognized that no canonical list or surviving ancient manuscripts combine or connect these two books together. But since Henry Cadbury proposed the singularity of these two works in both composition and message, the expression "Luke-Acts" has become commonplace and presumes the unity of these two biblical books.

Little external evidence offers definitive proof that these two books were written as two companion volumes of a larger work by a single author. On the one hand, these two texts deal with divergent material that is consistent with their respective canonical placement. The Gospel of Luke depicts Jesus's life and ministry, whereas the Acts of the Apostles deals with the early church, especially the characters of Peter (chs. 1–12) and Paul (chs. 13–28). The similarities between the Gospel of Luke and the other Synoptic Gospels suggest that these three Gospels be placed together, whereas the significant role of Paul in Acts provides a useful historical outline of the early church within which to place the Pauline corpus.

On the other hand, such basic differences do not eclipse the literary links between the Lukan Gospel and Acts. Both books name "Theophilus" as the recipient. The book of Acts reminds him about the author's "first book" regarding Jesus (1:1, NRSV), which is likely a reference to the Gospel of Luke. The overlap between the ending of the Third Gospel and the beginning of Acts joins these books together: the promise of the Father (Luke 24:49; Acts 1:4), the description of Jesus's followers as "witnesses" and the role of "power" that would come upon them (Luke 24:48; Acts 1:8, NRSV), the distinctly Lukan inclusion of Jesus's ascension to heaven (Luke 24:51; Acts 1:9-11), and so on. The narrative often depicts characters and journeys in Acts similarly to what readers find in the Lukan Gospel. Much of these two books share a common theological perspective. Most scholars think that the scarcity of external evidence for linking these two books together is overcome by the internal (or literary) evidence for doing so.

Approaching Luke-Acts as a single work rather than two separate works has significant ramifications for biblical study in general. Rather than approaching the Gospel of Luke as one voice among the Evangelists, and the Acts of the Apostles as another voice and work that serves as an introduction to Paul's letters, Luke-Acts should be understood on its own terms as the largest single NT contribution, composing more than one-fourth of the entire collection. Thus, although not long ago NT theologians often passed over Luke-Acts in favor of Pauline or Johannine texts, the Lukan contribution to the thought of the NT has increasingly become the focus of scholarly attention.

Luke's work as an historian did not prevent him from shaping the narrative theologically. Luke (unlikely the physician and Paul's ministry companion) went about his theological task very differently from what one finds in, for example, Paul's letter to the Romans. There is little doubt, however, that Luke offers a "theological history," in which God functions as the primary mover behind narrated historical persons and events. Throughout Luke-Acts, what orients everything are the will and purposes of the God of Israel. However, the Lukan theological perspective stands out among the other Evangelists because he included not only the story of Jesus as God's Messiah but also the story of the earliest Christians.

The addition of Acts as a second volume creates something very different from the other Gospels. Some suggest this addition reflects the delay of the parousia (Jesus's second coming)—that is, Luke relinquishes the view that Christians were living in the last days in favor of a salvation-historical understanding of the Jesus event as the midpoint between the time of Israel and the time of the church. Others understand Luke as seeing a time of God's promise followed by a protracted time of fulfillment. Such interpretations of Luke's theological perspective, however, often reflect contemporary theological concerns as much as they do the narrative of Luke-Acts. Nonetheless, several aspects of the theology in Luke-Acts emerge from a careful reading of that narrative.

1. The Plan and Purposes of God

The most important aspect of the theology of Luke-Acts is how this narrative describes God. The plan of God guides what takes place, with regard to both Jesus and the early church. The first two chapters of Luke's Gospel announce the births of John the Baptist and Jesus, emphasizing God's purposes and role. God's activities are described here and throughout Luke-Acts with the backdrop of the LXX in mind; the God at work here is the God of Israel.

The purposes of God, first seen in the stories of Israel, are now seen in the stories of Luke-Acts and its characters. Jesus's reading from the scroll of Isaiah in the synagogue of Nazareth affirmed God's plan through Jesus (Luke 4:18-19). Often, people praised God for what God had done through Jesus (e.g., 13:13; 17:15; 18:43; 19:37). In his Pentecost speech, Peter explained that Jesus was handed over to the Jews in Jerusalem according to God's plan (Acts 2:23). God vindicated Jesus from those who crucified him, raising him from the dead (vv. 24, 32; 3:15; 13:37).

God's guidance was responsible for notable narrative shifts in the story of the early church's ministry (10:1-48; 16:6-10). Throughout both books, God used various means—notably angels, visions, dreams, Scripture, and even events—to reveal and enact that divine plan. All this was what God had promised to God's people. So what God was doing is the fulfillment of God's promises to Israel.

2. Jesus and Christology

What is also noteworthy is Luke's distinct portrayal of Jesus. Although all NT Gospels depict Jesus as Messiah or Christ, Luke described him uniquely as the promised Messiah in fulfillment of Scripture (Luke 4:18-19) who embodied the good news that he proclaimed about God's salvation. Jesus offered forgiveness of sin, deliverance from disease and demonic oppression, and inclusion to the outcast. A unique title given him in the Third Gospel is "Savior," as he extended salvation through his ministry. Unlike other NT Gospels, the focus here is not so much on the cross of Jesus for redemption but on what began with the birth of Jesus (2:11), since God's saving work is seen in Jesus as Savior from the beginning and extends to "today" (19:9, NRSV).

Alongside Jesus's role as Savior is also that of **prophet**. Jesus proclaimed God's message, the good news of God's saving activity that extended beyond the established categories defined by Jewish thought and practice (see salvation below). As prophet, Jesus served as God's spokesperson in offering this message of deliverance to the oppressed and to those considered outsiders by the Jewish religious establishment. This prophetic role served as a model for the early church. Descriptions of leaders such as Peter and Paul mirror Jesus's ministry and have their ministries legitimized as they serve as he did.

An additional aspect of Luke's Christology is the depiction of Jesus as "Lord." In the latter chapters of the Third Gospel, LXX quotations mention "Lord" (20:41-44), which replaced the wording of the MT referring to Yahweh with the Greek *kyrios* (since Jews did not pronounce God's personal name but replaced it with a form of "Lord"). Such quotations are in the same general context as parables where Jesus is also portrayed as Lord (19:16-25; 20:13-15), thereby equating Jesus with God. Jesus is identified similarly after his encounter with two disciples in Emmaus (24:34).

In his Pentecost speech, Peter identified God's **resurrection** and exaltation of Jesus through the ascension as evidence of God's validation of Jesus and his ministry, as well as a sign of Jesus's lordship. This exalted Jesus, validated as both Lord and Christ (Acts 2:36), served as the agent who poured out the Spirit upon the believers at Pentecost (vv. 32-33).

3. The Role of the Holy Spirit

The **Holy Spirit** had a prominent role in the early church, beginning with Pentecost. The Spirit's outpouring on the believers was understood as the fulfillment of God's promises to Israel (Acts 2:17-21) and as the result of Jesus's resurrection and exaltation by the hand of God (vv. 22-36). Through the Holy Spirit, the community of believers came together in worship and fellowship (vv. 42-47; 4:32-35). Through the Holy Spirit, believers were empowered as witnesses in the face of increasing opposition (4:8, 31; 7:55), which fulfilled Jesus's promise that the Spirit would come to empower his followers as his witnesses (1:8).

Later in Acts, the role of the Spirit shifts, as the Spirit is mentioned less in describing empowerment for witness and more in describing guidance of the church and her **mission** (13:1-3; 16:6-10). Thus the Lukan depiction of the Spirit and power focuses on how the Spirit enabled the church to fulfill her mission and role as witness, not on how the Spirit empowered individuals in their personal lives as believers.

The Holy Spirit also has a distinctive role in the Third Gospel when compared to other NT Gospels. The Holy Spirit is associated with John the Baptist, marking him as a prophet of God (Luke 1:15). The conception of Jesus is linked to the activity of the Holy Spirit (v. 35), and this links Jesus's identity with God. Even Simeon was directed by the Spirit to go to the temple at the time of Jesus's presentation, where he then offered a prophetic message about the infant Jesus (2:25-32). This same Spirit anointed Jesus at his baptism (3:21-22), led him during his time of temptation in the **wilderness** (4:1-13), and then went with Jesus as he began his ministry in Galilee (v. 14). This Spirit that empowered and guided Jesus in his ministry has a similar role in the church in Acts.

4. Salvation and Its Scope

An essential element in Luke's theology is his perspective on salvation. From Luke's perspective, salvation broadly includes deliverance and restoration. It includes healing from disease, release from **demonic** domination, **forgiveness** of **sin**, and even deliverance from economic oppression. In what has been called the Magnificat (Luke 1:46-55), Mary described what God was doing through her "low status" (v. 48, CEB) as bringing down powerful rulers and lifting up the lowly. This is one example of what is known as the Lukan reversal, in which the evidence of God's saving activity was the opposite of what the people of that day would have expected.

In the Gospel of Luke, Jesus's ministry included those considered outside the realm of God's work and, therefore, outsiders to the historic people of God: tax collectors, "sinners," the disenfranchised, and the diseased (5:27-39; 8:40-56). The religious establishment made certain that the lost remained lost, the sinful remained sinful, and the outsiders remained outside. By welcoming them, Jesus's embodiment of the good news brought salvation and redemption to them and their status in relation to the people of God.

In Acts, the focus of the scope of salvation is on the inclusion of both Jews and non-Jews (Gentiles) as composing the one people of God. The initial post-Pentecost stories in Acts ground the believers' faith in Jesus's resurrection and God's ongoing story on behalf of God's people. Luke borrowed LXX images and vocabulary to depict the Christian movement in ways that suggest continuity with Israel. For example, in Peter's Pentecost speech, the quotation from the prophet Joel interprets the Pentecost phenomena as God's fulfillment to Israel. The use of the Greek term *ekklēsia* (usually translated "church" in the NT) usurps the concept found in the LXX of the assembly of Israel as God's people.

Thus, on the one hand, there is a theme of continuity. At the center of the action is the God of the Jewish people. On the other hand, this same God also coaxed believers to go to non-Jews, first to the Godfearer Cornelius (ch. 10) and to those in Antioch of Syria (ch. 11), before heading into the eastern half of the Mediterranean world. What Acts depicts throughout the second half of the narrative is the mission of the church that extended the message of salvation to both Jews and Gentiles. This also means the church is inclusive of both.

5. The Church and Israel

Since the LXX uses the term translated "church" (*ekklēsia*) to refer to Israel, the links between the Jewish community and the church are many. It is doubtful that Luke intended to present Pentecost as the birth of the Christian church, because the believers remained faithful in their Jewish practices throughout Acts. The descriptions of the church in Jerusalem consistently contrast with the Jewish religious leaders. Luke thus offers contrasting images of what it means to be the people of God. God's presence and blessing were found with the church. In a sense, there was division among the Jewish people or Israel over what God had done and was doing. Tensions arose repeatedly in temple and synagogue settings (4:1-22; 5:17-42; 18:1-17), as well as among Jewish believers, over the ongoing role of Jewish **law** and practices (21:18-26). Such questions arise throughout Luke-Acts and pertain to the relation of Jesus and the church to the heritage and legacy of Israel as the people of God.

6. Judaism and the Jewish People

One additional consideration about Luke's theology is the depiction of Judaism and Jewish people in Luke-Acts. Significant attention has been given to the different ways that Luke described Judaism as a religion and cultural system, the Jewish people more generally, Jewish individuals, and smaller groups of individuals. A general consensus among scholars sees the Lukan portrayal of Jewish persons and customs to be somewhat negative. The harshness of the accusations by Peter against the inhabitants of Jerusalem (Acts 2:23) and the ongoing role of "the Jews" as Paul's opponents in the latter half of Acts highlight and add to this negative portrayal.

This evidence contrasts with the inclusion of Gentiles into the realm of God's salvation. Some conclude that Luke's perspective on the Jewish people was very negative due to a crisis in Luke's church over the inclusion of Gentiles that Jewish Christians opposed. According to this view, such Jewish opposition led to the division between Judaism and Christianity, with the result that the Gentile church ultimately replaced Israel as the people of God.

Some scholars have asked if the Lukan perspective should be considered anti-Semitic. Others evaluate the evidence from a literary perspective and see the image as mixed, albeit more negative than positive. Still others conclude the negative images of Jews and Judaism in Acts are confined to unbelieving Jews, and Israel is actually divided over the **gospel** message. According to this latter view, Paul's mission was not to Gentiles in Acts but mostly to Jews, and Gentiles received salvation in contexts where Jewish persons did as well.

RICHARD P. THOMPSON, PHD

Mm

MARRIAGE

Although the OT does not have separate words for marriage, husband, or wife, the importance of marriage for human life is demonstrated from the **creation** accounts culminating with a marriage covenant between a man and a woman (Gen. 2:18-25; cf. 1:28). Because of its placement within the Christian canon, this marriage account, whether considered historically accurate or not, is given primary importance in forming one's understanding of the biblical concept of marriage and serves as a lens through which all marriages in the Bible are evaluated and critiqued.

First Marriage

While Genesis 1:26-28 speaks of humans in general as *(a)* created in the **image of God** as male and female, *(b)* given mutual responsibility to take charge of all the living creatures, and *(c)* blessed by God with fertility, Genesis 2:7-25 focuses on humans as they relate to God and each other. God personally gave life to the first human being, created a garden to provide for him (vv. 7-8), assigned him responsibilities within the garden, and educated him about rules of the "household" he created and ordered (vv. 15-17). As the Father, God took personal interest in the human. He observed that "it's not good that the human is alone" and addressed the need by making "a **helper** that is perfect for him" (v. 18, CEB), which literally means "corresponding to him," carrying the idea of equality and complementarity without subordination. This divine commentary is unexpected when compared to Genesis 1, which repeats seven times that God's creation was (very) good, and identifies the true reason for the creation of a "helper" and for marriage, which is companionship.

The human's loneliness is emphasized further when a "helper" cannot be found among the animals and birds that God formed from the "fertile land" as he did the human (2:19-20, CEB; cf. v. 7). Only when God fashioned the

woman from the human's own rib and brought her to him could the human poetically identify her as his perfect "helper"—that is, his kin, without whom he was incomplete. It is not surprising that the man declared upon seeing the woman that she is "bone from my bones and flesh from my flesh" (v. 23, CEB). By means of marriage, man and woman, and their respective **households**, were united as kinfolk with a reciprocal relationship of mutual privileges and obligations (24:49), and this was a common way of identifying one's kin (29:14; Judg. 9:2; 2 Sam. 5:1; 19:12-13). Neither is it surprising that the human identified himself as a "man" (Hebr., 'îš) and his helper as a "woman" (Hebr., 'iššâ), using similar-sounding words and further emphasizing her kinship to himself.

However, Genesis 2:24, as a prescription for all marriages, calls a man to "leave" or "forsake" (Hebr., 'āzab) his father and mother and to "cleave" (Hebr., dābaq) to his woman or wife in order to become one flesh. This is surprising because in both early Jewish and Greco-Roman societies *(a)* women left their households to join those of their husbands and *(b)* marriages were created to secure the well-being of households. Thus one could expect that the needs of the household and the man's kinship ties to his parents would always trump the woman's needs and the man's kinship ties to his wife. However, verse 24 turns this cultural expectation on its head, proclaiming the man's relationship to the woman as the most important of all his relationships. The language of leaving and cleaving has further significance, for elsewhere 'āzab is used in references to Israel leaving its **covenant** with YHWH (Isa. 1:4, 28) or in commands not to leave the marginalized (Deut. 14:27). Dābaq is used in passages that encourage Israel to cleave to YHWH alone (10:20; 2 Kings 18:6; Jer. 13:11). This language not only helps identify marriage as a covenant with aspects of passion and permanence (Gen. 34:3) but also correlates marriage and YHWH's relationship with Israel in the OT, foreshadowing Jesus's relationship with the **church** (Eph. 5:21-33).

Man and Woman as One Flesh

In Genesis 2:21-22 the woman is fashioned by God out of man's rib and is to be reunited with him as one flesh. The language of "one flesh" affirms kinship rather than sexual union, as verse 23 seems to indicate. Against a cultural background that valued procreation and viewed marriages as unions that could foster **love** (24:67; 29:18; cf. 1 Sam. 18:20) and bring sexual pleasure to both men (Prov. 5:15-20) and women (Gen. 18:12; Song of Sol.; 1 Cor. 7:1-5), this seems unusual—especially since Genesis 1:28 speaks of God blessing men and women to be fruitful. Moreover, the progression from one human (2:7) to man and woman (vv. 21-23) to one flesh can be puzzling (v. 24). One may wonder why the human needed a companion and why two were to become "one" (Hebr., 'eḥād), just as God is said to be one in Deuteronomy 6:4. The answer might be found in Genesis 1:26-27, which speaks of

God (Hebr., *ĕlōhîm*, pl.) contemplating (Hebr., *wayyō'mer*, sg.) the creation of humanity (Hebr., *'ādām*, sg.) in "our image to resemble us" (pl.) and creating humanity (sg.) as male and female (CEB). Here the plurality and singularity of God correlates with the plurality and singularity of humanity. Somehow humanity is created in the image of God and that image is reflected in them being male and female. Thus to have a holistic image of God, diversity in humanity has to be united, and being alone is somehow incomplete; humans require the companionship of the other.

Problems and Solution

Since YHWH vowed to keep his covenantal faithfulness to Israel forever, one might assume that marriages between men and women were to last forever as well. This was Jesus's position when he based his teaching against divorce on Genesis 2:24, concluding, "Humans must not pull apart what God has put together" (Matt. 19:6; Mark 10:9, CEB). However, signs of deterioration of marriage between Adam and Eve appear in Genesis 3:12, when the man, in order to justify himself, turned away from God and failed to cleave to his wife. Consequently, their being as one flesh was jeopardized and their descendants' attempts at forming successful marriages continued to be far from the ideal of Genesis 2, displaying issues such as polygyny, adultery, and divorce. Only in submission to Christ as the head of the **church** and in **sacrificial** submission to each other, modeled by Jesus in his love and death for the church, can spouses aspire to have one-flesh marriages (Eph. 5:21-33).

See also Fall, The; Matriarchs; Obedience; Women in the Old Testament; Women Leaders.

Resources

Campbell, Ken M., ed. *Marriage and Family in the Biblical World.* Downers Grove, IL: InterVarsity Press, 2003.
Wenham, Gordon J. *Genesis 1–15.* WBC, vol. 1. Waco, TX: Word Books, 1987.

NINA HENRICHS-TARASENKOVA, PHD

MATRIARCHS

Nine women in Genesis are known as matriarchs in Israel. The primary wives of the founding family's first three generations (Sarah, Rebekah, Leah, and Rachel), together with five others, mothered three nations (Israel, Edom, and the Ishmaelites) and established the royal line. As founding mothers, they are elevated in the traditions of both Testaments. The prominence of barrenness in these stories highlights Yahweh's life-giving power and notice of women.

Matriarchs of Genesis

Sarai or *Sarah* was the "first mother of Israel." After ninety years, a lifetime of barrenness and mishaps, Yahweh granted Sarah the miracle of bearing Isaac (Gen. 21:1-7). Sarah was a primary element of the promise of countless descendants (13:16).

Rebekah married Isaac, after the servant of Abram or Abraham took tremendous effort to procure a wife for Isaac from Abraham's family in Haran (ch. 24). Despite all her virtues as a bride, Rebekah was barren. After twenty years, Yahweh interceded and Rebekah bore twins—Esau and Jacob (25:21-26)—through whom she became grandmother of two nations: Israel and Edom.

Sisters *Leah* and *Rachel* gave Jacob the sons who founded the twelve tribes (29:15–30:24; 35:16-26). To compensate Leah for Jacob's neglect, Yahweh gave fertility: she bore Reuben, Simeon, Levi, and Judah in quick succession. Frustrated by her own barrenness, Rachel sent her maid Bilhah to Jacob; Bilhah conceived Dan, then Naphtali. Having ceased bearing, Leah sent her maid Zilpah to Jacob; Zilpah conceived Gad, then Asher. Leah's fertility returned, and she bore Issachar, Zebulun, and the only recorded daughter, Dinah. Rachel's womb was finally opened; she bore Joseph and Benjamin, whose birth en route from Bethel killed her. Leah's and Rachel's efforts established the nation.

Minor Matriarchs

Hagar was Sarai's Egyptian maid, sent to Abram before Sarai conceived (Gen. 16). Hagar's pregnancy induced contempt and jealousy. She was cast out, but Yahweh met Hagar in the wilderness, blessing *her* with the promise of numerous descendants. She returned to Abram's camp and gave birth, but the presence of her son Ishmael eventually led to great turmoil. Hagar and Ishmael were cast out permanently, but again Yahweh met them, saving their lives and giving them a future (21:8-21). Ishmael *also* had twelve sons, who settled in the Arabian Peninsula, well attested in extrabiblical sources as powerful, Arab tribes (25:12-18). Hagar became grandmother of the Ishmaelite people.

Bilhah and *Zilpah* bore four of Jacob's sons. They fit a pattern known from ANE marriage contracts: a maid given by the bride's family, in case the bride was infertile (29:24, 29). In these sources, children conceived thus were attributed to the wife; the maid did not usually assume wifehood or even become a permanent concubine. Bilhah and Zilpah are called "maid" (Hebr., *šipḥâ*) even after bearing sons (30:7, 10, 12, 18; 32:22 [23 HB]; 33:1-2, 6; 35:25-26) but rarely "wife" (Hebr., *ʾiššâ*; 30:4, 9; 37:2); Bilhah is once called "concubine" (Hebr., *pîlegeš*; 35:22). Their secondary status under Rachel and Leah explains why Bilhah and Zilpah were considered minor matriarchs.

Asenath was the Egyptian who gave Joseph two sons, Manasseh and Ephraim (41:45, 50-52; 46:20), whom Jacob elevated to take Joseph's place beside their eleven uncles (chs. 48–49). In Israel's first census, Asenath's descendants were the half-tribes called Ephraim and Manasseh (Num. 1:32-35). However, her pagan heritage—daughter of an Egyptian priest of Re, the sun god—has diminished her legacy. Ignored by other biblical writers, Asenath became a proper convert in the Pseudepigrapha and rabbinic writings.

Tamar was the Canaanite whose devotion to her father-in-law's lineage earned her a place in history (ch. 38). Judah's first son failed to impregnate Tamar before he died; against Judah's orders, his second son refused. Judah sent Tamar away to await the adulthood of his third son but neglected to recall her. When Tamar heard Judah was nearby, she took the extraordinary step of posing as a prostitute to sleep with him, during which encounter she conceived twins: Perez and Zerah. Tamar's loyalty was extolled in contrast with Judah's negligence, and she became, through Perez, ancestor and preserver of the royal line. This line (Judah-Perez) became primary in Israelite history.

The Matriarchs beyond Genesis

These women gained esteem beyond their own lifetimes; most reappear outside the Pentateuch. Isaiah upheld Sarah as an example of the improbable origins of Israel and hope for their restoration (Isa. 51:1-3). Paul cited Sarah's barrenness as an example of God's overcoming insurmountable obstacles (Rom. 4:19). He also used Sarah and Rebekah to illustrate Abraham's physical and spiritual descendants (9:1-18). In Galatians, Sarah and Hagar's story becomes an allegory about the old and new covenants (4:21-31). Hebrews uses Sarah's barrenness as a potential obstacle to Abraham's faithfulness (11:11). In a less flattering instance, Peter cites Sarah's "**obedience**" to Abraham ironically to commend trust in Christ instead of fear for Christian women married to nonbelievers (1 Pet. 3:3-6). Abraham was actually the one who "obeyed" Sarah's fearful demands, and her fear threatened great harm (Gen. 16:2, 6; 21:11-12).

Rachel, Leah, and Tamar all feature in Bethlehem's blessing of Ruth, invoking hopes for Ruth's fruitfulness and loyalty and bringing this Moabite into Israel's story (Ruth 4:11-12). Rachel's tomb became an early landmark, recorded carefully in Genesis 35:19-20 and 48:7 and specified in Samuel's instructions after anointing Saul (1 Sam. 10:2). Jeremiah imagined Rachel as a mother mourning the destruction of her descendants (Jer. 31:15), and this same imagery is cited in Matthew's account of Herod slaughtering Bethlehem's boys (2:18). Clearly, Rachel's disappointed hopes resonated in later losses.

Bilhah appears in the Chronicler's genealogy of Naphtali (1 Chron. 7:13), an odd inclusion, since Leah, Rachel, and Zilpah are absent. In fact, Zilpah never appears outside Genesis. Neither does Asenath, but she, Bilhah, and Zilpah were all given attention in rabbinic midrash.

Tamar appears in two important lineages. The Chronicler's genealogy mentions very few mothers, but Tamar is one of them (1 Chron. 2:4). Likewise, Matthew's genealogy of Jesus includes five women, but just one matriarch: Tamar (1:3).

These early mothers of Israel are only one example of the Bible's attention to the women among God's people. Their stories are sometimes fraught, but their legacy is sure.

See also Household Codes; Women in the Old Testament; Women Leaders; Women's Roles in the Church.

Resources

Bellis, Alice Ogden. *Helpmates, Harlots, and Heroes: Women's Stories in the Hebrew Bible.* 2nd ed. Louisville, KY: Westminster John Knox Press, 2007.

Mark, Elizabeth Wyner. "The Four Wives of Jacob: Matriarchs Seen and Unseen." *Reconstructionist* 63, no. 1 (September 1998): 22-35.

Meyers, Carol, ed. *Women in Scripture.* Grand Rapids: Eerdmans, 2001.

Reiss, Moshe, and David Zucker. "Co-opting the Secondary Matriarchs: Bilhah, Zilpah, Tamar, and Aseneth." *BibInt* 22, no. 3 (January 2014): 307-24.

SARAH B. C. DERCK, PHD

MERCY (*eleos, eleeō*)

The concept of mercy is relational throughout both the OT and NT. Mercy is a gift extended from God to humans, from one human to another, and even from humans to animals under their care. What these relationships have in common is that one party has some measure of control over the life of the other. One who is "merciful" recognizes the disparity in the relationship, acts in a way that promotes the life and welfare of the vulnerable party, and/or refrains from taking advantage of an opportunity to do the other harm through violence or other means of control.

The concept of mercy (Hebr., *ḥesed*; Gk., *eleos*) in the Bible is closely related to the concepts of **compassion** (Hebr., noun *raḥămîm*, verb *rāḥam*, and adjective *rāḥûm*; Gk., *splanchnon* and *oiktirmos*) and **graciousness** (Hebr., *ḥen* and *ḥānan*; Gk., *charis*), and translations of the Bible may use these terms interchangeably. In the OT, these terms may be paired with the Hebrew covenantal term, also *ḥesed*, often translated "steadfast love." These terms appear together in songs and prayers, including laments, praise, and petitions to God. The latter may be a request for general welfare, for salvation from military threat, or, especially in the NT, for a miraculous act of healing.

Mercy in the Old Testament

Mercy is attributed to God throughout the OT, especially in **Isaiah**, **Jeremiah**, and the Psalms. God's mercy toward humans is often described as "abundant," yet the manner and extent to which God extends mercy to us can be difficult for humans to comprehend. When God granted Moses's extraordinary request for God's **glory** to pass by him, God stated, "I will be gracious to whomever I will be gracious, and I will extend mercy to whomever I will extend mercy" (Exod. 33:19*b*, AT). God's merciful act—the gift of God's particular presence to Moses—was not an activity that could be predicted or expected. While humans can be assured that mercy is a characteristic of God, we do not always know how or when God's mercy will be made evident.

In the OT, this divine characteristic functions within the covenantal relationship between God and God's people, Israel. In the ANE, the relationship between a political ruler and those seeking his protection was sometimes formalized through a treaty (**covenant**). The treaty clearly defined expectations for the relationship: the ruler would stipulate the terms of expected behavior on both sides, the benefits (blessings) for those who remained loyal to the ruler, and the punishments (curses) on those who failed to observe the covenantal treaty. In the covenantal relationship, the ruler had the opportunity to be merciful and extend his protection or to enact the stipulated punishments against those who broke the treaty.

God established this type of covenant with Abraham (Gen. 15:18; 17:1-8) and the people Israel (Exod. 19–24). The book of Deuteronomy describes the giving of the **law** in terms of this covenantal relationship between the people and God. When the people agreed to the terms of the covenant with its blessings, they also accepted the possibility of punishment (curses) from God if they failed to uphold the covenant.

The OT describes the cyclical behavior of the people: following God during times of obedience and then rebelling against God and breaking the covenant by turning to other gods and failing to observe God's laws. Instead of immediately exercising the covenantal right to punish, God called the people to confess and turn from their **sins** in order that they might receive God's mercy—that is, the reestablishment of the proper relationship between God and God's people, and God's continued protection of the people (Prov. 28:13; Isa. 55:7; Dan. 9:9).

When mercy is withheld by God or by humans, the results can be devastatingly violent. Old Testament military accounts describe conquering leaders as acting "without mercy" when they slaughtered entire villages with no concern for life. Citizens of **Jerusalem** and the villages in Judah experienced firsthand the carnage of a merciless invasion by the Babylonians. The composer of a song of lament, expressing deep grief, accuses God of slaughtering "without mercy" by inviting Jerusalem's enemies to devastate them (Lam. 2:21-22). The **prophets** also speak of the removal of God's mercy from Israel after generations of rebellion, which ultimately allowed their enemies to invade (Jer. 16:5; cf. Isa. 60:10). In these cases, the removal of God's mercy is equated with the removal of God's protection of a people vulnerable to attack.

God's mercy in the OT has additional implications beyond protection from military invasion. **Wisdom**, instruction, and revelation are described as gifts of God's mercy (Ps. 119:77; Dan. 2:18). Other prayers ask that God be merciful by influencing those in a position to give economic or political aid (Gen. 43:14; Neh. 1:11). These prayers indicate that human acts of **compassion** can be extensions of God's mercy.

Though human mercy receives less attention in the OT than divine, God's people are instructed to be merciful when they have a position of control over the life of a human or animal (Prov. 12:10; Zech. 7:9). Often this command is combined with exhortations to graciousness and steadfast **love**. Those who have acted without mercy, such as the Babylonians in their violent conquest of Jerusalem, will receive **judgment** from God (Isa. 47:6-11).

Other passages promise, petition, and report the return of God's mercy. Petitions for a return of God's mercy are offered on behalf of the **community** (Zech. 1:12) and individuals (Ps. 51:1 [3 HB]). Alongside prophecies of the removal of God's mercy are the promises that God's mercy will be greater than God's anger (Isa. 60:10; Jer. 31:20). A prayer of communal confession in the book of Daniel (ch. 9) includes a report that God had extended mercy to the people in spite of their previous rebellion against God.

Mercy in the New Testament

The NT echoes the OT call to show mercy (Gk., *eleos, eleeō*) to others when one is in a position of power or control over them. Jesus used the example of forgiving a debt of money (Matt. 18:33). As the language of debts had become a common way to refer to **sin**, this command may be broadened to include offering mercy when one is sinned against by others. God has extended mercy to God's people, and God's people are expected, in turn, to extend mercy to others (Jude vv. 22-23); if God's people withhold mercy from others, God will withhold mercy when judging God's people (James 2:13).

That the work of God through Christ Jesus was extended to the Gentiles is attributed to God's mercy (Rom. 15:9; 1 Pet. 2:10). Paul and Timothy state that their ministry existed because of the mercy of God (2 Cor. 4:1). While praising God's gift of mercy to the Gentiles, Paul questioned why only some Jews were able to recognize Jesus as the **Messiah** (Rom. 9:14-18). In his wrestling, he quoted Exodus 33:19, acknowledging the ultimately inscrutable nature of God's mercy.

God's mercy is evident through the gifts of **incarnation**, baptism, and the **Holy Spirit** (Titus 3:5). Both the Song of Mary and Zechariah's prophecy declare that God has extended mercy by remembering the covenant with the people of Israel (Luke 1:50-55, 72-79). Throughout the **Gospels**, individuals with ailments and diseases call out to Jesus for mercy to heal them (Matt. 9:27; 15:22; 17:15; 20:30-31). They recognized that Jesus had the power to bring life and promote their well-being. Ultimately, the mercy of Jesus Christ leads to eternal life (Jude v. 21).

See also Forgiveness, The Art and Necessity of.

STEPHANIE SMITH MATTHEWS, MTS

MESSIAH/CHRIST

The various uses of the term "messiah" and the numerous messianic passages in the OT present a multifaceted Messiah (father, prophet, priest, king) who is not only a divinely appointed representative but also the Lord himself, the Father of his people.

The Hebrew term "messiah" (*māšîaḥ*) means "anointed" or "anointed one," corresponding to the Greek *christos*. The term "messiah" is used of the fathers or patriarchs (1 Chron. 16:22; Ps. 105:15), **prophets** (Elisha in 1 Kings 19:16), Aaronic priests (Lev. 4:3, 5, 16), kings (Saul in 1 Sam. 12:3, 5; David in 2 Sam. 3:39; 22:51; Ps. 20:6 [7 HB]), Davidic kings (2 Chron. 6:42; Pss. 18:50 [51 HB]; 84:9 [10 HB]), and an ideal ruler in the future (Ps. 2:2; Dan. 9:25-26). The term is also applied to Cyrus the Great (Isa. 45:1).

The "anointed" were those who had been anointed with holy oil, empowering and elevating them to priestly (Exod. 40:15) or royal (1 Sam. 16:13) status. Others were divinely appointed or symbolically anointed (with the Spirit of God) to fulfill the divine purposes on a national or international scale.

The theological significance of these "anointed ones" illuminates the identity and mission of the future Messiah. A pattern of fatherhood with prophetic, priestly, and kingly rule is observed in Abraham (e.g., Gen. 12:1-2; 14:11-16; 15:1-5, 9-10). Father Abraham received an eternal **covenant** in which all nations would be blessed through him and his descendants (22:16-18; 18:18).

The Abrahamic covenant has the far-reaching theological implication of a new era of comprehensive blessing that overcomes the evil effects of the **fall** (3:14-19, 22-24). This blessing connects with the promise of the woman's offspring who would crush the serpent's head, defeat **evil** (v. 15), and make possible a reentry into the garden of God. Because Father Abraham ushered in the messianic, redemptive work of God and because his "anointing" included the other three anointed functions, he could be understood provisionally as the woman's offspring. But the OT also awaits a Messiah who would complete the redemption of all **creation** (Isa. 11:1-9; 65:17-25) that God began with Abraham.

The promise of a new prophet like Moses (Deut. 18:15-22) raised a messianic hope of a multifaceted leader, particularly that of a revealer of God. Moses revealed God's identity (Exod. 3:15), character (33:18-19), power, supremacy, justice, and redemption (chs. 7–14). As a covenant mediator, Moses gave and taught the **law** of God (chs. 19–24). As a friend of God, Moses fulfilled priestly, intercessory functions (24:6-8; Num. 14:10-20). Moses also

performed kingly functions as the supreme governor, chief justice (Exod.
18:19-26), and occasional military leader (Num. 21:21-35).

The anointed priests embodied "HOLINESS TO THE LORD" (Exod. 28:36;
39:30, KJV). They bore the iniquity of the people and made atonement
(Lev. 16:32-34), enabling the continuation of the Lord's presence among his
people. The priests also had a prophetic function as teachers of the covenant
laws and a kingly role as judiciaries (10:11; Deut. 16:18–17:20).

The anointed kings of Israel were divinely authorized and commissioned (1 Sam. 10:6, 9-10; 16:13) to defend the people from their enemies
(e.g., 11:6-14) and to administer **justice** and **righteousness**. The kings were
required to lead the people in **covenant obedience** and faithfulness (Deut.
17:18-20) like shepherds to their people.

A few messianic texts envision a victorious king who would shepherd
his flock in universal, everlasting rule (Mic. 5:2-4; Zech. 9:9-10). Others
speak of a divine Son-King at the Lord's right hand, who judges the nations
(Pss. 2; 110). Isaiah 40:10-11 describes the future rule of the Lord himself
in language elsewhere used for the messianic Shepherd (cf. Ezek. 37:21-28).

Daniel 9:26, however, predicts that "the Anointed One will be put to
death" (NIV). The context suggests that this death is priestly, "to put an
end to sin, to atone for wickedness, to bring in everlasting righteousness" (v.
24, NIV). The priestly messianic Servant would suffer a vicarious death as a
sin offering to "justify many" (Isa. 53:11, NIV; see vv. 10-12). This Suffering
Servant is called "the arm of the LORD" (v. 1, NIV), which refers to the Lord
himself in saving action (51:5-10; 52:8-10).

The OT presents the coming Messiah as one who is simultaneously the
Lord's representative and the Lord himself. This is seen with clarity in two
of the names given to the promised "son" and Messiah in Isaiah 9:6: "Mighty
God" and "Everlasting Father" (NIV). These names point to the divine nature
of the coming Messiah. In addition, they speak of the Messiah as a perfect
embodiment of the compassionate and merciful fatherhood of God (63:16;
Ps. 103:13; Exod. 34:6-7) and the nature of his prophet-priest-king ministry
as the exact representation of divine fatherhood (cf. John 14:9).

In conclusion, the Messiah of the OT would be a prophet, priest, and
king all at once, reunifying and fulfilling the characteristics and functions
that were partially embodied in Abraham and Moses and were later specialized in segregated offices in the institutions of Israel. The coming Messiah
would embody to the fullest extent these leadership functions, expressing
God's own fathering of Israel and ultimately all peoples of the earth. This
Messiah would be at once an ideal human representative of God and the
Lord himself, the notion of which can be reconciled only in the mystery of
the **incarnation** and the manifold ministries of the Messiah in his first and
second comings.

See also Compassion; Holy Spirit; Mercy.

H. JUNIA POKRIFKA, PHD

MIRACLES OF JESUS

In addition to healing many with various diseases (e.g., Mark 1:32-34), the Gospels record thirty-two specific miracles performed by Jesus. They include casting out demons, healing the blind and afflicted, raising the dead, and commanding nature.

While in the modern world such events are often considered suspect, in the Greco-Roman and Jewish worlds they were not. Other individuals before Jesus had performed similar deeds, but none as varied or as numerous. During the ministry of Jesus, many afflicted persons flocked to him. They looked to him as a miracle worker.

The miracles that Jesus performed were expressions of the presence and power of the kingdom and should not be separated from his teachings about the **kingdom of God**.

There are four terms or phrases the Gospel writers used to refer to a miracle. (How the Greek words are translated varies from version to version.) The NIV translates *dynamis* nine times as "miracle[s]" and twice as "miraculous power[s]" (Matt. 13:54; Mark 6:14). The most common word used to signify a miracle is *sēmeion*, "a sign": Matthew, eleven times; Mark, six times; Luke, ten times; and John, sixteen times. The phrase "signs and wonders" (*sēmeion kai terata*) occurs three times: Matthew 24:24 (to refer to acts of false prophets); Mark 13:22; and John 4:48. *Ergon*, "work," is translated once as "miracle" (John 7:21), eleven times as "work[s]" (e.g., v. 3), and twice as "deed[s]" (Matt. 11:2; Luke 24:19).

Driving Out Demons

The Gospels record seven times that Jesus drove out an impure or demonic spirit, often with different reactions. On the Sabbath at Capernaum, Jesus drove out the spirit who recognized him as the "Holy One of God" and people were amazed (Mark 1:23-25, NIV; cf. 3:11). When Jesus cast out the demon of the blind and mute man, the people inquired, "Could this be the Son of David?" (Matt. 12:22-23, NIV). Jesus disembarked at the region of the Gerasenes and was confronted by a demon-possessed man of great strength (Mark 5:1-17; Matt. 8:28-34 reads two men); his healing of the man frightened the town's people (Mark 5:15). When Jesus drove out the demon of a man who was mute, the people were amazed, but the authorities claimed that he did it by the power of the "prince of demons" (Matt 9:32-34, NIV; Luke 11:14). The leader of the synagogue was indignant that Jesus would on the Sabbath cast out the spirit that had crippled a woman for eighteen years (Luke 13:10-14). Jesus's healing of the daughter of a Greek mother depended upon her wit and of the child with an impure spirit upon the faith of the father (Mark 7:25-30; 9:14-27).

Jesus's exorcisms demonstrated the breaking in of the kingdom and his authority and power over the forces of evil.

Old Testament Background

A number of Jesus's miracles reflect those recorded in the OT. Jesus's raising of the widow's son and his raising of Jairus's daughter (Luke 7:11-15; 8:40-56) parallel Elijah's restoring the widow's son at Zarephath (1 Kings 17:17-24) and Elisha's raising the Shunammite's son (2 Kings 4:32-37).

Isaiah viewed the restoration of the Israelites as a time when the blind would see, the deaf hear, the lame leap, and the mute speak (Isa. 35:5-6). When John the Baptist inquired whether Jesus was "the one who is to come," Jesus sent John's disciples back to him with this message: "The blind receive sight, the lame walk, those who have leprosy are cleansed, the deaf hear, the dead are raised, and the good news is proclaimed to the poor" (Matt. 11:3-5, NIV).

On two occasions Jesus healed two blind men who recognized him as the "Son of David" (Matt. 9:27-31; 20:29-34, NIV; for the latter, Mark has only one, Bartimaeus, 10:46-52). He also enabled the paralyzed to walk (Mark 2:1-12; John 5:1-8), cleansed those with leprosy (Luke 5:12-13; 17:11-19), and enabled a deaf and mute man to hear and speak (Mark 7:32-33). John would have recognized these deeds as the work of the **Messiah**.

Resurrection

There are three accounts of Jesus raising someone from the dead: the daughter of Jairus (Mark 5:22-24, 35-43), the son of the widow of Nain (Luke 7:11-15), and Lazarus (John 11:38-44). It has been suggested that the first two were resuscitations, the reviving of someone who was apparently dead. But the accounts describe them as being dead, and Jesus did not apply any medical procedures to revive them (although he did take the daughter by the hand). In both cases, he simply told them to "get up" (a present active imperative of *egeirō* to the daughter, and an aorist passive imperative to the son). By the authority of his word, Jesus brought all three back to life.

This imagery anticipates the resurrection of Jesus. The God who was "well pleased" with his Son (Matt. 17:5, NIV) would raise him from the dead. It also prefigures the resurrection of those who have faith in Jesus.

Nature Miracles

Each of Jesus's acts of healing could be considered nature miracles in that they changed the physical body of the person. However, usually this classification is restricted to changes in nature itself. Twice Jesus demonstrated his authority over the waters of the sea, when he stilled a storm (Mark 4:35-41) and when he walked on water (John 6:18-21). His command over the water echoes God's authority over the waters in creation (Gen. 1:6-9).

Twice Jesus fed the multitude: five thousand (John 6:5-13, the only miracle recorded in all four Gospels) and four thousand (Mark 8:1-9). These events have both a backward and forward reference: the manna that fed Israel in the **wilderness** (Exod. 16) and the Eucharist, which points to the messianic banquet.

After feeding the five thousand, the people wanted to make Jesus king (John 6:15). Jesus had faced this temptation before and rejected it because this was not the way the kingdom of God was to be ushered in (Luke 4:2-8).

Conclusion

For the writers of the Gospels, and the early church, the miracles that Jesus performed indicated that he was the Messiah who was to come. He healed the sick, changed water into wine, fed the multitudes, commanded the forces of nature, and raised the dead.

However, he was not the type of Messiah the people were expecting or that the leaders wanted. He was not a powerful commander of military forces, as was his ancestor David. Rather, he went to the cross as an authoritative teacher who possessed miraculous power. His vision of the kingdom of God was one of redemption and service, not the power of the sword.

Resources

Achtemeier, Paul J., Joel B. Green, and Marianne Meye Thompson. *Introducing the New Testament: Its Literature and Theology.* Grand Rapids: Eerdmans, 2001.
Childs, Brevard S. *Biblical Theology of the Old and New Testaments: Theological Reflection on the Christian Bible.* Minneapolis: Fortress Press, 1992.
Cotter, Wendy. "Miracle." Pages 99-106 in vol.4 of *NIDB.*
Richardson, Alan. *An Introduction to the Theology of the New Testament.* New York: Harper and Row, 1958.

ROBERT D. BRANSON, PHD

MISSIONAL HERMENEUTICS

The term "missional hermeneutics" describes a way of reading Scripture in light of the mission of the triune God, the *missio Dei*, and as a people engaged in that mission. It is grounded in the conviction that the whole of Scripture bears witness to a missional God, a God who is on a mission: to reconcile all people to himself, as well as to one another, and ultimately to restore the whole of **creation** in Jesus Christ (Col. 1:15-23; Rev. 21–22). Furthermore, missional interpretation seeks to articulate the church's role in the *missio Dei*, as a people called and empowered to participate in God's loving mission.

Why Missional Hermeneutics?

Several factors have come together in recent decades to trigger fresh interest in missional hermeneutics. The first has to do with the understanding of mission itself. Missiologists and biblical scholars have increasingly embraced a comprehensive understanding of mission, which involves more than the cross-cultural outreach of the **church**. Mission is anchored in God's purpose to bring about salvation at every level.

Second, biblical interpretation has seen significant movement away from purely historical readings of the Bible and toward those more open to the theological and missional dimensions of Scripture for the people of God.

Third, Christianity's "center of gravity" has shifted dramatically to the global South and East, leading the West to a heightened awareness that it now finds itself in a missionary context. At the same time, fresh voices from the majority world tend to be more sensitive to Scripture's missional character.

Fourth, missiologists, biblical scholars, and church leaders have begun to reflect seriously on missional interpretation. Leading voices include missiologists David Bosch and Michael Goheen and biblical scholars Christopher J. H. Wright, N. T. Wright, and Michael Gorman (see the bibliography in Goheen 2016).

The Character of Missional Hermeneutics

No consensus has yet emerged about what missional interpretation entails. George Hunsberger identifies four complementary understandings of missional hermeneutics that arose from a series of meetings sponsored by the Gospel and Our Culture Network in North America (see Goheen 2016, 45-67). The first spotlights the missional character of the biblical narrative, which is about God's mission and the church's participation in it. The second highlights how Scripture equips and enables the church to engage in the *missio Dei*. The third focuses on the missional location of the communities that read Scripture, and the fourth concerns how Scripture engages different cultures and social contexts.

All four of these dimensions contribute to the practice of missional interpretation. Nevertheless, the first two seem to be foundational, since they emphasize the message and purpose of Scripture itself for the people of God. They affirm Scripture's role as both a *witness* and an *instrument* of God's mission.

Scripture as a Witness to God's Mission

Missional interpretation consciously reads both the OT and NT as bearing witness to the story of God's gracious mission. Rather than seeing mission as a single theme alongside many others in Scripture, it views mission as a coherent framework for understanding the entire biblical story. Instead of trying to root out occasional "missionary texts" within the Bible (e.g., Matt. 28:18-20), it views the whole of Scripture as a "mission text."

A missional reading of the OT, then, recognizes that God called and blessed Israel not only for its own sake but also for the sake of all peoples by becoming an instrument of blessing (Gen. 12:1-3), a "light to the nations" (Isa. 42:6; 49:6, NRSV). In other words, Israel's very identity is missional. Likewise, the NT bears witness to the focus of God's mission, Jesus Christ, whom the Father sends in the power of the **Holy Spirit** to bring about God's restoring purpose in every dimension. What's more, the church, the redeemed and sent community, participates in and is defined by the *missio Dei*. The NT letters, for example, show the outworking of God's missional purpose in relation to concrete communities of **faith**.

Scripture as an Instrument of God's Mission

The Bible not only tells the *story* of God's comprehensive mission but also functions as an *instrument* of that mission. Many texts in the OT seek to shape Israel into a holy people, whose distinctive way of life was both visible to the surrounding nations and a means of bringing them to God (Exod. 19:4-6; Deut. 4:6-8). Even more directly, the NT writings address Christian communities already caught up in the mission of God. The Gospels, letters, and other NT writings proclaim and unpack the good news in ways that equip and nurture those communities for faithful witness in their settings.

This is also true of churches today. To read Scripture missionally involves hearing its call into fellowship with God, as a people who embody the mission of God. Missional interpretation beckons us to ask, How do these texts form and energize the church to bear witness, through word, deed, and character, to the ongoing story of God's loving mission in the world? What that looks like in practice will differ in various global settings. A missional interpretation will sing the **gospel** story in many different keys. New circumstances bring fresh questions and different ears for hearing biblical texts.

Missional Reading in Practice

As an example of reading Scripture missionally, consider John's vision of the new **Jerusalem** in Revelation 21–22. This text reveals the goal of God's mission. It represents the climax of God's purpose—to redeem people from every nation and to restore the whole of **creation**—with Christ, the slaughtered Lamb, at the center of that story. At the same time, John's vision of the new Jerusalem serves to shape and renew the missional communities that encounter this text. Through Revelation's apocalyptic images, John invites readers to *reimagine* their world from the perspective of God's future.

For John's first-century audience, this end-time perspective challenged the idolatrous and deceptive worldview of Rome. They were to bear witness in advance to a different empire, one characterized by **justice, holiness**, and hospitality. Similarly, by embracing God's future, Christian communities today receive the **grace** to live now as a foretaste of God's coming rule. For example, in the midst of the city stands the Tree of Life, whose leaves "are for the healing of the nations" (Rev. 22:2, NIV). If such healing represents the mission of the new Jerusalem, then the church leans into that mission when it becomes an instrument of healing and **reconciliation** among the world's nations.

Conclusion

Missional interpretation represents more than a passing hermeneutical fad. It offers Christians an overarching framework for reading Scripture: the sweeping mission of God. At the same time, it enables Christian communities to recognize more fully Scripture's function as an instrument of the *missio Dei*. Missional hermeneutics cannot claim to be the only lens through which to read biblical texts. It does affirm, however, that we read Scripture more faithfully when we read it with our ears finely tuned to the music of God's mission.

See also Church, Mission of the; Church, The.

Resources

Flemming, Dean. *Why Mission?* Nashville: Abingdon Press, 2015.
Goheen, Michael W., ed. *Reading the Bible Missionally.* Grand Rapids: Eerdmans, 2016.
Wright, Christopher J. H. *The Mission of God: Unlocking the Bible's Grand Narrative.* Downers Grove, IL: IVP Academic, 2006.

DEAN FLEMMING, PHD

Nn

NAMES OF GOD

Both Judaism and Christianity cherish the commandment against taking the Lord's name in vain. To keep this commandment one must know, above all, what precisely the name of God is. The OT gives God a variety of names, not the least of which is the term "god" itself, which functions not only as a proper name but also as a general noun for divine figures (along with "goddess" for female deities).

When the OT uses a particular name for God, this serves to place emphasis on one or another characteristic of God. The Hebrew OT uses four principal names for God: The first, *yhwh*, occurs more than 6800 times. Second, *ʾēl* and *ʾĕlōhîm* considered together occur more than 2800 times; these serve as both the common word for a deity and the name of Israel's God. Third, *ʾădōnāy* occurs 439 times including compounds; it means "Lord." Finally, *šadday* occurs 48 times including compounds; translators usually use "Almighty." One may find them alone or in combination, either with each other or with some other term.

This article will deal with these four terms in descending order of frequency. In addition, the article will list several of the compound names formed with *ʾĕlōhîm* and *yhwh*. This article will not include the many metaphors and similes employed particularly by poetic books (e.g., "You are my hiding place and my shield" [Ps. 119:114, NRSV]; "The name of the LORD is a strong tower" [Prov. 18:10, NRSV]).

YHWH (and Compounds)

For centuries, many Jews and Christians have refused to pronounce the revealed personal name of God, Yahweh. When and why Judaism established this practice remains unclear. The Bible never specifically prohibits pronouncing God's name; however, by the time of the Masoretes (sixth to tenth century AD), this was established practice. As to the reason, several possibilities present themselves. First, if one never said the name of God, one could not possibly misuse the name of God. Thus the practice built a fence around the commandment. Second, not speaking the name of God could avoid its accidental mistreatment or erasure. The other gods had to be removed from the promised land, but the true God must not be (Deut. 12:3-4). Third, the rabbis may have been counteracting the belief of some in the Jewish mystical tradition who held that magical power rested in knowing the name of God.

In keeping with the practice, the Masoretes suggested the substitution of another term when reading, usually *ădōnāy* (Lord) or *ĕlōhîm* (God). The pronunciation "Jehovah" combines the consonants of *yhwh* with the vowels of *ădōnāy*, making it, for some, an acceptable alternative. English versions typically represent the name—often called the Tetragrammaton because it consists of four Hebrew consonants—with small caps, "LORD" or, in a few cases, "GOD" (e.g., Jer. 1:6, NRSV).

The OT gives at least three traditions for the revelation of this name. In one, God revealed the name to Moses at the burning bush (Exod. 3:13-15). However, Abram used the name as far back as Genesis 13:4. Even further back, Genesis 4:26 states, "People began to invoke the name of the LORD" (NRSV). This ambiguity about the origins of *yhwh* surely indicates something of its ancientness. Exodus 3 posits an origin most directly. Genesis 15 seems to assume Genesis 4:26, whereas the latter remains uninterested in the origin of the name.

The name *yhwh* occurs in a number of compound phrases that express different aspects of God's nature. First, two names are often combined to form the phrase *yhwh ĕlōhîm*, translated "the LORD God" or something similar. This compound name first appears in Genesis 2:4. A variation of this is *yhwh ĕlōhênû*, translated "the LORD our God," the most famous example of which comes in the pivotal confession of faith known as the Shema (see Deut. 6:4-5). A second important compound joins *yhwh and ădōnāy*, the word often read in place of *yhwh*. When this happens (Jer. 1:6), the Masoretes usually suggested the pronunciation *ĕlōhîm* for *yhwh*.

Other compounds with *yhwh* emphasize various aspects of God's character and arise out of experiences in the tradition. Many occur only once in the OT:

Yhwh ṣĕbā'ôt means "YHWH of hosts" and has military connotations. Many English versions translate this phrase "the LORD Almighty," which unfortunately confuses *yhwh ṣĕbā'ôt* with *ĕl šaddāy* (see below). *Yhwh ṣĕbā'ôt* occurs several times in the OT, especially among the Prophets (both Major and Minor). In fact, the prophet Jeremiah prefers a much longer form, *yhwh ṣĕbā'ôt ĕlōhê yiśrā'ēl*, translated "the LORD of hosts, God of Israel" (Jer. 7:3).

Yhwh nissî (Exod. 17:15) means "YHWH is my banner." According to the tradition, Moses proclaimed this name when the Israelites defeated the Amalekites. Moses had to keep his arms raised during the battle; hence, he proclaimed God as the one who lifts Godself over God's followers.

Yhwh rōpē' (Exod. 15:26) means "YHWH who heals" and emphasizes God's protection from disease (see also Ps. 103:3).

Yhwh rō'î (Ps. 23:1) means "YHWH is my shepherd" and speaks to the care God has for God's people and to the assurance worshippers can feel in God's presence.

Yhwh šāmmâ (Ezek. 48:35) means "YHWH is there." It originally occurs in the context of an eschatological **hope** but also speaks to a constant awareness of the presence of God (see also Ps. 139).

Yhwh ṣidqēnû (Jer. 23:6; 33:16), meaning "YHWH is our **righteousness**," also has some eschatological (or at least future-oriented) overtones, for with this phrase Jeremiah looks forward to the restoration of God's people after the exile.

Finally, *yhwh měqadiškem* (Exod. 31:13) means "YHWH who sanctifies you" and emphasizes how God sanctifies God's people through God's commandments, for example keeping the Sabbath **holy**. Many Jewish prayers begin with a phrase recalling this and several other biblical names for God: *Bārûk 'attâ yhwh 'ělōhênû melek hā'ôlām, 'ăšer qidděšānû běmiṣwōtāyw wiṣiwānû l . . .*, translated "Praised art Thou, O Lord* our God, Ruler of the universe, who hast sanctified us through Thy commandments . . ." (Leviant 2008, 143).

El, Elohim, and Compounds

In the vast majority of OT occurrences, this name refers to the God of Israel. However, in some Canaanite traditions, El was the high god of the pantheon. A bull stood as a symbol for El, earning this god the epithet Bull-El. The shrines of the northern kingdom at Bethel and Dan, famous for their bull figurines so disapproved by the Deuteronomists, may have found their inspiration in these El traditions.

The use of *'ēl* includes various compound phrases such as *'ēl 'elyôn*, possessive pronouns ("my God," "our God," etc.), and phrases such as "the God of Bethel" (Gen. 31:13). Another singular form, *'ělôah*, occurs mainly in the book of Job, with scattered examples elsewhere. This version of the singular may lie behind Jesus's Aramaic words on the cross (Matt. 27:46, quoting Ps. 22:1 [2 HB]). The plural *'ělōhîm* occurs about three times as often, sometimes referring to the gods of other nations but usually to the God of Israel (e.g., Gen. 1:1). In the latter case, the plural noun occurs alongside singular verbs, thus yielding a "plural of majesty." Theologically, a plural of majesty may make a statement such as Psalm 97:9, where *'ělōhîm* refers to the gods of other nations, far above whom Israel's God is exalted.

Like *yhwh*, *ʾēl* occurs also in compound forms. The compound form *ʾēl* *ʾelyôn*, or "God Most High," occurs twenty-eight times in the OT. In Genesis 14:18-22, Abram identifies *ʾēl* *ʾelyôn*, whom the priest Melchizedek served, with Yahweh. Sometimes *ʾelyôn* occurs by itself or with the **covenant** name *yhwh*, as in Psalm 97:9.

Another form is *ʾēl šaddāy*, usually translated "God Almighty." This compound occurs seven times in the OT. The Priestly source of the Pentateuch argued that God was known by this name prior to revealing the name "Yahweh" to Moses (Exod. 6:3).

A third compound form is *ʾēl ʿôlām*, translated "Everlasting God" (Gen. 21:33; Isa. 40:28; implicitly in Pss. 90:1-3; 93:2; Isa. 26:4). The word *ʿôlām* appears with *melek*, "king," as a name in Jeremiah 10:10, referring to God as the King of the universe.

Other compound forms of *ʾēl* occur in the OT with varying frequency. Though many are more properly titles than names, each contributes to a more complete understanding of God. The following is a list of these other compounds, each with the author's translation and an OT verse as an example:

ʾēl ʾeḥād, "the one God" (Mal. 2:10)
ʾēl hanneʾĕmān, "the faithful God" (Deut. 7:9)
ʾēl ʾĕmet, "God of truth" (Ps. 31:5 [6 HB])
ʾēl ṣaddîq, "the righteous God" (Isa. 45:21)
ʾēl rŏʾî, "God who sees me" (Gen. 16:13)
ʾēl yĕšurûn, "God of the upright" (Deut. 33:26)
ʾēl gibbôr, "the mighty God" (Isa. 9:6[5])
ʾēl dēʿôt, "God of knowledge" (1 Sam. 2:3)
ʾēl haggādōl, "the great God" (Deut. 10:17)
ʾēl-hakkābôd, "God of **glory**" (Ps. 29:3)
ʾēl haqqādôš, "the **holy** God" (Isa. 5:16)
ʾēl haššāmāyim, "God of heaven" (Ps. 136:26)
ʾēl ḥayyāy, "God of my life" (Ps. 42:8 [9 HB])
ʾēl-ḥannûn, "the gracious God" (Jon. 4:2)
ʾēl yiśrāʾēl, "God of Israel" (Ps. 68:35 [36 HB])
ʾēl salĕʿî, "God of my strength" (Ps. 42:9 [10 HB])
ʾēl raḥûm, "God of **compassion**" (Deut. 4:31)
ʾēl yĕšûʿātēnû, "God of our salvation" (Ps. 68:19 [20 HB])
ʾēl qannāʾ, "the jealous God" (Exod. 20:5)
ʾēl hannôrāʾ, "the awesome God" (Neh. 9:32)

Adonai

The term *ʾădōnāy* simply means "lord," and, like *ʾēl*, it sometimes functions as the proper name of Israel's God. It also occurs as part of some humans' names. One notable example comes in Solomon's rival to the throne

Adonijah (1 Kings 1–2), whose name combines *ădōnāy* and *yhwh*. Isaiah's great vision in the temple (Isa. 6:1-8) is of the "Lord"—that is, *ădōnāy*. Isaiah 3:17 places *ădōnāy* and *yhwh* in parallel with each other, clearly indicating that *ădōnāy* could function as a proper name for God. Further evidence for this comes in the Septuagint, which consistently translates *yhwh* with *kyrios*, the Greek equivalent of *ădōnāy*.

Shaddai

Aside from the compound expression *'ēl šadday* (see above), *šadday* occurs thirty-six times by itself. Sometimes appearing in poetic parallelism with other names for God, *šadday* occurs most often in the book of Job (29x). It also occurs twice in Ruth and Psalms and once each in Genesis, Numbers, and Isaiah.

The precise meaning of this term remains unclear. Many translations render it "almighty," though this creates some confusion with *yhwh ṣĕbā'ôt*. An alternative reading derives from Genesis 49:25, which connects *šadday* to the word meaning "breasts." The resulting translation, "the Breasted One," emphasizes the nurturing and motherly aspect of God. A third option, from the Jewish sages, highlights the meaning "enough," suggesting that God created the world while leaving a little bit unfinished for humans to complete through the commandments.

Conclusion

Each of the varied names for God in the OT speaks to a different aspect of Israel's experience with God. Although most occur only once or twice in the Bible, each contributes to the vast significance of the term "God" and to our understanding of the importance of God in Israel's history. No human language can describe God fully; indeed, attempts at defining the infinite are bound to fail. The second commandment forbids worship of engraved or sculpted images, but even language employs imagery and the imagination, for it cannot function otherwise.

Resource
Leviant, Curt, ed. *Masterpieces of Hebrew Literature: A Treasury of 2000 Years of Jewish Creativity.* 2nd ed. Philadelphia: Jewish Publication Society, 2008.

MITCHEL MODINE, PHD

Oo

OBEDIENCE

The biblical idea of obedience is expressed as the expected relationship between the Creator and creatures. It is also extended to human relationships, such as rulers and their subjects, parents and their offspring, and masters and their slaves. The Hebrew word *šāma* means "to hear, listen to" and is often accompanied by the object "voice" (e.g., Deut. 4:30). The NT uses the Greek *hypakouō*, "to hear" or "to listen to," and *tēreō*, "to keep." To obey, then, is to engage in the relational act of listening to another's voice and heeding what is said or valuing and holding on to what one has been given. This vocabulary frames obedience as an act of love rather than as a matter of subjection or legalism.

The OT concept is first seen in Creator-creature relationships. God saw every part of the **creation** as good (Gen. 1). However, from early times, with the giving of the commandment not to eat of the Tree of the Knowledge of Good and **Evil**, humankind faced the choice of obedience or disobedience (ch. 3). God's command set boundaries for anticipated obedience. The account of Adam and Eve's deception and their partaking of the forbidden "fruit from the tree that is in the middle of the garden" (v. 3, NIV) reveals at least three acts of creaturely disobedience: the serpent's "crafty" deception (v. 1, NIV), Eve's eating of the fruit, and Adam's eating of it. These acts resulted in broken relationships with God and between themselves. Our Creator requires obedience in order to sustain the Creator-creature and creature-creature relationships.

By the time of Noah, obedience was rare: "Every inclination of the thoughts of the human heart was only **evil** all the time" (6:5*b*, NIV). However, "Noah was a **righteous** man, blameless among the people of his time, and he walked faithfully with God" (v. 9, NIV). In his obedience, "Noah did all that the LORD commanded him" (7:5, NIV).

Abraham's descendants were promised blessings for obeying God. Abraham was assured that through his offspring God would bless all nations (22:18). Later, Moses urged the Israelites toward a fully embodied obedience, "to **fear the** Lord your God, to walk in obedience to him, to love him, to serve the Lord your God with all your heart and with all your soul," reminding them that observing "the Lord's commands and decrees" was for their "own good" (Deut. 10:12-13, NIV).

This idea of relationship expressed in obedience carries over into the NT. Jesus revealed this dynamic within the Trinity, indicating he received commandments from the Father (John 10:18). Thereafter, he applied this to his followers, saying, "Whoever has my commands and keeps [*tēreō*] them is the one who loves me. The one who loves me will be loved by my Father, and I too will **love** them and show myself to them" (14:21, NIV). Obedience is a love relationship kept within these boundaries.

Jesus celebrated Abraham's obedience but accused the unbelieving Jews, saying, "If you were Abraham's children . . . then you would do what Abraham did" (8:39, NIV). Furthermore, they could not claim God as their Father, since they did not love Jesus, whom God sent to them. Despite their obedience to the **law**, their rejection of Jesus proved their "father [was] the **devil**" (v. 44, NIV). Paul acknowledged the gravity of obedience by speaking in terms of warfare, reminding the Corinthians that one must "take captive every thought to make it obedient [*hypakoē*] to Christ" (2 Cor. 10:5, NIV).

Obedience to one's rulers is expected in both Testaments. In the OT some rulers were recognized for having special relationships with God. For example, during a troubled period, the pharaoh of Egypt promoted Joseph because he was "one in whom is the spirit of God" (Gen. 41:38, NIV). He made him second-in-command, decreeing, "All . . . people are to submit to your orders" (v. 40, NIV). In the NT, Jesus acknowledged both religious and political rulers. First, he paid the temple tax even while acknowledging the inequity of the system (Matt. 17:24-27). Second, he admonished his challengers, "Give back to Caesar what is Caesar's, and to God what is God's" (22:21, NIV). Paul also practiced obedience to both religious (Acts 23:1-5) and political rulers (chs. 23–26).

Parents exercise authority over their offspring, and obedience to this authority is commanded by God. It is to be expressed as "**honor** [Hebr., *kābēd*] . . . so that you may live long and that it may go well with you" (Deut. 5:16, NIV). The NT admonishes children, "Obey your parents in everything, for this pleases the Lord" (Col. 3:20, NIV).

Slavery was a pervasive ancient reality. It therefore occasioned practical advice on obedience. In Paul's **household codes**, slaves were admonished to obey their masters as an act of love, "just as you would obey Christ" (Eph. 6:5-6, NIV; Col. 3:22; 1 Tim. 6:2). Slavery is also a prominent metaphor for obedience (Ps. 123:2; Mal. 1:6). Paul and Peter both speak of Christian obedience as slavery (Rom. 6–7; 1 Cor. 7:21-22; 1 Pet. 2:16).

See also Fall, The.

DARYLL GORDON STANTON, EDD

Pp

PAROUSIA (*parousia*)

The basic meaning of the Greek word *parousia* is "coming" or "presence" and referred, in classical Greek, to the arrival of a ruler, dignitary, or god. Occasionally, Paul employed *parousia* in the classical sense for the presence or arrival of the apostles or other Christian leaders (1 Cor. 16:17; 2 Cor. 7:6-7; 10:10; Phil. 1:26).

More recently, the biblical category has been expanded to become a catchall category, incorporating a number of other biblical terms that describe the coming or presence of Christ. This broadened category includes the first coming of Christ in the **incarnation**:

"For the **grace** of God has appeared [*epiphainō*] . . ." (Titus 2:11, ESV).

"Do not think that I have come [*erchomai*] to abolish the **Law** or the **Prophets**" (Matt. 5:17, ESV; cf. 10:34).

"He . . . descended [*katabainō*] from heaven, the Son of Man" (John 3:13, ESV).

"He has appeared [*phaneroō*] once for all at the end of the ages" (Heb. 9:26, ESV; cf. 1 John 3:5, 8).

The following terms also occur in reference to the second coming: "come" (*erchomai*; Matt. 10:23; 16:27; 24:30, 44; 25:31; 26:64; John 14:3); "descend" (*katabainō*; 1 Thess. 4:16); "appears" (*phaneroō*; Col. 3:4; 1 Pet. 5:4; 1 John 2:28; 3:2); "appearance" (*epiphaneia*; 1 Tim. 6:14; 2 Tim. 1:10; 4:1, 8; Titus 2:13); and "revelation" (*apokalypsis*; 1 Cor. 1:7; 2 Thess. 1:7; 1 Pet. 4:13).

This broadened category includes references to "the day": "the day" (*hē hēmera*; Luke 17:30; Rom. 13:12; 1 Cor. 3:13; 1 Thess. 5:5, 8); "day of the Lord" (*hēmera kyriou*; 1 Cor. 5:5; 1 Thess. 5:2; 2 Thess. 2:2; 2 Pet. 3:10); "day of Christ" (*hēmera Christou*; Phil. 1:10; 2:16); "day of Christ Jesus" (*hēmera Christou Iēsou*; 1:6); "day of our Lord Jesus" (*hēmera tou kypiou hēmōn Iēsou*; 2 Cor. 1:14; cf. 1 Cor. 1:8); and "day of God" (*hēmera theou*; 2 Pet. 3:12).

The OT depicts the presence or coming of God in numerous ways: theophanies to human beings (Gen. 3:8; 18:1-33; 32:22-32; Josh. 5:13-15); the **glory** of God (Exod. 13:20-22); and the appearance of the cloud over the **mercy** seat of the ark of the **covenant** (Lev. 16:2). Such disclosures anticipate the presence or coming of God in the NT that reaches its apex in the coming of Jesus Christ (John 1:1-18).

The Greek word *parousia* appears twenty-four times in the NT. In twenty-two of the twenty-four occurrences, the noun is translated "coming," but it has also been translated twice as "presence" (2 Cor. 10:10; Phil. 2:12, ESV).

When the disciples raised questions about the sign of the *parousia* "and of the end of the age" (Matt. 24:3, ESV), Jesus replied with three references to the term *parousia*, comparing it with various phenomena (vv. 27, 37, 39). The context of the first comparison is significant. Jesus warned against deception by false messiahs. He contrasted the manner of the coming or appearance of the false messiahs to that of the true **Messiah** (vv. 5, 23-28). The Messiah's coming would not be private or localized but, like the flash of lightning passing from the east to the west, visible universally (v. 27).

In the second and third comparisons, Jesus stressed the unexpected nature of the *parousia*, whose timing is known only to the Father (vv. 36-37). The *parousia* of Christ is likened to the flood during the days of Noah (vv. 37-39), which will surprise people who are preoccupied with the affairs of daily living (vv. 38, 40-41). The comparison with the flood of Noah's day stresses the unexpectedness of the *parousia* and the need for the readiness of all (vv. 42-44).

In 1 Thessalonians 4:15, Paul identified himself with those "who are alive" at the *parousia* (ESV), which implies the anticipation of an imminent *parousia*. Either a letter purported to be from Paul or perhaps his own emphasis on the imminence of Christ's return led the Thessalonian believers to a heightened anticipation of the *parousia*, to the degree that he wrote a second letter to quell their concerns (2 Thess. 2:1-2). He wrote to clarify that the second coming will be preceded by the "rebellion" and the *parousia* of the "man of lawlessness" (v. 3, ESV). Paul provided the order of events that will occur at the *parousia*: "The Lord himself will descend from heaven with a cry of command, with the voice of an archangel, and with the sound of the trumpet of God. And the dead in Christ will rise first" (1 Thess. 4:16, ESV). Subsequently, those who are alive and remain "will be caught up together with them in the clouds" (v. 17, ESV).

While these earliest written letters stress the imminent *parousia*, other later writings of the NT mention the delay of the *parousia*. The parable of the ten virgins warns against the unpreparedness of the five virgins when the bridegroom was delayed (Matt. 25:1-13). In another of Jesus's stories, a servant, reasoning that his master had delayed returning, had behaved in a manner inconsistent with his master's expectations, but **judgment** occurred when the master arrived unexpectedly (Luke 12:42-48). The central point of these parables is that one must be prepared at any moment for the return of Christ. The unexpectedness of the return of Christ forms the basis for the command: "Watch therefore, for you know neither the day nor the hour" (Matt. 25:13, ESV).

Despite the unexpectedness of the return, the *parousia* is the "blessed hope" (Titus 2:13, ESV) of the believers because it ushers in the saving benefits of the *eschaton* (end [time]) in redressing wrongs and bringing about the judgment of the wicked. John the Revelator expressed the prayer of believers: "Come, Lord Jesus!" (Rev. 22:20, ESV).

See also Eschatology.

Resources

Braumann, G. "παρουσία." Pages 898-901 in vol. 2 of *NIDNTT*.
Ladd, George Eldon. *A Theology of the New Testament*. Grand Rapids: Eerdmans, 1974.
Oepke, Albrecht. "παρουσία, πάρειμι." Pages 858-71 in vol. 5 of *TDNT*.
Radl, W. "παρουσία." Pages 43-44 in vol. 3 of *EDNT*.
Scobie, Charles H. H. *The Ways of Our God: An Approach to Biblical Theology*. Grand Rapids: Eerdmans, 2003.

J. RUSSELL FRAZIER, PHD

PATRONAGE SYSTEM

In the **Sermon on the Mount**, Jesus challenges his audience: "If you love those who love you, what reward do you have? Do not even the tax collectors do the same? And if you greet only your brothers and sisters, what more are you doing than others? Do not even the Gentiles do the same?" (Matt. 5:46-47, NRSV). In addressing the tendency to **love** and greet only select people with whom one shares a reciprocal relationship, Jesus is describing the phenomenon of patronage.

In ancient Greco-Roman culture, the patronage system normally linked together people of unequal status and consisted of a series of give-and-take exchanges across time. Patrons with superior status provided their socially inferior clients with access to resources and services that the clients were largely unable to obtain. Money, position, land, protection, and influence were variously at the disposal of the patron, to be meted out to his or her clients at will. In exchange for these gifts, clients were expected to express gratitude in the form of public ascriptions of honor to the patron, to embody an enduring loyalty to the patron, and to fulfill the patron's wishes when called upon later.

The patronage system was a complex network of particular relationships within society. Often individuals were simultaneously enmeshed in multiple patronage relationships, some as patrons and others as clients, depending on relative social status.

For example, Herod the Great served as a potential patron to his sub-jects and could lavish gifts upon particular individuals at will. He could also perform works of benefaction for the greater public good. Herod's recon-struction and expansion of the **Jerusalem** temple and his development of Je-rusalem's water resources both constituted such works of public benefaction. At the same time, Herod himself was a client of Caesar Augustus, who not only granted Herod his royal title but also expanded Herod's territory and supported him politically. According to Josephus, Augustus even arranged **marriages** and provided comfortable dowries for two of Herod's daughters after Herod's death (*Ant.* 17.11.5).

Augustus's continued faithfulness to the extended family of his deceased client Herod illustrates another characteristic of ancient Roman patronage: patronage was inextricably bound together with the categories of **honor and shame**. In most cases, patronage obligations were not legally enforceable. What motivated patrons and clients to perpetuate their exchanges was in-stead a collectively embedded sense of honor. A client who failed to help a patron risked being remembered as ungrateful and subsequently cut off from future benefits. Likewise, a patron who habitually neglected clients could suffer a loss of reputation and status and, ultimately, a loss of political power. These potentially disgraceful consequences ensured that both patrons and clients were sufficiently encouraged to maintain their patronage networks by means of gifts, favors, invitations, honors, and other forms of beneficence.

Acts of patronage and references to patron-client relationships appear several times in the pages of the NT. (1) A Roman centurion reportedly financed the construction of a synagogue for the residents of Capernaum (Luke 7:1-10). Later, when this centurion wanted to contact Jesus, he sent some synagogue elders as his personal messengers, who readily testified to his generosity. (2) When Paul was imprisoned in Caesarea under Antonius Felix's authority, Felix routinely summoned him because he wanted Paul to offer a bribe in exchange for freedom (Acts 24:26-27). When Felix could not get anything from Paul, he instead used his power to leave Paul imprisoned; this constituted a favor to Paul's opponents, who then became indebted to Felix. (3) Pontius Pilate customarily pardoned a prisoner during Passover in accordance with the crowd's request (Mark 15:6). This favor was intended to generate public goodwill, reinforcing Pilate's power and position.

The NT authors very often depict Jesus himself as an actant within pa-tronage relationships as well as a commentator on issues of patronage. Jesus's status with regard to God is frequently constructed as that of client: he is sent by God (John 13), he is given authority by God for completing particu-lar tasks (ch. 5), and he defers to God's will (e.g., as he prays in Gethsemane [Mark 14:32-42; Matt. 26:36-46; Luke 22:39-46]). God in turn resurrects Jesus (Rom. 1:1-7) and exalts him (Phil. 2:1-11).

People often treated Jesus as a patron who provided access to God's power in the form of healing miracles. Some of those healed are subsequently depicted as engaging in client-like acts of reciprocity. For example, Simon's mother-in-law began to serve Jesus and the disciples (Mark 1:29-31). Even Jesus's disciples viewed him through the lens of mutuality, most prominently James and John, who shamelessly asked Jesus for positions of political power (10:35-40).

While Jesus did not fully reject patronage, his tendency was to subvert its customary form. Unlike Gentile rulers who abused their power, Jesus served without seeking rewards (v. 45). Repeatedly Jesus attempted to remain anonymous and secretive in the aftermath of his miraculous acts. He washed his disciples' feet (John 13:2-17).

In a variety of ways, Jesus instructed his disciples in this very form of patronage. He said that instead of inviting clients or potential clients, people who throw banquets should invite the **poor**, who are unable to repay (Luke 14:12-14). He told a story about a Samaritan who, with no expectation of return, generously helped a stranger beaten by robbers (10:29-37).

Most subversive of all, Jesus taught his disciples to love their enemies in the same way that God loves those who are God's enemies (Matt. 5:44-45; Luke 6:35-36). This, finally, was Jesus's answer to the question he raised in the Sermon on the Mount. The essence of the pagan patronage system was returning love for love. But Jesus claimed that loving one's enemies and persecutors reveals that one has truly become a child—and a client—of the Father in heaven.

Classical Resources
Cicero. *De officiis* [Regarding obligations].
Seneca. *De beneficiis* [Regarding favors].

Contemporary Resources
deSilva, David A. *Honor, Patronage, Kinship and Purity: Unlocking New Testament Culture.* Downers Grove, IL: IVP Academic, 2000.
Hanson, K. C., and Douglas E. Oakman. *Palestine in the Time of Jesus: Social Structures and Social Conflicts.* 2nd ed. Minneapolis: Fortress Press, 2008.
Heen, Erik M. "Radical Patronage in Luke-Acts." *CurTM* 33, no. 6 (2006): 445-58.
Malina, Bruce J. *The New Testament World: Insights from Cultural Anthropology.* 3rd ed. Louisville, KY: Westminster John Knox Press, 2001.

JON MANNING, MA

PAULINE THEOLOGY

Paul's letters reflect his personal missionary activities and responses to specific situations in his churches; they were not written as a systematic theology. As such, scholars have difficulty determining the center of Pauline theology. Any center advanced must be based on limited information. Our primary sources are Paul's extant writings. Acts 13–28 give merely the gist of his missionary activities, and the proclamations attributed to Paul in Acts are heavily filtered through a Lukan perspective.

A moderate endeavor is attempted here: to collect important thoughts, especially those from Paul's undisputed letters (Rom.; 1–2 Cor.; Gal.; Phil.; 1 Thess.; Phlm.), and relate them to prominent theological motifs—without attempting to privilege one **belief** over the others. At the same time, this study admits the possibility that the order in which Paul's letters were written might assist in explaining possible developments of some of his ideas (see, e.g., Beker 1990).

We start with the God whom Paul attempted to serve even prior to his transformation in Christ: the God of the Jews and their Scriptures. The existence of this God is self-evident for Paul, who assumed that the recipients of his letters served this same Deity. In agreement with the Jewish Shema (Deut. 6:4), he affirmed that there is only one true God, the creator of all things in heaven and on earth (1 Cor. 8:4-6; Gal 3:20; cf. 1 Tim 1:17; 2:5). Such attributes of God as being eternal, righteous, and faithful, as revealed in the Hebrew Scriptures, were axiomatic for Paul (Rom. 1:17, 20; 11:33-36; 16:26; 1 Cor. 1:9).

Although Paul maintained there are no other gods by nature but one (Gal. 4:8), he considered that idolatry could be exploited by **demonic** powers (1 Cor. 10:19-21); Satan and his primary human ruler are identified as temporal "gods" (2 Cor. 4:4; 2 Thess. 2:3-4). A number of his Gentile converts once served idols before turning to the living God (1 Cor. 12:2; 1 Thess. 1:9).

As a Pharisee and persecutor of the **church**, Paul's life was radically changed when the risen Christ revealed himself to Paul on the way to Damascus (1 Cor. 9:1; 15:8-9; Gal. 1:11-16; Phil. 3:4-8; cf. Acts 9). This encounter transformed him into a devout believer proclaiming Jesus as the Christ, the Davidic **Messiah** who would be **Savior** to his people Israel (Rom. 1:3-4; 15:12; cf. 2 Tim. 2:8). As Christ's ambassador, following the teachings and prayers of Jesus, Paul emphasized God as Abba (i.e., Father) (Rom 1:7; 8:15; Gal. 4:4-6; cf., e.g., Matt. 26:39; Luke 11:2) and believed that God's sovereignty was now being manifested through Jesus Christ (Rom. 1:7, 20; 11:33-36; 16:26; 1 Cor. 1:9; 15:24-28). He came to believe that Christ followers belong to a family that loves, honors, obeys, and communicates with their heavenly Father.

Paul proclaimed Jesus as Lord (Gk., *kyrios*). This title identified him as God's vizier over the entire world, an idea that (whether overtly, subversively, or unintentionally) challenged the Roman emperor as the world's ruler under Jupiter, the most powerful god of the Roman pantheon. Paul attached Christ's lordship to the Shema: Christ is viewed in solidarity with God the Father (1 Cor. 8:4-6). Moreover, since God's sacred name as Yahweh in the

Hebrew Scriptures was translated in the Septuagint as *kyrios* (Lord), Paul associated Christ with the sacred name.

For Paul, the Lord Jesus preexisted his earthly life, whether as Yahweh or divine **wisdom** and is regarded as Deity (Rom. 9:5; 1 Cor. 10:4; 2 Cor. 8:9; Phil. 2:6-11; Col. 1:15-20; 2:9; cf. Titus 2:13). Prayers to Jesus as Lord are evident in 1 Corinthians 1:2 and 16:22.

Jesus's **title** as Son of God is used by Paul to refer to a royal and pro-phetic sonship as God's representative anticipated in Jewish Scripture and promised to David (Rom. 1:3-4; 1 Cor. 15:24-28; cf. Ps. 2; 2 Sam. 7:12-16; Isa. 9:4-7). Although creedal statements about God as the Trinity would not appear until centuries later, we find precursors to such language when Paul has God, Christ, and the **Holy Spirit** working together as personal entities transforming and empowering the church (1 Cor. 12:4-6, 11; 2 Cor. 1:20-22; 13:14 [13]). The Spirit, among other things, is called "Lord" by Paul (2 Cor. 3:17), discloses the mind of God (1 Cor. 2:10-11), and, along with the Father, raises Jesus from the dead (Rom. 8:11; cf. Gal. 1:1).

The **gospel** Paul proclaimed stemmed from his revelatory calling, his in-terpretation of Jewish Scripture, and the traditions he received from earlier apostles. He interpreted his mission primarily as an apostle to the Gentiles, someone appointed by Christ as envoy to the nations (Rom. 1:5-6; 15:15-21; Gal. 1:16; 2:1-10; cf. Acts 26:12-18). His gospel consisted of the good news that Jesus is Messiah and Lord, that he died on the cross for humankind, and that he rose again from the dead as the first fruit of a new **creation** reaching its zenith at the second coming (1 Cor. 15:3-4, 20-23; 2 Cor 5:17; 1 Thess. 4:14).

Paul taught that the blood of Jesus (i.e., his death) atones and redeems humans from the power of **sin** that enslaves them (Rom. 3:23-26; 5:7-11; 2 Cor. 5:14-15, 21; Eph. 1:7; Col. 2:13-14). Sin is associated with Adam's disobedience and is thereby inbred in all humans, contaminates the entire person, and separates fellowship between creature and divine Creator. Its hallmark is **idolatry**, which leads to self-gratification at the expense of dis-torting and denying the person and character God. Sin ends in death and condemnation (Rom. 1:20-32; 5:12-14; 6:20-23). Those who place their **faith** in Christ (who was himself faithful to the purposes of God) are forgiven of sin, delivered from its enslavement, and saved from the **wrath** to come. Whether Jews or Gentiles, they become part of the new created order in Christ. This salvific experience is viewed as an act of **grace**, a gift initiated by God's giving of his Son to undeserving humans (Rom. 1:17; 4:16-25; 5:15-21; 10:9-13; 2 Cor. 5:17-21; Gal. 2:16; Eph. 2:8). God's saving act in Christ pro-vides reconciliation and will result in restoration for the entire cosmos under divine dominion (Rom. 8:19-23; 1 Cor. 15:23-28; 2 Cor. 5:18-20).

The nature of the believer's **justification-righteousness** (Gk., *dikaiosynē*) has been, and is, much debated. Does justification come by faith alone as

Luther taught (Westerholm 2004), or does one become righteous by God's grace and remain in **covenant** relationship with God by **works** as taught in the new perspective (Sanders 1977)? Does justification entail God's forensic acquittal—that is, declaring the believer "not guilty," or does it mean that the believer is "righteoused" as a participant in Christ? Other positions are likewise possible: the post–new perspective tends to mitigate the importance of justification theory, and the "Paul within Judaism" perspective mitigates differences between Paul and ancient Jewish views (e.g., Campbell and Nanos, respectively, in Bird 2012). One mediating view on justification stresses a corporate and eschatological focus in which the covenant people are declared not guilty by God on **judgment** day (Wright 2013). If so, then along with **eschatology**, justification may be viewed as "now and not yet." Hence, the rectified people of God must behave righteously in the present so as to be fit for judgment day, and corporate righteousness does not make its members exempt from doing what is righteous. For Paul, baptism brings the convert into solidarity with Christ and imitates his death, burial, and **resurrection**. If converts have been raised to a new life in Christ via baptism, they must live in a way that corresponds with their new identity and become who they really are in Christ; as such, their old sinful ways must be abandoned (Rom. 6:4-19; 12:1-2; 1 Cor. 6:9-11). Spirit baptism has ushered them into the corporate body of Christ to become a **holy** community of **"saints"** and members of the metaphoric sanctuary of God. They are now expected to respond to the favors of their divine benefactor by showing gratitude and loyalty and by becoming more Christlike as they anticipate complete **sanctification** at his return (1 Cor. 12:13; cf. 1:2; 3:16; 6:19; 2 Cor. 6:16; 7:1; 1 Thess. 5:23).

For Paul, however, **holiness** is not accomplished by merely human determination but alliance with God's Spirit, who prompts and empowers believers to live in a way that pleases God. They are to "walk" in accordance with the Spirit's guidance, which among other things produces the "fruit of the Spirit" (moral virtues), especially loving one's neighbor as oneself, which sums up for Paul the essence of Mosaic law (Gal. 5:14–6:2).

Paul otherwise discouraged Gentile converts from keeping the works of the law, especially circumcision, dietary rules, and sacred days (Rom. 14:1-5, 14; 1 Cor. 7:18-19; Gal. 4:8-11; 5:1-4; 6:12-15; Col. 2:16-17). Although the **law** identifies and punishes sin, it cannot ultimately defeat it and is now set aside through the Christ event and faith (Rom. 3:20-27; 7:1-6; 1 Cor. 15:56; 2 Cor. 3:3-16; Gal. 2:16; 3:19-25). Through the Spirit those who are in Christ must now resist the desires of the "flesh," the sinful nature inherited through Adam and characterized by vices (Rom. 8:2-16; 13:8-10; Gal. 5:14–6:2).

Paul's preaching of the cross emphasizes not only Jesus's **sacrificial** death but also an attitude exemplary for Christian living. The cruciform life finds its strength in weakness, humility, and **wisdom** revealed by God's Spirit; these stand over against the wisdom of this age, arrogance, worldly power, and prestige (1 Cor. 1–2, 4). Paul's own hardships and afflictions for the gospel's sake functioned as a way to imitate Christ (4:16; 11:1; 2 Cor. 4:7-15; 6:3-10; 11:22–12:10; Rom. 8:34-38). Believers are encouraged to persevere in faith, endure affliction, and die to sinful ways. Paul warns that salvation may be rejected, and a life characterized by vice is tantamount to committing apostasy (Rom. 8:13; 1 Cor. 10:1-12; Gal. 5:3-4, 19-21; 1 Thess. 3:5).

Paul's churches comprised assemblies that regularly gathered together for worship, teaching, and spiritual edification and to commemorate the Lord's Supper. Members had been adopted into the spiritual family of God to become spiritual brothers and sisters (Rom. 8:14-16; 1 Cor. 6:8; Gal. 4:4-7; Phlm. vv. 1-2, 16). To be identified "in Christ" is to live in a sphere wherein fellowship with God, connection with God's Spirit, and salvific life is experienced in solidarity with other members identified as the corporate body of Christ (Rom. 8:1; 1 Cor. 12:12-20; Gal. 3:26-28; Phil. 1:1).

There were positions of leadership and ministry in Pauline congregations; these included apostles, **prophets**, teachers, evangelists, pastors or overseers, and other workers (1 Cor. 12:28-29; Eph. 4:11-13; Phil. 1:1; cf. 1 Tim. 4:14). Even so, Paul taught that every church member has **spiritual gifts** that the Spirit diversely and generously distributes in the corporate body to edify other members in love and to function as a witness to unbelieving visitors (Rom. 12:6-8; 1 Cor. 12:7-11, 28-31; 14:1, 20-26). The church is to do good to everyone and not hinder anyone from coming to or remaining in faith (1 Cor. 10:32-33; Gal. 6:10; Col. 3:17).

Paul recognized and accepted the Christian leadership of those who were apostles before him (1 Cor. 9:2-5; 15:4-7; Gal. 1–2), while he was not hesitant to correct Cephas (Peter) for hypocrisy when eating with and then separating from uncircumcised believers in Antioch (Gal. 2:11-14). He also considered certain teachers and missionaries who claimed to follow Christ to be teaching a false gospel (Rom. 16:17-18; 2 Cor. 11:2-14; Gal. 2:4; Phil. 3:2, 18-19). Some of these opponents encouraged Paul's Gentile converts to be circumcised and follow the entire Mosaic law, but Paul had multiple rivals who did not all teach and practice the same things (see Oropeza 2012).

Gentile followers of Christ did not become the new people of God themselves; they were added to God's elect people, the Jews. Paul saw his predominantly Gentile churches as fulfilling prophetic promises (Rom. 15:8-12), especially God's promise to make faithful Abraham the father of many nations (Gal. 3:6-18, 29; Rom. 4). At the same time, although Paul affirmed Israel's election and believed she would come to faith in her Messiah, he expressed sorrow over her present condition of unbelief (Rom. 9–11). God's **election** and **predestination** has a corporate emphasis pertaining to Israel and the church in Christ; Paul never affirmed the individual as being elected and predestined to final salvation independent of belonging to God's people.

The (now) **evil** age contrasts the (not yet) age to come when Christ returns (Gal. 1:4; Eph. 1:21). Paul viewed the second coming as imminent, and yet he was uncertain about its timing (1 Cor. 1:8; 3:13; Phil. 1:10; 1 Thess. 5:2). Paul included himself among those who would be alive at the event (notice "we" in 1 Thess. 4:15-17), and yet he recognized the real possibility of dying before that time (2 Cor. 4:14; Phil. 1:20-24). This may be an admission that he ultimately did not know whether he would be alive at that time, a perspective comparable with other traditions that may have informed him (Matt. 24:36; Mark 13:32; Luke 12:39-40; Acts 1:7; cf. 1 Thess. 5:2). However, apparently to curb the tide of extremism, Paul added that before the end, a great apostasy must first take place and a lawless ruler who will be deified in God's temple must appear (2 Thess. 2:1-12).

At Christ's return, the dead in Christ will be raised to immortality and transformed along with other believers who are still alive at that time. The resurrection will consist of a glorious body fully animated by God's Spirit and comparable with Christ's own risen body (Rom 8:23; 1 Cor. 15:12-56; 2 Cor. 4:14; Phil. 3:20-21; 1 Thess. 4:15-17). (Note: Paul believed that the human person has a "spirit," a self-aware "I" distinct from God's Spirit and related to but not equated with the mind [Rom. 8:16; 1 Cor. 14:14-15]. Upon death in the present age, this inner self apparently survives and is aware of its own existence even apart from the earthly body [2 Cor. 5:1-8; cf. 12:2-4]. Paul, however, did not clearly explicate how the inner self is transformed or unified again with the body at resurrection.)

Judgment day also will take place when Christ returns. God in Christ will judge everyone according to his or her deeds (Rom. 2:16; 14:10-12; 1 Cor. 4:3-5; 2 Cor. 5:10). The expected outcome for Christians is to be blameless (1 Cor. 1:8; Phil. 2:14-16; 1 Thess. 5:23), but Paul expresses apprehension that some might not be prepared for that day (2 Cor. 5:10-11).

Satan is viewed as an opponent of the faithful (2 Cor. 2:11; 1 Thess. 3:5) along with hostile angels, principalities, and powers (Rom. 8:38-39; 1 Cor. 6:3; 10:20-21; Eph. 6:11-12; Col. 2:15). Such forces are ultimately defeated at the Lord's return (1 Cor. 15:24-25; 2 Thess. 2:8). Death is the final enemy to be destroyed before the complete renovation of the cosmos takes place and God in Christ reigns undisputed over all (1 Cor. 15:26-28, 54-57; Rom. 8:19-23; Phil. 2:9-11).

See also Fall, The; Honor-Shame Culture; Obedience.

Resources

Barrett, C. K. *Paul: An Introduction to His Thought*. Louisville, KY: Westminster John Knox Press, 1994.

Bassler, Jouette M., David M. Hay, and E. Elizabeth Johnson, eds. *Pauline Theology.* 4 vols. Minneapolis: Fortress Press; Atlanta: Scholars Press, 1991-97.

Becker, Jürgen. *Paul: Apostle to the Gentiles.* Translated by O. C. Dean Jr. Louisville, KY: Westminster John Knox Press, 1993.

Beker, Johan Christiaan. *The Triumph of God: The Essence of Paul's Thought.* Minneapolis: Fortress Press, 1990.

Bird, Michael F., Thomas R. Schreiner, Luke Timothy Johnson, Douglas A. Campbell, and Mark D. Nanos. *Four Views on the Apostle Paul.* Edited by Michael F. Bird. Grand Rapids: Zondervan, 2012.

Bruce, F. F. *Paul: Apostle of the Free Spirit.* Carlisle, UK: Paternoster Press, 1977.

Dunn, James D. G. *The Theology of Paul the Apostle.* Grand Rapids: Eerdmans, 1998.

Gorman, Michael J. *Apostle of the Crucified Lord: A Theological Introduction to Paul and His Letters.* Grand Rapids: Eerdmans, 2004.

Harris, Timothy J. "Pauline Theology." Pages 353-91 in *All Things to All Cultures: Paul among Jews, Greeks, and Romans.* Edited by Mark Harding and Alanna Nobbs. Grand Rapids: Eerdmans, 2013.

Hawthorne, Gerald F., Ralph P. Martin, and Daniel G. Reid, eds. *Dictionary of Paul and His Letters.* Downers Grove, IL: InterVarsity Press, 1993.

Horrell, David G. *An Introduction to the Study of Paul.* 3rd ed. London: Bloomsbury, 2015.

Oropeza, B. J. *Jews, Gentiles, and the Opponents of Paul: The Pauline Letters.* Vol. 2 of *Apostasy in the New Testament Communities.* Eugene, OR: Cascade Books, 2012.

Porter, Stanley E. *The Apostle Paul: His Life, Thought, and Letters.* Grand Rapids: Eerdmans, 2016.

Sanders, E. P. *Paul and Palestinian Judaism: A Comparison of Patterns of Religion.* Minneapolis: Fortress Press, 1977.

Schnelle, Udo. *Apostle Paul: His Life and Theology.* Translated by M. Eugene Boring. Grand Rapids: Baker Academic, 2005.

Westerholm, Stephen. *Perspectives Old and New on Paul: The "Lutheran" Paul and His Critics.* Grand Rapids: Eerdmans, 2004.

Wright, N. T. *Paul and the Faithfulness of God.* 2 vols. Minneapolis: Fortress Press, 2013.

Yinger, Kent L. *The New Perspective on Paul: An Introduction.* Eugene, OR: Cascade Books, 2011.

B. J. OROPEZA, PHD

PEACE

In the OT the Hebrew noun *šālôm* (shalom), and forms of the verb *šālēm*, most often convey the theological concept of "peace." The noun *šālôm* occurs 250 times, the majority of which the English versions translate as "peace"; a number of occurrences, however, are translated differently, indicating the breadth of nuances of *šālôm*.

Theologically significant is that God is the giver of *šālôm*, both corporately and individually. God promised peace to Israel "in the **land**" (Lev. 26:6, NASB), contingent on the people's **obedience** to his commandments (v. 3). Such peace included physical protection from "harmful beasts" and "enemies," and it included "fruitful[ness]" of both offspring and crops (vv. 4-10, NASB). David, identifying himself to be a "godly man" (*ḥāsîd*; Ps. 4:3 [4 HB], NASB), sleeps in "peace" and "security" (*beṭaḥ*), which comes only from Yahweh (v. 8 [9 HB]). Jacob affirmed that it is Yahweh who gives "safety" (*šālôm*) on one's journey (Gen. 28:20-21, NASB).

The **prophets** and psalmists teach that only when **justice** (*mišpāṭ*), **righteousness** (*ṣĕdāqâ*), and truth (*ʾĕmet*) are practiced "in the gates" (in ancient Israel the place for legal matters to be decided [Zech. 8:16]), all of which are God given, can there be true peace (Isa. 32:16-17; 54:13; 59:8; 60:17, 21; Pss. 72:7; 85:8-13 [9-14 HB]).

Šālôm expresses conditions of well-being and physical health. David enquired of Uriah "concerning the welfare [*šālôm*] of Joab and the welfare [*šālôm*] of the people and the progress [*šālôm*] of the war" (2 Sam. 11:7, AT). Upon meeting Rachel at the well, Jacob asked concerning Laban, "Is it well with him?" (*hăšālôm lô*; Gen. 29:6, NASB). Concerning his own physical **suffering**, David laments, "There is no health [*šālôm*] in my bones" (Ps. 38:3 [4 HB], NASB).

A relationship of goodwill between human parties is expressed with *šālôm*, often accompanied with oaths or a **covenant**. During the conquest period, even though the Gibeonites duped the Israelites at Gilgal, Joshua "made peace" and "a covenant" (*bĕrît*) with them (Josh. 9:15, NASB). In the days of the united kingdom, excellent trade between King Solomon and King Hiram of Tyre resulted from "peace" and a "covenant" made between the two of them (1 Kings 5:12 [26], NASB).

On three occasions God promised a "covenant of peace" (*bĕrît šālôm*): with priest Phineas after he had both preserved God's **honor** and prevented **God's wrath** against Israel in the Moabite sexual misconduct affair (Num. 25:12); with resettled barren **Jerusalem** and cities of Judah, where *bĕrît šālôm* is paralleled with God's "lovingkindness" (*hesed*) (Isa. 54:10, NASB); and with his people regathered under his "servant David" (Ezek. 34:24-25, NASB).

Peace often signifies the absence of hostilities between nations, kingdoms, or tribes. Such peace might represent a long-standing agreement of nonaggression. In the Israelite-Canaanite war in the time of Deborah's judgeship, Canaanite commander Sisera sought safety in the tent of a Kenite (Kenites were a quasi-Israelite tribe), because he knew that there was "peace between Jabin the [Canaanite] king of Hazor and the house of Heber the Kenite" (Judg. 4:17, NASB). Or peace might indicate an offer to cease aggression so that normal relationships may be restored. After the majority of Israel had made war on the one tribe of Benjamin, nearly wiping it out, "the whole congregation" came to "the sons of Benjamin" and "proclaimed peace to them" (21:13, NASB).

The outward evidence of peace in relationships is determined by the attitude of the human heart. A psalmist cried out that he was "for peace," but when he spoke of it, others "who hate peace" "are for war" (Ps. 120:6-7, NASB). Joseph's brothers, overcome by jealousy, "so hated him [*yiśnĕʾû ʾōtô*] they were unable to speak to him in peace [*lĕšālōm*]" (Gen. 37:4, AT). Jeremiah decried the deceitful person who "with his mouth speaks peace to his friend, but in his inner being sets a trap for him" (Jer. 9:8[7], AT).

In the NT "peace" is expressed primarily by the Greek noun *eirēnē*, which occurs 91 times. A starting point in grasping the NT concept of peace may well be Paul's point of reference. True peace originates with God, evidenced to us in Christ. He assured the Philippians that "the God of peace [*theos tēs eirēnēs*] shall be with you" (4:9, AT; Rom. 15:33; 16:20; 1 Cor. 14:33; 2 Cor. 13:11; 1 Thess. 5:23; Heb. 13:20). Of Christ he declared to the Ephesians, "He Himself is our peace" (2:14, NASB). In 2 Thessalonians 3:16, Paul calls Christ "the Lord of peace [*ho kyrios tēs eirēnēs*]," who gives "peace in every circumstance" (NASB). In a turn of the phrase, Paul assured the Philippians that "the peace of God [*hē eirēnē tou theou*]" would guard from unnecessary anxiety the hearts and minds of those who are "in Christ Jesus" (4:6-7, NASB). In the context of preserving unity in the body of Christ, he urged the Colossians, "Let the peace of Christ [*hē eirēnē tou Christou*] rule [*brabeuetō*, "act as arbiter"] in your hearts" (3:15, NASB). That is, when the potential for strife among the members of Christ's body arises, it is Christ's peace that must regulate their relationships.

Paul made no distinction between God the Father and the Son Jesus Christ as the source of "peace" in his greetings to both churches and individuals (Rom. 1:7; 1 Tim. 1:2; etc.). Paul associated this peace with "**grace**" (*charis*; e.g., Rom. 1:7) and "the God of **love**" (*theos tēs agapēs*; 2 Cor. 13:11). In Romans 5 he insists that it is "through our Lord Jesus Christ" that we obtain "peace with God" (v. 1, NASB). This is made possible because of "the love of God" (v. 5, NASB), which caused Christ to die for us (v. 8). It is then because of our **faith** in Christ's "death" and "life" (i.e., **resurrection**) (vv. 1, 10, NASB) and because of God's love "poured out within our hearts through the **Holy Spirit**" that we are "justified" (vv. 1, 5, 9, NASB). This **justification** is "reconciliation" with God "through our Lord Jesus Christ" (v. 11, NASB). Peace, then, is reconciliation; we are no longer God's "enemies" (vv. 1, 10-11, NASB).

In Acts 10 Luke records Peter's experience at Gentile Cornelius's house, which led Peter to a new theological understanding: "God is not one to show partiality, but in every nation the man who fears Him and does what is right is welcome to Him" (vv. 34-35, NASB). He defines this theology as "the word . . . preaching peace through Jesus Christ" (vv. 36, NASB). The content of the preaching of this peace was Christ's death and **resurrection** (vv. 39-41). The sought-after result of this preaching was **belief** in Christ and "**forgiveness of sins**," to which "all the prophets bear witness" (v. 43, NASB).

Paul urged the Ephesians to clothe themselves fully in the strength of the Lord against "the schemes of the **devil**" (Eph. 6:10-11, NASB). Among the several pieces of spiritual clothing one was to don in order to be fully prepared is "the **gospel** of peace" (v.15, NASB). Paul was referencing Isaiah 52:7, where the prophet speaks of a messenger announcing to redeemed Jerusalem (v. 9) "good news" (*mĕbaśēr*) of "peace" (*šālôm*), "good" (*ṭôb*), and "salvation" (*yĕšûʿâ*). The prophet concluded that this good news was also for "the nations" and "the ends of the earth," who would see God's "salvation" (v. 10, NASB). The goal, then, of preaching "the gospel of peace," both for the OT prophets and NT apostles, was the salvation of their hearers.

Paul wrote to the church at Corinth concerning issues that were both actual and potential causes of disorder within the body of believers (1 Cor. 14). He reminded them of an overriding theological principle by which to regulate their conduct: "God is not a God of confusion but of peace [*eirēnēs*]" (v. 33, NASB). Thus, if a body of believers adhered to this principal, "all things [can] be done properly and in an orderly manner" (v. 40, NASB).

Paul also viewed peace to be the goal of the Christ follower in relationships outside the body of Christ. He urged the believers at Rome, "If possible, so far as it depends on you, be at peace with all men" (Rom. 12:18, NASB). Such conduct requires restraint: "Never pay back **evil** for evil to anyone" (v. 17, NASB), and "Never take your own revenge" (v. 19, NASB). Positively, it demands illogical action: give food and drink to "your enemy" (v. 20, NASB).

In both OT and NT, peace is spoken in greetings and farewells. An old man of Gibeah welcomed a Levite from Ephraim to his home with "Peace to you" (Judg. 19:20, NASB); after accepting a gift from Abigail, David sent her home with, "Go up in peace to your house" (1 Sam. 25:35, AT). Jesus dismissed the **woman** who had received healing by touching his robe with, "Go in peace" (Mark 5:34; Luke 8:48, NASB). Likewise, Jesus forgave a woman her sins, dismissing her with, "Go in peace" (Luke 7:50, NASB). On the evening of his resurrection, Jesus greeted his gathered disciples with the OT form, "Peace to you" (John 20:19-20, 26, AT).

See also Belief/Believe; Fear of the Lord/God.

Resources

Beck, H., and C. Brown. "Peace." Pages 776-83 in vol. 2 of *NIDNTT*.
Nel, Philip J. "שׁלם." Pages 130-35 in vol. 4 of *NIDOTTE*.

BARRY L. ROSS, PHD

PETER, 1 AND 2, THEOLOGY OF

Two letters in the New Testament claim to be written and sent from Peter, the fisherman whom Jesus called to be his disciple. Peter indeed became the most prominent disciple in Christian tradition and a significant figure in early Christianity, as specific references to him in Matthew, Mark, Luke, John, Acts, Galatians, and 1 Corinthians indicate. As such, the prominence of Peter commands authority, and with it any works attributed to him. All Christian groups recognize Peter as disciple and apostle and accept the two letters attributed to him as authoritative Scripture.

First Peter

The author of 1 Peter claimed to be "Peter, an apostle of Jesus Christ" (1 Pet. 1:1, NRSV). Almost all modern scholars believe the work is pseudonymous; nevertheless, the name "Peter" is a useful way of referring to the author.

First Peter is addressed to the "exiles of the Dispersion in Pontus, Galatia, Cappadocia, Asia, and Bithynia" (v. 1, NRSV). This letter was written in response to various problems and challenges faced by these early Christian believers.

The recipients were in the precarious position of living in a place not their own, as the designation of them as "aliens and exiles" indicates (2:11, NRSV). They had left behind their former life of ignorance (1:14) with its "futile ways inherited from [their] ancestors" (v. 18, NRSV). They now refrain from their former conduct marked by "debauchery, lust, drunkenness, orgies, carousing and detestable idolatry" (4:3, NIV). They have been born again (1:3, 23) and now live a new life of **holiness** (vv. 15-16) and **love** (v. 22) as Christians (4:16). Peter devoted much of his letter to instructing them how to live this new life (2:11–3:12).

As with many converts who leave behind family, friends, and associates, these Christians needed reassurance to validate their drastic and painful decision to leave their old life behind. In his capacity as an apostle of Jesus Christ, Peter wrote to them and confirmed and legitimated them (5:10) as living stones in God's spiritual house (2:4-8) and as God's very own chosen people who had moved out of darkness into light (vv. 9-10).

Breaking from their old life, these Christians experienced prejudice and verbal abuse (vv. 12, 15; 3:9, 16; 4:14-16) from detractors who could not understand their new life (4:4). These Christians were **suffering**, but Peter assured them that their trials were temporary (1:6-7; 4:7, 17; 5:10), and he exhorted them to set their **hope** upon the **grace** that would be brought to them at the revelation of Jesus Christ (1:13) and to be ready to provide an explanation to their detractors for this hope (3:15). Peter assured them that their suffering was within the will of God (4:19) and confirmed them as Christians, since Christ also suffered (1:11; 2:21-24; 3:18; 4:1, 13; 5:1). He also assured them that they were blessed in their suffering (3:13; 4:14), since their suffering like that of Christ would bring **glory** and **honor** to them and their God at the coming of Jesus Christ (1:7-8, 11; 2:12; 4:13; 5:1, 4, 6, 10).

Their experience of suffering and social alienation left these believers needing assurance of salvation, and Peter developed several salvific metaphors to reassure them of the legitimacy of their new life. Similar to the Johannine "birth from above" (Gk., *gennaō anōthen*; John 3:1-10) and the Matthean and Pauline "birth again" (Gk., *palingenesia*; Matt. 19:28; Titus 3:5), Peter developed the salvific metaphor of "**rebirth**" or "new birth" (Gk., *anagennaō*; 1 Pet. 1:3, 23). He described it as originating, not from a perishable sowing of an earthly father's seed, but from the imperishable sowing of the eternal **word (*logos*) of God** (vv. 23-25). When used in the context of generation, the Greek term *logos* approximates what moderns call DNA (see Aristotle, *Gen. an.* 1.1 [715a]; 2.4 [739b]; *Part. an.* 1.1 [639b]). Thus Peter assured these Christians that they had been generated anew with an imperishable DNA that enabled them to be saved from death through the **resurrection** of Jesus Christ from the dead (1 Pet. 1:3).

Peter exhorted them as "newborn babies" to desire "pure spiritual milk" in order that they might grow up into the salvation (2:2-3, NIV) that was prophesied by the **prophets** (1:10-12) and "that is ready to be revealed in the last time" (v. 5, NIV).

This new birth metaphor stands in some tension with the redemption metaphor that Peter also developed to explain salvation as a transfer from one house to another (vv. 18-19). The ancient household provided the basic social structure, and almost everyone belonged to a household as a result of being house-born or money-bought from a different household. Peter described the previous household of these exiles and aliens in terms of ignorance, futility, darkness, moral depravity, and **idolatry** (vv. 14, 18; 4:3-4); he stated that they have been released (Gk., *elutrōthēte*) from this household not with money but "with the precious blood" of Jesus Christ (1:18-19, NIV).

Peter thus developed two seemingly incompatible salvific metaphors to describe these exiles and aliens as both house-born and blood-bought; they were most certainly legitimate members of God's house (2:4-9; 4:17) and beloved siblings of one another (1:22; 2:11, 17; 4:12; 5:9). In addition to these two salvific metaphors, Peter also presented salvation in the more usual way: Christ's bearing **sins** (2:24) and dying for sins (3:18) so that these exiles and aliens might live in **righteousness**.

The theologically dense letter of 1 Peter contains many other theological ideas and themes. But almost all respond in some way to Peter's attempt to legitimate the standing of these Christians, to alleviate their suffering, and to confirm the salvation of their lives in the end.

Second Peter

The author of 2 Peter claimed to be "Simeon Peter, a servant and apostle of Jesus Christ" (2 Pet. 1:1, AT). Almost all modern scholars believe the work is pseudonymous; nevertheless, the name "Peter" is a useful way of referring to the author.

Peter says the recipients already know the teaching contained within the letter. However, the author wanted to refresh their memory (v. 13; 3:1-2) so they would always be able to recall what they had been taught (1:15). God has provided them with everything they need "for life and **godliness**" (v. 3, NRSV) so that they might escape "the corruption . . . in the world" and "become participants of the divine nature" (v. 4, NRSV).

The recipients were hearing a teaching contrary to what they first received, and Peter warned that false teachers among them would lead them astray (2:1-3, 10, 12-15, 18-19; 3:3-4, 17). Peter therefore claimed superior authority so the community would abide by the original teaching they received. The superior authority of Peter and the other apostles lay in their being eyewitnesses of Jesus's transfiguration (1:16-19). Further, Peter urged the community to remember the words of the holy prophets of the past and the commandment of Jesus spoken through the apostles (3:2), including himself and the other original evangelists of the community.

The false teachers were accused of a long list of sins, including being licentious (2:2, 18), being greedy (vv. 3, 14), being deceptive (v. 3), being lustful (vv. 10, 18; 3:3), and despising authority (2:10). For Peter's purposes, his greatest worry was that the false teachers baited people who were unsteady in their faith (v. 14) or who were new to the **faith** and did not yet know better (v. 18). Thus these false teachers lured them into incorrect **belief**. Peter declared that whatever the present success of the false teachers, their condemnation had already been assured (v. 3). Just as the sinful angels who once had God's favor were "cast into hell" (Gk., *tartarōsas*; v. 4), just as God did not spare the ancient world and destroyed all but eight people in the flood (v. 5), and just as Sodom and Gomorrah were destroyed and only Lot and family were spared (vv. 6-8), so also Peter assured that the false teachers and those who followed them would perish and that the righteous would be spared (vv. 9-10) when God consumes the whole earth in flames and thus eradicates wickedness forever (3:7, 10-12).

The theology of 2 Peter centers on the difficult task of explaining why one must maintain righteousness and how a generous (1:3-4) and forgiving (v. 9) God could have already destroyed the world once through a flood and will destroy it again with fire (3:5-7) and why Jesus had not yet returned. The struggle between the two ways of righteousness and unrighteousness is at the heart of this theology. The ancient sinners of the past were unrighteous (2:15), just like the false teachers in this community (vv. 9, 13). Those whom God spared in the past (Noah, Lot) were righteous (vv. 5, 7-8), and God will spare the righteous from the coming conflagration, for after the conflagration there will be "new heavens and a new earth" in which "righteousness is at home" (3:13, NRSV). To follow in the ways of the false teachers, therefore, was to be unrighteous and ungodly and ultimately to find one's end in destruction—just as the wicked did in the past. God's previous destruction of the world through the flood and future destruction of the world by fire seem contrary to the concept of a forgiving God. Peter, however, used these events to explain the delay of Jesus's return.

By this time, the Christian community had seen generations of Christians die without the promised return of Jesus. Peter put the challenge on the lips of those who would lead the faithful astray by saying, "Where is this 'coming' he promised? Ever since our ancestors died, everything goes on as it has since the beginning of creation" (v. 4, NIV). Peter assured the recipients that God is not slow but rather "is patient with you, not wanting anyone to perish, but everyone to come to repentance" (v. 9, NIV). Thus Peter explained that the delay of the **parousia** is because God's **mercy** is so great that God does not want anyone to perish. Therefore, we should "bear in mind that our Lord's patience means salvation" (v. 15, NIV).

Peter reasserts what the community was originally taught, namely, that despite God's mercy, the wicked cannot presume upon God's **forgiveness** forever. God is waiting patiently for the wicked to **repent**, not wanting anyone to perish. Further, those who have already received the knowledge of Jesus Christ must remain faithful and righteous, no matter how long it takes for Jesus to return.

See also Discipleship; Election; Evil; Providence of God.

TROY W. MARTIN, PHD, AND JENNY DEVIVO, PHD

POOR/POVERTY

Old Testament

The OT understood poverty as (1) the lack of material resources and goods and (2) the lack of political power in the face of oppression. The main contributors to poverty were the loss of familial **land** (Lev. 25:25), borrowing (Deut. 15:7-11), oppression (Eccles. 5:8; Isa 3:14-15), and laziness (Prov. 20:13).

The OT employs several Hebrew words for "poor" and "poverty." The most common word was *'ānî*, which describes those without their own land and in need of economic protection (80x). It is often paired with *'ebyôn* to speak of the destitute and those dependent on others for their daily survival (61x). The term *'ānāw*, pious "poor," designates a person who was made poor by another of greater power and prestige (24x). The term *dal* speaks of impoverished farmers who were helpless in the face of cruel oppression by rich landowners (48x). The **Wisdom** literature employs the terms *rîš* (22x) and *miskēn* (4x); poverty was presented as honorable and preferable to the life of the wicked oppressors. The last term was lazy "poor" *maḥsôr*, which spoke of poverty that came from indolence and mismanagement of one's resources (13x).

Old Testament books develop a theology of the poor. The narratives of the Pentateuch do not mention the issue, but laws in the Pentateuch protected the rights of the poor and marginalized because their lack of financial means made them vulnerable to abuse (Exod. 22:25; Lev. 19:9-10; 23:22; Deut. 15:11; 24:14-15). The Jubilee **laws** (Lev. 25) aimed at reversing the conditions of the destitute, enabling them to regain ownership of the land

and freedom from debt and, ultimately, to restore their **honor** as fully participating members of the community.

Deuteronomy 15 presents a tension between God's will that "there need be no poor people among you" (v. 4, NIV) and the acknowledgment that "there will always be poor people in the land" (v. 11, NIV). The solution that would eradicate poverty among the people was **obedience** to God (v. 5). The persistence of poverty and oppression in the land was regarded as a manifestation of **sin**.

The books of Ruth (3:10), Esther (9:22), and Daniel (4:27) mention poverty as an existing reality. However, Nehemiah (5:1-13) addressed the issue of poverty as part of his reforms in postexilic Israel.

The Wisdom literature writers accepted the existence of the poor as a class of society and described the miserable conditions of the needy (Prov. 15:15; Job 24:4, 9, 14). However, they refused to treat them within the accepted societal norms of **honor and shame**. Obedience to God and wise living bring honor in God's eyes (Prov. 31:20; Job 29:12), thus making economic status irrelevant as far as honor and shame are concerned (Eccles. 4:13; 9:14-16).

Through financial difficulties, the poor learn humility and complete dependence on God as their provider. The Psalms as well as the Wisdom writers saw this attitude of **humility** as leading to piety. Humbling oneself before the Lord displays the person's awareness of his or her true place in the cosmic order as compared to the creator, **covenant** God (Pss. 86:1; 109:22). The sages defended the needy and the poor as a way to please God (72:12-14; Prov. 31:8-9), who defends their case (Job 36:6, 15; Pss. 35:10; 82:3). Such teachings took the stigma of shame away from the state of poverty caused by economic oppression and injustice.

The **prophets** were vocal about the economic exploitation of the poor and the marginalized by the ruling elite of Israel. When describing the plight of this societal class, the prophets spoke of the insecurity and homelessness that surrounded the poor (Isa. 14:30; 25:4; Amos 8:4). They bemoaned the experiences of hunger and thirst that the needy had to endure (Isa. 32:6-7; Ezek. 16:49). The prophets exposed instances of unjust treatment by the rulers and the wicked (Isa. 3:14; 26:6; 29:19; Jer. 2:34; 20:13; Ezek. 22:29; Amos 2:7; 4:1). They condemned the wealthy for the unfair treatment of the afflicted in legal matters (Isa. 10:2; 32:7; Jer. 5:28; Amos 5:11-12; 8:6).

The prophetic answer to the problem of poverty in Israel was God's intervention in the life of the established society. The prophets saw a close relationship between the absence of **justice** and **mercy** in the land and the emptiness of the spirituality displayed by the ruling elite. God himself had to raise a new type of king, a **Messiah**, who would act on behalf of the poor and the oppressed with **righteousness**, mercy, and humility (Isa. 11:1-16;

14:32; Ezek. 34:11-31). God judges the oppressors (Isa. 29:17-21; Ezek. 34:1-10; Amos 4:1-3) and vindicates his people, the poor. The prophets presented God as the one who acts on behalf of the poor and the oppressed to protect and liberate them, to feed and empower them. It is his very nature to listen to the cries of the poor and the needy and to offer extra measures of protection to the most powerless.

New Testament

The NT uses the Greek term *ptōchos* for "poor, needy, beggar" (34x). *Penēs*, "poor, needy," is used only in 2 Cor. 9:9; *penichros*, "destitute," in Luke 21:2; and *endeēs*, "needy," in Acts 4:34.

Poverty is understood not only in terms of lacking economic means but also in terms of being oppressed and marginalized by society (Luke 18:2-8). While it was shameful to be poor in the eyes of the ruling class (Matt. 19:21-22; Mark 10:21-22), a humble existence in **obedience** to God brings honor and blessing from God (Matt. 26:10-12). Blessedness of the poor does not stem from their lack of financial resources but from their attitude of dependence on God, which connects Jesus's teaching with the OT view of humility and trust in the Lord (Matt. 5:3; Mark 12:41-44; Luke 6:20; 21:1-4; cf. Ps. 126:5-6; Isa. 57:15; 61:1). Jesus presented himself as the promised Messiah who fulfilled the OT expectations by bringing "good news to the poor" (Luke 4:18, NIV; cf. Isa. 61:1-3).

In Luke's **Gospel** "good news to the poor" is demonstrated in bringing the poor and the outcasts from the margins and including them into the community affairs (Luke 14:12-14, 21; 16:20, 22). The story of Zacchaeus, a rich but ostracized tax collector, served as a case in point. Jesus restored him to the **community**, and he, in turn, used his resources to support the poor (Luke 19:9-10).

Without using the term *ptōchos*, the Gospels depicted Jesus's lifestyle as one of poverty: he was homeless (Matt. 8:20); he and his disciples experienced hunger (12:1); he spoke of himself as belonging to the lowest classes of society (25:35-36). In portraying Jesus in this way, the Gospel writers emphasized his nature as the Son of God, who protected and cared for the ostracized. Jesus's choice to identify with the poor connected his ministry to the ministry of the OT prophets, who spoke on behalf of the needy and the oppressed.

The disciples followed Christ's example in leaving their own families to embrace the lifestyle of the poor (4:18-22). They shared their possessions so that there would be no needy in their midst (Acts 2:45). Obedience to Jesus's teaching and care of the needs in the community resulted in God blessing the work of the early church (2:46-47; 4:32-35; 6:1-6).

Paul's concern for the poor in Jerusalem was demonstrated in raising a contribution through the Asia Minor churches (Rom. 15:26; Gal. 2:10).

Christ's example of choosing poverty for believers' sake (2 Cor. 8:8-9) should inspire cheerful giving to the poor as a natural response of obedience and gratitude (9:6-7).

James demanded equal honor for the poor because God has chosen them and because mercy is the main criterion in the final judgment (James 2:2-6, 13).

In the book of Revelation, the letters to the churches of Smyrna and Laodicea (2:9; 3:17) juxtaposed material and spiritual poverty. Spiritual poverty was demonstrated as detrimental to one's eternal condition. According to Revelation 13:16, everybody, including the poor, will fall prey to the power of the beast. It is only at the second coming of Christ that every kind of pain and need, including those of the poor, will be eliminated (21:4-6).

See also Discipleship; Judgment; Parousia.

Resources

Domeris, W. R. "אבינן." Pages 228-32 in vol. 1 of *NIDOTTE*.
———. "מסכן." Pages 1001-2 in vol. 2 of *NIDOTTE*.
———. "רוש." Pages 1085-87 in vol. 3 of *NIDOTTE*.
Dumbrell, W. J. "ענו." Pages 454-64 in vol. 3 of *NIDOTTE*.
Hanks, Thomas D. "Poor, poverty." Pages 414-42 in vol. 5 of *ABD*.
Pleins, J. David. "Poor, poverty." Pages 402-14 in vol. 5 of *ABD*.
Silva, Moisés, ed. "πτωχός." Pages 704-6 in vol. 3 of *NIDNTTE*.
———, ed. "πενης." Pages 181-87 in vol. 4 of *NIDNTTE*.

LARISA LEVICHEVA, PHD

PREDESTINATION

Predestination is not a speculative enterprise but a biblical doctrine. As such, basic Wesleyan hermeneutics necessarily provides the interpretive framework of understanding, especially these two principles: (1) The biblical message, which is seen throughout the entire canon, is spoken consistently, if not identically in all of Scripture. (2) The literal reading of Scripture is primary, unless it veers toward conclusions that contradict the character of God, which is holy **love**.

From beginning to end, John Wesley preached a God of free grace. Wesley experienced **grace**, the equivalent of divine love, as "free in all, and free for all" (1986, 544). He found a theological ally in his mother Susanna, who saw strict Calvinists impugning God as the author of **sin**.

The inescapable biblical quality of predestination has not led to an orthodox consensus on its meaning. Its many shades of meaning remain contentious and divisive. The undoubted fault line between an Arminian approach, endorsed by Wesleyans, and the Calvinistic is simply stated. Wesleyan-Arminians never limit the scope, depth, and penetration of God's grace. Prevenient grace is freely given, not humanly deserved.

If the singular message of Scripture is divine love, impressed on human consciousness as grace and appropriated by **faith** (Eph. 2:8), then this scriptural principle is profoundly violated when the alien idea of God's "horrible decrees" is introduced; in these "terrifying" or "awesome" decrees, "the divine sovereignty decides one's eternal destiny without recourse to the human will" (Calvin 1960, 2:955). Is this not to hold God hostage to the decrees? So it has seemed to the Wesleyan way. The tidy logic of determinism is not in keeping with the providentialism reflected in the entire Bible. God's sovereign **providence** allows for human freedom and responsibility.

Known for its commitment to practical divinity, Wesleyan theology finds in predestination a description of God's intentions for all of humanity, not just a preselected slice, and indeed for the entire cosmos. The apostle Paul, so Wesley argued, took divine foreknowledge to be not a description of "a chain of causes and effects," but rather a simple showing of "the method in which God works," or the order of salvation (1985, 416).

When predestination is described as "simply the doctrine of **justification** stated in the active voice" (Jenson 1984, 134), Wesleyans can provisionally agree, provided that God's activity never obliterates human responsibility, but rather calls it to account. When Aquinas called predestination a "division of providence" (quoted in Jenson 1984, 134), this serves as a reminder that providence is, at least in its outworking, a cooperative venture between the divine and the human.

For Paul, God "desires everyone to be saved" (1 Tim. 2:4, NRSV). Wesleyans believe that God's desires may be frustrated by human inertia but can never be drained of divine passion and forbearance. Furthermore, Jesus Christ as the **Savior** of the world is the primary showing of how God predestines. Here Wesley may be anticipating Karl Barth, who saw in Jesus Christ God's predestinating intentions for the entire human race and indeed all of **creation**.

Wesley took direct aim at what so deeply disturbed him about Calvinistic predestination. Since all of God's attributes work together, with divine anger and **judgment** serving love's ultimate purposes to heal and redeem, how could God's arbitrary damnation of select souls be reconciled to God's love? It never could be. Predestination wrongly conceived vitiated Christian proclamation, missions, ethics, and spirituality.

The universal offer of redemption, reaching to every depth and stratum of existence, will yet not be met with universal acceptance. God's chosen elect are those who respond, by grace through faith. Ephesians 1:3-14, written to believers, speaks boldly about God's choosing "us in Christ," even "before the foundation of the world" (v. 4, NRSV), destined to be "marked with the seal of the promised **Holy Spirit**" (v. 13, NRSV).

A divine sovereignty humble enough to encourage human responsibility works to ground and solidify Christian assurance, which remains a hallmark of the Wesleyan proclamation. Wesleyans agree with the Lutheran theologian Robert Jenson, that "God's absolute freedom does not diminish our creaturely freedom" (1984, 136). The breathtaking panorama of biblical redemption is beautifully sequenced: "predestined . . . called . . . justified . . . glorified" (Rom. 8:30, NRSV).

Ponderings about predestination are an inevitable plunge into theology, how to think about God, and anthropology, the human question. The Wesleyan stress on the yoked necessity of both divine sovereignty and human responsibility centers Wesleyan advocacy at the vital heart of what the Christian **gospel** stands for.

See also Election; Free Will.

Resources

Calvin, John. *Institutes of the Christian Religion.* 2 vols. Edited by John T. McNeill. Translated by Ford L. Battles. Philadlphia: Westminster Press, 1960.
Jenson, Robert W. "The Holy Spirit." Pages 101-78 in vol 2 of *Christian Dogmatics.* Edited by Carl E. Braaten and Robert W. Jenson. Philadelphia: Fortress Press, 1984.
Wesley, John. "Free Grace." Sermon 110. Pages 542-63 in vol. 3 of *The Bicentennial Edition of the Works of John Wesley.* Edited by Albert C. Outler. Nashville: Abingdon Press, 1986.
———. "On Predestination." Sermon 58. Pages 413-21 in vol. 2 of *The Bicentennial Edition of the Works of John Wesley.* Edited by Albert C. Outler. Nashville: Abingdon Press, 1985.

RODERICK T. LEUPP, PHD

PROGRESSIVE REVELATION

The Christian **faith** affirms the reality of progressive revelation. Without it, the NT would be, not new, but only a different version of the OT. For Christians, the NT bears witness to a revelation that is more complete than what we find in the OT. Even in the NT we can see some developing insight into revelation, as when the **church**, after considerable discussion, came to see that God does not require male Gentile converts to be circumcised.

What usually worries us about the idea of progressive revelation is the possibility that there could be a revelation more ultimate than Jesus Christ or a witness to revelation more ultimate than the NT. The Church of Jesus Christ of Latter-day Saints, for instance, professes to have a revelation that goes beyond and adds to the revelation of Christ to which the NT bears witness. Muslim theology claims that Muhammad received from God the ultimate revelation that gives the true interpretation of Jesus Christ's significance. It is these sorts of **beliefs** that make the idea of progressive revelation problematic.

It is a bedrock element of the Christian faith that there is no revelation more ultimate than Jesus Christ and no witness to that revelation more ultimate than the NT. The basis of this belief is the affirmation that Jesus Christ is the Logos, the **Word of God incarnate.** Before Jesus Christ there were many preliminary expressions of the Word of God, such as Moses's **law** or the declarations of the OT's prophets. However, Jesus Christ is the Word of God itself and not merely an expression of that Word. It is also a fundamental conviction of the Christian faith that the NT is the unsurpassable witness to the revelation of Jesus Christ. This is so because it rests on the testimony of Jesus's apostles.

Revelation is not only something sent but also something received. Revelation that is not received by human eyes and ears and minds is not yet revelation. Thus there can be a development in the human understanding of revelation—a growing awareness of the implications of revelation. Although in one sense no revelation can surpass Jesus Christ and the NT's witness to Jesus Christ, there is a developing history in which God's revelation is understood with increasing insight.

The possibility of such a developing history is grounded in the fact that the revelation of Jesus requires the illumination of the **Holy Spirit**. The Spirit teaches disciples (John 14:26) and guides them into the truth (16:13). This Johannine theme reminds us that revelation must be received and that our minds must be suitably disposed by the Spirit to receive it. History shows us that the Spirit's attempt to lead the church into truth is progressive, even if the pace of progress is frustratingly slow and uneven.

For example, take the practice of **slavery**. Paul wrote that in Christ there is neither slave nor free person (Gal. 3:28). The revelation of Jesus Christ, in other words, means that God is overcoming the distinction between slave and free person. Yet the NT writers took slavery as a fact of life. They did not and, in their cultural situation, could not envision an end to slavery. Over the centuries, the Christian church came to understand that slavery is contrary to God's revelation in Jesus Christ. It took more than eighteen hundred years, but the Spirit finally succeeded in helping the church grasp this important truth. There has thus been progressive insight in the meaning and implications of revelation.

Another example is the ordination of **women** into the ministry of the church. It took Christian churches more than eighteen hundred years to grasp the point that the oneness of men and women in Christ implies the propriety of ordaining women. Most churches still do not acknowledge this point, but some do.

Finally, consider the centuries-long Christian belief that the Bible teaches that the earth lies at the center of the universe. It took the labors of astronomers to convince the Christian community otherwise. In this case, astronomy was useful in helping Christians gain insight into what God's revelation teaches and what it does not teach.

These examples show us that revelation is one thing and that the human understanding of revelation, of its meaning, significance, and consequences, is another thing. It is good for us not to confuse the two. When we forget this distinction, we identify our finite, fallible interpretations of Scripture with the declaration of Scripture itself. We think that our understanding of revelation is revelation itself.

What about the phenomenon of Christian prophecy? We read of **prophets** in the NT (Acts 11:27; 13:1; 15:32; 21:9-11; 1 Cor. 14:29). These prophets may have delivered a revelation (1 Cor. 14:6, 26, 30). Do these new revelations transcend the revelation of Jesus Christ? The book of Revelation shows us that such utterances of Christian prophets are new revelations but are not thereby progressive revelations. They do not constitute a revelation beyond Jesus Christ. They are fresh occasions of revelation in new contexts.

Because revelation must be received and because this reception always takes place in particular historical and cultural circumstances, there is no such thing as generic revelation. Revelation is always the intersection of God's speech and human situation. That is why we read the repeated refrain that we are to listen to "what the Spirit is saying to the churches" (Rev. 2:7, 11, 17, 29; 3:6, 13, 22, NRSV).

The revelation of Jesus Christ is, in a sense, a treasure. Those who are trained for the **kingdom of God** can bring from it both what is new and what is old (Matt. 13:52). Expressed differently, the Spirit of God may have a new word to speak to the church—new because the church dwells in ever-changing contexts that require fresh adaptations of the revelation of Jesus Christ.

See also Cosmology; Household Codes.

SAMUEL M. POWELL, PHD

PROPHETS/PROPHECY

Biblical prophets were individuals called by God. Moses at the burning bush (Exod. 3:1-10) was called by God to free his people from bondage. An **unclean** Isaiah stood before the **holy** God in awe and was asked, "Whom shall I send?" (Isa. 6:8, NIV). While a dramatic call story is not documented for all prophets, the common introduction "the word of the LORD that came to . . ." (Hos. 1:1; Joel 1:1; Jon. 1:1, NIV) affirms God's initiation of the prophets' ministries.

Scripture also shows that the acceptance of the prophetic call often included the prophet's angst, doubt, or even rebellion. Jonah ran from his call, for he knew that God would forgive the Ninevites and take away their punishment if they repented and turned from their sinful ways (Jon. 4:2). Moses raised the question "Who am I . . . ?" as he argued that he was unprepared and unqualified to deliver God's message to Pharaoh (Exod. 3:11, NIV).

Besides their own shortcomings, prophets who faithfully delivered God's message faced the reality that their audience could be hostile toward them and their message. Amos, a Judean shepherd and farmer, was rebuked and told to leave when he attempted to deliver God's message in Bethel, a center of **idolatry** in the northern kingdom (Amos 7:10-15). Ezekiel was called to preach to an obstinate, stubborn, and rebellious people (chs. 2–3). The prophets' acceptance of and **obedience** to the **call of God** despite their personal fears and doubts and the difficulties that would most likely ensue demonstrated the magnitude of the prophets' actions and their faithfulness to God.

Scripture highlights several functions that prophets fulfilled. One primary role of a prophet was to stand in the gap between a holy God and an unclean people. Moses delivered messages from God to the people and vice versa. On Mount Sinai, the Lord through Moses gave the **law** and commandments that the Israelites were to obey (Exod. 19:3-8; Deut. 5:1-5). The Israelites, in turn, often petitioned Moses to pray to the Lord on their behalf, such as when they were attacked by venomous snakes in the **wilderness** (Num. 21:6-9). Later, King Hezekiah sought the prophet Isaiah in hopes that God would hear the prayers of the prophet, who would communicate back to the king the proper course of action concerning the Assyrian attack on **Jerusalem** (Isa. 37:1-7). In the case of the prophet Ezekiel, it was the elders, rather than the king, who approached the prophet to inquire of the Lord (Ezek. 20:1). Habakkuk also served as the people's voice to God, crying out about his concerns of the **sufferings** of the Judeans and their anxieties that inevitably were representative of a society facing oppression (Hab. 1:2-4; 1:12–2:1).

Another primary role of a prophet was to deliver a message from God to a specific audience, most often the nation of Israel or Judah, but also to other countries, such as Jonah and Nahum to Assyria, and Obadiah to Edom. The prophetic message typically included both forthtelling and foretelling. Forthtelling addressed the present, directing accusations against the sinful acts in which the people were currently participating. The biblical audiences were often accused of not living in a covenantal relationship with God, prioritizing their lives around selfish interests and thereby neglecting their relationship with God and failing to **love** their neighbor. In this way and many more, the audiences were guilty of disobedience to the law.

Besides forthtelling, a prophet also foretold what would happen in the future if the audience chose to continue in its current sinful path. It is important to note that over 90 percent of the future predictions found in OT prophetic literature were fulfilled in the lives of the prophets or shortly thereafter. In comparison, very few OT prophecies were messianic ("less than 2 percent") or reflective of a new **covenant** age ("less than 5 percent"), and fewer still have yet to be fulfilled ("less than 1 percent") (Fee and Stuart 2003, 182).

With these messages of future punishment, it is easy for a reader of the OT Prophetic Books to come to the conclusion that the God of the prophetic message is simply one of **judgment**, destruction, and **wrath**. Indeed, the majority of the prophetic corpus does focus on the current **sins** of the audience and the consequences that would come about if the audience chose not to change its ways. Therefore, wrath was evident as humans regularly failed to repent of their sinful actions.

A closer reading of the Prophets, however, reveals a message of **hope**. There was hope in the very fact that God sent prophets to warn the people of their rebelliousness and to call them back to a covenantal relationship. If destruction was indeed God's ultimate intent, then there would have been no need to send prophets to call the people to **repentance**. It was not simply the prophets' existence that expressed hope. Their messages also spoke against the negative characterization of God and instilled the hope that he was instead a "gracious and **compassionate** God, slow to anger and abounding in love, a God who relents from sending calamity" (Jon. 4:2, NIV; see also Joel 2:14).

These are the attributes of God that were clearly on display when he took away the judgment on Nineveh following their repentance (Jon. 3:10). God's **love, mercy,** and **grace** are available for all those who seek him and follow in his ways. While the sins of a fallen humanity and the consequences of those sins consume most of the pages of the Prophetic Books, the key theological themes remain God's willingness to forgive a repentant people and his desire to restore the broken relationship with humanity.

See also Forgiveness, The Art and Necessity of; Word of God/Yahweh, The.

Resources

Chalmers, Aaron. *Interpreting the Prophets*. Downers Grove, IL: InterVarsity Press, 2015.
Fee, Gordon D., and Douglas Stuart. *How to Read the Bible for All Its Worth*. 3rd ed. Grand Rapids: Zondervan, 2003.

BRIAN T. BERNIUS, PHD

PROVIDENCE OF GOD

Providence (Gk., *pronoeō,* "perceive beforehand" [Wis. 14:3; 17:2]; Lat., *provideo,* "attend to") refers to God's constant and eternal superintendence (control) of the **creation,** and governance of human affairs. The Bible assumes and explicitly affirms divine providence (Pss. 104:4; 119:89-91; Prov. 16:33; 21:1). Providence applies to individuals (Ps. 71:1-24), to corporate entities (e.g., Israel), and to general (preservation) and special (miracles) divine activity.

Unlike the "gods" of the surrounding nations, a biblical concept of providence rests upon the belief that *in being,* God the Creator radically transcends his creation, even while being continuously and intricately active in it. The creation is *finally* dependent upon him in all respects and hence subsumed under governance incomprehensible outside radical monotheism. While creaturely dependence finally circumscribes creaturely autonomy, it also levies upon the Creator a responsibility not required by polytheism, a responsibility that, paradoxically, inspires both trust and bitter lament.

Consequently, sometimes people of the old covenant lamented perceived failures by Yahweh to act providentially (Pss. 10:1; 13:2 [3 HB]; 44:1-26 [2-27 HB]; 60:1-12 [3-14 HB]). But they never completely doubted God's sovereignty over his creation and his providential execution of that sovereignty, even when "the heathen raged" (Ps. 46:6 [7 HB], KJV) and Judah was led into captivity (Lam. 3:19-24; 5:1-22). The Hebrew term *hesed* ("steadfast love" or "faithfulness") anchors Hebrew faith against doubts about God's providence (Pss. 44:23-26 [24-27 HB]; 103:11; Isa. 54:10; Jer. 31:3; Dan. 9:3-4).

Classical Christian faith (e.g., Augustine, Thomas Aquinas, Luther, and Calvin) is in harmony with Hebrew convictions, with the eminent addition that God's faithful providence was manifestly exhibited in the person of Jesus Christ. In him God's long-anticipated reign upon earth was inaugurated. But even then, some NT writers recognized powers that challenge God's reign (Matt. 13:25-40; Eph. 6:12), a challenge negated on the cross (Col. 1:15-20; 2:9-15).

Human freedom, whatever its meaning, is finally fenced in by God's sovereign providence. The sixteenth-century Reformers had no doubt about God's sovereign governance, even when they could not precisely chart its pathway through religious and civic complexities.

In the modern era, Christian confidence in God's providence continues. However, for some Christians the term is used tentatively and its practical meaning is uncertain. Developments in modern philosophy have placed increased confidence in human autonomy and responsibility—intellectual, moral, and political. Secular institutions such as universities, democratic governments, and market economies have dislodged deity as a required explanation. Increased knowledge of the natural order, generated by the natural sciences, explains the world in ways that make God's active involvement less and less comprehensible. Fossil and genetic records seem to place human emergence outside any divine plan. Geological records trace a series of five catastrophic events in which species became extinct, followed by gradual evolutionary recovery. The modern era has in its memory demonic ideologies harnessing technology to unleash incomprehensible horrors upon entire population segments, all without a trace of divine restriction. Because of such events, many thoughtful people find it very difficult to speak meaningfully of divine providence. Others, such as Jewish theologian Richard Rubenstein, argue that continuing to believe in divine providence is irrational if not immoral (1966).

Today, many Christians hold to more traditional views of God's providence. But some forms of theology, such as process theology and open theism, have redefined providence in terms that work in conjunction with the "relative autonomy" of humanity and nature. Many faithful Christians, aware they know far more about nature and historical dynamics than their ancient kinsmen, are content to affirm God's providence and the anticipated consummation of his **kingdom** without claiming more.

See also Cosmology; Free Will; Idolatry.

Resources

Jowers, Dennis W., ed. *Four Views on Divine Providence.* Grand Rapids: Zondervan, 2011.
"Providence." Jewish Virtual Library. https://www.jewishvirtuallibrary.org/providence.
Rubenstein, Richard L. *After Auschwitz: History, Theology, and Contemporary Judaism.* Indianapolis: Bobbs-Merrill, 1966.
Sanders, John. *The God Who Risks: A Theology of Divine Providence.* 2nd ed. Downers Grove, IL: IVP Academic, 2007.

AL TRUESDALE, PHD

Rr

READER-RESPONSE HERMENEUTICS

The interpretation of a biblical text considers what that text may mean and where such meaning may be located. Most interpretive approaches begin with a basic assumption: an author (or authors) wrote the respective biblical text for an implied audience (or reader).

| Author ⟶ Text ⟶ Audience (or Reader) |

1. Three Interpretive Approaches

Interpretive approaches complement one another but differ in where they look for the biblical text's meaning. Some approaches are more *author centered*, considering the author's intention to be determinative of the text's meaning. So awareness of the author's world, the situation that prompted the text's writing, and the historical setting leads the interpreter to discover the text's meaning. Other approaches are more *text centered*, focusing on the text as a literary work. So the text's meaning resides within the text itself. That meaning may be found within a developing plot with its cast of characters or discovered in the way a letter lays out its argument to its church audience. In both cases, the text's meaning may be traced to specific features—structures, word connections, rhetoric, literary devices, and so on—within that text.

Still other approaches are more *audience* or *reader centered*, considering the role of the audience or readers in the construal or creation of a biblical text's meaning. Since a text's meaning is only potential in nature until the reading of that text, reader-centered approaches focus on the reader's role in determining that text's meaning. Readers often may interpret the same text differently. Such approaches recognize that no one reads neutrally but that each reads from a nuanced, "shaped" perspective. Because the role and perspective of readers in the interpretive process are often unrecognized in relation to the text's meaning, reader-response hermeneutics also considers what readers bring to the table and influences how they construe meaning.

2. Readers and the Reading Process

Reader-response hermeneutics appropriates and values traditional exegetical methods, but the scope of the interpretive process is broadened to include critical consideration of influences upon interpreters. Most interpreters recognize the problems in making specific connections between an author's intention and the text's meaning. So although the text reflects the historical (original) context, reader-response hermeneutics focuses attention on the active role of readers in the reading and interpretation of that text.

Given that the text itself may guide the reader to make some interpretive conclusions over others, reader-centered approaches recognize the reader is not passive in this process. While reading, the reader makes decisions about how specific textual features may relate together. He or she builds consistency throughout the reading process with what *is* and *is not* stated. As the reader encounters new things in the sequential reading process that vary from earlier conclusions, he or she revises those conclusions to account for new discoveries. Reader-response hermeneutics shines a spotlight on these activities that readers themselves often do not consciously realize to be at work. Yet such interpretive activities bring a (biblical) text to life, and the text remains meaningless without them. Since meaning is found in the *convergence* of the text and reader in this interpretive (creative) activity, reader-response hermeneutics understands meaning *as a product of the reader's interaction with the text*, not merely something self-contained within the text that may be extracted from it.

3. Readers and Presuppositions

Generations past assumed exegesis was done objectively and without the influence of the interpreter's presuppositions. Yet almost a century ago, Rudolf Bultmann challenged this assumption with a question, "Is Exegesis without Presuppositions Possible?" ([1957] 1984). His answer, which predated reader-centered approaches, suggested that more attention must be given to interpreters' preunderstandings or presuppositions, since they influence how readers see and read biblical texts.

Just as biblical authors wrote within their social location, which includes their *own* presuppositions and understandings (personal, cultural, social, religious, etc.), readers of biblical texts interpret within *their own* social location, within which they think, discern, and understand. Readers never perform their roles as interpreters of biblical texts by stepping outside their social location or these influences on the interpretive process. Presuppositions and preunderstandings provide the lenses through which these texts are read and interpreted. Thus reader-response hermeneutics contends that interpretation is incomplete without attention given to what the reader brings to the table.

4. Wesleyan Readers, the Church, and the Holy Spirit

As part of the **church**, Christian readers come to biblical texts with canonical presuppositions: these texts should be read and interpreted in the context of the church. Readings thus assume certain preunderstandings (e.g., the creeds) as they are heard and interpreted in this **faith** context. Responses to these texts also assume this faith community and her mission. Although traditional approaches to biblical exegesis and **biblical theology** have typically ignored such issues, reader-centered hermeneutics considers them central to the purposes of the biblical texts, to the Christian canon, and to the interpretive task.

Wesleyan readers read the Bible differently than other Christians do. Among the distinctive features of the Wesleyan tradition (e.g., its optimistic view of **grace**, its understanding of Scripture as salvific in nature, etc.) is the understanding of the role of the **Holy Spirit** in the church's reading and interpretation of Scripture—an understanding supported by John Wesley's comments on 2 Timothy 3:16 (1755). Most other approaches to studying biblical texts in the last couple of centuries do not consider such matters as relevant, since such approaches are either author centered or text centered and focus on more "objective" approaches to biblical study. But since reader-response hermeneutics considers what (church) readers bring to their readings of biblical texts as Scripture, this family of biblical interpretation offers a window through which Wesleyans may explore the dynamics of the Spirit at work within the church when reading Scripture together.

Resources

Bultmann, Rudolf. "Is Exegesis without Presuppositions Possible?" 1957. Pages 145-53 in *New Testament and Mythology and Other Basic Writings*. Edited by Schubert M. Ogden. Philadelphia: Fortress Press, 1984.
Wesley, John. *Explanatory Notes upon the New Testament*. London: William Bowyer, 1755.

RICHARD P. THOMPSON, PHD

RECONCILIATION

The Bible describes reconciliation between humans and, most significantly, restoration of the broken relationship between God and humanity. While the concept is developed most explicitly in the Pauline letters, it is prominent throughout the Bible.

Reconciliation in the Hebrew Scriptures

The Hebrew Scriptures speak of reconciliation in several ways. In 1 Samuel, as the Philistines prepare for battle against Saul's army, the Philistine commanders fear that David will try to "reconcile [*rāṣâ*] himself to" Saul by turning against the Philistines (29:4, NRSV). While the NRSV here translates the Hebrew *rāṣâ* as "reconcile," the word might just as accurately be translated as "become acceptable." The idea seems to be that David, on his own initiative, may try to restore his relationship with Saul by earning Saul's favor.

In Leviticus 26, the broken relationship is not between two human beings but between God and his people. There God says that if his people become humble under the weight of his judgment and "make amends [*rāṣâ*] for their iniquity" (v. 41, NRSV), he will remember his covenant (vv. 40-45). The phrase "make amends" occurs twice in this passage (vv. 41, 43, NRSV), both times translating the Hebrew *rāṣâ*. One party to a broken relationship may restore the relationship by earning the favor of the other. Here, however, while God's people must make amends, the initiative is God's.

The situation in Isaiah 44:22 is similar. God has sent judgment in the form of King Cyrus of Persia and has called his people to "return" (*šûb*) to him, assuring them that he has "swept away" (*māḥâ*) their sins and "redeemed" (*gā'al*) them (NRSV). The Hebrew verb *šûb* carries the idea of **repentance**. Here, as in Leviticus 26, God has sent judgment and called his people to respond with repentance and to enjoy a renewed relationship with him.

Reconciliation in the Septuagint and the Deuterocanonical Works

The Septuagint (LXX) speaks of reconciliation mainly by means of two Greek verbs, *diallassomai* and *katēllagēn*, both of which can be translated as "become reconciled"; the related nouns are *diallagē* and *katallagē*.

In 1 Samuel 29:4 (see above), the LXX uses *diallassomai* to translate *rāṣâ*. The Philistines fear that David will attempt to reconcile himself to Saul.

The author of 2 Maccabees uses the verb *katallassō* three times (1:5; 7:33; 8:29) to speak of the restoration of the relationship between God and his people. In 1:5, the author expresses his **hope** that God will hear the prayers of his people and "be reconciled" to them (NRSV). In 7:32-33, the youngest of seven Jewish brothers, all martyred for their faithfulness to God, says, "We are **suffering** because of our own sins. And if our living Lord is angry for a little while, to rebuke and discipline us, he will again be reconciled with his own servants" (NRSV). In verses 37-38, the same brother hopes that he and his brothers, by bearing **God's wrath** against the people, can bring that wrath to an end.

Judas Maccabeus and his men ask God to "be wholly reconciled with his servants" (8:29, NRSV). The author believes that God has withdrawn his favor from his people because of their sin; the relationship has been broken. It is hoped that God can be persuaded to return to the relationship.

Reconciliation in the New Testament

Paul's understanding of the reconciliation between God and human beings is less like that of 2 Maccabees and more like that of Leviticus 26 and

Isaiah 44. In 2 Corinthians 5:16-21, the key NT passage on reconciliation, four important elements of Paul's view stand out: (1) While 2 Maccabees hopes that God will be reconciled to his people, Paul states that God has reconciled (*katallassō*) people to himself (2 Cor. 5:18-19). (2) While 2 Maccabees hopes that the people's **suffering** will facilitate reconciliation, Paul proclaims that God's **work** of reconciliation is facilitated by what God has already done "through Christ" and "in Christ" (2 Cor. 5:18-20, NRSV)— "not counting their trespasses against them" (v. 19, NRSV) and making "him to be **sin** who knew no sin" (v. 21, NRSV). (3) For Paul, the God who has taken the initiative has also set the terms on which reconciliation can occur. It occurs through Christ and only through Christ. As God's envoy, Paul has been sent to announce the terms of reconciliation (*katallagē*) and call people to accept them (vv. 19c-20). (4) While reconciliation is facilitated by God's prior act, it requires a human response (v. 20).

Romans 5:9-10 provides three important details about reconciliation: (1) It occurs through the death of Christ. (2) Before reconciliation, human beings are enemies of God. (3) It is closely related to **justification**. These verses offer two parallel statements. Logically, in the second statement (v. 10) the verb "reconciled" (*katallassō*) occupies the same position that "justified" (*dikaioō*) occupies in the first (v. 9), and both justification and reconciliation are seen as the basis for future salvation. Paul does not make clear the precise relationship between the two. Perhaps we should understand them as inseparable though not identical, with "justification" belonging to forensic imagery and "reconciliation" to relational imagery.

Two references to reconciliation in other letters round out our understanding. Colossians 1:20 states that "through [Christ] God was pleased to reconcile [*apokatallassō*] to himself all things" (NRSV). (The debate over the significance of "all things" cannot be settled here. It must suffice to note that again reconciliation is seen as occurring through Christ.) In vv. 21-22, the author goes on to say that those who have been reconciled (*apokatallassō*) to God were once "estranged and hostile" (NRSV). Finally, Ephesians 2:16 states that through Christ, God has reconciled (*apokatallassō*) Jews and Gentiles.

See also Confession; Forgiveness, The Art and Necessity of; Regeneration/Rebirth.

Resource
Danker, Frederick William, ed. *A Greek-English Lexicon of the New Testament and Other Early Christian Literature.* 3rd ed. Chicago: University of Chicago Press, 2000.

J. EDWARD ELLIS, PHD

REDEEM/REDEEMER

Throughout the Bible, the concept of redemption is uniformly presented, in general terms, as the deliverance of a person or people group from a dangerous situation to a secure one. However, this idea is present in various contexts that nuance this simplified definition. In particular, the Old and New Testaments each have their own understandings of this concept. Moreover, the setting of redemption ranges from the social to the economic to the theological. The extent to which God is presented as a redeemer can only be properly understood once we examine the concept of redemption in the pragmatic, everyday environments of ancient persons.

The Use of the Root *Pādâ* for "Redeem/Redeemer"

In the OT, one Hebrew term commonly translated as "redeem," *pādâ* (58x), frequently carries the sense of being released from death. This is seen in cultic contexts (see Exod. 13:13; Num. 18:15), where firstborn children and some animals are pardoned from **sacrifice**. This sense also applies to individuals who are spared the fate of death (1 Sam. 14:45). Less frequently, and only in the passive voice, *pādâ* refers to release from a legal (Lev. 19:20) or cultic (27:29) obligation.

In this word's theological sense, God is viewed as the redeemer of both individuals and Israel. Here *pādâ* is always concerned with escape from imminent danger. God redeems persons from the power of death (e.g., Ps. 26:11) and from one's enemies (e.g., 69:18 [19 HB]). In a specific usage, God is frequently seen as the redeemer of Israel from the hand of **slavery** in Egypt (e.g., Deut. 7:8). This latter example is the most frequent context of the verbal root *pādâ*, appearing throughout the OT in various literary contexts.

The Use of the Root *Gā'al* for "Redeem/Redeemer"

The second Hebrew term often translated as "redeem" or "redeemer" in the OT is *gā'al*. This root appears more frequently than *pādâ* (102x). The root *gā'al* carries a number of socioeconomic meanings, but it is also significant theologically.

The one who fulfills the obligation of levirate **marriage** by taking the wife of his deceased brother as his own or the one who saves a **woman** from childlessness is known as a redeemer. Thus in the book of Ruth, Boaz is frequently referred to as a redeemer for Ruth (see ch. 4). Further, this term can carry a violent connotation, as one who avenges a death is known as a redeemer (e.g., Josh. 20:3).

In Leviticus, *gā'al* is used to describe the action of reclaiming lost property. Hence this term appears when someone buys back a house (25:33) or an individual retakes possession of an animal unfit for sacrifice (27:13). It is also used when a person is released from a debt obligation (25:47-55), thereby reclaiming his or her freedom.

It is this latter sense of reclaiming lost property that OT authors consistently attribute to God, with Israel designated as God's property. The root *gā'al* refers to God's actions in the exodus (Exod. 6:6; 15:13; Ps. 77:15 [16

HB]), as well as the prophetic hope for rescue from exile (Isa. 43:1; Jer. 31:11; Mic. 4:10). Thus *gāʾal*, like *pādâ*, frequently refers not only to God's rescue of his people from slavery but also to other similar contexts in which God reclaims his people lost in peril. Whereas the emphasis of *pādâ* is God's rescue of Israel from certain death in such situations, the stress of *gāʾal* is that God has reclaimed his people lost to other nations.

In summary, the OT usage of "redeem" or "redeemer" consistently bears a physical connotation. In every instance, it describes the rescue of property, an animal, a person, or a people group from some type of harm. In the OT, redemption does not yet refer to release from moral danger, a meaning that develops only in the NT.

"Redeem/Redeemer" in NT Narrative

Words in the NT expressing the concept of redemption appear less frequently (only 16x) than they do in the OT (160x). Nevertheless, the concept is pivotal in the NT for understanding God's work in Christ.

The Greek verbs often translated "to redeem" are *luō* (3x), *apoluō* (5x), and *exagorazō* (2x). The first two terms share the same root and thus often approximate one another in meaning. Whereas *apoluō* emphasizes a release *from* a person or situation, *luō* more generally expresses the concept of release. In several other **Gospel** passages, these verbs are used in similar contexts, specifically releasing someone from a particular place (e.g., the presence of Jesus or prison) without a burden to bear (Matt. 15:23; 18:27; 27:15-17; Acts 4:23).

Luke twice uses *apoluō* in a slightly different manner from what we have seen. In one instance, it refers to releasing someone from the burdens of **sin** through **forgiveness** (6:37), and in another instance, it refers to Jesus healing a woman with an illness (13:12). Both instances show that this verb has a wide variety of applications in the original Greek, though with the general sense of release from a difficult state to a liberating one.

Luke also introduces the nominal form of this root, *apolutrōsis*, in 21:28. Here the meaning is more cryptic, since it appears in an apocalyptic passage referring to the result of the Son of Man's coming. Given Luke's clearer definition elsewhere of the verbal form, *apoluō*, we can assume that the "redemption" believers will see at the coming of the Son of Man will also involve salvific actions such as forgiveness and healing.

"Redeem/Redeemer" in NT Epistles

The verb *exagorazō* is only translated to express the concept of redemption in Galatians 3:13 and 4:5 (it also appears in Eph. 5:16 and Col. 4:5 with the entirely different meaning about maximizing the use of time). In both instances in Galatians, *exagorazō* refers to how the work of Christ releases believers from the burdens of the Jewish **law**. This is an especially important concept in Galatians, where Paul addresses the tension faced by new Christians concerning the extent to which the Torah should be strictly followed by those who claim Jesus as the **Messiah**. Therefore, *exagorazō* has a moral import, much as *apoluō* does in Luke 6:37.

The nominal form *apolutrōsis* appears five times in the epistolary literature, each time referring to the saving work of Jesus. In 1 Corinthians 1:30, Paul claims "redemption" as a characteristic of Jesus in parallel with "**wisdom**," "**righteousness**," and "**sanctification**" (NRSV). Three times (Rom. 3:24; Eph. 1:7; Heb. 9:15) the author clearly connects redemption with forgiveness from sin.

In Romans 8:23, Paul refers to "the redemption of our bodies" (NRSV), which recalls the aspect of physical healing inherent in redemption (see also Luke 13:12). This suggests that any redemption from God is not just spiritual or psychological, but holistic. Indeed for Paul, it is God's desire to redeem all of **creation**.

In both Romans 8:23 and Galatians 4:5, Paul links redemption to the concept of adoption. The believer's redemption involves his or her claim to belong to the family of God. This underscores the importance of the idea of release inherent in the verbs *luō* and *apoluō* studied above. That is, one is always released *from* some place *to* another. There is no true independence for human beings. Rather, the human condition will always drive us to be dependent on something (or someone) else. The Christian who accepts the salvation of Jesus is released *from* the world of sin and death *to* God's household.

The Theological Significance of "Redemption" Shared by the OT and NT

In light of our study, we see that the concept of redemption has theologically significant understandings in both the OT and NT. Both Testaments borrow these theological meanings from pragmatic contexts, especially from social and economic interactions, and transform them to speak of the saving actions of God. In the OT, God is seen as the redeemer of Israel from material harm, rescuing them from captivity and death. In the NT, the threats from which God liberates God's people include not only death but also its companion force of sin.

Resources
Fentress-Williams, Judy. *Ruth*. AOTC. Nashville: Abingdon Press, 2012.

Hays, Richard B. *The Faith of Jesus Christ: The Narrative Substructure of Galatians 3:1–4:11*. 2nd ed. Grand Rapids: Eerdmans, 2002.

Wainwright, Geoffrey. *For Our Salvation: Two Approaches to the Work of Christ*. Grand Rapids: Eerdmans, 1997.

DREW S. HOLLAND, MDIV

REGENERATION/REBIRTH

The biblical concept of regeneration or rebirth is represented in various ways and with varying language in the NT. In general, it speaks of individual, corporate, and cosmic transformation and renewal of a kind that can only be attributed to the mighty work of God.

The Greek noun *palingenesia*, usually translated "regeneration," is found twice in the NT. In Matthew 19:28, Jesus's words have a cosmic emphasis connecting regeneration to the eschatological age and more specifically to the consummation of this age; when referencing disciples and other believers, it is in relation to their roles and rewards within the new age. To the disciples who follow Jesus "in the regeneration" (v. 28, NASB), they will join with him in imparting **judgment** (cf. 1 Cor. 6:2), and all followers will inherit eternal life.

Titus 3:5-6 emphasizes the work of the triune God who saved us "by the washing of regeneration and renewing by the **Holy Spirit**, whom He poured out upon us richly through Jesus Christ our Savior" (NASB). Regeneration is closely linked to the work of **justification** and adoption, with the expected outcome being transformation and **holiness** in the life of all believers (vv. 7-8; cf. Rom. 12:2).

With reference to rebirth, also translated "born again," the Johannine writings utilize multiple phrases that include a passive form of the Greek verb *gennaō* ("to beget" or "to give birth to") and a qualifier: "of God" (*ek [tou] theou*; John 1:13; 1 John 3:9; 4:7; 5:1, 4, 18; cf. 2:29); "from above" (*anōthen*; John 3:3, 7); or "of the Spirit" (*ek tou pneumatos*; vv. 5, 8). This rebirth is corporate, since it refers to a state or location in which all believers find themselves—namely, eternal life. In this sense, it is akin to the Synoptic Gospels' use of the **kingdom of God** or **kingdom of heaven**. Nevertheless, John's emphasis appears more individual or personal. The familial language of birth or begetting coupled with the significant stress on God as Father highlights the relational reality of John's rebirth language. Through **faith**, individuals enter into a relationship with the Father through the Son by way of the Spirit and thus become children of God (1:12; 11:52; 1 John 3:1-2, 10). Associated with rebirth is the phenomenon of coming to or walking in the light (John 3:21; 8:12; 12:36; 1 John 1:7; 2:9-10). To be born of God is to be with God and like God; it is a process of total transformation, a moving away from **sin** and darkness and toward God's glorious light.

Rebirth language is also used in 1 Peter. It is God the Father who has "caused us to be born again [*anagennēsas*] to a living **hope**" (1:3, NASB), making us "obedient children" (v. 14, NASB). Peter exhorts "Be **holy** yourselves also in all your behavior; because it is written, 'YOU SHALL BE HOLY, FOR I AM HOLY'" (vv. 15-16, NASB; quoting Lev. 19:2), which is bound to the imperative "Fervently love one another from the heart" (v. 22, NASB). Peter also connects this rebirth to the "living and enduring **word of God**" (v. 23,

NASB; cf. 2:2), which is a reference to the proclaimed **gospel** (1:12). A similar connotation is found in James 1:18, where God is said to have "brought us forth [*apekyēsen*] by the word of truth" (NASB).

The language of newness or renewal can convey similar ideas to that of regeneration and rebirth and is especially prevalent in the Pauline corpus. It is through Christ's faithfulness that believers are able to "walk in newness of life" (Rom. 6:4, NASB), to "serve in newness of the Spirit" (7:6, NASB), to "be transformed by the renewing of . . . mind" (12:2, NASB), to have their inner being "renewed day by day" (2 Cor. 4:16, NASB; cf. Titus 3:5), and to "put on the new self, which in the likeness of God has been created in **righteousness** and holiness of the truth" (Eph. 4:24, NASB; cf. Col. 3:10). For Paul, each of these realities is tied to the "already, but not yet" eschatological age brought about through Christ.

Those "in Christ" participate in the new creation (2 Cor. 5:17, NASB; Gal. 6:15; cf. Rom. 8:18-25) and are called to emulate Christ and share in his mission (2 Cor. 5:18-20); they are being transformed and are participating in the present transformation of this world. Herein we see the corporate and cosmic ramifications of God's actions through Christ and through his **church** as a result of the Holy Spirit at work in the life of the believing community.

This cosmic renewal is also found in Revelation 21:1 and 2 Peter 3:13 with their references to a new heaven and new earth, which are strong allusions to Isaiah 65:17 and 66:22. It is important to note that Isaiah is not the only OT book to highlight such eschatological regeneration. It is seen in Ezekiel's vision of the dry bones being made alive again by the indwelling of God's Spirit (Ezek. 37:1-14; cf. Joel 2:28-29) and in Jeremiah's promise of a new **covenant** written on the hearts of God's people (Jer. 31:31-34; cf. Deut. 30:6; Ps. 51:10 [12 HB]; Ezek. 36:26). In these few examples, we see that the NT concepts of regeneration, rebirth, and renewal are grounded in the OT promises of God. The NT writers were experiencing the beginnings of and anticipating the fulfillment of God's full salvation and restoration of all **creation**.

Although the language and ideas vary slightly from writer to writer, three measured conclusions can be drawn concerning the biblical concept of regeneration and rebirth. First and foremost, it is an act of the triune God—Father, Son, and Spirit. Second, it is based in a sustained relationship with this triune God. Third, its end goal is wholeness and holiness in the individual, the corporate church, and all the created order.

See also Eschatology; Gospel of John, Theology of.

Resources

Hubbard, Moyer V. *New Creation in Paul's Letters and Thought*. SNTSMS 119. Cambridge, UK: Cambridge University Press, 2002.

Rainbow, Paul A. *Johannine Theology: The Gospel, the Epistles and the Apocalypse*. Downers Grove, IL: InterVarsity Press, 2014.

ROB A. FRINGER, PHD

REMEMBERING

The English words "remember" and "remembrance" translate the Hebrew words *zākar, zēker*, and *zikkārôn* and the Greek words *mimnēskomai, mnēmoneuō*, and *mneia*, together with prefixed forms *anamimnēskō, hypomimnēskō*, and *anamnēsis*. Remembering in the biblical sense may be described as recall that moves to action. Prior forgetfulness is not necessarily implied. While these biblical words can be used to express the recall of facts (Num. 11:5), the biblical concept of remembering usually carries significant theological content. Three aspects are particularly noteworthy.

Properly Ordered Worldview

Five times in Deuteronomy the people of Israel were commanded to remember their **slavery** in Egypt. This remembrance undergirds the vision for community life in the Mosaic **law**. As the Israelites recall their former status and the freeing activity of God, their worldview is transformed from subservience to freedom and from self-importance to **compassion**. God is the protector of the powerless. He remembers those whom the world prefers to forget, and he expects those whom he remembers to remember others. God cares not only how people relate to him but also how they relate to one another.

Scripture also speaks about the remembrance of **sins**. Remembering sins means bringing the sinner to **judgment**. To forget sins means to forgive. This language of forgetting sins is reserved in the OT for God, a fact that may have influenced the scribes of Mark 2:7 to claim that God alone forgives sins. In Ezekiel 18:21-32, the prophet records a divine self-defense wherein God declares that the sins of a repentant wicked person will not be remembered, while the opposite is true for a **righteous** person who begins to **sin**. God's perspective on human sinfulness is the definitive one. Thus remembering involves aligning one's perspective with God's.

The remembrance of the destruction of **Jerusalem** in Psalm 137 is also instructive. This Psalm captures the emotions of a world turned upside down. The people of Israel were confident that God would protect them. But when they were exiled, that confidence failed. This conundrum forced the people to reevaluate their assumptions and realign their worldview.

Isaiah 65:17 says that the former things will not be remembered. God intends to bring reality into alignment with his desires. Past events that appeared to challenge God's sovereignty will lose significance when they are overshadowed by the consummation of his purposes.

Properly Aligned Interpersonal Relations

Remembering God and others invites us to properly order our relationships. Here it is helpful to recall the role and function of **patronage** in the ancient world. Patronage was a system of exchange wherein persons of dissimilar resources and social standing entered into an ongoing relationship. The person with greater resources (the patron) provided benefits, such as protection from foreign powers, to the person with fewer resources (the client). In exchange, the client regularly declared the praises of the patron, thereby increasing the patron's **honor**. The language of remembrance could be employed as a way of entering into a patronage relationship. Thus, when the crucified criminal asked Jesus to remember him (Luke 23:42), he may have been asking Jesus to become his patron.

The **covenant** relationship between God and his people may be understood in the context of patronage. God may be called upon to remember his people (Ps. 74:2), and vice versa (Deut. 8:18). The Scriptures also record calls to remember the covenant itself (1 Chron. 16:15). When the people are asked to remember, they are being encouraged to offer praises to God (patron) for his deeds on behalf of his people (clients). Prayers for God to remember his covenant with Israel are pleas for God to make good on his commitments for the benefit of his people. Such prayers can be offered in confidence based on God's past faithfulness.

In the same way, when people remember one another, they are to act in faithfulness to their commitments. To remember someone, therefore, requires an understanding of the dynamics of interpersonal proprieties.

Proper Responses in the Present

Remembering is a way of bringing the past powerfully into the present. Remembrance affects proper relationships in the present, but it also implies right action. When Paul said that he had been exhorted to remember the **poor** (Gal. 2:10), this clearly involves more than the "Go in **peace**" inaction of the **faith**-without-**works** individual of James 2:16 (NIV).

The much-discussed "Do this in remembrance of me" from the Lord's Supper similarly entails present action informed by the past. Remembering Jesus implies more than a cognitive rehearsal of his character; it also means renewing one's passion for Christ and one's resolve to follow his example. Paul highlighted one aspect of Jesus's example when he placed Jesus's charge to remember him in the context of a discussion about **church** unity. When Paul said that failure to consider the body of Christ during Communion brings judgment (1 Cor. 11:29), he reminded the Corinthians that Christ put the needs of others before his own.

When God remembers, he also acts. In Genesis 8:1, for example, when God is said to have remembered Noah and the creatures on the ark, we are not to understand that an absentminded God suddenly recalled a hapless family. Rather, the remembrance was of God's ongoing covenantal commitment to Noah, which caused God to act on his behalf.

Notice that God's remembrance implies his action in and reaction to historical events. The God of the Bible, therefore, is not the impassive god of Greek philosophy, but the impassioned lover of his people and the joyful caretaker of his **creation** who both initiates and responds to their activities.

See also Discipleship; Forgiveness, The Art and Necessity of; Providence of God.

Resources

Bubbers, Susan I. *A Scriptural Theology of Eucharistic Blessings.* London: Bloomsbury T and T Clark, 2013.

Keshgegian, Flora A. *Redeeming Memories: A Theology of Healing and Transformation.* Nashville: Abingdon Press, 2000.

Longenecker, Bruce W. *Remember the Poor: Paul, Poverty, and the Greco-Roman World.* Grand Rapids: Eerdmans, 2010.

Smith, Gordon T. *A Holy Meal: The Lord's Supper in the Life of the Church.* Grand Rapids: Baker Academic, 2005.

DARIN H. LAND, PHD

REMNANT

Remnant connotes what remains or survives after the whole has been used up or destroyed. In the OT, the word "remnant" may represent different Hebrew terms, although it is usually based on derivatives of *š'r*. From an early date, the religious texts of Israel's neighbors attest the motif of a remnant that survives a divinely decreed destruction as indicating **hope** for human existence. A similar theme is found in the story of Israel's calling as God's people. This account is grounded in God's **creation** intentions for humankind (*'ādām*), represented by a single pair in the divine **image** (Gen. 1:26-28) who were charged to be benevolent caretakers of God's creation (2:15). After the flood, humankind was reduced to a remnant (*wayiššā'er*; Gen. 7:23; cf. Sir. 44:17), and this blessing is renewed in God's **covenant** with Noah's family and all creation (Gen. 9:1-17).

Israel's **election** and vocation begins with the patriarchs and **matriarchs** (chs. 12–50) as the forbears of a divinely called remnant on earth (*šě'ērît bā'āreṣ*; 45:7). God entered into a covenant with this community as a bearer of God's blessing, which it was responsible to convey to all the peoples of the earth (12:1-3; 17:1-22; 28:13-14). In the Sinai covenant preamble, Israel's vocation is represented as a priesthood, dedicated and set apart to minister God's blessing to the rest of creation (Exod. 19:2-6).

Remnant may have either positive or negative connotations depending on how God's people were living up to their calling to glorify God as a community of **justice** and **righteousness** for the sake of all creation. Israel was warned that if it broke faith with YHWH, it would be destroyed by enemies and would be unable to defend or reestablish itself through the surviving remnant (*wĕhanniš'ārîm*; Lev. 26:36). This is the same hopeless situation facing nations threatened by divine **judgment** (e.g., Amos 1:6-8).

Israel's **prophets** challenged the leaders who had grown complacent and who considered themselves the divinely elected and favored remnant despite their unfaithfulness to their vocation. In the eighth century, Amos indicated that Israel's calling as the remnant of Joseph required it to establish a just community (5:14-15). Israel's **election** did not entitle this remnant to special privilege; it would be especially accountable for its **sins** (3:1-2). Amos announced a reduction of Israel to a remnant, signifying defeat (5:3; 6:8-9) or total destruction (3:9-12). Yet by God's **grace** even the remnant of Israel's enemies might become partakers with Israel in a divine covenant (9:11-12).

Isaiah employed the term "remnant" in multiple ways. When Judah's leaders pursued trusting in foreign alliances rather than in YHWH, Isaiah announced that not even a remnant of these nations would survive (Isa. 14:22-23, 28-31; 15:1-9). Yet later there would be salvation for the remnant of Judah's enemies (11:16). Positive and negative connotations for the fate of Judah are signified in the name of Isaiah's son Shear-jashub (meaning "a remnant will return or repent"; 7:3), as attested in the mixed messages of 6:11-13 and 10:20-23. On the one hand, it connotes a threat when depicting the reduction of the once great people of God to bare survival after their battles (10:22). On the other hand, a faithful remnant who repented would by God's grace return from captivity and carry on the election and calling of God (11:11; 37:31-32; cf. Lev. 26:40-45). In summary, the elect were not simply identical to the entire people of Israel (or Judah); rather, the elect would be a faithful remnant from Israel.

The seventh-century prophets confirmed Isaiah's message that even a reduced and struggling remnant of Israel could fulfill God's calling. After Zephaniah threatened the total destruction of the **Jerusalem** community (depicted as a cosmic judgment; see Zeph. 1:2-18), he announced that for the humble faithful who submitted to YHWH, there might be an opportunity to **repent** and survive God's judgment (2:1-2). Initially, this humble remnant would not fare well, since all that the prophet could promise was a subsistence-level existence to this urban Jerusalem **poor** as they fled to live as refugees in the ruins of foreign cities (vv. 5-7, 9). Yet through God's grace this scattered remnant would influence the nations to worship and depend upon the God of Israel (v. 11; 3:9-11). YHWH would then gather, shepherd, and reestablish the humble outcasts of **Jerusalem** as the beginning of a restoration of the created order (3:12-13; 19-20).

The Judeans who returned from the exile to restore the Jerusalem community considered themselves the elect remnant of Israel (Ezra 9:5-9; Hag. 1:12-14; see Isa. 11:11). Yet as some leaders began to abuse their power and exclude others, the prophets had to once again warn the leaders that only the faithful who establish **justice** qualified as God's true servants and that God's grace knows no ethnic boundaries (Isa. 56:1-8; 65:8-16).

The remnant theme does not appear as explicitly in the NT as it does in the OT. It is probably reflected in Jesus's teaching that "many are called, but few are chosen" (Matt. 22:14, NRSV). It is also suggested by Jesus's critique of unfaithful religious leaders and by his **compassion** for and calling of the outcast and excluded—including **women**, the poor, the ritually **unclean**, and Gentiles. The apostle Paul employed the idea of a faithful remnant as he struggled with the theological problem of Israel's (i.e., the Jews') continued place in the community of faith after God's **revelation** in Christ (Rom. 9–11). Through the quotation of OT passages (9:25-33; 11:1-6), Paul demonstrated that God's purposes have always been accomplished by a remnant that is called by grace and responds in **faith**. In Christ this remnant includes both faithful Israelites (like Paul) and Gentiles (9:23-24; 10:11-13; cf. 1:16-17; 3:29-30).

In conclusion, the idea of a remnant attests to the unrelenting "faithfulness" (*ḥesed*) of YHWH, who, for the sake of the entire creation, refuses to abandon divine promises. God's people can rest assured that even though they suffer hardships, God will not abandon them. God's creation purposes will be accomplished with a divinely called, empowered, and faithful remnant. But this remnant must not take their election status for granted. Rather, they must respond faithfully to **God's call** so that in the power of the Spirit they may bring **glory** to God and fulfill their vocation to convey the divine blessing to all of God's creation.

Resources

Hasel, Gerhard F. "Remnant." Pages 735-36 of *IDBSup*.

———. *The Remnant: The History and Theology of the Remnant Idea from Genesis to Isaiah*. 3rd ed. Andrews University Monographs, Studies in Religion 5. Berrien Springs, MI: Andrews University Press, 1980.

Vaux, Roland de. "The 'Remnant of Israel' according to the Prophets." Pages 15-30 in *The Bible and the Ancient Near East*. Translated by Damian McHugh. Garden City, NY: Doubleday, 1971.

LAURIE J. BRAATEN, PHD

REPENTANCE

The Hebrew word *šûb*, which means "change of mind" or "change of moral **judgment**," is often translated in English as "repent" or "repentance." *Šûb* is translated in the LXX by the Greek words *epistrephō* (return) and *apostrephō* (turn away), both of which stress the positive side of conversion—namely, turning toward God. The Hebrew word *nāḥam* is usually translated in Greek as *metanoeō* ("feel remorse," "repent") or *metamelomai* ("regret," "repent").

Repentance speaks of Israel's or a person's return to God (Jer. 4:1) and of God's turn to Israel (Josh. 24:20). Turning away from **evil** is synonymous with keeping YHWH's commandments. The two ideas evident in *šûb* are turning from evil and toward the good.

Repentance was often accompanied by physical externals such as **fasting**, rending clothes, and putting on sackcloth and ashes. The **prophets** of Israel were not deluded by these penitential exercises. For them, penitence must lead to an encounter with God. Israel often thought that God needed penitential exercises, hence the tendency to overdo them. The prophets, however, were not opposed to penitential exercises. Isaiah described true fasting as characterized by repentance, which entails addressing issues of **justice**, sharing bread with the hungry and homeless (Isa. 58:6-7). Joel admonished the people, "Return to me with all your heart, with fasting and weeping and with mourning" (Joel 2:12, NIV).

Even though the NT uses *metanoeō* (repent) frequently, the usage is more the notion of *šûb* than *nāḥam*. The majority of occurrences of *metanoeō* are found in the Synoptic **Gospels**. Both John the Baptizer and Jesus utilized it. Repentance for John was the only possible response in light of the impending **kingdom of God** and the only way to avoid judgment. *Metanoeō* was required of all, the sinners and the righteous, the Gentiles and the Jews. The transformation John called for must be accompanied by "fruit worthy of repentance" (Matt. 3:8, NRSV). The baptism of repentance marked the break with the past (Mark 1:4).

Jesus's message of the kingdom also required repentance. To enter the kingdom of God, repentance was not a suggestion but an imperative (v. 15). Like Israel's prophets, Jesus did not have patience for the externals. What Jesus required was a radical break with the past resulting in transformation. For Jesus, one who repents has to become humble like a child in order to enter the kingdom of God (Matt. 18:3). **Discipleship** is the natural outcome of repentance. Those who follow Jesus "must deny themselves and take up their cross and follow [him]" (16:24, NIV; Luke 9:23). Both turning from **sin** and turning to God are required in Jesus's call for repentance.

The apostles declared before the Sanhedrin that God exalted Jesus to his right hand in order to bring repentance to Israel and **forgiveness** of sins (Acts 5:30-31). Gentiles were also granted repentance leading to life (11:18). When Paul spoke to disciples in Ephesus, he found out that they knew only John's baptism of repentance. He then urged them to be baptized in the name of Jesus and receive the **Holy Spirit** (19:1-7). Paul's preaching included a call to repentance and faith in Jesus (20:21).

Both Jesus and Paul maintained that faith must be accompanied by "deeds [**works**] consistent with repentance" (26:20, NRSV). For Paul, the demand for repentance was as irrevocable as were the gifts and callings of

God that were given to Israel (Rom. 11:29). Though repentance is demanded of sinners, it is the kindness and will of God that leads to repentance (2:4; 2 Tim. 2:25).

The writer of Hebrews notes that repentance belongs to an earlier realm of God's work in a believer's life; something one should not have to go back and redo (6:1). For those who fall away from the **faith**, it "is impossible to restore [them] again to repentance" (vv. 4-6, NRSV). This is a pastoral rather than doctrinal injunction. Those who continue to crucify and hold in contempt the Son of God are not ready to repent. Conviction by the Holy Spirit must bring them to repentance. It is possible, as Peter states, that God even delays the **parousia**, the second coming of Christ, so that no one should perish but that all should "come to repentance" (2 Pet. 3:9, NRSV).

See also Justification; Reconciliation; Righteousness.

Resources

Behm, Johannes, and Ernst Würthwein. "μετανοέω." Pages 975-1009 in vol. 4 of *TDNT*.
Fabry, Heinz-Josef. "שׁוּב (šûb)." Pages 461-522 in vol. 14 of *TDOT*.
Hamilton, Victor P. "שׁוּב shûb." Pages 909-10 in vol. 2 of *TWOT*.
Kennedy, Brendan. "Repentance." In *LBD*.
Lunde, Jonathan M. "Repentance." Pages 669-73 in *Dictionary of Jesus and the Gospels*. Edited by Joel B. Green and Scot McKnight. Downers Grove, IL: InterVarsity Press, 1992.

GIFT MTUKWA, MA

REST

The most common Hebrew word for "rest" is *šābat*, which shares the same root as "Sabbath." It has the connotation of ceasing from activity (Josh. 22:25). A synonym, *nûah*, can mean the security of being settled or in physical relief (Job 3:13). *Šāqaṭ* is the rest, tranquility, and quietness that come with peace after a disturbance, such as a battle (1 Chron. 22:9). The less common *rāgaʿ* refers to physical or spiritual rest associated with peace (Jer. 50:34). The NT transliterates the Hebrew with *sabbaton* in reference to God's plan of rest on the Sabbath. Other Greek words are built on the *pauō* stem, to stop or rest from activity.

The cycle of work and rest has been designed as part of **creation**. The ancient Israelites traced their practice of Sabbath observance back to the creation account. God set the pattern by ceasing his creative activity after forming man and woman on the sixth day (Gen. 2:2). The seventh day of the week was designated as holy in reflection of God's character.

In the priestly understanding, the seventh day was sanctified as a blessing for renewed strength and a covenantal reminder of God's own **holiness** (Exod. 31:13-17; Mark 2:27). The fourth commandment dedicated this day to God for rest from labor (Exod. 20:8-11; Jer. 17:21-27).

Physical rest became necessary to counterbalance the pain of work that resulted from Adam and Eve's sin (Gen. 3:17). All of creation groans against the forces of death (Rom. 8:20-21) and requires times of physical renewal. Animals and land should not be denied rest; they need rest to fulfill their purposes in creation and for human sustenance (Exod. 23:12; Lev. 25:3-5). The promise of rest was a significant motivation for Joshua and the Israelites in conquering the land of Canaan (Josh. 1:13). Rest allows people to cease their struggle to survive and causes them to rely on God's **grace** and sovereignty (Lev. 25:4-7). Holidays were special times to celebrate God's grace and goodness to his people and to remind the people of God's holiness.

Physical rest is representative of the deeper, spiritual **peace** that comes in keeping covenant. When Israel looked to God in worship and **obedience**, it experienced the presence of God that brought rest (Exod. 33:12-14). Solomon's reign experienced peace and rest as long as he worshipped God (1 Chron. 22:9). The presence of the Lord among his people, particularly symbolized in the temple, brought a sense of security and peace (Ps. 132:8, 14), experienced vividly in security against enemies and in economic prosperity. The soul at rest with God will experience the **hope** of salvation (62:5 [6 HB]). God's Spirit will rest upon those who are **righteous** before him (51:10-12 [12-14 HB]) and persevere through **suffering** (1 Pet. 4:14).

Since the keeping of covenant results in rest, breaking of covenant brings physical and spiritual struggle (Lev. 26). Israel was warned that disobedience would bring war and afflictions (vv. 17, 21). Even the land would rebel when the people sinned by not observing the seventh-year Sabbath (vv. 2, 20).

Wickedness is a significant obstacle to experiencing God's rest (Isa. 57:20-21). However, too much rest to the point of laziness can be detrimental (Prov. 24:33-34). Ecclesiastes warns of the futility of seeking rest without fear of the Lord (2:22-23). Those who reject God's ways will struggle (Jer. 6:16).

Physical and spiritual rests are connected. Jesus's need for physical rest (Mark 4:38; John 4:6) revealed his humanity and need to spend time with the Father (Matt. 14:23). Jesus invited his weary disciples also to take time away from ministry to rest (Mark 6:31). The body may be overcome with fatigue, and this may create opportunity for **temptation** (Matt. 26:40-46).

The promise for rest in the OT finds fulfillment in the NT with Jesus Christ. Jesus invited people to take his yoke of discipleship upon them and experience rest for their souls (11:28). The author of Hebrews reflected on the wilderness experience of ancient Israel and spiritualized its struggle to enter the promised land because of a lack of **faith** (3:7-11, 19). The promise of participation in God's own Sabbath rest of holiness is experienced in the new covenant of Christ (4:3, 9-10). Pressing on to this holy rest of faith is not optional, and to reject it results in exclusion from the promises of God (v. 11). The promised holy rest of faith brings an end to the struggle against **sin** and the flesh (Gal. 5:24; Rom. 6). The coming of the **Holy Spirit** upon believers on the day of Pentecost (Acts 2:3; Ezek. 36:26-27; Joel 2:28-29) makes this new covenant promise available "today" (Heb. 3:13, NRSV). Those who trust in Christ experience perfect rest in death (Rev. 14:13), when all struggles against the flesh, pain, conflict, suffering, and temptation will cease.

See also Evil; Fall, The; Jerusalem.

DAVID A. ACKERMAN, PHD

RESURRECTION

The apostle Paul stated that if Christ is not risen, the **faith** of Christians is futile and they are still in their **sins** (1 Cor. 15:17). No idea, event, or theme is more central to NT theology than is the resurrection. Jesus's resurrection, his delivery from death, is the lynchpin of Christian theology. Without the resurrection, there is no NT theology. But what does "resurrection" mean?

The concept of resurrection plays a minor role in the OT. A few verses from late in the OT period can be interpreted to foreshadow a doctrine of resurrection (Job 19:25-27; Isa. 26:19; Dan. 12:1-2). Unfortunately, these and similar verses can hardly be used to create a coherent doctrine of resurrection. Rather, the notion of resurrection did not emerge within Jewish thought until the period between the OT and the NT. However, by the NT era, the idea of resurrection was widely known among Jews. Acts tells us that Pharisees expected a general resurrection of the dead, while the Sadducees rejected this **belief** (23:8; 26:8).

In the NT, the noun "resurrection" (Gk., *anastasis*) is used exclusively in relation to persons (1) who were (or are) dead, (2) who were (or will be) brought back to life, and (3) who will never die again. The Gospels and Acts report that several people were brought back to life by Jesus or the apostles (Mark 5:21-43; Luke 7:11-17; John 11:24-25; Acts 9:36-42; 20:7-12), but not one of these people was truly resurrected. All eventually died again. Resurrected persons are no longer subject to death. Thus Jesus's resurrection is unique within the NT and all human history. Only Jesus was raised from the dead and forever freed from death.

Jesus's resurrection is central to all of the NT, but the Easter event itself—Jesus's resurrection—was witnessed by no one. Instead, people were witnesses to the aftermath of the resurrection: the empty tomb and the resurrected Christ. In the immediate wake of Jesus's resurrection on Easter morning, the **Gospels** agree that both the empty tomb and the resurrected Jesus were first witnessed by a group of **women**, including Mary Magdalene, Mary the mother of James, and possibly another woman named Mary (Matt. 28:1; 27:56; Mark 16:1; Luke 24:10; John 20:1), as well as Salome and Joanna (Mark 16:1; Luke 24:10). Eventually Peter and the other apostles also visited the empty tomb and ultimately interacted with the resurrected Jesus (Matt.

28:16-20; Luke 24:12; John 20:19-23; Acts 1:3-11; 1 Cor. 15:5). Cleopas and another unnamed disciple encountered the resurrected Jesus while walking on the road to Emmaus (Luke 24:13-35). Many others also saw the resurrected Jesus, although some doubted what they had seen (Matt. 28:17).

The resurrection was crucial to the early church's proclamation and authority. Therefore, when the apostles sought to replace Judas, the candidates were those who had seen the resurrected Christ (Acts 1:22). The apostle Paul similarly defended his apostleship by claiming to have seen the resurrected Jesus (1 Cor. 9:1). According to Paul, he was the last person to see the resurrected Jesus and be called to apostleship (15:8).

Jesus's resurrection has the "firstfruits" of the general resurrection; the resurrection which all believers will experience upon Christ's return (v. 23, NIV). The resurrection of Jesus illustrates the life that awaits Christians postdeath. Paul explained that in this life, Christians have a "perishable" body but that they shall be raised with an "imperishable" body (v. 42, NIV). Using the analogy of planting a seed, Paul assured believers that the physical body that is sown in "dishonor" and "weakness" as a "natural body" will be raised in "glory" and "power" as a "spiritual body" (vv. 43-44, NIV).

On the one hand, Paul warned that "If for this life only we have hoped in Christ, we are of all people most to be pitied" (v. 19, NRSV). On the other hand, Paul warned that "flesh and blood cannot inherit the kingdom of God" (v. 50, NASB). According to Paul, like the resurrected body of Christ, future resurrected bodies of believers will experience a transformation so that they are no longer subject to death or decay (vv. 51-52). The people who inhabit these resurrected bodies will be the same persons but somehow different (2 Cor. 5:1-10; 1 Thess. 4:13-18). This depiction of resurrected bodies as both similar and dissimilar to persons' current physical bodies is consistent with the Gospel accounts where Jesus could walk, eat, talk, breathe, and be touched (Luke 24:15, 17, 30, 42-43; John 20:13, 22, 27) but could also appear, disappear, walk through walls, and disguise his identity (Luke 24:16; John 20:26; Acts 1:9). Resurrected bodies have appropriately been called transphysical—that is, transformed physical bodies that defy many physical limitations.

Because of the centrality of resurrection for Christian belief and witness, baptism is often explained using the imagery of death and resurrection. Believers experience a symbolic death as they are submerged in the water (and cease breathing); as they are then raised from the water (and resume breathing), they experience "newness of life" (Rom. 6:4, NRSV; see vv. 3-7; Col. 2:12). Likewise, believers live renewed lives of righteousness through the "power of [the] resurrection" that operates in them by faith (Phil. 3:10, NRSV). The entirety of the book of Revelation celebrates the death and resurrection of the Lamb in anticipation of his return to gather believers to himself.

In the NT the resurrection is the basis of all Christian **hope**. It is the process that brought Jesus back from the dead, left the tomb empty, and freed Jesus from the power of death. It is also the power that Christians experience through baptism and their ongoing faith in Christ.

See also Parousia; Regeneration/Rebirth.

Resources

Finney, Mark T. *Resurrection, Hell and the Afterlife: Body and Soul in Antiquity, Judaism and Early Christianity.* New York: Routledge, 2016.

Matera, Frank J. *Resurrection: The Origin and Goal of the Christian Life.* Collegeville, MN: Liturgical Press, 2015.

Riley, Gregory J. *Resurrection Reconsidered: Thomas and John in Controversy.* Minneapolis: Augsburg Fortress, 1995.

Smith, Dennis A. *Revisiting the Empty Tomb: The Early History of Easter.* Minneapolis: Fortress Press, 2010.

Wright, N. T. *The Resurrection of the Son of God.* Minneapolis: Fortress Press, 2003.

THOMAS E. PHILLIPS, PHD

RETRIBUTION

Retribution may be defined as the distributing of a reward or punishment in response to another's actions. While this article deals mainly with the concept of punishment, it must be remembered that God's **justice** does not work separately from his **love** and **mercy**. Those who obey God's commandments and "sow to the **Spirit** . . . reap eternal life" (Gal. 6:8, NRSV).

God's punishment is related to his justice. God promised in the OT not only to preserve and bless his faithful people but also to punish the unfaithful. Thus God is just in administrating justice.

God's punishment has a twofold goal—to redress past **sin** and to prevent future violations. Because God is relational, he uses retribution to turn his people back to him. Punishment may be immediate (Num. 16:1-35; Acts 5:1-11) or delayed (Gen. 15:16; Isa. 48:8-9; Rom. 3:25). Yet God's **judgments** are **holy** because they are always justified by the actions of those who sinned (Ps. 103:6-15).

God's retribution may be collective (Gen. 6–9) as well as individual (Num. 12:1-10). God used his people as an instrument of retribution against other nations (Gen. 15:16; Deut. 7:1-5, 16), and Assyria and Babylon against his own people (2 Kings 17:1-23; 25:1-21).

While God's **righteousness** is revealed through the gospel, his **wrath** is revealed "from heaven against all the godlessness and wickedness of people" (Rom. 1:17-18, NIV). Thus all are included and will receive from God either righteousness or wrath, according to their **obedience** to God's standards.

Even believers pass through difficult times. This does not mean that God is punishing them for some disobedience. Yet some still think Deuteronomy 28:1-68 teaches that if people are suffering, they have sinned and that if they are prospering, they are righteous. Life is never this black and white. Job's friends wrongly explained his situation as the result of **sin** (Job 4:7-8; 22:5). David understood that while God's absence made him vulnerable to **suffering** at the hands of his enemies, he also knew that God was not the cause of his suffering (Ps. 31:14-24 [15-25 HB]). When Jesus was asked why some people suffered, he explained that the suffering of others may be a warning not to follow their example (Luke 13:1-5) or that it may be an opportunity for God to display his works of **mercy** (John 9:1-3). Still the principle of sowing and reaping cannot be denied (Gal. 6:7).

Many people today reject the doctrine of eternal punishment, believing that God's **mercy** will have the last word. Others believe in annihilation. **God's Word** clearly states that there will be a day of **judgment** and **wrath** for those who refuse to **repent** and accept Christ as their **Savior** (Matt. 13:49-50; Luke 12:5; Rom. 2:5-6).

Resources

Bavinck, Herman. *Sin and Salvation in Christ*. Vol. 3 of *Reformed Dogmatics*. Edited by John Bolt. Translated by John Vriend. Grand Rapids: Baker Academic, 2006.

Greathouse, William. *Romans 1–8*. NBBC. Kansas City: Beacon Hill Press of Kansas City, 2008.

Preisker, Herbert. "μισθός." Page 717 in vol. 4 of *TDNT*.

MAWIYAH KHAZER HALASA, MA

RIGHTEOUSNESS

Righteousness in biblical texts and theology is an attribute or activity that can be possessed or performed by both God and humans. Most characteristically, righteousness is not about being morally, legally, or ethically correct according to a set of rules (i.e., not doing wrong) but about living rightly within a relationship and its obligations. Predominantly in Scripture, *righteousness* is "right relationship," and *to be righteous* is "to be rightly related."

The Terms

English translations use "righteousness" to translate several terms related to the Hebrew root *ṣdq* and the Greek element *dik-*. These terms include verbs meaning "to do right" or "to be or make right," as well as nouns ("righteousness," *ṣedeq*, *ṣĕdāqâ*, *dikaiosynē*; "righteous one," *ṣaddîq*) and adjectives ("righteous," *ṣaddîq*, *dikaios*). The roots of these biblical words also appear in other ancient languages, such as Ugaritic, Aramaic, and Arabic, with several nuances of meaning. In the OT, terms derived from the Hebrew root *ṣdq* occur more than five hundred times (in thirty of the thirty-nine OT books), with special prominence of the noun "righteousness" (*ṣedeq*, *ṣĕdāqâ*) and with the most occurrences in the Prophets, Psalms, and Wisdom literature. The related Greek terms in the NT (often translated "**justice**" and "**justification**") occur approximately three hundred times, most frequently in the letters attributed to Paul (especially Romans, which has more than seventy occurrences).

In the most basic sense, the root words for righteousness carry the meanings of conforming to a standard or norm in the sense of straightness, rightness, and order and of doing what is right and proper. However, the biblical texts use righteousness in a variety of ways that have different nuances of meaning depending on the specific contexts.

Old Testament Uses

In some OT texts, righteousness carries the legal meaning of fairness, innocence, and right standing before God and the **law**. Some of the earliest uses of *ṣedeq* and *ṣĕdāqâ* in the biblical canon relate to the proper work of judges in rendering fair decisions and due process in legal cases, especially for the **poor**, immigrants, and the vulnerable: "With righteousness [*ṣedeq*] you shall judge your neighbor" (Lev. 19:15, AT; see also Deut. 1:16-17; 16:18-20). Weights, measures, and balances that are fair, accurate, and just are described as righteous (Lev. 19:36; Job 31:6). In other legal contexts, righteousness terminology carries the meaning "to justify, acquit, declare right" in a dispute (Exod. 23:7; Deut. 25:1). Some passages use righteousness to describe God's fairness as a righteous judge (Pss. 7:11 [12 HB]; 9:4 [5 HB]), while others declare that all God's law (*tôrâ*) is righteous (Ps. 119). Wisdom literature often contrasts the "righteous" with the "wicked" (Prov. 10:24; 12:21), and Job uses righteousness as innocence or vindication before God (Job 13:18; 34:5).

Even these legal uses of righteousness terminology are based on the premise of relationships and the obligations entailed by them. Most interpreters have therefore concluded that righteousness in Scripture is predominantly a relational concept; rather than being about conformity to rules or the avoidance of wrongdoing (similar to innocence), righteousness in Scripture is about the proper fulfillment of the expectations and demands of the relationship of which one is a part (similar to faithfulness). Righteousness presupposes a relationship between two parties, by virtue of which each party has certain claims on the other. To be righteous is to live in right relationship with, or be rightly related to, one's relationship partners—that is, God, persons, or communities. To act righteously is to "do right by" those with whom one stands in relationship, to act in ways that **honor** the relationship and respect the claims it makes on its participants.

The notion of righteousness as right relationship is rooted especially in the **covenant** God established with the Israelites at Mount Sinai as the defining relationship meant to govern all their actions (Exod. 19:1-6). Accordingly, God is the source of righteousness (right relatedness); any and all righteousness is made possible by God's gracious initiative taken with God's people (and with all living beings; see Gen. 9:8-11). God has established a life-giving order, a governing relationship that should encompass conduct in every area of life (social, legal, ritual, etc.).

Of special note here is that righteousness not only pertains to human beings but also is an attribute and activity of God. Various OT texts describe God as righteous (Ps. 11:7; Lam. 1:18). More frequently, OT texts, especially the Psalms and **Prophets**, use righteousness terminology to describe God's acts of intervention, deliverance, and restoration for the covenant people (particularly the plural "righteous deeds," ṣidĕqôt, often translated as "saving acts"). Psalm 103:6 proclaims, "The LORD performs righteousness and justice for all who are oppressed" (AT). Psalm 71 repeatedly recalls the Lord's "righteousness" that provided deliverance in the past (vv. 15-16, 19, 24; see also Pss. 7:10-11 [11-12 HB]; 48:10 [11 HB]; 51:14 [16 HB]; 145:17). In Micah 6:5, the Lord asks the people to **remember** the past acts of divine deliverance and provision so they will know the Lord's "righteous deeds" (AT; "saving acts" [NRSV]; see also Judg. 5:11; 1 Sam. 12:7; Jer. 9:24; Joel 2:23). By labeling these saving deeds as "righteousnesses" (right-relationship actions), the texts define them as ways in which God fulfilled God's covenant obligations toward the people, acting in rightly related ways in accord with their relationship.

God's righteousness then provides the basis for the OT's numerous calls to God's people to be righteous, to live and act in right relationship with God and others. In an early canonical example, the Lord regards Abram's act of trusting in the divine promise as "righteousness" (Gen. 15:6, NRSV). Abram believed what the Lord asked him to **believe** in the context of covenant promises. Likewise, Deuteronomy 24:10-13 states that when an Israelite properly returns by sunset a garment taken as a pledge for a loan from a poor neighbor, so the poor neighbor may sleep in it at night, the act will be considered "righteousness" (v. 13, AT; "to your credit" [NRSV]). The lender will have done right by his or her obligations to provide for the well-being of the poor neighbor (cf. Amos 2:8).

Perhaps the most striking example of this relational meaning of righteousness occurs in Genesis 38. After Tamar's father-in-law refused to follow the legal requirement and provide her with a **marriage** that would produce children (by his youngest son), she posed as a prostitute, tricked her father-in-law into sexual intercourse, and became pregnant by him. Even though these actions would typically be considered improper, unethical, or at least questionable, Judah acknowledged, "She is more righteous [ṣĕdāqâ] than me" (v. 26, AT). Tamar had acted appropriately according to the just demands of the relationship, unlike Judah. Righteousness is defined by relationships more than by laws, morals, or **ethics**.

In the Psalms, references to the psalmist's own righteousness appear alongside references to God's righteousness, particularly in prayers for divine protection (7:8-9 [9-10 HB]; 92:12-15 [13-16 HB]). Similarly, OT Wisdom literature contrasts the righteous and the wicked, with righteousness often tied to **wisdom** (e.g., Prov. 1:2-3; Eccles. 7:15-17). The Prophetic Books employ righteousness terminology (with the highest concentration in Isaiah) to insist that the covenant people deal loyally and justly with God and others (Isa. 5:7; Amos 5:24). There is a special vision of righteousness prefigured by kings, rulers, and others in power, ultimately fulfilled by God's own rule (Isa. 9:7; 11:4-5).

Throughout the OT, but especially in the Prophetic Books, the term "righteousness" appears together in a parallel construction with other key Hebrew terms. "Righteousness" appears with the Hebrew term *ḥesed*, often translated "steadfast love" (Hos. 2:19; 10:12). Even more frequently, "righteousness" stands alongside *mišpāṭ*, translated "justice" (Isa. 5:7; 56:1; Amos 5:24). In both cases, the pairs likely function with a single meaning, indicating God's desire for proper order and right relationship.

New Testament Uses

Scholars have debated whether the meaning of a faithful right relationship is operative in the NT use of righteousness terminology, especially in Paul's writings. In Greek culture outside of the Bible, terms such as *dikaiosynē* carried the legal meaning of innocence or conformity to customs or religious obligations (virtue). However, many interpreters have suggested that Paul, influenced by the OT, understood righteousness as right actions done faithfully in accordance with a relationship (debate continues: see Irons 2015; Soards, in *NIDB*, 4:813-18). Seen in this way, righteousness in the NT can refer to faithful and proper actions within the relationship between God and humanity, and between fellow human beings, though different passages employ the terminology in different ways. In Paul's writings, the notions of "God's righteousness" and "righteousness that comes by **faith**" occupy central positions in the argument (esp. Romans; see 5:1-5; 8:3-4, 10-11).

The phrase "the righteousness of God" has played a key role in the larger theological debate over the nature of salvation (Rom. 1:17; 3:5, 21-22, 25-26; 10:3). At issue is whether righteousness here belongs to God and is extended (imputed) to human beings, who are simply declared to be righteous (innocent), or whether it describes God's saving actions undertaken in faithfulness to the covenant, wherein God gives (imparts) righteousness as a gift that transforms the character of believers. The meaning of righteousness in these contexts has implications for a Wesleyan interpretation of God's saving work, since Wesley emphasized the **grace**-empowered response of believers and God's sanctifying work of transformation into the **image** of Christ and perfection in **love**.

Resources

Irons, Charles Lee. *The Righteousness of God: A Lexical Examination of the Covenant-Faithfulness Interpretation.* WUNT 2.386. Tübingen, DEU: Mohr Siebeck, 2015.

Scullion, J. J. "Righteousness: Old Testament." Pages 724-36 in vol. 5 of *ABD*.
Soards, Marion L. "Righteousness in the NT." Pages 813-18 in vol. 4 of *NIDB*.

BRAD E. KELLE, PHD

Ss

SACRED PERSONS

Every person is sacred, since humans are made in the **image of God**. However, in Scripture there are a few unique persons (or roles for some individuals and groups) that receive esteemed status as sacred persons.

Highlighted here is Jesus as preeminent among those in sacred roles, then follows a listing from Melchizedek to Aaron and his family lineage as priests, to the Levites, Nazirites, and apostles.

Jesus

The book of Hebrews emphasizes the sacred role of the priesthood, including that of Jesus, with these words: "Every high priest is selected from among the people and is appointed to represent the people in matters related to God, to offer gifts and sacrifices for **sins**" (5:1, NIV). "Jesus, has entered on our behalf. He has become a high priest forever, in the order of Melchizedek" (6:20, NIV).

In these verses, key aspects of Jesus as a sacred person include roles in which sacred persons (1) are set apart from among people, (2) connect people (not just themselves) with God, (3) offer gifts to God in the service of achieving atonement for sins by means of sacrifice, and (4) work to restore relationships. While the OT priests fulfilled temporary roles during their earthly lifetime, Jesus alone is priest forever.

Melchizedek

Melchizedek (Gen. 14; Ps. 110:4; Heb. 5:6; 7:1-17) is the first person described as presenting offerings for God. He predates the Bible's presentation of other sacred persons and is not easily compared to their roles, which receive more textual space in the Bible.

Moses, Aaron, and Aaron's Sons

As the Hebrew slaves emerged from Egypt to become God's holy nation and priestly kingdom (Exod. 19:5-6), the Lord established persons to mediate God's presence in the midst of the people. While Moses, the key conduit of God's work, was set apart, the office of priest was given to Aaron.

Leviticus clarifies roles for Aaron and his sons as priests. Priests both participated in and gave oversight to sacrifices and offerings (chs. 1–7). They were, in a particular ceremony, ordained with set roles (chs. 8–9). These passages outline the set-apartness and uniqueness of priests and the priestly office. The sacred role of performing set functions (offerings and sacrifices) allowed the priests to help the people (1) be reconciled with God, (2) rest in God's favor, (3) remember God's good work, and (4) give reverence to God for God's gifts of salvation and sustenance.

Leviticus 10:8-11 in the **Torah** gives a list of roles for these sacred persons that included (1) overseeing sacrifices and offerings; (2) being uniquely ordained, even by special initiation into their office; (3) avoiding fermented drink; (4) distinguishing between the unclean and clean, the profane and pure; and (5) teaching the Israelites the decrees of the Lord.

Ezekiel 44 gives a similar list for the roles of priests. The comparison of this list with the list in Leviticus demonstrates the continuing synonymous responsibilities of priests, which included (1) abstaining from intoxicating beverages (v. 21), (2) distinguishing between the **clean and unclean** (v. 23), and (3) teaching the people (v. 23). Additional roles included (4) acting as judges (v. 24) and (5) keeping the Lord's commands (v. 24).

Levites

Alongside Aaron and his family were the Levites, who (1) were uniquely set apart for God's purpose among the tribes of Israel (Deut. 12:12), including service with sacrifices and offerings; (2) had roles, with Aaron's lineage, in the service of the ark of the **covenant**, tabernacle, and temple as places mediating God's presence in the world (Num. 1:50-53; 31:30, 47; Ezra 3:8-11); (3) had special property designations of pastureland (Num. 35); (4) received as their allotment special tithes for their service (Deut. 12:11-12; 18:1-8); and (5) had oversight for reconciling relationships and adjudicating disputes, including interpreting Torah with respect to governance over the cities of refuge (Num. 35:1-12; Deut. 17:8-18). Levites, at times, are described as using Urim and Thummim for discerning oracles (Deut. 33:8).

Nazirites

Nazirites were unique for their set-apartness insofar as a Nazirite did not derive from a lineage set at birth. (Though the Bible has no account of female Nazirites, women were not restricted from being set apart as Nazirites.)

According to Numbers 6, persons who elected to become Nazirites had to comply with the following provisions and prohibitions: (1) abstain from fermented drink and the fruit of the vine in any form, (2) forgo cutting their hair, and (3) avoid nearness to any dead body in order to protect ceremonial cleanliness.

The person so committed was "throughout the period of their dedication . . . consecrated to the LORD" (6:8, NIV). Unlike Aaron's sons or Levites, Nazirites could enter into set-apart sacred status and, later, resume their normal lives. Samson, Samuel, and probably John the Baptist (Luke 1:15) are examples of Nazirites.

Apostles

The final category of sacred persons to be noted here are the apostles of the NT. To be sure, the apostles played a role very different from other sacred persons in Scripture. In the period of the NT, as identified with the claims made about Jesus as Chief High Priest forever, and with the absence of the temple, apostles as sacred persons did not oversee any **sacrificial** offerings. Apostles were set apart to help govern and give **leadership** to the emerging work of God made known through the **work** of Jesus. First Corinthians 12:28 gives priority to the apostles as those set apart to lead God's people.

Scripture affirms that all persons are sacred to God (Gal. 3:28; cf. Gen. 1), even while some are set apart for unique roles (Rom. 1:1).

Ephesians emphasizes the roles of all believers in Christ having equal status, with the need for some still to have the unique status of being set apart (2:19-22). While set apart, the apostles were also to be among God's people in shared service: "So Christ himself gave the apostles . . . so that the body of Christ may be built up . . . attaining to the whole measure of the fullness of Christ" (4:11-13, NIV).

Summary

The Bible affirms a unique sacred status for every human person. Yet particular people take on the office or role of a sacred person in set periods of history, as demonstrated in Scripture. The canonical witness testifies to unique persons set apart at special **times**, while affirming that any person among God's people can serve the Chief Priest until all people of **faith** reach the unity of service.

See also Sacred Space; Sacred Times; Slavery.

MARTY ALAN MICHELSON, PHD

SACRED SPACE

Sacred spaces in the ancient world were understood as places where the divine and human realms intersected. Ancient people, including the Israelites, held a tripartite conception of the world: the heavens were the gods' domain, earth was the human realm, and the underworld or **afterlife** was peopled by the dead and/or divine spirits. Any physical space that witnessed an eruption of the divine into the human realm thus became sacred. Some geographical features were perceived as facilitating access to the sacred by virtue of proximity and extraordinary topography: mountains and trees raised people and thoughts toward the heavens; caves lowered them toward the underworld.

The erection of monuments and shrines at sacred places is an early feature of human culture. These range from simple stone piles to elaborate temple complexes. According to the biblical witness, anywhere God is present is made sacred. However, "sacred" space infers "profane," or common, space. Although religious activity (prayers, sacrifices, etc.) often occurred in these spaces, the spaces themselves were not necessarily part of official or organized cultic systems. This article will explore the types of sacred spaces in the Bible and their functions.

Sacred Presence

Theophanies, physical encounters with God, turned a particular place sacred. The people in these cases memorialized such encounters by naming the place, building a memorial (altars, stones, or pillars), or both. Abram, Isaac, Manoah, and Gideon each built altars (*mizbēaḥ*) after visits from Yahweh (Gen. 12:7; 26:23-26; Judg. 6:11-27; 13:15-20). Hagar's theophany led to the desert spring to which she fled being named Beer Lahai Roi, meaning "well of the Living One who sees me" (Gen. 16:14, NIV note).

Jacob's theophanies prompted both memorial constructions and namings. His heavenly stairway dream led him to set up and anoint a pillar (Hebr., *maṣṣēbâ*; some forms were associated with idol worship and outlawed [Lev. 26:1; Deut. 16:22]) and to call the place Bethel, meaning "house of God" (Gen. 28:19, NIV note; see vv. 10-22). Meeting Yahweh's angels en route to Esau, Jacob named the place Mahanaim, meaning "two camps," signifying the presence of his divine guardians (32:2, NIV note). He named the site of his nighttime wrestling with God Peniel, meaning "face of God" (v. 30, NIV note; see vv. 22-32).

One mountain was early identified with Yahweh's presence: Sinai-Horeb. Moses "discovered" Yahweh in the burning bush, and Yahweh declared he had entered sacred space: "Do not come any closer. . . . Take off your sandals, for the place where you are standing is **holy** ground" (Exod. 3:5, NIV). Similar boundaries were in place when the Israelites returned to Sinai-Horeb to receive the **covenant** (19:12-13, 21-24; 34:3). On this mountain, extraordinary phenomena displayed Yahweh's presence: unconsuming fire (3:2-3); a dense cloud to protect the people from exposure (19:9, 16; 24:15-18); thunder, lightning, divine trumpets, smoke, and quaking (19:16, 18). Yahweh is identified by the holy mountain in Moses's song of blessing (Deut. 33:1-29) and Deborah's song of victory (Judg. 5:5, paralleled in Ps.

68:8 [9 HB]). Elijah hid from Jezebel at Sinai-Horeb, where Yahweh rebuked his self-pity, using familiar phenomena (great wind, quaking earth, and fire) before speaking in a voice of silence (1 Kings 19:1-18).

Yahweh traveled with Israel from Egypt to Sinai to Canaan. The pillar of cloud and fire was the sacred manifestation en route (Exod. 13:21), and before the tabernacle was constructed, Yahweh spoke from the pillar to Moses at the tent of meeting (33:7-11). After the Israelites left Sinai-Horeb, the pillar showed them when to walk and when to make camp and it settled over the tabernacle in camp (40:34-38). This sign of Yahweh's presence made sacred space of every place it sojourned.

The concentrated presence of God was also associated with the ark of the covenant, which resided in the access-restricted holy of holies in the tabernacle (25:10-22) and from which it could be said that holiness radiated outward, at least spatially.

Sacred Memory

Near Jericho, Joshua was visited by a divine messenger, who repeated almost verbatim Yahweh's words to Moses: "Take off your sandals, for the place where you are standing is holy" (Josh. 5:15, NIV). However, most of his experience of sacred space involved commemorating Yahweh's saving actions rather than responding to theophanies. After leading the people across the Jordan, he erected twelve stones as a memorial at Gilgal (ch. 4), which were landmarks in the judges' era (Judg. 3:19). He built memorials on Mount Ebal (Deut. 27:1-8; Josh. 8:30-35) and at Shechem (Josh. 24) and allowed one in Gilead (22:10-34).

Samuel's memorial stone Ebenezer, meaning "stone of help," commemorated victory over Philistia (1 Sam. 7:12, NIV note). These memorials preserved the traditions of Israel's early generations and perpetuated the stories of Yahweh's involvement in the nation's history. The divine-human encounters preserved in these memorials rendered them sacred spaces of prayer, worship, and remembrance.

Sacred Altars

Though the tabernacle and temple were the official places of **sacrifice** in certain periods of Israel's history, many people built sacrificial altars spontaneously to celebrate or request Yahweh's intervention. Thus a place was made sacred, at least temporarily, as a witness to communication between Yahweh and humans. Commemorative altars include Noah's on Ararat (Gen. 8:20); Abram's at Hebron (13:18); Jacob's at Shechem, called El-Elohe-Israel, meaning "God, the God of Israel" (33:18-20, NRSV note). Moses built one at Rephidim, called "The LORD is my Banner" (Exod. 17:15, NIV). A large fieldstone served as an altar at Beth-shemesh when the ark returned from Philistia (1 Sam. 6:1-18).

Altars were also built to petition for immediate help or favor. In his quest to curse Israel, Balak built twenty-one altars at Bamoth-baal, Pisgah, and Peor (Num. 22:41–24:25). After slaughtering the Benjaminites to purge Gibeah's sin against the Levite's concubine, Israel built another altar at Bethel (Judg. 21:4). Saul built an altar after fighting the Philistines to compensate for having made his soldiers **fast** (1 Sam. 14:35). David built an altar on the threshing floor of Aruanah to stop the plague resulting from his census (2 Sam. 24:18-25). It became the site of Solomon's temple (1 Chron. 21:28–22:1).

Sacred Shrines

More permanent sacred spaces allowed communities to approach Yahweh through the cultic practices of the covenant by keeping the sacrificial and purity rituals and the many **festivals** and holy days. During Israel's early residence in the **land**, the tabernacle resided in Shiloh (Josh. 18:1). Many Israelites traveled there to worship and sacrifice (1 Sam. 1–2). However, 1 Samuel shows regional altars and high places (Hebr., *bāmôt*) also in use (e.g., Ramah [7:17], Zuph [9:5-25], Gibeath-elohim [10:5-13], Gilgal [15:12]). During the reigns of David and Solomon, Gibeon's high place was prominent. Eventually the tabernacle was relocated there, while the ark was installed at David's **Jerusalem** threshing floor (1 Kings 3:2-4; 1 Chron. 16:39; 21:29; 2 Chron. 1:3).

Once built, Solomon's temple embodied the Israelite ideal of sacred space. It was explicitly viewed as the dwelling place of Yahweh (1 Kings 6:1, 12-13). As the cloud had signified Yahweh's presence in the wilderness, so it filled the temple at its dedication (8:10-13). All the symbolism of Mount Sinai-Horeb and the tabernacle was subsumed into this locale: the temple, built in the Holy City, atop Mount Zion. The heights of satisfaction and rightness with God were to be found in the temple, the house of the Lord (Pss. 26:8; 27:4; 84). In the devastation of exile, restoration was symbolized by this house-mountain-Zion cluster of imagery (Isa. 66:20; Ezek. 43:1-12).

Sacred Households

Even after Israelite worship was centralized in the temple, and despite Deuteronomy's insistence upon restricting worship to Yahweh's chosen dwelling (12:1-28), local shrines were operative. Indeed, most of an Israelite family's worship in an average year occurred in and around the **household**. Purity laws were acts of devotion centered in the family fields, home, and table. The dedication of resources to the **poor** through gleaning, **redemption**, and tithing occurred in villages (Lev. 19:9-10; 25; Deut. 14:28-29).

Sabbath was a household observance, not a worship service. The demands of agrarian life, and the archaeological remains of Iron Age Israelite villages, suggest most Israelites worshipped at household and village shrines, even for the monthly new-moon feasts and annual pilgrimage festivals.

Some biblical narratives support this conclusion: Elkanah sacrificed at Shiloh only once a year, not the required three (1 Sam. 1–2; Exod. 23:14-17); no one in Ruth's Bethlehem is mentioned as going to Shiloh for Pentecost, even though the story's action centers on that season (Ruth 1:22). The Israelite household was itself sacred space.

New Testament Sacred Space

Given the historical, political, and religious realities of the postexilic and intertestamental eras—no less the **incarnation** vis-à-vis divine presence—it is no surprise that sacred space is represented very differently in the NT. The angels' visits surrounding Jesus's birth were preserved in narratives, not monuments or shrines (Matt. 1:20-24; 2:13-15, 19-23; Luke 1:11-20, 26-38). Likewise were the theophanies at Jesus's baptism (Matt. 3:13-17 and parallels), transfiguration (17:1-8 and parallels), and ascension (Acts 1:10-11) and the various apostolic visions (7:54-60; 9:1-19; 10:1-32, etc.).

Even setting aside the complex implications of Diaspora, the Second Temple in the NT era was deeply compromised as sacred space, as shown by Jesus's "cleansing" it (Matt. 21:12-17 and parallels) and by the frequent portrayals of temple personnel as corrupt (vv. 33-46). For the **church**, the dwelling place of God began to be relocated conceptually.

Stephen argued against the primacy of the Jerusalem temple, describing all of **creation** as the Most High's habitation (Acts 7:44-50). Paul's letters encouraged believers to view themselves as God's temple, insomuch as they are indwelled by the **Holy Spirit** (1 Cor. 3:16-17; 6:19). Corporately, too, the people of God form the temple (2 Cor. 6:16-18; Eph. 2:19-22). Christians, then, encounter the divine in the sacred spaces of gathered worship (Matt. 18:20) and service to those in need (25:31-46).

See also Sacred Persons; Sacred Times.

Resources

Albertz, Rainer, Beth Alpert Nakhai, Saul M. Olyan, and Rüdiger Schmitt, eds. *Family and Household Religion: Toward a Synthesis of Old Testament Studies, Archaeology, Epigraphy, and Cultural Studies*. Winona Lake, IN: Eisenbrauns, 2014.

Eliade, Mircea. *The Sacred and the Profane: The Nature of Religion*. Translated by Willard R. Trask. New York: Harcourt, Brace, and World, 1959.

Gittlen, Barry M., ed. *Sacred Time, Sacred Place: Archaeology and the Religion of Israel*. Winona Lake, IN: Eisenbrauns, 2002.

Isaacs, Marie E. *Sacred Space: An Approach to the Theology of the Epistle to the Hebrews*. JSNTSup 73. Sheffield, UK: Sheffield Academic Press, 1992.

SARAH B. C. DERCK, PHD

SACRED TIMES

Like other religions, ancient Judaism understood certain things to be sacred: time (e.g., festivals), space (e.g., temple), objects (e.g., ark of the covenant), people (e.g., priests), and actions (e.g., circumcision). The sacred has been set apart from the ordinary for divine purposes, and it gains the quality of transcendence, connecting earth and heaven. Although the understanding of the sacred changes from the OT to the NT, the concept remains. It continues into the medieval period but gradually diminishes in significance through the modern era in Western cultures.

Sacred Time in the Old Testament

Sacred times were set apart for the Israelites to commemorate divine actions—either regular and seasonal (e.g., the grain harvest) or exceptional (e.g., the exodus from Egypt). The recognition of such times reminded Israel of Yahweh's help, reactualized the reality of such events, encouraged the Israelites to view all time as belonging to Yahweh, and heightened Israel's collective identity.

The most important example of sacred time for the ancient Israelites was the seventh day of the week, or Sabbath. The only **holy** day commanded in the Decalogue (Exod. 20:8-11), the Sabbath was to be observed in perpetuity as a day of rest (23:12). Violators were subject to the severest punishments (16:23-30; 31:14-15; 35:2-3; Num. 15:32-36), but the day was to be a source of great delight (Isa. 58:13-14).

The Sabbath served several purposes for the Israelites:
1. As a reminder and an opportunity to renew Yahweh's lordship over **creation** and the individual worshipper
2. As a reminder of Israel's **slavery** in Egypt and a celebration of freedom
3. As an opportunity to express **compassion** to oneself and others
4. To increase fertility by allowing **rest** for the **land** and animals
5. To anticipate Yahweh's coming **kingdom**
6. To celebrate the Israelites' special relationship with Yahweh, who had revealed to them the special nature of the seventh day

Yahweh also instructed the Israelites to set apart several other days throughout the year. Some of these **festivals** celebrated the harvest (e.g., Pentecost), others celebrated his intervention on Israel's behalf (e.g., Passover, Tabernacles), and still others marked moments of spiritual recalibration (e.g., Rosh Hashanah, Day of Atonement).

Sacred Time in the New Testament

Although the **Gospels** contain numerous examples of the observance of sacred time as seen in the OT (Luke 2:21-24, 41), they also provide clear hints that a change was underway. Jesus spoke of himself as having fulfilled the **Law** (Matt. 5:17-20) and as Lord of the Sabbath (12:8 and parallels). He also described himself using symbols associated with the Passover (26:17-30 and parallels).

The early **church**, no doubt drawing out the implications of such comments and reflecting something of the Jew-Gentile tensions of the first century, reenvisioned sacred time as more symbolic than literal. Paul challenged the Corinthian Christians to rid themselves of the old yeast and become a batch of unleavened bread. "For Christ, our Passover lamb, has been sacrificed. Therefore let us keep the Festival, not with the old bread . . . but with the unleavened bread of sincerity and truth" (1 Cor. 5:7-8, NIV).

Paul also discouraged his churches from undue attention to the observance of the sacred times observed by Jews (Rom. 14:5-23; Gal. 4:8-11; Col. 2:16-17). For the author of Hebrews, the Jewish festivals had been fulfilled in the life and ministry of Jesus (chs. 8–10). The spiritualization of the Jewish festivals continued in the post-NT church, as evidenced by Barnabas's explanation of the **fasting** and scapegoat of Yom Kippur as types of Jesus (*Epistle of Barnabas*, ch. 7).

While we have no passage that commands Christians to replace the observance of the seventh day with the observance of the first, the Lord's Day eventually eclipsed the Sabbath in importance (Acts 20:7; 1 Cor. 16:2; Rev. 1:10). New Testament Christians tended to spiritualize the Sabbath as they had the Jewish festivals. As one example, the writer of Hebrews described the Sabbath in highly symbolic terms (4:1-6). Increased Jew-Gentile tensions in the post-NT period exacerbated the shift. Writers such as Ignatius and Tertullian sharply contrasted the two days: the Sabbath was part of the old and temporary, while the Lord's Day was associated with the new and permanent (Ignatius, *Epistle to the Magnesians*, ch. 9; Tertullian, *An Answer to the Jews*, ch. 4).

Significance for Contemporary Christians

While modern Western culture has largely ignored the sacred, the concept remains very much alive in other parts of the world, including among Christians. Some, such as philosopher Charles Taylor, have made the case that the concept of the sacred continues in the secular West, but in ways not associated with religion.

Given the persistent reality of the sacred throughout history and in most of the world, Christians would be wise to make a place for it in their reading of Scripture and their worship. The NT's shift toward a more symbolic understanding does not negate the reality of the sacred but highlights the Christ event as transposing the sacred into something much more rich. While all time is God's time, some times are more particularly endowed with the transcendent.

See also Holiness; Sacred Persons; Sacred Space.

Resources

Eliade, Mircea. *The Sacred and the Profane: The Nature of Religion.* Translated by Willard R. Trask. San Diego: Harcourt, 1959.

Epistle of Barnabas. In vol. 1 of *Ante-Nicene Fathers.* Edited by Alexander Roberts and James Donaldson. 10 vols. Reprint of the 1885 edition. Christian Classics Ethereal Library. http://www.ccel.org/ccel/schaff/anf01.vi.ii.vii.html.

Ignatius. *Epistle to the Magnesians.* In vol. 1 of *Ante-Nicene Fathers.* http://www.ccel.org /ccel/schaff/anf01.v.iii.ix.html.

Otto, Rudolf. *The Idea of the Holy.* Translated by John W. Harvey. London: Oxford University Press, 1923.

Taylor, Charles. *A Secular Age.* Cambridge, MA: Belknap Press of Harvard University Press, 2007.

Tertullian. *An Answer to the Jews.* In vol. 3 of *Ante-Nicene Fathers.* Edited by Allan Menzies. http://www.ccel.org/ccel/schaff/anf03.iv.ix.iv.html.

STEPHEN J. LENNOX, PHD

SACRIFICIAL SYSTEM

Continual Offerings

Leviticus 1–7 provides instructions for the five main sacrifices within the sacrificial system of ancient Israel. In addition to these, three types of sacrifices were to be presented continually: the dedication of the firstborn (continually in the sense of each generation), the daily morning and evening offerings, and the continual incense offering.

The *dedication of the firstborn* is introduced in response to the exodus. When Pharaoh refused to release the children of Israel from **slavery**, the Lord killed all the firstborn in the final plague against Egypt. Consequently, Israel was commanded to sacrifice to the Lord every firstborn among its own offspring (Exod. 13:15). However, only animals eligible for the altar were actually to be presented in sacrifice. Donkeys had to be redeemed with an animal from the flock (lamb or goat), and of course human children were also to be redeemed (vv. 13, 15; 34:20).

The Levites took the place of Israel's firstborn children (Num. 3:11-12, 41; 8:16-18). The Levites were dedicated to God, not on the altar, but as servants to do the work of the sanctuary (8:15). The dedication of the firstborn served as a reminder of God's great act of deliverance from slavery in Egypt (Exod. 13:14-16). This event also induced the broader directive that all firstborn belonged to the Lord (vv. 2, 12; 22:29-30; 34:19; Num. 3:13; 8:17).

The principle underlying the dedication of the firstborn is extended in the firstfruits offerings (Exod. 23:19; 34:26; Lev. 2:12, 14; 23:10-11, 17; Num. 15:20-21; Deut. 26:1-11; 2 Chron. 31:5). Dedicating the first of one's progeny, belongings, and produce represents giving back to God a token of the bounty God had provided. It is recognition that God owns all things. In gratitude, God's people returned the first portion of that which God had bestowed.

The *daily morning and evening offerings* consisted of two lambs that were to be presented as continual burnt offerings. One lamb was to be offered each morning, and a second lamb each evening (Exod. 29:38-39; Num. 28:3-4). These offerings, in Hebrew, were designated as *tāmîd*, "continual," reflecting their presentation every day and night (Exod. 29:38, 42; Num. 28:3, 6). They contributed to maintaining a constant fire, burning on the outer altar at all times (Lev. 6:9, 12-13 [2, 5-6 HB]). The endless burning of the fire upon the altar reflected the constant presence of God, whose divine fire provided the original flame for the altar (9:24). The daily morning and evening offerings suggested uninterrupted worship as the people of God were symbolically attendant upon God without ceasing. The sacrificial system kept the people's relationship with God continually before them.

The same term applied to the daily morning and evening offerings was used to indicate the "continual" (*tāmîd*) burning of incense upon the inner altar each morning and each evening (Exod. 30:7-8). Incense is likened to prayers, which ascend before God (Ps. 141:2; Rev. 5:8; 8:3-4). Like the daily morning and evening offerings, the *continual incense offering* is a perpetual reminder that the community lives in relation to God.

Voluntary Offerings

Five main sacrifices made up the sacrificial system in ancient Israel. The first three types of sacrifices are recognized as voluntary. These are the burnt offering (Lev. 1), the grain offering (ch. 2), and the well-being offering (ch. 3).

A distinctive feature of the *burnt offering* is that it was incinerated entirely on the altar. Consequently, it is sometimes referred to as the *whole* burnt offering. The main purposes of the burnt offering included invoking the presence of God, expressing the entire devotion of the offerer, celebrating significant events in the life of an individual or the community (Gen. 8:20; Lev. 22:18; Num. 15:3; 1 Sam. 6:14; 2 Sam. 6:17), and contributing to atonement (Lev. 1:4). Among these, the expression of complete commitment to God stands out in the context of an agrarian economy; wholly and voluntarily sacrificing a valuable animal without deriving any personal, physical benefit from its great worth signified the offerer's full surrender to God. Along with the functions of invoking God's presence and expressing joyous celebration, the devotion conveyed by the *whole* burnt offering highlights the foundational purpose of the sacrificial system: enriching relationship with God.

The *grain offering* reflects the basic purpose of a gift or tribute. It was offered independently or as an accompaniment to other sacrifices (Lev. 23:18; Num. 6:15; 8:8; 15:24). The grain offering exhibits a similar range of functions as the burnt offering. In fact, the grain offering may have served as an alternative to the burnt offering for the poor who could not afford the sacrifice of an animal or a bird (Milgrom 1991, 195-96). Unlike the burnt offering, however, the grain offering was eaten by the priests, after a portion was burnt on the altar to the Lord (Lev. 2:3, 10; 6:16-18 [9-11 HB]). This sharing of the offered food represented an intimate communion between God and humans; once again the relational foundation of the sacrificial system is evident. Provision was made so the **poor** were not excluded from opportunities to offer their gifts to God, and the procedure for the grain offering included a manifestation of fellowship with God through the sharing of bread.

Fellowship with God and others is especially embodied in the procedure for the *well-being offerings*, the final category of voluntary sacrifices. The well-being offerings, sometimes translated "peace offerings," were offered in three forms: as a thanksgiving offering (Lev. 7:12-15), as a votive offering, or as a freewill offering (vv. 16-17). The purpose of these offerings is clear from their titles. A thanksgiving offering was presented in order to express thanks to God for whatever blessing the offerer may have experienced (deliverance, healing, provision, etc.). The votive offering was presented in celebration of the successful completion of a vow. The freewill offering provided the opportunity for the offerer to express spontaneous praise to God. These manifestations of the well-being offering demonstrate that the sacrificial system included expressions of joyous celebration and thanksgiving.

Uniquely, the procedure for the well-being offerings included the worshipper and family among those who shared in eating the sacrificial meat. The well-being offerings represented a shared meal between God, the priests, and the people (1 Sam. 9:12-25). The meals related to well-being offerings were occasions of "unrestrained joy" with "sumptuous food and drink, and the experience of the divine presence and of blessing" (Gerstenberger 1996, 46).

The offerings discussed to this point (continual and voluntary) demonstrate that the sacrificial system encompassed much more than just seeking expiation from **sin** and release from guilt by means of a morose process of bloody sacrifice. The sacrificial system included joyous expressions of devotion, thanksgiving, celebration, praise, and fellowship. Such demonstrations contribute to the theological concept of relationship (with God and neighbor), which is foundational for understanding the purpose of the sacrificial system.

Required Sacrifices

The remaining two sacrifices in the main sacrificial system for ancient Israel were required ones. These are the purification offering (often translated "sin offering") and the guilt offering.

The procedure for the *purification offering* varied depending on the offerer. If a priest or the whole congregation of Israel sinned, the procedure was the same and required a bull from the herd (Lev. 4:3, 13-14). In these two instances, the blood from the bull was brought into the holy place to be sprinkled before the curtain hiding the holy of holies and applied to the horns of the incense altar (vv. 5-7, 16-18). In the case of a clan or tribal leader who sinned, a male goat was required, and the blood was applied to the outer altar of burnt offering (vv. 22-25). A common member of the community who sinned could bring for sacrifice a female goat or female lamb (vv. 27-28, 32). As with the leader's sacrifice, the blood of a common person's purification offering was applied to the outer altar of burnt offering (vv. 30, 34).

A person's act of sin generates impurity, which defiles both the person and the sanctuary of God's presence. Such imagery reinforces the relational character of the sacrificial system. The defilement of **sin** interferes with right relationships between people and God. Thus the pollution of sin must be cleansed from persons and from the places representing the presence of God. The instructions for the Day of Atonement make this clear (atonement for persons [16:6, 11, 17]; atonement for sanctuary objects [vv. 16, 18, 20]). The gradation of animals—from a bull for the priest and congregation to male goats for leaders to female goats and lambs for common persons—represents the degree of consequence attached to the sin of the disparate offenders. This reflects the principle of additional accountability for those with greater influence over the larger community (cf. James 3:1).

In addition to purging the defilement of sin, the purification sacrifice represents the offerer's own commitment to dedicate his or her life to God through **righteous** and **holy** living. The offerer placed a hand on the animal (Lev. 4:4, 15, 24, 29, 33), signifying that he or she identified with the sacrifice. The intent was to compel the person truly to dedicate his or her own life to God, even as the blood of the sacrifice was offered upon the altar before the Lord. Ancient Israel's **prophets** highlighted this understanding through their critique of the sacrificial system. They "proclaim that proper fulfillment of the sacrificial system should result in justice, care for the needy, loyalty, knowledge of God, righteousness, kindness, and a humble walk with the Lord (Isa 1:11-19; Hos 6:6; Amos 5:21-24; Mic 6:6-8)" (King 2013, 63).

The *guilt offering* is required for acts of unfaithfulness, especially in relation to the holy things of God (including people, who bear the **image of God**). Sins against "the holy things of the LORD" (Lev. 5:15, NRSV) might include eating sacrificial meat designated only for the altar or the priests, failing to offer a required sacrifice, presenting a sacrifice that was blemished or inferior in some way, and abusing sacred property, such as **land**, clothing, temple furniture, tithes, or items belonging to the temple treasury. Sins against other people (one's neighbor) include deceit, robbery, cheating, and lying (6:2-3 [5:21-22 HB]).

The guilt offering requires not only the appropriate sacrifice, and the restoration of the value of that which was taken or misused, but also an additional 20 percent of the value of the loss to provide full restitution (5:16; 6:5 [5:24 HB]). This reinforced the foundational theology of relationship in the sacrificial system. Atonement was secured between God and persons, and **reconciliation** was made between a person and his or her neighbor.

See also Clean/Unclean; Sacred Persons; Sacred Times.

Resources

Budd, Philip J. *Leviticus*. New Century Bible Commentary. Grand Rapids: Eerdmans, 1996.

Gane, Roy E. *Cult and Character: Purification Offerings, Day of Atonement, and Theodicy*. Winona Lake, IN: Eisenbrauns, 2005.

Gerstenberger, Erhard S. *Leviticus: A Commentary*. The Old Testament Library. Translated by Douglas W. Stott. Louisville, KY: Westminster John Knox Press, 1996.

Hartley, John E. *Leviticus*. WBC, vol. 4. Dallas: Word Books, 1992.

Kaiser, Walter C., Jr. "Leviticus." In vol. 1 of *NIB*. Nashville: Abingdon Press, 1994.

King, Thomas J. *Leviticus*. NBBC. Kansas City: Beacon Hill Press of Kansas City, 2013.

Levine, Baruch A. *Leviticus*. JPSTC. Philadelphia: Jewish Publication Society, 1989.

Marx, Alfred. "The Theology of the Sacrifice according to Leviticus 1–7." Pages 103-20 in *The Book of Leviticus: Composition and Reception*. VTSup 93. Edited by Rolf Rendtorff and Robert A. Kugler. Leiden, NL: Brill, 2003.

Milgrom, Jacob. *Leviticus 1–16*. AB. New York: Doubleday, 1991.

THOMAS J. KING, PHD

SAINTS/HOLY ONES

In the NT, the term "holy" (Gk., *hagios*) appears 221 times. This term most often applies to God, either in reference to the **Holy Spirit** or to Jesus as the "Holy One" (Mark 1:24; John 6:69; Acts 3:14). This term also refers to the temple as the holy place. The plural of "holy" (*hagioi*) frequently speaks of Christians as "saints" or "holy ones."

The use of *hagios* for Jesus's followers has its roots in God's **holy**, chosen people in the OT. The concept of **holiness** in the OT generally means "separation." People, animals, and things are "set apart" for God and his service. In Luke 2:23, Jesus is dedicated at the temple because the **Law** requires every firstborn male to be designated as *holy* to the Lord (Exod. 13:2). The NT use of *hagioi*, however, does not seem to carry this same level of separation, except as a way of distinguishing Christians from nonbelievers. The foundation for the holiness of Christian believers is God's command to the people of Israel to be holy as he is holy (Lev. 11:44-45; 19:2). Peter expresses this thought: "But now you must be holy in everything you do, just as God who chose you is holy" (1 Pet. 1:15, NLT). Paul also expressed the importance of Christians being holy (Eph. 5:27; Col. 1:22; 3:12).

Paul is the most frequent employer of *hagioi* in reference to Christians. He addressed Romans, 1 and 2 Corinthians, Ephesians, Philippians, and Colossians to the "saints" in each of these cities. He also sent greetings to and from "saints" in his letters (Rom 16:15; 2 Cor 13:12; Heb. 13:24). He did not always employ the term in the same manner, however. He often wrote of "saints" in reference to the believers in **Jerusalem** specifically as a part of his efforts to take up a collection for them from other Christian communities (Rom. 12:13; 15:25, 31; 1 Cor. 16:1; 2 Cor. 8:4; 9:1, 12). Along with the Jerusalem believers, the Jewish believers in Lydda and Joppa were also called "saints" (Acts 9:13, 32, 41). Paul's application of the term *hagioi* to the Jerusalem Christians reflected the Jewish concept of God's holy people. This viewpoint, that the Jewish Christians were God's true holy people, likely continued to circulate in some circles of the early church.

Paul, however, did not limit his concept of God's holy people to Jewish Christians. He encouraged Gentile Christians to see themselves as God's holy people (Proksch, in *TDNT*, 106-7). God has broken down the dividing wall of hostility so that both Jews and Gentiles have access to the Father by the one Spirit. Gentile believers are no longer strangers to God's household but rather co-citizens with the saints (Eph. 2:14-21).

Paul also wrote about the *hagioi* at the second coming of Christ (1 Thess. 3:13; 2 Thess. 1:10). Paul seemed to have used Jewish notions of the Lord's coming with his holy angels. Jude referenced Enoch's prophecy that the Lord will come with thousands of "holy ones," or angels (Jude v. 14). Also, Jesus said the holy angels would accompany him at his second coming (Mark 8:38; Luke 9:26). The above texts from 1 and 2 Thessalonians, which often translate *hagioi* as "saints," suggest that Jesus's followers will also accompany him at his second coming. However, since early Jewish literature often translated *hagioi* as "angels," it may also be Paul's meaning there (Aune 1997, 359).

Paul also wrote to the "saints" with an ethical thrust. The saints are those with the Spirit (Rom. 8:27). He expected them to show hospitality (16:2), and his congregations were to minister to the saints (1 Cor. 16:15; cf. Heb. 6:10). He praised those who loved the saints (Eph. 1:15; Col. 1:4; Phlm. v. 5). He expected respectful conduct in all churches (1 Cor. 14:33).

Paul's strongest ethical teaching comes from Ephesians (the letter with the most references to the saints). He started his letter with the reminder that God had called his people "to be holy and blameless before him" (1:4, NRSV; see also Col. 1:22). This calling was Paul's foundation for exhorting the Ephesian believers to live ethically in a way that is appropriate for the saints (Eph. 5:3), including the sacrificial love of husbands for their wives (v. 28). He also exhorted the believers to understand their identity as citizens with the saints (2:19; 3:18), for God has gifted them for ministry (4:12). In humility, Paul called himself the least of all saints (3:8).

The book of Revelation employs *hagioi* more than any book in the NT (13x). The ethical teaching in the letters to the seven churches (chs. 1–3) calls for faithfulness. Jesus is called "the Holy One" (*ho hagios*) in 3:7. That the writer of Revelation made such frequent use of the term "saints" suggests that holiness is a mark of believers who remain faithful to Christ. The saints are present at God's throne in heaven, and he listens to their prayers (5:8;

8:3-4). The theme of faithfulness in the midst of persecution is important for understanding the role of the saints in Revelation. The beast in chapter 13 is allowed to make war on the saints (vv. 7, 10), and the woman becomes drunk on the blood of the saints and martyrs (17:6; cf. 16:6). In the midst of persecutions and the temptation to worship the beast (14:9-11), 14:12 issues a call for the endurance of the saints, who are defined as those who keep God's commands and faith in Jesus. The saints will be rewarded because they fear God's name (11:18), and they will rejoice over God's destruction of Babylon (18:20). The bride of the Lamb in 19:8 is said to be clothed in "the righteous deeds of the saints" (NRSV), and God protects the saints from Satan's attack (20:9).

See also Holy Spirit.

Resources

Aune, David E. *Revelation 1-5.* WBC, vol. 52A. Dallas: Word Books, 1997.
Proksch, Otto. "ἅγιος in the NT." Pages 100-115 in vol. 1 of *TDNT*.

THOMAS GRAFTON, MA

SANCTIFICATION

Few words in the NT have been discussed and examined as thoroughly as those related to "**holiness**" or "sanctification." The Greek verb most often translated "to sanctify" or "to make **holy**" is *hagiazō*. The interpretation of this word generally falls into one or two categories, cleansing or separation, except in instances where the context indicates the author is combining both meanings into one.

Hagiazō, along with related words *hagiasmos* and *hagiotēs* (sanctification), is derived from *hagios*, which means "holy" or "holy one." It belongs to a family of Greek words referring to purity, including *hagnos* (pure), *hagnizō* (to purify), *hagneia* (purity), and *hagnismos* (purification). The primary meaning of *hagiazō*, therefore, is founded on the idea of purity or cleanliness. Related Hellenistic words such as the verb *hazō* (to shrink from) suggest that the meaning of *hagiazō* was also intertwined with the concept of separation from a very early stage.

Variants of *hagiazō* were used by translators of the LXX for the Hebrew root *qdš*, a word related to cultic purity (cf. Exod. 3:5; Josh. 5:15; 1 Sam. 21:5; Isa. 64:10). The adjectival form was also used in reference to God or people. Therefore, the idea of purity came to have a broader meaning for the OT writers than simply the purity or separation required in cultic practices. In later Judaism and into the NT period, it refers to persons and their devotion to God, demonstrated by observing particular religious practices. Herein is where we find the two basic strands of the word's meaning.

The first is the concept of "purity" or "cleanliness" that was derived from temple and cultic practices in Israel's pre-prophetic period. Procksch calls this stream of meaning the "priestly-cultic." This reading is not as well attested in the NT as the OT but is still present. Several Scriptures relate holiness to the idea of purity or cleanliness. One example is Ephesians 5:25-26: "Husbands, love your wives, just as Christ loved the church and gave himself up for her to make her holy, cleansing her by the washing with water through the word" (NIV). "To make her holy" could be translated "to sanctify her" (NASB). *Hagiazō* is parallel here with *katharizō* (to cleanse), making a clear reference to the priestly-cultic stream of meaning.

There is also a similarity to the way Paul uses *hagiazō* in 1 Corinthian 7:14. There it describes the action of a believing spouse covering the unbelieving spouse and "sanctifying" the unbeliever. The implication seems similar here. There is something about the husband's sacrifice in loving his wife as Christ loved the **church** that will cleanse her through his actions. Another instance of the word is found in 1 Thessalonians 5:23 where the idea of "sanctification" is related to being "blameless." This sets the meaning within the context of purity or cleansing from sin, especially in light of verses 21-22.

Not surprisingly, the priestly-cultic meaning of *hagiazō* is especially evident in the book of Hebrews. Hebrews 9:13 connects the cultic practice of sacrifice with holiness or sanctification. The parallel use of the phrase "cleanse our **consciences** from acts that lead to death" (v. 14, NIV) indicates that this holiness is not only physical but also spiritual. We also find this connection in 10:10 and 13:12.

The prophetic-ethical stream of meaning is the more common usage of the word for the NT writers. This meaning is grounded in the idea of being set apart for God, not by physical cleansing, but by a spiritual one resulting in "holy" behavior. In a few places a person or group is said to be "set apart" for God's purposes. In some Scriptures the meaning is quite direct, as in John 10:35-36, where the "set apart" one is Jesus himself. Here the prophetic-ethical meaning is surely intended. Elsewhere the idea of being set apart also encompasses the priestly-cultic sense of the words, bringing these two streams together to flow as one.

Romans 15:16 refers to the Gentile who is "sanctified" or "set apart" by the **Holy Spirit** as "an offering acceptable to God" (NIV), drawing a direct connection between the priestly and **prophetic** uses. Another instance of the two streams converging is 2 Timothy 2:20-21, where believers are compared to household articles designated for common use and not ceremonial use. "Those who cleanse themselves from" the dirt and defilement of being common objects "will be instruments for special purposes, made holy, useful to the Master and prepared to do any good work" (v. 21, NIV). So the idea of ritual cleansing and being holy or set apart for God's use are directly connected. It is the cleansing itself that makes the object worthy to be set apart. This is reinforced by verse 19, which affirms that "the Lord knows those who are his" (the "set apart" meaning) and that "everyone who confesses the name of the Lord must turn away from wickedness" (the "cleansing" meaning). Similar direct correlations can be found in Acts 26:18; Hebrews 10:10, 14, 29; 1 Timothy 4:5; and Revelation 22:11.

See also Biblical Ethics; Clean/Unclean; Household Codes; Sacrificial System; Sin.

Resources

Procksch, Otto, and Karl Georg Kuhn. "ἅγιος, ἁγιάζω, ἁγιασμός, ἁγιότης, ἁγιωσύνη." Pages 88-115 in vol. 1 of *TDNT*.

RHONDA G. CRUTCHER, PHD

SAVIOR

The Bible describes both God and Jesus as the Savior of humanity as well as the whole **creation**. God's work of creation ended with the declaration that all was good (Gen. 1:31). There was harmony between God, humanity, and the whole creation. However, because of **sin**, those relationships were disrupted. The consequences of Adam and Eve's sin were greater than what they could have imagined. Their disobedience resulted in death, alienation from God, and the disruption of creation. God's good creation itself became infected with **evil**.

Adam and Eve immediately recognized that they could not save themselves from pain, **suffering**, and death without a savior. Since they could not restore themselves to be whole again, they hid themselves from God. God who **loves** and cares for his creation had to redeem humanity. Genesis 3 marks the beginning of God's **work** as a savior. He assured Adam and Eve that despite their disobedience, and while recognizing the pain and suffering that came to the world as a result of sin, he would not abandon his creation. Instead, he would reconcile humanity to himself.

Humanity has been corrupted by the evil powers that permeate all spheres of life. Throughout the Scriptures we find various examples of humanity crying out to be rescued and delivered from evil and its symptoms (Exod. 2:23-24; Judg. 4:3; 2 Sam. 22:4-7; Pss. 27:9; 85:4 [5 HB]). Humanity has recognized the need of a savior to restore wholeness and **justice** in God's creation.

The consequences of sin are so great that no one can be his or her own savior. God must reorient and reorder creation. He is the only Savior who can rescue and deliver from sin and evil. In the OT, God revealed himself as Yahweh, *the Savior*. The Hebrew verb *yāša'* means "to save," "to deliver," or "to rescue," and the noun *môšîa'*, "the one who saves." In the NT, God revealed himself as Jesus, *the Savior* (Gk., *sōtēr*, "the deliverer," from the verb *sōzō*, "to save" or "to rescue").

While the **title** "Savior" is primarily used for God and Jesus Christ, it is evident that in God's plan to reorient and reorder his creation, he invites and empowers those who are reconciled with him to participate in the mission of bringing salvation to others and the world. Therefore, even when the Bible refers to certain individuals or groups as saviors or "deliverers" (Judg. 3:9, 15; 2 Kings 13:5; Neh. 9:27), these roles are only possible through the power of God, who sends and empowers the deliverers. Humanity can be an instrument of God for the redemption of the world, but ultimately God must save. Salvation emanates from God.

The exodus story is indispensable for the understanding of the revelation and declaration of God as a savior. The people of Israel could not rescue themselves. They cried out to Yahweh for their deliverance from Egypt and the powers thereof (Exod. 2:23-24). The exodus reveals God as the one who condemns and sets out to destroy the evil powers and to restore the **peace** (Hebr., šālôm) that he intended at creation. The deliverance of Israel from Egypt means more than just deliverance from **slavery**. It represents the work of a savior who rescues and delivers humanity from all the forces of evil, which manifest themselves in such ways as slavery, greed, and corruption.

Exodus illustrates that there is nothing—neither the gods nor the evil powers of this world—that can stop God's redemptive work. He is ultimately the only Savior, and he will accomplish his work of redemption (15:1-21). Accordingly, God will not rest until his commitment to reconcile the world to himself is accomplished. Throughout the OT and NT, we are reminded of the greatness of God and his saving power as demonstrated in the exodus account (Deut. 1:27; Josh. 2:10; Ps. 78:12-14; Acts 7:36).

The prophet Isaiah also incorporated the theme of a God who will not give up on his creation but will continue to work toward delivering his people from evil and death (Isa. 43:11; 49:26; 60:16). The **prophets** Micah (Mic. 5:2) and Zechariah (Zech. 9:9-10) also proclaimed that God would send another savior, a savior who would bring healing to the **land** and **forgiveness** of sin. They announced the coming of the Savior, Jesus. The people of God (Israel) are called to join and participate in the work of the world's only true Savior (Isa. 43:11).

The followers of God are invited to participate in the mission to demonstrate to the world God's **righteousness** and to showcase what it means to be united with and transformed by God, the Savior, even while they live in the world dominated by sin and evil. God calls his people to live a life of **hope** that declares the coming of the Savior to redeem and heal his creation.

The NT introduces us to the coming of the **kingdom of God** in Jesus Christ. Jesus is the Savior who rescues, delivers, heals, and forgives sins (Matt. 1:21; Acts 13:23; 2 Tim. 1:10). He is a savior like God the Father. There is nothing that can stop his salvific work. The coming of the **Messiah** was the final declaration that sin and evil will not be victorious. The Savior has come in the form of humanity to save and deliver. Thus the devil, the evil powers, and even death are not capable of stopping Jesus's mission of bringing **forgiveness** of sins, **reconciliation** with God, and ultimately even the liberation of God's creation from the bondage of decay (Rom. 8:19-21).

The coming of Jesus to the world is the pivotal revelation of God as a savior. God's kingdom brings life into the world, which is dominated by evil and death. With the coming of Jesus, the world is being transformed by God's offer of redemption, resulting in communities of transformed people, who are also invited to participate in the mission of rescuing the lost. Those who are part of God's kingdom are invited to live lives marked by **repentance** and **faith**. Redeemed from evil and its powers, they live new lives by the power of the Savior.

The kingdom of God invites believers to live with confidence and **hope** in God, the Savior, who is working to redeem his world and who will accomplish this at Christ's second coming, the **parousia**. Only God through the life, death, and resurrection of Jesus can save. People become righteousness through God's work of reconciliation as they are brought back into a right relationship with God. It is the **Holy Spirit** who awakens people spiritually and enables them to respond to God's saving **grace**. As they respond to his grace, by means of his authority and power exhibited in the resurrection of Jesus, God transforms them from death to life. The forces of death may manifest themselves in multiple ways: wars, famine, unrest, poverty, calamities, addictions, pain, suffering, and injustice. Yet Jesus Christ has been given the power to defeat death in its various forms (1 Cor. 15:54-57).

The people of God (Israel and the church) are those who have been rescued by God from sin and delivered from death. Once because of sin they were not a people of God. Now they are a **community** of God, the **saints**, priests, and **prophets** of God who bear witness to the world of God's redemptive powers. These redeemed communities model to the world what it means to be a rescued, delivered, saved people, while yet living in a world that continues to be plagued by evil powers (Eph. 2:13-22).

God wants to save human beings to bring them to his intended creation—people who live in harmony with God, other people, and his creation.

See also Demonic/Devil; Fall, The; Obedience.

Resources

Green, Joel B. *Why Salvation?* Reframing New Testament Theology. Nashville: Abingdon Press, 2013.

Scandrett, Joel, and Howard A. Snyder. *Salvation Means Creation Healed*. Eugene, OR: Cascade Books, 2011.

Wright, N. T. *Evil and the Justice of God*. Downers Grove, IL: InterVarsity Press, 2006.

FILIMÃO M. CHAMBO, DLITT ET PHIL

SERMON ON THE MOUNT

The Sermon on the Mount, found in Matthew 5:1–7:29, has been one of the most influential sections of Scripture during the history of the church. It was the most quoted portion of the Bible by the ante-Nicene writers, was debated over in the Reformation, and has been the subject of expositions in recent times by luminaries such as Dietrich Bonhoeffer, John Howard Yoder, and John Stott. John Wesley turned to the Sermon on the Mount more than any other Scripture in his sermons. The familiar contents of the Beatitudes, Lord's Prayer, and Golden Rule are a treasure for Christians.

Contents

There has been almost no end of proposed outlines of the Sermon on the Mount (hereafter designated SM). However, the contents can be described as follows:

Introduction	5:1-2
Beatitudes	5:3-12
Salt and Light	5:13-16
Interpretation of the **Torah**	5:17-48
Acts of Piety	6:1-18
The Life of Trust	6:19-34
Relation to the Community	7:1-12
The Narrow Entry	7:13-27
Conclusion	7:28-29

We can discern some internal patterns. In both the introduction and conclusion, there are references to "the crowds." There are numerous references to "**righteousness**" or "righteous" (5:6, 20; 6:1, 33) and to God's kingdom or the "kingdom of heaven" (5:3, 19; 6:10; 7:21). It has been proposed that the Lord's Prayer is the structural center of the SM. Regardless of structure, the SM presents life in the **kingdom of God/heaven**.

Sources

A careful reader of the SM who gives attention to the traditions of the Hebrew Bible readily notices its echoes of the OT. For example, the Beatitudes clearly reflect Psalm 37 (with concepts of righteousness, meekness, and inheriting the earth) and Isaiah 61:1-3 (the **poor** and the mourning). **Wisdom** and **prophetic** streams merge in the contents of the SM.

In addition, sources in early Judaism show clear continuity of thought. Scholars have long noted the "reverse golden rule" of Tobit 4:15, "What you hate, do not do to anyone" (NRSV). Sirach 7:14*b*, "Do not repeat yourself when you pray" (NRSV), has an echo in Matthew 6:7, "When you pray, do not use meaningless repetition, as the Gentiles do, for they suppose they will be heard by their many words" (AT). Clearly, the SM builds upon the piety of the OT and early Judaism.

Another issue in regard to sources has been the relation to Luke 6:20-49 and the Sermon on the Plain. Two-source theories of synoptic relations assume the hypothetical document Q. How does this, however, relate to the actual teaching of Jesus?

More recent theories of orality have noted that Jesus likely preached and taught similar things in a number of locations. Likely, the Lord's Prayer, for example, was taught in different forms in a variety of village settings. It is not hard to conceive that Jesus uttered beatitudes in a variety of forms in multiple places. Different forms, then, of the sayings of the SM do not necessarily oppose the proposal that the SM is an authentic message of Jesus, given in one setting at one time. It need not be something a redactor or editor collected and supplemented. It would seem unnecessary to advocate a multiple-stage reworking of the words of Jesus.

Ethics

It is clear that the SM presents the **ethics** of the kingdom. The ethical challenge of the SM, however, has led to multiple proposals for the ways Christians are to live out the SM. Aquinas proposed a difference between the "counsels of perfection" for the elite few and the things necessary for salvation for the masses. Anabaptists in Reformation times were literalists and said, for example, that the SM prohibits all vows. Luther distinguished between the kingdoms of the world and the kingdom of Christ. Those responsible for keeping order in society, such as soldiers, do not need to "turn the other cheek." Bonhoeffer taught the SM as a pattern of resistance in the context of a small believing community surrounded by Nazi powers. John Howard Yoder, influential to Stanley Hauerwas, further developed the Anabaptist vision in his presentation of the SM.

In recent years, Hans Dieter Betz proposed that the SM was not law but rather theology that must be internalized and creatively developed in the concrete situations of life. Many evangelical and Wesleyan interpreters have followed similar lines of thinking. For example, in the same section about not judging, Jesus says to watch out for wolves in sheep's clothing! The SM was intended to be reflected on and then lived out.

Community

The SM is not meant to be directed to individuals on the lonely path of **discipleship** but rather to believing communities seeking first God's kingdom and righteousness. The plural pronouns in the SM are a clue to this:

- "You [plural] are the salt of the earth" (5:13, NRSV).
- "You [plural] are the light of the world" (5:14, NRSV).
- "Unless your [plural] righteousness exceeds that of the scribes and Pharisees, you [plural] will never enter the kingdom of heaven" (5:20, NRSV).

- "Watch out not to do your [plural] righteousness before people" (6:1, AT).
- "Our Father, who is in heaven" (6:9, AT).
- "Do not lay up your [plural] treasures on earth" (6:19, AT).

The assumption is that community members have chosen to follow Christ together and will correct and challenge each other as they listen to the **Spirit** together. Discernment will place the SM in the full context of the words and actions of Jesus, the letters of the NT, and the biblical canon as a whole. Faithful communities will want to return again and again to the SM for their guidance and communal life.

Resources

Betz, Hans Dieter. *The Sermon on the Mount.* Hermeneia: A Critical and Historical Commentary on the Bible. Minneapolis: Fortress Press, 1995.

Greenman, Jeffrey P., Timothy Larsen, and Stephen R. Spencer. *The Sermon on the Mount through the Centuries.* Grand Rapids: Brazos Press, 2007.

Stott, John R. W. *Christian Counter-Culture: The Message of the Sermon on the Mount.* Downers Grove, IL: InterVarsity Press, 1978.

TIMOTHY DWYER, PHD

SIN (*ḥāṭāʾ, pāšaʾ, ʾāwōn, hamartia, adikia*)

"Sin . . . is an exclusively biblical concept" (Rutledge 2015, 174). Walter Brueggemann explains that in the Old Testament an "all-pervading conviction about God . . . precedes any thought of sin" (2002, 195). For Christians this means God as triune—Father, Son, and Holy Spirit.

Three convictions underlie a biblical understanding of sin. First is the reality of an original departure by humankind from the will of God, what Cardinal John Henry Newman called a "vast primordial catastrophe" (Rutledge 2015, 185n46). Second, the departure is evidenced and experienced in human solidarity—individually and corporately—as bondage to sin (Rom. 7:24). Third, there exists a forceful cosmic alliance or kingdom composed of sin, evil, and death (the world, the flesh, and the devil) (Acts 26:18; 2 Cor. 4:4; Eph. 2:2; Col. 1:13). The alliance is irrevocably set against God's reign. The apostle Paul uses the language of "powers" (Gk., *exousia*, pl. *exousiai*) to identify sin's structured character. The "powers" may refer to superhuman entities. But as structured evil they refer to instituted dimensions of earthly existence co-opted and distorted by evil.

These three convictions identify the "mystery of iniquity" (2 Thess. 2:7, KJV).

For Christians, most accurately, knowledge of sin happens by knowing Jesus Christ. As the definitive revelation of God, he is also the definitive revelation of sin. He exposes spiritual darkness (Gk., *skotia*). As the "light of the world" (John 8:12, NIV), Jesus shines in the darkness and the darkness cannot overcome him (1:5). His work is also that of the Father (5:30-32; 14:10-11) and the Holy Spirit (15:26-27; 16:5-11).

Knowledge of sin is both a matter of revelation and faith. We begin to know the nature of sin, including its despair (Rom. 3:9-20), when we have heard the gospel of Jesus Christ.

Sin as Unbelief and Idolatry

Sin manifests itself in external deeds. But the Bible first looks into the "depth of the heart with all its powers" (Luther 1961, 22). Instead of worshipping God in trusting obedience, unbelief "exalts the flesh, and gives the desire to do works that are plainly wrong" (22). This was the sin of our first parents. Christ singled out unbelief and called it sin (John 16:8ff.).

Unbelief gives rise to idolatry. Idolatry elevates what is finite into the realm of deity. It involves serving and worshipping the creature instead of the Creator. Idolatry distorts what is essentially good—God's creation. It claims a power it cannot sustain (1 Kings 18:20-29).

Sin as a Powerful, Ubiquitous Kingdom

Not only is sin unbelief and the rupture of relation, but it is also "the experience of an active power that lays hold of man." It is a "reality" (Ricoeur 1967, 70). Sin is more than simply the sum total of all human wrongdoing; it is the "result of idolatry, in which humans hand over their God-given powers to other 'forces,' which then enslave them" (Wright 2016, 280). According to Paul, death and sin rule powerfully by pressing compliant humans into their service (Rom. 5:12-19).

How the Old Testament Understands Sin

Walter Brueggemann says that in the Old Testament, knowledge of sin comes through knowledge of God who "creates, governs and wills a world of well-being with and for all of God's creatures" (2002, 196).

The Old Testament focuses on three terms for sin: (1) *ḥāṭāʾ*, meaning "to be deficient," "to fail," "to make a mistake," or "to go wrong" (e.g., Gen. 20:6, 9; 31:39); (2) *pāšaʿ*, meaning "to transgress" or "to rebel" (e.g., 1 Kings 8:50; 12:19; 2 Kings 3:5); and (3) *ʿāwōn*, meaning "moral violation," "guilt," or "iniquity" (e.g., Gen. 4:13; 15:16; Exod. 20:5). Although each term has a different root, for practical purposes they can be treated as synonymous (Exod. 34:7).

Brueggemann (2002) treats sin in the OT from three perspectives.

1. *Sin as God centered.* Sin is profoundly God centered. Humans are created by God and for God. They are meant to live in "glad, obedient responsiveness to God." Sin involves a "distortion or violation" of God's ordering of creation. It is "a refusal to be in a relationship of glad praise, thanks, and obedience" (196).

Sin is understood within the context of covenant. God is unfailingly faithful (righteous), and Israel is expected to be also. "The basis of a covenantal existence with God is the premise that obedient living leads to well-being and disobedience leads to trouble and death" (Deut. 30:15-20) (196). God keeps sin from becoming the defining reality of creation. "God's capacity to deal effectively with sin is a celebrated certitude in the Old Testament" (197). By a sovereign act, God is willing and able to pardon and forgive sins (Jer. 31:34; Ps. 51:1, 10).

2. *Life as Ordered by Torah.* The proper relationship between God and his creation is ordered and guided by Torah, the Law, as summarized in the Decalogue (the Ten Commandments). Violation of Torah, of worshipful relationship with God, is spelled out in all human life. It yields disorder, disruption, judgment, guilt, and death.

Broadly, Torah has two foci. First, "a relationship with the Creator God evokes a concern for holiness (purity, cleanness)" (Lev. 19:2) (196). Second, worship of God and a right relationship with him must be expressed by enacting societal justice in political and economic terms; "love of God" necessarily manifests itself as concern for the neighbor's well-being, "particularly for the disadvantaged or needy neighbors" (Prov. 17:5; Amos 6:21-24; Mark 12:28-31) (196). Sin rejects moral coherence, and it rejects coherence between true worship of God, moral wholeness, and love for one's neighbor (Amos 5:15).

3. *Sin as an Intruder.* Sin is as an intruder into God's good creation. It is "neither the defining mark of human personality nor the defining characteristic of life with God" (197). "Creatureliness may have within it the seeds of sin, but the Old Testament is clear that sin is not an inescapable product of creatureliness" (196). The creation, including humans, is *essentially* good (Gen. 1:4, 10, 12, 18, 21, 25) and "very good" (1:31, NIV).

The Old Testament never denies the presence of evil in God's creation. But evil is always present as disobedience and as a distortion of what God created as "good." It has no independent metaphysical status, no independent source of being. Evil derives its "life" from what it distorts.

How the New Testament Understands Sin

The apostle Paul insists that individual sins proceed as instances of a universal condition. Sin is a "racial" (the human race) problem. All humans are "in" Adam (Rom. 5:18). Fallen, all humans have in themselves confirmed Adam's rebellion. There is a solidarity of disobedience, idolatry, and justifiable "condemnation for all people" (v. 18, NIV). "The fraternity of Adam is the most comprehensive community of all" (Rutledge 2015, 178).

The major New Testament terms for sin are *hamartia* and *adikia* (Günther, in NIDNTT, 3:573-85).

Hamartia. *Hamartia* is the word from which we derive the word hamartiology, the doctrine of sin. *Hamartia* means "missing the mark." The Hebrew equivalent is *ḥāṭāʾ*. It is the comprehensive expression for everything opposed to God. All other concepts and synonyms are overshadowed by *hamartia* and are to be understood in its light. Along with its cognates, *hamartia* refers to offenses against morals, laws, people, and gods. In its verb form, *hamartia* means "to miss the mark," "to sin." In it noun form, it means a "sin," "transgression," or "sinner." As an adjective, *hamartia* means "sinful."

In the Johannine literature *hamartia* is used in the context of the incarnation, which holds together heaven and earth. Jesus, who is without sin, comes into the world and, as the Lamb of God, sheds his precious blood for the sin of the world (John 1:29; 1 John 3:5). Everything that opposes Jesus is sin. The Holy Spirit truly reveals sin and righteousness (God's faithfulness to his covenant and his world) (Wright 2016, 81-82) (John 16:4*b*-11).

Adikia. *Adikia* is less specific and more varied than *hamartia*. It describes the outwardly visible characteristics of what stands under the power of sin. James 3:6 is an example; "injustice" (*adikia* [unrighteousness]) is perpetuated by an unruly tongue. Similarly, Luke 16:1-9 refers to unjust mammon. In Romans 1:18-32, where Paul describes the sins of the Gentiles, he uses *adikia* and *asebeia* ("wickedness," "ungodly," "impiety"), not *hamartia*.

Adikia is the opposite of righteousness. It denotes "unrighteousness," "dealing unjustly," "unjust deeds," "wrong doing," and "injuring." It can mean behavior that does not conform to the moral norm (Matt. 5:45; Luke 18:11; John 7:18; 2 Thess. 2:12). *Adikia* mostly occurs in the singular, which indicates its attention to the whole phenomenon of transgression, not upon individual acts.

Paul and John contrast *adikia* with *alētheia* (truth) (John 7:18; Rom. 1:18; 2:8).

Parabasis is a synonym for *adikia*. *Parabasis* and its cognates refer to a transgression of the law. They shed light on *adikia*.

Paraptōma, which comes from *parapiptō*, means a "false step," a "falling down beside, a "losing of one's way," an "error," and a "trespass." Generally, it means a moral lapse and a willful offense for which one is responsible.

Additional Concepts. Additional concepts that belong to the wider range of sin are (1) *anomia* ("lawlessness"; from *nomos* [law]); (2) *ptaiō* ("stumble," "come to grief"); (3) *hēttēma* (defeat); (4) *hysterēma* ("lack," "fault"); (5) *planaō* ("go astray," "deceive oneself"); (6) *agnoeō* ("not know," "not understand"); (7) *opheilō* (be under obligation); and (8) *parakoē* (disobedience). Three terms are associated with guilt: (1) *aitia* ("cause," "accusation"); (2) *elenchō* (convict); and (3) *enochos* (guilty).

See also Demonic/Devil; Election; Evil; Fall, The; Sanctification.

Resources

Brueggemann, Walter. *Reverberations of Faith: A Theological Handbook of Old Testament Themes.* Louisville, KY: Westminster John Knox Press, 2002.

Günther, W. "Sin." Pages 573-85 in vol. 3 of *NIDNTT.*

Luther, Martin. *Preface to the Epistle of St. Paul to the Romans.* In *Martin Luther: Selections from His Writings.* Edited by John Dillenberger. Garden City, NY: Doubleday, 1961.

Ricoeur, Paul. *The Symbolism of Evil.* Translated by Emerson Buchanan. Boston: Beacon Press, 1967.

Rutledge, Fleming. *The Crucifixion: Understanding the Death of Jesus Christ.* Grand Rapids: Eerdmans, 2015.

Wright, N. T. *The Day the Revolution Began: Reconsidering the Meaning of Jesus's Crucifixion.* San Francisco: HarperOne, 2016.

AL TRUESDALE, PHD

SLAVERY

There is no definition of the term "slavery" that crosses all times and cultural realities. We must carefully distinguish ancient and first-century slavery from that which was practiced later in the New World. First, race played almost no role and a slave could not be identified by mere appearance. Second, many slaves held positions of authority in their master's household (Phil. 4:22) that might include owning their own property and slaves. They could worship with their master and even marry. However, the children of the slave would remain the property of the owner even after the slave was freed. Third, many persons sold themselves into servitude to receive a better standard of living in the homes of wealthy masters, thus effectively climbing socially and economically. Fourth, education was encouraged and provided to many slaves, since they often became teachers of slaveholders' children. Finally, a large number of domestic slaves could anticipate being set free (manumission) by the age of thirty and sometimes earlier.

However, one must be careful not to attribute positive moral value to slavery. In a world socially centered on honor, slaves could not rise above the shame that indelibly marked their situation in life. Ancient slavery was of a wholly different order from that of Brazil, the Caribbean, or other places of the New World. What the different forms of slavery had in common were the economic benefits they brought. Thus slaveholding in the Greco-Roman world was fundamental to the existence of many in agricultural and urban areas.

During the late Roman Republic, the largest contribution to the slave population came as spoils of war. Estimates project that up to 30 percent of the Roman world were slaves.

Ancient Near East, Greece, and Rome

According to ANE law codes, slaves were identified as property. Aristotle referred to slaves as mere "human tools." Slavery in the Greek world seemed to be more onerous than in the subsequent Roman culture. Even once freed in Athenian society, ex-slaves were forbidden to hold citizenship or own land, thus excluding them from political and public life. An alternative way of defining slavery is "social death," since the culture withheld from a person the dignity ascribed by it. One may have had physical existence but was socially excluded from the free population. This could amount to a sense of shame worse than death itself.

By contrast, the biblical text pays closer attention to the relationship between master and slave, putting the focus on the slave's human value. The Bible acknowledges the master's authority over the slave, yet it clearly restricts any excessive use of power or punishment.

Biblical Understanding of Slavery

Old Testament. Persons were thrust into slavery in many ways. At birth, if their parents were slaves, they became slaves. Due to extreme poverty, parents would sell their children into slavery. There were many unresolvable life circumstances for which slavery was the legal and social recourse, such as indebtedness or crimes that called for restitution to an injured party.

In the Hebrew civilization ruled by the Law or **Torah**, there were societal limits that put boundaries around the practice of slavery, such as prohibiting beating slaves to death (Exod. 21:20). Israelites were even commanded to provide refuge for abused slaves (Deut. 23:15). Families were to share the sacred Passover meal with their slaves and were required to let them rest on the Sabbath. Enslavement of a Hebrew for debt was limited to six years (Exod. 21:2; Deut. 15:12; Jer. 34:14).

Additionally, upon receiving freedom, slaves were to be given gifts by their former owner (Deut. 15:14) or to receive back their inheritance (Lev. 25:28) to enable them to successfully navigate this transition to a new life. Finally, the length of servitude of self-enslaved Hebrews ended with the year of Jubilee (vv. 13, 40). The Hebrew law code provided a more humane side to slavery. The slave was usually referred to as a second person in a social-cultural relationship, not merely property. Also, the code gave slaves hope for the future possibility of freedom.

New Testament. In the Greco-Roman world, which was principally brokered on relationships of power and compliance (e.g., **honor-shame**; **patron**-client), the most severe arrangement was slavery. Because the fledgling church was ingrained with this worldview, the institution of slavery was prominent, with the roles of masters and slaves being frequently referenced in Jesus's parables (Matt. 18:23-34; 24:45-51; Luke 16:1-13; 17:7-10) and in other NT texts (Eph. 6:5-9; Col. 3:22-25; 1 Tim. 1:10; Rev. 18:13). These references never directly approved or condemned slavery's stance in society; they merely recognized its existence.

The most revealing NT material indicating its attitude toward slavery occurs in the book of Philemon. Paul carefully navigated the real-life challenges of slavery as he called upon the return of Onesimus to Philemon as his legal owner. Yet he prominently identified the new standing of the slave Onesimus as both a son (v. 10) to Paul and a brother (v. 16) to Philemon. Paul did not exercise apostolic authority by calling for Philemon to release Onesimus (v. 8); rather, Paul appealed to Philemon to love (v. 9) out of his own free will (v. 14). Thus, given Paul's understated language, he submerged his call to end slavery beneath the gospel's new two-fold priority: the *missio Dei* and the equality of all people in the body of Christ, regardless of social status.

The Pauline household codes (Eph. 5:21–6:9; Col. 3:18–4:1) gave additional didactic instructions for living in "God's household" (1 Tim. 3:15, NIV), which was a whole new order of life. Even though the command to servants was to "obey [their] masters" (Eph. 6:5; Col. 3:22, NIV), there was an unprecedented reciprocal call to the masters to "treat [their] slaves in the same way" (Eph. 6:9, NIV; see Col. 4:1). Relationships were being renewed. They may not have been fully equal, but they were clearly heading in that direction so that societies based upon kingdom principles would look increasingly like the "commonwealth" of heaven (Phil. 3:20, RSV) rather than the shame-based culture of earth. The NT writers more than subtly identified slavery as part of a kingdom that was passing away.

See also Festivals; Marriage; Poor/Poverty; Sacred Times.

Resources

Bartchy, S. S. "Slave, Slavery." Pages 1098-102 in *DLNT*.
Harrill, J. A. "Slavery." Pages 1124-27 in *Dictionary of New Testament Background*. Edited by C. A. Evans and S. E. Porter. Downers Grove, IL: InterVarsity Press, 2000. Logos Bible Software.
Rupprecht, A. A. "Slave, Slavery." Pages 881-83 in *DPL*.

DAVID F. SMITH, PHD

SUFFERING

The Etiology of Suffering

The Genesis account of the fall of the first humans (ch. 3) is an etiological account that helps us to understand various aspects of human suffering. Just as Genesis explains the origin of creation, it also explains the origin of suffering, pain, and hostility. The curse against Adam and Eve fell not only on them but also on all their descendants. All are born into a world that is vulnerable to suffering. Suffering was not God's initial plan. Rather, it is an intruder into God's world.

The Reasons for Suffering

The causes of suffering are complex. Its biblical explanations are diverse and at points even contradictory. A main reason for human suffering is punishment for sin. People may suffer because they make wrong and sinful choices (Deut. 30:15-20). Although God's love and mercy extend to many generations, "he does not leave the guilty unpunished" (Exod. 34:6-7, NIV).

God's punishment falls on the immediate offenders and may also fall on "the third and fourth generation" (20:5-7; Num. 14:18; Deut. 5:9-10, NIV). The Bible in these passages views the people as a collective, the extended family perpetuating the same sins.

The book of Judges has a four-phase pattern of sin, suffering, crying out to God, and deliverance. Because the people sinned, God allowed a foreign nation to oppress them. God raised a judge who delivered them from the sufferings inflicted by the foreign nations. But the sin-suffering cycle continued on and so did the retributive **justice** of God.

An individual's sin may have far-reaching consequences. Achan's greed (Josh. 7) led to the defeat of the Israelite army, a loss of thirty-six lives (v. 5). His punishment for such a loss of life included the destruction of his family. While the punishment for breaking God's laws is rarely that inclusive, the sin of one individual may lead to the suffering of many others, such as causing a fire that destroys the houses of others.

According to the concept of corporate responsibility, God holds a family responsible for the sins of an individual, or a tribe for the sins of a few. When Israel was taken into exile, the people complained that God's justice was unfair; they were suffering for the sins of their ancestors. Ezekiel moved beyond the corporate concept to make it clear that they were not suffering for the sins of their fathers but for their own (Ezek. 18). Yet while God holds only the sinner accountable, other innocent persons may also suffer. The death of a father might plunge a family into poverty.

Though sin invites punishment, it is not the only reason people suffer. The righteous also were caught up in the suffering of the sinful nation when it was taken into exile (2 Kings 25). Enemies sought to destroy the righteous (Ps. 69:4 [5]). Jeremiah was placed in the stocks for speaking the **word of God** (Jer. 20:1-2).

Jesus did not condemn those killed in the collapse of the Siloam Tower, nor did he accuse the victims of Pilate's cruelty of being greater sinners than others (Luke 13:1-5). He also excluded sin as the cause of the man being born blind (John 9:1-5).

Suffering need not be the direct punishment by God for sinful acts. According to the **wisdom** tradition, the principle of rewards and punishments is built into the system of a moral universe. God does not have to punish directly the offender for doing wrong; the consequences of our actions sometimes automatically follow. For example, the lazy person will go hungry because laziness and hunger have a causal relationship (Prov. 6:9-11).

Why the righteous suffer eludes even the best minds. Job and his friends debated the issue in three cycles of arguments without finding an acceptable answer. Job found no satisfactory answer even from God for why the righteous also suffer.

Vicarious Suffering

The concept of vicarious suffering means that an innocent person may suffer willingly on behalf of others. Just as individual sins may have corporate and transgenerational consequences, the reverse is also possible. An individual as representative of a people may embrace suffering, as depicted in Isaiah 53, where an individual takes upon himself the punishment for the sins of his people. Christians have interpreted this passage as foreshadowing Christ's suffering on behalf of the human race. As suffering for sin entered the world through one man, Adam, so by Christ came **grace** and **righteousness** (Rom. 5:15-21).

Response to Suffering

The suffering of God's people is not always to be considered **evil**, but at times instructive; it is God disciplining his people (Deut. 8:5; Heb. 12:5-13). Although the exile brought punishment for the sins of the nation, it also meant **hope** (Isa. 43:14-15). The nation as God's people was a light to the Gentiles (42:6-7). The suffering of the Servant brought forth **forgiveness** (53:12*c*).

Hope in Suffering. There are two types of laments in the Bible. One accepts the situation and expresses sorrow and grief over it. David lamented the death of Saul and Jonathan (2 Sam. 1:17-27). The second is a plaintive prayer, examples of which are in Psalms and Lamentations; this type of lament refuses to take adversity as given and turns to God for answers and deliverance (Ps. 73; see also Hab. 3). Renewed **faith** can evolve out of suffering and pain.

The **prophets** looked beyond their present suffering to a time when suffering would be removed from this world and harmony and **peace** would reign (Isa. 2:2-4; Amos 9:11-15; Mic. 4:1-4). Both Daniel (Dan. 12:1-3) and John (Rev. 21) looked beyond the distress of this world to a time of renewed life and a new heaven and earth.

Suffering and the Lament Tradition. As noted above, human responses to suffering can be seen in the laments of the Psalms. They question God, demand answers, and pray for the reversal of situations. They are truly struggles of the human soul to be relieved of the pain. They also acknowledge that God knows the reasons why people suffer, that he is in control, and that he has the power to reverse the situations. This tradition is not limited to the OT. It can also be found in the NT, such as in the prayer of the **church** against its enemies (Acts 4:23-31) and in the prayer of the martyrs for revenge in the book of Revelation (6:9-11).

Christ's Suffering. Christ's suffering and death only made sense to early Christians because they read the OT. In Jewish thinking it was not possible to imagine a suffering and dying **Messiah**. Rather he was thought even by Jesus's disciples to be an invincible warrior. The encounter of the risen Jesus with his disciples on the road to Emmaus marked a new turn even in their understanding. Jesus asked them, "Did not the Messiah have to suffer these things . . . ?" (Luke 24:26, NIV). Then he began to explain to them from the Prophets and Moses what the Scriptures meant (v. 27). On the day of Pentecost Peter boldly proclaimed that Jesus the Messiah was raised by God from the dead and that by his suffering brought forgiveness of sins (Acts 2:36-39).

Christians' Suffering

As a new religious movement that challenged Jewish beliefs as well as the Roman imperial cult, the early Christians went through immense persecution. In the face of such severe persecution and martyrdom, the new believers drew strength from their Master's example and teaching.

Jesus's teaching embraced suffering rather than shunned it. In the Beatitudes he taught that suffering was not the evidence of evil but the evidence that God was pleased with his people (Matt. 5:3-12). They suffered for the sake of the **gospel** (16:24-25). The early Christians understood that God would stand by them in the time of suffering (Rom. 5:3-5) and that the promise of **resurrection** and eternal life offered a new hope for them in their struggle (1 Cor. 15). God does not desert his people. He stands with them in this age and welcomes them home in the next.

See also Progressive Revelation; Sermon on the Mount.

PAULSON PULIKOTTIL, PHD

Tt

TEMPTATION/TEST

The idea of trials and testing is widely used in the Bible, but the rendering of the term "testing" as "tempting" appears only in the NT in the context of Satan attempting to lead people into **sin**.

Two main OT Hebrew terms denote the idea of testing: *bāḥan* and *nāsâ*. *Bāḥan* appears mostly in poetic texts and refers to determining the dependability and value of something—namely, the purity of metal (Job 23:10; Zech. 13:9) or the truthfulness of words (Gen. 42:15-16; Job 12:11; 34:3). This term usually carries positive overtones when Yahweh does the testing. While there is no prescribed procedure, Yahweh examines the hearts and minds of his people to determine their spiritual health (Deut. 8:2; 13:3; 1 Chron. 29:17; Pss. 7:9 [10 HB]; 139:23; Jer. 12:3). On occasion, persons invite the Lord to examine or test their hearts and minds in prayer, to verify their devotion and dedication to him (Pss. 17:3; 26:2; Jer. 11:20). The Lord uses the testing process in formative ways to cleanse and purify human character through trials (Job 23:10; Prov. 17:3; Jer. 9:7; 17:10).

Bāḥan is also used negatively in several ways. At times, these tests seem oppressive and taxing (Job 7:18; Jer. 20:12). At other times, God's people fail his tests and receive punishment (Jer. 6:27-30; Lam. 3:40-42; Ezek. 21:13); however, when the people persevere through the testing, they are able to praise Yahweh for the lessons learned (Pss. 66:10; 81:7 [8 HB]). *Bāḥan* also has negative overtones when Yahweh is the object of the testing (Ps. 95:9; Mal. 3:15). Putting God and his faithfulness to the test results in punishment, unless he invites such testing to demonstrate his power and faithfulness to unbelievers (Mal. 3:10).

The second term, *nāsâ*, appears predominantly in narrative texts to denote a rather concrete type of testing, both religious and secular. *Nāsâ* captures the idea of testing to determine the truth or value of a person or thing. Having heard about Solomon's reputation, the queen of Sheba tested his **wisdom** (1 Kings 10:1; 2 Chron. 9:1). David had not tested Saul's armor and did not feel safe in it (1 Sam. 17:39). In Ecclesiastes, the Preacher tested pleasure and wisdom to find their value in life (2:1; 7:23). A Babylonian official tested Daniel's diet to determine its benefits for Daniel and his friends (Dan. 1:12, 14).

In the religious realm, *nāsâ* is used when people test God or vice versa. Although people are not supposed to test Yahweh, one finds instances when it happens, such as the incident at Rephidim—renamed Massah (testing) and Meribah (quarreling)—demonstrates (Exod. 17:2-7). Subsequent reflections on this episode condemn the people's testing of Yahweh as an example of disobedience (Deut. 6:16; Ps. 95:8). People tested Yahweh by questioning his faithfulness and rebelling against him (Num. 14:22; Pss. 78:18, 41, 56; 106:14).

When Yahweh tests people, he does so in a particular way for a particular goal. Isaac's near-sacrifice tested Abraham's **obedience** (Gen. 22:1). Thirst, hunger, false **prophets**, and pagan nations in the promised land were tests to measure the people's willingness to obey Yahweh (Exod. 15:25; 16:4; Deut. 8:2, 16; 13:3; Judg. 2:22; 3:1, 4). The Sinai theophany instilled the reverent **fear of God** in the Israelites (Exod. 20:20). Testing evaluates and shapes the character.

The NT uses two Greek verbs to reflect the idea of testing: *dokimazō* and *peirazō*, along with their cognates. In the LXX *dokimazō* corresponds to the Hebrew *bāḥan* mostly in the religious setting with Yahweh as the subject. In the NT it is used of testing buildings (1 Cor. 3:12-13), precious metals (1 Pet. 1:7), weather or signs of the time (Luke 12:56), "the spirits" (1 John 4:1), and deacons or bishops (1 Tim. 3:10; 2 Tim. 2:15). These tests are in order to evaluate, examine, approve of, or disapprove of that which is tested (Rom. 1:28; 1 Cor. 11:28; 2 Cor. 13:5-7; 1 Thess. 5:21). *Dokimazō* appears most often with God as the subject and human beings as the objects of testing.

Following the OT tradition, NT writers speak of human actions being tested by fire (1 Cor. 3:13) and of such testing producing **hope** and perseverance (Rom. 5:4; James 1:3, 12). Testing in affliction brings joy and sheds lights on those who are approved by God (2 Cor. 8:2). God tests the heart to find his servants approved (1 Thess. 2:4; 2 Cor. 10:18). Testing involves critical examination, reflection, and the actions of faithful obedience on the part of the believer, which are recognized by a larger body of Christ.

The second Greek term, *peirazō*, corresponds to the Hebrew *nāsâ* and means to examine critically (John 6:6; Rev. 2:2; 3:10), to burden with a test (Heb. 2:18; Rev. 2:10), and to purify (1 Pet. 4:12). Some may break under testing (Luke 8:13), but those who persevere are blessed (James 1:12).

In the Synoptics, Jesus's conflicts with the religious leaders are identified as "tests" that question Jesus's faithfulness to God's will (Matt. 16:1; 19:3; 22:18, 35). Testing Jesus (1 Cor. 10:9), God (Acts 15:10), or the **Spirit** (5:9) in this way is presented negatively. The Synoptics also recount Jesus's temptation (Matt. 4:1-11; Mark 1:12-13; Luke 4:1-13). Jesus's temptations by Satan (adversary)—called "tempter" in Matthew's account—are parallel to

Adam and Eve's and to Israel's testing in the **wilderness** and are focused on whether Jesus would remain faithful to God's will for his life and ministry. While the first humans and Israel failed the tests, Jesus persevered and overcame them.

Peirazō is rendered "tempt" only when Satan, the "tempter," tries to mislead people away from living in obedience to the Lord (1 Cor. 7:5; Gal. 6:1; 1 Thess. 3:5) or when people, choosing not to be content with God's provision for them, follow their own **evil** desires (1 Tim. 6:9; James 1:14). God does not tempt and cannot be tempted (James 1:13); rather, God is present with his people through trials, offering comfort and strength to endure (1 Cor. 10:13).

See also Demonic/Devil; Fall, The; Suffering.

Resources

Brensinger, Terry L. "*bāḥan.*" Pages 636-38 in vol. 1 of *NIDOTTE*.

———. "*nāsâ.*" Pages 111-12 in vol. 3 of *NIDOTTE*.

Carter, Warren. "Tempt, Temptation." Pages 515-17 in vol. 5 of *NIDB*.

Popkes, W. "πειραζω." Pages 64-67 in vol. 3 of *EDNT*.

Schunack, G. "δοκιμαζω." Pages 341-43 in vol. 1 of *EDNT*.

Silva, Moisés, ed. "δοκιμαζω." Pages 757-59 in vol. 1 of *NIDNTTE*.

———, ed. "πειραζω." Pages 694-703 in vol. 3 of *NIDNTTE*.

LARISA LEVICHEVA, PHD

THEOLOGICAL INTERPRETATION

Since the mid-1990s, interest in the nature and practice of the theological interpretation of Scripture (TIS) has been rekindled, with no final consensus on its particular shape having yet emerged.

Rather than being demarcated by methodological boundaries, the TIS is characterized more by a particular orientation toward Scripture, involving a self-conscious decision to locate oneself and one's interpretations within an ecclesial framework. Theological interpreters of Scripture assume that canonical considerations, doctrinal commitments and concerns, and ecclesial practices may illuminate and deepen the understanding of Scripture, even as Scripture may also illuminate and deepen the understanding of the church's doctrine and practices.

The TIS aims to engender critical reflection on the church's beliefs and practices and to facilitate the church's ongoing formation into the body of the cruciform, resurrected Christ, through whom God continues his mission in the world.

The TIS focuses primarily on the received form of the canonical documents in their literary wholeness (rather than the various aspects of their composition history), affirming that they are already theology in the form of the genre in which they appear. That is, they do not just "contain" theological nuggets waiting to be mined for contemporary purposes. Rather, the writers and editors of the canonical books were already engaged in doing theology within their particular social, cultural, and political contexts.

For example, the four **Gospels** are theologically driven narrative representations of past events trying to persuade their hearers to reorient their lives based on their depictions of Jesus's identity and significance. Familiarity with basic sociocultural and political assumptions, taken for granted in the ANE and in the first-century Jewish and Greco-Roman settings, is important for understanding how the writers and editors of the canonical documents utilized, represented, critiqued, and transformed such assumptions in attempting to shape the audiences into greater conformity to God's purposes.

The TIS assumes that a text may have more than a single meaning intended by the human author. This is because the triune God is assumed to be the ultimate author of Scripture, the one who has been at work before, during, and after the writing and editing of the canonical documents, engendering a wider interpretive framework for their interpretation. This includes the church's canon(s) of Scripture, its doctrinal confessions, and its ecclesial practices, including the history of scriptural interpretation itself. The primary authorial intention of the triune God is to form a people who reflect God's **holy** character as they witness to and participate in his mission to redeem humanity and all **creation**. Within this wider interpretive framework, Scripture passages may have multiple senses that go beyond the purview of their original human writers and hearers.

In practice, the TIS may employ an array of methods that facilitate a fruitful engagement with Scripture. Hence, one cannot simply list every endeavor that might count as the TIS. What follows describes some expressions of reading Scripture theologically under the headings of the particular commitments that undergird them.

The Christian Canon(s) as an Interpretive Framework

Practicing the TIS may involve seeking interconnecting and associated correspondences that span both Testaments.

One might, for example, explore the interconnection between Genesis 1, where God takes great care to create the world as his cosmic temple to become a theatre of his glory, and Revelation 21–22, where all of creation is soaked with God's unmediated holy, life-giving presence or **glory**, making all of it God's now completed holy temple (Rev. 21:11, 22; 22:3-5; cf. 1 Cor. 15:28).

Or one might engage in an ancient form of interpreting the Gospels by highlighting typological correspondences between OT events and Jesus's story, such as the correspondences between the **temptation** of Jesus in the wilderness and that of Israel in the wilderness, as well as Adam's temptation in the garden (Luke 4:1-13; 3:22, 38). Such correspondences signal that Jesus's temptation is part of an overarching narrative in which God, by calling Israel to be his **obedient** son (Hos. 11:1), endeavors to reverse what Adam's disobedience did to his good creation. In Luke's narrative typology, whereas Israel ultimately fails, Jesus becomes the true Son and true human through whom God begins redeeming creation from the consequences of Adam's trespass. When the Christian canon is an interpretive framework for interpreting Luke, this interpretation becomes plausible, whether or not the Gospel's human author intended it. (We should add, however, that Luke and other scriptural authors may well have assumed a similar canonical framework.)

The Nicene Tradition and Doctrinal Discussions as Clarifying Lenses

Scholarship in the modern era tended to assume that doctrinal commitments and concerns obscure biblical interpretation. The TIS acknowledges this as a possibility but maintains that doctrinal commitments sketched out in the Nicene tradition, along with doctrinal discussions carried on within its bounds, may also have a potentially clarifying effect on the interpretation of Scripture. These creedal and doctrinal commitments structure the theological interpreter's most basic convictions as well as the primary questions he or she brings to Scripture.

Refusing to rule out creedal commitments a priori has led some theological interpreters to challenge assertions that NT Christology is inconsistent with the pattern of judgments about Jesus in the Nicene tradition. Using the category of identity, they argue that the pattern of judgments evident throughout the NT sews together Jesus and Israel's God in a shared identity as Lord, reflecting a similar pattern of judgments made about Jesus in the creeds.

Refusing to rule out creedal commitments at the start might also entail bringing a particular orienting concern of a confessional tradition to bear on the interpretive task as a potentially clarifying lens for certain scriptural texts. For example, Wesleyan theological interpreters might orient their approach to Scripture with the primary question of how we and our communities might become a more sanctified people, embodying the holy character of the triune God.

Theological interpreters would insist that these confessional commitments also remain subject to the scriptural texts being interpreted. For example, the TIS would maintain that the bare framework of the Nicene Creed's three articles needs to be filled out and explained with careful readings of a variety of scriptural texts, which then essentially function as commentary on the creed. In this dialogical process, attempting to further explicate the bare bones of the creed's second article on Jesus might entail an engagement of Gospel texts in which Jesus either quotes or alludes to large numbers of OT references to Israel's story that prefigure his actions and teachings in ways that create theologically significant patterns of meaning. Noting this would, in turn, call for a critical reflection on the fact that the creed never explicitly mentions the story of Israel and would underscore the importance of filling out the story of the God of the Nicene tradition with greater reference to the story of Israel.

Christian Practices and Missional Formation as Clarifying Lenses

Since the triune God is, by nature, a sending, missional God, a primary aim of the Christian TIS is to facilitate the ongoing formation of the **church** into the body of Christ, enabling it to participate in the life and mission of God. Hence, the TIS is best carried out in communities open to being shaped by Scripture, whose practices indicate that they intend to lead lives analogous to that of Jesus. The practices of such communities might fit interpreters with lenses that sensitize them to particular missional aspects of scriptural texts.

For example, given the parallel sequence of verbs in Luke's Gospel describing what Jesus does with the bread in the feeding of the multitude (9:10-17) and in the Last Supper (22:19), a **community** that regularly practices the Eucharist might readily discern eucharistic overtones in the former passage when it is read in a worship service where the church is being fed at the Communion table.

Such overtones also connect the Lord's Supper with the physical hunger of the world, reminding the church of God's rich resources and spurring its participation in God's continuing mission, which includes providing food for hungry people. The subsequent missional practice of feeding the hungry, together with a regular celebration of the Eucharist, continues the provision of a clarifying lens that sensitizes interpreters to the potential missional implications of other biblical texts related to God's provision of food for his people.

The TIS is neither methodologically monolithic nor free of disagreements among its practitioners. Theological interpreters use a variety of methods and approaches; they do so within an ecclesial framework of commitments to canon, creeds and doctrinal orientations, and ecclesial practices. If these interpretive endeavors facilitate the church's ongoing formation into the body of the cruciform, **resurrected** Christ, through whom God continues his mission in the world, theological interpreters will have achieved their interpretive aim.

See also Cosmology; Fall, The; Sanctification.

Resources

Billings, J. Todd. *The Word of God for the People of God: An Entryway to the Theological Interpretation of Scripture*. Grand Rapids: Eerdmans, 2010.

Fowl, Stephen E. *Theological Interpretation of Scripture*. Eugene, OR: Cascade Books, 2009.

Green, Joel B. *Practicing Theological Interpretation: Engaging Biblical Texts for Faith and Formation*. Grand Rapids: Baker Academic, 2011.

Treier, Daniel J. *Introducing Theological Interpretation of Scripture: Recovering a Christian Practice*. Grand Rapids: Baker Academic, 2008.

Vanhoozer, Kevin J., ed. *Dictionary for Theological Interpretation of the Bible*. Grand Rapids: Baker Academic, 2005.

ANDY JOHNSON, PHD

TITLES OF JESUS

Hebrews 1:4 declares that Jesus is "as much superior to the angels as the name he has inherited is superior to theirs" (NIV). This chapter proceeds to identify, quoting OT texts, seven of the titles he bears. Four are explicit: Son of God (v. 5), Firstborn (v. 6), God (v. 8), and Lord (v. 10). Three are implicit: King (v. 8), **Messiah** (v. 9), and Creator (v. 10). This list is not exclusive but illustrative. More than one hundred explicit titles are attributed to Jesus in the Bible. These include the following four selections.

Savior

This title is used worldwide throughout all branches of the Christian **church** today. It is often coupled with another title, confessing Jesus as Lord and **Savior**.

The title "Savior" has strong biblical foundations. At his birth, heavenly messengers announced, "To you is born this day in the city of David a Savior, who is the Messiah, the Lord" (Luke 2:11, NRSV). The apostle John asserted, "And we have seen and testify that the Father has sent his Son to be the Savior of the world" (1 John 4:14, NIV). Fellow villagers of the woman whom Jesus met at the well of Jacob in Samaria declared, "We know that this man really is the Savior of the world" (John 4:42, NIV).

The name "Jesus," which means "God saves," is closely linked to this title. Prior to the birth of the Christ child, Joseph is told that Mary "will give birth to a son, and you are to give him the name Jesus, because he will save his people from their sins" (Matt. 1:21, NIV).

The title "**Savior**" and the name "Jesus" contribute significantly to the doctrine of salvation in Wesleyan theology. They undergird the proclamation that "there is salvation in no one else, for there is no other name under heaven given among mortals by which we must be saved" (Acts 4:12, NRSV).

Lord

This title, which is used globally in the twenty-first century, has a significant role in the Christian faith.

Biblical scholars have concluded that the declaration "Jesus is Lord" constituted one of the earliest **confessions** of the faith. Paul asserts, "If you confess with your lips that Jesus is Lord and **believe** in your heart that God raised him from the dead, you will be saved. For one believes with the heart and so is justified, and one confesses with the mouth and so is saved" (Rom. 10:9-10, NRSV). To paraphrase, the confession "Jesus is Lord," coupled with genuine **faith**, is the basis of salvation.

The Roman emperor required all subjects, as a testimony of their allegiance, to declare, "Caesar is Lord!" This brought believers in the first centuries of the Christian **church** into direct conflict with the government. One of those put to death for refusing to declare Caesar (rather than Jesus) as Lord was Polycarp, a bishop of Asia Minor. According to a text from the second century, after arresting the aged bishop, the provincial governor pressed him hard and said,

"Swear by Caesar, deny Christ, and I will release you."

[Polycarp responded,] "For eighty-six years I have been his servant, and he has done me no wrong. How then can I blaspheme my Lord who saved me?"

[When the governor persisted, Polycarp further declared,] "You vainly suppose that I will swear by Caesar; hear me plainly, I am a Christian." (*Mart. Pol.* 9.3–10.1, AT)

Because of his commitment to the lordship of Jesus in his life and his refusal to swear allegiance to Caesar in the manner prescribed, Polycarp was burned to death.

The confession of Jesus as Lord is a powerful declaration, particularly in the face of other (worldly) claims to power and sovereignty. The final affirmation of Scripture declares that Jesus is the "KING OF KINGS AND LORD OF LORDS" (Rev. 19:16, NIV).

Son of God

The declaration "Jesus is the Son of God" also constituted one of the earliest confessions of the Christian church. John states, "Whoever confesses that Jesus is the Son of God, God abides in him, and he in God" (1 John 4:15, NKJV). In other words, a personal, intimate, and living relationship with God is based on the acknowledgment that "Jesus is the Son of God." Hebrews 4:14 exhorts us, "Therefore, since we have a great high priest who has passed through the heavens, Jesus the Son of God, let us hold fast our confession" (NASB).

The **Gospel** writers make extensive usage of this title. **Mark** introduces his account of Jesus's life and ministry with these words: "The beginning of the good news about Jesus the Messiah, the Son of God" (Mark 1:1, NIV). **Matthew**, Mark, and **Luke** all report that at Jesus's baptism, a voice from heaven declared, "This is [You are] my Son, whom I **love**" (Matt. 3:17; Mark 1:11; Luke 3:22, NIV). This title describes Jesus's special relationship with God the Father.

At the climax of the Gospel narrative, when Jesus asked his disciples, "Who do you say I am?" (Matt. 16:15, NIV), Peter answered, "You are the Messiah, the Son of the living God" (v. 16, NIV). At the end of Jesus's life, we find another witness: "When the centurion, who stood there in front of Jesus, saw how he died, he said, 'Surely this man was the Son of God!'" (Mark 15:39, NIV).

For John, this title represents the key to believing in Jesus and experiencing eternal life. John describes the purpose for his Gospel in these words: "These are written that you may believe that Jesus is the Messiah, the Son of

God, and that by believing you may have life in his name" (20:31, NIV). He describes the purpose for 1 John in a parallel statement: "I write these things to you who believe in the name of the Son of God so that you may know that you have eternal life" (5:13, NIV).

Christ (Messiah)

This is the most frequently used title, both historically and globally. So commonplace is the phrase "Jesus Christ" that many believers have lost sight of its meaning.

Christos is a Greek term meaning "anointed one" (see Ps. 2:2 quoted in Acts 4:26). *Māšîaḥ*, or "messiah," is the corresponding Hebrew term, also meaning "anointed one." In two texts, John in his Gospel equates these Hebrew and Greek terms: "The first thing Andrew did was to find his brother Simon and tell him, 'We have found the Messiah' (that is, the Christ)" (1:41, NIV); "The woman said, 'I know that Messiah' (called Christ) 'is coming'" (4:25, NIV). In translations the two terms are interchangeable.

To name Jesus as "Christ" is to refer to him as the Messiah. Thus this title invokes all the messianic prophecies of the OT, declaring them fulfilled in Jesus as the Christ. While others may be described as anointed, Jesus is the Anointed One. About the crucifixion, Luke in his Gospel reports, "The people stood watching, and the rulers even sneered at him. They said, 'He saved others; let him save himself if he is God's Messiah, the Chosen One'" (23:35, NIV).

We read concerning John the Baptist, "He did not fail to confess, but confessed freely, 'I am not the Messiah'" (John 1:20, NIV). Several times, Jesus was asked whether he was the Christ, the Messiah. "The Jews . . . gathered around him, saying, 'How long will you keep us in suspense? If you are the Messiah, tell us plainly.' Jesus answered, 'I did tell you, but you do not believe'" (10:24-25, NIV). The council of elders pressed Jesus on this issue during his trial: "'If you are the Messiah,' they said, 'tell us.'" Again "Jesus answered, 'If I tell you, you will not believe me'" (Luke 22:67, NIV). Matthew reports in his Gospel, "Then the high priest said to him, 'I order you to tell us under oath before the living God whether you are the Messiah, the Son of God.' Jesus said to him in reply, 'You have said so.'" (26:63-64, NABRE).

Paul uses the title "Christ" more than 350 times in his thirteen Epistles, most often in the same ways we use it today: as a term interchangeable with "Jesus," referring to our Lord as either Christ or Jesus, and as a term alongside "Jesus," in either order, as Jesus Christ or Christ Jesus.

"Christ" is the most frequently used title in the NT, occurring more than 500 times. This level of frequency signifies its importance in the Bible. It also suggests its continuing importance for us as Christian believers in the twenty-first century.

These four titles of Jesus were selected on the basis of their importance in the NT and in the contemporary Christian church globally. Each is deserving of more in-depth study. And there are many more than these four awaiting our attention. No one title is adequate to express the fullness of our Lord and Savior. Each contributes to a more complete understanding and appreciation of his person and/or ministry.

See also Gospel; Jesus's Victory over Sin and Death.

Resource

The Martyrdom of Polycarb. In vol. 2 of *The Apostolic Fathers*. Translated by Kirsopp Lake. 2 vols. Loeb Classical Library. 1913. Reprint, Cambridge, MA: Harvard University Press, 1959.

WAYNE MCCOWN, PHD

TORAH (LAW, INSTRUCTION)

Divine instructions are central to the vision of Israelite religion described in the Hebrew Bible, or Old Testament, particularly in the Pentateuch. These divine instructions are regularly formulated in legal language and, taken together with their accompanying narratives, came to be known early in Jewish tradition and, subsequently, in Christianity as "Law" or "Torah" (teaching). Modern critical scholarship has demonstrated that there are three originally independent legal collections in the Pentateuch: the Elohistic covenant collection (Exod. 20:23–23:19, 33), the Priestly laws (scattered across Exod., Lev., and Num.), and the Deuteronomic laws (primarily in Deut. 12–26).

The larger narrative contexts in which these pentateuchal laws appear—and especially the characterization of the Deity within them—clarify the legal conceptualization of the religion they espouse: Yahweh, the God of Israel, is a great king who rules over his people on earth. This divine-human relationship is informed by ANE models of human kingship and its legal instruments (e.g., laws and treaties). It is the divine-human relationship defined by royal hierarchy (i.e., between sovereign and subject) that justifies the Deity's commands and demanded loyalties (e.g., Deut. 6:5).

Most significant for understanding the Pentateuch's theological notions of law are its claims regarding the purpose of divine legislation, the receptivity of Yahweh's subjects to his commands, and Yahweh's preparation of his people for keeping his laws. The pentateuchal Priestly source presents the fulfillment of the divine commands as the requisite for Yahweh's presence in the world and, particularly, in the midst of Israel. In the Priestly view, Yahweh did not create the world as a place where he himself intended to dwell (Gen. 1:1–2:4*a*). The world is thus not, of itself, **holy** or pure—qualities that Yahweh required for his environs (Exod. 29:42-46; Lev. 4; 16).

When Yahweh chose to inhabit the world, the specific locale and environs where he would reside required modifications. These modifications included the construction and inauguration of the sanctuary (according to Yahweh's detailed specifications), its proper staffing (priests and Levites) and operation (the sacrificial cult), and its ongoing maintenance (purification). Also included were specific behavioral requirements for the Israelite laypeople who would dwell in close proximity to Yahweh. In each of these cases, **obedience** to Yahweh's laws was presented as a concrete expression of hospitality toward the Deity who desired to live among his people, a hospitality that could overcome, at least to the extent necessary for their proximity, the fundamental differences between Yahweh and his created world.

If in Priestly texts the laws are properly for Yahweh's benefit, in the Deuteronomic perspective they are explicitly meant to benefit Israel. This claim appears repeatedly in Deuteronomy (4:1; 5:33; 6:24; 8:1, 3; 16:20; 30:16, 19). Deuteronomy 28:1-14 enumerates the specific blessings that the Israelites would enjoy if they were obedient to Yahweh's commands. These blessings included **land**, progeny, health, wealth, fertility, protection, and preeminence among the nations (cf. Exod. 23:20-33). Moreover, failure to keep Yahweh's laws would put the Israelites in jeopardy of calamity, plague, loss of land, enslavement, and utter destruction (Deut. 28:15-68). According to 4:6-8, the divine laws were not only proof of Yahweh's commitment to Israel but also a marker of Israel's **wisdom** that would be recognized as such by other nations.

Pentateuchal texts present conflicting views of Israel's receptivity to the divine commands. The Priestly source has a primarily optimistic perspective, which corresponds well with its royal characterization of Yahweh. When the Deity gives a command, it is assumed that his subjects will obey. On the occasion that Israel did not heed, it was assumed that a specific reason motivated their response. For example, in Exodus 6:9, it was "because of their exhaustion and heavy labor" that the Israelites failed to listen to Moses's prophetic message (AT). Had they not been so encumbered, they would have been receptive. In this view, then, Israel was well suited to a legal religion.

In the Deuteronomic perspective, by contrast, the Israelites were highly rebellious and thus ill matched to Yahweh's expectations for them. For example, in Deuteronomy 9:24, Moses scolded the Israelites for their unrelenting rebellion (cf. 9:7). Israel is also characterized repeatedly in the Deuteronomic source as a "stiff-necked people" (9:6, 13, NIV; cf. 10:16; 31:27) who, even after taming their obstinacy, must ever stand on guard against reverting to their former ways (6:10-15; 8:12-14).

Yet in each text that depicts Yahweh's revelation of law, Yahweh actively worked to facilitate the Israelites' successful obedience to his commands. In response to the Israelites' exhaustion reported in the Priestly source, Yahweh provided the Israelites respite from their labor (Exod. 10:21-23), after which they were again dutifully responsive to his commands (12:28). Moreover,

392 · TORAH (LAW, INSTRUCTION)

should the Israelites rebel, the Priestly authors imagined a series of punishments meant to induce them to obey once again (Lev. 26:14-45). In the Elohistic source, prior to communicating his laws to Moses, Yahweh gave the Israelites a onetime experience of the mechanics of revelation. He did so in order that the Israelites might never **sin** because they doubted the divine origin of the commands that Moses claimed came from the Deity (Exod. 19:9*a*; 20:20).

Even more striking is the Deuteronomic characterization of Yahweh's facilitation of Israel's obedience. In its reimagination of the Israelite wilderness era, Deuteronomy 8:2-5 portrays this forty-year sojourn not as a period of *punishment* for the Exodus generation (cf. Num. 14:22-23, 29-34) but as a period of *training in obedience*. The image of Yahweh in this text is parental and benevolent. He undertook a program of disciplinary preparation so that the Israelites would be best positioned to successfully obey when Moses finally conveyed the laws to them (Deut. 1:5; 5:31).

To this end, Yahweh induced hunger in the Israelites and then gave them specific instructions for satiating it (cf. Exod. 16:4-5, 26-30). He thus taught Israel "that a human does not live by bread alone but by every issuance of Yahweh's command" (Deut. 8:3, AT). To make this extended catechesis possible, and in so doing to demonstrate his commitment to his people, Yahweh miraculously sustained the Israelites across their forty-year wilderness sojourn. He ensured that the peoples' clothing and footwear were extraordinarily durable. He caused them to enjoy exceptional health. He assured that they were never in want (2:7; 8:4; 29:4).

As the foregoing discussion suggests, there is an integral connection between the pentateuchal laws and the narratives in which they are embedded. Indeed, these narratives offer essential theological contextualization for the laws and their imagined role in ancient Israelite society. The distinctive religious visions expressed in each of these works—and the particular legal perspectives that they advance—also help to clarify what these texts are, namely, constructive theological projects. As such, these texts tend to compete with each other, not least because their differing details stand unreconciled in the compiled Pentateuch.

This competition apparently once existed only or primarily in the marketplace of ideas, a claim that is consistent with the lack of extrabiblical evidence for the real practice of pentateuchal law in ancient Israel or Judah. Yet it is clear that pentateuchal laws came to be regarded as normative for Jewish life sometime during the Second Temple period. An early example of harmonistic legal exegesis that suggests the real practice of pentateuchal laws appears in 2 Chronicles 35:13. This verse describes the specific procedure of the Passover observance of the Judean king Josiah. It states that the cultic officials "boiled the Passover in fire, *according to the rule*" (AT, emphasis added).

This verse combines the conflicting legal claims found in Deuteronomy 16:7 and Exodus 12:9. The former verse commands Israel to *boil* the Passover sacrifice, but the latter instructs Israel *not* to boil it but to roast it *in fire*. The Chronicler sought a single practice ("according to the rule") from these two laws and did so by drawing partially from each.

Examples of such legal harmonization proliferate in early Jewish texts, sometimes in combination with additional interpretive interventions. For example, 4Q394, a compendium of halakhic perspectives found at Qumran, deliberately harmonizes the instructions concerning the place of sacrifice in Leviticus 17 and Deuteronomy 12. It also updates and specifies their geographical claims to match its contemporary context. While the two texts agree that there should be a single site for Israelite sacrifice, they refer to this site in different ways. Leviticus 17 refers to the place of sacrifice as the tent of meeting at the center of the Israelite camp (vv. 3-4, 6, 9). Deuteronomy 12, by contrast, refers to "the place that Yahweh (your God) will choose (from among all your tribes) to set his name" (vv. 5, 11, 14, 18, 21, 26). Neither text designates a specific locale for its cultic site, and in the case of Leviticus 17, the camp and sanctuary are intentionally mobile. Qumran text 4Q394 equates "the place that Yahweh will choose" in Deuteronomy 12 with the Israelite camp in Leviticus 17 and identifies these locations as **Jerusalem**. It further clarifies that the "tent of meeting" in Leviticus 17 refers to the Jerusalem temple, an equation that may already appear in Chronicles (e.g., 2 Chron. 24:6; cf. 5:5). With 4Q394's harmonization, any potential discrepancy concerning the cult sites described in Leviticus 17 and Deuteronomy 12 is resolved. At the same time, with their references to Jerusalem, these texts' claims were made relevant to the contemporary context of the 4Q394 author.

The characteristic presentation of laws embedded in narratives in the Pentateuch created already in antiquity a perception of these narratives as "instruction" (*tôrâ*) alongside the laws. In some cases, early Jewish authors rewrote pentateuchal narratives to cast their characters in a more positive light, especially in relation to legal observance.

The *Genesis Apocryphon* from Qumran contains a rewritten version of the wife-sister stories of Abraham and Sarah in Genesis 12 and 20 (cols. 19-20). In its retelling, Abraham could not be seen as selling Sarah to the Egyptian king, as might be construed from Genesis 12:16. The *Genesis Apocryphon* also depicts Abraham as a pious man of prayer who pleaded at length with God for Sarah's safe return. Scrubbed of his questionable behavior and credited with acts of piety, Abraham is cast as a figure worthy of emulation.

The authors of the early Jewish book of *Jubilees*, uncomfortable with the revelation of law only once the Israelites arrived at Sinai, inserted Sinai legislation into earlier pentateuchal narratives and associated the laws with important Jewish ancestors. For example, *Jubilees* reports that Noah followed sacrificial rules that, in the Pentateuch, were only later revealed at Sinai (6:2-3; 7:3-5). Noah and his family, as well as the angels before him and the patriarchs after him, also observed Shavuot (the Feast of Weeks) (6:17-19). *Jubilees* presents Abraham as the first observer of Sukkot (the Feast of Tabernacles) (15:2) and Jacob as the first observer of Yom Kippur (the Day of Atonement) (34:12-13). In each of these cases, the pentateuchal laws were understood to be normative for Jewish practice. Written into the distant past, they were also related to the heroes of Israel's history. Through such chronological rearrangement, the Israelite ancestors were rendered celebrated figures of legal observance, and a timeless quality was suggested for the Torah as a whole.

See also Cosmology; Creation; Sacred Persons; Sacred Space; Sacred Times; Sacrificial System.

Resources

Blum, Erhard. *Studien zur Komposition des Pentateuch*. Beihefte zur Zeitschrift für die alttestamentliche Wissenschaft 189. Berlin: Walter de Gruyter, 1990.

Chavel, Simḥah (Simeon). "The Legal Literature of the Hebrew Bible." Pages 227-72 in vol. 1 of *The Literature of the Hebrew Bible: Introductions and Studies*. Edited by Zipora Talshir. 2 vols. Jerusalem: Yad Ben-Zvi Press, 2011 (in Hebrew).

Fishbane, Michael. *Biblical Interpretation in Ancient Israel*. Oxford, UK: Clarendon Press, 1985.

Knohl, Israel. *The Sanctuary of Silence: The Priestly Torah and the Holiness School*. Translated by Jackie Feldman and Peretz Rodman. Minneapolis: Fortress Press, 1995.

Lohfink, Norbert. *Theology of the Pentateuch: Themes of the Priestly Narrative and Deuteronomy*. Translated by Linda M. Maloney. Edinburgh: T and T Clark, 1994.

Nihan, Christophe. *From Priestly Torah to Pentateuch: A Study in the Composition of the Book of Leviticus*. FAT 2.25. Tübingen, DEU: Mohr Siebeck, 2007.

Stackert, Jeffrey. *A Prophet like Moses: Prophecy, Law, and Israelite Religion*. New York: Oxford University Press, 2014.

———. *Rewriting the Torah: Literary Revision in Deuteronomy and the Holiness Legislation*. FAT 52. Tübingen, DEU: Mohr Siebeck, 2007.

JEFFREY STACKERT, PHD

Ww

WESLEYAN HERMENEUTICS

The term "Wesleyan hermeneutics" refers not only to biblical interpretation that can be labeled Wesleyan but also to an exegetical form of theological reflection set within a Wesleyan (or Methodist) way of life. To the extent that Wesleyan hermeneutics is connected to the hermeneutics of John Wesley, Wesleyan hermeneutics evinces both continuity and discontinuity with Methodism's founder. Either way, Wesleyan hermeneutics appropriates from Wesley, borrowing, modifying, and discarding elements of his hermeneutics based on the different aims and assumptions that have arisen about Scripture and theology since the eighteenth century when Wesley lived.

Generally, hermeneutics has to do with the interpretation of texts, but recently theologians and biblical scholars have widened the hermeneutical conversation to include "theological hermeneutics," "theological exegesis," and "**theological interpretation**." These terms, roughly synonymous, locate hermeneutics in a moment when academic theology and biblical studies, long parted and developing along different paths, have begun to reintegrate. This is not interdisciplinarity, since theological hermeneutics does not assume the integrity of biblical studies and systematic theology as discreet disciplines. Rather, theological hermeneutics revises theology's aims and practice and relocates theology within the **church** as its primary context. Theological hermeneutics in this sense is not an intermediate step between biblical exegesis and systematic theology; it is doing theology through biblical interpretation, set within the life and **faith** of the church.

Theological hermeneutics reads the Bible as Scripture. Regarding the church as the native context of the Bible, theological hermeneutics brings creedal, ethical, and sacramental commitments to interpretation. It does not discount "critical" strategies like those found in academia, but it assumes that Christian concerns discipline the use of these strategies. Neither is theological hermeneutics a method like that a systematic theologian might propose. Instead, it is a living interaction with the biblical text within the Christian tradition that has no clear starting point and whose end is not to execute a methodology, but to know God.

From Wesley to Wesleyans

To speak of Wesleyan hermeneutics today entails both continuity and discontinuity with John Wesley. Those who bear the name "Wesleyan" are following a trajectory Wesley initiated. However, over time the Wesleyan tradition has evolved in ways its founder could not have anticipated, making differences inevitable between Wesley and Wesleyans. Similarly, the advent of the modern university, where the present division of academic disciplines solidified—as well as the changing aims, assumptions, and practices of biblical interpretation and theology that context fosters—contributed to the gap between modern-day Wesleyans and their founding father.

This gap is reflected in how Wesleyan scholars approach Wesley's writings. Since Albert Outler, scholars have tended to read Wesley through the lenses of either systematic theology or historical studies. In the first case, theologians distill essential doctrines from Wesley's occasional writings, systematize them, and undergird them with a theological method (e.g., the "Wesleyan quadrilateral"). In the second case, historians sift Wesley's writings to uncover their sources, trace the pedigrees of successive editions of those writings, and reconstruct the contextual background of their composition. Both ventures have their strengths, but neither results in a theological practice similar to Wesley's.

However, the gap between Wesley and Wesleyans is also reflected in how modern scholarship has changed our regard for the Bible as Scripture and what we find within it. Whereas Wesley accepted Scripture in the form he received it within the Church of England, modern scholarship has been more archaeological, reading through the Bible in search of its sources in antiquity. More recently, theorists have seen the Bible as the site of play for the reader's subjectivity. Neither approach reads the Bible as Scripture, since the Bible is not taken at face value as the text through which God shapes the life and faith of the church. Additionally, Wesley assumed **justification** by faith was the center of the Bible's message of salvation. Today, justification is relegated to a Pauline teaching, with Paul's voice counted as one among many in the Bible, and the meaning of justification has been revised in the light of "new perspective" scholarship. Wesleyan hermeneutics must account for these changes.

One facet of theological hermeneutics is its interest in premodern forms of theological reflection, especially of the exegetical, nonscholastic variety, such as John Wesley's. To begin with, then, instead of reading Wesley through the agendas of systematic theology or historical studies, Wesley-

WESLEYAN HERMENEUTICS · 397

ans interested in hermeneutics might approach their founder's writings with the purpose of learning the craft of theological hermeneutics from Wesley. While studying and appropriating what they find, they nurture an awareness of what separates them from Wesley but carry forward the tradition in a way that can still be called Wesleyan. Within a tradition, adherents become practitioners when they learn the skills necessary to extend the tradition over time, navigating problems that could threaten to terminate the tradition but that could also become opportunities to break new ground. Reading Wesley this way allows his hermeneutics to emerge more on its own terms: we see that for Wesley, reading Scripture is theology.

The next step is to learn from Wesley the practice of reading Scripture.

Wesleyan Reading Practices

Theological hermeneutics highlights and explores reading practices that bridge naturally with Wesley's hermeneutics, particularly the literal sense, ruled reading, and the unity of Scripture.

Hermeneutics today differs from that of Wesley and his time because it sees meaning not as the property of the text but as the result of the interaction of at least three elements: reader, text, and context. In the end it might come to the same point—to know and **love** God through **holy** living—but the difference between textual property in Wesley's day and the production of meaning in our own must be grasped by those who wish to develop a Wesleyan hermeneutics. This is especially so if readers want continuity with John Wesley that accounts for differences between his context and theirs. For Wesleyans the work of appropriation can begin here.

Wesley was committed to the literal sense of Scripture, which for him was found in the words on the page, neither "behind" the text in the history of its composition nor "before" the text in the subjectivity of the reader. He would depart from the literal sense into a "spiritual" sense when a literal interpretation threatened to contradict Christian confession or another part of Scripture or when the interpretation resulted in an absurdity. But the literal sense was more than the words on the page for Wesley. The literal sense was also the soteriological sense of Scripture, because for Wesley every part of the Bible could be brought to bear on one's salvation. The literal sense was the instrument through which God addressed readers, transfiguring their identities from slaves to **sin** to children of God.

Contemporary hermeneutics views the literal sense formally, as a type of reading or interaction with Scripture, or how a community customarily reads. It is not a property of the Bible but the result produced by reader, text, and context acting upon one another through the interpretive process. What stands as the literal reading for one community might not be the same for another. Consider how a contemporary biblical scholar might read a given passage of Scripture differently than Wesley did. But texts cannot mean just anything. The language on the page of the text, the context in which a reader approaches the text, the reader's knowledge base—all place limits on the meaning of a text. Within these circumstances, the literal sense is the soteriological way Wesleyans read the Bible. In other words, Wesleyans read the Bible to come to know and love the God revealed through its pages and to become more like him through the work of the **Holy Spirit**.

Wesley could see Scripture's message of salvation because he read the Bible through the analogy of faith. The analogy of faith was what he called the "grand scheme of doctrine" that ran through Scripture from beginning to end. It was shorthand for the message of salvation, or *ordo salutis*: original sin, justification by faith, **sanctification**, and Christian perfection. The analogy of faith guided Wesley's reading of Scripture and structured how he talked about the message of salvation when he would expound on it. Both of these aspects of the analogy of faith have been revived in contemporary hermeneutics under the concept of "ruled reading."

The "rule" in a ruled reading is the logic or grammar by which the reader reads; it is the reader's assumption about how the text works within its own and the reader's context. Although typically the reader assumes this rule or grammar, he or she can make it explicit when required. Consider how grammar governs our use of language every day, but we rarely talk about grammar. Only when we need to, do we make our knowledge of grammar explicit. For Wesley, the analogy of faith was the rule by which he read Scripture. It was also the logic or grammar that guided how he talked about his faith. He could spell out the analogy of faith, but he always assumed it in his theological hermeneutics.

In hermeneutics today, many regard ruled readings as standard for the theological interpretation of the Bible. Research has shown how early Christians such as Origen, Irenaeus, and Augustine all appealed to the rule of faith to guide what they took to be the faithful interpretation of Scripture. The rule, or canon, of faith was an early Trinitarian articulation of Christian faith similar to the Nicene and Apostles' Creeds. It functioned as a "hypothesis" or outline of the plot of Scripture, as well as a grammar that shaped Christian speech. Wesley's analogy of faith functions the same way as the old rule of faith, although its articulation reflects his Protestant heritage of the justification of the individual before God.

Through the analogy of faith and the literal sense, Wesley saw Scripture as a unified whole, or its "general tenor." The general tenor included both the Bible's canonical coherence from Genesis to Revelation and the soteriological content of that coherence. The analogy of faith revealed the general tenor of Scripture, with its message of salvation, communicated from **creation** to new creation. One aspect of this unity was Wesley's use of typology. Typology allowed Wesley, following Christian tradition, to see OT theophanies as preincarnate appearances of Christ. In fact, for Wesley the OT was replete with "types" of Christ, whether foreshadowings fully revealed in Christ, or **prophecies** Christ later fulfilled. Typology also permitted Wesley to understand himself and other Christians as addressed by the Bible and identified by its markers. Methodists were children of God and joint heirs with Christ, as the Scriptures taught.

Modern scholarship stresses diversity in the Bible over unity, which is one reason Wesleyan hermeneutics today will have to appropriate from Wesley, not repeat him. For instance, one place contemporary biblical studies might press the Wesleyan interpreter to depart from Wesley is over the centrality of justification by faith. In line with his Protestant heritage, Wesley's understanding of justification, reflected in the analogy of faith, gave a Pauline flavor to his hermeneutics. Today, on the one hand, the traditional Protestant understanding of justification has been challenged by recent scholarship; and on the other hand, the different voices of Scripture are now allowed to speak for themselves, without the Pauline filter. Paul's view of salvation may not be that of the Fourth Gospel or 1 Peter, and these other voices should be heard on their own terms.

Due to these changes in our understanding of the Bible, Wesley's analogy of faith might now appear too narrow, privileging as it does the Pauline terminology of justification. Recent recoveries of the rule of faith, mentioned above, have led scholars to suggest the Nicene Creed as a viable grammar of the faith that can both structure Christian language and rule biblical interpretation. As an ecumenical statement about the Christian faith, the creed casts a wide net that encompasses the particular emphases of many Christian traditions, the Wesleyan tradition included, and is just as soteriological as Wesley's analogy of faith, only it sets salvation within the church's confession of the Father, Son, and Holy Spirit.

We must also revise what we mean by the unity of Scripture. For Wesley, the unity of Scripture was a self-evident property of the Bible. Today we would say the analogy of faith, as a hypothesis of Scripture's essential logic, allowed him to perceive the unity of Scripture. Unity in this sense emerges from reading the Bible a certain way, and this reading assumes the canonical form of the Bible as it has been handed down in the church. Historical-critical and reader-oriented approaches have their place, but the final form of the received text must be respected for the Bible to be read as Scripture. The canonical form of the Bible—the particular books that compose it, arranged as they are—contributes to the conception of unity. But the true point of unity in the Bible is theological: Scripture everywhere attests to the same God. Christian interpretation from its earliest days read Israel's Scriptures typologically, seeing the preincarnate Christ appearing in Israel's past. The church's clear confession of the Trinity came after the biblical canon was basically complete, but that confession stems from a line of Christian belief already reflected in the NT. The same Christians who confess this one God also read the Bible as Scripture, and it is this same God, met through interpretation, which unifies Scripture. Unity is a theological reading of the Bible and a theological statement about its nature as Scripture in the church.

The Wesleyan Reader

In *The Character of a Methodist*, Wesley claimed it is not a particular opinion or doctrine that defines Methodists. It is the love of God shed abroad in the heart—a love the Methodist reciprocates by loving God completely and loving neighbor as self. This end is also the beginning for Wesleyan hermeneutics, and what follows are suggested characteristics that further flesh out the Wesleyan identity.

One characteristic is that the Wesleyan reader is reading the Bible soteriologically, reading to know and love God. Interpreting Scripture will take the reader (or the community of readers) through the spectrum of salvation from sin, to adoption as children of God, and on to entire sanctification. The Wesleyan identity is rooted in and shaped by this commitment, because it is ultimately a commitment to the God revealed through Scripture: the Father, the Son, and the Holy Spirit. And since this Trinitarian God is revealed through Jesus, the filial identity of Wesleyans is encompassed and nourished within Jesus's own divine-human identity as revealed in Scripture. Whether or not Wesleyans continue to privilege justification by faith as the preeminent expression of salvation in Scripture, it is Christ and the Trinity Christ reveals that determine the identity of the Wesleyan interpreter through the soteriological interpretation of the Bible.

Closely related to this characteristic is theological interpretation as a means of **grace**. When interpreting Scripture, the reader opens to the sanctifying work of the Holy Spirit, who reinterprets the reader's identity from **slave** to sin to child of God. If, as Wesley knew, the **gospel** demands response from the reader, and if meaning arises dynamically from the interaction of reader, text, and context, then the true meaning of Scripture is the life of the Wesleyan reader. To put it differently, the meaning of Scripture that arises through its interpretation is not only, or even primarily, "exegesis" as we often think of it but rather the **holiness** of the interpreter's life. Regarding theological hermeneutics as a means of grace, the Wesleyan reader seeks out holiness as the meaning of Scripture.

If theological interpretation is a means of grace, then it is set within the web of practices by which Christians are sanctified, the foremost of which are the sacraments, and therefore the proper context of Wesleyan hermeneutics is the church. Wesley did not reflect much on what we would call ecclesiology, but even though he often cast his doctrine of salvation in mostly individual terms, he assumed a rich ecclesial life in his theology and tried to pass on to Wesleyans communal structures and practices to frame their life as "real Christians." The Christian Bible arises from the church and in turn impacts the life of the church through its ongoing interpretation. Within this context Wesleyan hermeneutics is not merely a concept but also a concrete practice within a Wesleyan way of life.

This article offers a baseline of issues Wesleyan hermeneutics today should address. Along with the issues of continuity and discontinuity between Wesley and Wesleyans, we can also expect Wesleyan hermeneutics to vary between different Wesleyan traditions that have emerged since Wesley's day. United Methodists and Free Methodists, for example, doubtless will have peculiarities that distinguish them from one another. Granting these distinctions, to the extent that the heirs of John Wesley practice theological interpretation to know and love God through holy living, their hermeneutics can be labeled accurately as Wesleyan.

Resources
Callen, Barry L., and Richard P. Thompson, eds. *Reading the Bible in Wesleyan Ways: Some Constructive Proposals*. Kansas City: Beacon Hill Press of Kansas City, 2004.

Green, Joel B. *Reading Scripture as Wesleyans*. Nashville: Abingdon Press, 2010.

Green, Joel B., and David F. Watson, eds. *Wesley, Wesleyans, and Reading Bible as Scripture*. Waco, TX: Baylor University Press, 2012.

Koskie, Steven J., Jr. *Reading the Way to Heaven: A Wesleyan Theological Hermeneutic of Scripture*. Journal of Theological Interpretation Supplement 8. Warsaw, IN: Eisenbrauns, 2014.

Wesley, John. *The Character of a Methodist*. Pages 30-46 in vol. 9 of *The Bicentennial Edition of the Works of John Wesley*. Nashville: Abingdon Press, 1989.

STEVEN J. KOSKIE, PHD

WILDERNESS, THEOLOGY OF

Applicable terms appear more than four hundred times throughout the Old and New Testaments, establishing "wilderness" as a dominant motif and theological concept: ḥārābâ, yĕšîmôn, 'ărābâ, ṣiyâ, midbār, erēmos, and erēmia.

Wilderness is "cultural space." A "marginalized and intermediary, semi-natural space that is regarded as distanced or marginalized with regard to an inhabited or 'home' region, and which is ascribed cultural meanings and functions" (Feldt 2015a, 165). It was ambiguous in ANE minds—not only inimical and chaotic but also necessary and ripe with opportunity. It was both positive and negative.

In Scripture, wilderness manifests a duality, referring to particular regions in and around Syro-Palestine and a specific era of Israel's history—the wilderness wandering. It is associated with punishment and **judgment** as well as formation, intimacy, and **glory**.

The Duality of the Wilderness

The dominant paradigm for the duality of the wilderness begins in Exodus. At the burning bush, Yahweh revealed that Moses would lead Israel into the wilderness to worship him (3:18-19). Exodus 19 recounts the fulfillment. Yet, immediately before Israel arrived at Sinai, it succumbed to the difficulties, erroneously perceiving the wilderness as a place of death. This behavior is repeated after Israel's departure and climaxes with overt rebellion and the subsequent death of a generation (Num. 13–14). Thus the actions and attitudes of a generation transformed a place of intimacy and encounter into one defined equally by death and judgment.

This memory casts a long shadow across the OT. The wilderness was a time of provision, testing, and judgment (Deut. 8–9), and this memory was revisited strategically as a warning not to succumb to similar temptations and test God (Neh. 9:13-21). Paul (1 Cor. 10:1-13) and the writer to the Hebrews (Heb. 3:7-19) later employed this logic.

The duality of the wilderness was also personalized. Hagar was told that her and her son would be the recipient of a great blessing (Gen. 16), which was fulfilled after they were expelled from Abraham's household (21:14-21). The wilderness was David's refuge from Saul and Absalom, as well as the locus of consolidating his power before assuming the throne (1 Sam. 23–25; 2 Sam. 15). Elijah also fled to the wilderness, only to be encouraged by a personal encounter with Yahweh (1 Kings 19). Thus it was a place of personal banishment and isolation as well as salvation and revitalization.

Within the prophetic corpus, the wilderness would be the place of death for Israel's historic enemies (Ezek. 29:5-7; Joel 3:19) as well as the locus of Israel's redemption (Hos. 2:14). Yet most distinctive is the use of the wilderness in describing eschatological glory. Isaiah inverted traditional connotations to highlight future glory. The wilderness would yield a harvest (Isa. 32:14-15) and the dry land would blossom and overflow with water (ch. 35). The wilderness would testify to Israel's return from exile (40:3). Most powerfully, the wilderness would become like Eden (51:3).

Elements of the wilderness tradition were adopted in the NT. Stephen invoked elements in his diatribe against the religious elite (Acts 7). The most significant development of the concept was its association with the **gospel**. John the Baptist preached in the wilderness in preparation for the Messiah. Jesus went into the wilderness to be tempted, which signified it as a necessary locus of isolation and preparation (Matt. 4:1-11; Mark 1:12-13; Luke 4:1-13). A "return to the wilderness" was necessary for the reestablishment of Israel's broken relationship. Finally, Jesus himself recounted the manna to highlight its ultimate insignificance and its anticipation of Christ's death (John 6:30-59).

Constructing a Theology of Wilderness

Depending on a number of hermeneutical assumptions, a theology of wilderness can take a variety of forms. Fretheim uses the motif to address leadership, and Cleaver-Bartholomew the effectiveness of the contemporary

church. Leal has greatly considered the implications of wilderness for eco-theology.

When constructing a theology of wilderness there are a few points of emphasis. First, one must accommodate the complexity of the data. Scripture's understanding of wilderness is nuanced; it is neither completely positive nor completely negative. Second, the wilderness will enjoy a notable place within God's eschatological plans, which fundamentally informs much of ecotheology. Third, one should recognize personal responsibility. Just as the undercurrent in Scripture suggests that Israel's disobedient actions significantly shaped its perception of the wilderness, a person's willingness to live in accordance with God's expectations will significantly shape his or her experiences and perceptions surrounding similar ambiguous phenomena of life.

See also Eschatology; Obedience; Prophets/Prophecy.

Resources

Cleaver-Bartholomew, David. "First Testament Wilderness Traditions and the Contemporary Church." *International Congregational Journal* 10, no. 1 (2011): 29-46.

Feldt, Laura, ed. "Ancient Wilderness Mythologies—The Case of Space and Religious Identity Formation in the Gospel of Matthew." *Archiv für Religionsgeschichte* 16, no. 1 (2015a): 163-92.

———. "Religion, Nature, and Ambiguous Space in Ancient Mesopotamia: The Mountain Wilderness in Old Babylonian Religious Narratives." *Numen* 63, no. 4 (2015b): 1-36.

———. *Wilderness in Mythology and Religion*. Berlin: Walter de Gruyter, 2012.

Fretheim, Terence E. "Leading from the Wilderness." *International Congregational Journal* 10, no. 1 (2011): 15-28.

Funk, Robert W. "The Wilderness." *JBL* 78, no. 3 (1959): 205-14.

Kohls, Randall L. "The Gospel Begins in the Wilderness: An Examination of Mark 1:1-15." *International Congregational Journal* 10, no. 1 (2011): 61-73.

Leal, Robert Barry. "Negativity towards Wilderness in the Biblical Record." *Ecotheology* 10, no. 3 (2005): 364-81.

———. *Wilderness in the Bible: Toward a Theology of Wilderness*. New York: Peter Lang, 2004.

Lefebvre, Henri. *The Production of Space*. Oxford, UK: Blackwell, 1991.

Mauser, Ulrich. *Christ in the Wilderness: The Wilderness Theme in the Second Gospel and Its Basis in the Biblical Tradition*. Naperville, IL: Alec R. Allenson, 1963.

Oelschlaeger, Max. *The Idea of Wilderness: From Prehistory to the Age of Ecology*. New Haven, CT: Yale University Press, 1991.

Stegner, William Richard. "Wilderness and Testing in the Scrolls and in Matthew 4:1-11." *BR* 12 (1967): 18-27.

Talmon, Shemaryahu. "The 'Desert Motif' in the Bible and in Qumran Literature." Pages 31-63 in *Biblical Motifs: Origins and Transformations*. Edited by Alexander Altmann. Cambridge, MA: Harvard University Press, 1966.

DAVID B. SCHREINER, PHD

WISDOM, THEOLOGY OF

In the Western world, people usually associate wisdom with ancient Greek philosophers such as Plato and Aristotle (fourth century BC). In fact, the English word "philosophy" means "love of wisdom." However, the Greek input was really quite late. People in ancient Mesopotamia and Egypt were already producing wisdom literature as early as 2700 BC. The Israelite sages were aware of this earlier wisdom literature. They borrowed its forms—both short proverbs and longer essays—as well as many of its concepts, although they placed it in a monotheistic context.

Old Testament Wisdom

The family of Hebrew words referring to wisdom (*ḥākam* [be wise], *ḥākām* [wise], *ḥokmâ* [wisdom], and *ḥokmôt* [wisdom]) occurs over three hundred times in the OT. The usage is especially frequent in the three primary wisdom books—Job, Proverbs, and Ecclesiastes.

Wisdom in the OT refers primarily to the ability to understand life— that is, the ability to discover and comprehend the nature of things, especially as viewed from God's perspective. This knowledge can be passed on from one person to another, but it is never achieved through human efforts alone. It is always seen as a gift from God, who is the source of true wisdom (Prov. 2:6; Exod. 35:30-35). His wisdom is far superior to that of humans, but he is willing to share a measure of it with those who seek him and **fear** him (Job 28:20-28). This connection of wisdom with God means that it always has a religious connotation (Ps. 111:10).

Sometimes God endows specific persons with superior knowledge and skills that classifies them as wise. These people included the architects and builders of the tabernacle (Exod. 35:30–36:1), weavers (28:3; 35:25-26), goldsmiths and silversmiths (Jer. 10:9), sailors (Ps. 107:27-30; Ezek. 27:8), royal counselors (Gen. 41:8; Isa. 44:25), and **women** skilled in lamentation (Jer. 9:17). These wise people knew what to do in their particular field and were able to do it.

In a more general sense, kings, judges, and parents were always expected to be wise. They had to make important decisions that affected other people in significant ways. Thus they needed God's wisdom and guidance to do their assignments well. The greatest example of a wise person in the OT is Solomon, upon whom God bestowed an abundance of wisdom to enable him to rule his nation wisely (1 Kings 3:4-15; 4:29-34).

The sages drew upon two resources to gain their wisdom about life. First, they studied the natural world noting the profound order that God had embedded in his universe at the time of creation. This provided illustrations from nature that contributed insights into understanding God's view of the world (Job 38:39–39:30; Prov. 30:18-19, 24-31).

Second, the sages studied human behavior. They noted that certain attitudes and actions always seemed to produce success and well-being. At the same time, other behaviors always produced failure. Over time, many of these behavioral patterns, both good and bad, became framed in cleverly worded, short sayings that we call proverbs. These were short enough that they could be easily memorized and passed on to the next generation. Thus they became part of the curriculum used to educate children (Prov. 1:8-19). Certain topics were especially popular in Israelite proverbs—relationships with family, friends, and neighbors; proper speech; and fools.

The purpose of the Wisdom literature was basically practical and educational rather than speculative in its orientation. It sought to provide a guidebook to successful living, especially directed at young people. The book of Proverbs with its hundreds of rules for right living is the best example.

The Wisdom literature also attempted to alert people to the paradoxes and exceptions to the rules that exist in the world of morality and justice. Sometimes life is chaotic rather than peaceful. Innocent **suffering** is not supposed to exist in the ideal world of the sages, but it does; and most people have experienced it. Job's struggles with this issue and Qoheleth's questioning of the vanity that he saw all around him (Eccles. 1:2) are examples of the more difficult side of Wisdom literature that looked at life honestly. In doing so, the sages raised profound, universal questions about the meaning of human existence, such as, Who is God? What is my purpose in life? Is our world stable or chaotic? Why do good people sometimes suffer terribly, while bad people sometimes escape punishment?

The theology of wisdom in the OT can be summarized in the following two categories.

1. *A Way of Thinking.* The Wisdom literature looks at God through his **creation** rather than through his actions in human history. The universe is his handiwork. He planned it, created it, and ordered it using wisdom (personified as "Lady Wisdom") as his **helper** (Prov. 3:19-20; 8:22-31). He continues to sustain and govern it as seen in his control of the weather; the sun, moon, and stars; and the animal kingdom. God's ability to produce such a magnificent and complex universe reveals that he is a God of unlimited power and wisdom. This becomes more and more evident as one examines each part of nature, from the smallest ant to the vast expanse of the sky above.

Further, God likes the world he created. It is beautiful and good (Gen. 1). Even though humans may not understand all of its mysteries or be able to control all of its parts, God delights in every part of his creation (Job 38–41).

This way of looking at life is in marked contrast with other parts of the OT that emphasize God's relationship to humanity as a **covenant** partner and/or **savior**. There one reads of Israel's great heroes and great historical events. But in the Wisdom literature there is no mention of people such as Abraham, Moses, and David or of events such as the crossing of the Red Sea or the building of the temple. Neither is there any sense of an Israelite nationalism. All peoples can be wise by seeking God and following the way of life taught by the sages. Job, a non-Israelite, is praised by God as the most righteous person of his generation (Job 1:8; 2:3). Thus the Wisdom literature provides a different but complementary view of God and the world.

2. *A Way of Living.* The Wisdom literature also promotes a lifestyle—a way of living that is pleasing to God. Specific behavioral characteristics such as trust in God (Prov. 3:5-6), honest speech (24:26), self-discipline (16:32), **humility** (11:2), and generosity (22:9) are praised as qualities that God desires for humanity. Just as each object in the heavens has its regular patterns that it traces across the sky and each animal has its unique characteristics that separate it from the others and that fit its needs, so God has designed an order for human behavior. People are called wise if they practice this order and foolish if they follow their own selfish interests. The ideal lifestyle of the wise was exemplified by Job: "This man was blameless and upright; he **feared God** and shunned **evil**" (Job 1:1, NIV).

With this interest in behavior, there also developed a strong emphasis on a reward system to encourage wise living. People who live ordered, righteous lives are rewarded by God with long life, riches, respect from their community, **peace**, blessedness, and **hope** for the future (Prov. 3:16-18; 24:14). Those who reject God's behavioral standards experience his retributive **justice**. They reap what they sow (10:16; 11:19-21; 12:7, 21; 13:21). Thus people should seek wisdom as the highest goal in life because the benefits are so much better than those experienced by the fool.

New Testament Wisdom

In the NT, the concept of wisdom derives from three Greek words (*sophia* [wisdom], *sophizō* [make wise, teach], and *sophos* [wise]) that occur over seventy times. These words can refer to the knowledge that human beings gain through native intelligence and education (Acts 7:22; 1 Cor. 1:19; 2:6) or to a spiritual wisdom that originates with God. Paul describes this spiritual wisdom as available to all. Even the nonintellectual and uneducated may receive the wisdom that comes from God, is embodied in Christ, and is taught by the **Holy Spirit** (1 Cor. 1:24, 26-31; 2:12-13).

As mentioned earlier, Proverbs 8 personified wisdom as a being who existed prior to creation and who helped God in his acts of ordering the world. The NT directly borrows from and builds upon this concept in two passages that ascribe the same qualities to Christ (John 1:1-14; Col. 1:15-20). Christ existed before all things and participated with the Father in bringing the world into existence, and he continues to provide for humanity the wisdom that is needed to live an ordered life of **righteousness, holiness**, and **redemption** (1 Cor. 1:30).

A. WENDELL BOWES, PHD

WITNESS OF THE SPIRIT · 407

WITNESS OF THE SPIRIT

The witness of the Spirit concerns the **Holy Spirit**'s communication of God's **love**, **forgiveness**, and acceptance of the believer. This concept is found chiefly in Paul's letters but also is in other NT writings.

In Romans 8:15-17 Paul writes of the believer receiving a spirit of adoption by which one calls God "Father." Indeed, "it is that very Spirit bearing witness with [Gk., *symmartyrei*] our spirit that we are children of God" (v. 16, NRSV). In the context of Paul's argument in Romans, this "witness" (Gk., *martys*) of the Spirit is an assurance that God has forgiven, accepted, made alive, and put believers into right relationship with God and neighbors. Believers are assured that Jesus's **grace** has made them God's children, apart from any requirement of belonging by the Jewish **law** or any other standard exterior to God's grace. (See also Gal. 4:1-7.)

Though the most immediate NT passages for the witness of the Spirit are Pauline, it is striking how this concept is similarly traced through other streams of the tradition. In Acts, the apostles boldly declare the **resurrection** of Jesus as God's action for the forgiveness of **sins**. They conclude, "We are witnesses to these things, and so is the Holy Spirit" (5:32, NRSV). Later when discerning what requirements to place on the inclusion of Gentiles in the **church**, the apostles bear witness to the Holy Spirit ("For it has seemed good to the Holy Spirit and to us . . ." [15:28, NRSV]) as the evidence that the grace of Jesus is sufficient for entrance into the people of God.

In the Johannine tradition, the witness of the Spirit testifies of God's acceptance and forgiveness through Christ. John records Jesus's promises that the Spirit "will guide [believers] into all the truth" (John 16:13, NRSV; 1:17; 14:6). Later John testifies that it is the Spirit who "bears witness" (Gk., *martyroun*; 1 John 5:6) that "God gave us eternal life, and this life is in his Son" (v.11, NRSV). By this witness believers know that God has extended to them his love and forgiveness, claiming them as his own children.

Paul recognized that the human spirit bears witness to God's forgiveness as well as does the Holy Spirit, thus laying a basis for the doctrine of assurance. There is an objective witness, the Spirit's, and a subjective witness, the believer's personal experience, that testify to Christ's saving presence.

The objective and subjective aspects of this testimony are both important in the Wesleyan tradition. In two sermons John Wesley distilled his thinking on the Spirit's witness of God's work of salvation. The objective witness is "an inward impression" given by the Spirit that the believer is a child of God, loved by Jesus and reconciled to God through the death of Christ (Outler and Heitzenrater 1991, 149).

The Spirit's objective witness leads to the subjective witness, the felt understanding that one has been accepted by God through Christ. Wesley described such assurance as sure a reality as the sun while standing in its direct rays (Outler and Heitzenrater 1991, 150). There follows other evidence of the Spirit's witness, such as **repentance**, conversion, joy, the urgent desire to do God's will, love of God and neighbor, and the fruit of the Spirit evidenced in one's life. But these are outworkings of the prior conviction that the Spirit has borne witness to God's love in Christ. For Wesley, **holiness** was possible only if one loved God, but one could not love God unless convinced of God's love for him or her; hence the essential work of the witness of the Spirit in his vision of Christian perfection.

The witness of the Spirit should not be confused with the inability to question and doubt. One may at times experience a season when God's presence cannot be sensed—a period called the dark night of the soul, a concept traced back to John of the Cross (d. 1591). The complexity of experiences of spiritual struggle or depression often exists in creative tension alongside the Spirit's objective witness that God in Christ has reconciled with humanity.

See also Communal Holiness; Jesus and the Law; Torah (Law, Instruction).

Resource
Outler, Albert C., and Richard P. Heitzenrater, eds. *John Wesley's Sermons: An Anthology.* Nashville: Abingdon Press, 1991.

RYAN HANSEN, PHD

WOMEN IN THE OLD TESTAMENT

The position of women in the ANE is largely consistent with the consequences for sin pronounced in Genesis 3. Women were separated from the life-sustaining presence of God (as were men) and in a state of mutual hostility with the "serpent"; they were subservient to men in society and subjected to male rule in the home. The depictions of women in the OT, then, have been interpreted in the light of an understanding of women in the ANE that sometimes strengthened the androcentric theological conclusions of male superiority and power and female subordination and dependence. However, while many OT texts show the sorry state of things in the fallen world, they do not necessarily represent the original divine intention or the ultimate redemptive purpose for women in the **kingdom of God**.

Indeed, the overarching biblical-theological pattern moves from ideal humanity in **creation** to corrupt humanity in the **fall**, to restored humanity in progressive redemption, and finally to glorified humanity in **eschatological** consummation. This pattern shows us a clear redemptive trajectory. In addition, consideration of the parallelism between the ideal woman made in the **image of God** in creation and the glorified woman in the perfected image of Christ (Rom. 8:29-30) in consummation provides new interpretive insight for understanding the redeemed woman of the OT as a type of Christ. Seen in this way, certain remarkable women of the OT are not simply exceptions to the rule but rather redemptive prototypes for others to emulate. These prototypical women fall into a number of important commanding roles in the life of Israel.

Mothers

As society gradually deteriorated to an androcentric, patrilocal, and patriarchal society, women and their reproductive capacities were largely treated as male property to ensure patrilineal descent. In the creation account, childbearing is a God-given privilege, and fruitfulness is a divine blessing essential for having dominion. Accordingly, in redemptive history, women's role in childbearing is of paramount importance for the fulfillment of not only God's original mandate of fruitfulness (Gen. 1:28) but also God's promises to Abraham of prosperity and the blessing of all nations through Sarah's child.

It is therefore no surprise that the serpent would be hostile to women and their childbearing (3:15-16). But the seasons of barrenness experienced by the matriarchs of Israel (Sarah, Rebekah, and Rachel) and other women (Samson's mother and Hannah) turned into occasions for divine self-revelation, intervention, blessing, and **victory** over the hostile serpent that resisted God and his people. Sarah's supernatural childbearing is especially significant because it established for Israel that women and reproduction belong to God and that **covenant** promises pass down through patterns of matrilineal descent (17:16-21).

The OT affirms the utmost importance of the unique role of mothers in God's redemptive work. Some mothers stand out for their extraordinary **faith**, courage, and sacrifice in bringing forth children who played key roles in the deliverance of Israel; such mothers include Jochebed, Moses's mother (Exod. 2:1-10); Ruth, King David's great-grandmother (Ruth 4:13-17); and Hannah, Samuel's mother (1 Sam. 1:24-28).

Mothers played a critical role in Israel's covenant life. The commandment to **honor** both mother and father affirms both as primary teachers and interpreters of God's covenant laws (Deut. 4:9-10; 6:7; 11:19). The command to honor one's mother also implies the God-given authority of mothers to bless their children and determine the general direction of their descendants' lives. The book of Proverbs, although written from a male perspective to a male audience, also assumes that both fathers and mothers are teachers of **Torah** and that both males and females learn from their mothers. Jewish tradition holds that Huldah was a prophet who taught publicly in a school. It also associates the "Gates of Huldah" in the Second Temple with Huldah's schoolhouse. Ultimately, the collective role of mothers as teachers of the Law (Exod. 20:12; Deut. 6:7) would serve to guard the religion of Israel and determine the destiny of the nation.

Wives

The unfulfilled call to subdue and have dominion over creation appears to find its distorted outlet in human-to-human domination, epitomized in the typical postfall patriarchal order predicted in the divine pronouncement "he will rule over you" (Gen. 3:16b, NIV). However, there are cases in which mutual authority between wife and husband prevailed, with wives sometimes taking the lead. Abraham obeyed (Hebr., šĕma' bĕqōlâ) Sarah (16:2; 21:12). Jacob obeyed his wives by taking their maidservants to produce more children for them (30:3-4, 9). Rachel and Leah negotiated their conjugal rights over Jacob, who submitted to their decision (vv. 15-16). Jochebed successfully executed her rescue plan on her own (Exod. 2:2-3). Zipporah (not Moses) performed priestly rites to deter death (4:24-26). Deborah judged Israel without her husband's supervision (Judg. 4–5). Hannah made and fulfilled a vow to the Lord (1 Sam. 1:10-28). Through her diplomatic gift of appeasement and prophetic endorsement of David's kingship, Abigail deterred David from taking personal vengeance upon her foolish husband Nabal and saved her own household (1 Sam. 25).

The Israelites' legal system provided some protection of a wife from unrestrained androcentric legal procedures, although it still shows the wife's subordinate status under male authority and power. In a state of anarchy, some men deteriorated into utterly brutal treatment of a wife (Hebr., 'iššâ; Judg. 19).

Other OT texts recall the fundamental unity, **love**, and honor between the wife and the husband expressed in the original man's exuberant praise of the woman ("bone of my bones and flesh of my flesh" [Gen. 2:23, NIV]). Song of Songs portrays a paradigmatic love relationship in which the lover and her beloved enjoy mutual love as it was meant to be. Their relationship was completely free of male domination or concerns for gender roles, and honors the Edenic matrilocal marital norm from Genesis 2:24, in which the man leaves his parents and cleaves to his wife (Song of Sol. 3:4; 8:1-3). Proverbs 31 also celebrates the wife of strength who is like **wisdom** personified. She is kind, generous, wise, favored, industrious, prosperous, strong, independent, courageous, valued, and praised in the private and the public spheres. The wife and her husband respect, value, trust, and bless each other, showcasing an ideal covenantal **marriage** as intended by God.

Proprietors

A census taken on the fortieth year of the exodus for the purpose of dividing the promised land among the tribes indicates that the property was distributed to sons. Five unmarried young daughters of Zelophehad ("Mahlah, Noah, Hoglah, Milkah and Tirzah" [Num. 27:1, NIV]) boldly and effectively challenged this pre-Israelite law as being inadequate. Out of their honorable desires to keep alive their father's name among the Gileadites, they demanded a holding along with their five uncles. God granted their request and forever changed the Israelite property law. The new law allowed daughters to inherit the land in the absence of sons before the deceased's brothers or uncles were considered (vv. 1-11). This law triggered another new law that prohibited an inheritance from being passed from one tribe to the other by limiting the inheritress's marriage within her tribal clan (36:1-12). Once in the land, the five daughters inherited their own lot (Josh. 17:3-6) along with their father's five brothers.

Another notable proprietor is the woman of power in Proverbs 31:10-31. Although set in the context of a patriarchal culture in which public decision-makers (i.e., the elders at the city gate [v. 23]) were typically men, the woman had significant domestic and social power and influence (vv. 16-20). Furthermore, the poem calls for public praise of the woman: "Let her works bring her praise at the city gate" (v. 31, NIV). The daughters of Zelophehad and the woman of strength portray a glowingly redemptive portrait of women.

Authors/Composers

There are two OT books dedicated to heroic women, Ruth and Esther, composed after their time. There are other texts that were composed by extraordinary women. Proverbs 31:1-9, which includes an impressive acrostic poem, is attributed to the queen mother of King Lemuel. Deborah's song (Judg. 5), which celebrates a military victory gained with the help of two women, mentions Deborah as the composer (v. 7). Hannah celebrated her vindication and victory in her song (1 Sam. 2:1-10), which is echoed in Mary's Magnificat (Luke 1:46-55).

Exodus 15:1-18 is a song that celebrates Yahweh's supreme power over creation and sovereign rule over political superpowers. Because this song is introduced with Moses and the Israelites as singers (v. 1), many have assumed Moses to be the composer of the song and designated the song as the Song of Moses, as shown in the headings of many translations. However, the text does not name Moses as the composer, which contrasts with Moses's song in Deuteronomy 31:19-22.

There are compelling reasons for Miriam's authorship of this hymn. (1) Victory songs that celebrate and memorialize significant events of salvation belong to a genre associated with female rather than male musicians or singers (e.g., Deborah's song, Hannah's song, and the women's song for David's triumphs in 1 Sam. 18:7). (2) While some suggest that Miriam sang only the first line as a chorus, the expression "Miriam sang to them" (masculine plural; Exod. 15:21, NIV) likely indicates that Miriam composed and sang the entire song to all the Israelites. Then Moses and the Israelites sang after her, committing the song to their memory. The first line in verse 21 probably serves as the title of the song, and verse 1 asynchronously reports the fact that Moses and the Israelites sang the song they learned from Miriam.

Song of Songs was traditionally attributed to Solomon, but this position has been challenged for good reasons. The language and content of the book strongly point to it being "for" or dedicated "to" Solomon. The language also points to a woman poet. She is the primary lover in the song, with the young man as the beloved. The book is written from the woman's perspective. The "other" voice in the book addresses her six times and both the lover and the beloved once (5:1). Song of Songs opens (1:2-4) and closes (8:14) with her voice, and she is the dominant speaker.

While biblical texts are largely written and compiled by men, those written by women are highly sophisticated in their composition, contribute indispensable theological ideas, and/or celebrate significant historical events. Their inspired words about God, war, history, life, **love**, or marriage have been transmitted, received, studied, and applied as God's timeless, authoritative, trustworthy, and transformative words to God's people.

Rescuers

There were female rescuers mediating and foreshadowing God's character and acts, especially the deliverance of the vulnerable from oppression and death. These redemptive women fulfilled their roles as "**helpers**" (cf. Gen. 2:18) of the weak and oppressed, and thwarters of the plans and powers of formidable enemies of God. Several stories from early in the book of Exodus stand out. The midwives who feared God more than the murderous Pharaoh courageously upheld the sanctity of life and defied the powerful pagan king in their act of civil disobedience (Exod. 1:15-21). Jochebed, in keeping with her son's special destiny, devised and successfully carried out a risky but brilliant rescue plan for her son (2:2-6). The Egyptian princess, moved by deep **compassion** and maternal tenderness, and exercising her privilege to act independently of her father Pharaoh, saved and adopted an apparently abandoned Hebrew baby (vv. 5-10). Young Miriam, extremely discerning and bold, approached the Egyptian princess to suggest a wet nurse and then brought the baby's own mother.

Esther was a Jewish queen of Persia. When her people were faced with the threat of annihilation, she was willing to sacrifice everything, even her own life, to intercede for and save her people. Whether in the books of Exodus or Esther, the ruthless genocide campaigns against the people of God can be seen as an extension of the serpent's hostility against the "seed" of the woman. By contrast, the Israelite women's redemptive acts and God's employment of God's people in the **judgment** of their enemies can be seen as significant fulfillments of the "seed" of the woman "striking" the serpent's head (Gen. 3:15, AT).

Rahab was a non-Israelite woman with historical understanding, spiritual insight, practical wisdom, and moral courage (Josh. 2:1-16). By saving two Israelite spies and defecting to Israel, she saved herself and her immediate and extended family from destruction (6:22-26). Once prostitute or innkeeper (vv. 17, 25; cf. Heb. 11:31; James 2:25), Rahab apparently was given favor and honor to be married into one of the prestigious families in the tribe of Judah. This woman of indecorous and foreign origin in turn became the mother of Boaz, an ancestor of Jesus Christ (Matt. 1:5), adding to the scandalous nature of God's **grace**.

Prophets

Women served God-given purposes not only in private sectors but sometimes in public and religious domains. One of the prominent gifts and positions for women was **prophet**, who received, proclaimed, and interpreted divine **revelation**. This function is consistent with the fact that women are made in the image of God to commune with God and make God known to the people.

The first woman named "prophet" (Hebr., *něbî'â*) was Miriam (Exod. 15:20). The words of the queen mother of King Lemuel are called an "oracle" or "prophecy," indicating that she was a prophet (Prov. 31:1). Deborah's commanding prophetic leadership provided military impetus, strategy, and victory, ushering in a long period of *šālôm* in Israel (Judg. 4–5). At least two texts speak of a prophetic role for a larger number of women: "The Lord gives the word; the women who announce the news are a great host" (Ps. 68:11 [12 HB], ESV); "I will pour out my Spirit on all flesh; your sons and your daughters shall prophesy" (Joel 2:28*bc*, ESV). Abigail, though not called a prophet, uttered a profound prophecy about David's integrity, kingship, divine protection and victory over enemies, and lasting dynasty (1 Sam. 25:26-31).

Huldah's prophetic leadership should not be underestimated. It was instrumental in Josiah's massive religious reforms (2 Kings 22; 2 Chron. 34:14-33). Even as her living quarters ("the college" [KJV]; "in the Mishneh district" [NET]) and the gates dedicated to her (the "Gates of Huldah") would indicate, Huldah probably was highly esteemed not only as a prophet but also as an interpreter and teacher of the law. This would explain why the king's delegates sought her out with a document found in the temple, even above her prophetic contemporaries Jeremiah and Zephaniah, who also ministered during the reign of Josiah (Jer. 1:2; Zeph. 1:1). Huldah validated the authority of that document, making a major contribution to the development of the Bible.

Women did not always use the prophetic gift for good. Miriam used her claims to prophetic powers to falsely question Moses's unique authority and wrongfully subject his wife to racial discrimination (Num. 12:1-9). Noadiah apparently abused her prophetic gift and influence to conspire against Nehemiah (Neh. 6:14). Their abuse of the prophetic gift does not negate the legitimacy of the gift or the calling. But it shows that the gift can be misused, whether by men or by women, to oppose God and God's people or used to serve God and build up God's people.

Priestly Ministers

A few texts testify to the participation of female Levites in the ministry of the tabernacle. Exodus 38:8 takes for granted that there were women Levites "serving" (Hebr., ṣābāʾ) at the tent of meeting. First Samuel 2:22 shows women serving at the tent of meeting during the time of the premonarchical period. Thus the commandments concerning the consecration and service of the Levites (Num. 8:24-26) should be taken as applicable to both male and female Levites.

Levitical women who were priestly and prophetic ministers are also attested in other parts of Israel's history. Heman's three daughters during King David's time were renowned temple musicians (either in vocal or instrumental music or both; see 1 Chron. 25:1, 5-6). Men and women temple singers are also noted during Josiah's time (2 Chron. 35:25; also 23:13; 29:28) and until the return from exile (Ezra 2:65, 70; 7:7; Neh. 7:67, 73). The roles women had in tabernacle and temple worship offer parallels to the other better-known OT women who served in noncultic leadership roles related to prophetic ministry, military exploits, and religious reform (e.g., Deborah and Huldah).

Through the installation of priests, God taught Israel about the distinction between the **holy** and the unholy. This was not so much to emphasize or to perpetuate the division between the sacred and profane but to provoke all people to a life of **holiness** whereby they, too, might draw near to God and be consecrated unto God. Accordingly, a provision was made that non-Levitical women or men, if they so desired, could consecrate themselves entirely to the Lord as Nazirites (Num. 6:2-21). This provision foreshadows the expanded vision of priesthood in the new covenant in which women are included (1 Pet. 2:5-9).

Rulers

Although many may remember Eve as an uneducated gullible woman, she was created as the "queen" to rule over God's creation on earth. Yahweh formed the woman as the "**helper**" (an epithet often used of God as the deliverer [e.g., Exod. 18:4; Pss. 33:20; 70:5 (6 HB); 115:9-11; Hos. 13:9]) equal to the man (Gen. 2:18). She was to share the responsibility of subduing and having dominion on earth (1:26-28). Although Eve failed to subdue the serpent who deceived her (Gen. 3:13; 1 Tim. 2:14), and the infamous Jezebel (1 Kings 18:13; 21:8-16) and the Judean queen Athaliah (2 Kings 11:1-16; 2 Chron. 23:12-15) used their royal power to do great **evil**, there are others in

Israel's history who exercised their political power and spiritual authority to bring deliverance to their people. Deborah was a prophet and a judge (or ruler) who governed Israel during the twenty years of the Canaanites' cruel oppression and then for an additional forty years after a decisive victory over them (Judg. 5:31). Her rule is presented as an extension of Yahweh's reign over Israel, as Moses's leadership had been. Women who walk in a redemptive calling, position, and responsibility are not deviating from God's overall purpose for women; rather, they are fulfilling God's purposes for redeemed women as rulers (cf. Eph. 2:4-6; Rev. 20:4, 6), consistent with God's original intention for women before the fall. As such, they are types of Christ, the King of kings and the Lord of lords.

Conclusion

Patriarchy and its effects do not represent God's ultimate purpose for women in the OT. The lives of the extraordinary women of the OT—mothers, wives, proprietors, composers, rescuers, prophets, ministers, and rulers—are evidence of the measure of *šālôm* that God brought to women as members of his redeemed people. They demonstrate the restored image of God, living out who they are created and redeemed to be. They offer a foretaste of the future messianic age, in which *all* evil effects of the fall will be completely vanquished and all aspects of life lavishly blessed (Isa. 11:6-9; 65:17; 66:22).

See also Demonic/Devil; Jesus and the Law.

H. JUNIA POKRIFKA, PHD

WOMEN LEADERS (IN THE EARLY CHURCH AND 1 TIMOTHY 2)

At face value, 1 Timothy 2:9-15 stands in stark contrast with many other Pauline passages, such as Romans 16; 1 Corinthians 11:2-16; Galatians 3:26-28; and Philippians 4:1-3, and seems to restrict the teaching and leadership of women. Since the 1 Timothy passage seems to counter other writings of Paul and the central role of women in the Jesus movement as represented in the Gospels and Acts, deeper research is required to interpret the meaning of such a passage.

When studying a text, language, context, authorship, and other matters relevant to the text must be evaluated. In the case of 1 Timothy, such an approach helps readers understand and apply a difficult passage to contemporary life.

Women in Ministry

There is no shortage of named women who were central to the ministry of Jesus and the apostle Paul: Mary the Virgin, Mary Magdalene (the first herald of the resurrection), Susanna, Salome, Joanna (Chuza's wife), Prisca,

Phoebe, Claudia, Chloe, Euodia, Syntyche, Junia, Dorcas, Lydia, and Eunice and Lois (Timothy's mother and grandmother), to name a few. In a patriarchal society such as the first-century Roman Empire, the mere fact that women are named in the Jesus and early church narratives is in itself countercultural. If we are to understand by what means these texts have come to us, we must be clear about the process. These texts were the stories of men, recorded by men, and copied and transposed by men for posterity.

Issue of Authorship

Scholars have classified 1 Timothy as *Deutero-Pauline*, that is, attributed to Paul, for they are not certain of its Pauline authorship. In antiquity, it was entirely appropriate to write in the name of your teacher or leader—a practice called *pseudonymity*. First Timothy is not classified as authentic Pauline for several reasons. Linguistically the letter reads differently than do other authentic Pauline letters, using some sixty Greek words Paul never used elsewhere. The Greek is more complex than Paul's usual writing, reading more like Luke than Paul. It is possible this letter was written by an *amanuensis*, a scribe taking dictation from Paul. The problem is that the letter's content runs counter to what Paul has said elsewhere about women in leadership.

Culture of Ephesus

Culturally and contextually speaking, the first hearers must have known that the letter was written to Timothy, who was presiding over the church in Ephesus. The intended audience, then, had no small bearing on the message of the letter. Ephesus was a major center of the empire and also became an important site for the fledgling church. According to tradition, the apostle John and Mary, the mother of Jesus, relocated to Ephesus after Jesus's ascension. John had a considerable following, including early church fathers Polycarp and Ignatius of Antioch, who were then tutors of Irenaeus and Tertullian, the latter of whom arguing for the authenticity of 1 Timothy.

Ephesus in the first and second centuries was a cultural and economic center. The temple of Artemis was a religious and banking hub of the empire. The temple was also the heart of the city, with Artemis's priestesses, adorned with lavish braids and fine jewelry, providing worshippers communion with the goddess through sexual acts.

The goddess Artemis and the Phrygian Cybele became identified as one so that in the Ephesian worship of Artemis there was a confluence of Eastern and Western religious ideas and practices. Because the city served as a link between East and West, Paul knew that Ephesus would serve as a perfect launching spot for his missionary efforts. He would be able to reach people across Asia Minor and across the sea in Macedonia. After establishing the church in Ephesus, he left Prisca and Aquila, his trusted colaborers in the gospel of Christ, to lead in his stead while he traveled abroad and back to Jerusalem (Acts 18:18–21:17; cf. 1 Cor. 3:9).

In summary, the following is clear: (1) According to early tradition, the apostle John and Mary, the mother of Jesus, relocated to Ephesus. (2) The city was teeming with cultic associations with the goddess Artemis and her priestesses. And (3) at some point, Prisca and her husband, Aquila, were entrusted with oversight of the believers in the city.

In addition, about this same time there arose another cultural phenomenon, the "new women of Rome," as labeled by Bruce Winter (2000). These were women abandoned by husbands serving in the military in provinces across the empire. Their service kept them from Rome for several years at a time. Because of a law passed by Julius Caesar, these women had use of their dowries. According to ancient correspondence, these women liked to attend parties, spend time with each other and with poets and artists, and adorn themselves with lavish jewels and hair combs. This was much different behavior from the expected posture of the noble Roman woman, plainly dressed, relegated to the home, and quietly submissive to her husband.

Conclusion

Given the discussion above, it is easier to understand and apply 1 Timothy 2:9-15. This passage, long held up against educated, called, and ordained women in the contemporary church, was originally a restriction leveled at women in an effort to clarify the differences between the community of the baptized and the priestesses of Artemis. The author was also concerned about the confusion between the women who were followers of Jesus and the Roman women who were newly free to come and go as they pleased due to the absence of their husbands. The author wanted the women in the church to uphold the Roman **household codes.**

Clearly the restrictions on leadership and preaching in 1 Timothy do not follow the practices of Jesus, Paul, or the early church. Rather they have been imposed in a particular context for a particular reason and time.

See also Household Codes; Women in the Old Testament; Women's Roles in the Church.

Resources

Grassi, Joseph A. *Mary, Mother and Disciple: From the Scriptures to the Council of Ephesus.* Wilmington, DE: Michael Glazier, 1988.

Winter, Bruce. "The 'New' Roman Wife and 1 Timothy 2:9-15: The Search for a *Sitz im Leben.*" *TynBul* 51, no. 2 (2000): 285-94.

KIMBERLY S. MAJESKI, DMIN

WOMEN'S ROLES IN THE CHURCH

Much has been written about women in Christianity and their roles as leaders of Christ's living body throughout history. The relatively recent emergence of literature about women's roles as leaders in the church is surmised by investigating what women do throughout the world today to build up the body of Christ. It is also based on a reexamination of texts and artifacts that demonstrate how women have influenced the world, making disciples of all nations. This evidence includes examining legislation by **church** leaders against women serving, as well as criticisms of the role of women in Christianity by critics of the church. Although women have served communities of **faith** visibly, publically, and privately (in sequestered settings) for centuries, the service of women to Christ's church was only sporadically recorded after the first century.

Early Christian texts demonstrate that women were disciples of Christ and apostles of the **gospel** from the beginning of Jesus's ministry and in the churches activated by Paul. Women followed, supported, and conversed with Jesus (Luke 8:1-3; 11:27-28); they witnessed his **resurrection** and were sent by him to tell others (Matt. 28:7-10; Mark 16:7-11; Luke 24:10-11; John 4; 20:17-18). The NT also indicates that women received the Spirit and functioned as witnesses, teachers, preachers, prayers, missionaries, deacons, and coworkers of Paul (Acts 1:14-15; 2:17; 16:1-15; 18:26-28; 21:9; Rom. 16:1-16; 1 Cor. 11:2-16; 14:33-36; Phil. 4:2-3). The **Holy Spirit** endowed women with the gift of prophecy—the gift Christians should earnestly desire (1 Cor. 14:1-5). Paul emphasized, in Galatians 3:28, that there is no exclusion or division in Christ. Another early Christian text, *The Acts of Paul and Thecla*, which tells the story of a virgin from Iconium, drew fierce reactions from critics of the **church**. Though probably fictional, it shows that women were drawn to chastity and the freedom that the gospel offered. Ancient frescoes show women serving the Eucharist and preaching.

The NT is not innovative in featuring women as **prophets** and leaders of God's people. The OT conveys stories about the women who were used by God to preserve and challenge Israel as bearers of God's message and models of faithfulness. For example, Deborah in Judges 4–5 is described as a prophetess, judge, military deliverer, and singer of one of the oldest portions of Scripture. King Josiah consulted the prophet Huldah, who promptly pronounced the **word of Yahweh** (2 Kings 22:16-20). Zipporah, Rahab, Ruth, and Bathsheba aggressively preserved the lives of those they loved and are models for all of God's people.

At its inception, and during moments of renewal, the church was resoundingly inclusive of women. Hierarchies and exclusive practices were established when its officials emulated the empire of Constantine. When ordination became formalized, those in power ignored Scripture, tradition, and the experiences of women serving God and ruled that males only could be priests. In his 1891 work, *Ordaining Women*, Benjamin T. Roberts cited the second-century letter of Governor Pliny to the Roman emperor Trajan;

the letter describes the persecution of two women ministers. Roberts concluded, "Women, it seems, could be ministers of the church at this early age, while it was poor and persecuted, but afterwards, when it became rich and popular, they were set aside" (157).

Influential church leaders encouraged asceticism and celibacy for men and women. A few women, such as Macrina the Younger (sister of Gregory of Nyssa, Basil the Great, and Peter of Sebaste), were honored for attaining that ideal in the fourth century. Nonetheless, Tertullian (ca. AD 155–ca. AD 230) and Augustine (AD 354–430) expressed negative views of women that simulate Platonic and Neoplatonic matter and gender dualism. We have few records of women's involvement in theological formulations; from the fourth to the twentieth century, women were excluded from formal church **leadership**, with the notable exception of abbesses such as Héloïse (twelfth century).

Although mystics and other celibate women in convents gained a measure of freedom and autonomy during the Middle Ages, many other women were executed as witches because clergy believed they were morally weak, feebleminded, easily swayed, deceitful, lustful, and submitted to the sexual advances of the **devil** (Kramer, *Hammer of Witches* 1487, cited in Ruether 1974, 291). Church **law** permitted wife beating as a way to control female corruption and disobedience.

Changes began during the Protestant Reformation and subsequently when some women preached and taught in their homes and churches. Quakers promoted the equality of men and women. Women continued to be involved in initiating break-off movements within religious spheres, but leadership roles were usurped by men in those communities within a generation or less. In the wake of the revivalism of Whitefield, Edwards, and the Wesleys (nineteenth century), Christian women collaborated to combat **slavery**; establish domestic and international colleges, hospitals, missions, and orphanages; and champion temperance and women's equality (voting rights, education, and ordination).

Wesleyan, holiness, and Pentecostal evangelicals, including the Assemblies of God and the Church of God (Cleveland, Tennessee), ordained women and/or encouraged their preaching and evangelism efforts. Some mainline Protestant groups began ordaining women between 1950 and 1970, and more recently in Africa and Asia.

Nonetheless, to this day some evangelical Protestant churches restrict women from serving as pastors, preachers, and teachers. These self-designated "complementarians" interpret Genesis 2–3 as assigning strict gender roles within the **church** and family. They claim that 1 Timothy 2:8-15 restricts women from teaching men in the church and thus from being ordained and becoming pastors. Consequently, they interpret differently biblical support for the Spirit's indiscriminate empowering and calling of women to preach, speak, teach, lead, and serve in other ways.

The Roman Catholic Church restricts women from serving as priests for different reasons. The church claims that it has no authority to institute a change required for the ordination of women. According to the 1976 Vatican document *Inter Insigniores*, the priest is the **image**, sign, and representation of Christ before God; priests must be male because Jesus was male. A mysterious bond unites Christ, his maleness, and the priesthood. Maleness, according to *Inter Insigniores*, is a more fixed and significant aspect of Christ than his humanity, age, or race. Therefore, those who shepherd his flock as clergy must be limited to males.

The same document claims that the church relies on the natural symbolism of gender to signify the relationship between the priest and Christ, the head and bridegroom of the church. "The mystery of Christ and the Church is indissolubly bound to the mystery of humans as male and female. Furthermore, Christ, himself a man, only chose men to be his apostles. The Church must be faithful to the example of her Lord" (*Inter Insigniores*, quoted in National Conference of Catholic Bishops 1990, 11).

Nonetheless, the Women's Ordination Conference (WOC) has advocated since 1975 for the ordination of women. Since 2002, women have been ordained through Roman Catholic Womenpriests (RCWP). The Roman Catholic Church has rejected these ordinations and excommunicated everyone involved. Pope Francis stated in 2013 that the church had spoken and said no to the ordination of women, referring to Pope John Paul's 1994 document *Ordinatio Sacerdotalis* (McClory 2013). Nonetheless, women compose the majority of leaders and workers at the parish level. St. Clement Parish in Chicago is one example of a Catholic church whose pastors are women, respected and supported by priests and parishioners alike, albeit frustrated because they cannot administer the sacraments.

Across the ages, women of the church have crossed cities, nations, and seas; have stood before lecterns and pulpits; and have pastored from desks, tables, and bedsides. They continue to speak, write, work, and otherwise transmit and live the gospel. In spite of restrictions, women pray, prophesy, serve the **poor**, and make disciples of all nations. Increasing numbers of women in more and more denominations are baptizing those whom they have discipled.

See also Household Codes; Women in the Old Testament; Women Leaders.

Resources

Bynum, Caroline W. *Fragmentation and Redemption: Essays on Gender and the Human Body in Medieval Religion.* Cambridge, MA: Zone Books, 1991.

Carr, Anne E. *Transforming Grace: Christian Tradition and Women's Experience.* San Francisco: Harper and Row, 1988.

Congregation for the Doctrine of the Faith. "Declaration on the Question of the Admission of Women to the Ministerial Priesthood (*Inter Insigniores*)." October 15, 1976. *Origins* 6, no. 33 (February 3, 1977): 517-24.

DeConick, April D. *Holy Misogyny: Why the Sex and Gender Conflicts in the Early Church Still Matter.* New York: Continuum, 2011.

John Paul II. *Ordinatio sacerdotalis* [Priestly Ordination]. Vatican Website. May 22, 1994. http://w2.vatican.va/content/john-paul-ii/en/apost_letters/1994/documents/hf _jp-ii_apl_19940522_ordinatio-sacerdotalis.html.

MacHaffie, Barbara J. *Her Story: Women in Christian Tradition.* 2nd ed. Minneapolis: Fortress Press, 2006.

Mackay, Christopher S. *The Hammer of Witches: A Complete Translation of the Malleus Maleficarum.* Cambridge: Cambridge University Press, 2009.

McClory, Robert. "Pope Francis and Women's Ordination." *The Francis Chronicles* (blog). *The National Catholic Reporter,* September 16, 2013. https://www.ncronline.org /blogs/francis-chronicles/pope-francis-and-womens-ordination.

National Conference of Catholic Bishops. "One in Christ Jesus: A Pastoral Response to the Concerns of Women for Church and Society." *Orgins* 19, no. 44 (April 5, 1990): 717-40.

Roberts, Benjamin T. *Ordaining Women: Biblical and Historical Insights.* 1891. Reprint, Indianapolis: Light and Life, 1992.

Ruether, Rosemary. "Persecution of Witches: A Case of Ageism and Sexism?" *Christianity and Crisis* 34 (December 1974).

Russell, Letty M., Kwok Pui-lan, Ada María Isasi-Díaz, and Katie Geneva Cannon, eds. *Inheriting Our Mothers' Gardens: Feminist Theology in Third World Perspective.* Louisville, KY: Westminster Press, 1988.

Torjesen, Karen Jo. *When Women Were Priests: Women's Leadership in the Early Church and the Scandal of Their Subordination in the Rise of Christianity.* San Francisco: HarperSanFrancisco, 1993.

Tucker, Ruth A., and Walter L. Liefeld. *Daughters of the Church: Women and Ministry from New Testament Times to the Present.* Grand Rapids: Zondervan, 1987.

Winslow, Karen Strand. "Recovering Redemption for Women: Feminist Exegesis in North American Evangelicalism." Pages 269-89 in *Feminist Interpretation of the Hebrew Bible in Retrospect 2: Social Locations.* Edited by Rachel Magdalene, Susanne Scholz, and Alan J. Hauser. Sheffield, UK: Sheffield Phoenix Press, 2014.

KAREN STRAND WINSLOW, PHD

WORD OF GOD/YAHWEH, THE

The OT authors indicated that they were conveying God speech—that is, God's word—through such Hebrew terms as the following: *dibbēr* (speak), *dābār* ("speech," "word"), *'āmar* (say), *'ōmer* or *'imrâ* ("utterance," "speech," "word"), *nĕ'um* ("utterance," "declaration"), *ṣāwâ* (command), *miṣwâ* (commandment), *qārā'* (call), and *qôl* (voice).

The **prophets** addressed God's people with the claim that they did so, not with their own thoughts and words, but with a word received from Yahweh, the living God. Isaiah demanded of **Jerusalem**'s rulers, "Listen to the word of Yahweh! [*šim'û dĕbar yhwh*]" (Isa. 1:10, AT). "Word of Yahweh" (*dĕbar yhwh*) occurs 241 times in the OT, of which 221 occur in the prophetic books. A prophet's word is to be identified with Yahweh's word. Thus the prophets' claimed that, having heard Yahweh speak, they were repeating the very words of God to the people: "Thus says Yahweh [kôh 'āmar yhwh]" (e.g., Amos 1:6, 9, AT).

The biblical text, however, does not clearly indicate how the prophets received God's word. At times it is as though the word was viewed as an animate "something" that came from Yahweh to the prophet. "The word [haddābār] that came [lit., "was" or "became"] to Jeremiah from Yahweh" (e.g., Jer. 7:1; 11:1, AT). "The word [haddābār] of Yahweh came to me" (Ezek. 6:1; 12:1 [113x in the OT], AT). Occasionally, the prophet affirmed the deliverance of God's word with a final emphatic "Yahweh has said! ['āmar yhwh]" (Amos 1:5, 8; 2:3, AT) or "Declares Yahweh! [nĕ'um yhwh]" (2:16; 3:15, AT). God's word through his prophets contains warnings (Isa. 2:12-22; Ezek. 3:17-21), offers of salvation (Mic. 7:18-19), **hope** for the future (Jer. 33:1-11), healing for the nation (Mal. 4:1-3), and **judgment** (Hab. 1:14-17).

Yahweh's prophets indicated that at times they received God's word by hearing, as did the prophet-disciple, whose ear God opened every morning to give a "word" (dābār) to pass on to the weary (Isa. 50:4-5). At other times, the prophets metaphorically received God's word through the mouth, ate it, and ingested it into the stomach (6:7; Jer. 1:9; 15:16; Ezek. 2:8; 3:1-3).

Moses, God's prophet par excellence, conveyed God's "word" (dābār; Deut. 30:14) to God's people in the form of "commandments" (miṣôt; vv. 8, 11). He placed the commandments in their "mouth" and "heart" to govern their future life in the **land** of Canaan (v. 14, NASB). If they obeyed these commandments, God's people would experience long life in the land, would produce multiple offspring, and would receive Yahweh's abundant blessing (v. 16).

Psalm 119 equates God's "word" (e.g., vv. 9, 11) with God's "law" (e.g., vv. 1, 18, 29), which God's people were to obey. God's word becomes the overall system that sets the pattern for the lifelong behavior of God's people. The eternality of God's word is rooted in heaven (v. 89) with God. It is God, then, who opens a person's spiritual eyes (v. 18) so that God's word-law may be taken into the deepest recesses of the human heart. There it resides to guard one from sinning against God (vv. 11, 101). From the heart, that word shines outwardly, going ahead, to illuminate the steps of one's journey so that the snares of the wicked lying in one's path may be avoided (vv. 105, 110).

Among its many benefits, God' word, hidden in the heart, enables one to have a ready answer for that person who spiritually opposes (v. 42). It becomes a conduit for God's **grace** (vv. 58, 65), enables one to endure affliction (vv. 67, 71), gives hope (vv. 74, 114-16, 147), and enables one to sing of God's **righteousness** (v. 172).

The OT writers present God as one who "speaks" ('āmar; e.g., Gen. 1:3, 6, 9). In speaking, God's word both creates and brings consistent and ongoing order into that **creation** (ch. 1; Pss. 33:6, 9; 148:5-6). On occasion, God "called" (qārā') to ordinary people, and they heard and responded; for example, Adam

(Gen. 3:9) and Samuel (1 Sam. 3:4). God continues to speak into the process that is the outworking of his purpose in history (Isa. 55:10-11) and is seen, metaphorically, as speaking to his creation through natural phenomena. The psalmist speaks of hearing the power and majesty of Yahweh's "voice" (*qôl*) in the storm—in the thunder (Ps. 29:3) and lightning flashes (v. 7) that break cedar trees (v. 5), shake the **wilderness** (v. 8), and signal the forest animals to give birth (v. 9). The human response to this voice of Yahweh is not that of **fear**; rather, Yahweh's word in the storm evokes an exultant "**Glory!**" (v. 9, NASB).

For the author of the Elijah narrative, however, Yahweh is not heard in wind, earthquake, or fire. Rather, his voice (*qôl*) is heard in soft whisperings (1 Kings 19:11-13). It is Yahweh's "utterance" or "word" ('*imrâ* or *dābār*) that both sends the snow and melts the ice (Ps. 147:15-18).

New Testament authors denote God's word primarily with the Greek terms *logos* and *rhēma* ("word" and "utterance"). It was John who wrote of "Jesus Christ" (John 1:17, NASB) as preeminently "the Word" (*ho logos*; vv. 1, 14, NASB). Even prior to taking on human flesh and dwelling among humankind (v. 14), the Word was eternally both coexistent with God and identical with God. As divine Word, Jesus Christ was instrumental in causing all creation to come into existence (vv. 1-3). Just as God's written and spoken word of the OT, hidden in the heart, enlightens one's personal life's path (Ps. 119:105), the divine Word, in coming to dwell among humankind in human flesh, is both "life" and "light," dispelling the "darkness" for all of humankind (John 1:4-5, 9, NASB).

John further identified Jesus as both the "Word of Life" (*logou tēs zōēs*; 1 John 1:1, NASB) and the "Word of God" (*logos tou theou*; Rev. 19:13, NASB). As Word of Life, Jesus is "the eternal life," existing with God the Father before being made visible to humankind in human form (1 John 1:2, NASB). It is Jesus whom John declared that he had "heard," "seen," and "touched" (v. 1, NASB). As the human manifestation of the Word of God, when Jesus spoke, preached, and proclaimed, his words were the very words of God the Father (John 14:10, 24; 17:8).

One who hears Jesus's words, and in **faith** accepts them and believes them to be the words of the Father, obtains "eternal life" (5:24, NASB). Jesus at times prefaced his words with the authoritative expression, "Truly [*Amēn*] I say to you" (e.g., Mark 3:28; 8:12; 9:1, NASB). This expression is Jesus's declaration of his divine origin and the divine authority of his words. Following one of these occasions (10:15), Mark recorded Jesus's encounter with the man "who owned much property" (v. 22, NASB). Jesus offered him "eternal life" and "treasure in heaven" in exchange for his giving all his possessions to the **poor** (vv. 17, 21, NASB). Grievingly he turned away, refusing the offer (v. 22).

Paul wrote of "the word of God" (1 Cor. 14:36; 2 Cor. 2:17; 4:2; 1 Thess. 2:13, NASB), "the word" (Gal. 6:6; Phil. 1:14; 1 Thess. 1:6, NASB), "the word of the Lord" (1 Thess. 1:8, NASB), and "the word of life" (Phil. 2:16, NASB). He wrote to the Corinthians that he was sent "to preach the gospel," which he identified with "the word of the cross," which is "the power of God" (1 Cor. 1:17-18, NASB). This message of the cross, when "preached," has the power "to save those who **believe**" (v. 21, NASB). Thus, for Paul, to preach the word of the Lord was to preach "Jesus Christ, and Him crucified" (2:2, NASB). The word of the cross leads to "the word of life" (Phil 2:16, NASB), which is the "power of His resurrection" (3:10, NASB). When we "know Him"—that is, Jesus Christ—we, too, "may attain to the resurrection from the dead" (vv. 10-11, NASB).

Luke's account of the spread of the **church**, during the lifetimes of the apostles, follows Jesus's postresurrection, preascension command. His disciples were his "witnesses" (Acts 1:8, NASB), first in **Jerusalem** (chs. 1–7), then in Judea and Samaria (chs. 8–12), and onwards beyond Palestine (chs. 13–28), to the remotest part of the world.

The book of Acts closes with Paul in Rome insisting that the "salvation of God" was also for the Gentiles, and "preaching the **kingdom of God** and teaching concerning the Lord Jesus Christ" (28:28, 31, NASB). Earlier, at Pisidian Antioch, Paul had identified the message he and the other apostles were preaching as "the message of this salvation" (13:26, NASB)—"the good news of the promise made [earlier] to the fathers" (v. 32, NASB). Thus he affirmed that the word of the God of the OT had now been fulfilled in the resurrected Jesus (v. 33).

Luke identified "the word of the Lord," to which Peter and John were testifying in the villages of Samaria, with "the **gospel**" (8:25, NASB). Paul and Barnabas, after being sent out by the church at Antioch (of Syria), spoke of "the word of God" as that which gives "eternal life" (13:46, 48, NASB). However, the Jews at the Pisidian Antioch synagogue rejected it (vv. 44-46). This rejection convinced Paul, as he journeyed on to Iconium and the surrounding cities, that "the word of His grace" (14:3, NASB), which Luke again equates with the gospel, must be preached to both Jews and Gentiles. As they then journeyed homeward to the sending church at Antioch (of Syria), Paul and Barnabas continued to preach "the gospel" and speak "the word" in the cities through which they passed (vv. 21, 25, NASB).

From early on, following Jesus's ascension, Peter recognized that God's announcement "beforehand" or "from ancient time" through the OT prophets had now been fulfilled in Jesus (3:18, 20, NASB). It was by recognizing this fulfilled word from God that one could "**repent**" and have one's sins "wiped away" (v. 19, NASB). Later, writing to believers in Asia Minor, quoting from Isaiah 40:6-8, Peter reminded them that they "have been born again

. . . through the living and enduring word of God" (1 Pet. 1:23, NASB). The written word of the OT is alive in Jesus, the Living Word! In a later letter to other anonymous believers, Peter described "the prophetic word" as "a lamp shining in a dark place," waiting "until the day dawns and the morning star arises" (2 Pet. 1:19, NASB). Both "day" and "morning star" point metaphorically toward the second coming of Christ. Peter then urged his readers to recall to mind "the words" the (OT) "**holy** prophets" spoke and "the commandment" that Jesus, "the Lord and **Savior**," gave through the (NT) "apostles" (3:2, NASB). Both the prophets and apostles, wrote Peter, look toward "the promise of His coming," his "promise" that looks "for new heavens and a new earth, in which righteousness dwells" (vv. 4, 13, NASB).

See also Call of God; Incarnation; Parousia; Resurrection; Sin; Torah (Law, Instruction).

Resources
Edwards, Ruth B. "Word." Pages 1101-6 in vol. 4 of *ISBE*.
Haarbeck, H., G. Fries, B. Klappert, C. Brown, O. Betz, and A. C. Thiselton. "Word, Tongue, Utterance." Pages 1078-146 in vol. 3 of *NIDNTT*.
Toon, Peter. "Word." Pages 1068-69 in *New International Dictionary of the Bible*. Pictorial ed. Edited by James D. Douglas and Merrill C. Tenney. Grand Rapids: Regency Reference Library, 1987.

BARRY L. ROSS, PHD

WORKS

Since the Protestant Reformation, the relationship between **faith** and works has figured prominently into discussions about the nature of salvation. The central debate has focused on the roles of faith and works in establishing and maintaining one's salvation. Although this debate has gained prominence since the Reformation, conflicting interpretations of the respective roles for faith and works can be seen even within our earliest NT documents.

In Galatians, Paul asserted that "a person is justified not by the works of the law but through faith in Jesus Christ" and that Christians are justified (saved) "by faith in Christ, and not by doing the works of the law, because no one will be justified by the works of the law" (2:16, NRSV). In contrast, James asked, "What good is it, my brothers and sisters, if you say you have faith but do not have works? Can faith save you?" (James 2:14, NRSV). James answered this rhetorical question by asserting, "Faith by itself, if it has no works, is dead" (v. 17, NRSV). On the basis of this apparent conflict between Galatians and James, Martin Luther concluded that Galatians contained the "pure **gospel**" (1955–2016, 26:88), while James was an "epistle of straw" (35:362). However, before concurring with Luther, we should consider the theme of "works" more broadly in Scripture.

In the OT, most of the references to "work" and "works" convey meanings similar to the English words associated with manual labor or physical productions, uses similar to the English expressions of "working for a living" (Exod. 20:9; 35:29) and "a work of art" (31:5; 35:24; Judg. 5:30). In a less literal sense, human beings can be "workers of iniquity" (Job 31:3, NRSV; Ps. 141:4).

Animals can "work" (Deut. 21:3), as can God the Creator (Gen. 2:2). Typically, when God works or acts in the OT, God is working for the sake of human salvation (Ps. 74:12). The children of Israel fell into **sin** when they forgot the works of God (Josh. 24:31; Isa. 5:12). God's **judgment** is likewise commonly described as a "work" of God (Ps. 28:5; Isa. 5:19). The works of God are closely associated with the **words of God** (Ps. 33:6). Even in **creation**, the words of God are the tools through which divine work is completed (Gen. 1:6-7, 14-16, 20-21, 24-25, 26-27). Both God's words and works (deeds) are consistently redemptive in the OT—even when that redemption comes in the form of judgment. Importantly, human works are never the source of salvation in the OT.

In the OT, human works are viewed within the context of Israel's **covenant** with Yahweh. Within this system of *covenantal nomism*, that is, laws given within the covenant, human **obedience** and adherence to the terms and laws of the covenant were always a response to God's divine **election** of Israel (18:19; Deut. 7:6; 14:2). God, not human obedience to the **law**, is always the source of salvation. Salvation never results from human activity. Salvation comes entirely from divine initiative, with the anticipation of obedience as the human response to divinely and freely granted salvation. Thus both versions of the Ten Commandments begin with the theme of divine election (Exod. 20:2; Deut. 5:2-5).

The appropriate human response to the gift of salvation is beautifully summarized by Micah: "What does the LORD require of you but to do **justice**, and to **love** kindness, and to walk **humbly** with your God?" (Mic. 6:8, NRSV). Over time, the appropriate response to the covenant became codified in two types of law: commandments and case law. Commandments are simple commands either to perform or avoid a particular activity, such as keeping the Sabbath (Exod. 20:8-11) and not misusing the divine name (v. 7). Case law is more detailed and involves discussions both about the particular circumstances surrounding one's deed and about the consequences for the violation of particular laws. These laws typically take the form of "if" a particular event meets these criteria, "then" these consequences should follow (Lev. 25:25-28, 29-34; 27:14-15).

The NT largely presumes this system of covenantal nomism, but with one major difference. Entry into the covenant is no longer predicated on one's birth into the people of God. Rather, entry into the covenant is possible for all people, both Jews and Gentiles, through faith in Jesus Christ. As Paul explained, "There is no distinction between Jew and Greek [non-Jew];

the same Lord is Lord of all and is generous to all who call on him" (Rom. 10:12, NRSV; see Gal. 3:28-29). Of course, within the system of covenantal nomism, all persons of faith should on their entry into the covenant of salvation obey the divine law, a divine law now reinterpreted by Jesus solely as love for God and for neighbor (Matt. 22:36-40; Mark 12:28-31). Most early Christians, therefore, became convinced that sincere faith could always be recognized by the works of love and **compassion** that it produced in the people of God (Matt. 7:20; Rev. 2:2, 19; 3:1, 8, 15).

In the conflict between James and Paul, James was deeply disturbed by people who claimed to be living within the covenant, while ignoring the plight of the **poor** (James 2:15-16). James declared that such "faith" was "dead" (v. 17, NRSV). Paul was equally disturbed by pious disregard for the poor (Gal. 2:10), but he presumed that such "dead faith" was no faith at all. James was willing to concede that such people possessed a sort of faith, but not the saving faith that allows one to remain within the covenant. Within the NT's covenantal nomism, believers enter the covenant by faith and respond to their inclusion within the covenant by loving God and neighbor. It is "faith working through love" (Gal. 5:6, NRSV).

See also Justification; Torah (Law, Instruction).

Resources

Bassler, Jouette M. *Divine Impartiality: Paul and a Theological Axiom.* Society of Biblical Literature Dissertation Series 59. Atlanta: Scholars Press, 1982.

Blenkinsopp, Joseph. *Wisdom and Law in the Old Testament.* 2nd ed. New York: Oxford University Press, 1995.

Dunn, James D. G. *Jesus, Paul, and the Law.* Louisville, KY: Westminster John Knox Press, 1990.

Luther, Martin. *Luther's Works.* Edited by Jaroslav Pelikan, Helmut T. Lehmann, Christopher B. Brown, Benjamin T. G. Mayes. 78 vols. Saint Louis: Concordia, 1955–2016.

Sanders, E. P. *Paul and Palestinian Judaism.* Philadelphia: Fortress Press, 1977.

THOMAS E. PHILLIPS, PHD

WRATH OF GOD

While "God is **love**" (1 John 4:8, NIV) operates as a simple sentence describing God's essence, no one suggests that "God is wrath or anger" also so defines God. God's wrath (or vengeance and anger) is essential only as God's response to human **sin** or injustice. God's love within Christian practice is likely most popularized by the frequent use of John 3:16: "For God so loved the world . . ." (NIV). Although "love" is not operative as a word in creation, it is noticeable that God creates while living in relationship with the creation and humans that God has created, even attentively fixing the problem of the man's aloneness (Gen. 2:18). Where God responds to problems in creation, this is characterized as wrath, though this response might also be seen as making right what humans have made wrong in creation.

1. Wrath or divine anger is not God's essence, neither was it a characteristic means by which Jesus lived in the world.

2. When and where God operates in the world with anger or wrath, God's actions are characteristically qualified and explained as a response to human sinfulness or to a nation's usurping God's role in the world. God's anger is tied to God's **justice** to restore order to the world.

Divine and Human Wrath

Both God and humans are described in Scripture as angry, wrathful, or seeking vengeance. Although descriptions of the wrath of God and that of humans include similar terms and settings, the wrath of each is characterized differently. Scripture routinely permits divine wrath, while it proscribes or prohibits human emotional anger or wrath that reacts unjustly.

God commands humans to redirect their *emotional* anger so that God's ordered intention for **creation** can prevail. The Lord expects that justice and human **judgment** are warranted against evildoers. Those who seek to shed the blood of others need to be held in check and prevented from doing harm (Gen. 9:6; Zech. 1:15). And yet, God prohibits the self-seeking, personally vindictive wrath of humans against other humans (Prov. 14:29; 29:11; Matt. 5:21-26; Eph. 4:26). God's limitation on human wrath is not a prohibition on human justice when the work of justice is subservient to the rule of the Lord. The Lord works to empower just rule for human well-being in line with God's intention for a good world (Gen. 1), where young and old sit in the city parks free from even the threat of harm (Isa. 2:4; Mic. 4:3; Zech. 8; Rev. 22:2).

God's Restrictions on Human Wrath

An example of God's restriction on violence by humans includes the important *lex talionis* (Lat., "law of retaliation") found first in the **laws** given at Sinai (Exod. 21:24). Leviticus 24:19-20 states, "Anyone who injures their neighbor is to be injured in the same manner: fracture for fracture, eye for eye, tooth for tooth. The one who has inflicted the injury must **suffer** the same injury" (NIV). While this permits responses of violence for violence, it limits the extent of it to an equal measure, which functions as a check against unremitting violence. The provisions of lex talionis become yet more restricted by Jesus who encourages turning the other cheek (Matt. 5:38-39) and says to "love your enemies and pray for those who persecute you" (v. 44, NIV).

Paul's Restrictions

Paul's important theological writings in the book of Romans offer much about God's wrath and human violence. Paul calls for human transformation: "Do not repay anyone evil for evil. Be careful to do what is right in the eyes of everyone. If it is possible, as far as it depends on you, live at **peace** with everyone. Do not take revenge. . . . But overcome evil with good" (Rom. 12:17-19, 21, NASB). God as Sovereign Lord is both able and ready to respond to wrongdoing, and only the Lord can do so with perfect equity. God's sovereign rule does expect human participation in seeking to right wrongs and in working for justice (Mic. 6:6-8), including functioning as "God's servants" in punishing wrongdoers (Rom. 13:4, NIV; Gen. 9:6). This function though must always be in service to the rule of the Lord and, for Christians, be consistent with the life of love modeled in Jesus, the Christ.

Hebrew Scripture Terms for God's Wrath

Nahum 1:6 typifies God's wrath: "Who can withstand his indignation? Who can endure his fierce anger? His wrath is poured out like fire; the rocks are shattered before him" (NIV). The Hebrew term for "anger" or "wrath" derives from the expression of a face turning red, an inflamed or snorting nostril. What is translated as "fierce anger" could also be "burning wrath" or the "burning of his anger." This single verse captures a strong sense of the claim of Scripture that God can certainly be one who is enraged with hot indignation and scorching wrath.

Summary

While God is love, God may also become angry. This wrath, however, is not a pattern for humans. Their anger should be more restrained so as not to participate in violence. When God acts with wrath, it has restorative power in line with the intended rule of the Lord who reigns over all.

See also Jesus and the Law; Sermon on the Mount; Works.

MARTY ALAN MICHELSON, PHD

SCRIPTURE INDEX

Old Testament

30:16	Love
30:16, 19	Torah (Law, Instruction)
31:19-22	Women in OT
31:27	Torah (Law, Instruction)
32:4	Belief/Believe, Communal Holiness
32:17	Demonic/Devil
32:20	Faith
32:41	Hate
33:1-29	Sacred Space
33:7, 29	Helper
33:8	Completeness/Integrity, Divination, Sacred Persons
33:26	Names of God

Joshua

1:1-9, 8	Deuteronomic Theology
1:13	Rest
2	Asian Hermeneutics
2:1-16	Women in OT
2:10	Savior
2:12-14	Love
3:10	Jerusalem
4	Sacred Space
4:24-27	Corporate Responsibility
5–12	Holy Warfare
5:10-12	Festivals
5:13-15	Parousia
5:15	Clean/Unclean, Sacred Space, Sanctification
6	Holy Warfare
6:17, 22-26, 25	Women in OT
7	Biblical Ethics, Holy Warfare, Suffering
7:1, 19-26	Corporate Responsibility
7:5	Suffering
8:30-35	Deuteronomic Theology, Sacred Space
9:15	Peace
10	Creation
13–21	Inheritance
14:9	Inheritance
17:3-6	Women in OT
18:1	Sacred Space
20:3	Redeem/Redeemer
22:5	Communal Holiness, Love
22:10-34	Sacred Space
22:25	Rest
23:6	Deuteronomic Theology
24	Covenant, Sacred Space
24:15	Election, Idolatry
24:26	Deuteronomic Theology
24:20	Repentance
24:31	Works
24:25	Justice OT

Judges

1:21	Jerusalem
1:24	Love
2:12	Discipleship
2:22	Temptation/Test
3:1, 4	Temptation/Test
3:9, 15	Savior

3:19	Sacred Space
4–5	Women in OT, Women's Roles in the Church
4:3	Savior
4:4-5	Judgment
4:4-14	Leadership
4:17	Peace
5	Creation, Women in OT
5:5	Sacred Space
5:7, 31	Women in OT
5:11	Righteousness
5:30	Works
6:11-27	Sacred Space
6:25-32	Idolatry
6:36-40	Divination
7–8	Holy Warfare
8:35	Love
9:2	Marriage
9:16, 19	Communal Holiness
11:2	Inheritance
13:15-20	Sacred Space
15:1-2	Hate
19	Justice OT
19:1	Women in OT
19:10-11	Jerusalem
19:20	Peace
21:4	Sacred Space
21:13	Peace
21:25	Justice OT

Ruth

1:6	Creation
1:8	Grace
1:22	Sacred Space
2:20	Grace
3:10	Poor
4	Redeem/Redeemer
4:1-10, 5	Inheritance
4:11-12	Matriarchs
4:13	Creation
4:13-17	Women in OT

1 Samuel

1–2	Sacred Space
1:10-28, 24-28	Women in OT
2:1-10, 22	Women in OT
2:2	Communal Holiness
2:3	Names of God
2:6	Cosmology
2:8	Inheritance
2:25	Forgiveness
3	Call of God
3:4	Word of God
4:1-11	Holy Warfare
5:11	Glory
6:1-18	Sacred Space
6:14	Sacrificial System
7:3-17	Leadership
7:6	Forgiveness
7:12, 17	Sacred Space
9:5-25	Sacred Space
9:12, 19	Deuteronomic Theology
9:12-25	Sacrificial System

New Testament

14:6, 26, 29, 30	Revelation
14:33	Saints/Holy Ones
14:33, 40	Peace
14:34-35	Feminist Hermeneutics
14:36	Word of God
15	Suffering
15:1-4, 2-3	Gospel
15:3-4, 4-7, 8-9, 12-56, 20-23, 23-28, 24-25, 24-28, 26-28, 54-57, 56	Pauline Theology
15:5, 8, 17, 19, 23, 42, 43-44, 50, 51-52	Resurrection
15:20-23	Festivals
15:20-28	Demonic/Devil
15:22, 44-45	Fall
15:23	Afterlife
15:26	Victory
15:28	Theological Interpretation
15:34	Honor/Shame
15:54	Isaiah
15:54-57	Savior
16:1, 15	Saints/Holy Ones
16:1-4	Justice NT
16:2	Sacred Times
16:17	Parousia
16:22	Pauline Theology

2 Corinthians

1:12	Conscience
1:14	Parousia
1:20-22	Pauline Theology
2:11	Pauline Theology
2:12	Gospel
2:17	Word of God
3:3, 17	Holy Spirit
3:3-16, 17	Pauline Theology
3:4-18, 6, 7-18, 14	Covenant
3:18	Church's Mission, Holiness, Image of God
4:1	Mercy
4:2	Honor/Shame, Word of God
4:4	Image of God, Sin
4:4, 7-15, 14	Pauline Theology
4:16	Regeneration/Rebirth
5:1-8, 10, 10-11, 14-15, 17, 17-21, 18-20, 21	Pauline Theology
5:1-10	Resurrection
5:4-5	Holy Spirit
5:10	Judgment
5:15	Grace

5:16-21, 18-19, 18-20, 19, 19-20, 20, 21	Reconciliation
5:17, 18-20	Regeneration/Rebirth
5:18-21	Holiness
5:19	Evil, Justice NT
5:21	Justification
6:1	Grace
6:3-10, 16	Pauline Theology
6:16-18	Sacred Space
7:1	Pauline Theology
7:6-7	Parousia
8:1–9:5	Justice NT
8:2	Temptation/Test
8:4	Saints/Holy Ones
8:8-9	Poor
8:9	Grace, Pauline Theology
8:18	Gospel
9:1, 12	Saints/Holy Ones
9:4	Honor/Shame
9:6-7, 9	Poor
9:8	Grace
9:13	Gospel
10:5	Obedience
10:7	Call of God
10:10	Parousia
10:18	Temptation/Test
11:2-14, 22–12:10	Pauline Theology
11:3	Leadership
11:4	Gospel
11:14	Demonic/Devil
12:2-4	Pauline Theology
13:5-7	Temptation/Test
13:11	Peace
13:12	Saints/Holy Ones
13:14	Pauline Theology

Galatians

1-2	Pauline Theology
1:1, 4, 11-16, 16	Pauline Theology
1:4	Evil
1:7, 8-9, 11	Gospel
1:15	Call of God, Grace
2:1-9, 10, 14-17	Justice NT
2:1-10, 4, 11-14, 16	Pauline Theology
2:10	Poor, Remembering
2:10, 14, 16, 17	Works
2:14	Gospel
2:15-16, 16	Justification
2:16	Belief/Believe
2:16, 21	Grace
3:2	Holy Spirit
3:13	Redeem/Redeemer
3:14	Inheritance
3:14, 22	Belief/Believe

www.ingramcontent.com/pod-product-compliance
Lightning Source LLC
Chambersburg PA
CBHW071009140426
42814CB00004BA/171